WARRNAMBOOL TO MELBOURNE

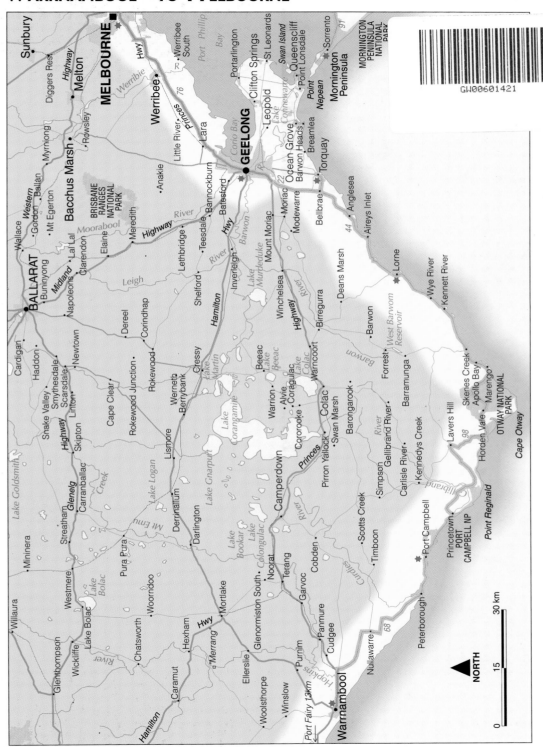

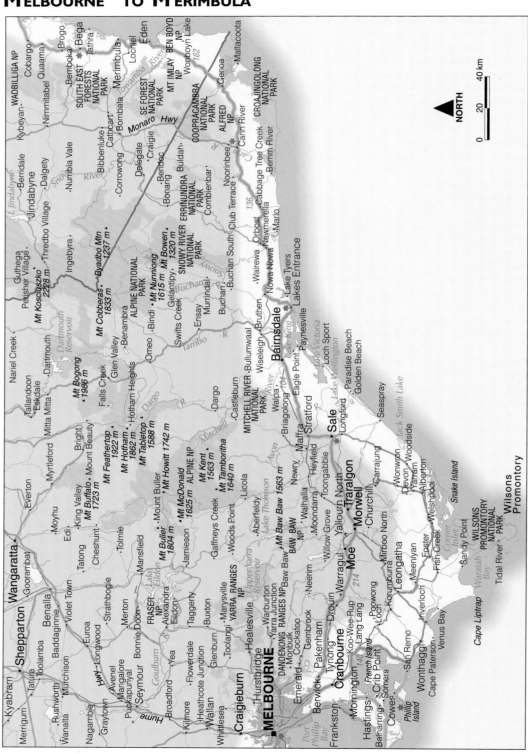

MERIMBULA TO SYDNEY

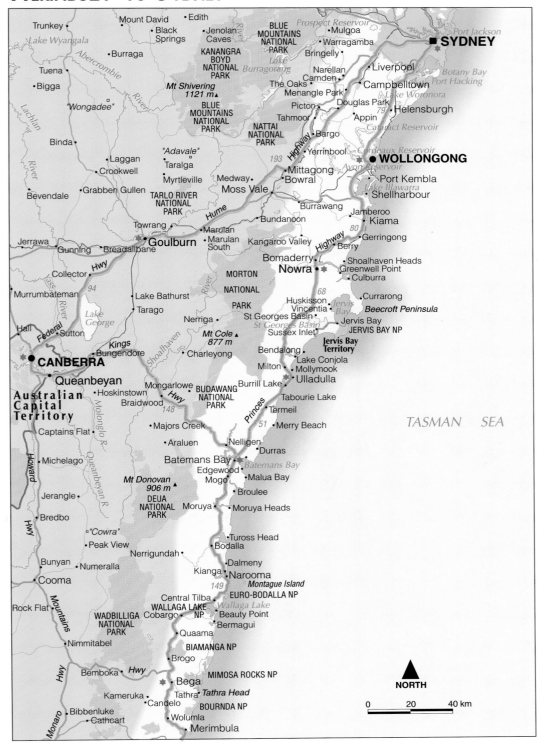

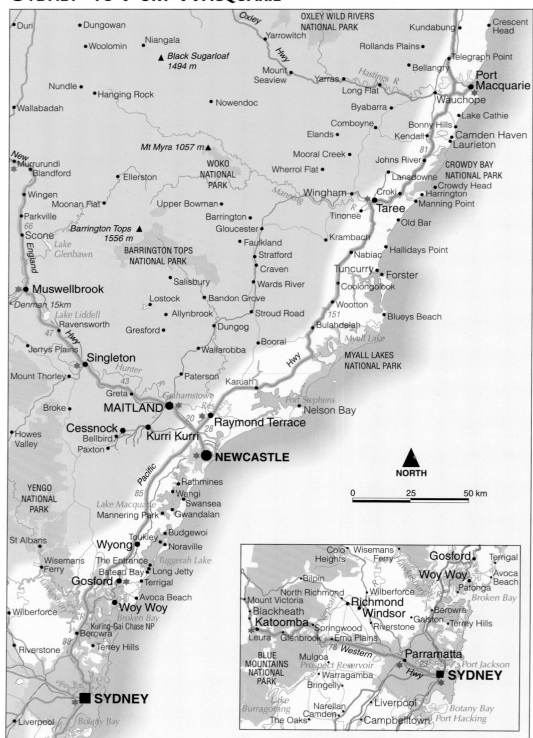

Sydney to Port Macquarie

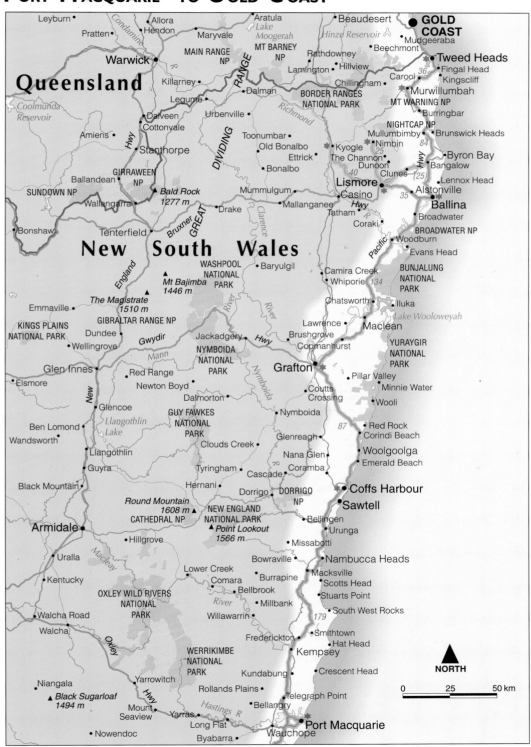

Port Macquarie to Gold Coast

GOLD COAST TO MARYBOROUGH

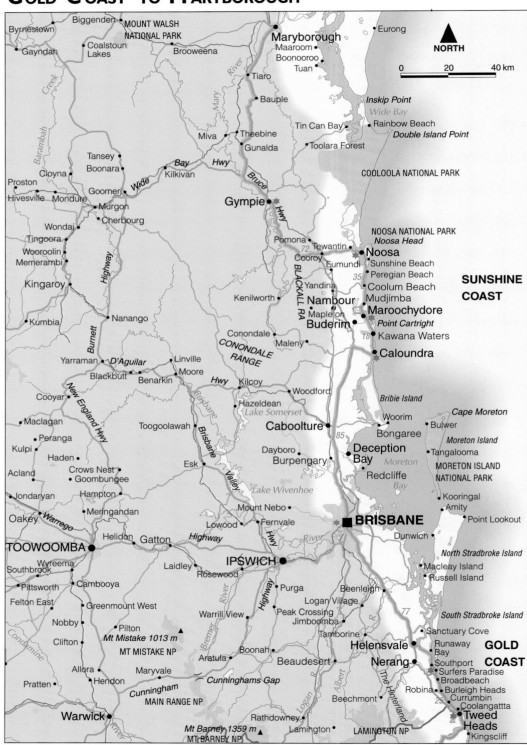

MARYBOROUGH TO MACKAY

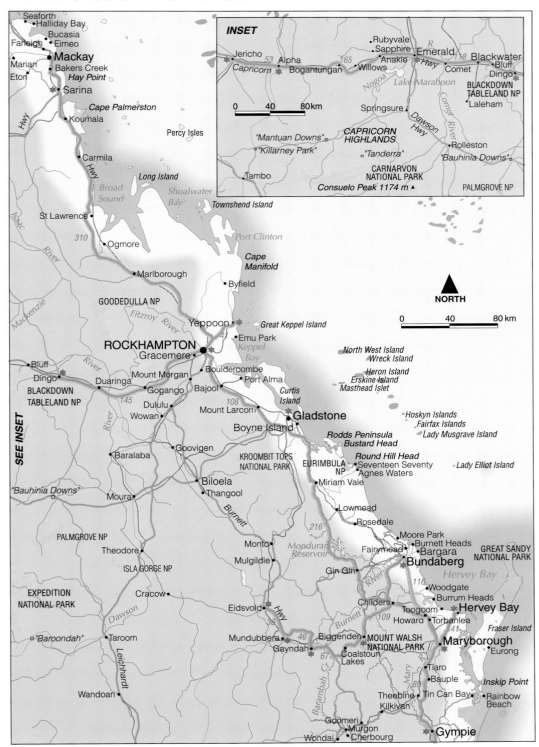

INSET

Jericho · 53 · Alpha · 165 · Rubyvale · Sapphire · Anakie · Emerald · 118 · Blackwater
Capricorn · Bogantungan · Willows · Hwy · Comet · Bluff · Dingo
Lake Maraboon · BLACKDOWN TABLELAND NP
Springsure · Laleham
CAPRICORN HIGHLANDS
"Mantuan Downs" · Dawson Hwy · Rolleston
"Killarney Park" · "Tanderra" · "Bauhinia Downs"
CARNARVON NATIONAL PARK
Tambo · Consuelo Peak 1174 m ▲ · PALMGROVE NP

0   40   80km

Seaforth
Halliday Bay
Bucasia
Farleigh · Eimeo
Mackay
Marian · Bakers Creek
Eton · *Hay Point*
Sarina
Cape Palmerston
Koumala
Carmila
Broad Sound · *Long Island* · *Shoalwater Bay*
St Lawrence · *Townshend Island*
310
Ogmore · *Port Clinton*
Marlborough · *Cape Manifold*
GOODEDULLA NP · Byfield
Fitzroy River
Yeppoon · *Great Keppel Island*
ROCKHAMPTON · 41 · Emu Park
Gracemere · *Keppel Bay*
Mackenzie · Bouldercombe
Bluff · Port Alma
Dingo · Duaringa · Gogango · Bajool · *Curtis Island*
BLACKDOWN TABLELAND NP · 145 · Dulula · Mount Larcom · 108
Wowan · **Gladstone**
Boyne Island
Baralaba · Goovigen · *Rodds Peninsula* · *Bustard Head*
KROOMBIT TOPS NATIONAL PARK · *Round Hill Head*
"Bauhinia Downs" · EURIMBULA NP · *Seventeen Seventy*
Moura · Biloela · Agnes Waters
Thangool · Miriam Vale
PALMGROVE NP · Lowmead
Theodore · Monto · *Monduran Reservoir* · Rosedale
ISLA GORGE NP · Mulgildie · 216 · Moore Park
Fairymead · Burnett Heads
EXPEDITION NATIONAL PARK · Cracow · Bargara
Eidsvold · **Bundaberg** · GREAT SANDY NATIONAL PARK
Hervey Bay
"Baroondah" · Childers · Woodgate
Taroom · Gin Gin · 116 · Burrum Heads
Toogoom · **Hervey Bay**
Mundubbera · 46 · Biggenden · 709 · Howard · Torbanlea
Gayndah · MOUNT WALSH NATIONAL PARK · 41 · *Fraser Island*
Wandoan · 67 · Coalstoun Lakes · **Maryborough**
Eurong
Tiaro · *Inskip Point*
Bauple
Theebine · Tin Can Bay · Rainbow Beach
Kilkivan
Goomeri · Murgon · **Gympie**
Wondai · Cherbourg

▲ NORTH

0   40   80 km

SEE INSET

North West Island
Wreck Island
Heron Island
Erskine Island
Masthead Islet
Hoskyn Islands
Fairfax Islands
Lady Musgrave Island
Lady Elliot Island

Percy Isles

Isaac River
Leichhardt
Dawson River
Burnett
Baramah Cr
Mary R

MACKAY TO CAIRNS

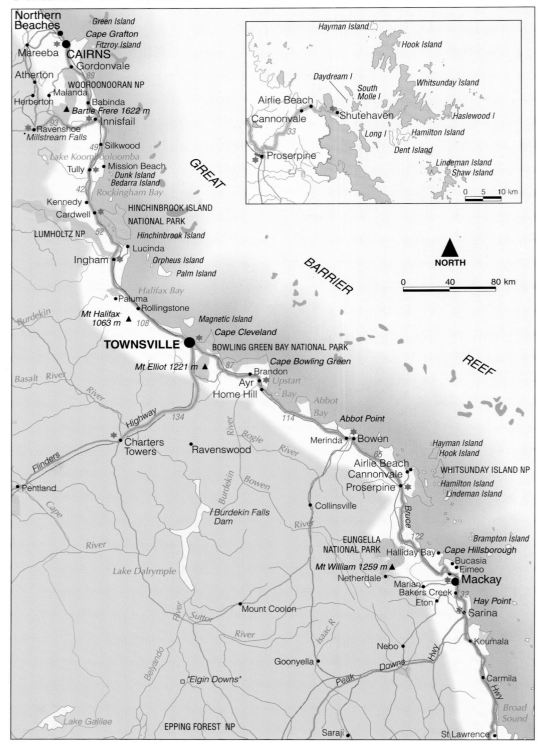

Cape York to Cairns

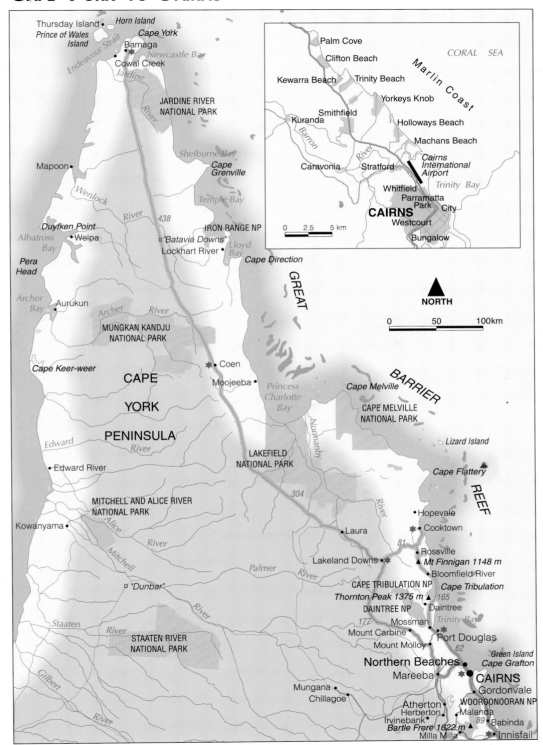

SYDNEY

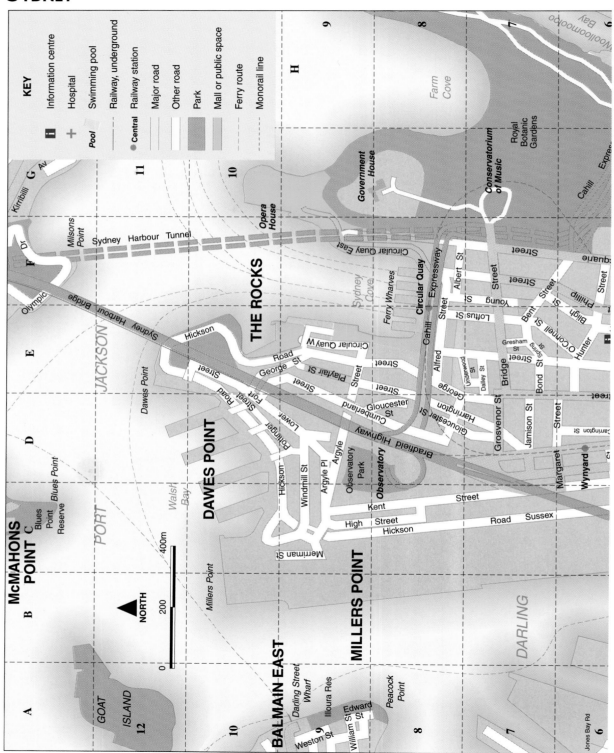

KEY

- **ℍ** Information centre
- **+** Hospital
- **Pool** Swimming pool
- Railway, underground
- **● Central** Railway station
- Major road
- Other road
- Park
- Mall or public space
- Ferry route
- Monorail line

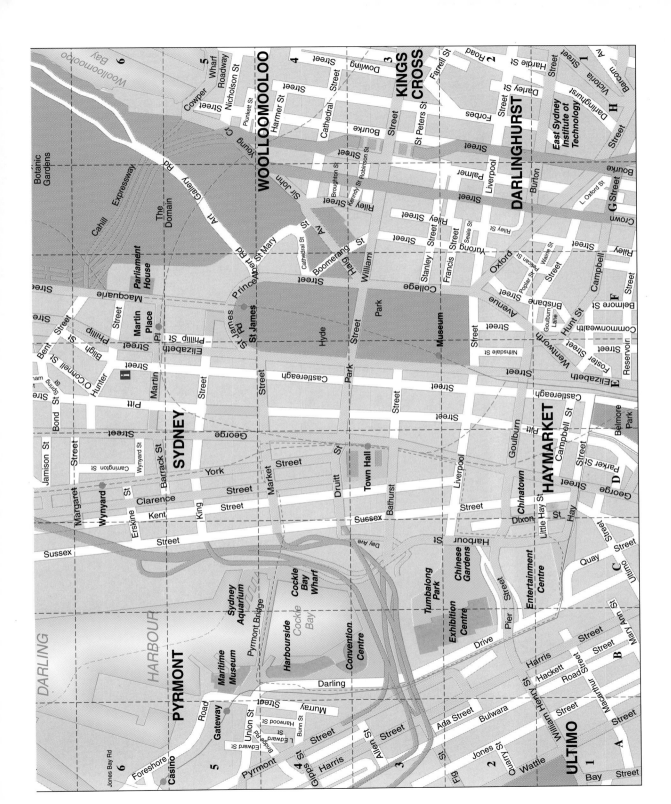

MELBOURNE

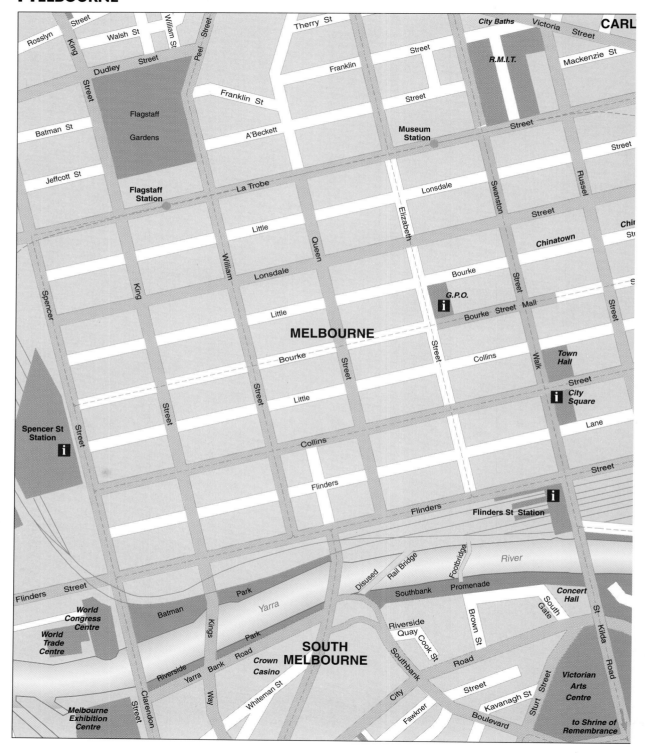

CARL

Rosslyn Street
King Street
Walsh St
William St
Peel Street
Therry St
Street
City Baths
Victoria Street

Dudley Street
Franklin Street
R.M.I.T.
Mackenzie St

Batman St
Franklin St
Flagstaff Gardens
A'Beckett
Street
Museum Station
Street

Jeffcott St
La Trobe
Lonsdale
Swanston
Russel

Flagstaff Station
Little
Elizabeth
Street

Spencer
William
Lonsdale
Queen
Bourke
Chinatown
Chi Str

King
Little
G.P.O.
Bourke Street Mall
Street

MELBOURNE
Bourke
Collins
Walk
Town Hall

Street
Little
Street
City Square

Collins
Lane

Spencer St Station
Flinders
Street

Flinders
Flinders St Station

River

Flinders Street
Disused Rail Bridge
Footbridge
Southbank Promenade
Concert Hall

World Congress Centre
Batman
Park
Yarra
Southbank
South Gate

World Trade Centre
Kings
Park
Riverside Quay
Brown St
Cook St

Riverside
Yarra Bank Road
Crown Casino
SOUTH MELBOURNE
Southbank
Road
Kavanagh St
Sturt Street
Victorian Arts Centre

Melbourne Exhibition Centre
Clarendon Street
Way
Whiteman St
City
Fawkner
Street
Boulevard
St Kilda Road
to Shrine of Remembrance

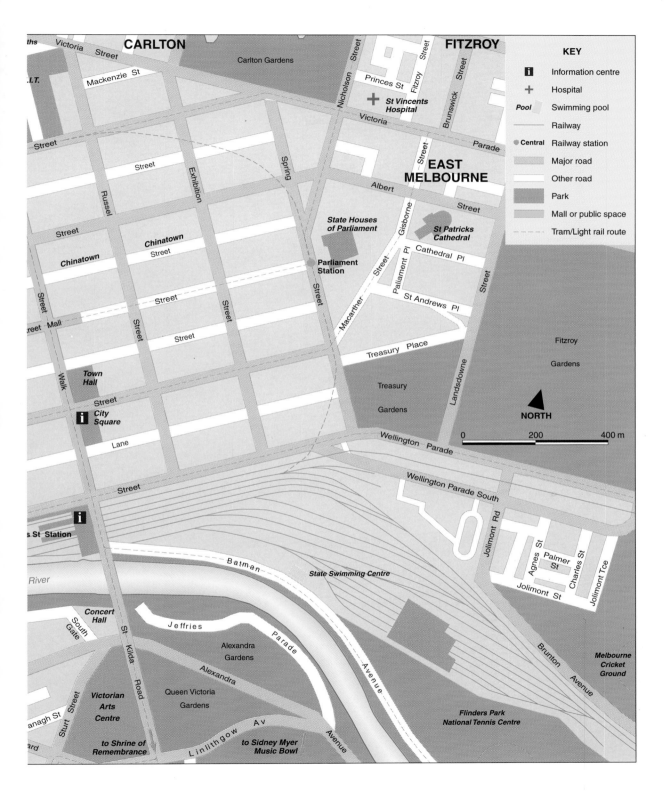

KEY

i	Information centre
+	Hospital
Pool	Swimming pool
———	Railway
● *Central*	Railway station
	Major road
	Other road
	Park
	Mall or public space
– – –	Tram/Light rail route

CARLTON

FITZROY

Carlton Gardens

Victoria Street

Mackenzie St

R.M.I.T.

Nicholson Street

Princes St

Fitzroy Street

Brunswick Street

+ St Vincents Hospital

Victoria Parade

Street

Street

Exhibition Street

Spring Street

Street

EAST MELBOURNE

Albert Street

Russel Street

Chinatown

Chinatown Street

Street

Gisborne Street

State Houses of Parliament

St Patricks Cathedral

Parliament Pl

Cathedral Pl

Street

Parliament Station

Macarthur Street

St Andrews Pl

Street

Street

Street

Street

Street

Street Mall

Walk

Town Hall

Street

i City Square

Treasury Place

Treasury Gardens

Landsdowne Street

Fitzroy Gardens

NORTH

Lane

Street

Wellington - Parade

0   200   400 m

i

s St Station

Wellington Parade South

Jolimont Rd

Jolimont Tce

Batman

State Swimming Centre

Agnes St

Palmer St

Charles St

River

Jolimont St

Concert Hall

South Gate

St Kilda Road

Jeffries

Parade

Brunton Avenue

Melbourne Cricket Ground

Alexandra Gardens

Alexandra

Sturt Street

Cavanagh St

Victorian Arts Centre

Queen Victoria Gardens

Avenue

Flinders Park National Tennis Centre

to Shrine of Remembrance

Linlithgow Av

to Sidney Myer Music Bowl

Avenue

BRISBANE

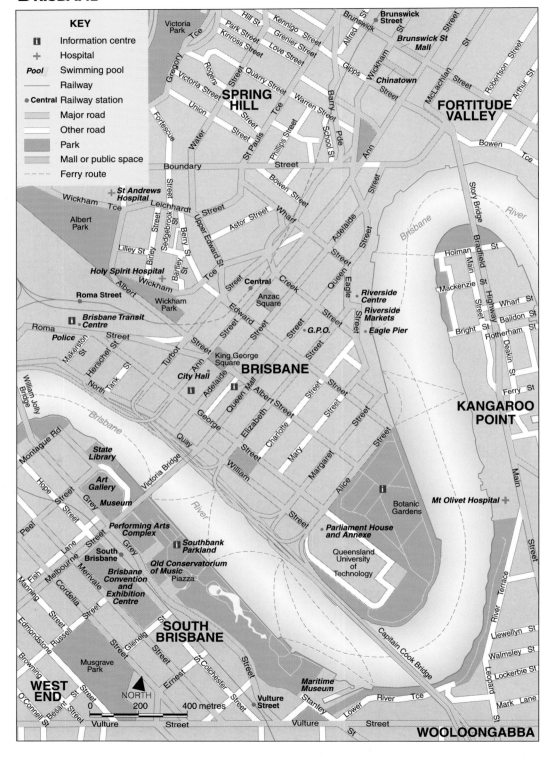

KEY

- ℹ️ Information centre
- ✚ Hospital
- *Pool* Swimming pool
- —— Railway
- • *Central* Railway station
- Major road
- Other road
- Park
- Mall or public space
- - - - Ferry route

SPRING HILL

FORTITUDE VALLEY

Victoria Park Tce
Hill St
Kennigo Street
Park Street
Brunswick Street
Brunswick St Mall
Alfred Street
Grenier Street
Love Street
Gipps
Wickham
Chinatown
Kinross Street
Quarry Street
Warren Street
Barry Pde
School St
Ann
McLachlan Street
Robertson Street
Arthur St
Rogers Street
Victoria Street
Gregory
Union
Fortescue
Water
St Pauls
Phillips Street
Street
Boundary
Street
Bowen Street
Bowen Tce

St Andrews Hospital
Wickham Tce
Leichhardt Street
Astor Street
Wharf
Adelaide
Street
Story Bridge
Brisbane River
Albert Park
Sedgebrook St
Berry St
Upper Edward St
Street
Street
Holman
Bradfield
Main
Mackenzie
St
Lilley St
Birley St
Bartley St
Street
Creek
Queen
Eagle
Street
Riverside Centre
Wharf St
Bright St
Baildon
Holy Spirit Hospital
Wickham
Central
Anzac Square
Riverside Markets
Eagle Pier
Rotherham St
Roma Street
Albert
Wickham Park
Edward Street
Street
Street
G.P.O.
Deakin St
Brisbane Transit Centre
Roma
Turbot Street
King George Square
BRISBANE
Ferry St
Police
Makerston St
Herschel St
Tank St
Ann Street
City Hall
Adelaide
Queen Mall
Albert Street
Street
Street
KANGAROO POINT
North
George
Elizabeth
Charlotte
Mary
Street
William Jolly Bridge
Brisbane
Quay
Victoria Bridge
William
Street
Margaret
Street
State Library
Montague Rd
Hope Street
Grey
Street
River
Alice
Main
Botanic Gardens
Mt Olivet Hospital
Art Gallery
Museum
Peel Street
Lane Street
Melbourne Street
Merivale Street
Grey
Performing Arts Complex
Southbank Parkland
Qld Conservatorium of Music
Piazza
Parliament House and Annexe
Llewellyn St
South Brisbane
Queensland University of Technology
Walmsley St
Manning Street
Fish Lane
Cordelia Street
Russell Street
Brisbane Convention and Exhibition Centre
River Terrace
Lockerbie St
Leopard St
Edmondstone Street
Browning
Glenelg Street
Ernest Street
SOUTH BRISBANE
Maritime Museum
Mark Lane
Musgrave Park
Colchester Street
Stanley
Capitan Cook Bridge
WEST END
O'Connell Street
Besant Street
Street
Vulture Street
Vulture
River Tce
Lower
Street
WOOLOONGABBA
Vulture Street

NORTH
0   200   400 metres

CANBERRA

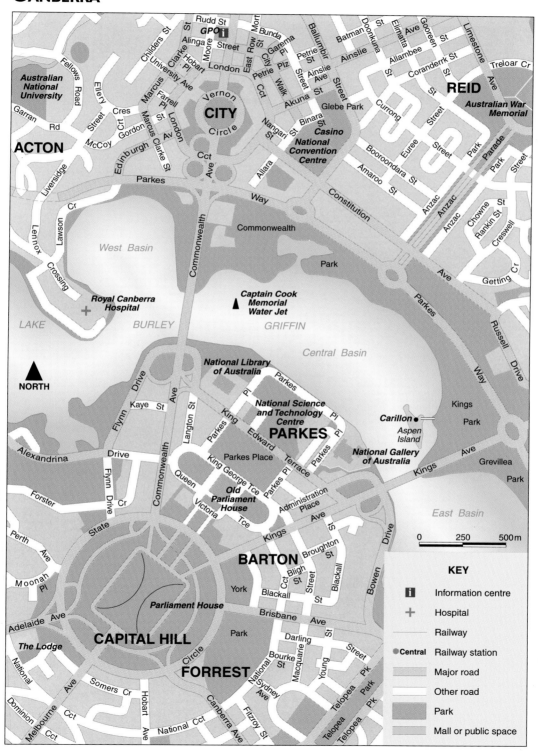

Doing the Coast

Travelling Australia's East Coast

Great Stay Guide

Doing the Coast

Travelling Australia's East Coast

 LITTLE HILLS·PRESS

Text © Little Hills Press, January 2002
Photographs © Little Hills Press, 2002
or printed with permission - see Photo Acknowledgements

Maps by MAPgraphics © Little Hills Press, 2000

Book conceived by Matthew Rice and Sam Lynch
Editor and designer: Mark Truman
Editorial assistant: Jerome Kattampallil
Publisher: Charles Burfitt

Printed in Singapore

Doing the Coast
Great Stay Guide
ISBN 1 86315 200 8

Little Hills Press
Sydney, Australia
www.littlehills.com
info@littlehills.com

DISCLAIMER

Whilst all care has been taken by the publisher and authors to ensure that the information is accurate and up to date, the publisher does not take responsibility for the information published herein or the consequences of its use. The recommendations are those of the writing team, and as things get better or worse, with places closing and others opening, some elements in the book may be inaccurate when you arrive. Please inform us of any discrepancies so that we can update subsequent editions.

Little Hills™ and are registered trademarks of Little Hills Press Pty Ltd.

CONTENTS

ACKNOWLEDGEMENTS

A special thanks to the helpful staff at the following Tourism outlets for assisting with the production of this book:

Tourism Queensland, Brisbane Tourism, Airlie Tourist Information Centre, Capricorn Coast Tourist Organisation, Fraser Coast Tourism, Gold Coast Tourism, Mackay Tourism and Development Bureau, Mission Beach Visitor Information Centre, Sunshine Coast Tourism, Tourism Tropical North Queensland, Ballina Visitor Information, Byron Bay Visitor Information, Coffs Harbour-Tourism Holiday Coast, Eurobodalla Visitor Information, Great Lakes Visitor Centre, Newcastle Tourism, Port Macquarie Visitor Information, Port Stephens Visitor Information, Sapphire Coast Tourism, Shoalhaven Visitor Information, Tourism Victoria, City of Melbourne, Geelong Tourism, Lakes & Wilderness Tourism, Lorne and Surfcoast Visitor Information Centre, Phillip Island Visitor Information, and Warrnambool Visitor Information.

Photo Credits

Photographs © Austral International Library - front and back covers

Photographs by Little Hills Press © Little Hills Press - 23, 24, 30, 34, 42, 45, 71, 75, 82, 95, 99, 108, 111, 187, 205, 227, 230, 231, 234, 239, 255, 256, 280, 295.

Photographs by Darren Hopton © Little Hills Press - 100, 102, 113, 114, 115, 119, 126, 130, 135, 137, 141, 144, 147, 154, 159, 161, 166, 168, 183, 190.

Photographs reproduced with the kind permission of Tourism Queensland ©Tourism Queensland - 204, 284, 300, 307, 322, 327, 335, 338, 340, 343.

Photographs reproduced with the kind permission of Gold Coast Tourism © Gold Coast Tourism Bureau - 214, 216, 221, 223.

Photographs reproduced with the kind permission of Newcastle Tourism © Newcastle Tourism - 173.

Photographs reproduced with the kind permission of Eurobodalla Coast Tourism © Eurobodalla Coast Tourism - title page, 53, 65, 67, 68.

PREFACE

Welcome to Australia's East Coast.

You may be part of a family looking for a different place to enjoy that annual holiday, a couple seeking a secluded romantic retreat, an adventurous local with a sense of discovery, an independent traveller intent on trekking through the hot spots, or an overseas visitor keen to visit the famous and popular tourist drawcards. There is a part of Australia's East Coast to meet every interest. This guide is intended to unlock the secrets and open up new possibilities.

A truly stunning stretch of landscape, the east coast of Australia takes in the Great Barrier Reef, the Gold and Sunshine Coasts, tropical northern New South Wales, the Sapphire Coast and Gippsland regions, the Great Ocean Road, and the state and national capitals along the way. There are also the less-well-known delights, such as the outlying regions you may have heard of but know nothing about, the many National Parks you had no idea existed, and the tiny villages with their heritage and individual charm that remain hidden.

Doing the Coast is designed to lead you through the best Australia's East Coast has to offer.

Safe travelling. We hope your stay is enjoyable and memorable.

HOW TO USE THIS BOOK

Symbols

Throughout the text you will find that symbols have been used to denote the information that follows, whether it be an admission price, opening time, phone number or web address. This will aid you in locating the specific details you desire more quickly.

Here is a list of the symbols used with an explanation of each:

 ℃ indicates a phone number
 ✪ indicates a price
 🕐 indicates opening times
 👁 indicates a web site
 ✗ indicates an email address

Goods and Services Tax

The prices quoted in this book include Australia's 10% GST. It should also be kept in mind that many products are exempt from the tax, including basic food items.

Accommodation and Eating Out

The Accommodation and Eating Out sections contain by no means an exhaustive list of what Australia's East Coast has to offer. We have tried to cater for a range of tastes and provide suggestions for your selection. They are designed to give you a basis for comparison and to act at the very least as a starting point for the planning of your holiday. All budgets from lavish to limited have been considered and included. With regard to eating out, remember that there are always cheaper meals available at fast food outlets and in the food courts of most shopping complexes; we have focused on listing only popular and recommendable restaurants. Again, the GST is excluded from any prices listed

Layout

The chapters of this book are laid out in order from south to north, beginning at Warrnambool, Victoria, and ending at Cape York, Queensland. You can access information on chosen locations easily, regardless of which direction you are heading, or what part of the coast your are covering.

From regional characteristics, how to get there, where to stay, and what to see, we have approached in detail every way a visitor might occupy his or her touring time, with the intention of helping to make the most of that limited time.

The headings are clear for ease of use, and our comprehensive Index will assist you in locatating your area of interest.

Internet Information

For your convenience you will find at the end of this book a list of transport and tourist information on the web, which can be used for the preliminary planning of a coastal holiday.

Maps

The colour maps at the front of this book cover Australia's East Coast from Warrnambool to Cape York. They contain additional information to make road travel easier. The main driving routes detailed in this guide are highlighted with a purple line that runs underneath the major roads and highways down the coastal length. Distances between selected major towns and cities along the way are shown in maroon, and a star has been placed beside the relevant locations to illustrate the start/end points of each given distance. Insets have been used on selected maps to show certain areas in greater detail or to feature a region that does not appear completely on the main map.

The capital cities of Sydney, Melbourne, Brisbane and Canberra have their own separate maps to assist in local orientation.

Throughout the book you will find Strip Maps which give distances between towns en route between major destinations. They are designed to be read both ways, depending on your travelling direction. Apart from the main route (following the major coastal highways) are additional 'Side Trips' offering unique regional sights.

Chapter 1
Australia: An Overview

Australia is an island continent in the South Pacific Ocean. It is the smallest continent and the largest island in the world with a coastline of 19,650km. Its nearest neighbours are New Zealand and Papua New Guinea, while East Timor and Indonesia are a little further away, off the north-western coast.

The country has an area of 7,682,300 square kilometres and is divided into six states - New South Wales, Queensland, Victoria, Tasmania, South Australia and Western Australia - and two territories - Northern Territory and Australian Capital Territory.

The capital of Australia is Canberra in the Australian Capital Territory (ACT). The capital cities of the states are as follows:

> New South Wales - Sydney
> Victoria - Melbourne
> Queensland - Brisbane
> Tasmania - Hobart
> South Australia - Adelaide
> Western Australia - Perth
> Northern Territory - Darwin.

History

It was generally accepted that the continent was first settled by Aborigines around 20,000 years ago, until recent discoveries suggested that they may have arrived much earlier. They were Stone Age people, and as the country had virtually no indigenous plants that could be cultivated for crops, and no animals that could be domesticated, they neither grew nor bred their food, but survived by hunting and gathering. In the interior of the country, this necessitated a nomadic way of life, but in the coastal areas they led a more settled lifestyle because of readily available food from the sea.

Their diet consisted of animals, snakes, birds, birds' eggs, fish, insects, berries and fruits. Their main weapons were the spear and woomera (a sort of spear launcher) and the boomerang. In the hot weather, they didn't bother with clothes, but in the colder regions they wore cloaks of possum or kangaroo skin.

The Aborigines were a peaceful race, and were deeply religious. Their mythology described the creation and explained the reasons for most human behaviour. It was passed from generation to generation in stories, songs and dances, as they had no written language. The dances were called corroborees, and there was one for every special occasion from praying for rain, to mourning death or celebrating a successful hunt.

Aboriginal art was mostly linked with their religion, but sometimes it was only a form of self-expression and not meant to be permanent. Intricate bark paintings were often made for a corroboree, and when it was finished they were simply thrown away.

European Discovery

Many Europeans visited Australia from the early 1600s, but the honour of discovering the continent goes to Captain James Cook, who in the ship *Endeavour* sailed into Botany Bay on April 29, 1770. Two boats went ashore, and tradition says that the first man to set foot on the land was Isaac Smith.

Cook and his party continued sailing northward, naming bays, capes, mountains and islands as they went, and reached a small island off Cape York where they went ashore on August 22, and took possession of the whole eastern coast in the name of King George III. Cook called the land New South Wales, and the island Possession Island.

European Settlement

The American War of Independence in 1783 was directly responsible for the settlement of Australia, as Britain then had nowhere to send her convicted criminals. In 1779, Joseph Banks, who had sailed with Cook, suggested that New South Wales would be a good place for a penal settlement, but nothing was done about it. By 1786 the situation was critical; old ships that had been converted into prison hulks were bulging at the seams, and the government decided to act. New

Part One
Introduction

**Australia:
An Overview**

South Wales was proclaimed a Crown Colony and Captain Arthur Phillip, RN, was appointed its first governor with orders to establish a penal settlement at Botany Bay.

The First Fleet sailed from England on May 13, 1787, and comprised HMS *Sirius*, the armed tender *Supply*, three storeships and six transports, with food clothing and other supplies sufficient for two years. They carried 1,044 people, comprising 568 male and 191 female convicts with 13 children, 206 marines with 27 wives and 19 children, and 20 officials. The ships moored in Botany Bay, but found the area unsuitable for settlement because of a lack of fresh water.

After exploring further north, Philip found the entrance to a large harbour, and decided the best spot for the new settlement was in the area he called Sydney Cove. In the afternoon of January 26, 1788, he and a party of officers and marines raised the Union Jack on the foreshore, drank toasts, fired volleys, and gave three cheers. The rest of the fleet arrived later in the day, and work on the new settlement began in earnest the following morning.

Expansion

The infant colony was not without its problems. The soil, except for a small area around Sydney Cove, was found to be of inferior quality. The majority of the convicts were city people, and so had no experience in farming or agriculture. The government in Britain was very good at giving orders about what should be done, but not very good at understanding the colony's problems and giving assistance to implement solutions. They simply kept sending more convicts, putting more strain on supplies.

Nevertheless the settlement survived and grew. Intrepid explorers discovered new areas, and other settlements were established - Parramatta in 1788, Newcastle in 1803, Hobart in 1804, Brisbane in 1824, Perth in 1829, Melbourne in 1835, Adelaide in 1836, and so on.

The last convict ship to reach Australia arrived in Fremantle on January 9, 1868.

In the 1850s, the discovery of gold brought a huge influx of migrants from all over the world in search of their fortune. Australia's population increased from a little over 400,000 to more than a million in ten years.

Federation

The campaign to form a federation of the colonies began on October 24, 1889, with a speech by Sir Henry Parkes, known as the Father of Federation, at Tenterfield. The movement grew rapidly under his leadership, and there was a meeting of colonial leaders early in 1890 and a convention in March 1891 in Sydney. Parkes died in April, 1896, and the reins were taken over by Edmund Barton, barrister and statesman. A second convention was held at Adelaide in March 1897, and a third conference in January 1898, when a draft constitution was accepted. The next step was to hold referendums in the various colonies. The first, in 1898, was defeated. The second, in 1899, saw the five eastern colonies vote in favour of federation and Western Australia abstain.

Barton then headed a delegation to London, where various objections raised by the Colonial Office were over-ruled. Western Australia agreed to join in after receiving a promise that a transcontinental railway would be built to link Perth with the east coast. On July 9, 1900, Queen Victoria gave her assent to the act which would unite the six colonies into a Commonwealth.

The Commonwealth of Australia was proclaimed and the first Governor-General, the Earl of Hopetoun, was sworn in at a ceremony in Centennial Park, Sydney, on January 1, 1901. About 60,000 people were present. On May 9, in the Exhibition Hall, Melbourne, the Duke of York (later King George V) officially opened the first parliament. The first Prime Minister was Edmund Barton.

In 1910, competitive designs were invited for the federal capital, to be built on a site of 2356 sq km, about 240km south-west of Sydney. The competition was won by Walter Burley Griffin, and after much discussion, it was decided to call the capital Canberra, an Aboriginal name for 'meeting place'. The first Parliament House, which was always considered to be a temporary building, was opened by the Duke and Duchess of York (later King George VI and Queen Elizabeth) in 1927. The present Parliament House was opened by Queen Elizabeth II in 1988.

Australians fought in World Wars I and II, Korea and Vietnam. The nation has lost over 100,000 in war this century, and of these, 60,000 were casualties of the first World War.

The legal system, public service and government structure of Australia are English-based.

Population

During the 1950s and 1960s, people wishing to migrate from Europe and the United States were provided with assisted passage by the Australian government. However, it was not until the late 1960s that restricted entry to Australia from Asia was eased. In the last 40 years Australian society has undergone a tremendous change with now one in four people being a migrant or the child of a migrant.

Australia since the 1970s has become aware of its presence in South-east Asia. The countries of the region are starting to have more of an impact on Australian life. Many new migrants are Asian, and society reflects this blend of European and Asian cultures.

Approximately 85 per cent of the 18,783,600 inhabitants live in urban areas. The east coast of Australia is the most populous because of the fertile plain east of the Great Dividing Range of mountains. The major cities are the state capitals, and the most populous state is New South Wales with 6,173,000 people, followed by Victoria with 4,533,300 people.

The social environment is heavily influenced by the US media and movies. California has a lot in common with Australia's east coast.

Language

Australians speak English, although due to the many people from other countries that have come to live in the country, it is not unusual to hear conversations in other languages when travelling by public transport. Melbourne, for instance, has the second largest Greek population of any city in the world, surpassed only by Athens.

Like the English, Australians call 'gas' petrol and 'fries' chips; but you will find links to the US are perhaps stronger, with McDonalds, Pizza Hut and KFC firmly established in every suburb. There are a few words and phrases that are unique to Australia and in common usage, and dictionaries of Australian slang are available at local bookshops. Australians do say "G'Day", and if stressing authenticity or the truth of a statement, they might say that something is "fair dinkum" or "dinky-di".

There is not much difference between the accents of people from different states, although the pronunciation of particular words sometimes makes the distinction clear. For example, New South Welshmen say the place where a king lives is a 'carsel', but Victorians say it is a 'cassel'. People who live in the cities tend to speak much quicker than those in isolated areas, and this becomes quite noticeable when travelling in the Outback.

Religion

The vast majority of Australians belong to the Christian Churches. There is only a slight margin between Roman Catholics and Anglicans, whose numbers hover around 26% each, reflecting the influence of migrating Irish and Italian Catholics, and the steady flow of English Anglicans into the country. All other religions and sects are present in Australia. Jews, Hindus and Buddhists are all represented strongly on account of the post World War II influx and other political developments since, which opened access to Australian shores. By and large there is peaceful co-existence, and the multicultural composition of society is typically celebrated and embraced.

Holidays

Christmas, New Year and Anzac Day (April 25) are the only holidays that are held at the same time throughout the country. Easter is a movable feast that can fall in either March or April. Australia Day is accepted by all as January 26, but some states have their public holiday on the exact day, and others choose the closest Monday, so as to have a long weekend break.

The whole of Australia stops for five minutes on the first Tuesday in November for the running of the Melbourne Cup horse race, but only people living in Melbourne have the day off work.

In additon, school holidays are different in each state, although the long Christmas break is the most popular holiday time, and runs roughly from the end of the second week in December to the end of January.

It is a good idea to check with the Visitor Information Centres in the cities and towns before or upon arrival, as prices and availability of services will be affected on public holidays.

Overseas Visitors

Entry Regulations

All travellers to Australia need a valid passport, and visitors of all nationalities, except New Zealand, must obtain a visa before arrival. These are available at Australian Embassies, High Commissions and Consular offices listed in local telephone directories. No vaccinations are required.

Before you land you will be given immigration forms as well as Customs and Agriculture declarations. As a general rule you must declare all goods of plant or animal origin. Quarantine officers will inspect these items and return them to you if no disease or pest risk is involved. Even if they are not prohibited, some may need to be treated before being allowed entry.

Each incoming traveller over the age of 18 years is allowed duty free goods to the value of $400, plus 1125mL of liquor and 250g of tobacco products. These items must not be intended for commercial purposes and you must carry them with you through customs.

Exit Regulations

There is a Passenger Movement Charge or Departure Tax of $30 for everyone over the age of 12 years, but this is generally pre-paid with inclusion in the price of an airline ticket. People taking money out of the country, above the value of A$10,000 in Australian and/or foreign currency, must file a report with Customs. For more information on Customs or Quarantine Regulations, visit the following web sites:

👁 www.aqis.gov.au for Quarantine
👁 www.customs.gov.au for Customs

GST Refund

Overseas visitors qualify for a part refund of any GST they pay for items bought in Australia, if the total purchases made at any one business exceeds $300, and the purchases were made no more than 30 days before the date of departure. Present the goods, a tax invoice, your passport and a boarding pass at the TRS (Tax Refund Scheme) booth in the international airport you are leaving from. The items on which you are allowed to claim back GST are only the handheld items you intend to carry with you onto the plane. Present your documents for verification and you will be given the refund to which you are entitled. If the total is less than $200 you can ask for the refund to be made in cash, otherwise it will be in the form of a mailed cheque or a credit arrangement. Foreign currency will also be accommodated in this transaction. Note that any general consumption purchases made within Australia (for example, hotel accommodation or meals) do not qualify for a refund claim.

Be aware that there is no GST imposed on dutyfree items sold in duty-free stores.

For further details and enquiries, phone the Australian Customs Information Line on ✆1300 363 263.

Embassies

Nearly seventy countries have diplomatic representation in Canberra. Some missions are called Embassies, and others who represent countries belonging to the Commonwealth, are called High Commissions. There are also Consuls in the State capitals, and their addresses can be found in the local White Pages telephone directory.

Following are the addresses of a few diplomatic missions in Canberra. The area code is (02).

New Zealand: Commonwealth Avenue, Canberra, ✆6270 4211.

👁www.passports.govt.nz

Canada: Commonwealth Avenue, Canberra, ✆6270 4000.

Britain: Commonwealth Avenue, Canberra, ✆6270 6666.

👁www.uk.emb.gov.au

USA: Moonah Place, Yarralumla, ✆6214 6600.

👁usembassy-australia.state.gov/embassy/

Singapore: Forster Crescent, Yarralumla, ✆6273 3944.

Japan: Empire Circuit, Yarralumla, ✆6273 3244.

👁www.japan.org.au

Money

The Australian Currency is decimal, with the dollar as the basic unit. Notes come in a colourful array of $100, $50, $20, $10 and $5 denominations, with minted coins for lesser amounts - gold $1 and $2 coins, and silver 50c, 20c, 10c and 5c.

Currency exchange facilities are available at international airports, and most banks and large hotels.

The Australian dollar tends to fluctuate quite frequently, but approximate rates of exchange at time of writing, which really must be used as a guide only, are:

NZ$	=	A$0.82
CAN$	=	A$1.26
UK£	=	A$2.85
US$	=	A$1.95
S$	=	A$1.09
Baht	=	A$0.04

For the most accurate and up-to-date currency conversions, it is recommended that you use the simple and easy facility at 👁www.xe.net/ucc

Travellers cheques are the most convenient way of carrying money when travelling, and these can be exchanged at any bank, large ho-

tels, and in large department stores. If you are intending to stay in Australia for any length of time, you might consider opening a bank account with automatic teller facilities. Automatic Teller Machines are widely available, both in the cities and in country towns, and most are open 24 hours a day. Different banks have different withdrawal limits, but it is generally about $1000 per day. All Australian banks operate this type of account.

GENERAL INFORMATION

Telephones

If you are calling any Sydney number from overseas, dial 61 for the country code and 2 for the area code, then the eight digit number.

Australia's recently revised area codes have simplified phone numbers across the country. Area codes now refer to states rather than districts. If calling from interstate, use the following prefix before any number you dial to:

New South Wales	- (02)
Australian Capital Territory	- (02)
Victoria	- (03)
Tasmania	- (03)
Queensland	- (07)
South Australia	- (08)
Western Australia	- (08)
Northern Territory	- (08)

Public telephones are easy to find in the cities and suburbs on street corners, in hotels, shops, cafes, and so on. A local call costs 40c from a phone box, but may be dearer from the privately leased phones outside shops. Emergency calls are free.

For international calls, you can dial direct to nearly 20 countries from almost any hotel, home, office or public phone in Australia. Simply dial 0011 + country code + area code + local number. Country Direct is the easiest way of making international telephone card and reverse charge (collect) calls. Upon dialling your Country Direct number, you are immediately put in touch with your own country's operator who will then connect the call. To find out your country's number ✆1800 801 800 (free call).

Newspapers

Morning and afternoon newspapers are available everywhere, with each state having their own press, as well as selling the national paper *The Australian*. There are also several local papers in city and suburban areas which have local news and advise on local events, such as *The Sydney Morning Herald* in Sydney and *The Age* in Melbourne.

Radio and Television

There is a national radio station and a national television channel, both of which are run by the Australian Broadcasting Commission (ABC). The capital cities have many AM and FM radio stations, and several free-to-air television channels. The television channels are: 2 (the national channel), 7 (commercial), 9 (commercial), 10 (commercial) and 0 (SBS, which is government sponsored and has mostly foreign language programs, with English sub-titles). Regional areas broadcast programs on these networks, so their may be slight differences in programming (eg. *WIN* (9) in Wollongong and *Prime* (7) in Newcastle). Cable television is also available.

Post

Australia has an efficient postal service, and postcards sent by airmail to overseas countries cost $1. To send a letter by Air Mail (weighing up to 50g) to the Asia Pacific Zone costs $1 and to the Rest of the World, $1.50.

Time Zones

Australia is divided into three time zones: Australian Eastern Standard Time, which covers Queensland, NSW, Victoria and Tasmania, is GMT plus 10 hours; Australian Central Standard Time, which covers South Australia and the Northern Territory, is GMT plus 9.5 hours; and Australian Western Standard Time, which covers Western Australia, is GMT plus 8 hours.

During summer, some of the states operate on daylight saving, putting their clocks ahead one hour on a designated Sunday morning in October, and back one hour on a Sunday in March. For NSW, Victoria and South Australia, it is the last Sunday in October and the first Sunday in March, but Tasmania remains on Summer Time until the end of March. Western Australia, Queensland and the Northern Territory do not have daylight saving, so at those times there are five different time zones in the country.

Credit Cards

American Express, Diners Club, Visa, JCB, Bank Card and MasterCard are widely accepted and usually signposted at participating retail outlets.

Electricity

Domestic electricity supply throughout Australia is 230-250 volts, AC 50 cycles. Standard three pin plugs are fitted to domestic appliances. 110v appliances, such as hairdryers and contact lens sterilisers, cannot be used without a transformer.

Videos

Australia uses the PAL system of videos. For the US market, tapes must be the NTSC system.

Internet General Information Sources

For general information on Australia, the best site to explore is ☞ www.australia.com which is the offical web page of the Australian Tourist Commission.

For phone numbers nationwide, go to:

☞ www.whitepages.com.au
☞ www.yellowpages.com.au
☞ www.colourpages.com.au

For additonal *Internet Information*, see the section at the back of the book.

Chapter 2
Travel Information

How To Get There

To reach Australia from overseas, visitors must come either by air or sea. Information on arrivals is contained in the *How To Get There* sections of the various cities that accept international flights. Contact details for a number of major airlines is included in the *Internet Information* chapter at the back of the book, including web addresses which will allow you to access current schedules and fares.

Before booking a flight, it is best to shop around for any cheaper fares that may be available. Your travel agent will be able to advise. You may also be able to find a Package Tour that meets all your requirements. These save you money because the companies that organise them can obtain cheaper fares and accommodation prices, as they are booking for groups. Again, your travel agent is the best person to ask.

Accommodation

Australia has well-developed hotel and motel accommodation in cities, resorts and rural areas. A typical room is usually spotlessly clean and has air-conditioning, a private bathroom, tea and coffee making facilities, a telephone, television, and a small refrigerator. Note that some small hotels may not have a private bathroom for every room, and it is best to enquire when booking. Because of the climate, many hotels and motels have small outdoor swimming pools.

Although the rooms are often the same, there is a difference between a hotel and a motel in Australia. A hotel must have a public bar among its facilities; motels often provide a bar for paying guests and invited friends, although they are not obliged to do this. Most hotels and motels have a dining room or restaurant.

Premier class hotels include names familiar throughout the world - Hilton, Sheraton, Hyatt, Nikko, Holiday Inn, Intercontinental, Marriott, Ibis and Mercure, can all be found in Australia's major cities.

Motels have generally been developed to meet the needs of travelling motorists and are located in cities, towns and resorts, and along the major highways.

The majority of hotels and motels offer accommodation on a room-only basis, but some include one or more meals in their tariff. Enquire about any meals that might be automatically included in the room price and check whether you can pay just for the room, if this suites your travel schedule better. For example, there is no point paying for lunch if you plan on leaving before daybreak, or for a dinner if you know you won't reach your destination until late.

Youth Hostels in most parts of the country offer an inexpensive alternative for budget conscious travellers. Membership of the Youth Hostels Association is required, ✆9261 1111. They have a comprehensive internet site showing all the hostel loctions at 👁www.yha.com.au and an email service at ✎yha@yhansw.org.au

Most towns and holiday resorts have caravan parks and camping grounds with shower and toilet facilities, at very reasonable rates. Caravan parks usually have some cabins or on-site vans available for overnight or longer stays. This is a comparatively inexpensive form of accommodation, but it usually means that you have to have your own bed linen, blankets and pillows.

Travelling Within Australia
By Air

The major interstate carrier is Qantas, ✆13 1313. Virgin Blue, ✆13 6789 and Ansett, ✆13 1300 offer limited services. All three offer reduced fares and 'specials' from time to time, and it is best to find out what is available when you intend to travel.

At the time of printing, the airlines listed above are in the process of significant changes, so it is best to check with an AFTA travel agent, listed in the phone book, about regional flights at the time of your trip.

By Rail

Train travel is possible between Brisbane, Syd-

Travel Information

ney and Melbourne, and from Sydney to Canberra. Most towns in between are also linked, as well as those in popular outlying areas of each state. Rail Australia offers two rail passes that can only be purchased *outside* of Australia:

Austrail Flexipass - 8 (✪$550), 15 (✪$800), 22 (✪$110) or 29 (✪$1440) days travel in 6 months with unlimited stopovers, in economy class.

Austrail Pass - unlimited travel for 14 (✪$660), 21 (✪$860) or 30 (✪$1035) days consecutively anywhere in Australia, including metropolitan services, in economy class.

Passes that are available *within* Australia include:

East Coast Discovery Pass - travel one-way with unlimited stopovers in a six month period: Brisbane to Cairns (✪$160); Sydney to Brisbane/Gold Coast (✪$94); Sydney to Cairns (✪$248); Melbourne to Sydney (✪$176); Melbourne to Brisbane/Gold Coast (✪$176); Melbourne to Cairns (✪$228). Note that the above rates apply to travel in the opposite direction.

Countrylink Discovery Pass - unlimited use of Countrylink trains and connecting coaches for 14 (✪$165), 30 (✪$198), 90 (✪$220), or 180 (✪$330) days.

Queensland Road Rail Pass - unlimited use of Queensland Rail services (long-distance) and McCaffertys Coaches for any 10 days over a 60 day period (✪$286) or any 20 days over a 90 day period (✪$374).

To get the latest prices, visit the Rail Australia web site at 👁www.railaustralia.com.au/pass_rates.htm

By Bus

The major interstate coach companies are Greyhound Pioneer and McCafferty's. Tickets for both companies are now interchangeable.

McCafferty's, ☎13 1499, 👁www.mcaffertys.com.au

Aussie Passes: a pre-selected travel route along which you can stop off at designated points.

All Australian
Validity: 365 days
Cost: ✪$2100 full fare, ✪$1790 concession.

Aussie Highlights
Route: Melbourne - Sydney - Brisbane - Cairns

- Uluru (Ayers Rock) - Adelaide - Canberra and many other outback, rural and coastal destinations in between.
Validity: 365 days
Cost: ✪$1255 full fare, ✪$1066 concession.

Sunseeker
Validity: 183 days
Cost: ✪$411 full fare, ✪$349 concession.

Best of the West
Validity: 365 days
Cost: ✪$1263 full fare, ✪$1074 concession.

Best of the East
Validity: 365 days
Cost: ✪$1026 full fare, ✪$872 concession.

Coast to Coast
Validity: 183 days
Cost: ✪$424 full fare, ✪$360 concession.

Western Explorer
Validity: 183 days
Cost: ✪$589 full fare, ✪$501 concession.

Reef & Rock
Validity: 183 days
Cost: ✪$596 full fare, ✪$507 concession.

Rock Track
Validity: 90 days
Cost: ✪$398 full fare, ✪$338 concession.

Outback & Reef
Validity: 183 days
Cost: ✪$726 full fare, ✪$617 concession.

An *Aussie Kilometre Pass*, valid for 12 months, allows you to 'bulk buy' the distance you think you will need to cover for your holiday, at a rate designed to increase your value for money with every kilometre purchased. Prices range from ✪$281 for 2000km to ✪$1077 for 10,000km to ✪$1975 for 20,000km.

By Road

Australians drive on the left-hand side of the road, and the speed limit in built-up areas is 50km/h or 60km/h, and on the open road up to 110km/h.

In an effort to cut the number of road fatalities, Australia has random breath testing which is carried out by police officers either from a standard police car or from what are known locally as 'booze buses'. The allowable blood alcohol level varies from state to state, but is generally around 0.05, or two standard drinks in the first hour and only one during every subsequent hour. But since body tolerance levels differ, it is best simply not to drink if you expect to drive soon after.

Eating Out

In every town and city in this guide we have included a selection of restaurants, and have stated whether they are licensed or unlicensed (BYO). Just to confuse everyone, some restaurants are both, so if you are unsure, check when reserving your table. Without going into the licensing laws of why this is so, here is a short explanation of how it will affect patrons.

A licensed restaurant has a wine list, and can provide beer, mixed drinks, ports, liqueurs, etc. Patrons are not allowed to provide their own drinks.

A BYO restaurant does not have a licence, so you Bring Your Own wine or beer or whatever. Glasses are provided, and a corkage fee (for opening the bottles!) may be charged, which is usually around $1.50 per bottle. The restaurant usually has a selection of soft drinks, mineral water and fruit juices.

A restaurant that is licensed and BYO can provide alcohol, but you have the choice of bringing your own wine (which works out cheaper), but you are not allowed to bring your own beer or mixed drinks.

Liquor stores in Australia are called 'bottle shops'. Many hotels have one, usually with its own street entrance, and there's one in every shopping centre.

Shopping

Toy kangaroos and koalas are high on everyone's shopping list, and are available everywhere. Everything Aboriginal is popular, and although it seems more appropriate to buy them in the Outback regions, they are available in the big cities in specialty shops.

Probably the most sought after articles, though, are opals. Australia produces more than 90% of the world's opals, and the three main areas where they are found are Lightning Ridge in western NSW, which produces the Black Opal; Quilpie, where the Queensland Boulder Opal originates; and Coober Pedy in South Australia, which has the White or Milk Opal.

When buying opals there are a few terms you should know:

Solid Opal - this is the most valuable, and good for investment purposes. The more colourful and complete, the greater its value.

Doublet - this is slices of opal glued together, and is of medium value. It has no investment value.

Triplet - this is slices of opal covered with quartz, perspex or glass, and is the least expensive. It has no investment value.

If your pocket can't stretch as far as a solid opal, but you still would like a piece of opal jewellery, remember that anything that is glued can come unstuck, and that condensation can form under perspex or glass. The less expensive types of opal are not suitable for rings, unless you are going to remember to take it off every time you wash your hands.

Beaches

Australian beaches are famous throughout the world, and they certainly live up to their reputation. All have white sandy shores, and rolling surf. Some offer better waves than others, and the bigger beaches are usually divided into sections for swimmers and for board riders.

The Surf Lifesaving Clubs which patrol the beaches during summer are staffed by voluntary workers, young people who give up their weekends and holidays to keep a watchful eye out for others. They put up flags to show which part of the beach is safest for swimmers, and there are usually signs requesting people to swim between the flags. This is good advice - don't ignore it.

Chapter 3
Warrnambool

Part Two
Australia's East Coast

Population 28,000

Warrnambool is situated on the coast, 263km (163 miles) south-west of Melbourne, where the Princes Highway meets the Great Ocean Road.

Climate

Average temperatures: January max 23C (73F) - min 13C (55F); July max 14C (57F) - min 6C (43F). Average hours of sunshine: summer 8, autumn 4, winter 3, spring 5. Wettest six months May-October.

Characteristics

Warrnambool was popular with the old whalers and sealers, as they could repair their boats and process their catches on its wide beaches. Due to reduced hunting, Warrnambool is now visited each year by a herd of the rare Southern Right whales, and a viewing platform has been erected at Logan's Beach to enable visitors to obtain a better view of the whales, which usually remain in the area for several weeks.

How to Get There

By Bus
Greyhound Pioneer, ✆13 2030, stop at Warrnambool on the Melbourne/Adelaide coastal route.

By Rail
There is a regular V/Line service between Melbourne and Warrnambool, ✆13 6196.

By Road
From Melbourne, travel to Geelong and then take the Princes Highway if you are in a hurry, but if you have more time, then take one of Australia's really beautiful roads, the Great Ocean Road which follows the coast and passes through Lorne.

Warrnambool is 263km (163 miles) from Melbourne via the Princes Highway, 211km (131 miles) from Mt Gambier, and 654km (406 miles) from Adelaide.

Visitor Information

The Tourist Information Office is at 600 Raglan Parade, ✆(03) 5564 7837, and it is ◷open daily 9am-5pm, or you can email the manager at ✉nan_adams@wcc.mav.asn.au

The website to visit is ☞www.warrnambool.org

In addition, Shipwreck Coast Tourism can be found at 174a Timor Street, ✆5561 7894.

Accommodation

Here is a selection of accommodation, with prices for a double room per night, which should be used as a guide only. The telephone area code is 03.

Guthrie Heights Apartment, 8/148 Merri Street, ✆5562 1600. 1 unit, 3 queen ensuites, sea views, barbecue - ✪$160.

Warrnambool Heritage Cottage, 26 MacDonald Street, ✆5562 6531. Private courtyard, barbecue - ✪$120-160.

Sundowner Chain Motor Inn, 525 Raglan Parade, ✆5562 3866. 60 units, licensed restaurant, swimming pool, spa - ✪$110-200.

Tudor Motel Warrnambool, 519 Raglan Parade, ✆5562 8877. 22 units, licensed restaurant (closed Sunday off-season), spa - ✪$100-150.

Olde Maritime Motor Inn, cnr Merri & Banyan Streets, ✆5561 1415. 37 units, licensed restaurant, spa - ✪$90-170.

Western Coast Motel, 349 Raglan Parade, ✆5562 2755. 21 units, restaurant - ✪$80-120.

Warrnambool Gateway Motor Inn, 69 Raglan Parade, ✆5562 8622. 26 units, *Quigley's* licensed restaurant (closed Sunday), barbecue, heated swimming pool - ✪$90-125.

Warrnambool Hotel, cnr Koroit & Keppler Streets, ✆5562 2377. 16 rooms, a la carte restaurant - ✪$70 including breakfast.

Motel Downtown Warrnambool, 620 Raglan Parade, ✆5562 1277. 58 units, heated swimming pool, spa - ✪$70-200.

Western Hotel, cnr Timor & Kepler Streets, ✆5562 2011. 20 units, standard facilities - ✪$60.

Bed and Breakfast

Merton Manor B&B, 62 Ardlie Street, ✆5562

0720. 6 rooms, barbecue - ✪$150-170.

Casa D'Oro B&B, 42 Shady's Lane, ✆5565 4243. 3 rooms, barbecue, comfortable rooms - ✪$90.

Whalesway, 6 Florence Street, ✆5661 2660. 2 rooms, barbecue - ✪$75-80.

Caravan Parks

Ocean Beach Holiday Village, Pertobe Road, ✆5561 4222. 58 sites, 26 cabins, no pets, barbecue, heated pool - powered sites ✪$19-24 for two. No on-site vans, but cabins are $52-115 for two.

Warrnambool Holiday Park, cnr Raglan Parade & Simpson Street, ✆5562 5031. 17 sites, 17 cabins, no dogs, barbecue, heated pool - powered sites ✪$16-22, on-site vans $45 for two, cabins $50-75.

Fig Tree Holiday Village, 33 Lava Street, ✆5561 1233. 72 sites, 23 cabins, no pets, barbecue - powered sites ✪$15-26 for two, cabins $46-80.

Caravarna Lodge, 81 Henna Street, ✆5562 3376. 42 sites, 4 cabins, barbecue, heated pool - powered sites ✪$12-15 for two, on-site vans $22-35 for two, cabins $27-45.

Hostels

Warrnambool Beach Backpackers, 17 Stanley Street, ✆5562 4874. 6 rooms, cooking facilities, guest dining - ✪$15.

Backpackers Barn, 90 Lava Street, ✆5562 2073. 15 rooms, cooking and dining - ✪$14.

Eating Out

There are over 50 places to have a meal in Warrnambool, from cafes to quality restaurants, and the Tourist Information Office will have details. Here is a selection.

Balenas Cafe, 158 Timor Street, ✆5562 0900. Contemporary Australian cuisine as well as seafood and steaks with Italian, Mediterranean and International influences. Open 7 days.

Jukes Cafe Restaurant, 525 Raglan Parade, ✆5562 3866. A-la-carte menu with entertainment on Saturday evening. Licensed, open seven days for breakfast and dinner.

Oriental Restaurant, 80-82 Liebig Street, ✆5562 7079. BYO, Chinese and Australian fare, lunch and dinner, open 7 days.

Mahogany Ship, 91 Merri Street, ✆5561 3866. Australian seafood steak and pasta is served in this Scottish themed restaurant. A-la-carte dining with sea views.

Bojangles, 61 Liebig Street, ✆5562 8751. Award-winning Italian restaurant offering wood-fire pizzas and pastas as a specialty. Licensed, open for dinner only.

Beach Babylon, 72 Liebig Street, ✆5562 3714. Seafood with Mediterranean and Australian flavours. Open every day.

Restaurant Malaysia, 69 Liebig Street, ✆5562 2051. Also has Thai, Indian and Chinese dishes, BYO, open 7 days, noon-2pm, 6pm to late. Yum Cha, Sun noon-2pm.

Freshwater, 78 Liebig Street, ✆5561 3188. Licensed restaurant serving modern Australian and International cuisine and offering local wines.

The Blues, 142 Timor Street, ✆5562 2033. Family oriented dining with live local music. Australian seafood and steaks.

Images, Liebig Street, ✆5562 4208. Licensed restaurant with a family atmosphere.

Breakers, 79 Banyan Street, ✆5561 3088. All types of seafood served in an Australian style.

Clovelly, cnr Banyan & Merri Streets, ✆5561 1415. A-la-carte menu with seafood, steak and pasta.

Dragon Inn, 219 Lava Street, ✆5562 1517. Chinese cuisine.

Points of Interest

Flagstaff Hill Maritime Museum, Merri Street, ✆5564 7841, recreates the atmosphere of an early Australian coastal port. The lighthouse and associated buildings, and the 1887 fortifications are the original features of the site, and around them the village has been created. The story of shipping and the sea unfolds for visitors as they tour the village. Each building portrays an important aspect of port life in the last century, whether it be the role of the Ship Chandler or the function of the Mission to Seamen Church. Among the relics on display there is the Loch Ard peacock: an 1851 Minton porcelain statue which was washed up (still in its packing case) in Loch Ard Gorge after a shipwreck. The mu-

Warrnambool

seum is ⏱open daily 9.00am-5.00pm. Admission is adults ✪$12, child $6, pensioner $10, family $30.

Lake Pertobe Park has causeways, walking tracks, a maze, a flying fox, paddle boats and a well-equipped Adventure Playground behind the surf beach of Lady Bay.

Fletcher Jones Gardens, cnr Flaxman Street and Raglan Parade, are a colourful advocate for Victoria's claim as the Garden State of Australia. Thousands of visitors come each year to see these gardens.

The Performing Arts and Conference Centre, 185 Timor Street, is a modern-style building situated in landscaped grounds in the heart of the business and restaurant district. It has three main venues suitable for stage presentations, conventions, dinners, cabarets, exhibitions, lectures, classes and meetings. Check the daily newspapers for programmes, or ✆5564 7904.

Warrnambool Art Gallery, 165 Timor Street, has a permanent collection of 19th and 20th century Australian and European paintings and graphics - ⏱open daily noon-5pm, ✆5564 7832. The **Warrnambool Botanic Gardens** are on the corner of Botanic and Queen Streets.

Tower Hill State Game Reserve, 14km (9 miles) from Warrnambool, is the remains of a volcano whose crater walls collapsed inward during its dying stages 6000 years ago. They blocked the 3km wide crater, which later filled with water. There is a sealed road leading to the main island, from where bushwalks radiate. There is also a **Natural History Centre**, ⏱open 9.00am-4.30pm daily, which conducts tours, ✆5565 9202.

Hopkins Falls, are 13km (8 miles) from Warrnambool, near Wangoom. Thousands of tiny eels (elvers) make their way up the falls to the quiet waters beyond, to grow to maturity before returning to the sea to breed.

There are several recommended **heritage walks** through the town and nearby regions, and the Tourist Centre can provide you with maps and other details.

Warrnambool also has **a mystery!** There have been several reported sightings of the wreck of a mahogany ship in the windswept sandhills west of the city. The last was in 1980, and several artefacts have been found in the area. It is said that the ship foundered 400 years ago with a complement of Dutch and Spanish sailors. If there is any substance to the story it means that Europeans set foot on Australian soil long before Captain Cook. In 1980 the City Council formed a Mahogany Ship Committee to compile all the known information, which is being fed into a computer in an endeavour to solve the mystery.

Festivals

Wunta Fiesta - February.
Racing Carnival - May
Melbourne-Warrnambool Cycling Classic - October.

Facilities

Aerobics, badminton, basketball, volleyball, bingo, boating, lawn bowls, indoor cricket, croquet, golf, greyhound racing, horse racing, swimming, mini golf, scuba diving, skin diving, squash, speedway, surfing, swimming, table tennis, tennis, ten pin bowling, waterskiing, windsurfing and yachting.

Here are a few specific activity venues:

Karting

Indoor Karting, Silverton Park, ✆5562 2422. Open Wed-Fri noon-late, Sat-Sun 11am-late.

Golf

Mini Golf Lake Pertobe, 47 Pertrobe Road, ✆5562 0644. Open Dec-Jan - 10am-close, Feb-Nov - noon-5pm.

Horse-riding

Rundells Mahagany Trail Rides, Millers Lane, Dennington via Warrnambool, ✆5529 2303. One and two hour trail rides, full day pub rides, twilight rides and riding lessons. Horse riding mainly along the beach.

Fishing

Warrnambool Trout Farm, 4km north of Warrnambool on Wollaston Road, ✆019 94 3396. Catches guaranteed, equipment supplied free, fish feeding, barbecue. ⏰Open every weekend 10.30am-5pm, 7 days during school holidays.

Tours

Regular tours on the new *Sprit of Warrnambool*, lasting from 1-1.5 hours return. ⏰Open 10am-6pm with nighttime charters available. Adults ✪$13, children $7.

Southern Right Charters and Diving, ✆5561 6222 or ✆5562 5044, offer fishing charters, diving charters, whale watching tours and scenic tours.

Seeall Tours, 13 Barham Avenue, ✆5562 5795, have six tours through various locations, costing between ✪$12 and $55.

Warrnambool River Cruises, 2 Simpson Street, can be contacted on ✆5562 7788.

Outlying Attractions

Port Fairy

The pretty town of Port Fairy is 29km (18 miles) from Warrnambool. The first stop for all visitors should be the Visitor Information Centre in 22 Bank Street, ✆(03) 5568 2682, as this historic town has many attractions. Over 50 buildings have been classified by the National Trust, and there many art, craft and antique shops, picnic and barbecue areas, and facilities for golf, tennis, squash, lawn bowls and boat trips. There are heritage buildings outlined in brochures available from the Visitor Centre, and the Port Fairy History Centre in Gipps Street should satisfy anyone interested in nineteenth-century memorabilia.

High on the list of attractions, though, is not man-made. It is the **Mutton Bird Rookery** on Griffiths Island. The bird gets its name from early settlers who utilised its fatty flesh for food, and as an oil source, but it is really the short-tailed shearwater (*puffinus tenuirostris*). They are not much to look at, but their lifestyle is fascinating. They arrive at Griffiths Island within three days of September 22 each year, returning to

A section of the craggy shipwreck coast

the nest burrow they had the previous year, with the same partner. They spend a few weeks renovating their homes, mate in early November, then fly out to sea for a couple of weeks. They return to Port Fairy about November 25, immediately lay their eggs (one per family), then both parents share in the incubation until the egg hatches in mid-January. After two or three days, the parents leave the chicks and forage at sea for food, firstly only for the day, regurgitating the food for the chicks at night, then gradually increasing the period and distance of food gathering until the chick has up to two weeks between meals. Nevertheless it gains weight rapidly and for a period becomes heavier than the adult birds. In mid-April the adult birds hear the call of the wild, commence their Pacific migration, and leave the young behind to fend for themselves. Hunger finally forces the chicks from the nest at night, and in early May they set off after the adults, somehow finding the migratory route with no help from mum or dad.

Obviously, the mortality rate is high, and it is not helped by stray dogs and cats, and visitors who do not stick to the formed tracks, and tramp through the burrows instead. In fact, one year 80% of the young chicks were lost because some people were careless while exploring the area.

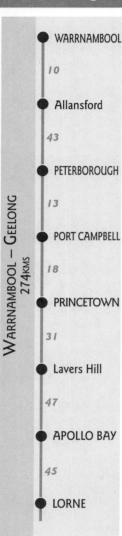
Chapter 4
Warrnambool to Geelong

Great Ocean Road

The spectacular Great Ocean Road follows the coastline for much of its 250 kilometre (156 miles) length from Torquay to Peterborough. In some parts it is the only thing separating the mountains from the surf beaches.

The road was built by 3000 First World War veterans, and was dedicated to the memory of all those who fought in that war. Using picks and shovels, the men commenced work in 1919 and the road was opened in 1932.

Fully sealed, though narrow in parts, it wends its scenic route through some of Victoria's most popular resorts. Pretty coastal towns like Lorne, Apollo Bay and Port Campbell swell to capacity in the high season. But it is in the winter, when massive breakers crash into the limestone cliffs, that the challenge which confronted the captains of the small coastal vessels can be understood. In the period to 1920, some 80 major shipping disasters were recorded between Port Fairy and Cape Otway. Of these the best known are the *Loch Ard* and the *Schomberg*, relics of

which can be seen in the Flagstaff Hill Maritime Village at Warrnambool.

The road also passes through some of the richest forests in Australia. The Angahook Forest Park, the Otway National Park and the Lorne Forest Park are all extensive forest systems with prolific fauna.

We will finish our trip along the Great Ocean Road at Lorne, which is 218km (135 miles) from Warrnambool, and less than 2 hours' drive from Melbourne.

As an additional resource, the website that covers the general area is ☞www.greatoceanrd.org.au

Peterborough

Population 200
Location and Characteristics
Situated at the mouth of the Curdie's River, Peterborough is a popular summer holiday town where you can get away from it all.

Accommodation and Services
Peterborough Motel, 9 Irvine Street, ✆5598 5251. 12 units, barbecue, heated pool, spa - ✪$65-100.
Schomberg Inn, Great Ocean Road, ✆5598 5285. 8 units, licensed restaurant, barbecue, minimal room facilities - ✪$55-75.
Great Ocean Road Tourist Park, Great Ocean Road, ✆5598 5477. (No pets allowed) 116 sites, barbecue, minimal facilities - powered sites ✪$16 for two, cabins $44-60 for two.

Points of Interest
River or beach swimming, and fishing for bream, mullet or crayfish are among the main pastimes, while the shipwrecks in the area provide good diving and aqualunging.

Port Campbell

Location and Characteristics
At the heart of one of Australia's most famed and photographed natural attractions, Port

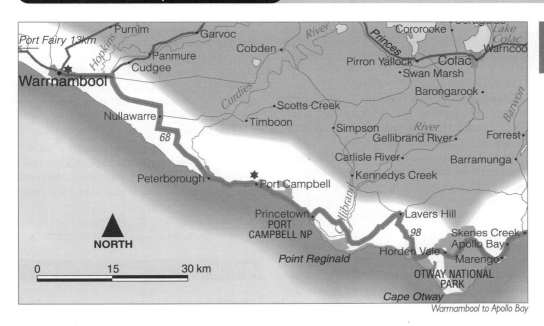

Warrnambool to Apollo Bay

Campbell is a very popular resort. Situated on Campbell's Creek, and named after Capt. Alexander Campbell, a Scotsman in charge of the Port Fairy whaling station, it began as a small fishing port with surrounding pastoral runs.

In 1964, 700ha (1729 acres) around Port Campbell was set aside as a National Park, and in 1981 the park was extended from Princetown through to Peterborough. Port Campbell is roughly at the centre of the park.

The town is a crayfishing port near the mouth of the river and has a safe, sandy beach ideal for family swimming. Restaurants and take-away foods are available and fresh local crayfish is the specialty.

Visitor Information
The Port Campbell Visitor Information Centre, is in 26 Morris Street, ✆5598 6089.

Accommodation and Services
Several motels and a caravan park provide accommodation, but it is wise to book well ahead.
Great Ocean Road Motor Inn, 10 Great Ocean Road, ✆5598 6522. 14 units, good room quality - ✪$120-175.
Southern Ocean Motor Inn, Lord Street, ✆5598 6231 or ✆1800 035 093. 1 unit, licensed restaurant, standard facilities, room service - ✪$105-175.
Port Campbell Caravan Park, Tregea Street, ✆5598 6492. (No pets allowed) 106 sites, minimal facilities - powered sites ✪$12-25 for two, cabins $50-80 for two.

There is a **Youth Hostel** in 18 Tregea Street, ✆5598 6305. It has 4 rooms at ✪$14 per person.

Points of Interest
Of course the **Port Campbell National Park** itself is the attraction (see entry overleaf), but whilst in Port Campbell you can take a trip to the old cemetery on the northern edge of the town. It has many old graves of interest, including that of Captain Scott and some of his crew, shipwrecked off the coast in the barque *Newfield* in 1892.

A look-out on the western side of the river offers a scenic panorama of the town and coastline.

Port Campbell National Park

Location and Characteristics
Recognised as one of Australia's most scenic sections of coastline, the 1750ha (4323 acres) Port Campbell National Park stretches 32km (20 miles) along the Great Ocean Road.

The best known features are the **Twelve Apostles**, **Loch Ard Gorge** and **London Bridge**. In early 1990 a span of London Bridge collapsed into the ocean, vividly demonstrating the ongoing erosion of wind and sea on the limestone cliffs of the park.

Gorges, arches, islands, blowholes and stark outcrops create a dramatic foreground to the stormy Southern Ocean which stretches to the Antarctic. Here and there a sandy beach glistens in sharp contrast to the sheer cliffs and deep inlets which offer some of the most interesting scenery and photography subjects you will find.

Camping
Dogs and cats are allowed in the park provided they remain in cars on main roads, however they are not permitted in the camping ground. All native plants and animals are protected and fires may only be lit in the fireplaces provided.

Further information on the park can be acquired by calling ©13 1963.

Princetown

Location and Characteristics
Situated on the La Trobe Creek near Gellibrand River, the surrounding limestone cliffs contain interesting fossils and formations. Gemstones can sometimes be found along the coastline, and the area is rich in flora and fauna. Princetown was named after Prince Alfred and was proclaimed in 1885.

Accommodation and Services
Twelve Apostles Motel & Country Retreat, 1435 Booringa Road, ©5598 8277 or ©1800 351 233 (toll free). 13 units, licensed restaurant, recreation room, playground, indoor heated pool - ✪$80-110.

Apostles Camping Park, Post Office Road, ©5598 8119. (Pets allowed) 40 sites, minimal facilities - powered sites ✪$12 for two.

Points of Interest
Given its location between the western boundary of the **Otway National Park** and the eastern boundary of the **Port Campbell National Park**, Princetown is ideal as a base for touring both.

Safe swimming, boating, fishing and water skiing are all features of this tiny settlement.

Apollo Bay

Population 2000
Location and Characteristics
Apollo Bay was first visited in 1840 by the Henty Brothers, founders of Portland and Mount Gambier. They established a small whaling station on what is now the golf course. One of the three major centres along the Great Ocean Road, it has all facilities to offer the visitor - motels, hotels, holiday flats, lodges and caravan parks; several restaurants and take-away food places.

Visitor Information
The Visitor Information Centre is on the Great Ocean Road, ©(03) 5237 6529.

Accommodation and Services
Apollo International, 37 Great Ocean Road, ©5237 6100. 24 units, pool, spa, basic room facilities - ✪$110-180.

Apollo Bay Motel, 2 Moore Street, ©5237 7577. 12 units, good room facilities, barbecue, playground, pool, spa, sauna - ✪$95-155.

Great Ocean View Motel, 1 Great Ocean Road, ©5237 6527. 11 units, minimal room facilities, barbecue - ✪$70-170.

Kooringal Holiday Park, 27 Kawood Street, ©5237 7111. (No pets allowed) 65 sites, playground, good facilities - powered sites ✪$18-

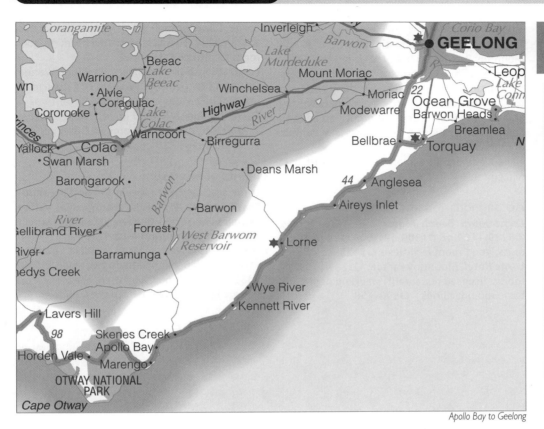

WARRNAMBOOL – GEELONG 274KMS

LORNE

18

Aireys Inlet

11

Anglesea

38

GEELONG

Apollo Bay to Geelong

27 for two, cabins $42-85 for two.
Recreation Reserve Caravan Park, Great Ocean Road, ℂ5237 6577. (Dogs allowed) 260 sites, minimal facilities - powered sites ✪$16.

There is a **Youth Hostel** on the corner of Great Ocean Road and Gambier Street, ℂ5237 7263 or ℂ1800 357 263 (toll free). It has 7 rooms at ✪$20 per person twin share.

There are also many guest houses, B&Bs and cottages in Apollo Bay, so if you prefer these cosy kinds of accommodation, the Information Centre can give you an idea of what is on offer.

Points of Interest
Apollo Bay is an ideal touring centre for the **Otway Ranges Forest Park**, **Otway National Park**, and **Melba Gully State Park**.

Lorne

Population 1200
Location and Characteristics
On the Erskine River, surrounded on three sides by forest ranges, and to the south by the Southern Ocean, Lorne was the first place declared an area of Special Significance and Natural Beauty by the Victorian Government.

On a bay named after Capt Louttit, who sought shelter there around 1840 while retrieving cargo from a shipwreck, Lorne was first settled by William Lindsay, a timber-cutter. Subdivision began in 1869 and the town was named after the Marquis of Lorne. Much of its colourful history is preserved in the gracious homes which remain.

Visitor Information

The Lorne Visitor Information Centre is at 144 Mountjoy Parade, ℂ5289 1152. It is ⏰open daily 9am-5pm. They can provide you with excellent information on absolutely everything you need to know to about this area, from where to stay and eat, to what to see and do. If you wish to contact them by email, the address is ✉lornevic @primus.com.au

The web page to explore is ☞www.surfcoast .vic.gov.au

Accommodation and Services

Lorne Main Beach Motor Inn, 3 Bay Street, ℂ5289 1199 or ℂ1800 681 008 (toll free). 34 units, good room facilities - ✪$125-265.
Lorne Hotel, Mountjoy Parade, ℂ5289 1409. 19 rooms, licensed restaurant, weekend nightclub, basic room facilities - ✪$90-150.

Lorne Coachman Inn, 1 Deans Marsh Road, ℂ5289 2244. 19 units, undercover parking, good room facilities - ✪$85-160.
Lorne Foreshore Reserves, Erskine Avenue, ℂ5289 1382. (No dogs allowed) 104 sites, minimal facilities - powered sites ✪$12 for two.
There is a **Youth Hostel** in 10 Erskine Avenue, ℂ5289 1809. It has 7 rooms at ✪$18 per person twin share.

Points of Interest

Lorne's attractions include **Lorne Angahook State Park**, **Erskine Falls**, **Pennyroyal Valley**, as well as numerous bushwalks leading through lush fauna to beautiful waterfalls.

Lorne is now serviced by an excellent bookshop - Lorne Beach Books on Mountjoy Parade, ℂ5289 2489. Meryl will spoil you rotten, one of the most knowledgeable booksellers in the country.

Chapter 5
Geelong

Population 145,300
Geelong is on the shores of Corio Bay, southwest of Melbourne.

Climate

Average temperatures: June max 25C (77F) - min 13C (55F); July max 14C (57F) - min 5C (41F).

Characteristics

Geelong is Victoria's premier regional city and, in fact, was a more important commercial centre than Melbourne in the 1840s. It is the natural gateway to the richest wool and wheat areas of the world. The city has many antique and arts and crafts shops.

How to Get There

By Air

Geelong has its own regional airport which can be contacted on ✆5264 1273.

By Rail

Trains run frequently between Melbourne and Geelong, ✆13 1368.

By Coach

V/Line services Geelong frequently, ✆13 6196.

By Car

From Melbourne, via the Princes Highway (74km-46miles).

Visitor Information

The Geelong and Great Ocean Road Tourist Information Centre is in Stead Park on the Princes Highway, ✆(03) 5275 5797. More information can be found at the Wool Museum on Moorabool Street, ✆5222 2900 or ✆1800 620 888 (free call).

The website to visit is ✎www.greatoceanrd. org.au (there are no email contact facilities).

The Melbourne website ✎www.melbourne. citysearch.com.au also lists information on Geelong.

If you are wandering around the city, keep in mind that there is an information outlet in the Market Square Shopping Centre in Moorabool Street. Another can be found on the corner of Princes Highway and St Georges Road, Corio.

Accommodation

Following is a selection of hotels, with prices for a double room per night. Please use this as a guide only. The telephone area code is 03.

Mercure Hotel Geelong, cnr Gheringhap & Myers Streets, ✆5221 6844. 142 units, 3 suites, licensed restaurant, pool, spa, sauna - ✪$140.

Sundowner Chain Motor Inn, 13 The Esplanade, ✆5222 3499. 35 units, licensed restaurant, sauna, pool - ✪$105-175.

Flag Inn Eastern Sands, 1 Bellerine Street, ✆5221 5577. 25 units, licensed restaurant, carport parking - ✪$95-125.

Rose Garden Motor Inn, 14 Settlement Road (Princes Highway), ✆5241 9441. 15 units, spas, carport parking - ✪$85-115.

Aristocrat Waurnvale Motel, 90 Princes Highway, ✆5241 8211. 14 units, spa bath, pool, playground - ✪$70-85.

Huntsman Innkeepers Motor Inn, 9 Aberdeen Street, ✆5221 2177. 36 units, licensed restaurant (closed Sunday), pool, spa, sauna - ✪$75-90.

Colonial Lodge Motel, 57 Fyans Street, ✆5223 2266. 10 units - ✪$65-75.

The Ponds Hotel Motel, Princes Highway, ✆5243 1244. 15 units, licensed restaurant - ✪$65-70.

Kangaroo Motel, 16 The Esplanade, ✆5221 4022. 10 units, licensed restaurant (closed Sunday) - ✪$70-75.

Caravan Parks

Barwon Caravan & Tourist Park, 153 Barrabool Road, ✆5243 3842. (No pets allowed) 191 sites, barbecue, playground - powered sites ✪$16 for two, cabins $45-55 for two.

City Southside Caravan Park, 87 Barrabool Road, ✆5243 3788. (No dogs allowed) 90 sites, barbecue, playground - powered sites ✪$15 for two, cabins $45-60 for two.

Billabong Caravan Park, 59 Barrabool Road,

Geelong

©5243 6225. (No pets allowed) 97 sites, barbecue, playground, pool - powered sites ✪$14-16 for two, cabins $45-60 for two.

Sherwood Forest Caravan Park, 70 Bailey Street, ©5243 1068. (Pets allowed at owner's discretion) 120 sites, pool, playground - self-contained sites ✪$12-14 for two, on-site vans $20-27 for two, cabins $32-38 for two.

Eating Out

Geelong has a good selection of restaurants, with all nationalities represented. Also remember that some of the motels have restaurants serving reasonably-priced meals. Recommended restaurants are:

Bamboleo, 86 Little Malop Street, ©5229 2548. Licensed restaurant with Spanish cuisine.

Rheingold Cellar, 9 Malop Street, ©5222 2557. Traditional German and Continental dishes. The restaurant has an historic theme and light entertainment to liven the atmosphere.

Le Parisien, 15 Eastern Beach Road, ©5229 3110. Licensed restaurant that has an extensive wine list boasting more than 350 selections. Waterside frontage and seafood specialities.

Empire Grill, 66 McKillop Street, ©5223 2132. Licensed restaurant with regional wines and a-la-carte dining.

Mexican Graffiti, 43 Yarra Street, ©5222 2036. All types of Californian-style Mexican food available. Fully licensed. Open from 11am daily.

Mei Ling, 169 Malop Street, ©5229 7505. Chinese food with dine-in, take-away or home delivery options.

Fisherman's Pier, Bay end of Yarra Street, ©5222 4100. Fully licensed seafood restaurant overlooking Corio Bay. Outside dining, family oriented menu. Open daily for both lunch and dinner.

King Edward VII, above the Sailors Rest Tavern, 3 Moorabool Street, ©5224 2241. Modern international cuisine with alfresco dining and water views.

Pastels by the Bay, 13 The Esplanade, ©5222 3499. Fully licensed, bay views, open daily for lunch and dinner.

Pearl of China Cafe, 154 Ryrie Street, ©5229

Part of the rocky southern Victorian coastline

8895. Take-away, home delivery or a-la-carte.

Sirinda, 93 Ryrie Street, ©5221 5797. Thai restaurant.

Koaki, Bell Parade, ©5272 1925. Traditional Japanese food.

Samraat, 137 Pakington Street, Geelong West, ©5229 7995. Indian cuisine.

McDonalds have branches on the corner of Ryrie and Yarra Streets, Geelong; 400 Melbourne Road, Geelong North; and 230-236 Autumn Street, Geelong West.

Points of Interest

Geelong was first settled in the 1930s and has several historic buildings within walking distance of the city centre. The Information Centre has details of a Heritage Walk that starts from the Post Office on the corner of Ryrie and Gheringhap Streets.

The National Wool Museum, cnr Moorabool & Brougham Streets, ©5227 0701, is housed in a bluestone wool store and traces the story of wool from the sheep's back to the finished garment. Wool auctions are still held here. ⏱Open daily 9.30am-5pm, and admission is ✪$8 adults, $4 children and $20 for families.

Geelong Art Gallery, Little Mallop Street, ©5229 3645, has some fine examples of early Australian painters and a good contemporary collection. ⏱Open Mon- Fri 10am-5pm, Sat-Sun 1-5pm. Admission is free.

Port of Geelong Maritime Museum, Eastern Beach Road, ©5277 2260, has displays depicting 150 years of shipping in Corio and Port Phillip Bays. The museum is ⏱closed on Tuesdays and

Thursdays, and opens from 10am-4pm every other day of the week. Entry fees are ✪$3 adults, $1 children and $6 for families.

The Ford Discovery Centre, on the corner of Gheringap & Brougham Streets, ✆5227 8700, features the history of car design and engineering, and offers insights into the impact of global influences and environmental change on automobiles in the future. It is ✹closed on Tuesdays but opens 10am-5pm every other day.

Gabbinbar Animal Wildlife Park, 654 Torquay Road, ✆5264 1455. Many types of animals, both native and foreign, can be found in the park ✹open daily 10am-5pm.

Beaches. Apart from the still-water beaches in Corio Bay-Eastern Beach and St Helen's - there are the nearby still-water beaches of Port Phillip Bay - Portarlington, Indented Head, St Leonards, Queenscliffe and Barwon Heads. Then you come to the ocean beaches of Point Londsdale, Ocean Grove, Torquay, Jan Juc, Anglesea, Point Addis, Airey's Inlet, Fairhaven, Lorne, and the famous surfing mecca, Bell's Beach.

Facilities

There are facilities for over 150 sports, including football, basketball, horse racing, greyhound racing, golf, tennis, and all water sports.

Geelong

Geelong to Melbourne

Chapter 6
Melbourne

Population 2,942,000

Melbourne, the capital of Victoria, is situated on the shores of Port Phillip Bay. The Yarra River flows through the city.

Settlers in Van Diemen's Land (Tasmania) had known for years that there was good grazing land in the Port Phillip area, but had been refused permission to settle there. In 1835, John Batman ignored the ban, landed with a party, and 'bought' 600,000 acres of land from the local Aborigines for a few axes and other trade goods. He then returned to Launceston and formed the Port Phillip Association. (On the north side of Flinders Street, between Market and William Streets, there is a small plaque in the pavement marking the place where Batman stood when he declared that it was a good place for a village.)

In 1836, Governor Bourke vetoed Batman's purchase, and appointed Captain William Lonsdale as resident magistrate of the rapidly-growing settlement. Bourke visited the site in the following year, named the place Melbourne, had a street plan drawn up, and offered lots for sale.

The Australian Colonies Government Act was passed in August 1850, and constituted the Port Phillip district as a separate colony, with La Trobe as its first Lieutenant-Governor. Soon after, gold was discovered near Ballarat, and people came from all over the world seeking their fortune. The consequent Eureka Uprising gave the new government its first major challenge.

Climate

Melbourne's climate is midway between maritime and continental, and is very changeable. Average temperatures: January max 26C (79F) - min 14C (57F); July max 13C (55F) - min 6C (43F). Average annual rainfall: 656mm (26 ins). The driest months are June to August.

Characteristics

Victoria is called the Garden State, and its capital city certainly does its share to live up to that reputation. Melbourne has tree-lined boulevards, acres of parkland on the banks of the Yarra River, and parks and gardens galore in the suburbs.

How to Get There

By Air

Melbourne International Airport, at Tullamarine, is serviced by over 20 international carriers.

The domestic lines of Qantas, ✆13 1313, Ansett, ✆13 1300, and Virgin Blue, ✆13 6789, have regular services from other cities in Australia. Aus-Air, ✆(03) 9580 6166, specialise in services to Tasmania and the southern islands of Flinders and King.

The airport is about 20km (12 miles) out of the city, and the Skybus operates between Tullamarine and the terminal at 58 Franklin Street, ✆9335 3066 or ✆9662 9275. The Frankston & Peninsula Airport Shuttle, ✆9783 1199, takes passengers to that area, and there are also shuttle buses for the eastern suburbs.

By Bus

Greyhound Pioneer, ✆13 2030, and McCaffertys, ✆13 1499, have regular services to/from Melbourne and Sydney, Adelaide, Canberra, Newcastle, Coolangatta, Brisbane, Alice Springs, Townsville, Perth, Cairns and Darwin.

By Rail

There are rail services from Sydney and Adelaide, with connections from other capital cities, ✆13 2232. The country and interstate terminal is Spencer Street Station.

V/Line

Rail and coach services operate from country Victoria to Melbourne daily. They also travel as far as Adelaide, Canberra and the Sapphire Coast of NSW. For further information, ✆136 196.

By Road

From Sydney, via the Hume Highway, 875km (544 miles); via the Princes Highway, 1058km (657 miles); via the Olympic Way, 961km (597 miles); via Canberra/Cooma/Cann River, 1038km (645 miles).

From Adelaide, via the Western and Dukes Highways, 726km (451 miles); via Princes Highway West, 910km (565 miles).

Visitor Information

The Victoria Visitor Information Centre is in the Melbourne Town Hall on the corner of Swanston Walk & Little Collins Street, ✆(03) 9658 9955. It is ⏱open Mon-Fri 8.30am-5.30pm and weekends and public holidays 9am-5pm. They can be emailed at:

✉ visitor@melbourne.vic.gov.au

There are information booths in Bourke Street Mall, between Elizabeth and Swanston Streets, and Flinders Street Station, on the corner of Flinders and Swanston Streets.

The Victorian Tourism Operators Association is on Level 2, Rialto North Tower, 525 Collins Street, ✆(03) 9614 8877 or email ✉ vtoa@vtoa.asn.au

Tourism Victoria is on Level 6, 55 Collins Street, ✆(03) 132 842.

City of Melbourne, is in Melbourne Town Hall, Swanston Street, ✆(03) 9658 9955.

The Travellers' Aid Society of Victoria is on the 2nd Floor at 169 Swanston Street, ✆(03) 9654 2600. They are ⏱open Mon-Fri 8am-6pm and Sat-Sun 10am-4pm. They also have a Rail Room at Spencer Street Railway Station, ✆(03) 9670 2873.

Melbourne also has an Information Line available 7 days a week from 8am-6pm - ✆13 28 42. The following websites will give you a detailed insight into the city of Melbourne, outlying regions and potential itineraries for travel around Victoria:

    👁melbourne.citysearch.com.au
    👁www.melbourne.org
    👁www.tourism.vic.gov.au
    👁www.theage.com.au
    👁www.victrip.vic.gov.au

Accommodation

For a complete list of accommodation, contact one of the Tourist Offices above or explore the web pages.

As with any big city, accommodation is usu-ally cheaper in the outer suburbs, and that is obviously where you find the caravan parks.

Here is a selection of city and inner suburban accommodation, with prices for a double room per night, which should be used as a guide only. The telephone area code is 03.

5-Star

Hotel Sofitel, 25 Collins Street, ✆9653 0000. 363 rooms, 52 suites, licensed restaurant, gym - ✪$310-1760.

Le Meridien at Rialto Melbourne, 495 Collins Street, ✆9620 9111. 242 rooms, 10 suites, licensed restaurant, swimming pool, spa, sauna, gym - ✪$425-1030.

Grand Hyatt Melbourne, cnr Exhibition & Lonsdale Streets, ✆9657 1234. 547 rooms, 26 suites, licensed restaurant, swimming pool, spa, sauna, gym, tennis - ✪$270-630.

Hilton on the Park Melbourne, 192 Wellington Parade, East Melbourne, ✆9419 2000. 398 rooms, 38 suites, licensed restaurant, swimming pool, spa, sauna, gym, barbecue - ✪$300-430.

4-Star

Rydges Melbourne, 186 Exhibition Street, ✆9662 0511. 363 rooms, 70 suites, licensed restaurant, undercover parking, pool, sauna, spa, gym - ✪$195.

Centra Melbourne, cnr Flinders & Spencer Streets, ✆9629 5111. 384 rooms, 13 suites, licensed restaurant, gym, heated swimming pool - ✪$195-275.

The Chifley on Flemington Melbourne, 5 Flemington Road, North Melbourne, ✆9329 9344. 227 rooms, 9 suites, licensed restaurant, bistro, swimming pool, gym, sauna - ✪$135-200.

3-Star

The Batmans Hill Hotel, 66 Spencer Street, ✆9614 6344. 85 rooms, licensed restaurant, undercover parking - ✪$140-160.

Hotel Ibis, 21 Therry Street, ✆9639 1988. 250 rooms, licensed restaurant - ✪$110-190.

Kingsway Motel, cnr Park Street & Eastern Road, South Melbourne, ✆9699 2533. 40 units - ✪$115-135.

Melbourne

Melbourne skyline

Treasury Motor Lodge, 179 Powlett Street, East Melbourne, ©9417 5281. 21 units - ✪$130-150.

Flagstaff City Motor Inn, 45 Dudley Street, West Melbourne, ©9329 5788. 39 units, spa - ✪$110-160.

Marco Polo Inn, cnr Harker Street & Flemington Road, North Melbourne, ©9329 1788. 70 units, licensed restaurant, swimming pool, sauna - ✪$110-200.

Hotel Enterprize, 44 Spencer Street, ©9629 6991. 150 rooms, licensed restaurant - ✪$100.

2-Star

City Square Motel, 67 Swanston Street, ©9654 7011. 24 units, basic facilities - ✪$105.

Melbourne Suburbs

Brunswick

Princes Park Motor Inn, 2 Sydney Road, ©9388 1000. 70 units - ✪$125-135.

Parkville Motel, 759 Park Street, ©9388 1500. 20 units - ✪$90.

Coburg

Coburg Motor Inn, 726 Sydney Road, Coburg North, ©9350 1855. 26 units, swimming pool, undercover parking - ✪$85-95.

Coburg Coach Motel, 846 Sydney Road, Coburg North, ©350 2844. 27 units, licensed restaurant (closed Sunday), swimming pool - ✪$75.

Footscray

Footscray Motor Inn, 90 Droop Street, ©9687 6877. 30 units, licensed restaurant (closed Sunday) - ✪$120-155.

Mid Gate Motor Lodge, 76 Droop Street, ©9689 2300. 25 units - ✪$85.

St Kilda

Cabana Court Motel, 46 Park Street, ©9534 0771. 16 units, 16 suites - ✪$100-120.

Crest on Barkly Hotel Melbourne, 47 Barkly Street, ©9537 1788. 60 units, sauna - ✪$110-160.

Serviced Apartments

South Yarra Place Apartments, 41 Margaret Street, South Yarra, ©9867 6595. 18 studio apartments - ✪$70-165.

Caravan Parks

Melbourne Holiday Park, 265 Elizabeth Street, Coburg East, ☎9354 3533. (No pets allowed), 120 sites, heated pool - powered sites ✪$20 for two, cabins $48 for two.

Ashley Gardens Holiday Village, 129 Ashley Street, Braybrook, ☎9318 6866. (No pets allowed) 106 sites, tennis, heated pool - powered sites ✪$20, cabins $49 for two.

Sylvan Caravan Park, 1780 Hume Highway, Campbellfield, ☎9357 0009. (No dogs or cats) 101 sites - powered sites ✪$16 for two.

There is a **Youth Hostel** in 78 Howard Street, North Melbourne, ☎9329 8599. It has 34 rooms at ✪$25-35 per person twin share. Another is at 76 Chapman Street, North Melbourne, ☎9328 3595. It has 59 rooms at ✪$18 per person twin share.

Local Transport

The Met, Melbourne's public transport system, covers trains, trams and buses, and is operated by the Public Transport Corporation. Melbourne is divided into three zones and your ticket type depends on which zone you are going to travel in, and for how long. Two-hour, daily, weekly, monthly or yearly tickets are available.

The routes of the various forms of transport are indicated on the Met map, available from railway stations, newsagencies and some book shops. Further information is available from the Met Transport Information Centre, 589 Collins Street, ☎13 1638 (☉open 7am-9pm), or from The Met Shop at 103 Elizabeth Street.

Melbourne's metropolitan public transport website for Bayside Trains is ☞www.met.vic. gov.au

Victoria's official public transport site, containing timetables and fares for trams, buses and trains, is ☞www.victrip.com.au

Trams

Trams are just about the 'symbol' of Melbourne, and are a big draw-card for visitors. These vehicles, some old-fashioned and some sleek and new, continue to provide transport for thousands of commuters.

They are an interesting, reliable and efficient way to see the city. The Visitor Centres can provide you with a brochure outlining the routes, stops, zones and fares, with explanations to assist your reading of tickets (Metcards) and timetables.

Here are a few hints: remember to take coins with you, as this is the only form of currency which ticket vending machines accept. You can purchase a daily ticket for around ✪$5, allowing you unlimited travel in Zone 1, which covers the city and immediate surrounds. Keep an eye out for retailers displaying the Metcard Sales Flag, because daily tickets must be pre-purchased. In the city centre, there is a free tram service, the Free City Circle, which skirts the rectangular perimeter of the CBD and may be useful for reducing your legwork while shopping or sightseeing.

Taxis

These can be hired off the street, at taxi ranks, major hotels, or by phoning one of the taxi companies.

Initial flagfall is ✪$3 and the meter clicks over at ✪$1 per kilometre, or at 41.6 cents per minute if the speed of the vehicle drops below 25km/h. There is a booking fee of $2 and also a late night surcharge of $2. Be aware that CityLink tolls will be added to the fare if you choose to travel on certain roads - both the Western and Southern Links are ✪$3 for taxis.

Following are some of the companies operating in Melbourne:
Arrow Taxi Service, ☎13 2211; Astoria Taxis, ☎9347 5511; Black Cabs Combined, ☎13 2227; Embassy Taxis, ☎13 1755; Frankston Radio Cabs, ☎9786 3322; North Suburban Taxis, ☎13 1119; Regal Corporate Cars, ☎9326 6600; Silver Top Taxi Service, ☎13 1008; West Suburban Taxi, ☎9689 1144; Yellow Cabs, ☎13 19 24.

Water taxis include:
River Yarra Water Taxis, ☎0416 06 8655; and Melbourne Circle Water Taxis, ☎9686 0914.

Car Hire

There are plenty of car rental agencies, and they

Melbourne

accept current international licences.

Airport Rent A Car, ☎9335 3355; All Cheap Car Rentals, ☎9429 6999; Atlas, ☎9633 6233; Avis, ☎9330 4011; Budget, ☎1300 362 848; Crown, ☎9682 2266; Delta, ☎9330 6122; Hertz, ☎13 3039; Murphy, ☎9602 2265; National, ☎9696 9000; Pacific, ☎9347 9600; Thrifty, ☎1300 367 2277.

When driving in Melbourne, there are a few rules about the trams. Drivers must not obstruct trams, and there are yellow lines on roadways indicating streets in which drivers must keep clear of the tracks when trams are approaching. Drivers must also stop when a tram is picking up or setting down passengers, if there is not a central traffic island. Making a right hand turn can sometimes be dicey in the city centre. If the intersection has a 'hook turn' sign, the turn has to be made from the left-hand lane when the lights change, to leave the centre of the inter-section clear for trams.

Tollways

Citylink is a system of roads that connects some of Melbourne's motorways together. At the time of writing, Citylink tolls are applicable on the Monash Freeway, Tullamarine Freeway and the Bolte Bridge. No other motorways in Melbourne have tolls on them.

Leave your change in your pocket, though, because tolls are collected electronically. Most people visiting Melbourne will only want to use Citylink a couple of times at most. It is possible to buy up to twelve day passes per year on Citylink. Day passes cost around ☉$5 and can be paid for with a Visa, Mastercard or Bankcard over the phone or bought at selected Shell service stations. Day passes can be bought up until 12pm the day after travel, but an extra fee for late day passes applies. The Citylink customer service number to pay for the pass is ☎13 26 29.

Bicycle Hire

Melbourne has quite a few bike tracks, and to hire a bike it is best to get in touch with Bicycle Victoria, 19 O'Connell Street, North Melbourne, ☎9328 3000.

Eating Out

Melbourne has over 3200 restaurants representing 70 national cuisines. The most plentiful choice of Asian restaurants is found in Chinatown's Little Bourke Street; for Italian food, try Lygon Street, Carlton; for Greek, Lonsdale Street; and for Vietnamese, Victoria Street, Richmond. South Yarra is another restaurant centre.

Here is a selection of highly recommended restaurants.

Asian

Flower Drum, 17 Market Lane, ☎9662 3655. This is the number one Chinese restaurant, with a legendary status in Melbourne culinary circles. The question, however, is whether the justifiable fame, outstanding cuisine and impeccable service are worth the average $150 bill for two. The Drum is open for dinner 7 days and lunch Mon-Sat, licensed.

Mask of China, 117 Little Bourke Street, ☎9662 2116. Licensed, excellent seafood and wine list, dinner served daily from 6pm, lunch on Sunday from midday.

Empress of China, 120 Little Bourke Street, ☎9663 1833. Open for dinner 6 days and lunch on Sundays.

Bamboo House, 47 Little Bourke Street, ☎9662 1565. Licensed. Peking duck and spicy seafoods are specialties. Open daily from 5.30pm and for lunch Mon-Fri.

King of Kings, 209 Russel Street, ☎9663 2895. Inexpensive meals of a good quality, open daily 11am-2.30am.

Isthmus of Kra, 50 Park Street, South Melbourne, ☎9690 3688. Gernerally considered one of the finest Thai restaurants in Melbourne. Licensed, wonderful wine list, varied menu, open for dinner 7 days and lunch Mon-Fri.

European

Austria Haus Edelweiss, 419 Spencer Street, ☎9329 5877. Licensed, open 7 days for lunch and dinner, with Viennese Sunday luncheon.

Casa Di Iorio, 141 Lygon Street, Carlton, ☎9347 2670. Italian cuisine restaurant and pizza house, plus takeaway.

Da Salvatore, 29 Gratton Street, Carlton, ☎9663 4778. Pizza, pasta and steaks, quick service, open 7 days for lunch and dinner.

Bonum, 2 Collins Street, City, ©9650 9387. Licensed, up-market restaurant with inventive and exotic dishes at prices around $25 for a main course. Open for dinner Mon-Sat and for lunch Mon-Fri.

2bc, 177 Greville Street, Prahran, ©9529 4922. Busy and trendy establishment that serves Mediterranean-style meals at reasonable prices. It is licensed and open for lunch 7 days and dinner Mon-Sat.

Akvavit, Ground Level 3a, 2 Southgate, Southbank, ©9699 9947. Swedish restaurant with views of the river and city. Licensed or BYO, open daily for lunch and dinner. Two people can escape here paying around $40 for meals plus drinks.

International

O'Connels, 407 Coventry Street, South Melbourne, ©9699 9600. A changing menu that ranges from North American to Middle Eastern cuisine. Licensed, open for lunch and dinner 7 days.

Blakes, Ground Level, 2 Southgate, Southbank, ©9699 4100. Extensive menu offering a variety of unique flavours. Wonderful views of the Yarra and city. Open daily for lunch and dinner.

Harvey's, 10 Murphy Street, South Yarra, ©9867 3605. Predominantly Asian and Italian flavours. Open daily for lunch and dinner, from 7am Mon-Fri.

Becco, 11-25 Crossley Street, ©9663 3000. Efficient service, strong wine list and an extensive menu. Open daily 9am-11pm.

Chinois, 176 Toorak Road, South Yarra, ©9826 3388. Expensive but elegant modern restaurant. Licensed, open for lunch and dinner Mon-Fri.

Abla's, 109 Elgin Street, Carlton, ©9347 0006. Considered to be the best Middle Eastern restaurant in Melbourne. Set menu with a variety of complementary flavours. Open Thu-Fri for lunch and Mon-Sat for dinner.

est est est, 440 Clarendon Street, South Melbourne, ©9682 5688. Short but innovative menu with good wines to match. An expensive venture. Licensed and open Mon-Sat from 6pm.

Theatre Restaurants

Hofbrauhaus, 18-24 Market Lane, Melbourne, ©9663 3361. Bavarian beerfest. Affordable lunch menu. Licensed, open daily midday to midnight.

Dirty Dick's Medieval Madness Restaurant, 45 Dudley Street, West Melbourne, ©9325 3999. Licensed, medieval banquet.

The Comedy Club, 380 Lygon Street, Carlton, ©9348 1622. Open 9am-5pm Mon-Fri. Fully, licensed, cabaret environment, dinner and show packages available.

Witches in Britches, 84 Dudley Street, West Melbourne, ©9329 9850. Bar, three course meal and a two-hour show to follow. Open 7pm-1am 7 days.

Dracula's Theatre Restaurant, 169 Exhibition Street, Melbourne, ©9663 1754. Comic Transylvanian theme. Centrally located in the city.

At the other end of the scale, KFC is at 201 Bourke Street and 37 Swanston Street. Pizza Hut is on the corner of Elizabeth and Bourke Streets (©13 1166 for delivery). There are no less than 11 McDonalds branches, with 4 on Bourke Street, 2 on Collins Street, 2 on Elizabeth Street, and one each on Lonsdale, Swanston and St Kilda. Of course, the suburbs are represented by additional branches of each of the above.

You will find many other types of fast food outlets in the city centre. Going hungry in Melbourne is almost impossible, except in cases when you remain indecisive for hours, overwhelmed by the wide choice of venues. But this seldom occurs.

Entertainment

Melbourne's nightlife conjures up images of excitement, colour, action and entertainment. There is a comprehensive range of nocturnal activities to select from including discos, wine bars, concerts, theatre, cinema, live bands, nightclubs and much more.

Here is a selection of entertainment venues in the city.

Cinemas

Hoyts Cinema Complex, 140 Bourke Street, ©9663 3303.

Melbourne

Village Centre, 206 Bourke Street, ✆9667 6565.
Chinatown Cinema, 200 Bourke Street, ✆9662 3465.
Crazy Horse Cinema, 34 Elizabeth Street, ✆9654 8796.
Greater Union, 131 Russell Street, ✆9654 8235.
Kino Cinemas, 45 Collins Street, ✆9650 2100.
Lumiere Cinemas, 108 Lonsdale Street, ✆9639 1055.
Moonlight Cinemas, Level 10, 140 Bourke Street, ✆9663 9555.

Theatres

The *Half-Tix* kiosk is in the Bourke Street Mall, ✆9650 9420.
Princess Theatre, 163 Spring Street, ✆9662 2911.
Victorian Arts Centre, 100 St Kilda Road, ✆9281 8000.
Athenaeum Theatre, 188 Collins Street, ✆9650 1500.
Comedy Theatre, 240 Exhibition Street, ✆9209 9000.
Playbox Theatre Company, 113 Sturt Street, South Melbourne, ✆9685 5111.
Melbourne Theatre Company, 129 Ferrars Street, Southbank, ✆13 6166.
Her Majesty's Theatre, 219 Exhibition Street, ✆9663 3211.
Forum Theatre, 154 Flinders Street, ✆9299 9700.
Princes Theatre, 163 Spring Street, ✆9299 9800.
Regent Theatre, 191 Collins Street, ✆9299 9860.
Sidney Myer Music Bowl, Kings Domain, ✆9281 8360.

Nightclubs

Chevron, 519 St Kilda Road, ✆9510 1281. ⏰Open Thu 9pm-5am, Friday midnight-10am. Cover charge ⊙$12.
Melbourne Metro, 20-30 Bourke Street, ✆9663 4288. ⏰Open Thu-Sat. Cover charge ⊙$6 Thursday, $10 Friday & Saturday.
Revolver Upstairs, 229 Chapel Street, Prahran, ✆9521 5985. ⏰Open Mon-Thu midnight-3am, Fri-Sun 24hrs.
The Dome, 19 Commercial Road, Prahran, ✆9529 8966. ⏰Opens daily from 10pm with a cover charge of ⊙$10.
Grainstore Tavern, 46 King Street, ✆9614 3570. Live acts upstairs, video dance club downstairs.
The Ivy, 145 Flinders Lane, ✆9650 1855. Open Thurs-Sat, four floors, dance, bar, band and VIP Bar upstairs.
Club V, 371 Chapel Street, South Yarra, ✆9827 1771. ⊙$10 cover charge.
Salt, 14a Claremont Street, South Yarra, ✆9827 8333. Melbourne's newest and most sophisticated nightclub.
Billboard, 170 Russell Street, ✆9639 4000. ⏰Open Mon, Thurs-Sat 9pm-7am.
Club UK, 169 Exhibition Street, ✆9663 2075. Geared towards the backpacker sector - perhaps those who are feeling a little homesick. ⏰Open Wed-Sun 5pm-3am and there is no cover charge.
Monsoon's, in the Grand Hyatt Melbourne, 123 Collins Street, ✆9653 4516.
P O D, 241 King Street, ✆9642 8100. As the name indicates, this venue is quite simply a 'Place Of Dance'.
Chaise Lounge, 105 Queen Street, Melbourne, ✆9670 6120. Good music, plenty of seating, vibrant atmosphere and post-modern decor. ⏰Open from 4pm Tue, Wed & Fri and from 9am on Saturday, closing at 3am.

Bars & Pubs

Up Top Bar, First Floor, 163 Russell Street, ✆9663 8990. ⏰Open from 4pm until late the following morning Wed-Sun. Nostalgic '50s decor revised in trendy style. Impressive list of alcoholic beverages. Entry is free.
Gin Palace, 191 Little Collins Street, ✆9654 0533. Characterised by an eclectic mix of furniture fashions and cocktail concoctions (try an 'Industrial Revolution', for example!). ⏰Open daily 4pm-3am.
Hairy Canary, 212 Little Collins Street, ✆9654 2471. An inviting complement of food is on offer for those who feel that they need something to wash down with their drink. ⏰Open 7.30am-3am 7 days.

The Bullring, 95 Johnston Street, Fitzroy, ✆9416 0022. Lively atmosphere with music and dance of Latin American derivation. ⏲Open from 6pm-late, entertainment begins at 10.30pm. ☉$5 cover charge.

Walters Wine Bar, Upper Level, Southgate, Southbank, ✆9690 1211. Popular after-dark venue with stunning city views across the Yarra River. Good meals also available. ⏲Open mid-day every day and closes Sun-Thu at 1am and Fri-Sat at 3am.

Bell's Hotel, 157 Moray Street, South Melbourne, ✆9690 4511. Meals from 6pm.

Redback Brewery, 75 Flemington Road, North Melbourne, ✆9329 9400. ⏲Open Mon-Thurs 11am-midnight, Fri-Sat 11am-1am, Sun 11am-11.30pm. Meals Mon-Sun noon-3pm and 6-10pm.

Edward's Tavern, 221 High Street, Prahran, ✆9510 9897. 3 main bars and live entertainment. ⏲Open from 7pm Fri-Sun & Tues, 9pm Mon & Thurs, closed Wednesdays.

Music Venues

Rock

Wayside Inn, 466 City Road, South Melbourne, ✆9699 8469.

Central Club Hotel, 246 Victoria Street, North Melbourne, ✆9329 7482.

Jazz

Dizzy's Jazz Bar, 90 Swan Street, Richmond, ✆9428 1233. A deservedly famous centre for jazz lovers. ⏲Open Thu-Sat 8pm-1am. Cover charges are ☉$10 on Thursday and $12 on Friday & Saturday.

Moylans, 384 Flinders Lane, Melbourne, ✆9629 1030. Smoke-free environment, and a magnet for talented jazz musicians.

Ozcat, at the Parkview, cnr Scotchmer Street & Georges Road, Fitzroy North, ✆9489 8811. This venue will be used only for special concerts, while the main features of the Australian Catalog of Independent Artists will be played at Moylans (*see above*).

Rhythm & Blues

The Next Blue, at the Crown Casino, 8 Whiteman Street, Southbank, ✆9292 7007.

Shopping

Melbourne is Australia's fashion capital, and has an enormous selection of clothes and accessories boutiques.

Collins Street has many designer label boutiques, and is linked to Bourke Street by a network of arcades and alleys with boutiques and specialty shops. Explore the sidewalks along Collins Street between Swanston and Spring Streets for some exclusive up-market clothing stores.

234 Collins, located at that address, is a complex dedicated to fashion.

Australia on Collins is another fashion mecca. It joins Collins and Little Collins Streets and boasts an elaborate food court.

The 19th century *Block Arcade*, with its high domed ceiling and mosaic tiled floor, runs from 282 Collins Street to Little Collins Street, or you can enter from Elizabeth Street.

The *Royal Arcade*, the oldest arcade in Melbourne, links Little Collins Street and Bourke Street Mall, and also has an entrance in Elizabeth Street.

The *Galleria Plaza* is a centre for fashion and also a good place to find gifts. It is on the corner of Elizabeth and Little Collins Streets.

The *Bourke Street Mall* in the heart of the city, between Swanston and Elizabeth Streets, offers very good shopping, and is dominated by David Jones and Myer Department Stores. Other arcades running off the Mall are the *Centrepoint Mall* and *The Walk*. Although the Mall is classed as a pedestrian area, trams do run through its centre.

Midtown Plaza is on the corner of Bourke & Swanston Streets.

If you are searching for **duty free** shopping, head to the stretch of Elizabeth Street between Bourke and Lonsdale Streets.

The bazaar-like character of: the *Queen Victoria Market*, cnr Victoria and Elizabeth Streets; the *Prahran Markets*, Commercial Road, just off Chapel Street; *South Melbourne Markets*, York Street, off Ferrars Street; and the *Victorian Arts Centre Sunday Markets*, 100 St Kilda Road, South Melbourne, each offer an alternative and entertaining shopping experience.

Toorak Village, in Toorak Road from Punt Road to Williams Road has restaurants, boutiques and expensive furniture stores.

A little further out in Campbellfield at 400 Mahoneys Road, just off the Hume Highway, is the *Pipeworks Fun Market*, ©9357 1155, with 600 shopping stalls, fun rides, live entertainment, mini-golf and bungee jumping.

Many **shopping tours** are available to factory outlets. Here are a few of the options:

Shopping Spree Tours, 2/77 Asling Street, Gardenvale, ©9596 6600. 8.30am-5pm daily, ✪$60 a head.

Special Buying Tours, 198 Cotham Road, Kew, ©9817 5985. 9am-5pm Mon-Sat, ✪$20-50 a head.

Melbourne Shopping Tours, 7 Almeida Crescent, South Yarra, ©9826 3722.

Points of Interest

City Explorer Bus. Taking a tour on the City Explorer Bus is a good way to get your bearings. This red and white double-decker leaves from Swanston Street, just outside the Visitor Information Centre, on the hour between ◷10am-4pm and visits most of the main city attractions with its 16 stops. There are discounts on entry into nominated venues and other perks that might appeal. The costs are ✪$25 adults, $12 children and $55 for families. For additional information, ©9650 7000. Enquire also about the evening City Lights Tour or the Half-Day Tours which include Australian Wildlife, Shrine of Remembrance & Botanical Gardens and All Around Melbourne.

Melbourne Museum. The Melbourne Museum replaced the Museum of Victoria, formerly in Swanston Street, which is now closed as a result. This $263 million project places Victoria's newest museum to the north of the Royal Exhibition Building in Carlton Gardens, off Nicholson Street. Its exhibits focus on the natural environment and new technologies. Among the many facilities are an Aboriginal Centre, a Forest Gallery, a Mind and Body Gallery, Technology Exhibitions and a Science Gallery, ©8341

7777. Adults ✪$15, children $7, families $34. Apart from the attractive garden surrounds, an **IMAX Theatre**, off Rathdowne Street, opened on the site in 1998, ©9663 5454. The nearby **Royal Exhibition Building**, built in 1880, is itself worth a visit for its history and architecture, ©9270 5000 for enquiries.

Immigration Museum. The museum is located in Old Customs House, on the corner of 400 Flinders Street and William Street, ©9927 2700. This musuem takes visitors through a cultural tour using interactive computer displays and permanent physical exhibits. Personal stories are recounted by immigrants themselves, providing insights into the emotions and memories of immigration experiences. The museum is ◷open between 10am and 5pm and admission is ✪$8 adults, $6 concession, $4 children and $23 for families. The best method of transport is the Free City Circle tram, which passes nearby on Flinders Street between 10am and 6pm.

Hellenic Antiquities Museum. Located on the second floor of Old Customs House, this museum is designed to host periodical exhibits of ancient Grecian and Byzantine treasures, and is a joint venture of the Victorian and Greek governments. It shares opening times and entry fees with the Immigration Museum on the ground floor, ©9927 2700 for current and upcoming showcases.

Scienceworks Museum. Scienceworks is a short 10 minute drive from the city centre, and occupies the futuristic cylindrical building in 2 Booker Street, Spotswood, which cannot be missed. Exhibitions include a detailed exploration of the human body and its mechanics (*Stayin' Alive*), and a 'behind-the-scenes' look at producing special effects for movies and television (*The Sequel*). Also included in the complex is the fascinating Melbourne Planetarium. Admission is ✪$9 adults, $7 concession and $5 children, and the museum is ◷open 10am-4.30pm, ©9392 4800 for more details.

State Library. The oldest public library in Australia, established in 1856, is on the corner of Swanston and La Trobe Streets. It contains over one million books and periodicals, as well as overseas manuscripts, maps, microfilms, a multimedia catalogue, paintings and photographs. The La Trobe Library is located in a special wing opened in 1965. It is ⊕open Mon-Thurs 10am-9pm, Fri-Sun 10am-6pm, ✆9669 9888.

Rialto Towers. An excursion to the top of Rialto Towers, 525 Collins Street, ✆9629 8222, is absolutely imperative for any visitor. The magnificent panoramic vista, completely unobstructed from mountain to ocean and everything in between, is undoubtedly the best way to see Melbourne and its surrounds. At 253m in height, it is the tallest office building in the Southern hemisphere. The Observation Deck is accessible ⊕Sun-Thu 10am-10pm and Fri-Sat 10am-11pm, adults ✪$8, children $6.

Old Melbourne Gaol. The National Trust has preserved one remaining cell block as a penal museum, which has a unique collection tracing the story of transportation, convicts, and the development of Victoria's penal system. It is believed that 104 hangings were carried out at the gaol, including that of Ned Kelly on November 11, 1880. The gaol is located in Russell Street, near Victoria Street, and ⊕opens daily 9.30am-4.30pm, with admission ✪$10 adults, $7 children and $28 for families, ✆9663 7228. For ✪$17 adults, $9 children and $43 families, shows are conducted on Wednesday and Sunday nights - but some may consider them to be suggestively violent in nature, so be warned if you plan to take young children.

Chinatown. Chinatown is in Little Bourke Street, and extends from Exhibition Street to Swanston Street. It contains many restaurants from the most economical to the extremely expensive. The **Chinese Museum** is in 22 Cohen Place, and is one of the best small museums in Melbourne. It is ⊕open Sat midday-4.30pm, Sun-Fri 10am-4.30pm, and entry fees are ✪$6 adult and $4 concession, ✆9662 2888.

Fire Services Museum Victoria. The museum, on the corner of 39 Gisborne Street and Victoria Parade, East Melbourne, was once the Eastern Hill Fire Station. Now it has displays of restored fire fighting equipment used by fire brigades throughout the city. The museum is ⊕open Fri 9am-3pm, Sun 10am-4pm, with admission ✪$6 adults, $3 children and $12 for families, ✆9662 2907.

Parliament House. The State Houses of Parliament in Spring Street, at the top of Bourke Street, were built in stages between 1856 and 1930, and have never actually been finished as the dome and facades to the side and rear were never added. Guided tours of this Victorian construction are available at 10am, 2pm and 3pm Mon-Fri when Parliament is in recess, ✆9651 8911.

The Old Treasury. This fine public building was restored, converted to a museum and re-opened in 1994. It is situated in Spring Street, at the top of Collins Street, ✆9651 2233. There are three permanent exhibitions which encompass the past history and contemporary life of the city, its art, culture and architecture. The layout of the museum is designed for self-guiding, but guided tours are offered at 1pm and 3pm. The Treasury is ⊕open 9am-5pm Mon-Fri and 10am-4pm on weekends and public holidays. Admission is ✪$6 adults, $4 children and $16 for families.

St Patrick's Cathedral. This Gothic Revival cathedral is in 1 Cathedral Place, which runs off Lansdowne Street, East Melbourne, and is constructed of Footscray bluestone. It was completed in 1897, except for the spires, which were added in 1936. There is a statue in the churchyard of the great Irish liberator, Daniel O'Connell, which is a replica of that which stands in O'Connell Street, Dublin. The Cathedral contains many beautiful works of art and is ⊕open 9am-5pm Mon-Fri, ✆9662 2233.

Fitzroy Gardens. Bounded by Albert, Clarendon, Lansdowne Streets and Wellington Parade in East Melbourne, Fitzroy Gardens are delightful nineteenth century gardens. The gardens contain **Cooks' Cottage**, ✆9419 4677, which was transported to Australia in 1934 and rebuilt block by block. It was originally built in the mid-eighteenth century by Captain James Cook's father. The cottage is ⊕open daily 9am-5pm. Also in the garden are the famous Fairy Tree and the miniature Tudor Village replica. Next to Fitzroy Gardens are the **Treasury Gardens**

containing the John F Kennedy Memorial.

Australian Gallery of Sport & Olympic Museum. The museum is outside the member's entrance to the **Melbourne Cricket Ground** in Yarra Park, Jolimont, and is Australia's first multi-sport museum. The three level building has priceless collections of memorabilia, which are displayed graphically in exhibitions aimed at entertaining and educating. The Australian Gallery of Sport now incorporates the Olympic Museum, which traces the history of the Olympics, from the ancient Greek games to the Modern Summer Olympics from 1896-1992. The museum is ⏱open daily 10am-4pm, ✆9657 8879. For tours of the adjoining MCG, which depart every day on the hour between 10am and 3pm, ✆9657 8879.

Queen Victoria Gardens and Kings Domain. These were originally the site of a gold-rush shantytown, and were proclaimed public parkland in 1854. The area contains Australian and English trees, and one of the most attractive sections of the Kings Domain is a garden of rockeries, tiny paths and waterfalls which commemorate the Pioneer Women of Victoria. The **Myer Music Bowl**, ✆9281 8360, venue for many of Melbourne's most popular entertainment events, is in the Kings Domain.

The **Shrine of Remembrance**, also in Kings Domain, is dedicated to the sacrifice made by Victorian men and women in the two World Wars. A feature is the Stone of Remembrance, the centre of which is illuminated by a shaft of sunlight at exactly 11am on Armistice Day, November 11 each year. It is ⏱open every day between 10am and 5pm. There is no charge, but a

donation box is located out the front if you wish to support the volunteers who give their time to conduct tours and answer your questions. For more information, ✆9654 8415.

The well-known **Floral Clock**, whose floral design is changed four times a year requiring the planting of over 30,000 flowers, is in the Queen Victoria Gardens.

La Trobe's Cottage. The Cottage, on the corner of Birdwood Road and Dallas Brooks Drive, in the Domain, South Yarra, was the colony's first Government House. La Trobe brought the house with him in the ship *Fergusson*, along with his family and possessions. The National Trust supervised the re-creation of the buildings, and they contain many of the original furnishings. The Cottage is ⏱open 11am-4pm Mon, Wed, Sat & Sun, ✆9654 4711.

Victorian Arts Centre Complex. On the banks of the Yarra River, at 100 St Kilda Road, the Centre comprises the theatres, the Melbourne Concert Hall, the Performing Arts Museum and the National Gallery of Victoria. As well as the performance and exhibition spaces, the Victorian Arts Centre has several restaurants. The **George Adams Gallery** has an extensive collection and is ⏱open Mon-Sat 9am-11pm, and Sun 10am-5pm, ✆9281 8194. The **Performing Arts Museum** has regularly changing exhibitions, free entry and is ⏱open Mon-Sat 9am-11pm, Sun 10am-5pm, ✆9281 8000. Guided tours of the Centre are available at limited times, ✆9281 8198.

Princes Bridge. The bridge is Melbourne's oldest and grandest, and is located at the point where Swanston Street becomes St Kilda Road. It was built around 1886, replacing a wooden bridge that had been opened by La Trobe in 1850.

Young & Jackson's Hotel. Also known as Princes Bridge Hotel, the pub is at 1 Swanston Street, ✆9650 3884. Its claim to fame is that the upstairs lounge is home to the infamous painting 'Chloe' which caused a scandalized public outcry when it was first hung in the Melbourne Art Gallery in the 1880s. She may have caused a stir then, but now she hardly manages to raise an eyebrow.

Shrine of Remembrance

St Paul's Cathedral. This Gothic Revival Anglican cathedral is on the corner of Swanston and Flinders Streets, on the site of the first official church service in Melbourne. The Cathedral was completed in 1891, and the spires added between 1926 and 1931. The doors are ◷open Mon-Fri 9am-5pm, ✆9650 3791.

Capitol Theatre. The astonishing ceiling of the theatre, at 113 Swanston Street, was designed by Walter Burley Griffin, the architect of the city of Canberra. Entry is ✪$9 adults, $5 children, ✆9654 4422.

Melbourne Town Hall. The Town Hall, in Swanston Street Walk, ✆9658 9779, was built between 1867 and 1870, and the portico added in 1887. It is worth going inside the main hall to see the chandeliers, murals and organ and the rest of its recenty restored interior. The Town Hall was one of the main venues for concerts before the advent of the Concert Hall in St Kilda Road.

Polly Woodside Maritime Museum. The barque *Polly Woodside*, in Lorimer Street East, Southbank, is a deepwater, square-rigged, commercial sailing ship built of riveted iron in 1885. Seventy years ago, she was one of the fast fleet of windjammers, today she is fully restored and the centrepiece of a display of Australia's maritime history. ◷Open 7 days 10am-4pm, admission ✪$8 adults, $5 concession and $18 for families, ✆9699 9760.

Melbourne Exhibition and Events Centre. At 28 Clarendon Street, South Melbourne, ✆9205 6400, this complex is the largest and most modern of its kind that Australia has to offer, and plays host to a wide range of exhibitions throughout the year. Its unique exterior design is worth a glance.

Crown Entertainment Complex. The complex is often described as 'the city under one roof', and indeed its restaurants, theatres, cinemas, Crown Towers Hotel, bars, nightclubs, showrooms, cocktail lounges, cafes, ballrooms, shopping boutiques and unabated gambling opportunities at the **Crown Casino**, do give the impression of a mini metropolis. The complex is in Southbank, and the Casino is at 8 Whiteman Street, ✆9292 8888.

Melbourne Aquarium. This Aquarium, situated on the corner of King Street and Queenswharf Road, City, ✆9620 0999, is a very sophisticated and impressive way to view ocean creatures. It has the enormous Oceanarium viewing tank, modern computer interactions, aquatic feeding facilities and a simulator. The complex is ◷open daily 9am-6pm (until 9pm during summer), and costs adults ✪$19, concession $14 and children $10.

Suburban Attractions

Royal Botanic Gardens. The Royal Botanic Gardens are in Birdwood Avenue, South Yarra, and have 41ha (101 acres) of lawns, gardens and ornamental lakes. The Gardens are regarded as one of the finest examples of landscape gardening in the world. Their development commenced in 1846 under the direction of the then Superintendent of the Colony, Charles Joseph La Trobe, and now features 12,000 plant species. Brochures are available on special seasonal walks through the Gardens. **Como House**, Como Park, is an elegant colonial mansion, built in 1847, which has been classified by the National Trust and is ◷open for inspection daily 10am-5pm, ✆9827 2500.

St Kilda

St Kilda is Melbourne's equivalent of Sydney's Kings Cross, only more so. Developers would like to move in and restore the area to the fashionable and wealthy resort it once was, but they are meeting resistance from long-established residents. From Swanston Street, there are many trams that run to St Kilda, including Tram 16 from Swanston Street, and from Bourke Street, Tram 96 goes through South Melbourne to St Kilda. From Richmond, take Tram 79, which travels along Church Street, and Chapel Street in Prahran, then continues on to St Kilda Esplanade. By road, St Kilda is reached by the West Gate Freeway from the west, Punt Road from the north. **The Esplanade** runs along the beach, which is not very inviting, and leads to the St Kilda Pier, which has a kiosk built in 1904 at the corner. The St Kilda hot sea baths are nearby, and are very popular. **Luna Park** is in 18 Lower Esplanade, next door to the Palais Theatre, and has been run as a fun palace since the 1920s. There is a restaurant behind the Palais that was originally a bathing shed. Rides such as the Mad Mouse, the Ghost Train and the Scenic Railway have been entertaining young ones for years. Entry is free into the Park but rides are priced at around ✪$3 or $4. It ⏰opens 11am daily and closes at 5pm Mon-Thu & Sun and 11pm Fri-Sat. **Rippon Lea**, 192 Hotham Street, Elsternwick, is a brick mansion built between 1868 and 1887, and has 33 rooms, iron carriage gates and a conservatory. It is set in a beautiful garden with a lake, and is one of the National Trust's pride and joys. It is ⏰open Tues-Sun 10am-5pm, ☎9523 6095. **Ripponlea Railway Station** is a fine example of early twentieth century architectural style.

Parkville

Parkville is a student area with colleges, halls of residence and student flats set amidst fashionable homes, office buildings and Victorian terraces. Its main attractions are the Melbourne Zoo and the nearby University of Melbourne.

The **Melbourne Zoo** is in Elliot Park, ☎9285 9300. It has a lion park, walk-through aviary and native fauna park, and a butterfly enclosure. More than 350 species are represented here in Australia's longest-standing zoo (since 1862). The *Lakeside Restaurant* serves 'meals with a view', looking out to Gibbon Island. Standard opening times are ⏰daily 9am-5pm, but some exhibits and special events have alternative times. It is recommended that you allow at least four hours to fully appreciate this attraction, and you can phone the above number for feeding times and other points of interest to better plan your visit. Admission is adults ✪$16, children $8 and $42 for families.

The **University of Melbourne**, Gratton Street, ☎9344 4000, dates back to the 1850s, and contains, among other interesting buildings, **The Grainger Museum**, Gate 13, Royal Parade, ☎9344 4270, which is ⏰open Mon 10am-1pm,

Tue 10am-4pm and Wed-Fri 10am-4pm.

Flemington

Flemington Racecourse is one of the most beautiful courses in the world, and is worth a visit even if you are not into betting. Unfortunately, it is only open to the public on race days, but the crowds add to the atmosphere anyway. The daily papers have details of race meetings in the sports pages. The famous Melbourne Cup is run here on the first Tuesday of November.

Tours

The Visitor Information Centre has details of all tours that are available in and around Melbourne. Here are some examples, with prices from around $50 to $140.

Melbourne Discovery Pass
Duration: ⏰12pm-5pm daily.
Attractions: Lunch at Rialto Towers, cruise on the *Melba Star* past Southbank and the Royal Botanic Gardens, Como Historic House, afternoon tea and return.
Operator: Rialto Towers Observation Deck, ☎9629 8222.
City Tour
Duration: ⏰9am-12pm daily.
Attractions: City, Chinatown, Parliament House, Fitzroy Gardens, Captain Cook's Cottage, Melbourne Cricket Ground, National Tennis Centre, Albert Park, Westgate Bridge, Botanic Gardens, Shrine of Remembrance and return.
Operator: Gray Line, ☎9663 4455.
Melbourne Highlights
Duration: ⏰1.30pm-5.30pm daily
Attractions: City, Chinatown, Shrine of Remembrance, South Yarra, Toorak, Dandenong Ranges, Sherbrooke Forest, Mt Dandenong and return.
Operator: Gray Line, ☎9663 4455.
Best of Melbourne
Duration: ⏰12.15pm-7.15pm daily
Attractions: Same as Melbourne Highlights but with the addition of dinner on the Colonial Tramcar Restaurant, which tours Melbourne streets at night while you eat.
Operator: Gray Line, ☎9663 4455.

Rowing on the Yarra

Penguin Parade and Seal Rocks
Duration: ⏱Fluctuates with season, daily.
Attractions: Phillip Island by coach, Koala Conservation Centre, dinner at Cowes (price not included), viewing of Penguin Parade, Seal Rocks Seal Life Centre and return.
Operator: Gray Line, ☏9663 4455.

Penguin Express
Duration: ⏱5.30-11.30 daily between March and November.
Attractions: Express coach to penguin viewing on Phillip Island then return.
Operator: Gray Line, 9663 4455.

Melbourne's Best Tours
Duration: ⏱Seasonal (late afternoon until late)
Attractions: Hotel pick-up in Melbourne, South Gippsland, Western Port Bay, Australian Wildlife, San Remo, tour of Phillip Island, Seal Rocks, Mutton Bird, Penguin Parade and return.
Operator: Melbourne's Best Tours, ☏1300 130 550.

Blue Dandenongs
Duration: ⏱8.40am-5.30pm daily.
Attractions: Dandenong Ranges, Puffing Billy train ride, lunch at Fergusson's Winery, Healsville Sanctuary and return.
Operator: Gray Line, ☏9663 4455.

Sovereign Hill
Duration: ⏱9am-5.30pm daily.
Attractions: Coach to Ballarat, Sovereign Hill Historical Park, gold panning, provincial town tour and return.
Operator: Gray Line, ☏9663 4455.

Winery Tour - Yarra Valley
Duration: ⏱8.30am-5pm daily.
Attractions: 3-6 wineries, lunch, Badger Weir Park and return.
Operator: Victorian Winery Tours, ☏9653 9749.
Additional tours of the Great Ocean Road, Grampians, Murray River and extended trips to Phillip Island are also available, and the Visitor Information Centre will supply you with details of all of them.

The **National Trust (Victoria)** produces a brochure which you can pick up at the Visitor Information Centre. It outlines buildings of particular historical significance and includes all the relevant details for visiting them.

Apart from their regular city service, the **City Explorer Bus** offers a number of different tours in the Melbourne area and to outlying regions, ✆9650 7000 to enquire further.

Cruises on the Yarra are also available. Here are a few companies which operate such services:
Melbourne River Cruises, Vault 18, Banana Alley Jetty, ✆9614 1215.
City River Cruises, 3 Princes Walk, Melbourne, ✆9650 2214.
Southgate River Tours, Southgate, Southbank, ✆9682 5711.

Festivals

The Moomba Festival is held in March each year. A parade is held before the Grand Final of the AFL competition in September.
The Melbourne Cup is held on the first Tuesday in November each year.

Sporting Facilities

Melbourne has four venues for horseracing - Flemington, ✆9258 4666; Caulfield in Station Street, ✆9257 7200; Moonee Valley in McPherson Street, Moonee Ponds, ✆9373 2222; and Sandown in Racecourse Drive, Springvale, ✆9546 9511.

In summer, many International Tests, one day International and state-based matches are played at the Melbourne Cricket Ground (MCG), Yarra Park, Jolimont.

There are two major venues for greyhound racing - Melbourne Park on Monday nights and Sandown Park on Thursday nights.

Harness Racing's main venue is Moonee Valley in Moonee Ponds, and races are held every Saturday and some Mondays.

Australian Rules Football (AFL) is played every Saturday during the season (March to September) at various grounds around the city, including the MCG.

Soccer's main venue is Melbourne Park, Swan Street, Melbourne, ✆9286 1600.

The Australian Tennis Open is held each year at the National Tennis Centre in Batman Avenue, East Melbourne, ✆9286 1600.

Calder Park Thunderdome, Calder Highway, Keilor, is Australia's only super speedway. For information on race meetings, ✆9217 8800.

The Australian Motorcycle Grand Prix is held at the Phillip Island Motor Racing Circuit, Back Beach Road, ✆5952 9400.

The Formula One Grand Prix is held at Albert Park in March, ✆9258 7100 for more information.

Melbourne has facilities for every type of sport, and venues and clubs are listed in the Yellow Pages telephone directory.

Chapter 7
Melbourne to Lakes Entrance

Dandenong Ranges

Location and Characteristics
The Dandenongs are only 35km (22 miles) east of Melbourne, and the area is ideal for picnics, bushwalks and wildlife observation. It is an extremely popular destination with Melbournians and tourists for both daytrips and weekend escapes. Mt Dandenong (630m - 2067 ft) offers a panoramic view of Melbourne from its strategic lookout points.

Visitor Information
The Dandenongs are covered in ☞www.melbourne.citysearch.com.au

Accommodation and Services
Tavlock Retreat B&B, Toorak Road, Mount Dandenong, ✆9751 2336. 2 rooms, barbecue, good facilities - ✪$145-180 including breakfast.
Emerald Golf & Country Resort, 48 Lakeside Drive, Emerald, ✆5968 4211. 6 rooms, basic facilities, tennis court, golf course - ✪$90 including breakfast.

Points of Interest
One of the most popular attractions is Puffing Billy, Old Monbulk Road, Belgrave, ✆9754 6800, an historic narrow gauge train that runs through 13km (8 miles) of mountain scenery between Belgrave and Lakeside (Emerald Lake) in the Dandenong Ranges every day of the year, except Christmas Day. Return fares are adults ✪$19, children $10 and $54 for families. The line opened in 1900, and it is the ideal way to view the Dandenongs at close range. The suburban trains from all stations connect with Puffing Billy at Belgrave, one hour's easy drive from Melbourne.
The famous **William Ricketts Sanctuary**, Mt Dandenong Tourist Road, ✆13 1963, is set in the lush surrounds of the Dandenong Ranges and comprises the inspired sculptures of one artist. Encapsulating the spirituality of Aboriginal culture and expressing an affinity with nature, these startling images bear a powerful mystique. The Sanctuary is ⏱open daily 10am-4pm and entry is ✪$6 adults, $3 children and $15 for families.

Mornington Peninsula

Location and Characteristics
The Nepean Highway follows the eastern shore of Port Phillip Bay for 97km (60 miles) to the seaside resort of Portsea. On the way it passes picturesque peninsula beaches such as Dromana, Rosebud and Sorrento.

Visitor Information
The Visitor Information Centre for Peninsula Tourism is at 359B Point Nepean Road, Dromana, ✆5978 3078. For web information: ☞www.melbourne.citysearch.com.au includes the Mornington Peninsula region.

Accommodation and Services
Sorrento on the Park, 15 Hotham Road, Sorrento, ✆5984 4777. 12 units, apartment facilities, playground - ✪$130-280.
Brooklands of Mornington, 93-101 Tanto Avenue, Mornington, ✆5975 1166. 36 units, licensed restaurant, good facilities, room service - ✪$90-180.
The Admiral, 799 Point Nepean Road, Rosebud, ✆5986 8933 or ✆1800 627 262. 12 units, basic facilities - ✪$90-145.
Blue Dolphin Motor Lodge, 86 Point Nepean Road, Dromana, ✆5987 2311. 15 units, basic facilities, playground - ✪$50-100.
Caravan Parks
Dromana Caravan & Tourist Park, 8 Nepean Highway, Dromana, ✆5981 0333. 109 sites, heated pool, tennis court, golf, kiosk, playground, recreation room, barbecue - powered sites ✪$15-20 for two, cabins $45-100 for two.
Mornington Caravan & Tourist Park, 98 Bungower Road, Mornington, ✆5975 7373. (No

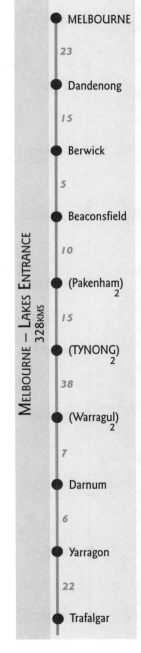

Melbourne to Lakes Entrance

MELBOURNE – LAKES ENTRANCE 328KMS

- ● MELBOURNE
- 23
- ● Dandenong
- 15
- ● Berwick
- 5
- ● Beaconsfield
- 10
- ● (Pakenham) 2
- 15
- ● (TYNONG) 2
- 38
- ● (Warragul) 2
- 7
- ● Darnum
- 6
- ● Yarragon
- 22
- ● Trafalgar

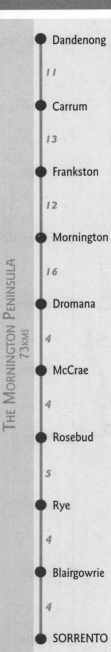

Melbourne to Lakes Entrance

THE MORNINGTON PENINSULA
73KMS

- Dandenong
- *11*
- Carrum
- *13*
- Frankston
- *12*
- Mornington
- *16*
- Dromana
- *4*
- McCrae
- *4*
- Rosebud
- *5*
- Rye
- *4*
- Blairgowrie
- *4*
- SORRENTO

pets allowed) 140 sites, barbecue, playground, recreation room - powered sites ✪$14 for two, cabins $60-70 for two.

Sunrise Caravan Park, 27 Rosebud Place, ✆5986 8977. 41 sites, playground, recreation, barbecue, minimal facilities - powered sites ✪$15 for two, cabins $45-60 for two.

There is a **Youth Hostel** in 3 Miranda Street, Sorrento, ✆5984 4323. It has 6 rooms at ✪$20 per person twin share.

Points of Interest

At Dromana, the **Arthur's Seat Scenic Chairlift** ride offers great views of Melbourne, Port Phillip Bay and the Mornington Peninsula. It ⏲opens at 11am daily September-April, and only on weekends and holidays during winter, ✆5987 2565.

The MV *Peninsula Princess*, a car passenger ferry, operates every day linking the Mornington and Bellarine Peninsulas, from Queenscliff to Sorrento.

Ashcombe Maze, Red Hill Road, Shoreham, ✆5989 8387, is a large hedge maze believed to be the only significant one of its type in Australia. There are tea rooms surrounded by extensive gardens. It ⏲open from 10 am every day and costs ✪$7 adults, $5 children.

Bass

Location and Characteristics

Bass is located on the Bass Highway and can be visited on the way to Phillip Island from Melbourne.

Points of Interest

The Giant Worm Museum, on the Bass Highway, is a unique attraction and education facility. They do actually have giant worms (including one you can walk through!), and many other historical and hands-on displays, ✆5678 2222.

Phillip Island

Population 2400

Location and Characteristics

Phillip Island is 129km (80 miles) from Melbourne, and is the home of the fairy penguins. At dusk, the famous penguins emerge from the surf, completely ignoring the thousands of curious onlookers. The island has a Phillip Island Nature Park, which is divided into a number of outlets for wildlife viewing and information, including koalas, fur seals, pelicans, mutton birds, and the famous fairy penguins.

Visitor Information

For more information on Phillip Island attractions, contact the Phillip Island Information Centre, ✆5956 7447, or drop into their outlet at Newhaven on Phillip Island Tourist Road. It is ⏲open 7 days a week, 9am-5pm.

You can take advantage of the comprehensive web page at ☞www.phillipisland.net.au, or the Centre's accommodation booking service on ✆1300 366 422. Contact them via email at: ✉info@phillipisland.net.au

Another good website for planning and attractions details is ☞www.penguins.org.au which includes an email form at ☞www.penguins.org.au/trip/index.html

Accommodation and Services

There are more than fifty places to stay in Cowes alone, the main tourist centre of Phillip Island. The districts of Newhaven, Rhyll and San Remo offer several alternatives. All types of accommodation are available. Here is a selection.

The Continental Phillip Island, 5-8 Esplanade, Cowes, ✆5952 2316. 67 units, licensed restaurant, good room facilities, squash, pool, room service - ✪$85-110.

Banfields, 192 Thompson Avenue, Cowes, ✆5952 2486. 34 units, licensed restaurant, room service, playground, heated pool, good facilities - ✪$90-170.

Quays Motel, Phillip Island Tourist Road, San Remo, ✆5678 5555. 12 units, basic facilities -

Melbourne to Sale

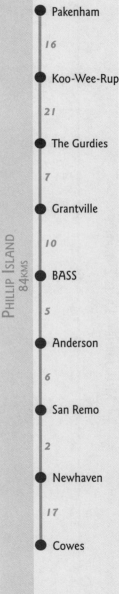

PHILLIP ISLAND
84KMS

- Pakenham
  16
- Koo-Wee-Rup
  21
- The Gurdies
  7
- Grantville
  10
- BASS
  5
- Anderson
  6
- San Remo
  2
- Newhaven
  17
- Cowes

✪$75-145.

Coleshill Lodge, 51 Rhyll-Newhaven Road, Rhyll, ✆5956 9304. 6 flats, cooking facilities - ✪$65-110.

Bridge Motel, 31 Forrest Avenue, Newhaven, ✆5956 7218. 9 units, basic facilities - ✪$60-130.

Koala Park Resort, Phillip Island Tourist Road, Cowes, ✆5952 2176. 18 units, licensed restaurant, pool, tennis court, playground - ✪$60-105.

Caravan Parks

Beach Park Tourist Caravan Park, McKenzie Road, Cowes, ✆5952 2113. (No pets allowed) 80 sites, kiosk, playground, heated pool - powered sites ✪$18-27 for two.

Kaloha Holiday Resort, cnr Chapel & Steele Streets, Cowes, ✆5952 2179 or ✆1800 060 277. 96 sites, heated pool, playground, recreation room, barbecue - powered sites ✪$15-25 for two, cabins $40-55 for two.

Beach Haven Caravan Park, 167 Marine Parade, ✆5678 5265. (No pets allowed) 95 sites,

minimal facilities - powered sites ✪$15-20 for two, cabins $35-45 for two.

The Islander Caravan Park, 137 Thompson Avenue, Cowes, ✆5952 2023. (No pets allowed) 95 sites, recreation room, playground, shop, pool - powered sites ✪$14-19 for two, cabins $55-80 for two, on-site vans $45-75 for two.

Newhaven Caravan Park, Phillip Island Road, Newhaven, ✆5956 7227. 150 sites, playground, recreation room - powered sites ✪$12-19 for two, cabins $45-80 for two, on-site vans $25-40 for two.

Swan Bay Caravan Park, 3 Lock Road, Rhyll, ✆5956 9220. 121 sites, playground, basic facilities - powered sites ✪$10-20 for two, cabins $41-64.

There is a **Youth Hostel** in 97 Church Street, Cowes, ✆5952 2548. It has 24 rooms at ✪$17 per person twin share.

Points of Interest

The **Penguin Parade Visitors Centre**, off Ventnor Road, ✆5956 8300, is ⏰open daily from

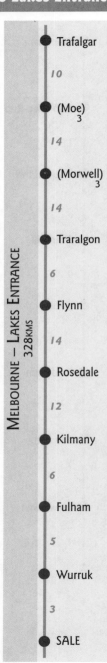

Trafalgar

10

(Moe)
3

14

(Morwell)
3

14

Traralgon

6

Flynn

14

Rosedale

12

Kilmany

6

Fulham

5

Wurruk

3

SALE

MELBOURNE – LAKES ENTRANCE
328KMS

10am and you can view the seasonal nightly pilgrimage of the cute creatures as they waddle their way onto the beach and up the sand dunes. It costs adults ✪$15, children $8 and families $34.

The Koala Conservation Centre is located at Fiveways on Phillip Island Road, ©5952 1307. It ⏱opens at 10am 7 days a week and costs ✪$6 adults, $3 children and $15 families.

Churchill Island, accessed via Newhaven, off Phillip Island Road, is popular for its tranquil gardens and stunning array of bird life. Costs are ✪$6 adults, $3 children and $15 for families.

The Seal Rocks Life Centre, Penguin Reserve, The Nobbies, ©9793 6767, has amazing educational displays and panoramic views. Entry is ✪$12 adults, $6 children and $32 for families.

A Four Park Pass gives access to all four attractions listed above for the one price: ✪$30 adults, $15 children and $73 for families.

At the **Australian Dairy Centre**, Phillip Island Road, Newhaven, there is a museum explaining the history of the dairying industry, and a cheese factory with sales section and tastings. The cafeteria sells dairy-based light meals and snacks, ©5956 7583.

Other attractions include great surfing beaches and restaurants.

French Island National Park, which can be reached by ferry either from Cowes at Phillip Island or from Stoney Point on the Mornington Peninsula, is larger than Phillip Island although less developed.

In Korumburra, on the South Gippsland Highway east of Phillip Island, is **Coal Creek Heritage Village**, a re-creation of an 1890s coal mining/railway town, with 40 buildings, including a mine, blacksmith, printer, stores, and a saw mill, ©5655 1811.

Tynong

Location and Characteristics

Tynong is a town on the Princes Highway, and can be visited on the way to Melbourne from Sale.

Points of Interest

Here you will find **Victoria's Farm Shed**, Australia's leading farm animal theatre featuring parades, milking, shearing and sheep dog displays. Show times are 10.30am and 2pm daily. For more information, ©5629 2840.

Also at Tynong is **Gumbuya Recreation and Leisure Park**, a 174ha (430 acres) recreation park with toboggan slide, minicars, pony coach and trail rides, mini golf, adventure playground, water slide, half court tennis, barbecue and picnic areas, and a restaurant, ©5629 2613. The park is ⏱open every day 10am-6pm (rides in operation 11am-4pm) and admission is ✪$7 adults, $4 children and $20 for families.

Sale

Population 13,900

Location and Characteristics

Situated on the Melbourne side of Lakes Entrance, Sale is the operations centre for the nearby Bass Strait oil fields of Esso-BHP. There is also a large RAAF training base located here.

Cullinen Park, off Foster Street, is the site of the historic Port of Sale where, in days of yore, steamers tied up after their long trip from Melbourne. From Sale there are roads leading to the southern end of Ninety Mile Beach.

Visitor Information

The Central Gippsland Visitor Information Centre can be found in 8 Foster Street, ©(03) 5144 1108. Email them at toursale@i-o.net.au

Accommodation and Services

The King Avenue Motor Inn, 20 Princes Highway, ©5143 2222. 33 units, licensed restaurant, room service, good facilities - ✪$160-240.

The Princeton Motor Lodge, 25 Princes Highway, ©5144 6599. 30 units, licensed restaurant, basic facilities - ✪$125-155.

Sale Hacienda International Motor Inn, Princes Highway & Raymond Street, ©5144 1422 or ©1800 035 356. 54 units, licensed restaurant (closed Sunday), good room facilities, room serv-

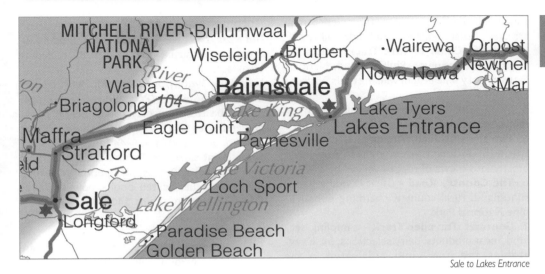

Sale to Lakes Entrance

ice, pool - ✪$95-100.
Sale Motor Village, Princes Highway, ✆5144
1366. 136 sites, kiosk, playground, barbecue -
powered sites ✪$16 for two, cabins $58-78 for
two.

Points of Interest
Apart from the historical interest of the town
centre, including the **Gippsland Art Gallery** (68
Foster Street, ✆5142 3372) and the **Historical
Museum** (Foster Street, ✆5144 5994), Sale is
surrounded by attractive natural areas which
include a **Wildlife Refuge** and the **David Mo-
rass State Game Reserve**.

Gippsland

Location and Characteristics
In general terms, the Gippsland area stretches
from the east of Bairnsdale to Phillip Island, and
north of Morwell and Traralgon down to Wilsons
Promontory and Ninety Mile Beach on the
southern coast, taking in just about everything
in between. It covers the beautiful landscapes
of fertile countryside and is full of various natural wonders from mountains and forests to rivers and beaches.

Visitor Information
Plenty of touring material is produced covering
the Gippsland region. There are detailed maps,
driving routes, accommodation listings and current news and events. Two information outlets
are:
Gippsland Country Tourism Information Centre,
Shop 1, Southside Central, Princes Highway,
Traralgon, ✆5174 3199 or ✆1800 621 409 (toll
free).
South Gippsland Visitor Information Centre, cnr
South Gippsland Highway & Silkstone Road,
Korumburra, ✆5655 2233 or ✆1800 630 704
(toll free).
For online information visit 👁www.gippsland
tourism.com.au or email ✎information@gipps
landtourism.com.au

Points of Interest
The best way to explore the Gippsland is by driving through it at a leisurely pace and absorbing
its scenic qualities.
The Visitor Centres can provide you with a range
of material comprising the eight uniquely-
themed drives listed below.
1. **Gippsland Heritage Track** - museums, historic buildings, shipwrecks, gold mines, antique
shops and more.
2. **Walhalla and Mountain Rivers Trail** - Long

Melbourne to Lakes Entrance

BAIRNSDALE - PAYNESVILLE
18KMS

● BAIRNSDALE

13

● EAGLE POINT

5

● PAYNESVILLE

Tunnel Extended Mine, Walhalla Cemetery, Stringers Creek Gorge, Walhalla Goldfields Railway.

3. **Wildlife Coast Nature Track** - Victoria's south coast including Phillip Island, National Parks, Ninety Mile Beach, walking trails, Wilsons Promontory.

4. **The Grand Ridge Road** - Strzelecki Ranges, rainforest and bushwakling areas.

5. **The High Country Adventure** - a journey through mountainous peaks providing breathaking views of rugged valleys below.

6. **The Country Road** - Great Dividing Range Hinterland, rural country, charming pubs, Alpine National Park.

7. **Gourmet Traveller Track** - sampling seafood, meat products, dairy selections, fresh vegetables and fine wines cultivated in the prosperous Gippsland soil.

8. **Power Track** - traces the history of coal mining in the region and takes you past the massive power generation facilities of the LaTrobe Valley.

Stratford

Population 1300
Location and Characteristics
Stratford is a town located on the Avon River 17km north of Sale.

Accommodation and Services
Stratford Motel, 26 Tyers Street (Princes Highway), ©5145 6500 - $55-75.

Points of Interest
A **Shakespearean Festival** is held here in April every year. For more details, ©(03) 5145 6133, email ✉dmccubb@netspace.net.au or visit the website at ●home.bicnet.au\~shakes

Eagle Point

Population 350
Location and Characteristics
Eagle Point is only 15 kilometres, following the coastline south then east, from Bairnsdale.

Accommodation and Services
Old Nats, 245 Lake Vcitoria Road, ©5156 6420. 1 cottage, good facilities- ✪$70-80 including breakfast.
Lake King Waterfront Caravan Park, 67 Bay Road, ©5156 6387. (Pets allowed by arrangement) 90 sites, shop, playground, heated pool - powered sites ✪$13-20 for two, cabins $39-57 for two, on-site vans $29-44 for two.
Eagle Point Caravan Park, ©5156 6232. (No pets allowed) 200 sites, playground, recreation room, barbecue, heated pool - powered sites ✪$13-18 for two, cabins $40-70 for two.

Points of Interest
The well known Mitchell River silt jetties are found at Eagle Point. Eagle Point is also known for its fishing, both in Lake King and the Mitchell River.

Paynesville

Population 2500
Location and Characteristics
Known as the boating capital of the Gippsland Lakes, Paynesville is 18km (11 miles) south-east of Bairnsdale, with a well-marked turn off the Princes Highway. McMillan Strait, Newlands Arm and canals provide sheltered moorings for many pleasure and commercial fishing boats.

Accommodation and Services
Mariners Cove Resort, The Esplanade, ©5156 7444. 15 units, good room facilities - ✪$85-140.
Sunlake Gardens, Toonalook Parade, ©5156 6261. 11 units, cooking facilities, recreation room, car parking, playground, mini golf, tennis court, sauna, spa, indoor heated pool - ✪$45-145.
Allawah Caravan & Boat Park, 13 Mitchell Street, ©5156 7777. (Pets allowed) 151 sites, kiosk, barbecue, playground, recreation room, pool - powered sites ✪$14-19 for two, cabins $39-70 for two, on-site vans $30-59 for two.

Points of Interest

From Paynesville there are many places to go by boat - the **Lakes National Park**, with its picnic grounds and kangaroos, the beautiful **Duck Arm**, and three of Victoria's best **bream rivers**: Mitchell, Nicholson and Tambo. There is also a ferry that runs from Paynesville to **Raymond Island**, which is inhabited by kangaroos, koalas and water and bush birds.

Bairnsdale

Population 10,700

Location and Characteristics

Bairnsdale, just over 30km west of Lakes Entrance, was the port for its pastoral hinterland in the days before road transport. Now it supports a number of secondary industries.

Visitor Information

The Tourist Information Centre is at 240 Main Street, ℰ(03) 5152 3444, and they have brochures and details of all attractions. You can email them at ✉ bairnsdale@lakesandwilderness .com.au

Accommodation and Services

Colonial Motor Inn, 335 Main Street, ℰ5152 1988. 14 units, good room facilities, sauna, pool, spa - ✪$95-125.

Bairnsdale Kansas City Motel, 310 Main Street, ℰ5152 6266. 20 units, licensed restaurant (closed Sunday), room service, playground, pool - ✪$70-85.

Bairnsdale Wander Inn Motel, 620 Main Street, ℰ5152 6477. 16 units, unlicensed restaurant, basic room facilities, pool - ✪$55-60.

Travelana Motel, 49 Main Street, ℰ5152 3200.

Fishing in the Lakes & Wilderness region

14 units, basic facilities - ✪$60-65.

Caravan Parks

Bairnsdale Tourist & Caravan Park, ℰ139 Princes Highway, ℰ5152 4066 or ℰ1800 062 885. (No pets allowed) 162 sites, recreation room, barbecue, playground, tennis court, golf putting green, pool, spa, sauna - powered sites ✪$17-21 for two, cabins $35-72 for two.

Mitchell Gardens Caravan Park, Main Street, ℰ5152 4654. (No pets allowed) 140 sites, playground, pool, barbecue - powered sites ✪$14-18 for two, cabins $55-85 for two.

Points of Interest

St Mary's Roman Catholic Church, ℰ5152 2942, built in 1913 and extended in 1937, has unique murals by Frank Floreani, an incredible painted ceiling and other works of art.

The **Court House**, built in 1893 and classified by the National Trust, has delightful architecture, but it can only be viewed from the street.

The Historical Museum, Macarthur Street, has some interesting memorabilia on display, ℰ5152 6363. It is ⏰open Wednesday, Thursday and Sunday 1-5pm.

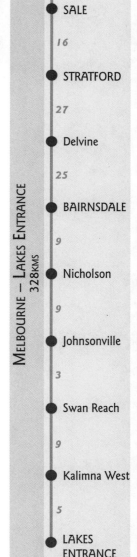

Melbourne to Lakes Entrance

MELBOURNE – LAKES ENTRANCE 328KMS

- SALE
  - 16
- STRATFORD
  - 27
- Delvine
  - 25
- BAIRNSDALE
  - 9
- Nicholson
  - 9
- Johnsonville
  - 3
- Swan Reach
  - 9
- Kalimna West
  - 5
- LAKES ENTRANCE

Chapter 8
Lakes Entrance

Population 4,600
Lakes Entrance is at the gateway to the Gippsland Lakes, Australia's largest inland water system. It is 360km (224 miles) east of Melbourne, 840km (522 miles) south of Sydney and 429km (267 miles) south-west of Canberra.

Climate

Lakes Entrance has a temperate climate. The average maximum temperature in summer is 33C (91F), in winter 21C (70F). There is some rain in July and August, and occasional overnight showers in summer.

Characteristics

The largest town on Ninety Mile Beach, Lakes Entrance is a popular holiday destination. It has a spectacular hinterland with mountains (snow in winter), rivers and forests.
   Wildlife in the area includes dolphins and water birds, kangaroos, wombats, koalas and bush birds.

How to Get There
By Bus
Greyhound Pioneer, ✆13 2030, provides interstate connections.
By Rail
V/Line, ✆13 6196, offer a road and rail combination to Lakes Entrance.
By Road
Access is via Princes Highway from Melbourne and Sydney, and the Cann Valley Highway from Canberra.
By Air
Flying is not the preferred method of access to this area, but regional connections can be made throughout the district and the Visitor Information Centre will be able to advise on the timetables and routes that suit your itinerary.

Visitor Information

The Lakes Entrance Visitor Information Centre is on the corner of Marine Parade and The Esplanade, ✆(03) 5155 1966. They are ⏱open 9am-5pm daily. Contact them over the internet at ✉lakes@lakesandwilderness.com.au or simply explore the web page at 👁www.lakesandwilderness.com.au

Accommodation

As mentioned, Lakes Entrance is a popular holiday spot, so there is plenty of accommodation from which to choose, in fact over 60 places in the town. The Information Centre has a complete list, but here are a few examples with prices for a double room per night, which should be used as a guide only. The telephone area code is 03.
Banjo Paterson Motor Inn, 131 Esplanade, ✆5155 2933. 22 units, licensed restaurant, heated swimming pool, barbecue - ✪$115-190.
Abel Tasman Motor Lodge, 643 Esplanade, ✆5155 1655. 11 units, heated swimming pool, barbecue - ✪$70-165.
Golden Beach Motor Inn, 607 Esplanade, ✆5155 1666. 29 units, swimming pool, unlicensed restaurant - ✪$55-100.
Lakes Central Hotel, 321-333 Esplanade, ✆5155 1977. 16 units, licensed bistro, swimming pool, spa, barbecue - ✪$55-95.
Albatross Motel, 661 Esplanade, ✆5155 1779. 8 units, heated swimming pool, barbecue - ✪$50-135.
Lakeside Motel, 164 Marine Parade, ✆5155 1811. 27 units - ✪$45-90.
The Esplanade Motel, 251 Esplanade, ✆5155 1933. 40 units, car wash, heated swimming pool, spa, barbecue - ✪$40-125.
Lakes Seaview Motel, 12 New Street, ✆5155 1318. 11 units, barbecue - ✪$40-80.
Caravan Parks
Silver Sands Tourist Park, 33 Myer Street, ✆5155 2343. (No pets allowed) 37 sites, spa, pool, barbecue - powered sites ✪$16-25 for two, on-site vans $26-70 for two.
Riviera Country Caravan Park, 29 Palmers

Road, ℗5155 1236. (No pets allowed) 62 sites, barbecue - powered sites ✪$15 for two, on-site vans $30-60 for two, cabins $35-80 for two.
Echo Beach Caravan Park, 33 Roadknight Street, ℗5155 2238. (Pets allowed under control) 25 sites - powered sites ✪$14-25 for two, cabins $40-95 for two.
Lake Haven Caravan Park & Flats, 3 Jemmeson Street, ℗5155 2254. (No pets allowed) 17 sites, barbecue - powered sites ✪$14-23 for two, cabins $30-68 for two, holiday flats $35- 85 for two, on-site vans $25-55 for two.
Lakes Entrance Tourist Park, 127 Princes Highway, ℗5155 1159. (Pets by arrangement) 100 sites, barbecue, heated pool - powered sites ✪$12-24 for two, cabins $20-85 for two.
There is a **Youth Hostel**, **Riviera Backpackers**, in 5 Clarkes Road, Lakes Entrance, ℗5155 2444. It has 19 rooms at ✪$15 per person twin share.

Eating Out

There is the usual range of takeaway outlets, and most hotels serve counter meals. Local seafood is often the specialty on the menu. Some of the motels have restaurants, but here are the addresses and phone numbers of other restaurants you might like to patronise.

For a special dining experience try **Nautilus Floating Dockside**, Western Boat Harbour, The Esplanade, ℗5155 1400. It is licensed, has a seafood specialty, and boasts an outstanding waterside location with views. This award-winning restaurant is open Mon-Sat from 6pm for dinner.
Egidio's Wood Oven, 573 The Esplanade, ℗5155 1411. Licensed, Italian menu.
Ocean Dragon, 601 The Esplanade, ℗5155 1349. Chinese cuisine.
Tres Amigos, 521 The Esplanade, ℗5155 2215. Authentic Mexican flavours.
Shang Hai Garden, 215 The Esplanade, ℗5155 2602.
Skippers, 481 The Esplanade, ℗5155 3551.
The Scallop Pot, 221 The Esplanade, ℗5155 1555.
Miriams, Shop 2, Level 1, 3 Bulmer Street, ℗5155 3999.
Cafe Pelicano, 171 The Esplanade, ℗5155 2166.
Pinocchio Inn, 569 The Esplanade, ℗5155 2565.
McDonalds is at 359 The Esplanade. Although there are no KFC or Pizza Hut branches here, you will find an abundance of alternative fast food outlets along The Esplanade.

Points of Interest

The artificial entrance of the lakes to the ocean was completed in 1889, and there are still visible signs of the equipment used to bring logs and rocks from inland for the construction.

A short walk across the footbridge brings you to the Entrance and Bass Strait, with **Ninety Mile Beach** stretching away into the distance. A section of the beach is patrolled by the Surf Lifesaving Club during the holidays.
Nyerimilang Park on Lake King, Kalimna West Road, Nungurner, overlooks Rigby, Fraser and Flannagan Islands. It has bullock driving demonstrations and field days, and there are bushwalks, as well as barbecue and picnic facilities, ℗5156 3253. Nyerimilang is Aboriginal for Chain of Lakes.
Kinkuna Country Fun Park & Zoo, Princes Highway, ℗5155 3000, has waterslides, a toboggan ride with electronic timing, kiosk, souvenirs, crafts and games room. It is ⏲open daily from 10am (weather permitting) and the entry fee includes barbecues, toddlers' pool, the jumping castle and wildlife area. The lions are hand-fed (not fed hands) at about 1pm on most days. Entry is ✪$8 adults, $6 children and toddlers under three are free.
Griffiths' Sea Shell Museum and Marine Display, 125 Esplanade, ℗5155 1538, also has a gift shop and a model railway display. Over 90,000 shells from around the world are featured, and there is also a model railway room for locomotive enthusiasts. The complex is ⏲open daily.
The Lakes Entrance Aboriginal Art & Crafts, 239 The Esplanade, ℗5155 3302, has genuine Aboriginal artefacts on display and for sale. ⏲Open 9am-5pm daily.

Festivals

Here are a few of the major events in the East Gippsland area:

January - the Metung Regatta, and the New Year's Eve fireworks at Lakes Entrance.

February - the Canni Creek Races near Buchan, the Cattlemen's Cup (every year in the high country, once every four years at Omeo).

March - the Marlay Point Overnight Yacht Race and the Bairnsdale Festival.

Easter - Rodeos at Omeo and Buchan, the Kinkuna Festival and Blessing of the Fleet at Lakes Entrance.

June - the Wildtrek at Dinner Plain.

November - the Flat Water Classic (windsurfing) at Paynesville.

Facilities

Boat cruises from Lakes Entrance, Metung, Lake Tyers, Paynesville. Sail and motor boat hire, daily or longer term, from Lakes Entrance, Metung, Paynesville, Lake Tyers, Johnstonville. Fishing from jetties, shoreline, from hired boats, or on organised fishing trips. Swimming in lakes and sea. Viewing the hot pools at Metung. Rafting and canoeing on rivers. Horse-riding - full day and extended trail rides. 4WD tours, bushwalking, tennis, lawn bowls, golf.

The Visitor Information Centre has all the information on times and locations, ©(03) 5155 1966.

Chapter 9
Lakes Entrance to Batemans Bay

Nowa Nowa

Location and Characteristics
Situated approximately 24km (15 miles) from Lakes Entrance, Nowa Nowa is predominantly a timber milling town.

Accommodation and Services
Nowa Nowa Caravan Park, Bruthen Street, ✆5155 7218. (Small dogs allowed) 20 sites, barbecue, minimal facilities - powered sites ✪$12 for two, on-site vans $25-32 for two.

Points of Interest
Numerous forest drives off the Princes Highway lead to delightful barbecue spots. Close by are the trestle bridge and the Mundic Creek waterfall at **Cosstick Weir**. The arm from **Lake Tyers** extends to the town, offering good fishing.

Buchan

Population 400
Location and Characteristics
In the foothills of Snowy River Country, 56km (35 miles) from Lakes Entrance, lies the town of Buchan which is probably best known for its limestone caves.

Visitor Information
The Visitor Centre in Lakes Entrance produces a very good pamphlet detailing activities and attractions in the area, including a comprehensive driving map, ✆5155 1966.

Accommodation and Services
Buchan Motel, off Main Street, ✆5155 9201. 8 units, unlicensed restaurant, barbecue, basic facilities - ✪$60-75.
Buchan Caves Caravan Park, Caves Road, ✆5155 9264. (No pets allowed) 93 sites, playground, kiosk, pool - powered sites ✪$14-17 for two, cabins $45-55.

Points of Interest
The **limestone caves** were discovered in 1907, and the reserve surrounding them has picnic facilities, barbecues, and lots of kangaroos. There is also a swimming pool fed by an extremely cool underground stream. The rangers conduct tours through the caves during the day.

Omeo

Population 300
Location and Characteristics
Omeo is on the way to the snowfields at Mt Hotham, about one-and-a-half hours drive from Bairnsdale. The town's history lies in timber, gold and cattle, and the town is like the backdrop for a movie set in the 1880s.

Visitor Information
Additional visitor information can be acquired by phoning ✆0500 877 477.

Accommodation and Services
The Omeo Golden Age Hotel, Great Alpine Road, ✆5159 1344. 15 rooms, licensed restaurant, good facilities - ✪$90.
Colonial Motel Omeo, Day Avenue, ✆5159 1388. 4 units, cooking facilities, barbecue - ✪$70-90.
Omeo Motel, Park Street, ✆5159 1297. 11 units, unlicensed restaurant (closed Sunday), playground - ✪$50-85.
Holston Tourist Park, Old Omeo Highway, ✆5159 1351. 160 sites, barbecue, kiosk, minimal facilities - powered sites ✪$13 for two, on-site vans $28-36 for two.

Points of Interest
Omeo is an ideal place to stop for a meal and to hire skis and chains during winter, and even close enough to stay in the town and visit the snow of Alpine National Park daily. Many people visit Omeo for trout fishing, bushwalking and canoeing.

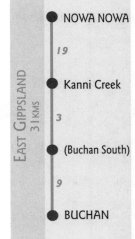

Lakes Entrance to Batemans Bay

EAST GIPPSLAND
31 KMS

NOWA NOWA

19

Kanni Creek

3

(Buchan South)

9

BUCHAN

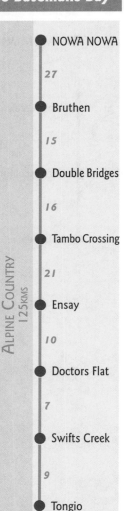

Lakes Entrance to Batemans Bay

ALPINE COUNTRY 125 KMS

NOWA NOWA

27

Bruthen

15

Double Bridges

16

Tambo Crossing

21

Ensay

10

Doctors Flat

7

Swifts Creek

9

Tongio

20

OMEO

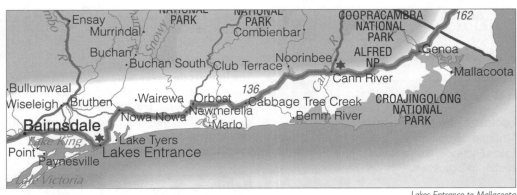

Lakes Entrance to Mallacoota

Orbost

Population 2500

Location and Characteristics
Orbost is the railhead for East Gippsland, and is situated on the Snowy River 16km from the coast. It is the gateway to Marlo where the Snowy meets the Brodribb River and where a sandbar allows the rivers to reach the sea.

Visitor Information
For ideas on the best places and routes to explore, the Snowy River Visitor Centre in Lochiel Street can be contacted on ✆(03) 5154 2424 or emailed at ✎ orbost@lakesandwilderness.com.au

Accommodation and Services
Orbost Country Roads Motor Inn, 94 Salisbury Street, ✆5154 2500. 14 units, basic room facilities, barbecue, pool - ✪$70-80.
Countryman Motor Inn, ✆5154 1311 or ✆1800 012 010. Licensed restaurant, basic facilities - ✪$55-60.
Orbost Caravan Park, cnr Lochiel & Nicholson Streets, ✆5154 1097. 120 sites, playground, minimal facilities - powered sites ✪$14-15 for two, on-site vans $25-30 for two.

Points of Interest
Scenic drives and walks are the main attraction of this stunning region. Cape Conran, reached via Marlo, has camping, picnic and walking facilities.

Mallacoota

Population 1000

Location and Characteristics
Reached via Genoa on the NSW/Vic border, Mallacoota is surrounded by the Croajinolong National Park.

Visitor Information
If you wish to explore the natural wonders here, contact the Park Office, Genoa Road, Mallacoota, ✆(03) 5158 0263 or the Information Centre in nearby Cann River, ✆(03) 5158 6351.

Accommodation and Services
Following is a list of accommodation in the area. The telephone code is 03.
Mallacoota Motor Inn, 15 Maurice Avenue, ✆5158 0544. 8 units, barbecue, playground, basic facilities - ✪$65-110.
Mallacoota Hotel/Motel, 51 Maurice Avenue, ✆5158 0455. 21 units, licensed restaurant, basic facilities, pool - ✪$55-80.
Mallacoota Shady Gully Caravan Park, Lot 5 Genoa Road, ✆5158 0362. (No pets allowed) 94 sites, barbecue, playground, heated pool - powered sites ✪$14-18 for two, cabins $40-55 for two, on site vans $22-36 for two.
Mallacoota Caravan Park, Allan Drive, ✆5158 0300. (Pets allowed by arrangement) 600 sites, playground, minimal facilities - powered sites ✪$14-20.
There is a **Youth Hostel** in 51-55 Maurice Av-

enue, ☏5158 0455. It has 4 rooms at ✪$15 per adult twin share.

Points of Interest

Mallacoota is situated in one of Victoria's most remote and peaceful lakeland settings. There are many walking tracks through the **Croajinolong National Park**, which has prolific birdlife.

Wonboyn Lake

Population 200

Location and Characteristics

The locals are proud of Wonboyn Lake, some 30km (19 miles) south of Eden, and surrounded by Ben Boyd National Park and Nadgee Nature Reserve.

Accommodation and Services

Wonboyn Lake Resort, 1 Oyster Lane, ☏6496 9162. 14 cottages, licensed restaurant, cooking facilities, recreation room, pool, spa - ✪$70-150.
Wonboyn Cabins & Caravan Park, Wonboyn Road, ☏6496 9131. 42 sites, playground, recreation room, playground, pool - powered sites ✪$15-22 for two, on-site vans $32-42 for two, cabins $50-85 for two.

Points of Interest

In addition to the stunning scenery of **Ben Boyd** and **Nadgee**, Wonboyn has a reputation for the finest lake fishing on the Sapphire Coast.

Heading north, we now cross into the state of New South Wales, where the telephone area code is (02).

Eden

Population 3100

Location and Characteristics

Eden is situated some 61km (38 miles) south of Bega, on Twofold Bay. A former whaling station, it is now a deep water fishing port, and the fishing and timber industries are of utmost importance to the survival of the town.

Visitor Information

For more information on accommodation and things to do, contact the Eden Tourist Information Office, Princes Highway (at the roundabout), ☏6496 1953. It is ⏱open Mon-Fri 10am-4pm, Sat-Sun 10am-noon.

Accommodation and Services

Twofold Bay Motor Inn, 166 Imlay Street, ☏6496 3111. 24 units, good facilities, room service, heated pool, spa - ✪$80-170.
Coachmans Rest Motor Inn, Princes Highway, ☏6496 1900. 26 units, licensed restaurant, room service, pool, spa - ✪$65-120.
Bayview Motor Inn, Princes Highway, ☏6496 1242. 30 units, licensed restaurants, playground, barbecue, spa, pool, room service - ✪$65-130.
Sapphire Coast Motel, 48 Princes Highway, ☏6496 1200. 19 units, licensed restaurant, barbecue, playground, car parking, spa, pool - ✪$50-90.
Caravan Parks
Garden of Eden Caravan Park, Princes Highway, ☏6496 1172. (Pets allowed by arrangement) 215 sites, tennis court, playground, pool - powered sites ✪$15-21 for two, cabins $26-95 for two.
Twofold Beach Resort, 731 Princes Highway, ☏6496 1572 or ☏1800 631 006. (No pets allowed) 330 sites, barbecue, kiosk, playground, tennis court, spa - powered sites ✪$14-20 for two, cabins $33-125 for two, on-site vans $28-40 for two.

Points of Interest

The town's **Killer Whale Museum**, 94 Imlay Street, ☏6496 2094, gives an overview of Eden's history, and houses the skeleton of 'Old Tom' a legendary whale from the area. Also featured is the **Seaman's Memorial Wall**, commemorating those lost at sea. The museum has limited opening times daily.
The **Ben Boyd National Park** flanks Twofold Bay to the north, with its famous Red Cliffs, and borders historic Boyd's Tower to the south. You can camp in the park, and at East Boyd Bay the

Lakes Entrance to Batemans Bay

LAKES ENTRANCE - BATEMANS BAY
590KMS

- LAKES ENTRANCE
  21
- NOWA NOWA
  10
- Tostatree
  23
- Newmerella
  6
- ORBOST
  11
- Brodribb River
  15
- Cabbage Tree Creek
  11
- Bellbird Creek
  34
- Tonghi Creek
  7
- Cann River

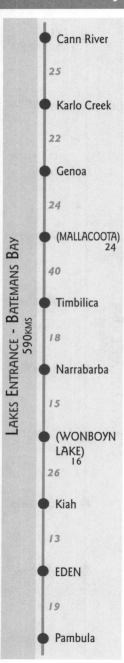

LAKES ENTRANCE - BATEMANS BAY
590KMS

- Cann River
- 25
- Karlo Creek
- 22
- Genoa
- 24
- (MALLACOOTA)
  24
- 40
- Timbilica
- 18
- Narrabarba
- 15
- (WONBOYN LAKE)
  16
- 26
- Kiah
- 13
- EDEN
- 19
- Pambula

Mallacoota to Cobargo

Forestry Commission runs the Edrom Lodge for students.

Merimbula

Population 4400

Location and Characteristics
This flourishing resort town on Lake Merimbula is 26km (16 miles) south of Bega.

Visitor Information
The Tourist Information Centre is on Beach Street, ©6495 1129, ⊙open Mon-Fri 9am-5pm, Sat-Sun 9am-1pm. This is the place to get all the information on available accommodation, of which there is plenty.

Accommodation and Services
Fairway Motor Inn, Lot 386 Princes Highway, ©6495 6000. 20 units, car parking, cooking facilities, barbecue, tennis, pool, spa - ✪$70-130.
Town Centre Motor Inn, 8 Merimbula Drive, ©6495 1163. 20 units, recreation room, cooking facilities, pool - ✪$65-115.
Pipers Lodge, 107 Princes Highway, ©6495 1440. 9 units, cooking facilities, pool, barbecue - ✪$50-85.
Merimbula Motor Lodge, 131 Merimbula Drive, ©6495 1748. 18 units, cooking facilities, playground, pool - ✪$55-110.
Merimbula Gardens Motel, Merimbula Drive, ©6495 1206. 22 units, basic facilities - ✪$60-95.
There is a **Youth Hostel** in 8 Marine Parade, ©6495 3503. It has 16 rooms at ✪$19 per person twin share.
Caravan Parks
South Haven Caravan Park, Elizabeth Street, ©6495 1304. 88 sites, barbecue, playground, sauna, tennis, indoor heated pool - powered sites ✪$16-35 for two, units $85-105 for two, cabins $55-95 for two.
Sapphire Valley Caravan Park, Sapphire Coast Drive, ©6495 1746. (No pets allowed) 150 sites, barbecue, recreation room, shop, playground, pool - powered sites ✪$16-32 for two, cabins $30-99 for two.
Merimbula Caravan Park, Cliff Street, ©6495 1269. (No dogs allowed) 334 sites, barbecue, tennis court, shop, heated pool - powered sites ✪$16-26 for two, cabins $45-65 for two, on-site vans $30-60 for two.

Points of Interest
Merimbula is an activity-based centre, with surfing on Main Beach, Short Point and Tura Beach, sailboarding and water skiing on Lake Merimbula,

golf at the 27-hole Pambula-Merimbula golf course, lawn bowls at the ubiquitous bowling clubs and a variety of other activities - tennis, canoeing, horseriding and cycling. It has an RSL club with 'pokies' and live entertainment.

The **Magic Mountain Family Recreation Park**, with its water slides, mini Grand Prix race track and mountain toboggan slide, is just north of the town on Coast Drive, ⌀6495 2299. The park ⏱opens at 10am and admission is ✪$25 adults, $16 children 5-7 years old and $20 children aged 8-11.

The area also boasts an **Aquarium** (Lake Street, ⌀6495 4446), **Yellow Pinch Wildlife Park** (Princes Highway, ⌀6494 9225), **Milingandi Leisure Farm** (⌀6495 6125) and a **Museum** in Main Street.

Tathra

Population 1700
Location and Characteristics
Tathra is a quiet seaside village 18km (11 miles) east of Bega, with a beautiful beach and great fishing spots.

Visitor Information
Tathra Tourist Centre on Tathra Wharf, Wharf Road, ⌀6494 4062, is the best place to find out what you wish to know. The local people are very friendly and helpful.

Accommodation and Services
Tathra Beach House Apartments, 57 Any Poole Drive, ⌀6494 1944. 6 units, cooking facilities, heated pool, spa - ✪$80-200.

Kianinny Cabins Resort, Tathra Road, ⌀6494 1990 or ⌀1800 064 225 (toll free). 25 cottages, playground, barbecue, cooking facilities, car parking, volleyball, canoeing, pool - ✪$90-180.

Seabreeze Holiday Park, Andy Poole Drive, ⌀6494 1350 or ⌀1800 614 444 (toll free). (No pets allowed) 124 sites, playground, barbecue, kiosk, heated pool - powered sites ✪$14-25 for two, cabins $45-128 for two, on-site vans $30-81 for two.

Tathra Beach Tourist Park, Andy Poole Drive,

⌀6494 1302. (No dogs allowed) 226 sites, playground, basic facilities - powered sites ✪$13-23 for two, cabins $36-130 for two, on-site vans $30-47 for two.

Points of Interest
Tathra offers the best of both worlds: beautiful beaches with ocean activities as well as the opportunity to explore the wildlife of nearby **Mimosa and Bournda National Parks**. There is a **campground** at Bournda National Park with very basic facilities for ✪$10-15 a night for two, ⌀6495 4130.

Bega

Population 4200
Location and Characteristics
The town of Bega is 170km (106 miles) south of Batemans Bay, and 80km (50 miles) south of Narooma. It is the commercial centre of the district with a population above 4000. The district is famous for its dairy industry and cheeses.

Visitor Information
The Sapphire Coast Tourist Information Centre, Office 2, 163 Auckland Street, Bega, ⌀(02) 6492 3313 or ⌀1800 663 012, tends to be the arrival and departure point for coaches, and is the place to obtain assistance for accommodation and suggestions on where to dine. If you have internet access, or are planning your holiday from home, contact them at ✉info@sapphire coast.com.au, or visit the web page at ⌨www.sapphirecoast.com.au

Accommodation and Services
Bega Village Motor Inn, Princes Highway, ⌀6492 2466. 27 units, indoor heated pool, spa - ✪$85-100.

Bega Downs Motel, cnr High & Gipps Streets, ⌀6492 2944. 27 units, licensed restaurants, room service, pool - ✪$90-120.

Northside Motel, Old Princes Highway, ⌀6492 1911. 21 units, licensed restaurant, basic facilities - ✪$60-90.

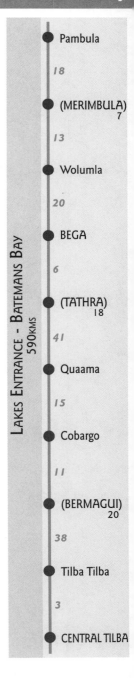

Lakes Entrance to Batemans Bay

LAKES ENTRANCE - BATEMANS BAY 590KMS

● Pambula

18

● (MERIMBULA) 7

13

● Wolumla

20

● BEGA

6

● (TATHRA) 18

41

● Quaama

15

● Cobargo

11

● (BERMAGUI) 20

38

● Tilba Tilba

3

● CENTRAL TILBA

Girraween B&B, 2 Girraween Crescent, ✆6492 1761. 2 rooms, cooking facilities, car parking, barbecue - ✪$60 including breakfast.

Bega Caravan Park, Princes Highway, ✆6492 2303. 50 sites, barbecue, playground, basic facilities - powered sites ✪$15-20 for two, holiday units, $44-60 for two, cabins $30-48 for two, on-site vans $25-38 for two.

There is a **Youth Hostel** in Kirland Crescent, ✆6492 3103. It has 4 rooms at ✪$17 per person twin share.

Points of Interest

The **Bega Cheese Heritage Centre** on the northern side of the Bega River, Lagoon Street, ✆6491 7777, is ⏱open for inspection and tasting daily 9am-5pm.

The Bega Family Museum, cnr Auckland and Bega Streets, is ⏱open Mon-Fri 10.30am-4pm, Sat 10am-12pm, ✆6492 1453.

Brogo Valley's Rotolactor is 23km (14 miles) north of Bega on Baldwin Road, Brogo, and is ⏱open to the public Mon & Wed 2-5pm, with milking at 3pm, ✆6493 8330.

The **Grevillea Estate** winery and vineyards is on the Buckajo Road, ✆6492 3006.

Mumbulla Falls Picnic Area, 20km (12 miles) north of Bega off the Princes Highway along a gravel road, is a very pleasant spot for picnics and a swim. Because of the gravel road, only try it in dry weather.

The largest farm in the Bega Valley is **Kameruka Estate** which is classified by the National Trust. The homestead is set in extensive gardens, with its own church and clock-tower. It is ⏱open daily, ✆6492 0509.

Candelo Village, situated 20km (12 miles) south-west, still retains its old world charm with galleries and restaurants. It is a pleasant place for afternoon tea after a short drive.

Mimosa Rocks National Park, sprawls across its 17km coastal stretch north of Tathra and east of Mt Gearge Mountain. It is a perfect site for a picnic, and for enjoying the natural wonders of landscape and wildlife. Camping areas are also available, and it is best to discuss plans and ideas with the Tourist Information Centre, ✆6492 3313.

Cobargo

Population 400
Location and Characteristics
This village is 19km from Central Tilba.

Accommodation and Services
Cobargo Hotel Motel, Princes Highway, ✆6493 6423. 7 units, licensed restaurant, basic room facilities - ✪$55-60.

Eilancroft B&B, County Boundary Road, ✆6493 7362. 2 rooms, car parking, fireplace - ✪$95-115 including breakfast.

Points of Interest
It has various cottage industries of pottery and leather, art and craft galleries, and a pub.

You can turn off here for Bermagui, or it can be reached by turning off at Tilba Tilba and going along the coast road and crossing Wallaga Lake.

Bermagui

Population 1200
Location and Characteristics
Located on the coast 18km (11 miles) from Cobargo, Bermagui is the mecca for big game fishing in New South Wales, and was made famous in the 1930s by the novelist Zane Grey. Today a large fishing fleet operates out of Bermagui, and game fishermen from all over come for the sport between November and May.

Accommodation and Services
There is enough accommodation in the area for a comfortable short stay in Bermagui.

Beach View Motel, 12 Lamont Street, ✆6493 4155. 8 units, car parking, barbecue, good room facilities - ✪$80-135.

Horseshoe Bay Hotel, Lamont Street, ✆6493 4206. 26 rooms, licensed restaurant, barbecue, recreation room, car parking - ✪$35-60.

Eastview Motor Inn, 46 Coluga Street, ✆6493 4777. 9 units, cooking facilities, pool - ✪$80-130.

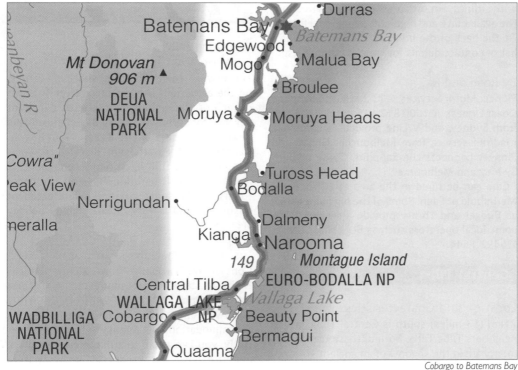

Cobargo to Batemans Bay

Caravan Parks

Wallaga Lake Park, Wallaga Lake Road, Wallaga Lake, ©6493 4655. (Dogs allowed on leash) 200 sites, recreation room, playground, kiosk, tennis court, pool - powered sites ✪$15-21 for two, cabins $30-75 for two.

Zane Grey Park, Lamont Street, ©6493 4382. (No dogs allowed) 186 sites, barbecue, playground, basic facilities - powered sites ✪$15-20, cabins $37-65.

Beauty Point Caravan Park, Beauty Point Road, Wallaga Lake, ©6493 4260. 33 sites, barbecue, basic facilities - powered sites ✪$15-17 for two, holiday flats $35-70 for two, on-site vans $28-43 for two.

Points of Interest

Charter boats are available (for example, Blue Water Charters, Endeavour Drive, ©6493 4540) for pleasure cruising or game fishing, and the harbour has a boat ramp and provision for trailer parking. Swimming and surfing are again the other main diversions - at Blue Pool, Horseshoe Bay and Wallaga Lake. Water skiing is the go on Wallaga Lake.

Sapphire Coast

Visitor Information

The best website covering this area, from Eden to Tilba, is at ☜www.sapphirecoast.com.au

Another website, taking in the Sapphire Coast and surrounding areas, is ☜www.acr.net.au

How to Get There
By Air

The airport near Merimbula, some 30km (19 miles) south of Bega, acts as the air link for the Sapphire Coast. After the turmoil in the aviation industry in late 2001, it is best to check

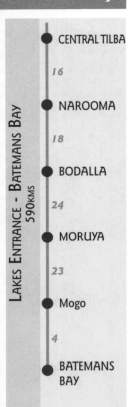

Lakes Entrance to Batemans Bay

LAKES ENTRANCE - BATEMANS BAY
590 KMS

- CENTRAL TILBA
- *16*
- NAROOMA
- *18*
- BODALLA
- *24*
- MORUYA
- *23*
- Mogo
- *4*
- BATEMANS BAY

with airlines, airports or your travel agent about the availability and regularity of regional flights. At the back of the book, in the Appendix, is a list of contact details for various companies.

By Road and Rail

Pioneer Motor Services, ©13 3410, and Sapphire Coast Express, ©1800 812 135, service the area from Sydney, and V/Line provides a combined road/rail service from Melbourne. Greyhound Pioneer connects the Sapphire Coast to both Sydney and Melbourne.

Cars can be hired in the area at either Bega, Merimbula or Eden. Some of the big names such as Budget and Thrifty provide a service as do some local operators such as Bega Hire Service, ©6492 1544.

Central Tilba

Location and Characteristics

21km (13 miles) south is Central Tilba, which neighbors Tilba Tilba. Both of these tiny settlements are in the shadow of an ancient volcano, Mount Dromedary.

Accommodation and Services

The Two Story B&B, Bate Street, ©4473 7290. 3 rooms, car parking - ✪$95-105 including breakfast.
Wirrina B&B, Blacksmiths Lane, ©4473 7279. 3 rooms, basic facilities - ✪$95 including breakfast.
Bellburra Cottages, 318 Ridge Road, ©4473 7157. 4 cottages, cooking facilities, barbecue - ✪$65-95.

Points of Interest

Situated in rather pleasant hilly country at the base of **Mt Dromedary**, Central Tilba has become a tourist spot with art and craft shops, an old wooden general store, a cobblers cottage, a pub, and a quaint restaurant with displays of the traditional crafts. A pleasant day excursion from Narooma.

Narooma

Population 3400
Location and Characteristics

This town is 44km (27 miles) south of Moruya, on the estuary of the Wagonga River. It is another popular fishing resort with excellent beaches for surfing (Mystery Bay, Handkerchief Beach, Narooma Main Beach, Bar Beach, Dalmeny Point, Potato Point, Blackfellows Point and Tuross Head). It has a narrow channel that leads to a small harbour. As with the other towns on the south coast, it offers excellent bushwalks and is very much a family holiday area.

Visitor Information

Contact the Narooma Visitors Centre, Princes Highway, ⏱open every day except Christmas Day 9am-5pm, ©(02) 4476 2881 or ©1800 802 528, with any queries, or to assist in booking accommodation, restaurants or tours. Alternatively, you can email them at ✉eurovcn@acr.net.au or visit the website at ◉www.naturecoasttourism.com.au

Accommodation and Services

For accommodation in Narooma, there are at least 10 motels and hotels, 15 sets of holiday units (✪$45-$130 double/day) and 4 caravan parks, as well as private holiday homes that you can book through an estate agent in the town.

Prices are similar to Batemans Bay, perhaps a little cheaper due to its distance from Sydney. As an indication for a double room per night:
Festival Motor Inn, 126 Princes Highway, ©4476 2099. 28 units, licensed restaurant, barbecue, pool - ✪$75-110.
Holiday Lodge Motel, Princes Highway, ©4476 2282. 12 units, pool - ✪$65-95.
Coastal Comfort Motel, cnr Tilba Street & Princes Highway, ©4476 2256. 12 units, cooking facilities, pool - ✪$70-100.
Olympic Lodge, 76 Princes Highway, ©4476 2379. 4 units, barbecue, cooking facilities, room service - ✪$55-90.

Caravan Parks
Island View Beach Resort, Princes Highway, ©4476 2600. (No pets allowed) 300 sites, barbecue, playground, kiosk, tennis court - powered sites ✪$15-26 for two, cabins $36-138 for two.
Easts Van Village Narooma, Princes Highway, ©4476 2161. (No pets allowed) 231 sites, playground, tennis court - powered sites ✪$16-20 for two, cabins $37-110 for two.
There is a **Youth Hostel** in 11 Riverside Drive, ©4476 4440. It has 7 rooms at ✪$17 per person twin share.

Points of Interest
Montague Island, 8km (5 miles) offshore, is a flora and fauna reserve, and the area around there is well known for its game fishing. The island is the halfway point in the Sydney to Hobart Yacht Race.

Bodalla

Population 300
Location and Characteristics
24km (15 miles) south along the Princes Highway is the town of Bodalla, made famous by Bega cheese which uses it as a brand name.

Accommodation and Services
The *Motel Bodalla* is on the Princes Highway, ©4473 5201. They have 9 units with basic facilities for ✪$55-70 a double per night.

Points of Interest
The **All Saints Church** is one of several photogenic buildings in this attractive little town.
Just before Bodalla is the turnoff to **Tuross Head**, where you can hire boats for fishing and boating on the lake of the same name. The *Tuross Beach Holiday Park*, ©4473 8236, has powered sites - ✪$16-25 for two.

Moruya

Population 2600
Location and Characteristics
The town of Moruya is 27km (17 miles) south of Batemans Bay on the Princes Highway. It has some fine old buildings, including the Wesleyan Church built in 1864 with local granite. The air-

port, which caters for the area, is on the north headland of the river entrance. South Moruya has a fine surf beach.

Accommodation and Services

Accommodation is not plentiful in the area, since Batemans Bay to the north and Narooma in the south provide such facilities. If you are planning to stay here, however, there are a limited number of motels, lodges, guesthouses and B&Bs to choose from. Most are along the Princes Highway, so keep an eye out as you drive through.

Moruya Motel, Princes Highway, ✆4474 2511. 12 units, barbecue - ✪$70-100.

Pearly Shells Motor Inn, Princes Highway, ✆4474 4399. 20 units, licensed restaurant (closed Monday), car parking, fireplace - ✪$45-70.

Monarch, 50 Vulcan Street, ✆4474 2433. 22 rooms, licensed restaurant, spa bath - ✪$40-70.

River Breeze Caravan Park, Princes Highway, ✆4474 2370. (No pets allowed) 126 sites, recreation room, playground, barbecue, tennis, pool - powered sites ✪$14-16 for two, cabins $35-72 for two, on-site vans $28-35 for two.

Points of Interest

The area has excellent **fishing** in the Deua River with its mangrove swamps, and along the various coastal headlands. **Surfing** is great from Moruya Heads to Congo, North Head, Broulee South, North Broulee, Pink Rocks (off the north face of Broulee Island - experienced riders only, 6m waves) and Mossy Point near the mouth of the Tomago River.

Behind Moruya, along the Araluen Road, is the 81,158 ha (200,460 acres) **Deua National Park** which extends up the coastal ranges to Batemans Bay. You can try hiking - good luck and be sure to let the ranger know your plans.

Moruya has an **Historical Museum** in 85 Campbell Street, ☉open Mon & Fri 11am-3pm and on Saturdays 11am-1pm (during peak Christmas and Easter seasons it open daily). Admission is ✪$3 adults and $1 for children, so drop in if you have time.

Each Saturday from 9am the **Moruya Country Markets** are held in Shore Street, and the **Congo Crafts Gallery**, ✆4474 2931, is ☉open Wed-Mon 11am-5pm during school holidays, but it's best to phone beforehand.

Kiora House, along the Araluen Road, is a National Trust classified building that offers quaint old world charm. There is no public access to this building, but its recollections of colonial heritage can be admired from the street.

Moruya boasts a speedway, and a horse racing complex together with golf courses, tennis and bowling clubs.

Chapter 10
Batemans Bay

Population 9600
Batemans Bay is situated on the Clyde River Estuary, at the foot of Clyde Mountain, 306 km (190 miles) south of Sydney.

Climate

Average temperatures: January max 23C (73F) - min 16C (61F); July max 16C (61F) - min 6C (43F). The average annual rainfall: 916mm (36 in). The hours of sunshine per day are 7 in summer and 6 in autumn, winter and spring.

Characteristics

Batemans Bay is a weekend and holiday retreat for people from Canberra. The beaches of the area are clear and clean with superb fishing. It has all the facilities of a beach resort but it is all very understated. It is the only place where the commercial fishing trawlers are permitted to sell their catch direct to the public. The general atmosphere is very friendly; strangers smile and say hello in the street.

How to Get There

By Air

Hazelton Airlines, ℂ13 1713, fly to Moruya and Merimbula from Sydney, Melbourne, Brisbane and Adelaide, with at least two flights daily.

By Bus

Priors Scenic Express operates between Sydney and the Eurobodalla Coast, with a focus on the sightseeing opportunities of the trip, ℂ1800 816 234.
Murrays offer daily services from Canberra, ℂ132 251.
V-Line have a combined road/rail service between Melbourne and Batemans Bay, ℂ132 232.

By Rail

The trains from Sydney, ℂ13 2232, terminate at Bombaderry, on the northern side of the Shoalhaven River, so you will have to organise an alternative form of transport to complete the trip south, be it a hire car or one of the coach services listed above.

By Car

From Sydney and Melbourne, via the Princes Highway - 279km (173 miles) from Sydney and 769km (478 miles) from Melbourne.
From Canberra it is 150km (93 miles) along the Kings Highway.

Visitor Information

The Eurobodalla Visitor Information Centre, cnr Princes Highway and Beach Road, Batemans Bay, ℂ(02) 4472 6900 or ℂ1800 802 528, is ⏱open daily 9am-5pm (closed Christmas Day). Email them at ✉info@naturecoast-tourism.com.au or visit their website at 👁www.naturecoast-tourism.com.au

Accommodation

Batemans Bay, as with most towns on the south coast of New South Wales, is well endowed with a variety of accommodation. Although motels and holiday units dominate, you can usually rent out cottages in the area at reasonable prices, outside of school holiday periods. Contact estate agents in the area or the local Visitor Centre.

Prices vary considerably depending on the standard of accommodation and the season. Here we have a selection, with prices for a double room per night, which should be used as a guide only. The telephone area code is 02.
Reef Motor Inn, 27 Clyde Street, ℂ4472 6000. 33 units, licensed restaurant, swimming pool, spa, barbecue - ✪$105-195.

Batemans Bay

Lincoln Downs Country Resort, Princes Highway, Surfside, ✆4472 6388. 33 units, 7 suites, licensed restaurant, pool, tennis courts, barbecue - ✪$100-160.

Argyle Terrace Motor Inn, 32 Beach Road, ✆4472 5022. 9 units, swimming pool, barbecue - ✪$155-160.

Hanging Rock Golf Club Family, Beach Road, ✆4472 4466. 27 units, playground, barbecue, swimming pool - ✪$55-60.

Holiday Units

These listed are self contained units with all the 'mod-cons'.

Del Costa Holiday Villas, 54 Beach Road, ✆4472 6260. 15 units - ✪$65-130.

The Beach House, 22 Myamba Parade, ✆4472 4086. 1 cottage - ✪$95-130.

Caravan Parks

Easts Riverside Holiday Park, Wharf Road, ✆4472 4048. (No dogs allowed) 47 sites - powered sites ✪$17-24, cabins $50-180.

Coachhouse Marina Resort, Beach Road, ✆4472 4392. (No dogs allowed) - powered sites ✪$16-28 for two, on-site vans $32-40 for two.

Batemans Bay Tourist Park, Old Princes Highway, ✆4472 4972. (Dogs may be permitted on application) - powered sites ✪$14-20 for two, on-site vans $30-55 for two, cabins $34-85 for two.

There is a **Youth Hostel** on the corner of Old Princes Highway and South Street, ✆4472 4972. It has 11 rooms at ✪$18 per person twin share.

Eating Out

The area boasts fine restaurants with particularly good fish dishes. Most of the larger motels have licensed restaurants which can be recommended. There are also a good number of Clubs - Bowling (✆4472 4502), Golf (✆4472 4967), Returned Servicemen (✆4472 4847) - that also contain restaurants. Here are some additional venues.

Briars, Lincoln Downs, Princess Highway, ✆4472 6388. Licensed, seafood and meat dishes, open daily.

Trappers Seafood Restaurant, 26 Princes Highway, ✆4472 5888. Licensed, a la carte but sea-

food specialty, open daily.

Gallery, Catalina Country Club, part of the golf club, ✆4472 4967. Licensed, a la carte, open daily. Also has the Garden Bistro, light snacks to grills with a kids' playground.

Innes' Boatshed, Clyde Street, ✆4472 4052. BYO, family restaurant, seafood caught by the chef, open daily.

Rafters, 28 Beach Road, ✆4472 4288. BYO, a la carte, open daily.

Mexican Munchies, Annetts Arcade, Orient Street, ✆4472 8746. Authentic Mexican dishes.

Raymond's, 19 Clyde Street, ✆4472 5700. Chinese cuisine, open daily.

Pinky's Pizza, 3 Clyde Street, ✆4472 3073.

Vietnamese, Thai & Malaysian, Shop 7, Bay Plaza Centre, Orient Street, ✆4472 7274.

McDonalds is on the corner of Hill and Vesper Streets and KFC is on the Princes Highway.

Points of Interest

The population increases to approximately 90,000 during the peak holiday season (from about mid December to early February). Batemans Bay has **16 golden beaches**, with some sheltered calm waters. McKenzie's Beach is a small beach that has consistent small to medium waves, with the best area at Malua Bay, south of the Surf Club. To the north, there are several good beaches including South Durras near Wasp Head, and Depot, Pebbly and Merry beaches accessible through **Murramarang National Park**

The **Clyde River**, which is quite a spectacular waterway, is navigable for 51km (32 miles) from

Batemans Bay up into the hills. Regular cruises are available up to **Nelligen**, which boasts a number of historically significant buildings.

The MV *Merinda* offers a great time out on the Clyde River (✆4472 4052), or you can hire a boat in the town for your own 'explore and see', combined with a little fishing.

The area is well known for its **fishing**. Durras Lake, to the north of Batemans Bay, has flathead, whiting and bream, and various points and bays between there and North Head offer other good spots. Up from the town near the oyster beds and the mangrove flats on the Clyde River, many people catch whiting, mulloway and bream. There is also quite a deal of fishing from the bank around the town. To the south, Malua Bay and Pretty Point are perhaps the most popular spots. There are many **National Parks** and **forests** in the region, and maps are available from the Visitors Centre. The nearest one to Batemans Bay is Murramarang, which lies between South Durras and North Head. Access is via the Princes Highway and Durras Road, and there are six well-defined walks beginning from the road.

Walks from the town include:

1. Beach walk from Clyde River to Cullendulla Creek - about 3 km (2 miles) long around the coast. Easy, okay for kids.

2. Guerilla Bay to the lighthouse - 1.5km (1 mile).

3. Along the Princes Highway to the Round Hill Fire Tower.

There are many other coastal walks recommended by the Visitors Centre.

The Birdland Animal Park at 55 Beach Road is ◷open 9.30am-4pm daily. It includes 'Wombat World', snake demonstrations, an animal nursery, a koala exhibit, and a scale model train. Admission is ✪$12 adults, $7 children and $22 for families, ✆4472 5364.

The **Historical Society Museum** is in the old court house, cnr Beach Road and Orient Street, and is ◷open Thu-Sat 1pm-4pm, ✆4472 8993.

The **Mogo Goldfields**, on the Tomakin Road near Mogo Village 15km (9 miles) from town, are ◷open weekend and school holidays, 10am-4pm. There is a guided tour of the old underground gold mine. You can camp here with all the amenities, ✆4471 7381. The Village is open most of the time and depicts a bygone era. It is well-known for its art and craft shops.

Festivals

The Neptune Festival is held each November.

Facilities

Boat, catamaran and sailboard hire, golf, tennis, lawn bowls and ten-pin bowling are all provided for in the area.

Chapter 11
Canberra

Population 308,000
Canberra, in the **Australian Capital Territory**, is situated in the southern tablelands of New South Wales, 100km (62 miles) from the coast. It is 300km (186 miles) from Sydney, 654km (406 miles) from Melbourne, 1654km (1028 miles) from Brisbane, and 1201km (746 miles) from Adelaide.

Climate
Average temperatures: January max 28C (82F) - min 13C (55F); July max 11C (52F) - min -1C (30F). Average annual rainfall is 650mm (25 ins).

Characteristics
Canberra, Australia's national capital was founded in 1913. From its inception it has been developed as a garden city and is unique in that it was planned from the outset. In 1912, an American, Walter Burley Griffin, won first prize in a world-wide competition to design the new capital.

Since 1915, thousands of trees have been planted annually and the variation in the shades and colours of the leaves during spring and autumn leave a lasting impression. Over half of the city is parkland and open space dotted with picnic areas.

The Commonwealth Parliament did not sit in Canberra until 1927, when the provisional Parliament House was opened. The new Parliament House was completed in 1988, the Bicentennial Year.

How to Get There
By Air
Qantas, ☎13 1313, service Canberra with their domestic lines, but you can check the availability of other regional flights with your agent.
By Bus
All the major coach companies have daily services from/to Sydney and Melbourne, and less frequent services from/to Adelaide, Brisbane, Wollongong, Cooma, Yass, Batemans Bay and Orange.
By Rail
Countrylink, ☎13 2232, has train services Sydney-Canberra three times a day.

From Melbourne there is no direct rail service to Canberra, but there are a few alternatives: train to Yass, then coach; train to Wodonga, then coach; train to Bairnsdale, then coach, ☎13 6196 or ☎13 1368.
By Car
From Sydney and Melbourne, via the Hume Highway. The trip takes just over 3 hours from Sydney and about 8 hours on a good run from Melbourne. To get around Canberra easily, you really need a car.

Visitor Information
The Canberra Visitor Information Centre can be found at 330 Northbourne Avenue in Dickson, and it is ⏰open 9am-5pm Mon-Fri and 8.30am-5pm on the weekend and public holidays.

Contact them on ☎(02) 6205 0044 or ☎1800 100 660, or by email at ✉canberravisitorcentre @msn.com.au. You can browse through their web page at 🌐www. canberratourism.com.au

Another web site worth exploring is 🌐canberra.citysearch.com.au

Canberra also has a Hire-A-Guide service which operates seven days a week, and can be contacted on ☎6288 7894 or visited at 4 Reveley Crescent, Stirling. The guides are available to individuals or coach parties.

Accommodation
The Tourist Centres have full details of accommodation in the city and suburbs, including apartments, cabins, on campus, hostels and farm stays.

Here is a selection of hotels and motels, with prices for a double room per night, which should be used as a guide only. The telephone area code is 02.

Rydges Lakeside Canberra, London Circuit, Canberra City, ⓒ6247 6244. 201 rooms, licensed restaurants, swimming pool - ✪$150-180.

Parkroyal Canberra, 1 Binara Street, Canberra City, ⓒ6247 8999. 293 rooms (private facilities), licensed restaurant, bistro, swimming pool, spa, sauna, gym - ✪$160-290.

Capital Executive Apartment Hotel, 108 Northbourne Avenue, Braddon, ⓒ6243 8333. 83 units, licensed restaurant, sauna, gym - ✪$140-155.

University House Motel at Australian National University, Balmain Crescent, Acton, ⓒ6249 5211. 100 rooms (private facilities), licensed restaurant - ✪$120-130.

Quality Inn Garden City, Jerrabomberra Avenue, Cooma Road, Narrabundah, ⓒ6295 3322. 69 units, licensed restaurant, swimming pool, spa - ✪$120-150.

Tall Trees Motel, 21 Stephen Street, Ainslie, ⓒ6247 9200. 50 units - ✪$95-130.

Quality Inn Downtown, 82 Northbourne Avenue, Braddon, ⓒ6249 1388. 65 units, licensed restaurant, gym - ✪$110-150.

Embassy Motel, cnr Hopetoun Circuit & Adelaide Avenue, Deakin, ⓒ6281 1322. 86 units, licensed restaurant, air conditioning, sauna, pool - ✪$125.

Acacia Motor Lodge, 65 Ainslie Avenue, Braddon, ⓒ6249 6955 - 53 units, barbecue - ✪$85-95.

Australian Capital Motor Inn, 193 Mouat Street, Lyneham, ⓒ6248 5111. 54 units, licensed restaurant (closed Sunday), swimming pool - ✪$65-85.

Canberra Central Apartments, cnr Northbourne Avenue & Barry Drive, Turner, ⓒ6230 4781. 158 units - ✪$110.

Caravan Parks

Canberra Motor Village, Kunzea Street, O'Connor, ⓒ6247 5466. (No pets allowed), licensed restaurant, barbecue, tennis, pool - powered sites ✪$20 for two, cabins $64-126 for two.

Canberra South Motor Park, Canberra Avenue, Symonston, ⓒ6280 6176. (No pets allowed), licensed restaurant - powered sites ✪$17-18 for two, cabins $45-75 for two.

Anzac Parade

Canberra Carotel Caravan Park, Federal Highway, Watson, ⓒ6241 1377. (No pets allowed) - powered sites ✪$12 for two, on-site vans $33 for two.

There is a **Youth Hostel** at 191 Dryandra Street, ⓒ6248 9155. It has 28 rooms at ✪$21-23 per person twin share.

Eating Out

Canberra's eateries cater for all tastes and pockets, and the Tourist Centres have complete lists. Here are some standard restaurants you may wish to try:

Charcoal, 61 London Circuit, Canberra City, ⓒ6248 8015. A quality steakhouse with seafood varieties available.

Great Wall, 113-119 Marcus Clarke Street, Canberra City, ⓒ6247 5423. Chinese food with yum cha lunches and a take-away option.

The Haig, cnr Northbourne Avenue & Girrahween Street, Canberra City, ⓒ6243 8121. Italian restaurant with al fresco dining.

Shalimar, Tasman House, Marcus Clarke Street, Canberra City, ⓒ6249 6784. Indian cuisine. A la carte and take-away options.

Tasuke, 122 Alinga Street, Canberra City, ⓒ6257 9711. Japanese selections.

Shogun, 70 Bunda Street, Gareema Centre, Gareema Place, Canberra City, ⓒ6248 8888. Traditional Japanese cooking with sashimi and sushi.

Batemans Bay to Canberra

BATEMANS BAY - CANBERRA 138KMS

- BATEMANS BAY
  - 5
- Nelligan
  - 34
- Mongalowe
  - 12
- Braidwood
  - 27
- Doughboy
  - 22
- Bungendore
  - 26
- Queanbeyan
  - 12
- CANBERRA

Tu Tu Tango, 124 Bunda Street, Canberra City, ©6257 7288. Cafe & bar, woodfire pizzas a specialty.

Anatolia, cnr Bunda & Mort Streets, Canberra City, ©6257 1100. Turkish cuisine.

Canberra Vietnamese Restaurant, 21 East Row, Canberra City, ©6247 4840.

Lemon Grass, 71 London Circuit, Canberra City, ©6247 2279. Traditional Thai.

Taj Mahal, 39 Northbourne Avenue (upstairs), Canberra City, ©6247 6528. Indian dining.

Zydeco, 173 City Walk, Canberra City, ©6248 8709.

Rincon Latino, 5 Garema Place, Canberra City, ©6247 0840.

Brindabella, 1 Binara Street, Canberra City, ©6274 5506.

Ardeche, cnr City Walk & Ainslie Avenue, Canberra City, ©6230 4800.

If you can't make up your mind what you fancy to eat, take a trip to Glebe Park in Coranderrk Street, Canberra City. There you will find eight food outlets - patisserie, hamburgers, refreshments bar, continental, Asian, Italian, carvery, seafood and bottle shop. The complex is open seven days, ©0412 626 7252.

As in other cities, the Clubs offer good value for money, and welcome visitors. Some examples are:

The Canberra Club, 45 West Row, Canberra City, ©6248 9000, has French cuisine in their restaurant.

Canberra Workers Club Bistro, cnr University Avenue & Childers Street, Canberra City, ©248 0399, have a budget-priced bistro.

Ainslie Function Centre in the Ainslie Football Club, 52 Wakefield Avenue, Ainslie, ©6248 8422, serves a Grand Seafood Buffet on Thursdays, but their extensive steak, seafood and salad menu should suffice on other days.

The *Canberra Labor Club*, Chandler Street, Belconnen, has an upmarket bistro at downmarket prices, ©6251 5522.

KFC outlets are at Shop B07, Bunda Street, Canberra City; Bengendore Street, Queanbeyan; and 151 Canberra Avenue, Fyshwick.

McDonald's are found at the corner of Badham Street & Dickson Place, Dickson; 20-24 Wanniassa Street, Queanbeyan; cnr Namatjira Drive & MacNalley Street, Weston. Pizza Hut is in Woolley Street, Dickson and the Kippax Centre, Holt, ©13 1166 for delivery.

Local Transport

Bus

Canberra has a public bus service, operated by Action Buses. The buses are large and orange and not easy to miss. The territory is divided into three zones, North, Central and South, and you will have to check your starting point against your destination to determine if you need a 'one zone' or 'all zone' ticket. The flat fares for adults are ✪$2 one zone and $4 all zone, but keep in mind that *Faresaver* tickets are available for extended use of this service.

Ticket agents can be found right across the area, and for more detailed information contact Action on ✆13 17 10 or for timetable information, either ✆6207 7611 or visit the website at ☞www.action.act.gov.au

Bicycle

Otherwise you can hire a bicycle at the Youth Hostel, Dryandra Street, O'Connor, ✆6248 9155; or Mr Spokes, near the Acton Ferry, Barrine Drive, ✆6257 1188.

Car Rental

Avis, 17 Londsdale Street, Braddon, ✆6249 6088; Rumbles, 11 Gladstone Street, Fyshwick. Using a car is a good idea in Canberra.

Organised Tour

Round About Tours, ✆6262 8389; Canberra Region Tours, ✆6247 7281; Grand Touring Coach Charter, ✆6299 1600.

Points of Interest

Canberra has five sign-posted **Tourist Drives** which take in most of the sights. Each begins at the City Hill Lookout, and three concentrate on the central area of Canberra, while the others take in the popular stops on the city outskirts and beyond. The Visitor Centre will give you detailed information on these Drives.

Three popular tourist attractions in Canberra are Parliament House, the War Memorial and the National Library.

Parliament House, in keeping with Walter Burley Griffin's original plan, is the central landmark of Canberra. The building took eight years to complete, and was opened in 1988. While some might not be taken with the 81m (266 ft) stainless steel flagpole that dominates the city, all have to agree that the interior of the building is magnificent. There are imposing marble columns and stairs, extravagant halls, outstanding collections of paintings, sculptures, photographs and ceramics and well-worked timber masonry. Two halls are open to the public. In the Great Hall hangs one of the largest tapestries in the world, based on a painting by Australian artist, Arthur Boyd, that has to be seen to be believed.

Public galleries overlook the House of Representatives Chamber at the eastern side of the building, and the Senate Chamber to the west. The colours of the decor in both chambers reflect the natural green and red tones in native Australian flora. Visitors are welcome to view the Chambers between ⏰9am-5pm, and at all times when Parliament is sitting, even in the early hours of the morning. Guides are at key areas throughout the public areas of the building, and are happy to answer questions. There are also free guided tours available every 30 minutes. Facilities for visitors include a theatrette, an exhibition area, a post office, and on the first floor there is a cafeteria. The bookshop in the Foyer has many publications on Parliament and Parliament House, and a wide range of souvenirs. Pedestrian access is through the northern entrance, the side which overlooks the lake. Access to the underground carpark, which incidentally has room for 2000 vehicles, is via the ramps running off Commonwealth Avenue and Kings Avenue. Details on sitting hours of either of the Houses are available at the information desk in the foyer, or ✆6277 7111.

The National Library, Parkes Place, is on the southern shores of Lake Burley Griffin. It has over 6 million books, periodicals and newspapers, thousands of paintings, maps, films, photographs, music scores, oral histories, and treasures. Exhibitions are held throughout the year, and tours of the Library are available on weekdays. The Library is ⏰open every day except Good Friday and Christmas Day, and hours for the reading rooms, licensed bistro, shop and exhibition areas vary. For further information, ✆6262 1111.

Australian War Memorial, Limestone Avenue, Campbell, commemorates the Australians who gave their lives for their country. The stylised Byzantine building houses a collection of relics, paintings, models, displays and records from all theatres of war. Exhibitions cover the history of Australians at war from Gallipoli to Vietnam. There is a free carpark and picnic areas, a licensed kiosk, and a shop selling a comprehensive range of military books, prints, posters and model kits and souvenirs. The memorial is ◷open daily 9am-4.45pm, ✆6243 4211.

The National Gallery opened in 1982 and houses the national art collection. Eleven galleries provide more than 7000 square metres (8372 sq yds) of exhibition space spread over three levels. Sculpture is displayed in the garden. Regular lectures, film screenings and guided tours are available, and there are frequent special exhibitions, including some from overseas. Facilities include a shop, restaurant and snack bar. ◷Open daily 10am-5pm, ✆6240 6502.

The High Court of Australia, Parkes Place, Parkes, is on the lake shore parallel to the Library. The building features extensive public areas, and is linked to the National Gallery by a pedestrian bridge. The three elegant courtrooms are open to the public. The court contains many interesting national murals and ceremonial plaques, and has a licensed cafeteria. ◷Open daily 10am-4pm. If you are in the mood for a meal, the *Sufficient Grounds* restaurant (✆6270 6820) can be found here - surely one of the most inventive theme names around!

Questacon, The National Science and Technology Centre, is located on the shores of Lake Burley Griffin, between the High Court and the Library. The Centre has over one hundred 'hands-on' exhibits, and visitors of all ages are entertained, intrigued and reassured about the science in our lives. Here you can experience an earthquake, operate a hovercraft, observe an active bee hive, and view a gallery of optical illusions, among other things. There is a cafe and science shop, and all are ◷open daily 10am-5pm, ✆6270 2800.

Seventy countries have diplomatic representation in Canberra, and most of their **Embassies** are in the suburbs of Yarralumla, Forrest and Red Hill. Two have special exhibitions open to visitors: Papua New Guinea, 39-41 Forster Crescent, ✆6273 3322 and Indonesia, 8 Darwin Avenue, ✆6252 8600. Some embassies are open for public inspection on occasions during the year, and the Visitor Information Centre has the details, as well as a brochure on all the embassies, and their addresses. Some of the embassies are built in their traditional style, including India, Thailand, Indonesia and China, and perhaps this explains the cattle that graze on the lawns of the New Zealand High Commission.

Government House, Dunrossil Drive, Yarralumla, the official residence of the Governor General, is not open for inspection, but there is a good view of the building from a lookout on Lady Denman Drive, south of Scrivener Dam.

The Prime Minister's Lodge is on the corner of Adelaide Avenue & National Circuit, Deakin, but it is not open to the public either.

Weston Park, Yarralumla, on the shores of the Lake, has picnic areas and gas barbecues. Features include a miniature railway, a mouse house and a maze. The maze takes about 15 minutes to negotiate and is suitable for all ages. ◷Open weekends and public and school holidays 11am-6pm. Miniature train rides are available 10.30am-5pm, ✆6282 2714.

Lake Burley Griffin is named after Canberra's designer, American architect Walter Burley Griffin. The lake was formed in 1963 by the construction of Scrivener Dam to hold back the waters of the Molonglo River. Over 400ha (988 acres) of parkland has been developed around the 35km (22 miles) foreshore, with numerous picnic areas and sailing boat launchings (power boats are prohibited). Swimming spots can be found at Black Mountain Peninsula, Yarralumla Bay and Springbank Island. Boat hire and cruises are available at Acton Terminal in West Basin, take Barrine Drive off Commonwealth Avenue.

The relatively inaccessible wetlands in East Basin, between Jerrabomberra Creek and the

Captain Cook Memorial Jet

Molonglo River, provide a sanctuary for a variety of bird life.

Although they appear tranquil, Canberra's lakes can be dangerous for small craft as wind gusts can attain a velocity of 25 knots. Weather bulletins issued by the media include wind forecasts, and boating enthusiasts should also heed orange spherical signals raised by water police, which indicate sailing conditions. The temperature of the water surface falls to 6.5C (44F) in winter, and obviously it is even colder below the surface, so this can also be a hazard.

The Captain Cook Memorial Water Jet, powered by two 560Kw motors, spurts a column of water 140m (459 ft) above central Lake Burley Griffin near Regatta Point. The jet and lakeshore Terrestrial Globe were built to mark the bicentenary of Captain Cook's discovery of eastern Australia in 1970. ☉Operating times are 10am-noon and 2pm-4pm, subject to weather conditions.

The National Capital Exhibition is at Regatta Point in Commonwealth Park, ☏6257 1068. There are audio-visual presentations, photographs and displays explaining the history and development of the Nation's capital. Regatta Point provides an excellent vantage point of Lake Burley Griffin, and from the observation area and terrace restaurant there are views of the Captain Cook Water Jet, the Lake's Central Basin, and the Parliamentary Triangle. The Planning Exhibition is ☉open daily 9am-5pm, and there is a gift and book shop.

St John's Church and **Schoolhouse**, Constitution Avenue, Reid, were built in the 1840s, and are Canberra's oldest surviving buildings. The schoolhouse features relics of Canberra's early history, ☏6248 8399. St John's is still an active parish.

Blundells Cottage is on Wendouree Drive, off Constitution Avenue, Parkes, and has a museum display of family life from the nineteenth century. The cottage was built about 1860 by Robert Campbell, and was part of his Duntroon Estate. The first long-term occupants were William and Mary Ginn, and their daughter, Gertrude, was the first child born in the cottage. Mr Ginn was the head ploughman on the Duntroon Estate. The farm house was occupied for 100 years until Mrs Oldfield, the final occupant, passed away on September 8, 1958. The cottage is ☉open Tue-Sun 10am-4pm, ☏6273 2667.

The Carillon, on Aspen Island, Lake Burley Griffin, Wendouree Drive, Parkes, is a three-column belltower, a gift from the British Government to mark Canberra's 50th jubilee. There are free 45 minute recitals in the afternoon daily, ☏6257 1068. The HMAS *Canberra* Memorial is nearby.

Royal Military College, Duntroon, is Australia's first military college and was founded in 1911. Tours of the grounds are available at limited times, ☏6265 9537 for details.

Civic Square is the civic heart of Canberra. Canberra Theatre Centre is at the head of the square and the famous old merry-go-round is in nearby Petrie Plaza. The statue of Ethos is in the foreground, flanked by government offices.

The **National Philatelic Exhibition**, Alinga Street, on the first floor of the GPO building, ☏6209 1680, has a gallery featuring Australia's largest and most valuable collection of stamps, including sheets of Australian stamps issued from Federation to the present.

The new, high-tech **National Museum of Aus-**

tralia is on the Acton Peninsula, ✆6208 5000. It houses a vast and impressive collection in five permanent exhibitions and other temporary displays. Themes include *First Australian's*, *Tangled Destinies*, *Nation* and *Eternity*. An emphasis is placed on the unique people of Australia – historically and in the contemporary era. A visit to the museum is an interactive and immersive experience. There's plenty to see and do, with a range of engaging multimedia that means you'll probably come away learning something new. Plan to spend at least three hours exploring. A restaurant, cafe and shop are part of the complex. Open 9am-5pm daily. Admission is free.

Scrivener Dam lookout is off Lady Denman Drive. Nearby is the National Aquarium & Wildlife Park, ✆6287 1211, with exhibitions of aquatic life, furry fauna and colourful birds. There is a walk-through oceanarium with sharks, rays, Barrier Reef fish, crocodiles, turtles and barracuda, though obviously not all in together. The complex also has a theatrette showing continuous films, a reasonably-priced Brasserie, seating 240 indoors and 300 outdoors, and a gift shop, all set in 5ha (12 acres) of landscaped grounds. It is ⏱open daily 10am-5.30pm and admission is ✪$12 adults, $7 children and $35 for families.

The Royal Australian Mint, Denison Street, Deakin, is responsible for the production of Australia's circulating and collector coinage. The Mint also manufactures medals and medallions, and supplies coinage for several overseas nations. There is a display of past and present Australian coins and old minting equipment, and the Coin Shop offers a wide range of collector's coins and associated products. Ample parking is available, and the grounds are perfect for a picnic. The Mint is ⏱open Mon-Fri 9am-4pm, Sat-Sun 10am-3pm, ✆1300 652 020 or ✆6202 6800.

St Christopher's Catholic Cathedral, 55 Manuka Street, near Manuka Park, ✆6295 9555, has a Byzantine flavour to it.

The Free Serbian Orthodox Church, 32 National Circuit, Forrest, has vivid murals covering the walls and ceiling, the work of the late Karl Matzek, who painted them at the age of 87. The Church is not open to visitors on Sunday mornings, ✆6295 1344.

The Telstra Tower is on the summit of Black Mountain, ✆6248 1911, and from its lookout platforms, kiosk and restaurants, there are panoramic views of the whole region. Black Mountain Drive, the road to the Tower, runs off Clunies Ross Street, near the Botanic Gardens. Telstra Tower is ⏱open daily 9am-10pm, adults ✪$4, concession $2. The kiosk and coffee shop provide refreshments and light meals, but for something special, the revolving restaurant in the Tower offers international cuisine for lunch and dinner seven days a week, ✆6248 6162.

Australian National Botanic Gardens, also off Clunies Ross Street, Black Mountain, are devoted to growing Australian native plants and have over 6000 species. Special features include the Rainforest Gully, Eucalypt lawn and the Rockery. The Visitor Centre has displays and leaflets on walks around the gardens, and there is a kiosk and bookshop. ⏱Open daily, 9am-5pm, ✆6250 9540.

All Saints Anglican Church, 1 Bonney Street, Ainslie, was for 80 years the mortuary railway station at Rookwood Cemetery, Sydney. It was re-erected here stone by stone as the Parish Church of Ainslie, and is ⏱open daily, with tour guides on duty, ✆6248 7420.

The Australian Institute of Sport, Leverrier Crescent, Bruce, was the training ground of many athletes who took part in the 2000 Olympic Games in Sydney. It has become a popular tourist destination, particularly in recent years. Some tours are led by the athletes themselves, and take the visitor through the modern facilities and sporting memorabilia, as well as provide an insight into gruelling training programs. Admission is ✪$10 adults, $5 children and $24 for families, ✆6214 1444.

Stromlo Exploratory, Cotter Road, Weston Creek, ✆6249 0232. This visitor centre is located in the Mt Stromlo Observatory and offers the latest in learning about outer space. Hands-on exhibits cover two floors, and there are giant-telescope tours and slides of spectacular solar system images. Admission into the Exhibition Hall is ✪$6 adults, $4 children and $14 for families. Public Observing Nights are only held once a month since they depend on the moon's phase, so phone the above number to check if this coincides with your trip and book your place.

Festivals

January - Multicultural Festival.
February - Royal Canberra Show. Canberra Travel Fair.
March - Canberra Festival. Autumn Flower Show. Black Opal Stakes. Canberra Antique Fair.
April - Canberra Marathon. ACT Heritage Week.
June - Trooping of the Colour - Duntroon. Embassy inspections.

Floriade Spring Festival - September
Canberra's parks and gardens come alive with spring colour during this very popular annual event. Talented gardeners and landscape architects create delightful patterns by plant-ing a range of thousands and thousands of flowers. For information, ✆6205 0044, or visit ✺www. floriadeaustralia.com

October - Octoberfest.
November - Spring Show.

Facilities

Special, clearly marked cycleways have been provided in Canberra to separate cyclists from other traffic. A map of the metropolitan cycleways is available from the Canberra Visitors Centre. Cycles can be hired for an hour or a day around the lake (see under *Local Transport*).

Windsurfers, catamarans and other sailing craft can also be hired (Lake Burley Griffin Boat Hire, Acton, ✆6249 6861).

Golfers can choose from five courses (including Royal Canberra in Bentham Street, Yarralumla, ✆6282 7000), and another in nearby Queanbeyan.

Tennis courts can be hired in almost every suburb. There are also croquet lawns, squash courts, ten-pin bowling lanes and an ice rink.

The Visitor Information Centre has details of these and other sporting facilities, ✆1800 100 660.

Fishing

The streams in the ACT are divided into two categories - Open Fishing Water, which comprises the Murrumbidgee and Molonglo River below Coppins Crossing; and Trout Fishing Waters, which comprise all of the other waters in the ACT and Lakes Burley Griffin and Ginninderra.

No licences are required, and fishing is permitted in open fishing waters all year round. But trout and bass caught out of season must be returned to the water with the least possible injury. The bag limit is 10 fish per day.

The Open Season for fishing in trout fishing waters extends from the Saturday nearest October 1 to the Sunday nearest May 31 the following year.

Outlying Attractions
Gold Creek Road

The Gold Creek Road, a tranquil rustic setting embracing the historic Ginninderra Village, is only ten minutes' drive from Canberra City, following the Barton Highway. There are several interesting places to visit in the area.
Cockington Green, 11 Gold Creek Road, Nicholls, is Canberra's piece of Great Britain, and has accurate one-twelfth scale model buildings spread in acres of colourful fairy-tale-like gardens. A high speed train flashes by a station and across bridges as a nearby crowd watches a village cricket game. Not far away the people of Braemer Castle are enjoying the morning sun. Each model is a precise reconstruction, and each flower bed, lawn and hedge has been carefully manicured by Cockington Green's gardeners. There's a miniature steamtrain and a playground, both big enough for the kids, and a licensed restaurant that is adequate for discerning adults. Other facilities include an outdoor kiosk, gas barbecues and picnic areas. ⏱Open daily, 9.30am-5pm. Admission is adults ✪$12, children $6 and families $32.

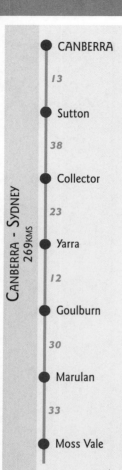

Canberra

CANBERRA

13

Sutton

38

Collector

23

Yarra

12

Goulburn

30

Marulan

33

Moss Vale

CANBERRA - SYDNEY
269 KMS

Gems Gallery, is opposite Gockington Green, ✆6230 2740. The display in this museum is the largest presentation of Australian opals, and there is also a priceless collection of Aboriginal artefacts, some pieces being over 70 thousand years old. The cafeteria is open for meals daily, and there is an opal and souvenir shop. ⏱Open daily 9.30am-4.30pm.

Gold Creek Cultural Centre, O'Hanlon Place, has locally made crafts, Australian souvenirs, hand painted clothing, unique garden pots and other accessories from a variety of shops. ⏱Open daily 10am-5pm, ✆6241 8811.

Nearby is the **Ginninderra Gallery**, with paintings, pottery, wood-turnings, glassware and leather works, all with an Australian theme. ⏱Open daily 10am-5pm, ✆6230 2922.

National Dinosaur Museum, on the corner of the Barton Highway, Gungahlin, ✆6230 2655. The museum houses more than 300 exhibits, including full-scale skeletal replicas and astonishing prehistoric facts. It is ⏱open daily 10am-5pm and admission is ✪$10 adults, $6 children and $25 for families.

George Harcourt Inn is an 'old English' pub, where you can dine outdoors, or in winter, inside before the open log fire. ⏱Open daily from 11am for lunch, and closes at midnight Thu-Sat, an hour earlier during the rest of the week. For further information, ✆6230 2484.

Canberra Walk-in Aviary, Federation Square, Gungahlin, ✆6230 2044. Hundreds of bird finches can be viewed in this unique environment, ⏱open daily 10am-4pm. Admission prices are ✪$6 adult, $3 children and $15 for families.

Bywong

Historic Bywong Mining Town is 33km (21 miles) north of Canberra, off the Federal Highway, Millyn Road, Gearys Gap. It is a gold mining village with areas classified by the Heritage Council. Guided tours of the village are available with an interesting commentary on geological and historical areas, including the open-cut mine shaft mines and batteries. Panning tools can be hired. There is a kiosk, barbe-

cue and picnic areas. ⏱Open daily 10am-4pm, ✆6236 9183.

Ginninderra Gorge and Falls

The Falls are in Parkwood Road, the continuation of Southern Cross Drive, West Belconnen (NSW). There are spectacular views of Ginninderra Gorge and the Falls, scenic nature trails, canoeing, picnic facilities and camping. ⏱Open daily 10am-5pm.

Cotter Dam

The source of Canberra's original water supply and first major construction work is located 22km (14 miles) west of the city, on Cotter Road. It is a very popular spot for picnics, camping and swimming in the river. There are playgrounds, a kiosk, shop, and licensed restaurant. ⏱Open daily.

Tidbinbilla Space Centre

Situated 40km (25 miles) south of Canberra, off Paddys River Road, still in the ACT, the space tracking station is one of three such facilities located around the world to provide complete 24-hour tracking coverage. The other two are in the United States and Spain. ⏱Open 9am-5pm, ✆6201 7838.

Tidbinbilla Nature Reserve

The Reserve is a wilderness area with marked trails and free-range wildlife enclosures, containing red and grey kangaroos, wallaroos, emus and water birds, and the occasional koala. The walking trails in the area are graded from easy to difficult, and you can walk 70m or 7km. The Reserve is off Paddys River Road and opens every day, except Christmas Day and days of total fire ban. At the Visitor Information Centre there are displays, audio visual presentations, literature and helpful staff who will answer your enquiries, ✆6205 1233. The Reserve is ⏱open 9am-6pm daily, with extended hours in season, and cars are charged at ✪$9 per day for entry.

Corin Forest Recreation Area & Ski Facility

Corin Forest is off Tidbinbilla Road, Smokers Gap,

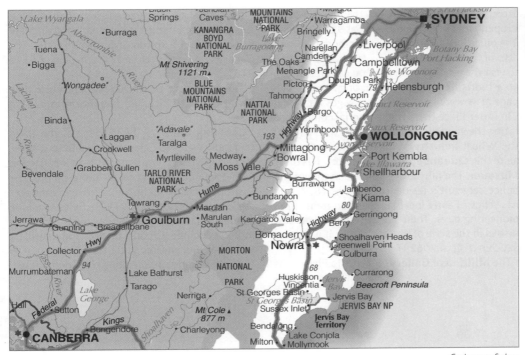

Canberra to Sydney

Moss Vale

8

Bowral

4

Mittagong

12

Yerrinbool

96

SYDNEY

---

a 30 to 40 minute drive from the city. It is home to Australia's longest bobsled/alpine slide (800m - 875 yds), which winds down through mountain forests, achieving a speed of up to 75km/h (47mph). During June through September, providing there is sufficient snow, there is skiing, ski hire and ski school, and snow toboganing. ☾Open every weekend 10am-5pm, and all school and public holidays. There is also a licensed restaurant. For further information, ℰ6247 2250.

Lanyon Historic Homestead

In Tharwa Drive, off Monaro Highway, Tharwa, the Homestead is classified by the National Trust, and is set in landscaped gardens and parklands on the banks of Murrumbidgee River. In the early days it assumed the proportions of a self-contained village. There is a coffee shop, gift shop, and the Sidney Nolan Art Gallery is close by. ☾Open Tues-Sun 10am-4pm, with 1

hour tours available, ℰ6237 5136. ✪$6 adults, $3 children and $14 families.

Cuppacumbalong Craft Centre

Another historic property in Naas Road, Tharwa, featuring three cottages, nine out-buildings and a private cemetery. There are craft galleries, studios, a restaurant, and picnic and barbecue areas near the river. ☾Open Wed-Sun and public holidays 11am-5pm, ℰ6236 5116.

Queanbeyan

Although Queanbeyan is in New South Wales, it is virtually a suburb of Canberra, with a population of around 25,700. The town has plenty of accommodation, and generally the prices are lower than in Canberra. Many people find it worthwhile to stay in Queanbeyan, and drive the 12km (7 miles) into the city to commence their sightseeing. The Queanbeyan Visitor Information Centre, 1 Farrer Place (cnr Lowe

Canberra

Street), ☎(02) 6298 0241 or ☎1800 026 192, is ⏰open Mon-Fri 8.30am-5pm, Sat 9am-1.00pm. The office has details of all accommodation, and also of tourist drives they have mapped for you to visit the interesting sights. You can email them at ✉tourist@qcc.nsw.gov.au, or go to the web page at 🖱www.queanbeyan.nsw.gov.au

In Farrer Place there is a memorial commemorating the valuable work carried by the Father of the Wheat Industry, William James Farrer, and also the **Queanbeyan & District Historic Museum**. The museum is housed in the former police sergeant's residence, built in 1877, and has relics of early local families and items from pioneering days. There are also two rooms furnished in the style of the late 1890s. It is ⏰open Sat-Sun 2-4pm, ☎6297 1978.

The **Millhouse Gallery**, 6 Trinculo Place, was built in 1883 and restored and reopened in 1983. It is a unique building with rooms housing rare books, antique furniture and arts and crafts. The Gallery is ⏰open Wed-Sun 10am-2pm, ☎6297 8181.

Lookouts in the area include **Bungendore Hill**, 4km east of the city, and **Jerrabomberra**, 5km west.

Googong Dam was built south of the town to supply water to Queanbeyan, and to supplement supplies to Canberra. The area is ⏰open 8am-5pm and it is a good idea to drop into the Visitor Centre by the entrance for maps and recreational ideas, ☎6207 2779. Activities include canoeing, sailing, fishing and walking. Points of interest include London Bridge Homestead, a woolshed and shearer's quarters. The turnoff to the dam is about 10km along the Cooma Road.

Chapter 12
Batemans Bay to Nowra

Burrill Lake

Population 1400
Location and Characteristics
Situated 5km (3 miles) south of Ulladulla, Burrill Lake is crossed by the Princes Highway at its eastern arm, but the main expanse reaches inland almost to the township of Milton.

The inlet and beach are to the east of the Highway, and if you take the road to Dolphin Point and follow Seaside Parade you will come to the picnic area, rock platforms and popular fishing spots.

Accommodation and Services
Accommodation is available in caravan parks, motels and holiday units close to the lake and beach.

Snuggle Inn, 155 Princes Highway, ✆4455 3577. 11 units, cooking facilities, fireplace, heated pool - ✪$70-120.

Edgewater Motel, Princess Avenue, ✆4455 2604. 10 units, barbecue - ✪$60-130.

Holiday Haven Lake Burrill Tourist Park, Princess Avenue South, ✆4455 2811. (No dogs allowed) 110 sites, barbecue, playground, heated pool - powered sites ✪$16-25 for two, cabins $50-100 for two, on-site tents $30-60 for two.

Points of Interest
Burrill Lake offers boating, sailing, lake and beach fishing, surfing, swimming, windsurfing and prawning in season. Boats can be hired, and there are three launching ramps.

A boat hire service, ✆4454 0951 operates from the reserve on the foreshores in Moore Street. At **Bungalow Park**, you can feed the lorikeets, which arrive at 8am and 3pm (during daylight saving 9am and 4pm), or play mini-golf on a course which is a replica of the Mollymook Hilltop Golf Course. There are also boats available for hire, ✆4455 1621.

Ulladulla

Population 8300
Location and Characteristics
Ulladulla is 68km (42 miles) south of Nowra, on the Princes Highway, and there is much to see around the harbour and wharf. Trawlers of the fishing fleet are anchored in the harbour behind the safety of the breakwater. Various small craft and the activity associated with fishing are fascinating. Each Easter Sunday, the traditional Blessing of the Fleet Ceremony is conducted on the harbour breakwater. This is a religious custom which has been practised by the Italian fishermen for many generations. Each year this ceremony has become quite a celebration which is worth seeing. Trawlers are decorated for the event and there is a carnival atmosphere.

One of Ulladulla's first settlers was the Rev Thomas Kendall, and his grandson, Henry Kendall was born in April 18, 1839, at the family property north of the present township of Milton. Henry Kendall remained at Ulladulla for only five years, after which he moved about the country, but the people of the town considered him to be Australia's poet laureate, and in March 1862 instigated the publishing by subscription of his poems and songs.

Visitor Information
The Ulladulla Visitors Centre, Civic Centre, Princes Highway, ✆4455 1269, is ✪open Mon-Fri 10am-5pm, Sat-Sun 9am-5pm, and should be your first port of call. There is no shortage of accommodation or restaurants in the town, and the Visitor Centre has all the details.

Accommodation and Services
Albacore Motel, Boree Street, ✆4455 1322. 19 units, cooking facilities, barbecue, pool - ✪$85-150.

Quiet Garden Motel, 2 Burrill Street North, ✆4455 1757. 9 units, barbecue, cooking facilities - ✪$60-140.

Top View, 72 South Street, ✆4455 1514. 12

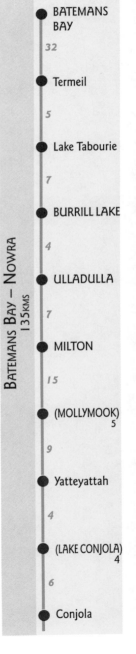

Batemans Bay to Nowra

BATEMANS BAY — NOWRA 135kms

- BATEMANS BAY
- 32
- Termeil
- 5
- Lake Tabourie
- 7
- BURRILL LAKE
- 4
- ULLADULLA
- 7
- MILTON
- 15
- (MOLLYMOOK)
- 5
- 9
- Yatteyattah
- 4
- (LAKE CONJOLA)
- 4
- 6
- Conjola

units, car parking, cook-ing facilities, playground, barbecue, pool - ✪$60-130.

Beach Haven Holiday Resort, Princes Highway, ✆4455 2110. (No pets allowed) 243 sites, recreation room, playground, heated pool, spa, sauna, tennis - powered sites ✪14-23 for two, cabins $32-82 for two, units $47-84 for two.

Ulladulla Tourist Park, South Street, ✆4455 2457. 240 sites, playground, barbecue, tennis, pool - powered sites ✪$16-25 for two, cabins $35 for two.

Points of Interest

The **Warrigal Dive Charter Vessel** leaves from the harbour, and for bookings ✆4455 5303.

The Royal Volunteer Coastal Patrol maintains full sea search and rescue facilities at Ulladulla, for the area from Jervis Bay to Batemans Bay. Radio cover is provided on 2182KHz, 2524KHz and VHF Channel 16 during weekends and holidays periods, and at any other time of day or night by arrangement. However, a continuous watch is maintained 7 days a week on 27880KHz. Pleasure craft owners are urged to lodge sailing plans with the Coastal Patrol Ulladulla either by telephone, ✆4455 3403, or by radio, to ensure they have an adequate radio cover while at sea, and then to advise the base of their safe arrival at their destination.

Pedal boats can be hired on the beach surrounding the harbour during holiday periods. On **Wardens Head**, the southern point of Ulladulla Harbour, is the lighthouse, and from there you can get an uninterrupted view of the coast. A track leads from the lighthouse to the beach where there is good fishing and surfing.

South Pacific Heathland Reserve stretches from Dowling Street to Pitman Avenue, and features the Chris Humphries Nature Walk covering 12ha (30 acres).

Funland, 93 Princes Highway, ✆4455 3053, is one of the largest indoor fun parks in New South Wales. There are three floors of attractions, including dodgems, the 'sizzler' thrill ride, controlla boats, air hockey, slot cars, kiddy rides, and more. ◷Open daily from 10am, closes 10pm Sat and school holidays, 5pm Sun-Fri.

Mollymook

Population 3000

Location and Characteristics

Mollymook is less than 5km (2 miles) south east of Milton, situated by the sea.

Accommodation and Services

Accommodation is available in motels, holiday units and the caravan park. The list below should be used as a guide only.

Bannisters Point Lodge, 191 Mitchell Parade, ✆4455 3044. 24 units, licensed restaurant, barbecue, pool - ✪$95-155.

Mollymook Seascape Motel, 22 Princes Highway, ✆4455 5777. 10 units, cooking facilities, barbecue, heated pool - ✪$65-200.

Mariners on Mollymook, 1 Golf Avenue, ✆4454 2011. 5 units, car parking, cooking facilities, spa bath - ✪$120-200.

Colonial Palms Motel, 15 Princes Highway, ✆4455 1777 or ✆1800 634 800. 13 units, playground, barbecue, pool - ✪$65-120.

Mollymook Caravan Park, Princes Highway, ✆4455 1939. 80 sites, kiosk, barbecue, playground, pool - powered sites ✪$14-18 for two, cabins $40-80 for two, on-site vans $30-45 for two.

Batemans Bay to Nowra

Points of Interest

The surfing beach at Mollymook is patrolled daily, and surf skis are available for hire during the Christmas school holidays from the Surf Life Saving Club. Next to the Club is an 'Exersite' outdoor exercise area with equipment and instructions for strengthening and stretching exercises.

Mollymook Golf Club's picturesque 9-hole beachside course has superb sea views from the clubhouse and restaurant. Visitors are welcome, ©4455 1911. In addition, an 18-hole championship hilltop course is located in Maisie Williams Memorial Drive, with a pro-shop and snack bar facilities. Visitors are welcome here also, ©4455 2055.

The **Bogey Hole**, a circular natural rock pool, and Collers Beach are reached via Golf Avenue and Riversdale Avenue.

The **Mollymook Beach Bowling & Recreation Club** in Forest Way, ©4455 2141, is another friendly place.

Milton

Population 1050

Location and Characteristics

Milton is 7km (4 miles) north of Ulladulla, and 61km (38 miles) south of Nowra. It was established in 1860, has many historic buildings, and in the Mick Ryan Park there is a giant fig tree that is estimated to be over 110 years old.

Accommodation and Services

Accommodation is available in motels, hotels and a caravan park.

Milton Village Motel, Princes Highway, ©4455 1944. 8 units, pool - ✪$60-105.

Batemans Bay to Nowra

JERVIS BAY TERRITORY 62 KMS

- Conjola
- 32
- ST. GEORGES BASIN
- 6
- VINCENTIA
- 10
- (JERVIS BAY)
- 10
- 14
- HUSKISSON

Milton B&B, 124 Princes Highway, ✆4455 4449. 3 rooms, car parking, fireplace, barbecue, pool - ✪$140-170 including breakfast.

Milton Tourist Park, Princes Highway, ✆4455 2028. (No dogs allowed) 164 sites, barbecue, cooking facilities, recreation room, playground, kiosk, pool, tennis - powered sites ✪$16 for two, cabins $30 for two.

Points of Interest

A flea market, featuring local crafts and second-hand goods, is held at the **Settlement Courtyard** on the first Saturday of the month.

Over the long weekend in October every year Milton celebrates the **Milton Settlers' Fair**, which consists of markets, art and craft exhibitions, music and dancing.

Lake Conjola

Population 400

Location and Characteristics

The town of Lake Conjola, is on the shores of the lake of the same name, about 55km (34 miles) south of Nowra.

Accommodation and Services

Accommodation is available in cabins, cottages and caravan parks.

Lake Conjola Entrance Tourist Park, Main Road, ✆4456 1141. (No dogs allowed) 332 sites playground, barbecue, tennis half-court - powered sites ✪$15-24 for two, cabins $45 for two.

Conjola Lakeside Van Park, Norman Street, ✆4456 1407. (No pets allowed) 304 sites, barbecue, playground - powered sites ✪$12-20 for two, cabins $40-80 for two.

Points of Interest

Boats can be hired at the Post Office and General Store, Carrol Avenue, ✆4456 1163, and at Conjola Boat Hire, ✆4456 1563 (school holidays only). There are tennis courts, a bowling club, fishing and water skiing.

The Craft Corner in the General Store specialises in needlework and tapestry supplies and books, ✆4456 1163.

The **Lake Conjola & District Bowling Club**, in Entrance Road, ✆4456 1272, welcomes visitors.

St Georges Basin

Location and Characteristics

Sanctuary Point and St Georges Basin have a combined estimated population of 6000.

Accommodation and Services

The *St Georges Basin Gold View* is at 49 Paradise Beach Road, ✆4443 9502. They have 10 units with basic facilities for ✪$60-100 per night for two.

Points of Interest

There are some lovely spots in and around both places for picnics and all water sports. Catamarans, sailboards and small canoes can be hired from **Sanctuary Point Sail Centre**, 272 Grenville Avenue, ✆4443 0205 (only available in Summer). The **St Georges Basin Country Club**, Paradise Beach Road, ✆4443 0666, is a licensed club that welcomes visitors.

Jervis Bay Territory

Location and Characteristics

This area is part of the Australian Capital Territory, and is 35km (22 miles) from Nowra. It contains the Royal Australian Naval College, HMAS Cresswell, the Jervis Bay Nature Reserve and Botanic Gardens Annex. The ruined lighthouse overlooking the ocean is quite interesting. It was built in the wrong place and proved to be a navigational hazard luring boats to their doom on the rocky coastline. The navy was requested to shell it!

Visitor Information

At Jervis Bay Village you will find a public telephone, police station, supermarket, general store and petrol station. The Administrative Office of Jervis Bay Territory is situated in the grounds of the village, ✆4442 1217.

Accommodation and Services

Booderee National Park is managed by Jervis Bay Administration, and there is a Visitors Centre on the left near the entrance, ©4443 0977. In keeping with the protection of the environment, spear guns, handspears, dogs and other domestic animals are not permitted in the reserve, and fires can only be lit in defined barbecue areas. For enquiries about camping in the park, call into the Visitor Centre, which is ⏱open 8.30am-5pm in the Christmas-Easter period, and 9am-4pm during the off-peak season. Entry into the park is ✪$6 per car weekly.

Green Patch is a camping and picnic area within the National Park, and has a sheltered beach, toilets, hot showers, wood barbecues and picnic tables. There is prolific birdlife, many interesting bush walks, and a camping ground that allows a maximum of three weeks' stay.

Murrays Beach, Summer Cloud Bay and Cave Beach are other popular spots within the Reserve.

Points of Interest

HMAS Cresswell was established as an officer training college in 1915, and visits to the grounds of the college are permitted on a limited basis (20 minutes on weekends and most public holidays), ©4429 7985 for details.

In the college is the **Royal Australian Naval College Historical Collection**, with a display of artefacts specifically related to the college and the Jervis Bay area, and Peter Webber's collection of model sailing ships. It is ⏱open on the last Sunday of each month, or by appointment, ©4429 7845.

The **Jervis Bay Annex** to the Australian National Botanic Gardens is 2km along the Cave Beach Road, and has a large variety of native plants collected from all parts of Australia. Facilities include nature walks, toilets and picnic area, but no barbecues are permitted. The annex is ⏱open Mon-Fri 8am-4pm, and the first Sunday of the month 10am-5pm. Hours may be extended during public and school holidays, ©4442 1122.

Vincentia

Location and Characteristics

Across the Moona-Moona Creek Bridge from Huskisson is the town of Vincentia, 30km (19 miles) south-east of Nowra. This is another holiday town, with shops, and a 9-hole golf course with superb views of Jervis Bay and the Pigeon House Mountain.

Accommodation and Services

Jervis Bay Dolphin Shores Motor Inn, 53 Beach Street, ©4441 6895. 16 units, cooking facilities, barbecue, heated pool, car parking - ✪$85-170.

Bay View, 306 Elizabeth Drive, ©4441 5805. 2 rooms, barbecue, car parking - ✪$100 including breakfast.

Points of Interest

Visitors are welcome at the local golf course and clubhouse at all times, ©4441 5264.

Plantation Point offers sweeping views of Jervis Bay to Bowen Island and Point Perpendicular, and there are barbecue and toilet facilities.

Huskisson

Population 3400

Location and Characteristics

The town of Huskisson, on the shores of Jervis Bay, is 24km (15 miles) south-east of Nowra, and has a shopping centre, a modern RSL club and bowling clubs. It is a real holiday spot, and during the Christmas holiday period a movie theatre and carnival operate in the town. The sands of Jervis Bay are renowned as the whitest in the world, and each Easter Huskisson hosts the White Sands Carnival.

Accommodation and Services

Accommodation is available in hotels, guest houses, motels, caravan parks and holiday units. **Anglesea Lodges**, 2 Admiralty Crescent, ©4441 5057. 3 units, cooking facilities, playground, pool - ✪$150-265.

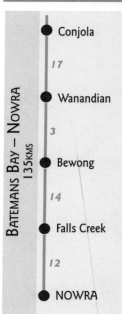

Batemans Bay to Nowra

BATEMANS BAY – NOWRA 135KMS

- Conjola
- 17
- Wanandian
- 3
- Bewong
- 14
- Falls Creek
- 12
- NOWRA

Huskisson Beach Motel, 41 Owen Street, ©4441 6387. 32 units, unlicensed restaurant - ✪$75-250.

Bayside Motor Inn, cnr Hawke & Bowen Streets, ©4441 5500. 32 units, licensed restaurant, cooking facilities, barbecue, room service, heated pool - ✪$65-200.

Huskisson Beach Tourist Resort, Beach Street, ©4441 5142. (No dogs allowed) 176 sites, kiosk, barbecue, playground, recreation room, pool, tennis court - powered sites ✪$17-25 for two, cabins $48-130.

Huskisson White Sands Tourist Park, cnr Nowra & Beach Streets, ©4441 6025. (No pets allowed) 196 sites, kiosk, playground, barbecue - powered sites ✪$13-25 for two, cabins $45-120 for two.

Points of Interest

The **Lady Denman Heritage Complex** in Dent Street is worth a visit. The *Lady Denman* is an old Sydney ferry which was originally built at Huskisson, and saw many years of service on Sydney Harbour. After she retired she was sailed back to Huskisson, placed in the park at the Heritage Complex, and now contains the **Museum of Jervis Bay, Science and The Sea**. The park is ◷open daily 9am-5pm, and the museum is ◷open Tues-Fri 1-5pm, Sat-Sun and school holidays 10am-5pm. Nearby is **Lady Timbery's Aboriginal Arts and Crafts Centre**, ©4441 5999.

Chapter 13
Nowra

Population 11,600
Nowra is situated on the banks of the Shoalhaven River, on the south coast of New South Wales.

Climate
Average temperatures: January max 26C (79F) - min 18C (64F); July max 17C (63F) - min 9C (48F). Average annual rainfall: 1275mm (50 ins).

Characteristics
Nowra is the hub of the City of Shoalhaven, which has a population of around 83,000. The city area stretches from Berry to Durras North, and has 109 ocean, bay and lakeside beaches, lush rolling pastures, craggy mountain haunts and bush trails.

The town has produced two Melbourne Cup winners - Archer and Arwon.

How to Get There
By Rail
Bomaderry is the terminus of the South Coast Railway, and there are train services daily from and to Sydney, ✆13 2232.

Pioneer Motor Service operates a daily bus service which connects with the train, ✆13 3410.

By Bus
Greyhound Pioneer, ✆13 2030, have daily services from Sydney/Melbourne/Sydney which stops at Nowra.

By Road
From Sydney, via the Princes Highway - 162km (100 miles).

Visitor Information
The Shoalhaven Visitor Information Centre, cnr Princess Highway & Pleasant Way, ✆4421 0778 or ✆1800 024 261, is ◷open 9am-4.30pm daily. Their internet details are ☞www.shoalhaven .nsw.gov.au for tourist information and ✉ beverlyc @shoalhaven.nsw.gov.au for email contact.

Accommodation
Here is a selection of available accommodation with prices for a double room per night, which should be used as a guide only. The telephone area code is 02.

Pleasant Way Motor Inn, Pleasant Way, ✆4421 5544. 22 units, swimming pool, spa, barbecue - ✪$95.

Parkhaven Motor Lodge, cnr Kinghorn & Douglas Streets, ✆4421 6444. 30 units, licensed restaurant, swimming pool - ✪$95-160.

Marriott Park, cnr Princes Highway & Douglas Street, ✆4421 6999. 16 units - ✪$70-85.

George Bass Motor Inn, 65 Bridge Road, ✆4421 6388. 10 units, comfortable rooms - ✪$80-100.

Cross Country Motel, 242 Kinghorn Street, ✆4421 7777. 18 units, swimming pool, barbecue - ✪$70-80.

Nowra Motor Inn, 202 Kinghorn Street, ✆4421 0555. 30 units, licensed restaurant, swimming pool - ✪$70-80.

Riverhaven Motel, Scenic Drive, ✆4421 2044. 22 units, licensed restaurant, indoor heated pool, barbecue - ✪$60-75.

Caravan Parks
Shoalhaven Caravan Village, Terara Road, ✆4423 0770. (Pets allowed under control) - powered sites ✪$15 for two, cabins $30-60 for two.

Rest Point Caravan Park, Browns Road, ✆4421 6856. (No pets allowed) 80 sites, playground, barbecue - powered sites ✪$14-18, cabins $35-55.

Eating Out
Nowra has a wide selection of restaurants, coffee shops, and four licensed clubs. Many of the motels also have restaurants. Some of the choices are:

Nowra Steak House, 16 Kinghorne Street, ✆4423 4193.

Captain's Table, 202 Kinghorne Street, ✆4421 0555.

Boatshed, Wharf Road, ✆4421 2419.

Nowra

Trevi Fountain, 223 Kinghorne Road, ✆4423 0285. Italian cuisine.

Riverhaven, Riverhaven Motel, I Scenic Drive, ✆4421 2044.

Shoreline, Parkhaven Motel, cnr Kinghorn & Douglas Streets, ✆4421 5444.

Nowra Palace, 54 Berry Street, ✆4421 4902. Malayasian and Chinese selection.

Theodore's Brasserie, 116 Kinghorne Street, ✆4421 0300.

Leong's Chinese Restaurant, 83 North Street, ✆4421 2131.

McDonald's is on the corner of Cambawarra Road, Bomaderry, and the Princes Highway & Browns Road, South Nowra, ✆4421 1099. KFC is in Lot 22, Princes Highway, South Nowra. Pizza Hut is on the corner of McLean Street and the Princes Highway in Nowra, ✆4421 4199.

Points of Interest

Cruises of the Shoalhaven River are available from Shoalhaven River Tours, 49 Greenwell Point Road, Greenwell Point, ✆4447 1978.

The old **Shoalhaven River bridge** was erected in 1881. To cope with the heavy volume of traffic across the River, a second bridge was erected in 1980.

In **Moorhouse Park**, Bridge Road, there is an old flood rescue boat from Terara.

Nowra Olympic Pool and **Nowra Waterways** are in Scenic Drive and are open from September to Easter, ✆4421 2093.

The Showground, in West Street, is the venue for the two-day agricultural show held in February each year. In the Showground there is the Council Youth Centre, and the Memorial gates, which were built to commemorate servicemen who died in action in the two World Wars.

At the western end of the Showground is **Hanging Rock**, a precariously positioned formation with views across the River and Nowra Golf Course.

Ben's Walk is a walking track which follows the river bank from the track head near Shoalhaven River Bridge to Nowra Creek, which is spanned by a suspension bridge.

On the corner of West and Worrigee Streets, is

Meroogal, an historic house built by Robert Taylor-Thorburn in 1886. It is now owned by the Historic Houses Trust of New South Wales, and is ⏱open Sat 1pm-5pm and Sun 10am-5pm. For further information, ✆4421 8150.

Shoalhaven Historical Museum, cnr Kinghorn & Plunkett Streets, is ⏱open Sat-Sun 1-4pm, and on Mon, Wed and Fri during school holidays 1pm-4pm, ✆4421 2021.

Werninck Craft Cottage, 102 Plunkett Street, is ⏱open Mon-Fri 9.30am-3.30pm, Sat-Sun 10am-4pm, ✆4423 2419.

Situated on the corner of Kinghorn & Kalandar Streets is a **Sea Venom Jet**, which has been donated by HMAS *Albatross*. A short history of the aircraft and type of service is on a plaque at the site.

HMAS Albatross

Travel south from Nowra along the Princes Highway to the Kalandar Street intersection, turn right at the traffic lights and follow the signs.

The **Royal Australian Naval Air Station**, HMAS Albatross, 9km (6 miles) south-west of Nowra, is the home of the Fleet Air Arm. The fixed-wing section at the base was disbanded, due to the lack of an aircraft carrier, and the station now concentrates on helicopters. Educational tours can be arranged, ✆4421 1211 for more information.

The **Naval Aviation Museum** at the Air Station has the finest collection of historic military aircraft in Australia, and a good collection of engines, aviation equipment, models, uniforms and memorabilia. Picnic, barbecue and toilet facilities are provided, and it is ⏱open daily 10am-4pm, ✆4421 1920.

Near the base is the **Nowra Hill Lookout**, with panoramic views of the Shoalhaven and Jervis Bay area. There is a pleasant stroll from there along Commodore's Walk to the Harry Sawkins Memorial Lookout.

Festivals

February - Nowra Agricultural Show.
November - The Shoalhaven Spring Festival.

Facilities

Lawn bowls, canoeing, fishing, golf, sailing, scenic drives, squash, swimming, tennis, water skiing, 4WD escapes and bushwalking tours. Check with the information centre.

Boats can be hired from the following outlets: Aquatique, 125 Junction Street, ©4421 8159 - canoes, scuba and diving gear, surf and wave skis. Shoalhaven Caravan Village, Terrara Road, ©4423 0770 - canoes.

**Nowra
to Wollongong**

● NOWRA

6

● BOMADERRY

13

● BERRI

23

● (SHOALHAVEN
HEADS)
32   15

● Gerrigong

8

● KIAMA

6

● Dunmore

4

● SHELLHARBOUR

NOWRA – WOLLONGONG
114KMS

Chapter 14
Nowra to Wollongong

Bomaderry/North Nowra

Location and Characteristics

The town of Bomaderry is really a northern suburb of Nowra, separated from it by the river. It has a large shopping centre, Narang Road Supergrass Tennis Centre, Shoalhaven Sporting Complex, and a Basketball Stadium. Bomaderry Railway Station is the terminus of the South Coast Railway Line, ©4423 6416.

Accommodation and Services

Avaleen Lodge Motor Inn, 317 Princes Highway, ©4421 8244. 6 units, cooking facilities, barbecue, heated pool - ✪$75-90.
Treehaven Tourist Village, 278 Princes Highway, ©4421 3494. (No pets allowed) - powered sites ✪$16-18 for two, on-site vans $30-40 for two.

Points of Interest

Bomaderry Creek Walk is a track that follows Bomaderry Creek from below the Ten Pin Bowling Centre in Narang Street. Walkers have a choice between a three hour walk and a one hour walk, and picnic and barbecue facilities are available at the track head.
Nowra Golf Club is situated under bush-covered escarpment, near the river in North Nowra, Greys Beach. The clubhouse has first class facilities, and the scenic 18-hole course offers a challenge. Visitors are welcome, ©4421 3900 (pro-shop ©4421 2249).
The **Grotto Walk**, west of the golf course, is an easy walk following the River, and beginning off Yurunga Drive.
From **Rockhill Lookout**, off McMahons Road, you can get a spectacular view of the river.
Nowra Wildlife Park is set in 6ha (16 acres) off Rockhill Road, North Nowra, overlooking the river. You can walk amongst the animals, and have your photo taken with the resident koalas.

The park has a well appointed picnic and barbecue area, a kiosk and a camping area, and is ⊕open daily 8am-5pm, ©4421 3949. Admission is ✪$7 adults, $4 children.

Shoalhaven Heads

Population 2500
Location and Characteristics

The township of Shoalhaven Heads is at the southern end of Seven Mile Beach, about 13km (8 miles) east of Bomaderry. It is a popular holiday spot near Seven Mile Beach National Park.

Accommodation and Services

Coolangatta Estate Resort, 1335 Bolong Road, ©4448 7131. 25 units, licensed restaurant, barbecue, recreation room, tennis, pool, golf - ✪$100-185.
Mountain View Caravan Park, 14 Shoalhaven Heads Road, ©4448 7281. (No pets allowed) 212 sites, playground, tennis, barbecue, mini golf - powered sites ✪$15-20 for two, cabins $50-120 for two.
Shoalhaven Heads Tourist Park, Shoalhaven Heads Road, ©4448 7178. (No dogs allowed) 324 sites, recreation room, playground, barbecue, mini golf, tennis half-court, cooking facilities - powered sites ✪$15-24, cabins $35-130.

Points of Interest

The town offers a bowling club, fishing facilities and a swimming pool. You can hire bicycles at Shoalhaven Heads Hardware Store, ©4448 7707. Nearby is **Coolangatta Estate Historic Village Resort**, 1335 Bolong Road, ©4448 7131, the site of the first settlement in the Shoalhaven district. The complex comprises buildings erected by the district's founder, Alexander Berry, that have been restored as motel units. There is also a 9-hole golf course, a winery, and picnic areas and barbecues.
The **Coolangatta Craft Centre**, 1180 Bolong Road, is housed in the original school house, established in 1861. It is ⊕open Wed-Mon 9am-5pm, and daily during school holidays, ©4448 7205.

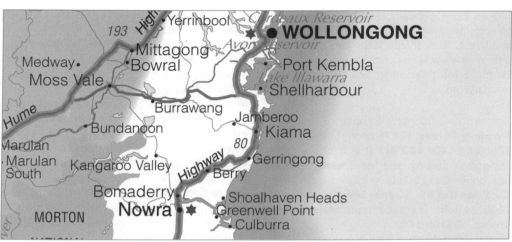

Nowra to Wollongong

Cambewarra Mountain Lookout. The lookout is on Tourist Road, Beamont, north of Bomaderry, and offers panoramic views of the Shoalhaven River Valley and the coastline. Picnic, barbecue and toilet facilities are provided. There is also a kiosk which is ⏰open Fri-Wed 9am-5pm and daily during the Christmas school holidays, ✆4465 1321.

Berry

Population 1600
Location and Characteristics
Called the Town of Trees, Berry more than lives up to its name, and is 16km (10 miles) north of Nowra. The town has a population of around 1600, with shopping facilities, motel and hotel accommodation, restaurants, and many antique and craft shops.

Visitor Information
Local information can be obtained from *Pottering Around*, on the corner of Queen and Alexandra Streets, ✆4464 2177.

Accommodation and Services
Abbeywood in the Fields, cnr Bryan & Hillandale Road, ✆4464 2148. 2 rooms, wood fire, - ✪$110-140 including breakfast.
Bangalee Motel, Princes Highway, ✆4464 1305. 10 units, pool, barbecue - ✪$65-115.
Berry Hotel, 120 Princes Highway, ✆4464 1011. 14 rooms, licensed restaurant, recreation room, room service, playground - ✪$50-80.

Points of Interest
The **Berry Historical Museum**, Queen Street, is ⏰open Sat 11am-2pm, Sun 11am-3pm and public holidays 11am-2pm, ✆4464 1551, and they can point out the other buildings in the town classified by the National Trust, such as the Court House and National Bank.
Berry Country Fair, featuring local crafts and second-hand goods, is held at Apex Park, cnr Princes Highway & Prince Alfred Street, on the first Sunday of the month.

Kiama

Population 11,700
Location and Characteristics
Kiama is a seaside town 36km (22 miles) south of Wollongong.

Visitor Information
The Kiama Visitors Centre is on Blowhole Point Road, ✆4232 3322 or ✆1300 654 262 (free call).

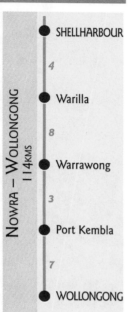

NOWRA – WOLLONGONG
114KMS

SHELLHARBOUR

4

Warilla

8

Warrawong

3

Port Kembla

7

WOLLONGONG

☼Open 9am-5pm daily, they have information on accommodation available, and all the places of interest. You can check the area out on the web at ☞www.kiama.com.au and email them for more information at ✉kiamatourism@ozemail.com.au

Accommodation and Services

Terralong Terrace, 129 Terralong Street, ☎4232 3711 or ☎1800 683 711 (toll free). 16 units, undercover parking, spa baths, cooking facilities, pool - ❂$115-260.

The Pines Flag Inn, 10 Bong Bong Street, ☎4232 1000. 29 units, licensed restaurant, pool, room service - ❂$100-180.

Kiama Ocean View, 9 Bong Bong Street, ☎4232 1966. 17 units, barbecue - ❂$45-140.

Surf Beach Holiday Park, Bourrool Street, ☎4232 1791. 91 sites, playground, barbecue - powered sites ❂$17-22 for two, cabins $55-140.

Blowhole Point Holiday Park, Lighthouse Road, ☎4232 2707. (No pets allowed) 102 sites, unlicensed restaurant, kiosk, playground, tennis, pool - powered sites ❂$16-20 for two, on-site vans $35-80 for two.

Points of Interest

The Blowhole is the main attraction, but nowadays it only seems to 'blow' in nasty weather. In any case, it is floodlit until 9.30pm.

The best way to explore Kiama is on foot, strolling around the foreshore area. First, visit the burial site of one of the members of the First Fleet, and then walk around the showground that overlooks Storm Bay's jagged rocks, to the town's popular Surf Beach. You can picnic in the adjoining park, or continue through the town centre taking in the historic grand old homes and commercial buildings on the way.

The Terraces, a row of historic timber cottages, are now gift and specialty stores, and a good place to pick up a bargain. Most of the stores are ☼open daily 10am-5pm.

The **Family History Centre**, 7 Railway Parade, ☎4233 1122, has comprehensive in-house microform and data inventory to enable people

to trace their family trees. The Centre is ☼open daily 9.30am-4.30pm.

The **Quarry Leisure Centre**, Havilah Place, ☎4232 1877, has a 25m heated swimming pool, a wading pool, sauna, spa, aerobics, and facilities for indoor sports.

Minnamurra Falls. The Falls are 15km (9 miles) west of Kiama, in a dense subtropical rainforest, and plunge some 50m (164 ft) into a deep gorge. There is a delightful walk from the parking area through the rainforest to the Falls, and the round trip takes about an hour.

Barren Grounds Nature Reserve. The Reserve is 25km (16 miles) west of Kiama on the Jamberoo Mountain Road, and affords magnificent views from the lookout. There is a unique hanging swamp and bird observatory, and picnic and barbecue facilities.

Shellharbour

Population 46,300
Location and Characteristics
The town of Shellharbour is around twenty minutes' drive south of Wollongong on the coastal road. There are caravan and camping areas, modern motels, one of the state's largest licensed clubs, an attractive corner pub, golf, bowls, great restaurants and beautiful beaches.

The name Shellharbour is derived from the many Aboriginal shell middens found here and at nearby Bass Point. The location is listed on the Heritage Commission Register, and is regarded as one of the two most important archaeological sites on the NSW coast.

Visitor Information
For more information contact the Shellharbour Visitor Information Centre, ☎4221 6169. They are located in Lamerton House, Lamerton Crescent, and are ☼open 8.30am-4.40pm Mon-Fri, closed weekends and public holidays.

They can be emailed at: ✉tourism@shellharbour.nsw.gov.au and the web address is ☞www.shellharbour.nsw.gov.au

Accommodation and Services

Shellharbour Resort, Shellharbour Road, ©4295 1317. 31 units, licensed restaurant, tennis court, car parking, pool, room service - ✪$105-135.

Windradene Seaside Guest House, 29 Addison Street, ©4295 1074. 4 rooms, car parking, barbecue, fireplace - ✪$110-130.

Shellharbour Beachside Tourist Park, John Street, ©4295 1123. (Dogs allowed by arrangement) 118 sites, barbecue, pool - powered sites ✪$15-25, cabins $60-110.

Points of Interest

Bass Point is a popular diving area, as part of its waters form a marine reserve. There is an airport at nearby Albion Park, and joy flights are offered. Nearby is the turnoff to Jamberoo Recreation Park, where you can play mini golf, go bobsledding, grass ski, or take the chairlift to the mountain top. There is also a maze, a licensed family restaurant, children's play area and a barbecue hut.

Southern Highlands

If you are interested in trekking westwards, the Southern Highlands Visitor Information Centre, ©(02) 4871 2888, located at 62-70 Main Street, Mittagong, will assist you with accommodation and attractions so that you can plan your visit to the area. They are ☺open 8am-5.30pm every day, and can also be emailed at ✒wingtour@ wsc.com.au

Mittagong, Bowral, Moss Vale and Kangaroo Valley are the most popular destinations in the Southern Highlands. Taking the Hume Highway through the Southern Highlands is the quickest route to Canberra in the ACT. See *Australian Road Trips* by Ian Read (Little Hills Press, 2001) for more detail of this area.

Nowra to Wollongong

Chapter 15
Wollongong

Population 219,800
Wollongong is situated on the coast of New South Wales, 80km (50 miles) from Sydney, and 238km (148 miles) from Canberra.

Climate
Average temperatures: January max 26C (79F) - min 18C (64F); July max 17C (63F) - min 9C (48F). Average annual rainfall: 1275mm (50 ins).

Characteristics
Wollongong is the seventh largest city in Australia, and the gateway to the Illawarra and Southern Highlands region. To its north, cosy mining villages dot the coastline against a dramatic backdrop of green escarpment. Here the Illawarra coastal plain is narrowest, at times reduced to nothing, as rocky sea cliffs reach right to the pounding waves.

In the seaside village of Thirroul, D.H. Lawrence wrote *Kangaroo*, and from Stanwell Park, aviator Lawrence Hargraves tested his kites.

How to Get There
By Rail
Electric trains run regularly between Sydney's Central Station and Wollongong, connecting with on-going services to Port Kembla and south to Bomaderry on Nowra's northern outskirts, ✆13 2232.
By Bus
Greyhound Pioneer, ✆13 2030, and McCaffertys, ✆13 1499, stop at Wollongong daily on their Sydney/Melbourne via the Princes Highway services.
By Road
From Sydney, via the Princes Highway to Waterfall and then the F6, or continue along the highway and turn off at the Stanwell Park signpost for a spectacular drive along the coast.

Another interesting route is via the National Park to Stanwell Park - turn off just past Sutherland.

Visitor Information
The Wollongong Visitor Information Centre, 93 Crown Street (corner of Kembla Street), ✆(02) 4277 5545 or ✆1800 240 737 (free call), is ⏰open seven days a week 9am-5pm Mon-Fri, 9am-4pm Sat and 10am-4pm Sun. They can be emailed at ✉tourism@wollongong.nsw.gov.au and the website to explore is ⌖www.wollongong.nsw.gov.au

Accommodation
The Illawarra coast boasts a comprehensive range of accommodation from caravan parks on many of the beaches and lakesides, to an international style resort hotel, leisure village, quality motels, hotels, holiday units and superb convention facilities. Here is a selection with prices for a double room per night, which should be used as a guide only. The telephone area code is 02.

Novotel Northbeach, 2 Cliff Road, ✆4226 3555. 203 rooms, 17 suites, licensed restaurants, swimming pool, spa, sauna, gym, tennis, bicycling - ✪$230-360.

City Pacific Boutique Hotel, 112 Burelli Street, ✆4229 7444. 61 rooms, licensed restaurant, swimming pool - ✪$75-250.

Boat Harbour Motel, 7 Campbell Street, ✆4228 9166. 42 units, licensed restaurant (closed Sun and public holidays) - ✪$115-140.

Golden Pacific North Beach, 16 Pleasant Avenue, North Wollongong, ✆4226 3000. 20 units, 2 suites - ✪$95-180.

Downtown Motel, 76 Crown Street, ✆4229 8344. 31 units, licensed restaurant (closed Sun) - ✪$75-100.

Beach Park Motor Inn, 10 Pleasant Avenue, North Wollongong, ✆4226 1577. 16 units, barbecue - ✪$60-170.

Caravan Parks

Corrimal Beach Tourist Park, Lake Parade, Corrimal, ✆4285 5688. 397 sites, barbecue - powered sites ✪$13-16 for two, cabins $52-140 for two.

Windang Beach Tourist Park, Fern Street, ✆4297 3166. (No pets) 259 sites, barbecue - powered sites ✪$16-20 for two, cabins $32-60 for two, bungalows $32-60 for two.

Bulli Beach Tourist Park, 1 Farrell Road, ©4285 5677. (No pets allowed), 269 sites - powered sites ✪$16-20 for two, cabins $52-140 for two.

Eating Out

Wollongong's cosmopolitan community offers you a wide choice of superb restaurants, snack bars and coffee lounges. Here are some you might like to try.

Fuji Yama Tepan Restaurant, 35 Flinders Street, ©4226 2609, specialise in Japanese barbecues.

Charcoal Tavern, 18 Regent Street, ©4229 7298. Modern Australian dining, seafood and steaks.

Nam, 4 Kenny Street, ©4228 3646. Vietnamese and Chinese food.

Beach House Seafood Restaurant, 16 Cliff Road, ©4228 5410.

Anchorage, cnr Campbell & Wilson Streets, ©4228 9166. A-la-carte menu and beach views.

Branches, Blackbutt Motel, Shellharbour Road, Shellharbour, ©4297 1323. Italian and seafood.

Zita's, 147-149 Corrimal Street, ©4227 1110. French, Italian and German cuisine with local seafood.

King's, 26 Flinders Street, North Wollongong, ©4228 6976. Chinese cuisine.

Amigos, 116 Keira Street, ©4229 8181. Mexican selection.

Bangkok Orchid Thai, Shop 1, 119 Corrimal Street, ©4229 6620.

Mammas Pizza Roma, 56 Crown Street, ©4229 9166.

Tandoori Village Indian Restaurant, Shop 2, 120 Corrimal Street, ©4225 7876.

During business hours a good place to eat is the Food Court, lower level of the Gateway on the Mall shopping complex, cnr Burelli & Keira Streets. They have tables in the centre and you can choose from Chinese, Italian, Austrian, Mexican, crepes, chicken, pies, kebabs, hamburgers, and so on.

McDonald's have outlets at 115 Corrimal Street and Wollongong Crown Central, Shop 97, 200 Crown Street. There are branches in all other Wollongong localities as well.

A southwards view of Wollongong from Bulli Lookout

Pizza Hut have outlets in localities surrounding Wollongong. You will find them on the corner of the Priness Highway and McGrath Street, Fairy Meadow, 32 Princes Highway, Dapto and on the corner of King Street and Kemblawarra Place in Warrawong.

KFC can be found at cnr Princes Highway & McGrath Street, Fairy Meadow; 74 Princes Highway, Unanderra; cnr Kemblawarra Road & King Street, Warrawong; 136 Princes Highway, Dapto; and Holm Place, Shellharbour Square.

Entertainment

For those who want to boogie the night away, there are many night clubs and discos, as well as the licensed clubs. The clubs in Wollongong itself are:

Collegians RLFC, 3A Charlotte Street,t, ©4229 7711.

Illawarra Master Builders, 61 Church Street, ©4229 6466.

Illawarra Leagues Club, 87 Church Street, ©4229 4611.

Wollongong Ex-Services, 82 Church Street, ©4228 8522.

For movie goers, Wollongong has two cinema complexes:

Regent Theatre, 197 Keira Street, ©4228 9238.

Town Cinemas, Burelli Street, ©4228 4888.

The ***Illawarra Performing Arts Centre***, Burelli Street, ©4226 3366, has live theatre and musical presentations.

Wollongong

Points of Interest

Most historic buildings can be visited on a **walking tour** commencing at Flagstaff Hill (parking available). The sights visited are: Wollongong Head Lighthouse; Breakwater Lighthouse; Belmore Basin; Drill Hall; Throsby's stockman's hut monument; Market Square; Illawarra Historical Museum; Congregational Church; Wollongong Courthouse; St Michael's Provisional Cathedral; Wollongong Uniting Church; The Town Hall; Wollongong East Post Office; Tourist Information office; St Francis Xavier's Provisional Cathedral; and Andrew Lysaght Park. **Mount Kembla Historic Village**, 7km (4 miles) from Wollongong was the site of the 1902 mining disaster, but it is full of art and craft centres today.

Wollongong Botanic Garden, in Keiraville, is a pleasant spot for picnics and quiet walks, and offers many areas of interest - Sir Joseph Banks Plant Houses, where plants from the wet tropics, deserts and temperate regions are displayed; The Rose Garden; Woodland Garden; Flowering Trees and Shrub Garden; Succulent Plants from South Africa and Central America; Australian Plant Habitats; and The Herb Garden. The Garden is ☉open daily 7am-4.45pm Mon-Fri and 10am-4.45pm Sat-Sun. During winter the gardens close at 6.45pm.

The **Wollongong City Art Gallery**, 85 Burelli Street, ☎4228 7500, has a fine collection of modern and traditional paintings, with changing exhibitions. It is ☉open Tue-Fri 10am-5pm, Sat-Sun noon-4pm.

Magnificent views of the coastline can be obtained from **Mount Kembla Lookout**, **Sublime Point** and **Bulli Lookout**, all of which are only about 15 to 20 minutes' drive from the centre of town.

Kelly's Falls, 2km off the Princes Highway at Stanwell Tops, has a picnic area and easy walking tracks to the falls. Flannel flowers are abundant in spring and early summer.

Nearby is **Symbio Wildlife Gardens**, 7 Lawrence Hargrave Drive, ☎4294 1088, which has native and exotic animals, free barbecues, swimming and wading pools and lunchtime demonstrations of activities from milking a cow to handling reptiles. The gardens are ☉open daily from 9.30am, and they advertise that feeding time is 'all the time'. To get to these attractions, take the old Princes Highway from Wollongong, not the F6.

While you are in the area, drive north for half an hour to **Bald Hill Lookout**, where there is a memorial to Lawrence Hargraves, and if the wind is favourable you will see many brightly coloured hang-gliders floating by.

Stanwell Park is in the valley below, and you can call in and browse through Articles Fine Arts Gallery, 111 Lawrence Hargrave Drive, ☎4294 2491, and have a Devonshire tea on the outdoor terrace. The hang-gliders land in the part next to the sea.

South of Wollongong is **Lake Illawarra**, renowned for fishing and prawning, and often ablaze with colourful sailing boats and sail boards. The lake is actually a lagoon covering an area of 35 sq km (14 sq miles), with its entrance at the foreshore suburb of Windang.

The **Illawarra Escarpment State Recreation Area** has many fine walking trails through the rainforest, ☎9585 6444 for details.

Australia's largest steel mill is located around the foreshores of **Port Kembla Harbour**. The harbour sees millions of tons of coal exported each year from the surrounding mines, as well as steel from the steelworks.

Wollongong has two **bicycle tracks**. The one to the north starts at North Beach and goes to Corrimal, 14km (9 miles) away. The southern one starts near the Windang bridge and skirts the shores of Lake Illawarra.

Festivals

The Festival of Wollongong is held each year in November.

Facilities

Ten-pin bowling (8 Commerce Drive, Warilla), car rental depots (Auto Rentals, ☎4229 7766; Avis, ☎4228 4111; Budget, ☎13 2727; Thrifty, ☎4227 3000), catamaran and sailboard hire (Lake Illawarra & Belmore Basin), tennis, squash,

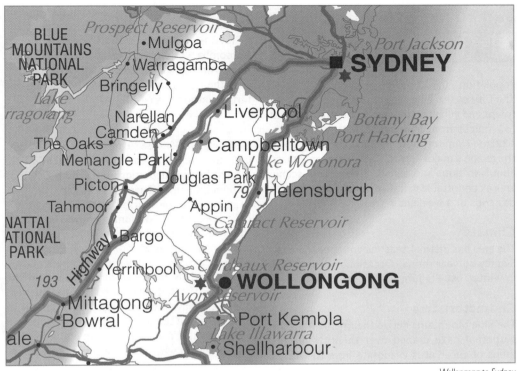

Wollongong to Sydney

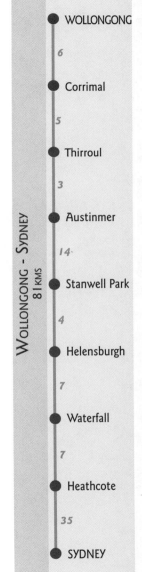

WOLLONGONG – SYDNEY 81 KMS

- WOLLONGONG
- *6*
- Corrimal
- *5*
- Thirroul
- *3*
- Austinmer
- *14·*
- Stanwell Park
- *4*
- Helensburgh
- *7*
- Waterfall
- *7*
- Heathcote
- *35*
- SYDNEY

horse riding (Otford Valley Farm, ©4294 2442), golf, joy flights (Albion Park Aerodrome), fishing, leisure centre with heated pools (Beaton Park, ©4229 6004), horse racing (Kembla Grange, ©4261 7211), greyhound racing (Bulli, ©4267 1467 and Dapto, ©4261 2449), harness racing (Bulli, ©4267 4224) and indoor cricket (Albion Park Rail, ©4256 6138 and Unanderra, ©4271 6685). Deep sea charter boats leave from Belmore Basin. Roller skating is available at Dapto, ©4261 6333.

Chapter 16
Blue Mountains

Population 70,800
The City of the Blue Mountains, comprising 26 towns and villages, stretches from Penrith, 53km (33 miles) from Sydney, to Mount Victoria, 122km (76 miles) from Sydney. The drive up to the region's major centre, Katoomba, only takes about an hour and a half, making this scenic area a comfortable distance from Sydney city for day trips or a weekend retreat.

Climate
The area has distinct seasons and is cooler than Sydney all year round. Occasionally snow falls in winter, usually July, but it does not last.

Characteristics
The Blue Mountains derive their name from the perpetual haze draped over them. Miniscule drops of eucalyptus evaporate from the leaves of the dense forest and are struck by the sunlight to produce this effect.

It was not until twenty-five years after the arrival of the First Fleet that the Blue Mountains were crossed in search of grazing land. The intrepid explorers who performed the feat in 1813 were Blaxland, Wentworth and Lawson, and three mountain towns bear their names.

In the 1920s and '30s, the Blue Mountains was the Holiday Capital of New South Wales, then it declined in popularity, as people travelled further afield. In recent years there has been a revival, and the Blue Mountains is once again a popular tourist centre.

How to Get There
By Rail
Electric trains depart from Central Station in Sydney every day with stops at Lapstone, Glenbrook, Blaxland, Warrimoo, Valley Heights, Springwood, Faulconbridge, Woodford, Hazelbrook, Lawson, Wentworth Falls, Leura, Katoomba, Medlow Bath, Blackheath and Mt Victoria.

CityRail have special off-peak fares to Katoomba - any train after 9am on weekdays, or any time at the weekend, with return before 4am the next morning, for ✪$11.80 adult. For further information ✆(02) 4782 1902.

By Bus
AAT Kings, ✆9666 3899, Newmans, ✆1300 300 036, and Australian Pacific Tours, ✆9247 7222, have daily tours departing from Sydney Day Tour Terminal, Circular Quay West at 9am.

Fantastic Aussie Tours, ✆9938 5714 (Sydney) or ✆4782 1366 (Katoomba) have three hour tours which connect with trains from Sydney at Katoomba Railway Station.

They also have full day tours of Jenolan Caves departing daily from Katoomba Station in the morning. The Blue Mountains Explorer Bus also operates daily and picks up and drops off in Katoomba and Leura at the main attractions and restaurants. It meets most trains from Sydney, and connects with trains returning to Sydney. On Wednesdays only, they offer trips to Australia's Wonderland, as well as Darling Harbour and the Olympic Site combined.

By Road
From Sydney, via Parramatta Road, the F4 Freeway and the Great Western Highway. From the west, the Great Western Highway.

Visitor Information
Echo Point Information Centre, ✆1300 653 408 and Glenbrook Visitor Information Centre, Great Western Highway, Glenbrook, ✆1300 653 408, are ⏰open Mon-Fri 9am-5pm, Sat-Sun 8.30am-4.30pm.

Contact them by email on ✉info@blue mountainstourism.org.au

The official website of Blue Mountains Tourism, ✆1300 653 408, is ☟www.bluemountains tourism.org.au but another one to visit is ☟www.bluemts.com.au

Accommodation

Here is a selection of accommodation, with prices for a double room per night, which should be used as a guide only. GST is included. The telephone area code is 02.

Katoomba

Alpine Motor Inn, cnr Great Western Highway & Orient Street, ✆4782 2011. 20 units, 4 suites, licensed restaurant, indoor heated swimming pool, sauna - ✪$200-255.

Mountain Heritage, cnr Lovel & Apex Streets, ✆4782 2155. 41 units, licensed restaurant, playground, swimming pool - ✪$180-420.

Katoomba Town Centre Motel, 218-220 Katoomba Street, ✆4782 1266. 18 units, spa - ✪$80-230.

The Cecil Traditional Blue Mountains Guest House, 108 Katoomba Street, ✆4782 1411. 23 rooms, unlicensed restaurant, barbecue, spa, playground tennis - B&B ✪$140-180.

Echo Point Motor Inn, Echo Point Road, ✆4782 2088. 37 units, licensed restaurant - ✪$70-130.

3 Sisters Motel, 348 Katoomba Street, ✆4782 2911. 20 units, unlicensed restaurant - ✪$65-120.

Leura

Peppers Fairmont Resort, 1 Sublime Point Road, ✆4782 5222. 210 rooms, 20 suites (private facilities), licensed restaurant, swimming pool, spa, sauna, gym, tennis, squash - ✪$240-340.

Mercure Resort Blue Mountains, Fitzroy Street, ✆4784 1331. 80 units, 9 suites, licensed restaurant, swimming pool, spa, sauna, gym, tennis, squash, putting green - ✪$130-170.

Medlow Bath

Hydro Majestic Hotel, Great Western Highway, ✆4788 1002. 63 rooms (private facilities), modern Art Deco and classic Edwardian style rooms available, very famous heritage hotel, licensed restaurant, swimming pool, tennis, spa (selected rooms) - ✪$220-1350.

Chalet Blue Mountains, 46 Portland Road, ✆4788 1122. 8 rooms, unlicensed restaurant, tennis, playground - ✪$130-150.

Mt Victoria

Mount Victoria Motor Inn, Station Street, ✆4787 1320. 12 units - ✪$95-160.

The Hotel Imperial, cnr Great Western Highway & Station Street, ✆4787 1233. 23 rooms, licensed restaurant - ✪$75-275 (a range of room standards offered).

Jenolan Caves

Caves House, ✆(02) 6359 3304. 50 rooms, licensed restaurant, playground, tennis, pool, barbecue - B&B ✪$80-200 a double; hotel section, 28 units - ✪$100-105 including breakfast.

Blackheath

Blackheath Motor Inn, 281 Great Western Highway, ✆4787 8788. 18 units, spa - ✪$90-135.

High Mountains Motor Inn, 193 Great Western Highway, ✆4787 8216. 21 units, unlicensed restaurant, swimming pool - ✪$70-120.

Caravan Parks

Katoomba Falls Caravan Park, Katoomba Falls Road, ✆4782 1835. (No pets), 68 sites, barbecue - powered sites ✪$25-30 for two, cabins $60-84 for two.

Leura Village Caravan Park, cnr Great Western Highway & The Mall, ✆4784 1552 (no pets) - powered sites ✪$13 for two, on-site vans $31-33 for two.

Blackheath Caravan Park, Prince Edward Street, ✆4787 8101. (No pets), 74 sites, - powered sites ✪$20-22 for two, cabins $38-55 for two.

Eating Out

If you would like a superb meal in a hotel, try: ***The Swiss Cottage Restaurant***, 132 Lurline Street, Katoomba, ✆4782 2281. Undoubtedly one of the best restaurants in the Blue Mountains, *The Swiss Cottage* offers excellent meals in a warm atmosphere. The steaks and fish are superb, the soup is thick and rich, and, for dessert, the melted-Lindt-chocolate-soaked pudding is unbeatable (look for 'Death By Chocolate' on the menu). Your lively host Monique will make you feel welcome and keep you chuckling as she serves up each course.

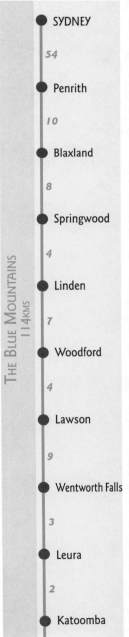

Blue Mountains

SYDNEY

54

Penrith

10

Blaxland

8

Springwood

4

Linden

7

Woodford

4

Lawson

9

Wentworth Falls

3

Leura

2

Katoomba

THE BLUE MOUNTAINS 114KMS

Blue Mountains

Blue Mountains area

Grand View, 174 Great Western Highway, Wentworth Falls, ©4757 1001.

Fairmont Resort, 1 Sublime Point Road, Leura, ©4782 5222.

Hydro Majestic Hotel, Great Western Highway, Medlow Bath, ©4788 1002.

The Imperial, Station Street, Mt Victoria, © 4787 1788.

Guest Houses which serve good meals include:

Felton Woods Manor, cnr Lurline Street & Merriwa Streets, Katoomba, ©4782 2055.

Clarendon, 68 Lurline Street, Katoomba, ©4782 1322.

Mountain Heritage, cnr Apex & Lovel Streets, Katoomba, ©4782 2155.

Cecil, 108 Katoomba Street, Katoomba, ©4782 1411.

St Mounts, 194 Great Western Highway, Blackheath, ©4787 6111.

The Victoria & Albert, 19 Station Street, Mt Victoria, ©4787 1241.

For a touch of nostalgia make sure you visit the National Trust classified **Paragon Cafe** at 65 Katoomba Street, Katoomba, ©4782 2928, which is fully licensed and is the home of the famous Paragon Chocolates.

Local Transport

Bus

Pearce Omnibus, ©4751 1077, have services connecting Faulcon-bridge and Penrith; Springwood and Winmalee; Blaxland and Mt Riverview.

Katoomba Woodford Bus Company, ©4782 4213, operate services between Katoomba, Leura and Wentworth Falls; Bullaburra and Lawson; Hazelbrook and Woodford; Katoomba Falls, Scenic Railway and Skyway. (No service on public holidays)

Katoomba Leura Bus Service, ©4782 3333 links Leura, Katoomba, Echo Point, North Katoomba, Blackheath, Medlow Bath and Mt Victoria. (No service Saturday afternoon, Sunday or public holidays)

Car Hire

Thrifty, 80 Megalong Street, Leura, ©4784 2888.

Taxi

Taxis Katoomba, ©4782 1311; Springwood Taxis, ©4751 1444; Blue Mountains Taxi Cabs, ©4759 3000; Lawson Taxis, ©4759 3000.

Points of Interest

Penrith

Situated on the Nepean River, less than an hour's drive from Sydney, Penrith is one of the most rapidly growing regions in Australia. The biggest tourist attraction is **Panthers**, set in 81ha (200 acres), where bona fide visitors are most welcome. The club has two cable water ski lakes, a miniature car racing track, swimming pool with water slides, tennis complex and a lake with canoes, windsurfers and paddle boats. It also has a motel, six restaurants, a huge variety of poker machines, cocktail bars and a Cabaret Room. It is located in Mulgoa Road, ©4720 5555.

Other major attractions Penrith offers are the **Nepean Belle Paddlewheeler** (©4733 1274), the **Museum of Fire** (©4731 3000), **Warragamba Dam** and **Wonderland Sydney** (©9830 9100). For more information on these and other places contact the Tourist Information Centre in the carpark at Panthers, Mulgoa Road, ©4732 7671. If you are in the mood for a show, there are two places you may wish to contact to find out what is on - the Q Theatre, ©4721 5735 and the Joan Sutherland Performing Arts Centre, ©4721 8832.

Lower Blue Mountains
Lapstone-Blaxland

Lapstone Zig-Zag Walking Track begins behind the RAAF base at Glenbrook, and follows the original railway cuttings with views of the arches of Knapsack Viaduct.

Blue Mountains National Park, Glenbrook Area, has bushwalking, picnicking and camping. Information and advice plus publications are available from the Visitors Information Centre, Great Western Highway, Glenbrook, ©1300 653 408.

Lennox Bridge, Mitchell's Pass Road, Glenbrook, was built in 1833 and is the oldest bridge on Australia's mainland. The bridge is well sign-posted from the Great Western Highway.

Wascoe Siding, 15 Grahame Street, Blaxland, ©4739 9701, has a miniature railway and picnic area, and is open on the first Sunday of each month, except January.

Springwood

Two extremely good **bushwalks** originate in Springwood: the first, an easy 90 minute walk to Birdwood Gully, starts from Bednall Road; the second, to Sassafras Gully, is rated medium, and access is either from Holmdale Street, Sassafras Gully Road or Bee Farm Road.

The **Local History Centre** and a **Community Art Gallery** are in Braemar, an early Federation home which is classified by the National Trust, as are the Frazer Memorial Presbyterian Church and Springwood Railway Station.

In the cemetery is the grave of Sir Henry Parkes, the Father of Federation.

Faulconbridge

Norman Lindsay Gallery and Museum, Chapman Parade, ©4751 1067, is the home of this famous Australian artist and writer. There are displays of his paintings, etchings, ship models and family mementos, and a special Magic Pudding room. The house is set in delightful gardens with dozens of statues, some of which are also 'delightful'. There is a shop and a good coffee shop. ©Open Fri-Sun and public holidays 10am-4pm.

Central Blue Mountains

Bull's Camp, Great Western Highway, Linden, was used as a camp for convicts working on the road across the Blue Mountains. It is now a good picnic spot.

Selwood Science & Puzzles, 41 Railway Parade, Hazelbrook, ©4758 6235, is a mid-Victorian house which has been classified by the National Trust. It is ©open Thurs-Mon 9am-5pm, and has a fine collection of art and science features.

There are two interesting **bushwalks** emanating from Lawson: one begins at South Lawson Park, Honour Avenue, and goes to Adelina, Junction, Federal and Cataract Falls - 90 minutes, easy; the other starts in North Lawson Park, Bernards Drive, and walks along Dantes Glen and Lucy's Glen to Frederica Falls - 180 minutes, easy.

Wentworth Falls

Yester Grange, Yester Road, ©4757 1110, is a 19th century house with a collection of 19th century water colours, Victoriana and ceramics. The house is set in bush and parkland and Devonshire teas and light lunches are available. ©Open Wed-Fri 10am-4pm, Sat-Sun and public holidays 10am-5pm.

Wentworth Falls Lake, Sinclair Crescent, is a pleasant picnic spot with a playground and tame ducks. Row boats are available for hire.

There are several **walks** with good views in this area. From Falls Road to Fletcher's Lookout, Undercliff Walk, to Den Fenella - easy walk with views and wildflowers, 90 minutes. To Princes Rock with views of Wentworth Falls and Jamison Valley, 20 minutes. To the top of the Falls, 30 minutes. To Undercliff Walk, Den Fenella, Overcliff Walk to Valley of the Waters with panoramic views, 150 minutes.

Upper Blue Mountains
Leura

Sublime Point, at the end of Sublime Point Road, has great views of the Three Sisters and the Jamison Valley.

The Everglades Gardens, 37 Everglades Avenue, ©4784 1938, is classified by the National Trust as one of the Great Gardens of Australia. There are unique sandstone terraces, magnificent mature trees and native flora, and a grotto pool, ©open daily 10am-5pm during spring and

Blue Mountains

THE BLUE MOUNTAINS 114KMS

- Katoomba
  - 6
- Medlow Bath
  - 4
- Blackheath
  - 3
- Mount Victoria

Blue Mountains

summer, and closing an hour earlier during the colder seasons. Admission is ✪$5 adults and $1 children.

Leuralla, 36 Olympian Parade, ✆4784 1169, is an historic art deco mansion with a collection of 19th century Australian art and a Memorial Museum to Dr H.V. Evatt, first President of the United Nations Organisation. There is also a toy and railway museum.

Gordons Falls Reserve is a pleasant picnic area with playground and toilets, and from it there is a walk to the Pool of Siloam and Lyrebird Dell.

Leura Cascades on Cliff Drive is another picnic area, and there are a number of bushwalks that start from this point, with the Round Walk taking about 40 minutes.

Katoomba

The best way to see the attractions of Katoomba is to follow **Cliff Drive**. From the Railway Station, take Lurline and Merriwa Streets to the Drive around the Jamison and Megalong Valleys. Along the drive there are many lookouts, all signposted, the most famous of which is undoubtedly **Echo Point**, from where there are the best views of **The Three Sisters**, Mennhi, Wimlah and Gunnedoo. These rock formations are very important in Aboriginal legend, and are floodlit at night. From the point you can also see the Ruined Castle and Mount Solitary, and it is possible to pick out many animal shapes on the mountains on the other side of the valley.

From Echo Point the **Giant Stairway** of almost 1000 steps leads to the floor of the Jamison Valley and the Federal Pass, and the Prince Henry

Three Sisters, Echo Point, Katoomba

Cliff Walk leads left towards Leura or right towards the Scenic Railway Complex.

The Point has picnic facilities, a restaurant and a takeaway food outlet.

Katoomba Falls Reserve is another picnic spot because the cascades, and several walking tracks begin behind the kiosk.

The Scenic Railway and Skyway on Cliff Drive, ✆4782 2699, offer a ride down to the Jamison Valley, which is not for the faint-hearted, or a ride over the valley in the Skyway. The complex also has the cafeteria-style restaurant, a fun parlour and a souvenir shop, and is ⏰open daily 9am-5pm. Fares are ✪$5 for adults and $2 for children.

Also on Cliff Drive is **Cahill's Lookout**, another picnic spot, this time with views of escarpment and valley, and of Boar's Head Rock. The Drive ends at the Great Western Highway, at Katoomba Holiday Caravan Park.

Explorers' Tree, on the highway 2km west of Katoomba, commemorates the crossing of the Blue Mountains by Blaxland, Wentworth and Lawson. From behind the tree a Katoomba to Jenolan Caves walk begins, which takes 2-3 days. More information is available from the Tourist Information Centres.

Blackheath

Evans Lookout, Evans Lookout Road, offers superb views of the Grose Valley.

Govett's Leap, Govett's Leap Road, also has views of Grose Valley and of Bridal Veil Falls, the longest single drop fall in the Blue Mountains.

National Parks & Wildlife Service Heritage Centre, Govett's Leap Road, ✆4787 8877, has an exhibition on natural features of the Blue Mountains, and nearby Fairfax Heritage Track is suitable for disabled people.

Blue Mounts Rhododendron Garden, Bacchante Street, is set in native bushland. It is ⏰open 9am-5pm and admission is by a donation. There are easy walking tracks and picnic facilities.

From **Anvil Rock** and Wind-eroded Cave, Hat Hill Road, Blackheath, you can get good views of the Grose Valley.

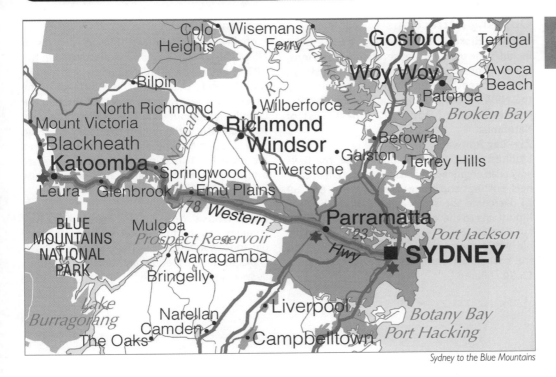

Sydney to the Blue Mountains

Mount Victoria

A visit to the village of Mt Victoria is like taking a step back in time, with buildings of sandstone and iron lace, and others of colonial weatherboard housing antiques, crafts and tearooms. Attractions include the Post Office, Toll House and Railway Station, the Scenic Drive and Mount York where explorers Blaxland, Lawson and Wentworth realised they'd crossed 'The Impenetrable Barrier'. Victoria Falls, Mount Piddington and Pulpit Rock Reserve are also worth a visit.

The Mounts Area

Rich volcanic soils and high rainfall produce the lush vegetation for which the Mounts are renowned. A beautiful area with famous gardens, lookouts and walks.

Cathedral of Ferns, Mount Wilson, is a beautiful rainforest with nearby picnic area.

Mount Tomah Botanic Garden, Bells Line Road, ©4567 2154, was a Bicentennial project of the Royal Botanic Gardens, Sydney. It features cool-climate planting with sections representing specific geographic areas of the world. There are panoramic views and picnic areas, and the gardens are ©open 10am-4pm March to September, and until 5pm during the other months.

Festivals

Lawson Festival - March;
Wentworth Falls Autumn Festival - April;
Yulefest - June/July;
Springtime in the Blue Mountains - September thru November;
Leura Gardens Festival - October;
Leura Village Fair - October;
Blackheath Rhododendron Festival - November;
Glenbrook Festival - November.

For dates and attractions for these festivals it is best to contact the Glenbrook Visitors Centre.

Facilities

Lawn bowls, bush walking, golf, horse riding, scenic drives, swimming pool, tennis, cinemas, squash, art galleries and craft shops.

Outlying Attractions

Hartley Historic Site, Hartley, ✆6355 2117 includes the old Courthouse, churches and inns. The site consists of a relatively small cluster of mid-nineteenth century buildings preserved by the NSW National Parks and Wildlife Service. Hartley is about 35km (22 miles) west of Katoomba.

Zig-Zag Railway

Situated about 7km east of Lithgow, the Railway is an engineering feat. It is a system of tunnels, cuttings and stone viaducts built 1866-69 to overcome the steep descent from the Blue Mountains to the Western Plains beyond. There are picnic areas, and rides are available on an old world steam train. Trains run ⏱daily and the cost of a return journey is ✪$13 adults, $6.50 children.

Jenolan Caves

Probably the best-known limestone caves in NSW, the Jenolan Caves were discovered in the 1830s when the victim of a bushranger tracked his attacker to this hideout. The entrance to the caves is in a narrow gorge accessed through the Grand Arch, about 24m (79 ft) high. The view from Carlotta Arch, which overlooks the Blue Lake, is superb. Nine of the twenty-two caves are open for inspection, and guided tours are available. Phone the Jenolan Caves Reserve Trust on, ✆6359 3311 for more information.

Caves House, ✆6359 3322, right at the caves complex, is a charming hotel, with a restaurant, bar and accommodation. There are several bush walks in the area, and daily tours are run from Sydney and Katoomba.

Chapter 17
Sydney

Population over 3,900,000
Location and Characteristics
Sydney is the capital city of the State of New South Wales, the birthplace of the Nation of Australia, and the largest city in the country.

It is located on the south-east coast of Australia, latitude 33' 53" south, longitude 151' 13" east, on the shores of Sydney Harbour, arguably the most beautiful harbour in the world. It is always busy with ferries, hydrofoils, charter cruisers and pleasure craft. Circular Quay, between the Harbour Bridge and the Opera House, is the ferry terminal, known locally simply as 'The Quay'. The area is always crowded with people arriving or departing on ferries, buskers competing for space, and culture buffs strolling towards the Opera House.

Australia's oldest city, Sydney began as a penal settlement clustered around what is now Circular Quay. The present city sprawls about 55km east-west from the Pacific Coast to the Great Dividing Range, and roughly 70km north-south.

The distance along the actual coastline, allowing for all the bays, is 350km, and in fact there are so many bays and beaches that even Sydneysiders who have lived here all their lives don't know every one by name, and probably haven't visited more than half of them. The ocean beaches have beautiful white sand and rolling surf.

Life in this cosmopolitan city is geared to outdoor activities, taking advantage of the long hours of sunshine and the moderate climate.

Climate
Sydney has a temperate climate, and the average temperatures are: January max 26C - min 19C; July max 17C - min 8C.
The Seasons are:
  Summer - December through February
  Autumn - March through May
  Winter - June through August
Spring - September through November.

The average annual rainfall is 1216mm, with the heaviest falls in the period from February to July. Sydney does not experience snow and only rarely sleet, and quite often the temperature on a winter's day is higher than that of London or San Francisco in the middle of their summers.

Lightweight clothing is necessary for the summer months, and medium to heavy for the winter months. A raincoat, or at least an umbrella, should be included in your suitcase whatever the season.

How to Get There
By Air

Airlines in Australia
Sydney is the major gateway to Australia from overseas, and all overseas airlines servicing Australia fly into Kingsford-Smith International Airport.

Qantas, ©13 13 13, is the major internal Australian airline, and there are a number of smaller ones servicing the country towns and some interstate destinations, such as Kendell Airlines and Hazelton, to name a few. Virgin Blue, ©13 6789, are the latest carriers flying to major centres.

Airport Facilities
Kingsford-Smith is situated in the suburb of Mascot, 10km from the city centre. The Domestic Terminals are 3km to the east, and taxis and express buses connect them with the International Terminal. The large green and gold Airport Express bus runs every 10 minutes, 7 days a week and costs ✪$3 adults, $1.50 children and $7 for families.

The Airport Express also operate services between the Airport and City (route 300), Kings Cross (route 350), and Darling Harbour & Glebe (route 352), from all passenger terminals to Central Railway and return.

Bus Route 300 travels between the Airport and Circular Quay, stopping at specially-identified places along George Street, and in Eddy Avenue near Central Railway. Bus Route 350 travels between the Airport and Elizabeth Bay, passing through Kings Cross. Buses run every ten minutes to and from Central Railway Station and every twenty minutes to the city and Kings Cross. No reservations are needed. Services run every day between, 6am and 11pm, ☎9667 3221 or ☎9667 0663. Fares are ✪$7 one way, $12 return, $4 for children under 12.

Other Sydney Buses routes that travel via the airport are Route 100 (Dee Why-Airport, every 30 minutes Mon-Fri), Route 305 (Railway Square-Airport, every 30 minutes Mon-Fri) and Route 400 (Bondi Junction-Airport-Burwood, every 20 minutes Mon-Fri, every 30 minutes Sat-Sun).

Major rental car companies have desks at the international and domestic terminals, but it is a good idea to book your car in advance - Hertz, ☎13 30 39; Avis, ☎13 6333; Budget, ☎13 27 27; Thrifty, ☎1300 367 227.

Taxis are readily available at the airport for transfer to the city, and the fare is at least ✪$25.

CityRail established a link between Sydney Airport and Central Station. It provides an efficient alternative method of transportation to the city. The line comprises four stops, running northwards from the International terminal to the Domestic terminal, then to Mascot and Green Square before joining the City Circle. Travelling southwards it connects with Wolli Creek. A single ticket to Central costs ✪$15 one-way from the domestic terminal and $20 from the international terminal. Trains operate at fifteen minute intervals between the four stations.

Sydney Airport has all the facilities expected of an international airport - money changing, information, hotel bookings, car hire, shops, cafes, bars, restrooms/showers.

International Airline Offices
Following is a selection of airline reservation and flight confirmation telephone numbers.

Qantas - ☎13 1313.
Ansett Airlines - ☎13 1300
Air New Zealand - ☎13 2476.
Canadian Airlines - ☎1300 655 767.
British Airways - ☎8904 8800.
Cathay Pacific - ☎13 1747.
Singapore Airlines - ☎13 1011.
United Airlines - ☎13 1777.

For further details of airline companies, refer to the *Internet Information* section at the back of the book.

By Bus
Following is a list of some of the bus companies that travel to/from Sydney and other cities and town in Australia. Many also offer day tours and package deals for touring the entire country.

Greyhound Pioneer - ☎13 2030 (see also *Internet Information*).
McCafferty's - ☎13 1499 (see also *Internet Information*).
AAT Kings - ☎ 9666 3899.
Mylon Motorways - ☎6056 3100.
Interline - ☎9605 1811.
Firefly Express - ☎9211 1644.
Murrays - ☎13 22 59.

By Rail
The State Rail Authority's Countrylink branch, ☎13 22 32, has XPT services between Sydney and Brisbane, Melbourne and Murwillumbah. The XPTs are fast, smooth and comfortable with air-conditioning, aircraft style seats and big panoramic windows.

There are overnight and daylight interstate services from/to Melbourne, frequent services to Canberra, an overnight service from/to Brisbane, and a motorail service from/to Murwillumbah with bus connection to the Gold Coast and Brisbane.

A *Countrylink East Coast Discovery Pass* may be a viable option if you plan to make rail your primary means of transport on your east coast holiday. This ticket offers travel one-way with unlimited stop-overs in a six month period from: ✪Brisbane to Cairns ($160); Sydney to Brisbane/Gold Coast ($94); Sydney to Cairns ($248); Melbourne to Sydney ($94); Melbourne to Brisbane/Gold Coast ($176); Melbourne to Cairns ($330). Note that the above rates apply for travel in the opposite direction.

Other extended travel passes are available, and the website is ☞www.countrylink.nsw.gov.au

By Road

From *Melbourne*, via the Hume Highway (867km), via the Princes Highway (1032km).
From *Brisbane*, via the Pacific Highway (975km), or via the New England and Cunningham Highways (1008km).
From *Adelaide*, via the Sturt Highway (1427km), or via the Princes Highway (1936km).
From *Darwin*, via Tennant Creek, Mount Isa, Toowoomba, then New England Highway (4262km).
From *Perth*, via Great Eastern Highway, Eyre Highway, Sturt Highway and Hume Highway (3128km).

Visitor Information

The *Travellers Information Service* at the Airport can make accommodation bookings, and also has a telephone information service that operates seven days a week between ⏱8am and 6pm, ☎9669 5111.
First stop in Sydney for all visitors should be the *Travel Centre of New South Wales*, 11-31 York Street, ☎13 20 77. The office is ⏱open Mon-Fri 9am-5pm, and has numerous brochures, maps, etc, and a large and very helpful staff. Pick up copies of all the current city information guides and you will have plenty of reading material, and good tips on what to see and where to go.
The AMP Sydney Tower Visitors Information and Booking Service is located at the top of the tower, ☎9229 7430. It is ⏱open seven days 9.30am-9.30pm (Sat till 11.30pm), and is a minefield of information for those people brave enough to take the lift to the top.
The *Sydney Convention and Visitors Bureau* has an information kiosk in Martin Place that is ⏱open Mon-Fri 9am- 5pm, ☎9235 2424.
The *Sydney Visitor Information Centre*, 106 George Street, The Rocks, is ⏱open seven days, 9am-5pm, ☎9255 1788. The website is 🖰www.tourism.nsw.gov.au
There are three recommended websites that will give you additional information about Sydney's highlights, from obscure clubs and pubs to major attractions and current events.

🖰www.sydneyvisitorcentre.com
🖰sydney.citysearch.com.au
🖰sydney.sidewalk.com.au
🖰www.cityofsydney.nsw.gov.au

Independent Traveller Information

The *Youth Hostels Association Membership & Travel Centre* is at 422 Kent Street, ☎9261 1111.
For information and travel advice, there is a Backpacker Travel Centre in Shop P33, Imperial Arcade, Pitt Street Mall, ☎9231 3699.
The website for the Youth Hostels Association Australia is 🖰www.yha.com.au and their email is ✉yha@nswyha.com.au

Accommodation

Sydney has a wide range of accommodation, from luxurious 5-star hotels such as the *ANA* and *Park Hyatt*, to small budget-priced establishments offering the basics. Something to keep in mind though: even if you opt for the lower-priced accommodation, you are still going to pay a significant amount for the quality you receive, as is common in major cities. Caravan parks, for example, are rare, and the closest you will find is in North Ryde, about half-an-hour's drive from the city centre. Simply put, if you wish to stay in the heart of Sydney you are going to have to pay for it - there are very few short-cuts.
If you are after something a little different, *Staying in Sydney* by Sam Lynch provides comprehensive details of those 'tucked-away' establishments in Sydney which offer a unique alternative to mainstream chains and well-known accommodation venues. Rates are listed and assessed by the author so that you have a good idea of the places with facilities, service-levels and an ambience to match their price tag. The information gives a valuable insight into this niche market.
Following is a selection of standard accommodation, with prices including the 10% GST, representing a double room per night, which should be used as a guide only. Establishments are listed initially by rating, and secondly from most expensive to least expensive (in terms of their base

rate). Considering that prices increase frequently and without notice, listing hotels in this way will at least give you the best foundation for comparison.

The telephone area code is 02.

City Accommodation
Hotels
5-Star

Even if you can't afford to stay in the places listed below, they *are* local icons in themselves, so if you find the time, have a quiet drink in the lounge or stroll through the foyer. The cocktail lounge of the *ANA* is recommended in particular for its panoramic views of Sydney from a stunning height; although here you will pay no less than $16 for a standard cocktail.

Park Hyatt Sydney, 7 Hickson Road, The Rocks, ✆9241 1234. 36 suites, 158 rooms, licensed restaurants (including the *harbourkitchen&bar*, Club Bar, rooftop heated swimming pool, spa, sauna, gym - ✪$600-5000.

Sir Stamford at Circular Quay, 93 Macquarie Street, ✆9252 4600. 13 suites, 106 rooms, licensed restaurants, cocktail lounge, heated swimming pool, sauna, gym - ✪$515-2000.

ANA Harbour Grand Hotel, 176 Cumberland Street, The Rocks, ✆9250 6000. 40 suites, 570 rooms, licensed restaurants, cocktail lounges, heated swimming pool, spa, sauna, gym - ✪$430-680.

Sheraton on the Park, 161 Elizabeth Street, ✆9286 6000. 48 suites, 558 rooms, licensed restaurants (*Botanica Brasserie* and *Gekko*), cocktail lounges, indoor heated swimming pool, sauna, gym - ✪$370-450.

Four Points Hotel Sheraton Sydney, 161 Sussex Street, ✆9299 1231. 47 suites, 645 rooms, licensed restaurants, cocktail bars, *Dundee Arms* pub, gym - ✪$315-340.

Hotel Inter-Continental Sydney, 117 Macquarie Street, ✆9696 9000. 29 suites, 498 rooms, licensed restaurants, cocktail lounges, heated swimming pool, sauna, gym - ✪$460-560.

Quay West Sydney, 98 Gloucester Street, ✆9240 6000. 132 suites, licensed restaurant, heated indoor pool, spa, sauna, gym - ✪$380-1650.

The Observatory Hotel

89-113 Kent Street, ✆9256 2222. 21 suites, 100 rooms, licensed restaurants, cocktail lounges, heated swimming pool, spa, sauna, gym - ✪$420-670.

"The Observatory is as good an example of a complete luxury hotel as can be found in Sydney. Located on the western edge of the Rocks area, the Observatory Hotel caters to every whim and caprice of its guests.

...The basement houses a fully equipped health centre including a pool with the most astonishing reproduction of the night sky. All the constellations are depicted by using optic fibres in its roof.

The Observatory is essentially an opulently luxurious hotel of the first order, every detail of which has been meticulously planned and cared for, without giving any impression of rigidity."

From *Staying in Sydney* by Sam Lynch

4-Star

The establishments below are centrally located and convenient for self-guided walking tours of the city.

All Seasons Premier Menzies Hotel Sydney, 14 Carrington Street, ✆9299 1000. 8 suites, 446 rooms, licensed restaurants, cocktail bars, heated indoor pool, spa, sauna, gym - ✪$200-350.

The Wentworth, 61 Phillip Street, ✆9230 0700. 29 suites, 384 rooms, licensed restaurants, cocktail lounges, gym, heated pool, sauna - ✪$300-720.

Sydney Hilton, 259 Pitt Street, ✆9266 0610. 28 suites, 585 rooms, licensed restaurants, cocktail bars, heated swimming pool, spa, sauna, gym - ✪$260-400.

Old Sydney Holiday Inn, 55 George Street, The Rocks, ✆9252 0524. 174 rooms, licensed restaurant, cocktail lounge, swimming pool, spa, sauna - ✪$255.

3-Star

The hotels listed below tend not to bear the frills and indulgences of the places mentioned above, but do provide you with good, clean accommodation, the occassional perk, and prices that are perhaps more reasonable for most travellers.

Harbour Rocks Hotel, 34-52 Harrington Street, The Rocks, ©9251 8944. 54 rooms, 1 unique suite, licensed restaurant, cocktail bar - ✪$220.

Sydney Vista Hotel, 7 York St, ©9274 1222. 120 units, 8 suites, pool - ✪$160-270.

Hyde Park Inn, 271 Elizabeth Street, ©9264 6001. 6 suites, 85 units, licensed restaurant (closed Sun), cocktail lounge - ✪$160.

Park Regis Hotel Sydney, cnr Castlereagh & Park Streets, ©9267 6511. 120 units, 8 suites, swimming pool - ✪$170.

Castlereagh Inn, 169 Castlereagh Street, ©9284 1000. 2 suites, 83 rooms, licensed restaurants - ✪$145-170.

Lower Rating

The Lord Nelson Brewery Hotel, cnr Kent & Argyle Streets, The Rocks, ©9251 4044. 9 rooms (no private facilities), licensed restaurant - ✪$120-180 including breakfast.

The Wynyard Hotel, cnr Clarence and Erskine Streets, ©9299 1330. 14 rooms, restaurant open Mon-Fri - ✪$105.

The Mercantile Hotel

25 George Street, ©9247 3570. 19 rooms, 4 higher-standard rooms, spa bath - ✪$100-130.

"The Mercantile is an Irish theme pub that makes itself the centre of St Patrick's Day celebrations in Sydney and is generally a very popular night spot with tourists and locals alike. Being in the Rocks, the Mercantile is close to every amenity you could want, including shops, restaurants, the harbour, attractions and night life.

...Guests should be aware that the Mercantile's bar and night life and live entertainment all contribute to a delightfully rowdy atmosphere, so those seeking an early night with a book in bed should go elsewhere."

From *Staying in Sydney* by Sam Lynch

Y on the Park

5-11 Wentworth Avenue, ©9264 2451. 122 rooms - ✪$135.

"The Y has recently been totally refurbished and offers a broad range of accommodation from dorm to deluxe. The main benefit of staying at the Y for budget travellers is feeling safe. It is not a roach-filled dive near the beach, but a modern, clean, secure location that insists on civilised behaviour. Dorm rooms also feature single beds rather than bunk beds for extra comfort.

...Each floor offers large communal living areas including a TV lounge and mini-kitchen on each floor and there is a guest laundry. The Y is just across from Hyde Park, and is only 200 metres from Museum railway station. Public transport in the form of buses is also plentiful, but the central business district, shopping centres, museums, The Rocks and other attractions are all within walking distance as well.

...The Y represents good value, clean and secure accommodation in the heart of the city for travellers ranging from backpackers to business travellers, to families on holiday. Members of the YWCA get a 10% discount."

From *Staying in Sydney* by Sam Lynch

Serviced Apartments

The places below are recommended for those who wish to opt for the extra space of an apartment-style room, and prefer a sense of self-sufficiency, even though the rooms are serviced in a fashion similar to hotels.

High Rating

Saville 2 Bond Street, cnr George & Bond Streets, ©9250 9555. 180 units, gym, heated pool, spa - ✪$245-1000.

The Waldorf Apartment Hotel, 57 Liverpool Street, ©9261 5355. 60 units, swimming pool, spa, sauna - ✪$195-470.

Carrington Sydney City Centre Apartments, 57 York St, ©9290 1577. 20 units - ✪$220-275.

The York Apartment Hotel, 5 York Street, ©9210 5000. 134 units, 101 suites, licensed restaurant, heated swimming pool, spa, sauna - ✪$260-400 (suites $380-610).

The Stafford, 75 Harrington Street, The Rocks, ©9251 6711. 40 units, 21 suites, swimming pool, spa, sauna, gym - ✪$240.

Metro Suites on King, 27-29 King St, ©9290 9200. 17 units, pool - ✪$160-180.

Lower Rating

The Savoy Apartments, cnr King & Kent Streets, ✆9267 9211. 72 units - ✪$170.

Metro Suites on Sussex, Beehive Tower, 132 Sussex Street, ✆9290 9200. 32 units - ✪$135-185.

Inner-Suburban Accommodation

The suburbs listed here are within a 10km radius of the CBD. Staying in one of these adjacent areas will give you a feel for Sydney different to what you would experience in its centre. The fringe suburbs have their own independent ambience - from beach life to night life - which may appeal to the visitor who has already seen it all and is searching for an alternative.

Bondi Beach (8km east of the city)

High Rating

Swiss-Grand Hotel Bondi Beach, cnr Campbell Parade & Beach Road, ✆9365 5666. 203 suites, licensed restaurant, heated swimming pool, spa, sauna, gym - ✪$230-720.

City Beach Motor Inn, 99 Curlewis Street, ✆9365 3100. 25 units, swimming pool - ✪$140-200.

Bondi Hotel, 178 Campbell Parade, ✆9130 3271. 50 rooms - ✪$95.

Lower Rating

Bondi Beachside Inn, 152 Campbell Parade, ✆9130 5311. 67 units, licensed restaurant - ✪$100-120.

Beach Road Hotel, 71 Beach Road, ✆9130 7247. 22 rooms, restaurant - ✪$90.

The Alice Motel, 30 Fletcher Street, ✆9130 5231. 31 units, swimming pool - ✪$100-120.

Coogee (8km east of the city)

High Rating

Crowne Plaza Coogee Beach, 242 Arden Street, ✆9315 7600. 207 rooms, licensed restaurant, heated swimming pool, gym, tennis - ✪$200-240.

Coogee Sands Apartments, 161 Dolphin Street, ✆9665 8588. 81 units - ✪$155-220.

Coogee Bay Boutique Hotel

9 Vicar St, ✆9665 0000. 52 rooms, *Selinas Night Club* - ✪$90-210.

"The Coogee Bay Boutique Hotel has been meticulously refurbished in contemporary mode and opened in 1998. Thoroughly modern, it is built with the business traveller in mind, and actively bids for the conference market. Business travellers will find special features such as in-room safes, private voice-mail, and modem connections for notebook computers cater to their special needs.

Decor is art deco styled, and rooms have a modern feel with shuttered balconies opening onto truly spectacular ocean views. Rooms are air conditioned and offer full kitchens and spa baths as options.

...The Coogee Bay Hotel is a well-known night spot and is very popular with the locals. It often hosts performers of international fame.

Coogee Bay Boutique Hotel offers a good alternative to the expensive city hotels with the added benefit of being pleasantly located at the beach. Business travellers won't miss any of the comforts or facilities that they would expect from larger hotels, are still reasonably close to the city, and stay in some luxury at a very reasonable price. Other travellers will appreciate the relaxed beach-side atmosphere which is less crowded than Bondi and not as remote as Manly."

From *Staying in Sydney* by Sam Lynch

Double Bay (4km east of the city)

High Rating

The Ritz-Carlton, 33 Cross Street, ✆9362 4455. 15 suites, 140 rooms, licensed restaurant, swimming pool, gym - ✪$190-3000.

Savoy Double Bay Hotel, 41 Knox Street, ✆9326 1411. 4 suites, 39 units - ✪$120-190.

Double Bay Bed & Breakfast, 63 Cross Street, ✆9363 4776. 3 rooms - ✪$145-190.

Elizabeth Bay (3km east of the city)

High Rating

Sebel of Sydney, 23 Elizabeth Bay Road, ✆9358 3244. 24 suites, 141 rooms, licensed restaurant, cocktail lounge, heated swimming pool, sauna, gym - ✪$280-340.

Gazebo Hotel, 2 Elizabeth Bay Road, ✆9358

1999. 11 suites, 395 units, licensed restaurant, cocktail lounge, heated swimming pool, sauna - ✪$125-255.

Seventeen at Elizabeth Bay Boutique Apartments, 17 Elizabeth Bay Road, ©9358 8999. 35 units - ✪$180.

Madison's Central City Hotel

6-8 Ward Avenue, ©9357 1155. 8 suites, 39 rooms - ✪$110.

"Madison's is tucked away from Kings Cross by a matter of a couple of streets and is consequently only a few minutes walk from Kings Cross restaurants & clubs. This modern, 5 storey hotel is designed around a central courtyard full of greenery that greets you as you enter. All the rooms face into this courtyard, which is open at the top.

...There are doors interconnecting adjacent rooms, so family groups can be accommodated. There are also some suite style rooms that have a small separate lounge area.

There is no public space such as a large lobby area, lounge or restaurant in the hotel apart from the room on the top floor where complimentary breakfast is served each day. Madisons stands out in its area as being a comfortable base to operate from for anyone in Sydney for a short stay, whether on business or pleasure."

From *Staying in Sydney* by Sam Lynch

Lower Rating

Roslyn Gardens Motor Inn, 4 Roslyn Gardens, ©9358 1944. 29 units - ✪$75-110.

Kings Cross (2km east of the city)

High Rating

Millenium Hotel Sydney, Top of William Street, ©9356 1234. 390 rooms, licensed restaurants, swimming pool, gym - ✪$135 including breakfast.

The Crescent on Bayswater, 33 Bayswater Road, ©9357 7266. 44 suites, 67 units, *Studebaker's Nightclub*, brasserie and bar, swimming pool, fitness centre - ✪$200 including breakfast.

The Crest Hotel, 111 Darlinghurst Road, ©9358 2755. 226 rooms, licensed restaurant, cocktail bar, swimming pool, spa, sauna, gym - ✪$140 including breakfast.

Kingsview Motel, 30 Darlinghurst Road, ©9358 5599. 67 units, unlicensed restaurant - ✪$75-110.

Lower Rating

Astoria Private Hotel, 9 Darlinghurst Road, ©9356 3666. 30 rooms - ✪$95.

Cross Court Tourist Hotel, 203 Brougham Street, ©9368 1822. 20 rooms, 2 suites - ✪$80.

North Sydney (4km north of the city)

High Rating

Rydges North Sydney, 54 McLaren Street, ©9922 1311. 46 suites, 166 rooms, licensed restaurant, cocktail bar - ✪$160-200.

North Sydney Harbour View Hotel, 17 Blue Street, ©9955 0499. 2 suites, 211 units, licensed restaurant, swimming pool - ✪$230.

Potts Point (3km east of the city)

High Rating

The Landmark Parkroyal Hotel, 81 Macleay Street, ©9368 3000. 10 suites, 470 rooms, licensed restaurant, cocktail lounge, swimming pool - ✪$195.

The Grantham, 1 Grantham street, ©9357 2377. 38 units, pool - ✪$120-180.

Macleay Serviced Apartments, 28 Macleay Street, ©9357 7755. 80 apartments, pool - ✪$110-150.

Simpsons of Potts Point

8 Challis Avenue, ©9356 2199. 14 rooms, ensuites - ✪$190.

The stately home which is now Simpsons was built as the residence of a prominent and wealthy parliamentarian in 1892. The current owners, Peter and Barbara Farris, have meticulously restored the building which gives the

Sydney

impression of being a vast and very beautifully decorated home, rather than a small hotel.

The House is elegant without giving an impression of its age ... A comfortably furnished drawing room at the front of the house, and a lovely conservatory at the rear where breakfast is served all help to give it an atmosphere that lovers of history and historic houses will appreciate greatly.

Rooms are generally very spacious and are likewise decorated and furnished beautifully ... All rooms are air-conditioned individually, as well as being equipped with ceiling fans, direct dial phones, mini-bar, and clock radio. Challis Avenue is a relatively quiet street several blocks away from the noise and lights of Kings Cross, and the house itself is drawn well back from the road, ensuring quiet.

Simpsons is located at Potts Point north of Kings Cross station in a street close to the harbourside. Potts Point being elevated well above the level of the harbour, strolling about in the leafy street rewards you with magnificent views of the city and harbour. Potts Point is also home to a good many restaurants, and multitudes of coffee shops."

From *Staying in Sydney* by Sam Lynch

Rushcutters Bay (3km east of the city)

High Rating

The Bayside Hotel, 85 New South Head Road, ©9327 8511. 99 rooms, licensed restaurant, cocktail lounge - ✪$140-160.

Budget Accommodation
Caravan Parks

These tend to be in the outer suburbs, but are generally good value for money.

The Grand Pines Tourist Park Ramsgate Beach, 289 The Grand Parade, Sans Souci, ©2529 7329. (No pets allowed), 73 sites, unlicensed restaurant, barbecue - powered sites ✪$25-35 for two, park cabins $60-120 for two, on-site vans $50-60 for two.

Lakeside Caravan Park, Lake Park Road, Narrabeen, ©9913 7845. (No pets allowed), 368

sites, playground, barbecue - powered sites ✪$20-22 for two, park cabins $70-135.

Lane Cove River Caravan Park, Plassey Road, North Ryde, ©9888 9133. (No dogs or cats allowed), 216 sites, playground, pool - powered sites ✪$20 for two, park cabins $65-75 for two.

La Mancha Cara-Park, 901 Pacific Highway, Berowra, ©9456 1766. (No pets allowed), 196 sites, sauna, squash, pool, playground - powered sites ✪$20-22 for two, park cabins $64-69 for two.

YHA Hostels

The following Sydney hostels are listed with prices for a double room per night.

Central Station, 11 Rawson Place (corner Pitt Street), ©9281 9111 - ✪$35

Glebe Point, 262 Glebe Point Road, ©9692 8418 - ✪$27.

Collaroy Beach, 4 Collaroy Street, ©9981 1177 - ✪$26.

Pittwater, via Halls Wharf, Morning Bay via Church Point, (ferry from Church Point), ©9999 2196 - ✪$21.

Local Transport

Sydney has an efficient public transport system, with buses, ferries and trains covering the city and the suburban areas. For information on all public transport contact the Infoline, ©131 500, ✪6am-10pm, 7 days.

Train

The railway network is the backbone of the Sydney transit system and is operated by State Rail. There are ten route systems, each with a different colour code, and all services travel on part of the City Circle underground system.

The main station is *Central (Railway Square)*. All country trains begin their journey from here. All suburban trains pass through Central and Town Hall stations, and you can change at either to link up with the City Circle; to cross over the Harbour Bridge; or to board the train for Bondi Junction, which passes through Martin Place, Kings Cross and Edgecliff.

Central Station can be entered from Eddy Avenue, Elizabeth Street (best for suburban trains), or from the entrance road that runs off Pitt Street (best for country trains) to the left after crossing Hay Street if you are coming by car.

The stations in the City are:
Town Hall, Wynyard, Circular Quay, St James, Museum and Martin Place. These stations are all part of the underground network. The first five form the City Circle.

Wynyard Station has three entrances - one in George Street and two in York Street (one accessed from the transport interchange in Wynyard Park).

Town Hall Station has two entrances on each side of George Street.

St James Station has entrances in Elizabeth Street and Queens Square.

Museum Station has entrances on both sides of Liverpool Street and one in Elizabeth Street.

Martin Place Station is well sign-posted, as is *Circular Quay Station*.

Tickets are purchased from a sales window before commencement of a journey, or you can use one of the machines on the city stations.

Bus

Details of the routes and schedules of Sydney Buses can be found by calling the Public Transport Infoline on ✆13 1500 or visiting the website at 👁www.sydneybuses.nsw.gov.au

Sydney Buses services radiate from the city, ferry wharves and railway stations, and connect the Sydney central business district with the suburbs.

Generally speaking, buses from the Eastern Suburbs terminate at either Central Railway or Circular Quay; those from the North-western and Western Suburbs terminate at York Street (near the Queen Victoria Building) or Circular Quay; and North Shore and Northern Suburbs bus routes end at Wynyard Park, near Wynyard Station, or outside the Queen Victoria Building.

Bus no. 888 runs between Wynyard Station, in George Street, and the Art Gallery of New South Wales in east Circular Quay every 10 minutes, Mon-Fri.

The Opera House and Harbour Bridge

The Sydney Explorer Bus

The red Sydney Explorer bus is a great way to get around the city. It travels a 35km (21 miles) circuit to 22 different stops from 9am-5.25pm, beginning at Circular Quay, every day except Christmas Day. You can get on anywhere along the route where there is a distinctive Sydney Explorer bus stop sign. Passengers can get off at any stop, stay as long as they like, then pick up the next bus that arrives. The buses run every 20 minutes, and the fares are ✪$30 adults, $15 children under 16, $75 families.

If you miss the last Explorer bus, don't worry because your ticket is good on any State Transit bus running along the Explorer route until midnight. **The Explorer stops are:**

1. Sydney Cove (Circular Quay)
2. Sydney Opera House
3. Royal Botanic Gardens/Museum of Sydney
4. State Library/The Mint
5. Mrs Macquarie's Chair
6. Art Gallery of NSW
7. Hard Rock Cafe
8. Kings Cross
9. Macleay Street
10. Elizabeth Bay House
11. Potts Point
12. Woolloomooloo Bay
13. Wynyard Station/Martin Place
14. Queen Victoria Building/Sydney Tower/ Planet Hollywood
15. Australian Museum
16. Central Station
17. Chinatown/Powerhouse Museum

Sydney

18. Darling Harbour/National Maritime Museum
19. The Chinese Gardens/Powerhouse Museum
20. Sydney Aquarium
21. Campbell's Cove/Dawes Point
22. The Rocks Visitors Centre

Tickets can be purchased when boarding the bus, or beforehand from the NSW Travel Centre, 11-31 York Street; Australian Pacific Tours, 102 George Street, City; CountryLink Rail Travel Centres; 11 York Street, City; or from a local travel agent.

Bondi & Bay Explorer

Blue and white buses clearly marked Bondi & Bay Explorer operate on a 35km circular route from the city centre through the eastern harbour and bayside areas. They run at 30 minute intervals from 9am-4pm every day, departing from Circular Quay. The fares are ✪$30 adults, $15 children under 16, $75 families.

Bondi & Bay buses stop at the following destinations:

1. Circular Quay
2. Kings Cross
3. Top of the Cross
4. Rushcutters Bay
5. Double Bay
6. Rose Bay Ferry
7. Rose Bay Convent
8. Vaucluse Bay
9. Watsons Bay
10. The Gap Park
11. Bondi Beach
12. Bronte Beach
13. Coogee Beach
14. Royal Randwick Racecourse
15. SCG/Football Stadium/Paddington
16. Oxford Street
17. Hyde Park
18. Martin Place

If it suits your itinerary you can purchase twin tickets for both buses: ✪$50 adults, $25 children, $125 families.

Olympic Explorer

This service departs from the Homebush Bay Visitors Centre between 9.20am and 5pm daily, at 10-15 minute intervals. This is the most efficient way to explore the sporting facilties, with ten stops along the route at which you can disembark, and join a later bus after viewing the attraction at your leisure. A ticket costs ✪$10 for adults and $5 for children, but the higher cost will come from making your way out to the Olympic site to take the tour. If you are in the city, the best choice is to take the RiverCat from Circular Quay and purchase an Olympic RiverCat Ticket for ✪$22 adults and $12 children - included in the price is access to the Olympic Explorer bus service.

Ferry

Providing undoubtedly the most scenic way to travel, Sydney's ferries and RiverCats ply the magnificent harbour.

Full information on routes and schedules can be obtained by phoning ✆131 500 or visiting the same site as for Sydney Buses (*see above*).

Ferry services operate daily, 6am-11pm, from Circular Quay up-harbour to Balmain, Long Nose Point, Hunters Hill and Greenwich.

Across-harbour ferries travel to Kirribilli, Neutral Bay, Cremorne, Mosman and Taronga Zoo. Ferries and hydrofoils also service Manly.

The wharves at Circular Quay are well signposted to indicate which area they service, but on weekends there are changes, and it is best to check before putting your ticket into the automatic turnstiles. Tickets can be purchased from machines on each wharf, or from the kiosk underneath the Circular Quay Station. This kiosk also sells tickets to harbour cruises run by Sydney Ferries, which leave at 10am daily, 1pm Mon-Fri, Sat-Sun 1.30pm, and 8pm Mon-Sat; and river cruises which leave at 10am daily.

For information on times, connections and fares for all government and private bus, rail and ferry services in Sydney, contact the Infoline on ©131 500 (daily 6am-10pm) - they can also advise on *Sydney Discovery Tours* tickets. Alternatively, visit the website listed above.

SydneyPass

If you are going to be in the city for at least a week, it will pay you to invest in a **SydneyPass**. It costs adults ✪$90 for 3 days, $120 for 5 days and $140 for 7 days. The Pass gives you unlimited use of the Sydney Explorer Bus, Manly ferries, harbour cruises run by Urban Transit, and all jetcat, ferry and bus services. These passes are available from the Travel Centre of NSW and State Transit ticket offices displaying the SydneyPass sign.

The Monorail

The monorail system runs anticlockwise and has seven stations - Harbourside (Darling Harbour), Convention Centre, Haymarket, Garden Plaza, World Square (Liverpool Street), Galeries Victoria (Pitt Street, near Park Street) and City Centre (Pitt Street, near Market Street).

It is the best way to get from the city centre to Darling Harbour, and if you are travelling to the city by car you can park in Pyrmont behind the Darling Harbour complex and take the monorail into the city.

The fare for the monorail is ✪$3.50 for everybody 6 and over, whether you are going one stop or the complete circuit. You are not permitted to stay aboard for more than one circuit.

An unlimited travel **Supervoucher Day Pass** can be obtained if you plan to use the monorail several times to make your way around the city (it also contains discount coupons for nearby attractions). The ticket costs $8 per person (there is no adult/child distinction) and is valid until closing on the same day. The alternative is the **Supervoucher Family Pass**, which costs $24 for 2 adults and 2 children (or 1 adult and 3 children).

The monorail runs 7am-10pm Mon-Thu, Fri-

Circular Quay

Sat 7am-midnight and 8am-10pm on Sundays, ©9552 2288 for further details. There is a website at ☞ www.metromonorail.com.au

Sydney Light Rail

This tram service begins at Central Station and takes you through Haymarket to Darling Harbour, up to Pyrmont, Star City, Fish Market, Wentworth Park, Glebe, Jubilee Park, Rozelle Bay and finally Lilyfield. It runs 24 hours a day and generally at 10 minute intervals. There are two zones for fares - Zone 1 (Central to Darling Harbour) and Zone 2 (Darling Harbour to Lilyfield). Fares per person are from ✪$2.50 to $4.80. Children are half fare. A ticket for unlimited weekly trips costs ✪$19 per person. This form of transport may prove useful as a quick and relatively cheap alternative for sightseeing. For further information, ©9660 5288 or visit the web page at ☞www.metrolightrail.com.au

Taxi

Sydney is well served by taxis, and charges are set by the Department of Motor Transport. The main cab companies are:
Taxis Combined Services, ©8332 8888;
RSL Cabs, ©13 22 11;
Legion Cabs, ©13 14 51;
ABC Taxis, ©13 25 22;
Specially outfitted cabs for people in wheelchairs are available, and must be booked in advance.

Taxis may be hailed in the street, hired at a taxi rank, or arranged over the phone for a pick-up, though there will be an extra fee. This service has vastly improved in recent years.

Taxi ranks in the city include Central Station, Circular Quay, Park Street opposite the Town Hall, and outside all the major hotels.

If you hire a taxi in the city to take you over the bridge, ✪$3 will be added to the bill even though there is no toll for travel south to north. This extra fee is added because the taxi driver has to pay the toll to travel over the bridge when returning to the city, and may not get a fare going back that way. Be aware of this for other destinations whose routes involve toll roads.

If you are travelling to the airport from the northern side of the Harbour Bridge, it is safest to predict a $6 surcharge on your fare to cover all tolls and rates.

Water Taxi

Several companies operate on the harbour, including **Taxis Afloat**, ℭ9955 3222; **Quay Water Taxis**, ℭ9922 4252; and **Water Taxis**, ℭ9755 4660. They will take you from one landing point to any other landing point on the harbour, and also offer scenic cruises.

Car

Renting a car is relatively cheap if you are travelling in a group, but driving in the city is not really recommended. The one-way streets take a bit of getting used to, and parking is a problem. Street parking is extremely hard to find, and the parking station fees add considerably to the cost of your day out. However, for travelling in the suburbs and outlying areas, a car is definitely the way to go.

Here are a few names of rental companies and their reservation phone numbers:

Avis, ℭ13 63 33;
Budget, ℭ13 27 27;
Hertz, ℭ13 30 39;
Thrifty, ℭ1300 367 227.

International and overseas drivers licences that are in English are accepted, and a deposit, or credit card details, are required before pick-up. Other car rental companies are found in the A-K Yellow Pages Telephone Directory.

The National Roads & Motorists Authority (NRMA) has reciprocal arrangements with over-

seas and interstate automobile associations. The head office is located at 151 Clarence Street, Sydney. The phone number for enquiries is ℭ13 2132, and for road service, ℭ13 1111.

Sydney Road Tolls

Both the Harbour Bridge (Bradfield Highway) and the Harbour Tunnel have a toll fee of ✪$3 for southbound cars. It should be mentioned that the Tunnel is not an alternative to the Bridge. It is for traffic heading for the airport and the eastern suburbs, and the Bridge is for traffic to the city and the Western Distributor.

The recently completed Eastern Distributor has cut travel time from the city to the airport dramatically, and for most tourists the ✪$3.20 toll (northbound) is worth paying to get to the hotel for a warm shower sooner.

If you are travelling out into the suburbs, the Motorways are the M4, (through mid-western Sydney out to Penrith) which costs ✪$1.60 both ways, and the M2 (to the Hills area in north mid-western Sydney) which will cost you ✪$3.30 east to west and ✪$1.70 from Seven Hills to Pennant Hills or $3.30 from Seven Hills right through to Lane Cove.

Eating Out

Sydney has a plethora of restaurants offering every type of cuisine imaginable. The harbour foreshores are liberally sprinkled with eating establishments, for there are not too many experiences that surpass, or for that matter match, a leisurely brunch on a sunny weekend with the harbour and all its craft as a backdrop.

Unfortunately, though, you often have to pay top prices for this indulgence. With so much competition, you would expect that prices would have to be kept to a minimum, but there are apparently enough people to ensure that each restaurant is well-patronised, and indeed bookings are essential when a water view is offered.

Restaurants are classified as **Licensed** or **BYO**.

Licensed means that the establishment has a licence to sell alcohol. **BYO** means 'bring your own' wine, etc, because the restaurant does not have a liquor licence.

Some restaurants, although licensed, allow patrons to supply their own wine (not beer or spirits), which is usually less expensive than paying the mark-up on the wines that the restaurant is legally allowed to add. In this case a **corkage fee** may be added, which will be per bottle or per person, but the end result is usually still less expensive.

Alcohol can be purchased from the bottle department of a hotel, or from one of the many bottle shops that abound in every suburb.

It is reasonable to say that the price of a bottle of wine in one of these shops would be less than half the price of the same wine in a restaurant.

Following is a list of recommended restaurants, rated:

Expensive (main course ✪$23+),
Moderate (main course ✪$15-$23)
Budget (main course under ✪$15).

Not included here are the restaurants in the 5-star hotels, as everyone knows that they exist and are much the same the world over with regard to menus and prices.

Credit card abbreviations are:

Amex = American Express; BC = Bankcard; DC = Diners Club; MC = MasterCard; V = Visa.

One of Sydney's best, and most expensive, restaurants is **Forty One**, Level 41 Chifley Tower, Chifley Square, ✆9221 2500. The view is magnificent, and complements rather than dominates the food. The cuisine is Modern Australian, and the presentation is first class. It is ⏱open for lunch Mon-Fri and for dinner Mon-Sat 6-10.30pm.

Running a close second, though some might say that it is a dead heat, is **The Rockpool**, 107 George Street, The Rocks, ✆9252 1888. The cuisine here is also Modern Australian, the presentation is excellent, and the prices are commensurate. ⏱Open for lunch Mon-Fri, dinner Mon-Sat.

Both the above are licensed and accept all credit cards.

At the other end of the scale is a Sydney landmark that has been around a very long time:

Harry's Cafe de Wheels, Cowper Wharf Roadway, Woolloomooloo, ✆9357 3074. It is not a restaurant, not even a cafe, just a roadside stall - but everyone knows *Harry's*. Their delicious real Aussie meat pies, peas and more, are handed to you on a paper serviette. Eating a pie in this fashion requires complex synchronisation of hand and mouth - an ability with which most Sydneysiders are already born, or one they develop with rapid evolution at weekend football matches. So, when in Rome...

The City and The Rocks

Bilson's, Upper Level, Overseas Passenger Terminal, Circular Quay West, ✆9251 5600. Licensed, good harbour views, French/Australian cuisine, **expensive**, ⏱open Sun-Fri noon-3pm and nightly 7pm-10pm, Amex, BC, DC, MC, V.

Doyle's at The Quay, Lower Level, Overseas Passenger Terminal, Circular Quay West, ✆9252 3400. Licensed, good harbour views, outside tables, seafood, **expensive**, ⏱open Mon-Sun 11.30am-2.45pm and Mon-Sat 5.30pm-9.30pm, Sun 5.30-9pm, BC, DC, MC, V.

Bennelong, Sydney Opera House, Circular Quay, ✆9250 7548. Licensed, good harbour views, Modern Australian cuisine, **expensive**, ⏱open Mon-Sat dinner from 5.30pm-11.30pm, Amex, BC, DC, MC, V.

Rossini Rosticceria, Shop W5, Circular Quay, ✆9247 8026. Licensed, good views, outside tables, Italian, cafeteria style, **budget**, ⏱open daily 7pm-10.30am, 11am-4pm, 5-10.30pm, no credit cards accepted.

MCA Fish Cafe, Museum of Contemporary Art, Quayside, Circular Quay, ✆9241 4253. Licensed, good harbour views, outdoor tables, seafood, **moderate**, ⏱open Mon-Fri 12pm-4pm, Sat-Sun 9am-4pm, Amex, BC, MC, V.

Imperial Peking Harbourside, 15 Circular Quay West, The Rocks, ✆9247 7073. Licensed, good views, outdoor tables, Chinese cuisine, **moderate**, ⏱open daily noon-3pm, Sun-Thurs 6pm-11pm and Fri-Sat 6pm-midnight, Amex, BC, DC, MC, V.

Sailors Thai, 106 George Street, The Rocks, ✆9251 2466. Licensed, Thai cuisine, **budget**,

Sydney

🕐open daily noon-2pm and 6pm-10am, Amex, BC, DC, MC, V.

The Summit, Level 47, Australia Square, 264 George Street, City, ✆9247 9777. Licensed, revolving restaurant, incredible views of the city its and outreaches, Modern Australian cuisine, **expensive**, 🕐open daily 6pm-10pm and Sun-Fri noon-3pm, Amex, BC, DC, MC, V.

Casa Asturiana, 77 Liverpool Street, City, ✆9264 1010. Licensed, Mediterranean cuisine, **budget**, 🕐open daily from 6pm and Tue-Fri noon-3pm, Amex, DC, MC, V.

Paragon Cafe, 1st Floor, Paragon Hotel, Circular Quay, ✆9241 3888. Licensed, Modern cuisine, **moderate**, 🕐open Mon-Fri noon-3pm and Mon-Sat 6.30pm-10pm, Amex, BC, MC, V.

Merrony's, 2 Albert Street, Circular Quay, ✆9247 9323. Licensed, Australian/French, **moderate**, 🕐open Mon-Fri noon-2.30pm, Mon-Sat 5.45pm-11pm, Amex, BC, DC, MC, V.

Caminetto, 13-17 Playfair Street, The Rocks, ✆9247 5787. Licensed, Italian cuisine, **moderate**, 🕐open Fri-Sat 10am- midnight and Sun-Thu 10am-10pm, Amex, BC, DC, MC, V.

Phillip's Foote, 101 George Street, The Rocks, ✆9241 1485. Licensed (it is actually a pub), cook-your-own steaks, good salad bar, outdoor tables, **budget**, 🕐open daily for lunch and dinner, Amex, BC, DC, MC, V.

Restaurant CBD, CBD Hotel, 75 York Street (cnr King Street), ✆9299 8911. Licensed, British/Modern Australian, **moderate**, 🕐open for lunch and dinner Mon-Fri, Amex, BC, DC, MC, V.

EJ's, 143 Macquarie Street, City (lower ground floor), ✆9247 8588. Licensed, cuisine includes a bit of everything from everywhere, **moderate**, 🕐open for lunch only Mon-Fri noon-2.30pm, Amex, BC, DC, MC, V.

Capitan Torres, 73 Liverpool Street, City, ✆9264 5574. Licensed, Spanish fare, **moderate**, 🕐open daily noon-3pm and 6pm-11pm, Amex, BC, DC, MC, V.

Botanic Gardens Restaurant, follow the signs once you are in the Gardens, ✆9241 2419. Licensed, good views, casual dining, outdoor tables, **moderate**, 🕐open daily noon-2.15pm, Amex, BC, MC, V.

Dendy Bar & Bistro, 19 Martin Place, ✆9221 1243. Licensed, extensive menu, **budget**, 🕐open daily 11am-midnight, Amex, BC, MC, V.

Zolie's Restaurant, 5 York Street, City, ✆9299 3276. European cuisine, **moderate**, 🕐open Mon-Fri noon-3pm and nightly 6pm-10pm, Amex, BC, DC, MC, V.

Restaurant Suntory, 529 Kent Street, City, ✆9267 2900. Licensed, traditional Japanese cuisine, **expensive**, 🕐open Mon-Fri noon-2pm, Mon-Sat 6.30pm-10pm and Sun 6pm-9pm, Amex, BC, DC, MC, V.

Papillon, 71 York Street, City, ✆9262 2624. Licensed, French cuisine, **expensive**, 🕐open Mon-Fri noon-3pm and Tues-Fri 6pm-9pm, Amex, BC, DC, MC, V.

Don Quixote, 1 Albion Place, City, ✆9264 5903. Licensed, Spanish cuisine, **expensive**, 🕐open Mon-Fri noon-3pm and Mon-Sat 6pm-11pm, Amex, BC, DC, MC, V.

Kamogawa, Corn Exchange Building, cnr Sussex & Market Streets, City, ✆9299 5533. Licensed, Japanese with teppan bar, traditional rooms and conventional dining area, **moderate to expensive** depending on locale, 🕐open daily 6.30pm-10am, 6pm-10pm and Mon-Sat noon-3pm, karaoke bar Mon-Fri 8.30pm-1am, Amex, BC, DC, MC, V.

Amar's, 44 Bridge Street, City, ✆9247 9930. Licensed, Indian cuisine, **moderate**, 🕐open Mon-Fri noon- 2.30pm and 5.30-10.30pm, Amex, BC, DC, MC, V.

Planet Hollywood, 600 George Street, ✆9267 7827. The 32nd link in this world-wide chain of movie themed restaurants. Licensed, **moderate**, 🕐open daily 11am-1am, does not take reservations.

Chinatown (Haymarket)

Golden Harbour, 31 Dixon Street, ✆9212 5987. Licensed & BYO (corkage fee per bottle), Cantonese, **budget**, 🕐open Mon-Fri 10am-4.30pm, 5.30pm-11pm and Sat-Sun 9am-4.30pm, 5.30pm-1am, Amex, BC, DC, MC, V.

House of Guang Zhou, 76 Ultimo Road, ✆9281 2205. Licensed, Chinese, **budget**, 🕐open Mon-

Fri 11.30am-3pm, Sat-Sun noon-3pm and daily 5.30pm-2am, Amex, BC, DC, MC, V.

Golden Century Seafood Restaurant, 393-399 Sussex Street, Haymarket, ✆9212 3901. Licensed, popular venue, fresh seafood with Asian influence, **expensive**, ⏲open daily noon-4am, Amex, BC, DC, MC, V.

Marigold, Levels 4 & 5, 683-689 George Street, ✆9281 3388. Licensed & BYO (corkage fee per person), Cantonese, **moderate**, ⏲open daily 10am-3pm and 5.30pm-midnight, Amex, BC, DC, MC, V.

Malaya, 761 George Street, ✆9211 0946. Licensed, Malaysian cuisine, **budget**, ⏲open daily noon-3pm, Mon-Sat 5-10pm and Sun 5-9pm, Amex, BC, DC, MC, V.

East Sydney

Beppi's, cnr Yurong & Stanley Streets, ✆9360 4558. Licensed, Italian cuisine, **expensive**, ⏲open Mon-Fri noon-3pm and Mon-Sat 6pm-11.30pm, Amex, BC, DC, MC, V.

Yutaka, 234 Crown Street, ✆9361 4804. Licensed & BYO (corkage fee per person), Japanese cuisine, **moderate**, ⏲open Mon-Fri noon-2.15pm, Mon-Sat 6-10.45pm and Sun 6-10pm, Amex, BC. MC, V.

Tre Scalini, 174 Liverpool Street, ✆9331 4358. Licensed, Italian cuisine, **expensive**, ⏲open Mon-Fri noon-2.30pm and Mon-Sat 6-10.30pm, Amex, BC, MC, V.

Ristorante Mario, 38 Yurong Street, ✆9331 4945. Licensed, Italian cuisine, **expensive**, ⏲open Mon-Fri noon-3pm and Mon-Sat 6.30-11pm, BC, MC, V.

No Name, 2 Chapel Street, Darlinghurst, ✆9130 4898. BYO, Italian pasta and minestrone, **budget**, ⏲open for lunch and dinner, no credit cards accepted. There are a few No Name restaurants around Sydney, but this is the original and most people think it is still the best.

Cruising Restaurants

Captain Cook Cruises, ✆9206 1111, have lunch and dinner options.

The *Luncheon Cruise* departs Circular Quay at 12.30pm, lasts one and a half hours and includes a Buffet Luncheon featuring Sydney rock oysters, Tasmanian trout, rare roast beef, ham, chicken, fresh salads, fruit platters and Australian cheeses - ✪$49 adult, $29 child.

The *Sunset Dinner Cruise* leaves from Wharf 6 Circular Quay at 5.15pm daily. The cruise offers a 2 course a la carte menu & wine or local beer. The cost is ✪$69 adult, $55 children. Reservations essential.

The John Cadman Dinner cruises every night of the year and departs Wharf 6 Circular Quay at 7.30pm. The a la carte menu is prepared by international chefs, and there is a selection of Australian and imported wines. Cost of the dinner cruise is ✪$97 adults, $55 children, and reservations are essential, ✆9206 6666.

Captain Cook Cruises also offer *Coffee* and *Explorer Cruises*.

Sail Venture Cruises have luncheon and dinner cruises on their Big Cats, with changing menus. The luncheon cruise departs Darling Harbour Aquarium Wharf at 12.15pm (returning at 2.25pm) and Campbells Cove, Circular Quay, at 12.35pm (returning at 2.05pm) - ✪$55 adult, $28 child.

The dinner cruise departs Darling Harbour at 7pm (returning at 10.10pm) and Campbells Cove at 7.30pm (returning at 9.45pm) - ✪$105 adult, $55 children.

For reservations and enquiries, ✆9262 3595.

Matilda Cruises serve lunch on their two-hour harbour cruises, which leave Darling Harbour Aquarium Wharf at 11.30am and 1.30pm, Campbells Cove Circular Quay at 11.45am and 1.45pm, and Taronga Zoo at 12.45pm and

2.45pm. The cruises cost ✪$56 adult, $28 children, and an Aussie BBQ lunch cooked on board. Reservations are necessary, ✆9264 7377.

Bounty Cruises have lunch and dinner cruises aboard the tall ship *Bounty*, and they always guarantee that part of the cruise will be under sail. The cruises leave from Campbells Cove Wharf, where you can also inspect the *Bounty*, which is a replica of the one that Captain Bligh sailed on and was built for the movie *Mutiny on The Bounty*. The lunch cruise departs every day at 12.30pm, and costs ✪$65 on weekdays and $95 on weekends. The dinner cruise begins at 7pm and costs ✪$99 for adults. Both cruises offer buffet-style meals. For reservations, ✆9247 1789.

Don't think for one moment that the above lists all the restaurants in Sydney. It is little more than the tip of the iceberg. Often you will find restaurants that we have not listed in the same street as the ones included above. Our list gives you somewhere to start and an idea of what is on offer.

On weekends, it is a wise idea to phone ahead and book a table.

In case you are wondering about the availability of a Big Mac, be reassured that there are 14 *McDonald's* in the city. *Pizza Hut* has two city branches; and *KFC* has one in the city and one at Darling Harbour.

Entertainment

As mentioned in the Introduction chapter, the Friday edition of *The Sydney Morning Herald* has 'Metro', and the Thursday edition of the *Daily Telegraph* has '7 Days' which list what's on at all of Sydney's night spots.

It would be lengthy and boring to list all the venues in the city and suburbs, so we took a survey amongst a group of Sydney ragers and the following are their favourites.

Night Clubs
City

Harbourside Brasserie, Pier One, Millers Point, ✆9252 3000. It has two cocktail bars and commands sweeping views of Sydney Harbour.

Paragon Hotel, 1 Macquarie Place, ✆9241 3522. Open ◷Mon-Thu 9.30am-1am, Fri-Sat, 9.30-5am, Sun 12pm-10pm.

Orient Hotel, cnr Argyle & George Streets, ✆9251 1255. Open ◷7 days 10am-3am (live bands every night of the week). Nightclub and live bands set out over three floors. Plenty of space. Tourist spot, very popular.

Retro Bar, 20 Sussex Street, City, ✆9212 4868. Open ◷Thursday to Saturday 6pm-5am. Popular for those who wish to re-live the eighties, or are still there.

Riche, Hilton International Hotel, 259 Pitt Street, ✆9266 0610. Open ◷Wed 9pm-2am, Fri-Sat 9pm-2am.

Bar Luna, Jackson's on George, 176 George Street, ✆9247 9334. Open ◷Tues-Sun, afternoon or evening until early the following morning (restaurant service ceases 9.30pm). Very popular. The beer flows freely here.

Riva, Sheraton On The Park, 130 Castlereagh Street, City, ✆9286 6666. Open ◷10pm to late Wednesday to Saturday. Excellent atmosphere for middle-aged crowds.

Darling Harbour/Pyrmont

The Cave, Star City, Pirrama Road, Pyrmont, ✆9566 4755. Open ◷9.00pm to late (24 hour licence) 7 days a week. If you're tired of losing money in the Casino nearby, this is a good place to go to forget about it - provided you can still afford the cover charge.

Kings Cross

Round Midnight, 2 Roslyn Street, ✆9356 4045. Open ◷Tue-Thu and Sun 8am-3pm, Fri-Sat 8am-5pm. Popular venue.

Sugareef, 20 Bayswater Road, Kings Cross, ✆9368 0763. Open ◷9pm to 6am every day. Popular and often crowded.

Darlinghurst

Kinselas, 383 Bourke Street, Darlinghurst, ✆9331 3100. Open ◷24 hours, 7 days. This building was once Kinsela's Funeral Parlour. You can find better.

The Cauldron, 207 Darlinghurst Road, ✆9331 1523. Open ◷Tues-Sat 10am-3am. Very popular venue with the smart, well-dressed crowd, bookings advised.

North Shore

Greenwood Hotel, 36 Blue Street, North Sydney, ✆9964 9477. Open ⏰Monday to Saturday 11am to late. A very good club/bar with a nice atmosphere.

Metropole Hotel, 287-305 Military Road, Cremorne, ✆9909 8888. Open ⏰10pm until 5am(ish) Friday/Saturday only. Very upmarket and popular.

Paddington

Fringe Bar, 106 Oxford Street, Paddington, ✆9360 3554. Open ⏰11.30am to midnight Monday to Thursday, 11.30am to 3am Friday to Saturday.

Bars & Bistros

City

Bridie O'Reilly's, corner Kent and Erskine Streets, ✆9279 3133. Open ⏰11am-midnight (Mon-Thurs), 11am-2am (Fri-Sat), 11am-10pm (Sun). Bistro. Light entertainment includes Irish bands.

Bridie O'Reilly's, cnr George and Hay Streets, ✆9212 2111. Open ⏰11am-midnight (Mon-Thurs), 11am-2am (Fri-Sat), 11am-10pm (Sun). Bistro. Light entertainment includes Irish bands.

Horizons Bar, ANA Hotel, 176 Cumberland Street, The Rocks, ✆9250 6000. Open ⏰Mon-Thu noon-1am, Sat noon-2am, Sun noon-midnight. Light lunch noon-2pm.

Lucy's Tavern, 54 Castlereagh Street, ✆9221 3908. Open ⏰Mon-Thurs 10.30am-10pm, Fri-Sat 10.30am-5am.

Marble Bar, Sydney Hilton Hotel, Pitt Street, ✆9266 2000. Open ⏰Mon-Fri noon-11pm, Sat 3pm-2am. The Marble Bar was part of the Adams Hotel, dating from 1893, which was built by George Adams, founder of Tatts Lotto. When the Hotel was being refurbished by the new owners, the Italian Renaissance Marble Bar was dismantled stone by stone and rebuilt on the completion of the Hotel that stands today. Dressy and posh venue.

Customs House, Sydney Renaissance Hotel, 31 Alfred Street, ✆9247 2285. Open ⏰Mon-Fri 11am-10pm (closed weekends). Lunch is served from noon-2pm, there is no dinner service. The bar is at the rear of the hotel and opens onto Macquarie Place Park where, in summer, a crowd of business movers and shakers spend their evenings. In operation since 1846, it has been said that should a bomb explode in this bar on any Friday evening, the Australian Stock Exchange would not open come Monday morning, not to mention the banking, legal and accounting professions.

Woolloomooloo Bay Hotel, 2 Bourke Street, ✆9357 1177. Open ⏰Mon-Sat 10am-11pm, Sun 11pm-9pm, bistro lunch and dinner 12pm-9pm. The Woolloomooloo is a great place to spend a Sunday afternoon in summer. The patrons spill onto the pavement outside whilst the band is playing.

Darling Harbour

Craig Brewery Bar & Grill, Festival Market Place, Darling Harbour, ✆9281 3926. Open ⏰Mon-Wed 10am-noon, Thurs-Sat 10am-3am. Dinner - cook your own steaks on the barbecue.

Pumphouse Restaurant & Bar, 17 Little Pier Street, Darling Harbour, ✆8217 4100. Open ⏰Mon-Fri 11am-late, dinner till 9pm, nightclub and live bands. The pumphouse is known for the fabulous boutique beers available on tap.

East of the city

Kings Cross

Bourbon & Beefsteak, 24 Darlinghurst Road, Kings Cross, ✆9358 1144. Open ⏰24 hours, 7 days a week, dinner 7.30-10.30pm The Bourbon and Beefsteak is an institution. Nearly every Sydneysider has visited the Bourbon at least once.

Darlinghurst

Burdekin Hotel, 2 Oxford Street, ✆9331 3066. Open ⏰11am-2pm, lunch & dinner 7.30-10.30pm.

Paddington

London Tavern & Restaurant, 85 Underwood Street, ✆9331 6192 (restaurant), 9331 3200. Open ⏰Mon-Thurs 11am-11pm, Fri-Sat 10am-11:15pm. Pool Tables and card machines available.

Pubs

City

Lord Nelson Brewery Hotel, 19 Kent Street, ℅9251 4044. Open ⏱7 days 11am-11pm. The Lord Nelson claims to be the oldest continually licensed hotel, and the only pub brewery in Sydney brewing natural ales.

Mercantile Hotel, 25 George Street, The Rocks, ℅9247 3570. Open ⏱Mon-Thurs 10am-midnight, Fri-Sat 10am-1am. The Mercantile is frequented by Irish travellers and is known as the Irish Pub. It has an Irish flavour and St Patrick's Day, March 17 is a big day for the Mercantile. They even serve green beer!

The Hero of Waterloo Hotel, 81 Lower Fort Street, ℅9252 4553. Open ⏱Mon-Sat 10am-11pm, Sun 10am-10pm. Bistro lunches and dinners available seven days. A museum downstairs shows a tunnel which runs down to the harbour. This pub is the oldest continuously trading pub in Sydney. Built in 1843.

Jazz Venues

The Basement, 29 Reiby Place, City, ℅9251 2797. Open ⏱open nightly for dinner, Mon-Fri for lunch. Features modern local and international artists and serves contemporary Australian food. Excellent music and food. Guaranteed to have a good time. For jazz lovers.

Soup Plus, 383 George Street, City, ℅9299 7728. Open ⏱Mon-Thu noon-midnight, Jazz 7:30-midnight; Fri-Sat noon-1am; Jazz 8pm-12.30am.

Strawberry Hills Hotel, 453 Elizabeth Street, Surry Hills, ℅9698 2997. Open ⏱Mon-Thurs 11am-midnight. Fri-Sat 11am-12.30am. Sun noon-10.30pm.

The Classics

The Sydney Opera House is *the* venue in Sydney for opera, ballet, and performances by the Sydney Symphony Orchestra.

The newly refurbished Sydney Town Hall is also the scene of musical evenings. The 'Metro' has the information on programs, locations and times.

Theatres

Sydney has a vibrant theatre scene, and the local talent compares favourably with the rest of the world.

The large theatres have cocktail bars for pre-show or intermission drinks, and most of them have banned smoking in these areas, as well as in the auditoriums themselves. Some theatres have restaurants attached, where service is geared to getting patrons into the theatre on time.

Then there are the small theatre groups, and local dramatic and musical societies, whose performances are quite professional and you may see a star in the making. For example, **NIDA**, the National Institute of Dramatic Art (where Mel Gibson learnt his craft) presents plays at **The Parade Theatre** at 215 Anzac Parade, Kensington, ℅9697 7613, opposite the main entrance to the University of New South Wales. Prices vary according to the production but range from ☺$17 to $20, not much more than you pay to see Mel in a movie.

Half-tix

Speaking of prices, Sydney has a **Half-tix booth** in Darling Park, 201 Sussex Street, at the base of the IBM building, and it sells tickets to major venues at half price on the day of the performance.

It is ⏱open between 9am and 5pm Monday to Friday, and 10am-3pm Saturday. The phone number for selections and reservations is ℅9286 3310 and for the head office, ℅9966 1723. All major credit cards are accepted. They have a website at ☞www.halftix.com.au

Major Theatres

The Sydney Opera House has two theatres - the *Drama Theatre*, which seats 544, and the *Playhouse*, which seats 398. The Box Office is ⏱open Mon-Sat 9am-8.30pm, and charge telephone bookings may be made, ℅9250 7777. There are several eateries at the Opera House itself, or you can choose from those in the area of Circular Quay.

Her Majesty's Theatre, 107 Quay Street, ℅9212 3411, is close to Central Railway Station and within walking distance of the restaurants of Chinatown.

Capitol Theatre, 13 Campbell Street, Haymarket, ©9320 5000 for recorded show information, or ©9266 4800 for bookings. The theatre is in Haymarket, near Chinatown.

The Theatre Royal, MLC Centre, King Street, ©9231 6111, is in the heart of the city.

The Ensemble Theatre, 78 McDougall Street, Milsons Point, ©9224 8444, is situated in the Lower North Shore and has its own restaurant.

The Wharf Theatre, Pier 4, Hickson Road, Millers Point (The Rocks), ©9250 1700, also has a restaurant, ©9250 1761.

Belvoir Street Theatre, 25 Belvoir Street, Surry Hills, ©9699 3444, doesn't have a restaurant, but does have a licensed bar offering light snacks before and after the show.

Seymour Theatre Centre, cnr Cleveland Street & City Road, Chippendale, ©9531 7940, has three theatres - the *York*, *Everest* and *Downstairs*, and a very good restaurant, ©9692 4138. There is also a coffee and snack bar in the upstairs foyer.

The Footbridge Theatre, Sydney University, Parramatta Road, Glebe, ©9692 9955 or 9266 4800 (bookings), is actually in the grounds of Sydney University. It doesn't have a restaurant of its own, but there are plenty in nearby Glebe.

Small Theatres

Stables Theatre, 10 Nimrod Street, Kings Cross, ©9361 3817.

Bay Street Theatre, 75 Bay Street, Glebe, ©9692 0977.

New Theatre, 542 King Street, Newtown, ©9519 3403.

Pilgrim Theatre, 262 Pitt Street, City, ©9261 8981.

Enmore Theatre, 116 Enmore Road, Enmore, ©9550 3666.

These small theatres may not have a current presentation when you are in town, and others not mentioned here may have something that you would be interested in seeing. Check 'Metro' for details. More live cinemas are found in the suburbs.

Rock Concerts

The main venue for these is the **Sydney Enter-tainment Centre**, near Chinatown, ©1900 957 333 for recorded information or ©9320 4200 for enquiries.

If the person or group is a big star, eg Michael Jackson, Billy Joel, Elton John, Madonna or U2, the promoters may opt to stage the concert at the Sydney Cricket Ground, even during the cricket season.

The Sydney Entertainment Centre is also used for ice shows, tennis tournaments, boxing matches, etc.

Cinemas

The main cinema area in the city is in George Street, between Park and Liverpool Streets. Here you will find:

Village Cinema City, 545 George Street, ©9264 6701; **Hoyts Centre**, 505 George Street, ©9273 7431; and **Greater Union**, 525 George Street, ©9267 8666.

There are also many cinemas in the large suburban restaurants.

An independent cinema in the city is **Dendy**, 19 Martin Place, ©9233 8558 and 261 King Street Newtown, ©9550 5699.

As a general rule, Tuesday is half-price night at all cinemas, although some offer discounts on other nights.

Gambling Venues

Star City Casino, 80 Pyrmont Street, Ultimo, ©9777 9000, is close to Darling Harbour, and can be reached by ferry and bus. There are the usual assortment of blackjack tables, roulette tables, and so on, and hundreds of poker machines where people queue up to lose their money 24 hours a day.

The complex contains a 352-room 5-star hotel, the Lyric Theatre seating 2000, a cabaret room seating 900, 14 restaurants, 12 bars, designer-name retail outlets, conference facilities, and 139 serviced apartments in the adjoining tower. It has its fair share of critics.

There are plenty of other places to go if you feel like a flutter. Firstly there are the **Clubs** - Leagues Clubs, RSL (Returned Servicemen's League) Clubs, Bowling Clubs, Worker's Clubs, Golf Clubs - which all have poker machines (that seem to offer better odds than those at the Casino), and most have keno.

Of course, it is not compulsory to play the pokies, and in fact, a lot of people don't - they go to the club to get a reasonably priced meal, and enjoy whatever entertainment is on offer. This varies from imported acts to cabaret shows with local talent, to movies, to chook raffles (yes, you do actually win a chook, or rather, a dead chicken).

Every suburb has one or more clubs, but if you are a first-time visitor to Sydney, I suggest that you stick to the suburban League Clubs. They are bigger, brighter, busier, and you can experience a good cross-section of Sydney life. Clubs are listed in the Yellow Pages Telephone Directory under *Clubs - Social and General*.

Although the clubs are there primarily for the use of members, visitors are always made welcome, as long as they are suitably dressed - no thongs, a collar with a shirt, and in the evening, long pants are preferred. Those dress rules are of course for men. Women must be 'decently' attired. Remember to sign the visitor's book in the foyer.

The clubs also have TAB facilities and SKY Channel television. This means that you can study the form guide in the comfort of a well-appointed club with a cold glass of whatever you fancy, place bets on your favourite horses, watch the race live, then collect your winnings (or tear up your ticket). Perhaps it should be mentioned that SKY Channel is only available to TAB agencies and licensed premises.

If you are not into the club scene you can, of course, place your bets at the local TAB agency, and they are in every suburb, but there is no atmosphere.

Alternatively you can venture outdoors and actually watch the horses, or dogs, go round at the track. Sydney's racetracks are very attractive, with good parking facilities, lots of grassed areas, plenty of bars, take-away food outlets, and restaurants, and the choice of investing your money on the Tote, or with a bookmaker. Children are welcome, and on a beautiful Sydney day it can be a great family day out.

The Horse-racing venues are:
Randwick Racecourse, Alison Road, Randwick, ©9663 8400.
Canterbury Racecourse, King Street, Canterbury, ©9930 4000.
Rosehill Gardens Racecourse, Grand Avenue (off James Ruse Drive), Rosehill, ©9930 4070.
Warwick Farm Racecourse, Hume Highway, Warwick Farm, ©9602 6199.
Races are held every Saturday and Wednesday at one of the above courses.

The first race is usually around 12.30, but during January and February the first race starts around 2.30pm. These are called *Twilight Meetings*, as the last race is around 6.30pm. The daily newspapers have details of race times, starters and jockeys, comprehensive form guides, TAB numbers and post positions.

Harness-racing venues are:
Harold Park Paceway, Ross Street, Glebe, ©9660 3688. Meetings are held on Tuesday and Friday nights, and first race is 7pm.
Bankstown City Paceway, 178 Eldridge Road, Bankstown, ©9708 4111. Meetings are held on Monday nights, and first race is 7pm.
Fairfield Paceway, Fairfield Showground, ©9604 4559.
Meetings are not held on a regular basis, so either phone the club or look in the newspapers for forthcoming races.

Greyhound racing is held at **Wentworth Park**, Wentworth Park Road, Glebe, ©9660 6232. Meetings are held every Monday and Saturday nights and the first race is 7.30pm.

Shopping
The City
Sydney has a large shopping area in the city, stretching from Park Street in the south to Hunter Street, with shops along George, Pitt, Castlereagh and Elizabeth Streets, which run south-north, and Market, King and Hunter Streets, which run roughly east-west. The section of Pitt Street between Market and King Streets is a pedestrian mall, with many arcades connecting it to both Castlereagh and George Streets. The closest railway stations to the shop-

ping areas are Town Hall, Wynyard, St James and Martin Place.

If on the day you have set aside to shop, the heavens open and the rain pours down, remember it is possible to walk from Town Hall Station to the MLC Centre in Martin Place without venturing out of doors. It is rather a convoluted route, but there are signs pointing you in the right direction. Basically, from the station take the arcade under the Queen Victoria Building to Grace Bros, then from the first floor of Grace Bros take the overpass to Centrepoint, then travel across the Imperial Arcade, Glasshouse and Skygarden shopping centres to the King Street overpass, and, *voila*, you are in the MLC Centre. Of course, if the weather is warm and sunny, forget this option and stroll through the Mall.

Shops are normally ⏱open Mon-Wed 9am-5.30pm, Thurs 9am-9pm, Fri 9am-6pm, Sat 9am-5pm, Sun 11am-4pm, but this is not a hard and fast rule. Some open earlier and close later, particularly on Sunday, and many suburban supermarkets are open until late at night six days a week, and until around 6pm on Sunday. The shops in the tourist areas are open every day, usually with extended hours.

Souvenirs

If you are only interested in buying souvenirs, such as cuddly koalas and kangaroos, T-shirts, etc, it is probably best to head for the tourist areas, such as The Rocks, Darling Harbour or Circular Quay.

Other 'typically Sydney' souvenirs are found in the range of goods at the Done Art & Design Shops at The Rocks, Darling Harbour, Queen Victoria Building and the departure level of the International Airport. Ken Done is a local artist who produces very colourful works of art featuring the harbour, the bridge, the opera house, koalas, kangaroos, etc. These paintings are reproduced on material and his wife, Judy, designs a spectacular range of sportswear, swimwear, homewares, bags, stationery - in fact, just about everything you can think of can be found in their shops.

Buying Opals

If you have your heart set on some opal jewellery, you should grab your passport and airline ticket and head for a duty free store, or a jewellery shop that has a 'Tax Free for Overseas Visitors' sign in the window. In the case of opals, which are mined in Australia and set in jewellery locally, there is no duty, therefore in both establishments you would avoid the 10% GST.

Australia produces more than 90% of the world's opals, and the three main areas where they are found are Lightning Ridge in NSW which produces the Black Opal; Quilpie, where the Queensland Boulder Opal originates; and Coober Pedy in South Australia, which has the White or Milk Opal.

When buying opals there are a few important terms you should know:

Solid Opal - this is the most valuable, and is good for investment purposes. The more colourful and complete, the greater its value.

Doublet - this is comprised of slices of opal glued together, and is of medium value. It has no investment value.

Triplet - slices of opal covered with quartz, perspex or glass. This is the least expensive with no investment value.

If your pocket can't stretch as far as a solid opal, but you still would like a piece of opal jewellery, remember that anything that is glued can come unstuck, and that condensation can form under perspex or glass. The less expensive types of opal are not suitable for rings, unless you are going to remember to take them off every time you wash your hands.

Department Stores

David Jones

David Jones has two stores in the city - one bounded by Elizabeth, Market and Castlereagh Streets, the other diagonally opposite on the corner of Market and Castlereagh Streets. The Elizabeth Street store is devoted mainly to ladies' wear, except for the Lower Ground Floor (haberdashery, books, records, CDs, pharmacy, confectionery, wool, fabrics and restaurant); the

Queen Victoria Building

5th Floor (toys, children's wear and sporting goods) and the 6th Floor (manchester).

The Market Street store is known as the men's store, but it also has the Food Hall on the lower ground floor, and stocks travel goods, and small and large electrical appliances and furniture. Both stores have the same phone number: ✆9266 5544.

David Jones was considered to be one of the most beautiful stores in the world, and was designed by the same person who later designed the refurbishment of Harrods in London, and there are similarities.

David Jones stores are ⏱open Mon-Fri 9am-5.30pm (Thurs to 9pm), Sat 9am-4pm, Sun 11am-5pm, and all major credit cards are accepted.

Grace Bros

Situated on the corner of George and Market Streets, Grace Bros is more of a family store and sells literally everything under one roof. It has seven floors of shopping and is ⏱open Mon-

Wed 9.30am-6pm, Thurs 9am-9pm, Fri 9.30am-6.00pm, Sat 9am-6pm, Sun 11am-5pm, ✆9238 9111.

Argyle Stores

Sydney's newest department store is situated in The Rocks. For more information see The Rocks section in the *City Sights* chapter.

City Shopping Centres

Town Hall Arcade

Situated underground in the Town Hall Station, there are two arcades of specialty shops. The shorter of the two from the station leads to Bathurst Street, near Kent Street, and the other continues under the Queen Victoria Building to Grace Bros.

The Queen Victoria Building

The QVB was built in 1898 in the Byzantine style, and originally housed the city markets. Bounded by George, Market, York and Druitt Streets, its prosperity was short-lived, and it fell into disrepair. At one stage it was used as part offices and part Municipal Library, and the partitions that succeeded in making the building into a rabbit warren were actually nailed onto the beautiful tiled floors. Both the inside and outside of the building were decidedly tacky, and in 1959 there was much debate about demolishing the entire structure and building another shrine to modern architecture. Fortunately, common sense prevailed and the wreckers were not allowed to move in, but it was not until 1982 that a 99-year lease was granted and over $75 million invested to restore the building to its original state.

It is a magnificent building, and Pierre Cardin, on a visit to Sydney, christened it 'the most beautiful shopping centre in the world'. But, it is not only a shopping centre, there are a lot of things to see, all with a royal theme, in keeping with the name of the building. It even has replicas of the Crown Jewels on the top level.

The Royal Automata Clock 'performs' on the hour between 9am and 9pm daily, and you need to get there early to see the moving Royal Pageant. (It is a good idea to keep a firm grip on your handbag and wallet while waiting in this crowd.)

The QVB is open seven days a week. Apart from the range of boutiques and specialty shops, there are several restaurants and cafes, both in the QVB and in the underground walkway to Grace Bros. These exclusive retail outlets are housed in a setting lavish enough to match the prices of their merchandise. However, stunning architecture, the imitation Crown Jewels, and various other monuments and displays ensure that a browse through the QVB does not have to involve shopping to be enjoyed.

Centrepoint

Known as 'the heart of the city', Centrepoint is located on Pitt Street Mall, beneath Sydney Tower, and connects Grace Bros with David Jones. It has over 170 shops on four levels, including hairdressers, beauticians, leather shops, jewellery and accessory outlets, boutiques, and several coffee shops and takeaways. The lifts for Sydney Tower are found on the elegant Gallery Level of Centrepoint.

The lower ground floor is the Centrepoint Tavern, a good spot for a quick lunch, or a happy-hour drink.

Centrepoint is open daily, but not all the shops are open outside normal shopping hours.

Imperial Arcade

The Imperial runs between the Pitt Street Mall and Castlereagh Street, and has 114 specialty shops on 3 levels. It is also connected to Centrepoint.

Glasshouse on The Mall

Located in the middle of the Pitt Street Mall, the Glasshouse has three floors of shopping, with the usual collection of boutiques.

Skygarden

A very up-market shopping experience, Skygarden has three levels of prestigious shops under a huge crystal dome. The mosaic entrance arch is made of thousands of Venetian glass tiles, and depicts the day and night theme of the complex. The top dining level is nothing to write home about.

Strand Arcade

The Strand opened in 1892 and is an *olde worlde* walk-through with mosaic tiled floor and Victorian architecture. It connects Pitt Street Mall with George Street and is ☉open Mon-Wed and Fri 9am-5.30pm, Thu 9am-9pm, Sat 9am-4pm and Sun 11am-4pm.

Mid City Centre

This centre connects Pitt Street Mall and George Street, and is between the Strand Arcade and Grace Bros, with an entrance from Grace Bros. It has four levels of shopping with over 40 fashion boutiques, more than 50 specialty shops, and first class restaurants and coffee shops.

MLC Centre

The MLC Centre has entrances from Martin Place, Castlereagh Street and King Street, and has fashion boutiques, coffee shops and restaurants, and the Theatre Royal. The outdoor cafes overlooking Martin Place are popular lunchtime places.

Royal Arcade

Located under the Sydney Hilton Hotel, the

Sydney

Royal Arcade is between Market and Park Streets, and connects Pitt and George Streets. It has a range of rather expensive shops, typical of those found in hotel arcades.

Piccadilly Arcade

The Piccadilly is near the Pitt Street Cinema Centre, and connects Pitt and Castlereagh Streets. It also has overhead walkway connections to the Sydney Hilton and Sheraton on the Park Hotels. This is another rather upmarket shopping experience.

At the other end of the shopping district, near Wynyard Station, there are a few more places waiting to be discovered.

Wynyard Arcade

Fairly recently renovated, this arcade is situated inside the station and has specialty shops of its own as well as access to Westpac Plaza and the Hunter Connection.

Chifley Plaza

Situated on Hunter, Elizabeth and Phillip Streets, Chifley Square is home to, among other not-so-well-known names, the local branch of *Tiffany's*. If after visiting all of the above you are still in a shopping mood, return to the city centre and hop on the monorail for Darling Harbour.

Harbourside, Darling Harbour

After undergoing an extensive renovation upgrade, the Harbourside Festival Marketplace has a new look for its 200 shops from boutiques to souvenirs, sportswear to art, and restaurants, cafes and bars. It is a bazaar for overseas visitors rather than for Sydneysiders, and the refit was no doubt pitched at attracting the Olympic crowds.

Markets

The Rocks Market

Every Saturday and Sunday, at the end of George Street in The Rocks, a sail-like canopy transforms the area into a Portobello Road. It is not an exceptionally large market, but it has many interesting articles for sale, and the Victorian terraces, pubs and old warehouses that surround it contribute to a holiday atmosphere year round. Nearby there are plenty of cafes, outdoor food stalls and restaurants.

Paddy's Markets

There are two locations:
The original Paddy's is in Haymarket, on the corner of Hay & Thomas Streets, near Chinatown. It is open Fri-Sun 9am-4pm.
The other is on Parramatta Road, Flemington, and it is open Fri 10am-4.30pm and Sun 9am-4.30pm.

There are over 1000 stalls in each location selling fashion garments, footwear, jewellery, household and electrical goods, takeaway foods, fresh fruit and vegetables, poultry, seafood, and heaps and heaps of souvenirs. Paddy's is the biggest market in Australia, and for further information, phone the Hotline - ©1300 361 589.

Paddington Bazaar

Located at the corner of Oxford and Newcombe Streets, Paddington, in the grounds of the Uniting Church, this bazaar is held on Saturdays 10am-4pm, ©9331 2646. There are over 250 stalls offering all types of clothing, crafts, jewellery and food.

While you are in Paddington you could visit *Coo-ee Aboriginal Art*, 98 Oxford Street, ©9332 1544. They have a large display of Aboriginal Art, and are agents for Tiwi Design fabrics.

Balmain Saturday Market

Held in the grounds of St Andrew's Congregational Church, corner Darling Street and Curtis Road, Balmain, every Saturday 8.30am-4pm, ©0418 765 736 (mobile).

Glebe Markets

These are held in Glebe Public School, cnr Glebe Point Road & Derby Place, on Saturday 9.30am-4.30pm. Many people think this Market has a lot of atmosphere.

City Sights

It is not possible to see the sights of the city of Sydney in one day on a walking tour, even if you are super-fit. Apart from the distance, Sydney is not a flat city, and the hills would slow you down. By taking advantage of **The Sydney Explorer** bus (see *Local Transport*) you could catch a glimpse of everything, but you still wouldn't have time to appreciate what you saw. It is best to allot at least a few days for the city itself before you spread your wings to the outer attractions. So this guide is set out in areas, perhaps you should allow one day per area. Note that all museums are closed on Christmas Day and Good Friday.

The grid references shown below refer to the colour map of Sydney at the front of the book.

Circular Quay Area

Sydney Harbour Bridge   E11

Affectionately known to Sydneysiders as 'The Coathanger' the Sydney Harbour Bridge dominates the city skyline. It is 503m long, and was completed in 1932 after nine years of construction. It was built from either shore, and when the two halves met they were only 7.6cm (3 inches in the old measurements) out of alignment! The Bridge opened with a piece of drama. The dignitaries were lined up, the Premier, Jack Lang, stepped forward to cut the ribbon, and up rode Captain de Groot on a noble steed. He slashed the ribbon with his sword, and all and sundry stood speechless, at least for a few seconds. The miscreant was apprehended, the ribbon was rejoined, and the ceremony continued.

In August, 1992, came the opening of the long-awaited harbour tunnel, which has lived up to its expectations in reducing peak hour traffic snarls on the bridge. You can't walk through the tunnel but you can walk over the bridge, and you can climb up the south-east pylon for some of the best harbour views. The pylon is ⊕open daily 10am-5pm and admission is around ✪$2 adult.

A recent enterprise which has proved extremely popular is offered by *BridgeClimb*, 5 Cumberland Street, The Rocks. Included in the three hour package is a safety briefing and a magnificent walk up and across the great steel span. From the top of the bridge, spectacular views of Sydney by day or night are the reward for making it to the top, ✆9252 0077 for tickets, ⊕7am-7pm, 7 days a week.

From the bridge there is a good view of Sydney's newest crossing, the Glebe Island Bridge with its many suspension cables. The bridge has improved the traffic flow into the city from the west.

Sydney Opera House   G10

This magnificent performing arts complex is situated on Bennelong Point, which was named by Governor Phillip after an Aboriginal he befriended, taught English, and actually took back to England. This spot is apparently where Bennelong resided in his humpy.

Shrouded in controversy during its construction, Sydney Opera House was finally completed in 1973, and has since become almost the symbol of Australia. Instantly recognisable anywhere because of its unique architecture, this extraordinary building can only really be appreciated when acknowledged as part of its surroundings. The design encapsulates the concept of architecture mimicking its environment: the white sails give the vague impression that the building is a cluster of vessels on the waters of Port Jackson.

The Opera House has four theatres, four restaurants and six bars, and is surrounded by wide walkways. Details of current programs are published in the daily newspapers, and the Box Office is ⊕open Mon-Sat 9am-8.30pm and two hours prior to the start of a Sunday performance. Phone bookings may be made up to seven days prior to the performance, and the booking clerk will advise when payment must be made, or you can use your credit card. Front of House tours are held ⊕daily from 9am-4pm, departing every 30 minutes, and cost ✪$15 adults, $10 concession, ✆9250 7111. There are also tours on some Sundays that take visitors backstage and cost ✪$23 per person with no concessions (the tour is unsuitable for children under 12). The availability of the backstage tours depends on whether there are rehearsals in the house. It is best to contact *Guided Tours*, on the Saturday before you would like your tour, on the above number.

Bus no 438 travels down George Street to the concourse. Circular Quay Railway Station is the closest stop for train passengers.

Surely one of the world's greatest marine back-

drops, the combination of Sydney's premier icons, the Opera House and the Sydney Harbour Bridge, must be appreciated at every angle. On any crystal morning, the white roof of the House is resplendant in the sunlight. Nearby, the impressive span of the Bridge arches over passing yachts and small cruisers carving their white trails across the harbour. The source of Sydney's beauty in a nutshell.

Circular Quay   F8

It doesn't seem to matter when you visit the Quay, there are always lots of people around, but it is on weekends and holidays that you have the added colour and noise of all the buskers. From men playing classical pieces on violins, to little kids belting it out on a range of brass instruments, to Aborigines and (non-Aborigines) playing didgeridoos and teaching people to perform kangaroo and emu dances - it's all captivating entertainment.

The Quay is the heart of the Sydney Ferry network. At any given time, at least one of these green-hulled vessels will be visible at the docks, either accepting passengers or waiting for them to disembark. They then make their way slowly to and from the middle harbour on routes that stretch north-east to Manly and west towards Parramatta River.

It is a real *mezcla* of people milling in anticipation of their ferry; people hurrying to catch their train at the railway station; some buying tickets for harbour cruises; some fishing in the doubtful water near Wharf 5; others, the well-dressed ones, beginning their walk around to the Opera House for a ballet or opera matinee.

A fairly recent and certainly controversial development has been established along the eastern promenade, stretching most of the way to the forefront of the Opera House. It is lined with up-market cafes, restaurants, shops and a movie cinema. The top levels are exclusive apartment residences. This imposing complex was initally dubbed 'The Toaster' by protesters who demonstrated on the steps of the Opera House in December 1996, during its construction, hoping to preserve the aesthetic quality of this landmark area. You can judge for yourself the final result.

Circular Quay Railway Station, although not underground, is part of the City Circle, and the Cahill Expressway on top of the railway takes traffic from the Bridge to the Eastern Suburbs and Macquarie Street.

Justice & Police Museum   F8

This museum, at 9 Phillip Street, ☏9252 1144, is almost directly opposite Wharf 5, and if you look across you will see figures of 'burglars' apparently trying to break into the building on the corner. It is only ⏰open Sunday 10am-5pm, but is worth a visit if you are in the area, and interested in phrenology or medieval-style weaponry. The collection began with the Police Exhibition that was an exhibit at the Royal Easter Show for many years. It is now housed in a former police station and court house, and has displays of relics from police investigations and trials, as well as record sheets of some of Sydney's most notorious felons. Admission is ✪$7 adults, $4 children.

Museum of Sydney   F7

Situated on the corner of Phillip and Bridge Streets, on the site of First Government House, this modern museum is ⏰open daily 10am-5pm and admission is ✪$7 adults, $4 children, $17 family, ☏9251 5988. It has an excellent cafe and a good bookshop, both of which can be visited without entering the museum. The bookshop specialises in architecture and design titles. There are also exhibits in the forecourt, and in the entrance foyer the foundations of Australia's first Government House are visible. Over the years there has been some controversy about the exhibits on show, and about the quotations of famous people that are on display throughout the galleries.

Museum of Contemporary Art (MCA)   E8

The MCA is the Art Deco building on the waterfront around from Wharf 5. It formerly housed the Maritime Services Board and when the board moved to new premises, there was some talk of levelling this imposing structure. Then somebody realised that it would be the perfect place for the J.W. Power collection of contemporary art, which had been left to the University of Sydney many years before. Now the museum is run as a non-profit company by a joint venture between Sydney University and the NSW Government. The museum's brochure proclaimed:

> "This is a museum about the beautiful under our noses, the unusual, the weird and wacky in the visual, electronic, sound and tactile world we all live in."

And that just about sums it up! The museum is ◷open daily 10am-5pm every day except Christmas. Admission is free. Entrance is from the Quay or from George Street. Volunteer-led guided tours are available for free, and curator-led tours cost $25 a head ad must be booked two weeks in advance. For details of current exhibitons phone ✆9252 4033 or the Infoline on ✆9241 5892.

The MCA Store in George Street has an incredible range of books, magazines, posters, etc, and the MCA Cafe next to the Quay entrance is worth a visit in itself. Why? It is managed by the people from the award-winning restaurant, *Rockpool*, which is nearby at 109 George Street, The Rocks.

Cadman's Cottage   E9

Continuing along the waterfront, the cottage is situated in a reserve on the corner of Argyle Street. It is the oldest remaining house in Sydney, and was home to John Cadman, the last Government Coxswain.

The two-storey sandstone cottage was finished in early 1816, and its building was possibly supervised by Francis Greenway, the convict architect, who lived nearby. At that time the house stood two metres from the water, on a small sandy beach, and had a wharf on its northern side. Its present position resulted in the late 1840s when ten acres of land were reclaimed to form Circular Quay. The lack of recorded history, artefacts or detailed plans of the cottage has stopped the National Parks & Wildlife Service (NPWS) from restoring the building as an historical museum.

It is presently an information centre for Sydney Harbour National Park, ✆9247 5033, and has plenty of brochures on walks and trips in Sydney parks and those further afield. It is open seven days a week.

The waterside walk continues around the back of the Overseas Terminal. There is a new upmarket bar and restaurant here over two levels, with great views. Continue on to Campbell's Cove, which has many restaurants in converted storehouses, and the wharf from which the *Bounty* and other cruise ships depart. Nearby is the Park Hyatt Sydney Hotel.

The Rocks   E9-E10

The Rocks nestles on the western edge of Circular Quay, the initial point of colonial settlement. Preservation of the area's heritage was the subject of conflict during the 1970s, but eventually common sense prevailed and the region has undergone restoration and improvement to become popular with both locals and tourists. The architecture transports the visitor to a previous era, and even products of modern consumerism attempt to blend in with the nostalgic theme.

The Sydney Visitor Centre   E9

Steps beside Cadman's Cottage lead up to George Street, and if you turn right at the top of the steps you will come to the old Sailors' Home which now houses The Rocks Visitor Centre, ✆9255 1788. The Centre is ◷open daily 9am-5pm, and has a very good video presentation on the first floor, of the growth of Sydney from a small penal colony to a thriving modern city. They carry brochures and maps for tourist attractions all over Sydney.

George Street   E9-E10

Continuing along George Street, there are many old historic buildings and pubs, and on the weekends the Bridge end of the street is closed off and The Rocks Markets are held (see *Shopping* section).

In the building on the right hand side of the markets there are some interesting craft displays and shops.

Westpac Museum E9

Retrace your steps along George Street, walk past the Old Sydney Parkroyal Hotel, then turn up Playfair Street. Here at no 6-8 is the Westpac Museum, ✆9763 5670, which traces the history of the bank from its beginnings in 1817 as the Bank of NSW, to the present day of technological banking. There are also temporary exhibitions featuring subjects as diverse as the Royal Flying Doctor Service and Antarctica. The museum is ✆open Tues-Fri 10.30am-4pm, Sat-Mon 1-4pm and admission is free.

By the way, Playfair Street bends to the left, and straight ahead from the museum is Atherden Place, with four terrace houses. It is the shortest street in Sydney.

The Rocks Square E9

The square is in the middle of Playfair Street (which is closed to traffic) and this area has many outdoor eateries, little shops, jazz or rock bands, and several lanes sprouting in all directions. Following Playfair Street to its end brings you to Argyle Street.

The Rocks Puppet Cottage E8

The cottage is situated in Kendall Lane, and can be reached from George Street through a lane at no 77. It is ✆open 10am-5pm Wed-Sun, ✆9241 2902. There are hundreds of puppets on display, and shows are held at 11am, 12.30pm, 2pm and 3.30pm on weekends, and other days during school holidays. Admission is free, and the cottage is sponsored by the Sydney Cove Authority.

Susannah Place D8

Situated at 58-64 Gloucester Street, Susannah Place, ✆ 9241 1893, is a terrace of four brick houses that was built in 1844. It is now a museum of the lifestyle in the area from the 1840s until the turn of the century. Included is a shop that stocks the type of goods that would have been available then.

The Rocks Centre E9

The centre is on the corner of Playfair & Argyle Streets and offers two floors of boutiques and eateries.

Argyle Stores E9

The Rocks' newest addition is Argyle Stores, 18-24 Argyle Street, ✆9251 4800, which has around 5000 square metres of upmarket shopping. Modelled along the lines of France's Galleries Lafeyette, the different departments are managed by individual operators, but blend to give the appearance of one entity.

The building was initially completed in 1828 using convict labour, and was the first Customs House in Australia. Over the years it has had several uses, and names, until in 1993 it was completely restored by the Sydney Cove Authority at a cost of around $9 million. In 1994 it was offered for lease as a department store, and back in October 1996 the Argyle opened its doors to customers.

A few doors up Argyle Street is *The Argyle Restaurant*, which is ✆open daily 11.30am-3pm, 7.30-10.30pm, ✆9247 7782. This is a real Aussie theatre-restaurant, that serves good old fashioned tucker (food) with large helpings of fun and laughter.

Clocktower Square E9

The square is the building on the corner of Argyle and Harrington Streets with the clocktower, and it contains several souvenir shops, a Japanese restaurant, and **The Rocks Opal Mine**, ✆9247 4974. Here you can not only buy tax-free opals, you can dig for them! There is a mine shaft elevator which really does seem to travel down to the depths of the earth, then the door opens and an old mine tunnel appears with 'miners' busy at work. It's good fun even if you are not interested in buying opals, and is ✆open seven days.

Millers Point E11

Millers Point is the suburb on the opposite side of the Harbour Bridge (and the Bradfield Highway which crosses it) to The Rocks. It can be reached by following Hickson Road from the Park Hyatt Sydney Hotel around the base of the south-east pylon of the Bridge to Dawes Point;

by following George Street to its end, then walking down steps to Hickson Road; or by continuing along Argyle Street and passing under the Bradfield Highway.

Holy Trinity (Garrison) Church　　D9

The Church is in Argyle Street. It was built in 1848 and is called the Garrison Church because it was compulsory for the soldiers of the 50th Regiment stationed at Dawes Point Battery to attend the morning service. There is a leaflet available for a small purchase fee at the rear of the church which details its complete history.

Argyle Place　　D9

The little park just up the street, is Sydney's oldest village green.

Sydney Observatory　　D8

The Observatory is on Watson Road, Observatory Hill, and can be reached by following Argyle Street, then walking up some steep steps. The Observatory, ✆9217 0485, has a regular program of exhibitions, films, talks and night viewings, and a hands-on exhibition. During the day it is ⏱open Mon-Fri 2-5pm, Sat-Sun 10am-5pm and admission is ✪free. It is also ⏱open nightly, except Wednesday, and has two programs in winter (6.15 and 8.15pm) and one in summer (8.15pm). Bookings are necessary for the night sessions, and charges are ✪$10 adults, $5 children, $25 family.

You may wonder about the ball on top of the building. It has been part of the synchronisation of time in Sydney since the building was erected in 1858. In the early days of the colony, a gun was fired at exactly 1pm from Dawes Point, and another from Fort Denison. These were for the ships in the harbour to check their chronometers. To enable the settlers in the colony to also check their time-pieces, the ball on the Observatory was hoisted by mechanical means to the top of the pole at approximately five minutes to one, then when the guns fired, the ball dropped back to the bottom. The ball still fulfils its function, but only on special occasions such as public holidays and during school holidays.

S.H. Ervin Gallery　　D8

The Gallery is in the National Trust Centre, almost next door to the Observatory. The building was erected in 1815 as a military hospital, then for many years was home to one of Sydney's leading girls' high schools.

The Gallery has changing exhibitions, and for current programs and entry charges, ✆9258 0173.

The Royal Botanical Gardens & Macquarie Street

The Gardens are a popular lunchtime spot for city workers, and weekends see many family picnics. They are situated on the edge of Farm Cove, where the early colonists first tried to grow vegetables.

As you enter through the gate near the Opera House and climb the slight slope, the astonishing building to your right is **Government House**. It is the state's finest example of sophisticated Gothic Revival and took eight years to build, finally completed in 1845. Although the battlements, turrets and arches present it for all intents and purposes as a castle, defence was not one of the building's intended functions, and it was instead given over to the administration of colonial affairs. Surrounded by scenic gardens in one of the city's finest corners, it now acts as a pleasant welcoming venue for the Governor's official receptions. It is ⏱open to the public Fri-Sun 10am-3pm, ✆9931 5222. The garden belonging to the House is ⏱open every day 10am-4pm.

The building at the end of the driveway leading from Government House is the **Conservatorium of Music**, which was originally the Governor's stables.

Signposts point the way to **Mrs Macquarie's Chair**, a rock outcrop where the Governor's wife apparently sat to watch for ships arriving from England.

The small remote island you can see in the centre of the harbour is **Fort Denison**. For a short time it was regarded notoriously among early convicts as the most inescapable gaol of the colony and the destination of wayward miscreants. The nickname 'Pinchgut' evolved from the starvation men unlucky enough to spend time on the island experienced. Poorly treated and unfit to attempt a fleeing swim, these criminals were naturally inappreciative of their otherwise superb location. Feared and despised in those times, the fort is now a prime location commanding one of the best views of the city and harbour. It was built as part of Sydney's defences, and has come under the jurisdiction of the National Parks and Wildlife Service, as part of Sydney Harbour National Park.

Tours of Fort Denison leave from Wharf 6, Circular Quay, but must be booked in advance, ✆9247 5033 (NPWS at *Cadman's Cottage*). The tour costs ✪$16 for adults, $10 for children and concession and $40 for families.

Back on land, the footpath by the sea wall leads to the Visitors Centre and shop, a kiosk, and a restaurant; and signposts show the way to the herbarium, the pyramid glasshouse and other exhibits. There are two exits near the pyramid, one on to Macquarie Street, the other leads to the Art Gallery. The Royal Botanical Gardens are ⊕open daily 8am to sunset, ✆9231 8125.

Art Gallery of New South Wales   G5

The Art Gallery is in Art Gallery Road, in the Botanical Gardens, and faces The Domain. It is a spectacular building, housing a vast contemporary collection of Australian, European and Asian Art, and a fine collection of Aboriginal paintings and artefacts. The names of famous artists are set in stone on the front of the building, upon the tier just below the roof level. Two statues of mounted horseman grace the patches of lawn on either side of the entrance.

Many special exhibitions are held at the Gallery, and for recorded information on current exhibits, ✆9225 1744 or ✆9225 1790. Free guided tours of the Gallery are available - check at the information desk on your left as you walk into the gallery through the vestibule. There is no charge for admission to the Gallery and its permanent collection, but a fee is levied for special exhibitions.

There is a restaurant and a coffee shop, and the Gallery is ⊕open daily, 10am-5pm.

In this enriching environment, you can immerse yourself in culture and history before relaxing and reflecting among the flora of the Domain across the road or in the Botanical Gardens nearby.

The Domain   G5

The Domain is the large grassed area between the Art Gallery and the Public Library. It is a peaceful park setting for soap box orators on Sundays, and the venue for a number of Sydney's free summertime open-air concerts, such as *Opera In The Park* and *Symphony in the Park*.

State Library of New South Wales   F6

The original, imposing building of the Library faces Shakespeare Place, on the corner of Macquarie Street. The new section has been built behind, but can also be accessed from Macquarie Street. The hushed ambience of the library envelops you upon entering.

The Library, commonly referred to as the Mitchell Library, contains the nation's finest collection of Australiana and an amazing wealth of historical records. The accumulation of this stored knowledge continues to grow with the obligation under law placed on all publishing houses to supply the library with a copy of each of their publications.

There is a magnificent reading room with wood panneling and tiered shelving, complete with matching stairs and narrow walkways. There is also an excellent Reference Library. The new wing contains the latest technology for reading and learning. The information desk has a self-guided tour sheet with information on every part of the library, and it is worth obtaining.

There is a restaurant and a bookshop, and the Library is ⊕open Mon-Fri 9am-9pm, Sat 9am-5pm, Sun 11am-5pm, and admission is of course free, ✆9230 1414. The Library has changing exhibitions, usually of an historic nature, and information on current programs can be obtained by calling the above number.

Parliament House   F6

Situated in Macquarie Street, Parliament House has experienced several additions, removals, renovations and upgrades since its initial construction in 1816. It is a combination of styles - from Georgian to Victorian to contemporary - which have been carefully designed over the years to blend the variety and preserve the pleasant small scale of the building despite necessary expansions. The most recent challenge was the attachment of a twelve-storey office block to the existing framework, and its relative obscurity was accomplished by setting part of it underground, so that the new floors are only visible from the Domain at the rear rather than spoiling the Macquarie Street frontage.

The House is open to visitors, and they can even attend a session. Parliament generally sits from mid-February to early May, and from mid-September to early December, on Tues, Wed and Thurs. ☉For information on hours, ✆9230 2111.

The Mint   F5

The Mint is further south of Parliament House and next to Sydney Hospital (which was once a wing of Governor Macquarie's Rum Hospital). Built in 1816, it was the 1850s that earned the building its name for it was here that gold sovereigns were coined. Visitors can visit the Mint's former vaults, strike their own souvenir coin, and learn how raw gold was turned into bullion and currency. The Mint is ☉open daily 9am-5pm and admission is free, ✆9217 0311.

Hyde Park Barracks   F5

The Barracks is a Georgian building designed by convict architect Francis Greenway, and was intended for convict accommodation when it was built in 1819. It now houses an impressive collection which shows how the convicts spent their daily lives; where and how they slept, ate and worked. The Barracks also has the Greenway Gallery, which has changing exhibitions of historical and cultural interest. The Barracks Cafe is in the original confinement cell area and has an imaginative menu, but it's a bit on the expensive side.

The Historic Houses Trust of New South Wales has control of the Barracks which is in Queens Square, adjacent to The Mint and north-east of Hyde Park itself. The museum ☉opens daily (except Christmas Day and Good Friday) 10am-5pm, ✆9223 8922. Admission is ✪$7 adults, $3 children, $17 family.

Francis Greenway also designed St James' Anglican Church on the other side of the street from the Barracks.

Archibald Fountain and St Mary's Cathedral

St Mary's Cathedral   F4

The Cathedral, on the corner of College Street and St Mary's Road, ✆9220 0400, is a magnificent example of revival Gothic architecture in Hawkesbury sandstone, outmatched in its style only by Government House.

Begun in 1866, after a fire destroyed the previous church, the workmen laid down their tools in 1928, standing back to admire the legacy of a 62-year project. The twin spires over the southern nave were added in early 2000, rectifying the unfinished look the exterior bore for seventy years.

Vaulted ceilings, intricate statues, period-piece gargoyles and crafted side altars make the church interior both beautiful and fascinating.

Perhaps the pinnacle of the labour is the outstanding stained-glass window features, depicting scenes from the life of the Blessed Virgin Mary, and the early days of the Catholic Church in Australia. Under the Cathedral is a crypt where the Catholic Archbishops of Sydney are interred, and there is also an exhibition on the background of the Cathedral and the plans for its future.

The Chapter Hall is the earliest building on the site. Built in Gothic Revival style between 1843 and 1845, it was to form part of a Benedictine Monastery planned to include the original cathedral. The monastery was never completed. The Chapter Hall was commissioned by John Bede Polding, the first Bishop of Sydney, and since its construction it has been used as a meeting hall, classics school and general purpose hall. It is classified by the National Trust.

Another attraction of the Cathedral is its world-famous choir which sings every Sunday at the 10.30am Mass.

Hyde Park   F5-F2

Opposite Hyde Park Barracks is Queen's Square with an imposing statue of Queen Victoria, and adjoining that is Hyde Park. Further south into the park is the impressive **Archibald Fountain**. Its fanning peacock-spray captures the attention of people strolling through the northern section of Hyde Park.

Hyde Park is bounded by Queen's Square, College Street, Liverpool Street and Elizabeth Street, with Park Street running through the centre, and changing its name to William Street as it crosses College Street. The western boundary of the park adjoins the hectic commerce-and-trade climate of Market and Elizabeth Streets while St Mary's Cathedral to the east encourages quiet contemplation and prayer.

At the Queen's Square end of the park there are entrances to the underground **St James Station** from Macquarie Street, Elizabeth Street (at the end of Market Street) and Queen's Square. At the Liverpool Street end of the park there are entrances to the underground **Museum Station** from Elizabeth Street (at the end of Bathurst Street) and near the corner of Elizabeth and Liverpool Streets.

The **Anzac War Memorial**, with the tomb of the Unknown Soldier and the Pool of Reflection, is in the southern section. Protruding from its lush surrounds, this enormous monument commemorates those Australians who gave their lives in wars - a significant proportion of the population each time. The poignant carvings on the Memorial pitch solemm order against the rage of battle, evoking a sense of reflection and an awareness of great loss. It is a remarkable feature with outstanding architecture that should be viewed.

The Australian Museum   F3

The Museum is at 6 College Street, and is ⏲open daily, except Christmas Day, 9.30am-5pm, ☏9230 6000. General admission to the museum is ✪$8 adult, $3 child (5-15), $19 family, but for special temporary exhibitions there may be an extra fee. There is no charge after 4pm each day. Phone the above number for all details of current attractions, special programs for children, information on guided tours and any other query you could possibly have.

The Australian Museum is recognised as one of the foremost museums of its type in the world. There is a bookshop and restaurant in the complex.

Parking

It is not really recommended that you take your car to the city if you intend to visit several places. Wherever you find a place to park, you will be walking quite a distance away from it, then have to retrace your steps to retrieve it. There is very limited long term street parking, and although there are parking stations in The Rocks area (behind the Regent Hotel), it could end up costing you more for the car than for your day out.

Another alternative is the council-run **Domain Parking Station**, which is entered from Sir John Young Crescent, east of St Mary's Cathedral. If a car is a necessity, ☏9232 6165 for current opening times and daily charges and flat rates. Take note of the closing time because a fee exceeding $50 will be levied against you if you are forced to call the emergency number on the ticket and call someone out to open the station for you to retreive the car.

There is a moving underground footway from the parking station to the intersection of St Mary's Road, Prince Albert Road and College Street, in the front of the Cathedral. Privately-owned parking stations in other parts of the city are more expensive than the Domain.

City Centre

Pedestrians flock through city centre thoroughfares for many reasons. Most shop at the many lavish malls, plazas, arcades and complexes. Others hunt for a snack in an elegant food court, a fresh seafood meal by the waterside, or dinner with a view at one of the upper-floor restaurants in the middle of the CBD. Still more stroll on their way to relax with friends over coffee at a promenade cafe. And all enjoy the sights and

CBD from Sydney Tower

sunshine of a remarkable city, drawn like moths to a flame.

Though this is principally a shopping area, here are a few sites worth visiting.

Martin Place   E6-F6

A traffic thoroughfare until 1973, Martin Place, or Martin Plaza as it is sometimes called, is a wide pedestrian mall that stretches for five blocks from George Street to Macquarie Street. At the George Street end near the GPO is the **Cenotaph**, where a Military Memorial Ceremony takes place on the last Thursday of the month at 12.30pm. On other Thursdays the Army Band plays near the monument. It is near the Cenotaph that Sydney's official Christmas Tree is erected (very tall and impressively decorated, it is disappointingly artificial nevertheless).

Between Pitt and Castlereagh Streets, near the *MLC Centre*, there is a sunken amphitheatre where free lunchtime entertainment is staged Mon-Fri, noon-2pm.

The entrance to Martin Place Railway Station is between Phillip and Macquarie Streets.

Sydney Tower   E5

Now burdened with the most overbearing advertisement visible, AMP Sydney Tower soars over 300m above the city, and is the highest public building in the Southern Hemisphere. It is located above the Centrepoint Shopping Complex, bounded by Pitt, Market and Castlereagh Streets. From the Market Street foyer take the lift to the Podium Level, then board one of three double-decker lifts that will take you to the Observation Level (Level 4). Here there are high-powered binoculars, an illuminated display of

Sydney Harbour's water traffic, a tourist booking and information service, audio and guided tours.

Level 3 has the highest coffee lounge in Australia; Level 2 has a self-service revolving restaurant; and Level 1 has an a-la-carte up-market restaurant.

The Observation Level is ⊙open daily 9am-10.30pm Sun-Fri and 9.30am-11pm on Saturday. A general tour is available, lasting between 30 and 45 minutes. The 76-floor ascension costs adults ⊙$20, children $14, and $55 for a family, ©9229 7444.

The Queen Victoria Building   D4

There is more information on this restored building in the *Shopping* chapter, but even if you aren't interested in shopping, you should call in and have a look. It is not just a shopping centre, it is a remarkable building, with style.

From the outside it gives a visually comparative insight into Sydney's architecture, which is an eclectic mix of old and new. The ostentatious towers, arches, angelic figureheads and pale green domes of the restored QVB contrast with the streamlined walls and dominant glass of the typical modern skyscrapers occupying the background. Yet somehow the clash pleasantly co-exists.

The QVB is located at 455 George Street, ©9264 9209.

Sydney Town Hall   D3

Situated on the corner of George and Druitt Streets, the Town Hall was built between 1868 and 1889 in French Renaissance style. Its concert hall houses a pipe organ which ranks with the biggest and best in the world. The Sydney City Council administrative offices occupy the modern tower block at the rear of the building. The Town Hall was given a facelift in time for Sydney's Sesquicentenary in 1992 (prior to 1842, Sydney had not received city status).

The steps of Town Hall are often crammed with people catching their breath, snacking on food, making a protest, selling something suspect or busking with limited talent. At night, the building's spires and recesses are aesthetically flood-lit.

Centrepoint Touring Company conduct tours of the building when there are no functions taking place, ✆8223 3815 for further information.

Town Hall Railway Station has entrances to the underground on both sides of George Street.

St Andrew's Cathedral   D3

The Cathedral has twin towers reminiscent of York Minster, and is the oldest cathedral in Australia. The foundation stone was laid on May 17, 1837 by Governor Bourke. Work stopped in 1842 due to lack of funds; a three year drought had caused the colony financial problems. The Cathedral was finally completed in 1868.

There was lot of drama during its construction, including a change of architects, and the complete reversal of the church's interior - the back door of which appeared on the original plans as opening onto George Street where the main entrace should have been. It is possible to buy a book detailing the history of this beautiful Cathedral.

St Andrew's is just south of Town Hall.

Cinema District   D3

The next block on George Street, between Bathurst and Liverpool Streets, has four cinema complexes, the local branch of Planet Hollywood, a couple of McDonald's, a Pizza Hut, and other varieties of fast food outlets. There are also arcade parlours, restaurants and coffee shops. In short, this is a very busy part of the city.

Chinatown   D2

Continue down George Street, turn right at Goulburn Street, and the first turn on the left will bring you to Chinatown, which has the usual amount of restaurants, delicatessens and herbalists.

From here it is a short walk to **Paddy's Markets**, the **Entertainment Centre** and the restored **Capitol Theatre**.

Darling Harbour

Darling Harbour is Sydney's newest area, and is nearly half the size of the Sydney Business District at 54ha (133 acres). It was originally a shipping and storage area for the Port of Sydney, but the advent of container ships sounded its death knoll and it became nothing more than an eye-sore. After years of planning, wrangling amongst civic authorities, and the investment of millions of dollars, Darling Harbour is rapidly becoming the entertainment hub of Sydney. The Conference Centre, Exhibition Centre, Maritime Museum, Aquarium, IMAX Theatre, Chinese Gardens and Sega World can all be found here. A short distance away is the Entertainment Centre, the penultimate venue for concerts. In recent years, the Harbourside Festival Marketplace upgrade and construction of Cockle Bay Wharf has raised the profile of the location further.

On weekends families can be seen strolling along the walkways, picnicing on the grass and having a pleasant time.

There is always something on at Darling Harbour. Every weekend there is a program of entertainment, and almost every yearly festival or show has changed its venue to this central area - the Home Show, the Boat Show, Navy Week, Music Festivals, Book Fairs, Antique Fairs, and the list goes on.

For information on special events when you are in town, phone the Darling Harbour Infoline on, ✆1902 260 568. Alternatively, you can visit the Darling Harbour Information Centre, situated between the IMAX Theatre and Sega World, or phone them directly on, ✆9286 0111. Their web site is at ☞www.darlingharbour.com.au

How to Get There

By Monorail, the closest station to the Pitt Street Mall is near the corner of Pitt and Market Streets. There is a stop on both sides of Darling Harbour: Darling Park Station on the city side and Harbourside Station on the other. The monorail operates 7am-10pm Mon-Thu, Fri-Sat 7am-midnight and 8am-10pm on Sundays (see also under *Local Transport*).

By Light Rail, which runs from Central Station to Darling Harbour, in the middle of the circuit.

By Bus no 456 from Circular Quay via Town Hall to Darling Harbour, Mon-Fri 10am-2.30pm, Sat-Sun 11.30am-5pm, every 30 minutes.

By Sydney Ferries from Wharf 5 at Circular Quay to the Aquarium via Pyrmont Bay (Casino and Maritime Museum).

By Sydney Explorer Bus, which stops at

Harbourside and the Chinese Gardens.

By Train, the nearest stations are Town Hall, from where you can walk down Market or Bathurst Streets then across Pyrmont Bridge; and Central Station, from where you can catch Bus 469, or take any bus travelling north along George Street and alight at Chinatown.

Parking

Although several thousand car parking spaces are available on the western side of Darling Harbour - off Quay Street, adjacent to the Sydney Entertainment Centre; off Murray Street behind Harbourside; off Darling Drive under the Sydney Exhibition Centre; and off Sussex Street underneath Darling Park through to Cockle Bay Wharf - it is an expensive operation to park your car for a whole day, so the best advice is to leave the car at home, or at a railway station on the outskirts of the city.

Getting around Darling Harbour

Of course, you can walk from attraction to attraction, but if you have small children, or elderly people with you, there is the *The People Mover* train, a 20-minute ride operating between 10am and 5pm daily, which stops at all the major attractions in Darling Harbour. It costs adults ☻$3.50 and children $2.50.

Taxis

If you have overstayed your visit and missed all the public transport available, there is always the option of grabbing a cab.

Taxi Ranks are located at the Convention Centre entrance (rear of Harbourside off Darling Drive), in front of Sydney Entertainment Centre, and at all the hotels.

Darling Harbour Super Ticket

Several of the attractions at Darling Harbour have banded together to offer reductions in the form of the Darling Harbour Super Ticket, which can be purchased at any of the information booths at Darling Harbour, the Sydney Aquarium, the Monorail, the Chinese Garden, or at Matilda Cruises. The cost is ☻$45 adults, $30 children under 12, which may sound a bit expensive, but this is what you receive:

A two hour Matilda Harbour Cruise.
Entry to Sydney Aquarium.

Discount entry to IMAX theatre.
Discount entry to the Powerhouse Museum.
A ride on the Monorail.
A visit to the Chinese Gardens.
Lunch at the Shark Bite Restaurant at the Aquarium.

When you add all that, the ticket is definitely worth considering. Also, all sections of the ticket can be used on the one day, or you can use some sections on that day, and the rest are good for one month from the date of issue. The ticket also has a few optional extras, such as discount on the People Mover and on the bus fare to Homebush Bay.

Now that you know how to get there, how to get around, how to leave, and all about the Super Ticket, let's see what there is to see and do.

Cockle Bay Wharf   C4

Located on the city side of Darling Harbour, this is the area's latest development. Modern, innovative and precise architecture is a feature of the construction, complemented by the space-age IMAX Theatre hovering at its southern end. Cockle Bay is worth visiting for its photogenic appeal alone, but there is much more.

During the lunch hour and in the evening, corporate types stream from their multi-windowed offices in Sussex Street, behind the wharf, to patronise the many cafes, bars and restaurants found along this trendy strip. At night, an influx of people eager to participate in the atmosphere ensures the area bustles with life. Both a nightclub and a pub can also be found along the promenade, and the restaurants are outstanding. It is definitely a recommended place to dine, and two excellent choices are *Coast*, ✆9267 6700, and *Nick's*, ✆9264 1212, if you don't mind lightening your wallet.

Sydney Aquarium   C5

The Aquarium is located near the city end of Pyrmont Bridge, and is one of the largest and most spectacular in the world. The numerous tanks and tunnels allow the visitor to experience life on the ocean floor, surrounded by hundreds of different species of marine life. There are also displays of river systems, crocodiles, rocky shores, and the Great Barrier Reef. A touch pool allows you to get your hands onto some rough and spiky creatures.

The Aquarium is ◷open daily 9.30am-9pm, and admission is ✪$22 adult, $10 child, $48 family (2 adults and up to 3 chil-dren), ✆9262 2300. The *Shark Bite Restaurant* has plenty to tempt your taste buds while you are here.

Australian National Maritime Museum B5

The museum, at the western end of Pyrmont Bridge, is dedicated to helping people understand and enjoy Australia's ongoing involvement with the sea. Among the craft moored at the museum are yachts, warships, tugboats, and a refugee boat.

Free guided tours of the Museum building are available at regular intervals throughout the day, and a booking must be made at the Information Counter on arrival. Audio tours are also available from the Information Counter - ✪$3 adults, $5 for 2 adults sharing, $2 children.

The museum has a program of changing exhibitions, and information can be obtained by phoning the recorded information line on, ✆1900 962 002, or for general information, ✆9298 3777. There is also a library, a kiosk on the waterfront, and a shop with a wide range of nautical gifts. The museum is ◷open daily 9am-5pm (closes at 6pm in January), and minimum general admission is ✪$10 adult, $6 child, $25 family. There are extra charges for special exhibitions.

Harbourside B4

Harbourside Darling Harbour is a shopping centre with 200 shops that include 54 waterfront restaurants and food places. There are no department stores, and many of the shops sell for the tourist trade although there are branches of fashion outlets that seem to find their way into every shopping centre in Sydney.

Harbourside shops have ◷longer trading hours than in any other complex in the city - Mon-Sat 10am-9pm, Sun 10am-6pm - the restaurants, of course, stay open even longer.

Harris Street Motor Museum A3

The building next to Harbourside is the **Convention Centre**, and for people that are interested in cars, motoring and associated

memorabilia, their next stop should be the **Motor World Museum Gallery**, Level 1, 320 Harris Street, a short walk from the Convention Centre Monorail Station, ✆9552 3375. Here you will find a spectacular array of classic machines from the earliest to the latest, with lots of hands-on exhibits, in an historic old Woolstore building. The museum and carpark cover almost 4ha on two levels. It even has a place where you can 'park' the kids for a while under supervision. *The Cadillac Cafe* is available for roadside snacks, and the bookshop stocks everything ever written about cars, and some out-of-the-ordinary souvenirs. The museum is ◷open Wed-Sun 10am-5pm, and admission is ✪$11 adults, $6 children, family $22, ✆9552 3375.

The Powerhouse Museum B2

While you are in Harris Street, you continue in the direction away from the water until you arrive at Australia's largest museum, The Powerhouse Museum, on your left. Created from the shell of an old Sydney power station, the museum is alive with dynamic exhibitions, hands-on fun and special performances. There is so much to see that some people spend the whole day wandering through this incredible exhibition. Tours, talks, films, performances, demonstrations and workshops are continually in progress, and there is the *Ken Done Restaurant* (painted by, guess who?) and a kiosk when you need sustenance. As always, there is a souvenir/book shop, but this one offers some unusual merchandise. The Powerhouse Museum is ◷open daily 10am-5pm. Admission is ✪$8 adults, $2 children, under 5 free, $18 family, and the first Saturday of every month is free, ✆9217 0100.

Back at Darling Harbour proper, the **Exhibition Centre** is the next group of buildings, and information on current shows is available from the Infoline.

In front of the centre is **Tumbalong Park**, and from there it is a short walk to the next attraction.

The Chinese Garden C2

The Garden was specially designed by landscape architects from Guangdong Province, and is the largest and most elaborate outside China. It

IMAX Theatre

and the Ocean to concerts, virtual roller-coaster rides and 3-dimensional cartoon features. Current showings are advertised in the daily newspapers on the same pages as the more conservative cinemas, or you can contact IMAX on ⓒ9281 3300. Admission is ✪$17.50 adults, $12.50 children, and $50 for a family pass.

The complex also contains the *Wockpool Noodle Bar*, ⓒ9211 9888.

Star City Casino
A5

An $867 million testament to the Aussie love affair with luck and misfortune, Star City coaxes punters inside with its glittering neon lights and extravagent surrounds. The exterior looks as if it has been airlifted to the site directly from Vegas; you will either be disgusted by its tackiness or impressed with its dazzling lavishness. A mecca for the nocturnal, this enormous complex sprawls over almost three-and-a-half hectares and consists of a five star hotel, an apartment complex, a huge gaming room, the Lyric Theatre, the Showroom, 20 bars and restaurants, shops and a nightclub. If you are going to lose your money, you might find some comfort in doing it here in style - and knowing you are not alone.

The casino is at 80 Pyrmont Street, Pyrmont, a short stroll from Darling Harbour, and its doors are open 24 hours, ⓒ 9777 9000.

Sydney Jewish Museum

Over in Darlinghurst to the east, the Sydney Jewish Museum is worth the trip across town. It is the corner of Darlinghurst Road and Burton Street, south of Kings Cross Station, and is ⓒopen Mon-Thurs 10am-4pm, Fri 10am-2pm, Sun 11am-5pm (closed Saturday and Jewish Holidays). Admission is ✪$7 adult, $5 child, $16 family, ⓒ9360 7999.

The exhibits are spread over three floors with six mezzanine levels. The ground floor has a re-creation of George Street in the 1840s, showing the homes and businesses of some of the Jewish settlers. There are also displays of elements of contemporary Jewish rituals, with guides available to answer any questions, and information on some famous Jewish Australians. The mezzanines contain the permanent exhibition

covers a full hectare, and has a two-storey pavilion above a system of lakes and waterfalls. It is a serene retreat from the mayhem of the waterfront.

The Garden is ⓒopen daily 9.30am-5pm and admission is ✪$4.50 adults, $2 children.

Across Pier Street from the Chinese Garden is the **Sydney Entertainment Centre**. Chinatown is opposite the main entrance to the Centre, in Harbour Street.

From the Chinese Garden walk back towards the waterfront, and you will come to **Darling Walk**, opened in 1997. It covers 20,000 square metres of mainly restaurants, bars, clubs and shops.

Panasonic IMAX Theatre
C3

There is no way you could miss this building - it is the strangely-shaped monolith painted with yellow and black squares. The theatre has a 900m² movie screen, the largest size in the world, and seating for over 500 people. Programs have varied from documentaries on Antarctica

of The Holocaust, and survivor volunteers are present on each level to offer a rare insight into the displays. However, Catholics argue that the role of the Vatican during World War II is inaccurately recounted by the Museum, and that the aid which Pius XII gave to thousands of Jews at the time unfortunately goes unacknowledged.

The museum has a shop with a wide range of souvenirs, and on the lower ground floor the excellent *Cafe Macc* offers traditional European and Israeli cuisine at reasonable prices.

Sydney Beaches

Sydney's coastline stretches for approximately 65km, from Palm Beach in the north, to Cronulla in the south. Most Sydneysiders have their 'favourite' beach, which is not necessarily the closest to their homes. Some people grew up living near one beach, then moved as an adult to another, but you will usually find them returning to their original haunt. The people who live here have a connection with the ocean that develops from a very early age; sand between the toes and watery foam lapping at the ankles are not cliches but sensations simply indicative of a way of life.

Most of the ocean beaches are patrolled during the summer months on the weekends and during school holidays. The lifesavers, who know what they are doing, erect flags in the safest part of the beaches, and people are requested to make sure they swim between these flags. If they don't, and get into difficulties, the lifesavers are not going to let them drown, but under reasonable circumstances it should not come to this point.

If the beach is considered unsafe, perhaps because of a strong undertow or a very high tide, the lifesavers will close it and erect a sign warning people not to enter the water. Take notice of such signs and decide to spend the day somewhere else.

Board riders are given their own stretch of beach, so that they don't interfere with swimmers, and swimmers should keep out of designated board areas.

Lifesavers in this country are not paid for the

hours they spend on duty. They are young people who give freely of their time to keep our beaches safe.

Harbour beaches are not patrolled. It must not be assumed that the harbour is one giant swimming pool. There are several places where sharknets have been strung across inlets, and these are the only places where you should venture into the water. You won't see one, but there are sharks in Sydney Harbour. It is generally believed that old sharks, unable to fend for themselves in the open sea, come into the harbour for easy feeding - and what could be easier than a human thrashing around? Of course, there are also sharks in the open ocean, but the surf patrols on these beaches keep a sharp lookout, and sound alarms if a shark is sighted. You may not have caught a wave all day, but if a shark alarm sounds it is incredible how quickly you can get yourself back on the beach.

Having said all that, there has not been a shark attack in Sydney since 1963, when two children were taken whilst swimming in Middle Harbour.

Ocean Beaches

Listed below are the beaches stretching from Palm Beach in the north to Bundeena in the south, with the closest main road, and the public transport that gives access.

Also included is the following information for each venue:

Dressing Shed - usually will include showers and toilets.

Patrolled - in summer on weekends and during school holidays, ie from the first weekend in October to Easter the following year.

Pool - rock pool suitable for children.

Board - surf is suitable for board riders.

Surfers - surf is suitable for body surfers.

Usually beaches back onto a park or a reserve, and there are clear directions on the major roads indicating the way to the beach. Most beaches tend to have some topless sunbathers during the hottest parts of the day.

North of the Harbour

Palm Beach, off Barrenjoey Road, was once

mainly frequented by the wealthy and yuppy set. It has now become very popular with British tourists because it is the setting for the TV series *Home and Away*. Dressing shed, patrolled, surfers and board, pool south end. About one-and-a-half hours drive from the city centre.
Bus no 190 from Wynyard.

Whale Beach, off Barrenjoey Road. Dressing shed, patrolled, surfers and board, pool south end.
Bus 190 from Wynyard, Bus 193 from Avalon (infrequent service).

Avalon Beach, off Barrenjoey Road. Dressing shed, patrolled, surfers and board, pool south end.
Bus 190 from Wynyard.

Bilgola Beach, off Barrenjoey Road. Dressing shed, patrolled, surfers and board.
Bus 190 from Wynyard.

Newport Beach, off Barrenjoey Road. Dressing shed, patrolled, surfers and board.
Bus 190 from Wynyard.

Bungan Beach, off Barrenjoey Road. Patrolled, board.
Bus 190 from Wynyard.

Mona Vale Beach, off Barrenjoey Road. Top end not patrolled (Bongin Bongin). Dressing shed, patrolled south end, surfers south end, board north end.
Bus 157 from Manly, Bus 184 from Wynyard (peak hour).

Warriewood Beach, off Pittwater Road. Dressing shed, patrolled surfers and board.
Bus 157 from Manly.

Turimetta Beach, off Pittwater Road. Not patrolled, board.
Buses 155 and 157 from Manly.

Narrabeen Beach, off Pittwater Road. Dressing shed, patrolled, surfers and board.
Buses 182 and 190 from Wynyard, Buses 155 and 157 from Manly.

Collaroy Beach, off Pittwater Road adjoining Narrabeen Beach. Dressing shed, patrolled, surfers and board, pool at southern end.
Buses 182 and 190 from Wynyard. Buses 155 and 157 from Manly.

Collaroy Basin, off Pittwater Road. Surfers, little swell.
Via Collaroy Beach.

Long Reef Beach, off Pittwater Road. Dressing shed, patrolled, surfers and board.
Bus 182 and 190 from Wynyard, Bus 155 and 157 from Manly.

Dee Why Beach, Howard Street, off Pittwater Road, adjoins Long Reef Beach. Dressing shed, patrolled, surfers and board, pool south end.
Bus 178 and 180 from Queen Victoria Building, Bus 190, 182, 184 from Wynyard.

Curl Curl Beach, Oliver Road, off Pittwater Road. Dressing shed, patrolled, surfers and board, pool south end.
Bus 136 from Manly.

Freshwater (Harbord) Beach, Oliver Road, via Pittwater Road. Dressing shed, patrolled, surfers and board, pool north end.
Bus 139 from Manly.

Queenscliff Beach, off Pittwater Road. Dressing shed, patrolled, surfers and board, pool north end.
Bus 136 and 139 from Manly.

North Steyne Beach, off Pittwater Road, adjoins Queenscliff Beach. Dressing shed, patrolled, surfers and board.
See Manly Beach for travel information.

Manly Beach, off Pittwater Road, adjoins North Steyne Beach. Dressing shed, patrolled, surfers and board.
Bus 169 from Wynyard or Buses 143 and 144 from Chatswood, ferry from Circular Quay, JetCat from Circular Quay. Peak hour bus services available from Wynyard.

Shelly Beach, off Darley Road. Sheltered area with little swell, suitable for swimmers. Between Shelly Beach and Manly Beach there is a pool at Fairy Bower.
Via Manly Beach.

South of the Harbour

Bondi Beach, via Bondi Road off Old South Head Road. Dressing shed, patrolled, surfers and board, sanctioned topless area south end, pool at south end.
Bus 380 and 389 from Circular Quay, 365 from Edgecliff.

An internationally famous beach, **Bondi** can attract more than 40,000 people on a sunny Sunday afternoon. Crowds filter through even

Bondi Beach

the farthest reaches of the city to stake their claim to a golden patch of sand for a few hours. Inviting ocean temperatures and the safety provided by an elite surf life-saving team have made this coastal stretch extremely popular during the summer months.

The 1km strip of beach has a long history of development, since the local government authority gained control of it in 1881. By 1907 it was very popular with the neck-to-knee fraternity, although bathing time was limited to half an hour to avoid loitering. In 1928, the Bondi Beach Pavilion was built and then contained changing rooms for 1200 people, turkish baths, shops, a gymnasium and a ballroom. Today it is a community centre.

Surf life saving had its origins here and at nearby Bronte, with these clubs claiming to be the world's oldest. Surf Carnivals are often held at the beach, but the standard of the surf depends on the wind, and can range from enormous waves one day to a mill-pond the next. In the event that the swell is disappointing, there

are plenty of cafes and restaurants to attend, or some casual street shopping to enjoy. Bondi has its own distinct lifestyle, and the pace slows as soon as you cross into its suburban boundary.

Tamarama Beach. Off Bronte Road. Dressing shed, surfers and board.
Bus 360 and 361 from Bondi Junction.

Bronte Beach, off Bronte Road. Squeezed between Tamarama and Clovelly it can experience some rough surf at times. Dressing shed, patrolled, surfers and board, pool south end.
Bus 378 from Railway Square.

Clovelly Beach, off Clovelly Road. Dressing shed, patrolled.
Bus 339 and 340 from Millers Point. Although Clovelly has a sandy foreshore, it is more like a swimming pool than a beach. Good for children.

Coogee Beach, off Coogee Bay Road. Dressing shed, patrolled, surfers and board, pool south end.
Bus 372 from Railway Square, Bus 373 from Circular Quay (Pitt Street).

Maroubra Beach, Fitzgerald Avenue, off Anzac

Parade. Dressing shed, patrolled, surfers and board.

Bus 395 from Railway Square, Bus 396 from Circular Quay.

Wanda Beach, off The Kingsway. Dressing shed, patrolled, surfers and board.

Catch a train to Cronulla and then make the short walk to beach.

Elouera Beach, adjoins Wanda Beach. Dressing shed, patrolled, surfers and board, pool south end.

Train to Cronulla, walk to beach.

North Cronulla Beach, adjoins Wanda and Elouera Beaches, off The Kingsway. Dressing shed, patrolled, surfers and board, pool south end.

Train to Cronulla, walk to beach.

South Cronulla Beach, off The Kingsway. Dressing shed, patrolled, surfers and board, pool north end.

Train to Cronulla, walk to beach.

Shelly Beach, off Cronulla Street. Dressing shed, patrolled, surfers and board, pool south end.

Train to Cronulla, walk to beach.

Harbour Beaches

There are hundreds of coves and bays around the harbour, but we are only including those that have shark-proof nets, changing facilities, takeaway food outlets, and picnic areas. Obviously the beaches on the harbour do not have waves.

Clifton Gardens, Chowder Bay. The bay is two bays north-east of Taronga Park Zoo, and not easy to get to by public transport.

Take Bus 228 from Milsons Point (Mon-Fri), Bus 247 from Wynyard/QVB to Taronga Zoo, alight at Thompson Street and follow the signs.

Balmoral, Hunter's Bay. This is quite a pretty beach and is divided into two by Rocky Point, a tree-covered outcrop. Balmoral is very popular and has takeaway food bars as well as coffee shops and an up-market restaurant. The rotunda on the beach is used for many shows on summer evenings, the 'Shakespeare on the Beach' programs in particular have a large following.

Bus 238 from Taronga Zoo, Bus 257 from Chatswood, or Bus 233 from Mosman Wharf.

Manly Cove, Manly. The swimming enclosure is adjacent to Manly Wharf, where the ferry from Circular Quay docks.

Travel by Ferry, or Bus 144 from Chatswood.

Nielsen Park, between Vaucluse Road and Greycliffe Avenue, Vaucluse, in the eastern suburbs. During the swimming season (October to April) a shark-proof net is erected at Shark Beach. Experience has shown that this net must be taken down during the colder months because it cannot withstand the winter storms and heavy seas. There are dressing sheds and showers for swimmers, and a kiosk is situated opposite the beach.

Ferry from Circular Quay, Bus 325 from Circular Quay.

Botany Bay Beaches

Botany Bay was where Captain James Cook landed, and where Captain Phillip was sent to begin the new colony. Phillip, unable to find a fresh water supply, sailed further north to Sydney Harbour. Nowadays Botany Bay is a densely populated area, and if you arrived in Sydney by air, you have already spotted it; Kingsford Smith Airport is situated on its shores.

The Bay also has its share of sharks, so if you feel like a swim, stick to:

Brighton-le-Sands Baths, off Grand Parade. It has wire netting for protection, although the rest of the Lady Robinson Beach is not protected and is frequented by swimmers. There are dressing sheds. Bus 302-303 from Circular Quay, Bus 478 from Rockdale.

Bundeena

South of Botany Bay is Port Hacking. Cronulla is on its northern side, and Bundeena on the southern side borders the Royal National Park. Access is by ferry from Cronulla.

Surrounding Bundeena are Hordens, Gunyah and Jobbons, pleasant but small beaches which have little swell and are suitable only for swimming. They have no safety nets and are not patrolled.

Inner-City Suburbs

As an introductory note, it is recommended that if you wish to explore the inner suburbs and outlying regions of Sydney by car, you should use a detailed Street Directory to find you way around. The directions listed in the *How To Get There* sections below are based on that premise; they are street-specific and really require the aid of a comprehensive map. Several Street Directories are available from book stores, newsagencies and information centres.

If you wish to explore a little further afield, the suburbs bounding the city may be worth visiting. Major city centres around the world are becoming increasingly similar, and the real distinctions can sometimes only be gleaned from the lifestyles exhibited on their perimeter, where the homogenising effect of commercialism is softened by the first stages of urban sprawl. Surry Hills, Paddington and Newtown are examples offering their own insights.

Terrace housing is a quaint and common feature of inner-suburban dwelling. Density of living in popular regions with close proximity to the CBD means that town houses, duplexes and apartments are basically the only form of accommodation on offer. Sometimes these linked buildings stretch the distance of a whole street, separated in appearance only by exterior colours and the barest architectural trimmings. Those craving a big backyard head into the outer suburbs while inner-suburbanites tend to their flower pots on two-square-metre balconies, choosing the lifestyle instead. Although the frontal facade of these places is standard and often unimpressive, the interior is typically where owner's exert their effort, and they are often breathtaking. A pleasant stroll through these quiet, leafy backstreets can be worth the trip.

You can also make your way through the flurry of the main thoroughfares nearby. The consistency of building styles in the inner-city is an instantly noticeable trait. Commercial outlets are crammed into and against terraces that match the homes lining residential streets nearby. While there are a few shopping centres and several walk-through arcades, the space restrictions and advertising value mean that most retail businesses have main street fronts, and the majority of local shopping is done outside.

The inner-suburban people will most likely draw your interest. The clash of fashion, status and ideology within a small geographical radius is fascinating. Paddington east of Sydney is known for its concentrated gay community while Newtown to the city's south is the cultural centre of liberal alternative youths epitomising New Age living. A half-hour walk can take you between worlds.

NORTH

Although the Lower North Shore harbour front now contains some of the most valuable and exclusive real estate in Australia, it was originally the burial ground of the infant colony because it was considered to be far enough away to prevent the spread of disease.

How To Get There

Whatever form of transport is used, visitors must first cross the Sydney Harbour Bridge.

By Train

Trains from Central Station pass through Town Hall, Wynyard and Milsons Point to North Sydney. If you are on a train that is going to travel the City Circle, you must change trains at Town Hall or Wynyard for one on the Northern Line.

After North Sydney, the service continues through many suburban stations to Hornsby, where it may terminate, or link up with the main northern line to Newcastle, Dungog and Scone.

There is no rail service to the Lower North Shore suburbs, but buses from the city stop at North Sydney Station.

By Bus

Buses to the Lower North Shore begin in Carrington Street, at Wynyard Station. There are several to choose from, but there is a route map there, and a ticket machine. Some buses travel via North Sydney Station, while others take the Freeway and exit the Bridge on Military Road.

By Car

There are signs on all roads leading to the city that direct you to the Bridge or the Cahill Expressway. Once on the Bridge, Lane 1 has an exit for Lavender Bay, Milsons Point, and access under the Bridge to Kirribilli; Lanes 1 and 2 allow cars to exit to North Sydney, and Lane 2 also allows travel to the next exit for Crows Nest and Manly. To reach Military Road, and the suburb of Neutral Bay, follow the signs leading to Manly. Lane 4 also has an exit for Neutral Bay and Kirribilli, but this is not as easy to follow.

By Ferry

Ferries leave from Circular Quay Wharf 4 for the Lower North Shore suburbs. Buses meet the ferries to take passengers to the main street, Military Road.

Attractions

On the western side of the Bridge are the suburbs of **Milsons Point** and **Lavender Bay**. Milsons Point is home to North Sydney Olympic Pool, and the now inoperative Luna Park. Lavender Bay has harbourside parkland, from where you can get great photographs of the harbour.

The suburb of **North Sydney** rivals the Sydney CBD for skyscraping office blocks, and has a few large shopping areas, and numerous restaurants. North Sydney is really a mid-week place, as the service industry is geared for the office worker rather than the resident. This, of course, does not apply to a few good quality night venues.

On the eastern side of the Bridge lies **Kirribilli** and the stately mansions, *Admiralty House*, Sydney residence of the Governor-General, and *Kirribilli House*, Sydney residence of the Prime Minister. These two imposing buildings can be seen from the Harbour, and about twice a year they are opened for public inspection. Even if you are lucky enough to be in Sydney that particular weekend, think twice about going to view them for the queues of locals extend for blocks. By the way, Admiralty House is the one closest to the Bridge. Also in Kirribilli is the *Ensemble Theatre*.

Neutral Bay is the first suburb over the Bridge if you have used the Expressway, and the main street is lined with designer shops and restaurants. The side streets on the right hand side lead to the Harbour and open parklands, and there are many interesting old Federation homes. The side streets on the left lead to the suburb of

Taronga Zoo

Cammeray, and Long Bay, part of Middle Harbour.

Military Road, still with door-to-door shops and restaurants, continues through the **Cremorne Junction** to **Spit Junction**, where Spit Road branches off towards **Manly**, and Military Road continues on its way to **Mosman**, where the biggest attraction has to be Taronga Zoo. There is a lovely walk along the foreshores of the Harbour between Cremorne Point Wharf and Mosman Bay Wharf.

Taronga Park Zoo

The Zoo, ©9969 2777, has Australia's best collection of native and exotic animals. Its main entrance (for car and bus access) is on Bradley's Head Road, but it is only a pleasant 12 minute ferry ride from Wharf 4 Circular Quay (leaving every half hour). Admission prices are ✪$21 adults, $15 children and $55 for families.

Taronga has Australia's best collection of native and exotic animals, and also offers some of the finest views of the city, particularly from near the giraffe enclosure. There are seal shows, a rainforest aviary, a nocturnal house, all the usual animals, and Friendship Farm, where children can pat baby animals. Throughout the park there are plenty of food outlets, and there is also a licensed restaurant.

Probably the best way to explore the exhibits is to take the air cable from the lower wharf to the main entrance at the top of the hill and work your way down to catch the ferry back at the end of your journey. Of course, if you use the main entrance to begin with, walk at your leisure to the bottom of the zoo and remember to catch the air cable back in order to save your legs.

A *ZooPass* ticket is available from the ticket office at Circular Quay, and it costs ❍$28 adult, $14 child, with no combination ticket for a family. The pass includes the ferry to the Zoo, a bus up to the main entrance, and the admission fee.

Taronga is ○open every day, including Christmas Day, 9am-5pm, ©9969 2777.

From Mosman, it is also a short drive, or bus ride, to **Balmoral Beach**. If you head back to Spit Junction, and turn right down Spit Road, you will come to The Spit, the entry to Middle Harbour and the famous, or infamous, Spit Bridge, which opens to allow tall-masted boats to pass through into Middle Harbour, where they moor. There are set times for the opening of the bridge, but for the unwary driver it seems to be a very time-consuming occasion. On the other hand, for people on harbour cruises, it is fascinating to see the giant piece of the bridge lift skyward.

Once through The Spit, the road goes up a sweeping hill, then a right turn leads through the suburb of **Balgowlah** to popular **Manly**.

Manly

The *Manly Visitor Information Centre*, ©9977 1088, is at North Steyne, on the beach opposite the Steyne Hotel. There are two websites to visit for this locality: ☞www.pcn.com.au and the official website of Manly Council, which is ☞www.manly.nsw.gov.au with an email address at ✉vic@manly.nsw.gov.au

Probably the most popular attraction at Manly is **Oceanworld**, West Esplanade, ©9949 2644. You have three options for getting close to the sea creatures: viewing them through the safety of glass, handling them in touch pools or - for the fearless - rubbing skin against scale with the sharks in the diving tank. Seals perform at 11.45am and 2pm. Oceanworld is open ○10am-5.30pm and entry fees are ❍$16 adults, $8 children.

EAST

Travelling to the inner eastern suburbs may seem

that you have never left the city. The reason for this is that you really haven't. It is just that most of the streets have changed their names.

How To Get There

By Train

The Eastern Suburbs line runs to Kings Cross, Edgecliff and Bondi Junction.

By Bus

Buses to the eastern suburbs leave from Circular Quay and Railway Square.

By Car

Drive up William Street from the Australian Museum. At the top of the street, turn left into Darlinghurst Road to tour Kings Cross, or continue straight ahead for New South Head Road.

To get to Paddington, follow Oxford Street from Hyde Park.

By Ferry

Ferries travel from Circular Quay Wharf 4 to Double Bay, Rose Bay and Watsons Bay.

Attractions

The first suburb on this trip is **Kings Cross**, probably one of the best-known Sydney areas. The Cross is sleazy, of that there is no doubt, with its strip joints, sex shops and ladies of the night. But, if you drive through during the day mid-week, it may seem like any other suburb. It is when the sun drops that it comes into its own. There are some excellent restaurants and night spots, and there are some places where you have to be brave to enter. It is not the type of place where you talk to strangers, and believe me, there are some strange people walking the streets. Nevertheless, there are people who would think they had not seen Sydney if they hadn't been to the Cross. It is a haven for backpackers because of the number of cheap hostels, and it is certainly a central area, but it is probably not a good idea to stay there if you are travelling with children.

Having said that, there are a couple of landmarks. The **El Alamein Fountain**, on the corner of Darlinghurst Road and Macleay Street, was built to commemorate the men of the Australian 9th Division who fought in North Africa during World War II. It is an unusually shaped ball of a fountain, and there are always hundreds of people in the park surrounding it.

A short walk away, although in a different suburb, is **Elizabeth Bay House**, at 7 Onslow Avenue, Elizabeth Bay, ✆9356 3022. It was built for the Colonial Secretary, Alexander Macleay and his wife Eliza, and is presently furnished to the period, 1839-1845. In its day it was considered to be the finest house in the colony, and its views over the harbour would have been even more impressive then than they are now. It is a two-storey house with a grand winding staircase, and is maintained by the Historic Houses Trust. It is ⏱open Tues-Sun (Monday when a public holiday) 10am-4.30pm (except Christmas Day and Good Friday) and admission is ✪$7 adult, $4 child, $17 family.

Paddington is another suburb that seems to be part of the city, but it is a charming part. It has many crooked streets lined with pretty terrace houses that are decorated with Paddington Lace, a distinctive wrought-iron trimming. The original village was established in the 1840s and housed the workers building the Victoria Barracks. Parts of the original little town can be seen in the area bounded by Shadforth, Prospect and Spring Streets.

Darlinghurst Road links Kings Cross with Paddington, or you can follow Oxford Street from the city.

Attractions in the area include numerous antique shops along Queen Street, and art galleries sprinkled along Oxford Street and the side streets. The Paddington Village Bazaar is held in the Uniting Church grounds every Saturday (see *Shopping*).

Victoria Barracks in Oxford Street, next to the Town Hall, ✆9339 3170, is a Georgian-style building (1841-1848) and a living history of Australia's military. The Army Museum is ⏱open on Sunday 10am-3pm.

The **Sydney Cricket Ground** is a little further south, in Driver Avenue, Moore Park, ✆9360 6601. This famous and historic site continues to play host to many notable sporting events. A *Sportspace Tour* is available, guiding visitors through the complex and its memorabilia for

✪$20 adults, $13 children and $52 for families, ✆9380 0383 (bookings essential).

Centennial Park in Oxford Street, was founded in 1888 to celebrate the centenary of the colony. The park is open daily sunrise-sunset, and there are facilities for hiring horses and bikes (see *Sport*).

Double Bay, one of the most up-market suburbs in Sydney, is reached in a car by following New South Head Road from Kings Cross; or by bus from Elizabeth Street; or by train to Edgecliff and walking down New South Head Road.

Known by Sydneysiders who can't afford to shop here as 'Double Pay', it is the most exclusive shopping area in Sydney, and all the well-known, top-class designers have outlets. The surrounding areas of Darling Point, Point Piper, Vaucluse, etc, are populated by people who *can* afford to shop here, and it is worth a visit.

New South Head Road continues through **Rose Bay** and on to **Vaucluse** where it is worth visiting **Vaucluse House**, which dates from 1803. It was the home of William Charles Wentworth, one of the intrepid trio who first crossed the Blue Mountains, and the father of the Australian Constitution. He, and his wife Sarah and their children, lived here from 1829 to 1853, and it's furnishings still recall that period. The house is set in 11ha with gardens, bushland and a harbour beach frontage, and has out-buildings and stables. The house is ⏱open Tues-Sun 10am-4.30pm and Monday if it is a public holiday. Admission is ✪$6.50 adults, $2.50 children, $15.50 family. There are tearooms in the grounds, and they serve a-la-carte lunches, and Devonshire teas that you would die for. If you are not driving, Bus 325 from Circular Quay stops at the front gate.

The end of New South Head road is **Watsons Bay**, which is on the Harbour, near South Head and the Harbour entrance. The area's most famous landmark is not, as some would say, the pub, nor is it Doyle's restaurant - it is **The Gap**, a cliff from which there are great views, and from where people have committed suicide by jumping into the ocean below. When things are not going too well for them, it is common for

Sydneysiders to say that they are going to throw themselves off The Gap, although fortunately not many do.

Nearby is the anchor from the ill-fated *Dunbar*, a barque which was to carry passengers and goods on a regular basis between Sydney and England, but was wrecked on the rocks of The Gap on its second voyage in August 1857. It was Sydney's worst shipping disaster, with 121 lives lost and only one survivor.

From Watsons Bay you can follow Old South Head Road to **Bondi Junction**, or turn off Old South Head Road left onto Military Road and head for **Bondi Beach** and the other beaches to the south. Bondi Junction is about 2km from the beach, and is the main bus/train link for public transport throughout this area. It is also quite a good shopping centre, and its branches of David Jones and Grace Bros are linked by the Oxford Street pedestrian Mall, which has many specialty shops. Bus no 280 runs between Bondi Beach and Bondi Junction.

SOUTH

The southern suburbs are for the most part either industrial or residential, and if you arrived by air, you have already travelled through parts of them. However, there are a few places that are historically interesting on the shores of Botany Bay. The two main areas are **La Perouse**, on the north head of Botany Head, and **Kurnell** on the south head.

How To Get There

By Train

There is no direct train route to *La Perouse*.
To get to *Kurnell*, take the train to Cronulla, then local Bus 67 from the depot opposite the station, near Munroe Park.

By Bus

Bus no 398 runs from Circular Quay to *La Perouse*.
The best transportation route to *Kurnell* is detailed above.

By Car

To get to *La Perouse*, follow Anzac Parade all the way from Taylor Square in Oxford Street.

To get *Kurnell* from there, drive around the foreshores of the bay, crossing Endeavour Bridge and Captain Cook Bridge.

It is difficult to get to both places in one trip without a car.

Attractions

La Perouse

La Perouse is named after Jean-Francois de Galaup, Comte de Laperouse, who was commissioned by Louis XVI in 1785, to set out on a voyage of discovery. The expedition consisted of two ships, *L'Astrolabe* and *La Boussole*. Two and a half years later, the two ships arrived in Botany Bay, a week after the arrival of the First Fleet. La Perouse and Captain Phillip apparently became good friends, and the Frenchman gave Phillip reports and letters to be sent back to his king. The French ships stayed in Botany Bay for a period of six weeks, then La Perouse set sail, never to be heard from again.

The whereabouts of the ships remained a mystery until the two wrecks were discovered on the reefs of Vanikoro, off the Solomon Islands, by Peter Dillon, an Irish trader and adventurer.

The **La Perouse Museum**, ☎9311 3379, is housed in the Cable Station, inside a circle formed by the end of Anzac Parade. It contains many artefacts from the wrecks, as well as relics from their time in the Bay.

The **Cable Station** was designed and built between 1880 and 1881 to provide accommodation, offices and telegraph facilities for the officers of the Eastern Extension Australasia and China Telegraph Company. The company's submarine cable between La Perouse and Wakapuaka in New Zealand terminated here.

On the bay foreshore, where La Perouse landed, there is an obelisk to commemorate his visit, and close by is the grave of Pere L.C. Receveur, a chaplain and naturalist with the expedition who has the honour of being the first Frenchman to be buried on the Australian continent.

The **Macquarie Watchtower**, also in the circle formed by the road, was built between 1820 and 1822, to prevent smugglers entering Botany Bay.

A causeway from the tip of the point leads to **Bare Island**, on which the fort was built in 1881, following Britain's decision to give self governing colonies the responsibility for their own defence. It only operated as a means of defence for 27 years, then it became a war veterans' home, then a museum with exhibits associated with its early history.

Kurnell

Kurnell has **Captain Cook's Landing Place**, an historic site of over 400ha. Cook landed at 3.00pm on April 28, 1770, and tradition maintains that the first person to step ashore was his wife's young cousin, Isaac Smith. The spot where he scrambled onto dry land is marked with a small obelisk, and there is a larger one dedicated to the discovery nearby.

The site is also a monument to the Gwiyagal People, the Aboriginal tribe who inhabited the area at the time of European discovery.

The **Discovery Centre**, in Captain Cook Drive, is ☉open Mon-Fri 11am-3pm and 10am-4pm on weekends and public holidays, ✆9668 9111. It is one of the major features of the site, with exhibits detailing Cook's life, exploits and achievements, including his notes and opinions on the country he had discovered.

There are also scenic walks, picnic and barbecue areas, and an historic walk, and the visitor centre has maps and leaflets on everything you can see and do.

WEST

The inner western suburbs were settled in the early days of the colony and therefore have many buildings and homes from a bygone era.

How To Get There

By Bus

Buses 438, 440, 470 travel south along George Street and pass the beginning of Glebe Point Road, Glebe, but the buses that actually drive down Glebe Point Road are 431, 433, and 434. Bus no 433 continues on to Balmain.

Bus 440 connects the city with Rozelle, passing through the suburbs of Camperdown, Annandale and Leichhardt.

By Road

To get to Glebe, drive south along George Street, which becomes Broadway, then turn right at the traffic lights on the corner of Glebe Point Road. Incidentally, at that point Broadway becomes Parramatta Road and the Great Western Highway.

Or, if you are crossing the Harbour Bridge, take the Western Distributor, stay in the left lane, follow the sign to the Western Suburbs, then take the first exit onto Bridge Road. The Fish Markets are off to the right and if you continue on you will find yourself in the heart of Glebe.

The best way to get to Balmain from the city is to drive south along George Street to Leichhardt, turn right at Norton Street, follow that street to its end, turn left, then right at the first traffic lights, and follow this street, which undergoes a few name changes before it becomes Darling Street and travels through the heart of Balmain.

If you are coming over the Harbour Bridge, take the Western Distributor, continue over the new Glebe Island Bridge, go with the major flow of traffic turning right into Victoria Road, then right into Darling Street, Balmain. This way by-passes Leichhardt.

By Ferry

Sydney Ferries travel between Circular Quay and three wharves in Balmain - Darling Street, Thames Street and Elliott Street.

Attractions

The word 'glebe' means 'a gift to the church', and the suburb of **Glebe** was first settled in the late 1700s as a church-owned estate. The church in question was St John's Church, and it still stands on the corner of Glebe Point Road and St John's Road. Apparently by the 1820s the church had fallen on hard times, and the land was sold and subdivided. The high portions of Glebe, away from the insect-ridden Blackwattle Swamp (now known as Blackwattle Bay) were purchased by wealthy families. Grand houses with names such as Hereford House, Forest Lodge, Toxteth House and Lyndhurst were built. The land that was not so valuable became as area for worker's cottages, many of which have recently been restored.

By 1861, Glebe was Sydney's largest suburb

and quite a stylish place to live, but by 1911 things had changed dramatically. The wealthier older families moved out, and the poor moved in, so by about 1930 there was nothing grand about giving your address as Glebe.

In a full turnaround, Glebe has become a trendy place to live again, and it has a small shopping centre with lots of art galleries and heritage shops. There are also many fine, cheap restaurants along Glebe Point Road, and a couple that are really up-market - *The Abbey*, ✆9660 4792, and *Darling Mills*, ✆9660 5666.

Unfortunately, many of the old historic homes are privately owned, so they are not open to the public, except on special tours arranged occasionally by the Glebe Society, ✆9660 7873.

If you are in Glebe on a Saturday or Sunday, you might like to visit the *Glebe Markets*, held in Glebe Public School, on the corner of Glebe Point Road and Derby Place. There are lots of stalls selling new clothes and jewellery, and others offering pre-loved treasures (see also under *Shopping*).

On Parramatta Road, opposite the start of Glebe Point Road, is Victoria Park, which has a wide expanse of lawns for picnics, and a public swimming pool, ✆9660 4181.

The University of Sydney, on Parramatta Road, adjoins Victoria Park, and is a sandstone blend of Tudor and Gothic architecture, with acres of green lawns. The Great Hall has a Royal Window which illustrates the monarchy from the Normans to Queen Victoria. The University's Fisher Library, ✆9351 2993, contains more than 400,000 volumes, and the Nicholson Museum has a quality collection of Egyptian, Etruscan, Greek and Roman art.

Leichhardt has a large Italian population, and consequently a large number of Italian restaurants are found in the main streets of Parramatta Road and Norton Street. Leichhardt Park, at the end of Mary Street, has several football ovals, acres of parkland, and an attractively sited public swimming complex, ✆9555 8344, with views over Iron Cove.

Trendy Norton Street's newest addition is the **Italian Forum**. Most residents used to think that the closest they would ever come to Italy on their own doorstep was to venture into Norton street and absorb the atmosphere of its Italian restaurant-lined sidewalk. Developers decided to go one step further. The Italian Forum is accessed through a narrow alley where buildings tower above and charming Tuscan flourishes grace the architecture. The end of the alley opens onto a stunning courtyard, surrounded by apartments, shops and restaurants, all mimicking something similar to the typical image of a quaint Italian village (except for the commercialism). This is no down-market immitation - the restaurants are top-class, the boutiques are expensive and the apartments exclusive. A statue of Dante, ornate waterscapes and a bright selection of flowers help to round off the European feel, and transport you - at least temporarily - out of Sydney's lifestyle and into another. The Forum is located 100 metres from the intersection of Parramatta Road on the right-hand side.

The suburb of **Balmain** gets its name from Dr Balmain, who received the whole of the peninsula as a land grant. To give some idea of the size of his grant, his house was situated in Johnson Street in the suburb of Annandale. Balmain is a trendy area now, rivalling Paddington with its quaint terraces, art galleries and alternative lifestyle shops, but it wins hands down in the restaurant department. There are also many pubs that have outdoor beer gardens and live entertainment.

When driving to Balmain from Victoria Avenue, the *Dawn Fraser Swimming Pool*, named after Australia's swimming legend because this is where she began her swimming career, is in Elkington Park, ✆9555 1903. The park is opposite Young Street, which runs off Darling Street to the left. Further along Darling Street, there is a set of traffic lights, and a left turn will take you into Rowntree Street and lead to the less outrageous waterfront suburb of **Birchgrove**.

Balmain Saturday Market is held in the grounds of St Andrew's Congregational Church, on the corner of Darling Street and Curtis Road, ⏱every Saturday 9am-4.30pm, ✆0418 765 736.

Darling Street continues to Darling Street Wharf, where there is a nice little park at Peacock Point, and from where the ferries leave for Circular Quay.

Outlying Attractions

Parramatta

Parramatta Road terminates at Parramatta, the second oldest settlement in the country. The area was first visited by Governor Phillip and a party of explorers on April 24, 1788. It had become obvious that the soil in the area of Sydney Cove would not produce sufficient crops to feed the infant settlement, and in September 1788, Governor Phillip announced his intention to found another settlement. On November 2, 1788, he chose this area, and named the settlement Rose Hill, but on June 4, 1791, he renamed it Parramatta.

Parramatta became the site of Australia's first orchard, vineyard, tannery, legal brewery, woollen mills, observatory, steam mill, market place and fair. It also was the terminating point of the first road, ferry and rail links out of Sydney. And, most importantly, it saw the beginning of Australia's wool industry.

Although, strictly speaking, Parramatta is a suburb of Sydney, it is a city in its own right with a population of about 130,000. The *Parramatta Visitors Centre* has been incorporated into the Parramatta Heritage Centre, 346 Church Street, ☏9630 3703, and is ⏰open Mon-Fri 10am-5pm, Sat-Sun 10am-4pm. The Centre has a wealth of information on the city, and a detailed brochure covering walking tours, restaurants, transport details and more, with good maps on the area. The brochure is produced annually and is called *Discover Parramatta*. The self-guided tours include a walk through the heart of the central business district with an excursion into Parramatta Park and Old Government House; and another which passes the outskirts of the old town to the important historic houses of *Experiment Farm Cottage*, *Elizabeth Farm* and *Hambledon Cottage*. To take both tours requires a full day, and a certain amount of fitness, as there are many points of interest.

At the end you will have a good idea of the historical importance of the city.

Parramatta Park is within easy walking distance of the central business area, and comprises about 85ha. In the Park are found Old Government House, the Governor's Bathhouse, The Tudor Gate House, Australia's first Observatory, and a kiosk with boat and cycle hire. Nearby are *Parramatta Stadium* and the *Swimming Centre*.

Parramatta has an enormous shopping complex located near the train station, and a section of the main street, Church Street, is a shopping mall with shrubs, trees, paved pedestrian areas, a fountain and an amphitheatre.

The beautiful picnic area of Lake Parramatta Reserve is at the northern edge of the city, and a regular bus service and a sealed road provide access. The reserve covers about 65ha (160 acres), and the Lake covers 9ha (23 acres) in area. Along the drive on both sides of the Lake, and giving shade to the parking and picnic areas are splendid specimens of Blackbutts, Grey Gums, Red Mahoganies, Bloodwoods, Turpentines, Rough-Barked Angophoras and Sydney Red Gums. The Lake is very deep in parts, so boating is prohibited, but there is a fenced swimming pool and an artificial sandy beach. There are also fireplaces, tables, toilets and a kiosk.

Parramatta has many sporting facilities, including Rosehill Racecourse (see under *Entertainment*), very good restaurants, three cinema complexes, and a wide range of accommodation.

The city's main festival is the Wistaria Garden Festival, held in September each year.

North of Parramatta, in the suburb of **West Pennant Hills**, is *Koala Park Sanctuary*, ☏9484 3141. Set in 4ha, the Park not only has plenty of koalas, there are also kangaroos, wallabies, wallaroos, wombats, dingoes, echidnas and emus. The Park is ⏰open daily 9am-5pm, and photo sessions with koalas are available at intervals throughout the day. Admission is ✪$14 adults, $8 children and $32 for families. The Sanctuary is on Castle Hill Road, and to get there from Parramatta follow Pennant Hills Road to the Castle Hill Road turn-off. To get there from Sydney by road, travel along Epping Road which

becomes Beecroft Road (or along the M2 to the Beecroft Road exit), to its end, then turn left onto Pennant Hills Road and a short distance along on the right is the Castle Hill Road turn-off. From Sydney by train, travel to the Pennant Hills Station, then take Bus 655 to the Park.

Ku-ring-gai Chase National Park

Located 24km (15 miles) north of the city, the Park has numerous bushwalks and some magnificent Aboriginal rock carvings in accessible spots. The higher parts of the park afford magnificent views across Pittwater.

On the edge of the park is *Waratah Park*, 13 Namba Road, Duffys Forest, home of 'Skippy the Bush Kangaroo' and many of her friends, including Tasmanian Devils, dingoes, wombats, wallabies, emus and koalas. Feeding times are on the hour between 11am and 4pm. There is a restaurant, a snack bar, and a souvenir shop, and the Park is ⏱open every day 10am-5pm, ©9450 2377. Admission is ✪$12.90 adults, $6.50 children and $34.90 for families. To get there by car, proceed north on the Pacific Highway to the suburb of Pymble, then turn right onto Mona Vale Road. Take the left turn to Duffy's Forest off Mona Vale Road at Terrey Hills, and follow the signs.

Wonderland Australia

Located near the M4, in outer western Sydney, Wonderland is 219ha (540 acres) of landscaped grounds in Wallgrove Road, Eastern Creek, and has Australia's longest wooden roller coaster, the Bush Beast. Other rides include The Demon,

Space Probe and Snowy River Rampage. There are also many different kinds of theme shops, live shows and picnic spots. It is ⏱open 10am-5pm every day, ©9830 9100 or ©9830 9106 (recorded information). Admission is adults ✪$39 and children $27.

The *Australian Wildlife Park*, ©9830 9187, also at Wonderland, is ⏱open daily 9am-5pm. Entry fees are ✪$18 adults, $12 children and $46 for families.

Shuttle buses run to the fun park from Mt Druitt, Fairfield, Blacktown and Rooty Hill train stations.

Also in Eastern Creek is the **Eastern Creek Raceway**, Brabham Drive, ©9672 1000. This venue has accommodated the 500cc Motor-bike Grand Prix, and hosts other races around the year.

Hawkesbury River

The River is 45km (28 miles) north of Sydney, and is dotted with historic towns such as Windsor, Richmond, Wilberforce, Pitt Town and Wisemans Ferry. It winds around Sydney's western outskirts through a natural forest area until finally meeting the sea at Brooklyn. One of the best ways to see it is to join the *Riverboat Postman* near the Hawkesbury River Railway Station in Brooklyn. This four hour cruise includes commentary and snacks. The cost is ✪$35 adults, $18 children and $72 for families, ©9985 7566.

An alternative is to hire a house boat from the many on offer at Brooklyn, at the southern end of the Hawkesbury Bridge. Two such companies are Holidays Afloat Houseboats, ©9985 7368, and House Boats Prestige, ©9985 7744.

Royal National Park

History

Royal National Park was gazetted in 1879 as 'The National Park', and was the first public reserve in Australia to be so termed. In fact, the Park can lay claim to being the first in the world, because although Yellowstone Park in the USA was established in 1872, it was not officially gazetted as a national park until 1883. When Queen Elizabeth II first visited Australia in 1954, she bestowed the title 'Royal', but most Sydneysiders still refer to it as 'The National Park'.

The Park is situated south of Port Hacking, about 29km from the centre of Sydney, and covers 16,000ha of vegetation and landscape typical of the Sydney Basin sandstone.

The original inhabitants of the area were the Aboriginal people of the Dharawal tribe, who used the sandstone caves for shelter and lived off the land and waterways. Little detail is known of their lifestyle as rock engravings, axe-grinding grooves, charcoal drawings and hand stencils are the only physical remains of the culture.

The Royal National Park was established by the then NSW Premier, Sir John Robertson, who saw a need for a recreation space for Sydney, many parts of which had become infested with vermin and disease.

Audley was the site of the first European settlement in the Park. The native mangroves and mudflats were replaced by grassed parkland and exotic trees, and added to the local fauna were deer, rabbits and foxes.

Park Features

The Park has been shaped from a sloping sandstone plateau, which rises from sea level at Jibbon Point in the north, to over 300m at Bulgo in the south.

The Park scenery is magnificent and varied. The waves from the open sea have produced majestic cliffs, broken every now and then by small creeks and beaches. Deep river valleys have been formed by streams flowing north to Port Hacking and east to the Pacific Ocean. The upper slopes have woodlands that merge with the heath vegetation on the plateaux. Gorges and valleys have forest and rainforest, the tidal channels of the rivers have mangrove, and the swamps are covered in sedges.

There are numerous grassy areas along the *Hacking River valley*, and from July to November the wildflowers on the plateaux provide a riot of colour. There are waterfalls at *Wattamolla, Curracurrong, Uloola* and *National Falls*.

How to Get There

By Rail

Trains on the Illawarra-Cronulla line stop at Loftus, Engadine, Heathcote, Waterfall and Otford, and from these stations there are walking tracks into the Park.

By Car

From Sydney, follow the signs toward the Airport, and then follow the signs to Wollongong (Princes Highway) or President Avenue at Brighton-le-Sands, turn right and at the end of the street turn left onto Princes Highway keep going until you are past Sutherland. The Audley entrance to the Royal National Park is well signposted. You take a left turn of the Princes Highway just south of Sutherland.

From Liverpool City, take the Heathcote Road exit from the M5 motorway (before the toll booth). Turn right into Heathcote Road so you cross over the M5 Motorway and follow it all the way to the Princes Highway (between Engadine and Heathcote).

You can then do one of two things:

> Turn left and go back about 3km to enter the Park south of Sutherland (Audley entrance); or
>
> Turn right and head south to Waterfall and enter the Park there.

From Wollongong, drive north along the Princes Highway. After reaching Bulli continue along Lawrence Hargraves Drive (don't go up the escarpment). Another way is to follow the Mt Ousley Road to the Princes Highway and turn right at Stanwell Tops to go to Stanwell Park. At the top of the Bluff, turn left along Lady Wakehurst Drive, then continue to the Otford entrance of the Park.

By Ferry

Cronulla National Park Ferry Cruises, ©9523 2990, have a service from the wharf near Cronulla railway station to Bundeena, and the trip takes 25-30 minutes. The first ferry from Cronulla leaves at 5.30am Mon-Fri on the hour to 6.30pm, 8.30am Sat-Sun and public holidays on the hour to 6.30pm. The last ferry leaves Bundeena daily at 7pm (summer), 6pm (winter).

It should be noted that Bundeena is *not* within the Royal National Park.

Tourist Information

A Visitor Centre and Wildlife Shop is on Farnell Avenue, Audley. Call into the centre for advice on all aspects of your park visit. Permits for camping are obtained here. It is ◷open daily 8.30am-4pm, ✆9542 0648. The shop sells books, film, maps, posters, gifts and souvenirs.

Park Entrance Fee

There is no charge for traffic travelling through and not stopping in the Park from Sutherland to places south of the Park.

For those that intend to stop within the park the following charges apply:

Bus - ✪$3.00 per adult, $1.00 for each school age child, under the age of 5 free, pensioners free. Must display pensioner card.

Cars - ✪$9.00 per vehicle.

Motor Bikes - ✪$3.00 per bike.

There is no charge for people who hike into the park for the day.

Park Regulations

All fauna, flora, Aboriginal sites and rock formations are protected.

Wildfires can destroy lives and property, so be careful, especially during the bushfire danger period (normally October to March). Use only the fireplaces provided and observe Total Fire Bans. Portable fuel stoves are required for camping.

Pets and Firearms are not permitted in national parks.

Vehicles, including motorbikes must keep to formed public roads. Drive carefully.

Please use rubbish bins if provided; or take rubbish with you when you leave the park.

Camping

Caravans and car camping are permitted at the camping ground at **Bonnie Vale**, off Bundeena

Road. It has toilet and shower blocks, but no powered sites. In fact, there are only 40 sites in all, and during school holidays and long weekends, ballots are held to allot them. There are so many applicants that this seems to be the fairest way. At other times there is not so much demand, and therefore there is a good chance of securing a site, but booking ahead is essential. For reservations, ✆9542 0648.

For site fees, you can expect to pay about ✪$10 per person for the first two people, and a couple of dollars per extra person. Children under 5 years of age are free.

There are lots of places for bush camping throughout the park, however booking and obtaining permits are essential. The permits must first be obtained from the Visitor Centre. They are free, but written on the back of them are the special conditions that apply to camping in a national park, and this is the best way of making sure that everyone is aware of them.

Activities

Weekends see many organised picnics arranged by sporting clubs, church groups and families with the addition of aunts, uncles, grandparents and third cousins, all taking advantage of the wide open expanse near the Audley causeway.

National Park Ranger guided activities are available. Bookings and more information can be obtained on ✆9542 0649.

Picnicking

There are many picnic areas dotted throughout the park, but there are only barbecue facilities at Audley, Warumbul, Wattamolla, Bonnie Vale and Garie. Kiosks are found at Audley, Wattamolla and Garie Beach.

Swimming

Safe saltwater swimming is available at *Bonnie Vale*, *Jibbon*, *Wattamolla* and *Little Marley* beaches, and these are favourite spots for families.

Surfers head for *Garie*, *Era* and *Burning Palms* beaches, which are patrolled by surf lifesavers on weekends and public holidays during summer.

Freshwater swimming is possible at *Blue Pools*, *Karloo Pool*, *Deer Pool*, *Curracurrang* and *Crystal Pools*, but care should be taken when swimming in rock pools. The water always tends to be cold, so it is easy to get cramps. It is not always easy to judge how deep a rock pool is, so never jump or dive into these pools. Spinal injury units of hospitals are always warning people about the dangers of leaping head-first into unknown waters.

Boating

The *Audley Boatshed*, ©9545 4967, has rowing boats, canoes, kayaks and aquabikes for hire, and only these may be used in Kangaroo Creek, and in the Hacking River above the causeway. Private boats can be used downstream from the Audley causeway.

The boat shed is ☉open Mon-Sat 9am-5pm, Sun and public holidays 9am-5.30pm. A small refundable deposit is required for each craft.

Walking

The Park has over 150km of walking tracks that provide access to the wide range of scenery available, and the Visitor Centre has track pamphlets. Bungoona, Governor Game and Otford Lookouts offer chances to take spectacular photos, and National, Winifred and Curracurrong Falls are easily accessible.

Cycling

The best route for cyclists is Lady Carrington Drive, which is closed to motor vehicles, and is relatively flat. Ask at the Visitor Centre for directions. Bicycles and mountain bikes are only allowed on management trails. They are not permitted on walking tracks.

Sydney Tramway Museum

If you are visiting the Royal National Park on a Sunday or Wednesday, you might like to check out the Sydney Tramway Museum in Pitt Street, Loftus, ©9542 3646. It is ☉open Sunday and Public Holidays 10am-5pm, Wednesday 9.30am-3.30pm, but no one is admitted in the hour prior to closing.

Trams operated in Sydney for one hundred years to 1961, and a fleet of over 1500 vehicles provided the city with an efficient transport service. The Sydney Tramway Museum has an excellent collection of Sydney trams, and others from Brisbane, Ballarat, Melbourne and San Francisco, and also a selection of the buses which replaced them in Sydney. This fleet includes the last remaining double-decker trolley bus.

Every open day, a number of the museum's trams operate along a kilometre of track, each return trip taking about 15 minutes, but the San Francisco PCC Streetcar only operates on the first Sunday of the month. There is also a tramway waiting shed from Railway Square, the unique counterweight dummy from the Balmain line, and an extensive range of photographs and artefacts.

The museum has a shop with a range of books, post cards, video tapes and souvenirs, as well as snacks and drinks. There are also picnic facilities within the Museum grounds.

Admission is ❖$12 adult, $6 child, and includes unlimited tram rides and use of facilities.

Festivals

The **Festival of Sydney** is held during the entire month of January each year, and features include twilight and open-air concerts in the Domain, contemporary music at Hyde Park and Darling Harbour, outdoor movies at the Opera House, bike rallies, street theatre, and classical theatre performances at the Opera House, the Belvoir Theatre and the Seymour Centre.

Australia Day, January 26, sees the city come alive, especially around the harbour, with all kinds of displays, and a Ferrython in which all the Sydney ferries compete.

The Mardi Gras is organised by representatives of the gay and lesbian community, and is held on the first Friday in February each year. It is actually part of a month-long festival that centres around the Oxford Street section of the city.

The main attraction of the Mardi Gras for the thousands of spectators is the colourful parade of extremely imaginative floats and performers.

For visitors who are new to this scene, be aware that the parade's participants are often very expressive. Nudity and sexual insinuation are always prevalent here.

The Royal Easter Show was held at the Showground in Moore Park beside the SCG for decades, but that land is now occupied by Fox Studios. 1997 marked its last appearance at that site and Shows are now held at Homebush Bay, the venue of the 2000 Olympics.

The Show begins on the Friday before Good Friday and finishes on Easter Tuesday.

Advertised as *"when the country comes to town"*, there's something for everyone, with displays of horticulture, livestock, crafts and hi-tech machinery. For kids, there are rides and sample bags, and for all ages there is non-stop entertainment in the show ring with livestock judging, trotting races, equestrian events, the Grand Parade, bands, sky divers, clowns, rodeos, and fireworks displays.

The Show is well patronised by Sydneysiders with attendances on the public holidays reaching 100,000.

Anzac Day commemorates the actions of Australian and New Zealand troops involved in the conflict of the First World War, and the lives they sacrificed. The day falls on the 25 April, the same date that the soldiers landed on the shores of Gallipoli in 1914 and were overwhelmed by the Turkish resistance. Originally conceived as a lightning campaign, the conflict soon developed into an 8 month conflict during which time both sides sustained heavy casualties. Anzac Day services are held around the country and involve parades, marches, laying wreaths, minutes of silence, playing *The Last Post* and reciting the poem, *For the Fallen*. The opportunity is taken to reflect on all military losses since WWI. It remains a solemn and important day of remembrance in the Australian psyche.

The **National Folkloric Festival** is an annual multicultural event featuring dancers and musicians from many ethnic backgrounds. It is held in June, and begins with a Sunday parade that terminates at the Opera House, the scene for the many events of the following weekend.

St Patrick's Day seems to be gaining momentum every year. On the 17 March, thousands don a green item of clothing, grab a clover in one hand, and trot down to the nearest pub for a few pints or more of Guiness. The day is intended to mark the death of Ireland's patron saint and to commemorate his lifetime work of converting the country's entire population to Catholicism, but how this ties in with flagrant alcoholism remains something of a mystery. There is plenty of fun and good cheer, though halos are in scarce supply and the behaviour is often less than saintly!

The Biennale of Sydney is an international exhibition of contemporary art held every two years. Since its inception in 1973, the Biennale has brought the world's leading artists to Sydney, and more than 800 of them from over 45 countries have been exhibited.

The Biennale is not only confined to Sydney as visiting artists travel giving lectures, workshops and artist-in-residence programs, and special lectures and displays are organised.

The Sydney to Hobart Yacht Race can hardly be classed as a festival, but it does generate a lot of excitement. Every Boxing Day thousands of people line the vantage spots around the harbour to watch the mini and maxi yachts set off on their adventure, and there are so many boats of all sorts on the harbour, farewelling the entrants, that it is a wonder they ever get through the Heads. The race is closely monitored by news crews in light aircraft, and hourly reports are given on TV and radio as to who is in the lead, and by how much. Meanwhile, the people in Hobart get ready for the big welcoming party.

The City to Surf Fun Run is another annual event. Held every year in August, thousands of people of all ages assemble for the start of the run to Bondi Beach, and as the starting gun goes off, Park Street becomes a sea of people. Of course, the race is always won by a professional marathon runner, but winning is not really what the spectacle is all about. Everyone who finishes receives a certificate, and their names are listed in the newspapers. Even those who don't finish are congratulated for entering, and there is a real spirit of comradeship as you watch people helping each other along the way.

In addition to the above, each municipal area of Sydney has its own festival, and there are other special annual events, such as the blessing of the fishing fleet.

Public Holidays

Christmas, Boxing Day, New Year and Easter are obviously celebrated at the same time as everywhere else in the world.

Other holidays that are enjoyed in Australia are:

Australia Day - January 26.
Anzac Day - April 25.
Queen's Birthday - the second Monday in June.
Labour Day - the first Monday in October.
Another day is *Bank Holiday*, which is held on the first Monday in August, but only banks, government offices, insurance companies and the like are closed.

Sport and Recreation

Boating

It should be noted that a licence is required to drive any mechanically driven vessel capable of 10 knots or more. There are several places around the harbour foreshores where bare boats can be hired. Here are a few names and addresses:

Abbotsford Point Boat Hire, 617 Great North Road, Abbotsford, ©9713 8621.
Australian Sailing School & Club, Parrawi Road, Mosman, ©9960 3077.
Balmoral Sailing and Kayaking School and Hire, 2 The Esplanade, Balmoral, ©9969 5344.
Eastsail, d'Albora Marinas, New Beach Road, Rushcutters Bay, ©9327 1166.
Rose Bay Marina, 594 New South Head Road, Rose Bay, ©9363 5930.

If you are a marine enthusiast and wish to admire the yachts in the harbour, there are several wharfs along the shoreline. The *Cruising Yacht Club* at Rushcutters Bay is close to the city. Since the best way to enjoy the spectacular scenery of Sydney Harbour is by drifting luxuriously in its centre, a sailing craft is almost a necessity for those who can afford one, and on weekends the water's surface is laced with the tranquil patterns of whitewash. For the rest of the week, while corporate owners are in the city earning the money needed to pay for them, these yachts

bob softly at the marina, their many masts forming an impressive sight against the skyscape.

Cycling

Australian Cycle Co., 28 Clovelly Road, Randwick, ©9399 3475, are ○open seven days and are close to Centennial Park. They hire out bikes at reasonable prices.

Golf

Although Sydney has about 40 public golf courses, few are located close to the city centre. Here is a selection:

Moore Park Golf Club, is on the corner of Cleveland Street and Anzac Parade, ©9663 1064. This is the closest course to the city. It comprises 18-holes and is par 71 for 5790m. Eighteen holes will cost you ○$24 on a weekday and $27 on weekends.

Cammeray Golf Course is located in Park Avenue, Cremorne, ©9953 2089. Another 9-hole course, at 2417m, par 33, Cammeray is built on quality terrain that is always well-kept. A nine-hole round is ○$11 and can be played between designated hours daily.

Bondi Golf Course, 5 Military Road, North Bondi, ©9130 7170. This course is only a 2500m nine-hole course, but its hills and freak peninsula winds provide some challenges. Famous Bondi Beach sprawls below - a soothing sight after a terrible shot. It costs adults ○$9 to play, and a further $9 to hire clubs. Children play for $5.

Balgowlah Golf Course, 506 Sydney Road, Balgowlah, ©9949 2057, is another terrific nine-holer. This popular spot is not far from Manly Beach and is difficult enough to test good golfers whilst not crushing the dreams of intermediates. It is green and lush and can make for a pleasant couple of hours. The course is par 34, 2321m long, and costs ✪$12 for nine holes. Non-members have access to the course daily at designated hours.

Wakehurst Golf Club is on Upper Clontarf Street, Seaforth, ✆9949 3188. This is a full 18 hole, par 72 course built in the middle of cleared scrubland and dotted with water hazards. Its length is just over 6100m and its terrain can be tricky for any golfer to negotiate. A round on this scenic course will set you back ✪$22 on weekdays and $25 on weekends. Club hire is an additional ✪$15 and you can pick up a golf cart for $25.

The Australian in Rosebery and **Royal Sydney** in Rose Bay are nearby, while the **New South Wales Golf Club** is in La Perouse further south. However, the only way to make a divot on these exclusive fairways is to quickly make friends with a member, if you can find one.

For further information on Sydney's courses, find the listing in the Yellow Pages Telephone Directory or use the golf guide at 👁sydney. sidewalk.com.au

Horse Riding

Superior Horse, Pavillion A, Driver Avenue, Moore Park, ✆9360 5650, has horses for hire daily 9am-5pm. Centennial Park and adjoining Queens Park have a combined area 220ha (543 acres) - more than enough room to have a decent ride.

Lawn Bowls

There are bowling clubs in almost every suburb of Sydney, and one in the city. Bowling clubs are famous for their hospitality, and visitors are warmly welcomed. It is necessary, of course, to phone ahead to find out what days are reserved for social play, and to organise for a set of bowls. Bowling clubs are listed in the Yellow Pages Telephone Directory under *Clubs - Bowling*. If you are not sure which club is the closest to where you are staying, you could contact the Royal NSW Bowling Association, ✆9283 4555.

Scuba Diving

Gear can be hired and dives arranged from the following places:

Dive 2000, 2 Military Road, Neutral Bay, ✆9953 7783.

Deep 6 Diving, 1057 Victoria Road, West Ryde, ✆9858 4299.

Pro Dive, Head Office, 34/330 Wattle Street, Ultimo, ✆9281 6166.

Swimming

The closest public swimming pools to the city centre are:

North Sydney Olympic Pool, Alfred South Street, Milsons Point, ✆9955 2309;

Andrew (Boy) Charlton Pool, The Domain, Woolloomooloo, ✆9358 6686;

Prince Alfred Park Swimming Pool, Chalmers Street, Surry Hills (near Central Railway Station), ✆9319 7045.

The new **Cook and Phillip Park Recreation Centre**, is on the corner of Haig & Boomerang Streets, near St Marys, ✆9326 0444. It has a 50m underground pool among its facilities.

The larger hotels have swimming pools, usually heated all year round.

Tennis

Tennis courts abound in Sydney's suburbs and most have lights for night play. Pages of available courts can be found in the L-Z Yellow Pages Telephone Directory, appropriately enough under *Tennis Courts For Hire*.

For spectators, the NSW Tennis Open is played at **White City** in Rushcutters Bay, ✆9360 4113.

Ten Pin Bowling

The bowling centres close to the city are:

Balgowlah Bowling Centre, Condamine Street, Balgowlah, ✆9948 7656. Other centres can be found in the A-K Yellow Pages Telephone Directory under *Ten Pin Bowling*.

Spectator Sports

Basketball (April-October)

Sydney's team in the National Basketball League (NBL) is *The Kings*, and they play their home games at the Superdome, Olympic Boulevard, Homebush. Phone ✆9764 1300 for dates of the Kings' games.

Baseball (October-February)

The Sydney Blues is the local team in the Na-

Stadium Australia, Homebush

tional Baseball League and their home games are played at the Parramatta Stadium. The teams in the local competition play at various suburban venues, and for information on games, times, etc, contact the NSW Baseball League on ©9552 4635.

Cricket (October-March)

The Sydney Cricket Ground, near the Showground, is home to International matches, and is NSW's home ground in the competition played between the states. Grade matches are played on suburban grounds.

Football (March-October)

Rugby League is played on Saturdays and Sundays at various suburban grounds and at the Sydney Football Stadium, near the Showground. *Rugby Union* is played on Saturdays at suburban grounds and at their headquarters at Concord Oval.

Soccer is played on Saturdays at various suburban grounds and Sydney Athletic Field, Anzac Parade, Kensington, ©9662 4390.

Australian Football is played on Saturdays at

suburban grounds, and the *Sydney Swans* play their home games in the Victorian competition at the Sydney Cricket Ground.

Horse Racing

See Entertainment.

Sydney Olympic Park

Situated roughly in the geographic heart of metropolitan Sydney, the Olympic Park is 14km from the CBD, in the suburb of Homebush.

Facilities include Stadium Australia, Bicentennial Park, the Sydney International Aquatic Centre, the State Sports Centre, as well as Tennis, Hockey and Archery facilities. Other features include a major metropolitan park, called Millennium Park, a golf driving range and an Olympic Village which accommodated 15,000 athletes.

A concentration on modern architecture is the definitive element of the Olympic site. From a distance the domes, arcs and cylindrical shapes of the venue seem to make it spring like a spaceport from science fiction out of its green surrounds.

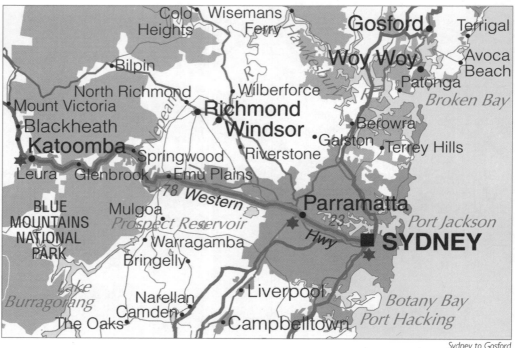

Sydney to Gosford

Stadium Australia

This enormous stadium was the venue for the Opening and Closing Ceremonies, and will host many other notable competition events into the future. It has a seating capacity of 100,000 people.

State Sports Centre

The Centre is a multi-purpose venue designed to present a full spectrum of events. The design enables the Centre to be used as: a competition venue for sporting events of State, National and International standard, and a training centre for these athletes; a sports education centre; and a venue for concerts, seminars and exhibitions.

The Arena, within the *Sports Hall*, is the focal point of the State Sports Centre, and is capable of staging a wide range of sports from gymnastics to showjumping, fencing to indoor cricket. It has seating for 5000, and a clear floor area of 57m x 38m.

Also in the Sports Hall is the *Hall of Champions* which honours Australia's champs in many sports.

The State Softball Centre has two floodlit fields, warm-up facilities and accommodation for 3000 spectators.

The State Hockey Centre has two synthetic pitches, flood lighting, and accommodation for 8000 spectators.

There are also outdoor netball courts, training centres and plans for many more sporting facilities.

For information about current programs at the Centre, phone the information line on, ✆9763 0111.

Transport to Homebush

Transport to the Olympic Site is by car, bus, river cat or rail (Olympic Park station).

Guided tours of the Olympic Site are available, and perhaps the best way to explore this venue and all of the others in close proximity, is on the Olympic Explorer Bus (see under *Local Transport*).

Chapter 18
Central Coast

The Central Coast is located north of Sydney. It begins at the Hawkesbury River and stretches northwards to the southern shores of Lake Macquarie, and westwards to historic St Albans.

The area is roughly divided into two - the City of Gosford with Brisbane Waters, and the Shire of Wyong with Tuggerah Lakes. Within these two districts there are many seaside and holiday centres.

Gosford City

Population 129,000

The City of Gosford is 88km (55 miles) north of Sydney. The natural beauty of the district and its close proximity to the major cities of Sydney and Newcastle has made it an attractive living and recreation area on the east coast of Australia. There are many popular surfing beaches and the Brisbane Waters are legendary for fishing, sailing and other recreational pursuits. Although for many years, it has been a popular holiday and retirement area, many young families are now settling in the district as an alternative to living in the outer suburbs of Sydney and Newcastle.

Climate

Average temperatures: summer max 25C (77F) - min 18C (64F); winter max 17C (63F) - min 10C (50F). Average annual rainfall is 1300mm (51 ins), average ocean temperature is 20C (68F).

How to Get There
By Bus
Interstate coachlines call at Gosford.
By Rail
There is a good electric train service from/to Sydney, and the State Rail Authority has mini-fares, family fares and combined rail/coach fares, ©131 500.

By Road
From Sydney via the Pacific Highway all the way to Gosford, or the F3 expressway from Hornsby to the Gosford turn-off, then the Pacific Highway.

Visitor Information

The Gosford Visitor Information Centre is in 200 Mann Street, Gosford, ©(02) 4385 4430 or ©1800 806 258, ©open Mon-Fri 9am-5pm, Sat-Sun 9am-2pm. Their email address is ✎thecoast @cctourism.com.au and the web page is at ⊕www.cctourism.com.au

If you are in Terrigal, the Visitor Information Centre is in Rotary Park, Terrigal Drive. It is ©open 9am-5pm Mon-Sat and 9am-3pm on Sunday during summer. They share contact details with the Gosford Centre.

The Centre has compiled some very good self-drive tours of the area, which encompass all the attractions. Visitors are well-advised to pick up these brochures.

Accommodation

Accommodation is not a problem in the area, although it is wise to book in advance during the summer holiday period. Here is a selection with prices for a double room per night, which should be used as a guide only. The telephone area code is 02.

Gosford

Metro Motor Inn Gosford, 512 Pacific Highway, ©4328 4666. 50 units, licensed restaurant, swimming pool, spa, barbecue - ✪$105.

Bermuda Motor Inn, cnr Henry Parry Drive & Pacific Highway, North Gosford, ©4324 4366. 17 units, swimming pool, barbecue - ✪$65-95.

Gosford Motor Inn, 23 Pacific Highway, ©4323 1333. 36 units, heated swimming pool, barbecue - ✪$70-100.

Rambler Motor Inn, 73 Pacific Highway, West Gosford, ©4324 6577. 55 units, playground, swimming pool, spa, barbecue - ✪$75-100.

Wyoming Caravan Park, 520 Pacific Highway, Wyoming, ©4328 4358. (No pets allowed) - powered sites ✪$19 for two, cabins $55 for two.

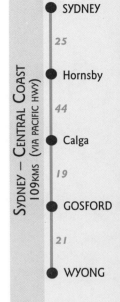

Central Coast

SYDNEY — CENTRAL COAST 109KMS (VIA PACIFIC HWY)

- ● SYDNEY
- *25*
- ● Hornsby
- *44*
- ● Calga
- *19*
- ● GOSFORD
- *21*
- ● WYONG

Woy Woy

Glades Country Club Motor Inn, 15 Dunban Road, ©4341 7374. 23 units, swimming pool, barbecue - ✪$80-120.

Ettalong

Motel Paradiso, cnr Schnapper & Ocean View Roads, ©4341 1999. 1 room, licensed restaurant - ✪$75-140.

Ettalong Beach Village, Fassifern Street, ©4344 2211. (No pets) - powered sites ✪$20-32 for two, cabins $60-110 for two.

Avoca

Bellbird Resort, 360 Avoca Drive, ©4382 2322. 36 units, licensed restaurant, swimming pool, tennis court - ✪$80-100.

The Palms at Avoca, Carolina Park Road off the Round Drive, ©4382 1227. (No pets allowed), barbecue, sauna, pool - cabins ✪$80-145 for two, villas $75-125 for two.

Terrigal

Country Comfort Terrigal, 154 Terrigal Drive, ©4384 1166. 40 units, 7 suites, licensed restaurant, swimming pool, spa, sauna, tennis, barbecue - ✪$175-220.

Clan Lakeside Lodge, 1 Ocean View Drive, ©4384 1566. 26 units, licensed restaurant (closed Sunday & Monday), barbecue - ✪$100-220.

Terrigal Beach House, 1 Painter Lane, ©4384 1423. 9 units - ✪$45-90.

Bellbird Caravan Park, 61-69 Terrigal Drive, ©4384 1883. (No dogs allowed) - unpowered sites ✪$20-25 for two, on-site vans $50-60for two, cabins $80-95.

Wamberal

Apollo Country Resort, 871 The Entrance Road, ©4385 2099. 42 units (private facilities), licensed restaurant, swimming pool, spa, barbecue, tennis, gym - ✪$95-160.

Kincumber

Figtree Cottages, 247 Avoca Drive, ©4368 3056. 2 rooms, unlicensed restaurant, solar heated saltwater pool, fireplace, spa - ✪$120-130.

Eating Out

No matter which locality of the Central Coast you choose to stay in, you will find excellent restaurants. Here is a brief list, and the Information Centre can advise you further if you desire.

Gosford

Gosford Shoreline, Masons Parade, ©4325 0644. Fully licensed seafood restaurant with an a-la-carte selection. Open midday-2pm and 6pm-8.30pm Mon-Sat, and until 9.30pm Friday and Saturday nights, lunch only on Sundays, closed Public Holidays.

Gee Kwong Chinese Restaurant, 197 Mann Street, ©4325 2489. Open 11.30am-3pm and 4.30pm-9pm Mon-Sat, and until 10pm on Friday and Saturday nights, closed Sunday and Public Holidays.

Tohn Oor Sian Classic Thai, 26 Adelaide Street, Gosford East, ©4324 2887. Take-away available, dine-in BYO wine only. Open midday-2.30pm and 5.30pm-10.30pm 7 days.

Jaceys, 45 Imperial Centre, ©4324 2558.

Da Vincis, 1-2 Brisbane Waters Drive, Gosford West, ©4322 8000.

Saltwater, Shop 6 Brisbane Waters Drive, West Gosford, ©4323 7744.

Curry House, 104 Mann Street, ©4322 0223.

Peking Garden, in the Central Coast Leagues Club, Dane Drive, ©4324 3788.

Surrounding Areas

Paceys, 172 Avoca Drive, Avoca Beach, ©4382 3588. Seafood, a-la-carte. Open 6pm-9pm 7 days and midday-3pm weekends and Public Holidays.

Sirens, 1 Kurrawyba Avenue, Terrigal, ©4385 2602. Open 5pm-midnight every day.

Pizza One, 80 Ocean View Drive, Wamberal, ©4385 3311.

Ghandi Indian Restaurant, 189 Ocean View Road, Ettalong, ©4341 1994.

The Don's Italian Restaurant, 28 Kincumber Village, Avoca Drive, Kincumber, ©4363 1900.

Fishermans Wharf, The Boulevarde, Woy Woy, ©4341 1171.

For Pizza Hut deliveries, ©13 1166. Branches of McDonalds and KFC are found in all the major towns.

Points of Interest

The town site of Gosford was first referred to as the Township at Point Frederick, then in February 1839, when the plan was sent to Governor Gipps for approval, as the Township of Brisbane Water. The plan was returned by the Governor in April marked as the Plan of Gosford, with no explanation to indicate the reason for its name. It was later discovered that the Governor had served with the Earl of Gosford in Canada, and had taken the opportunity to honour his friend.

Originally, timber cutting was the main economic product of the district, then from the 1880s, citrus orchards began to dominate the local farms in the Narara, Lisarow, Wyoming, Holgate and Ourimbah areas. These farms were close to the railway, but later as roads developed, farming spread on to Somersby plateau. By 1928-29, the district supplied 34% of the state's citrus crop.

The 1880s also saw the Gosford area become a tourist venue, with the completion of the railway in 1887, and visitors coming for the fishing, and for hunting trips.

In recent times Gosford's development has been influenced by other factors, such as the metropolitan expansion of Sydney, improvements to the roads, and changes in lifestyles.

The majority of people visit the area now for the surf, sun and sand, but there are quite a few attractions worth visiting.

Old Sydney Town, Pacific Highway, Somersby (west of Gosford) is the largest heritage park in New South Wales, and is a faithful re-creation of Sydney as it was 200 years ago. There is live street theatre, and demonstrations of different crafts take visitors back to the 18th and 19th centuries. The park has many eateries, from fine restaurants to damper and billy tea places, or you can take your own food and make use of the barbecue facilities. Old Sydney Town is open Wed-Sun and all state school and public holidays, 10am-5pm, ☎4340 1104. Admission fees are adults ✪$20, children $13. A family pass can be obtained for $55.

Henry Kendall Cottage & Historical Museum, 218 Gertrude Street, Gosford, ☎4325 2270, was built for the famous poet in 1836 by Peter Fagan. It is now an historical museum with displays of various items from the past. Open Wed, Sat & Sun, and public and school holidays, 10am-4pm.

The Australian Reptile Park was the first major tourist attraction on the Central Coast, and is a popular science exhibit. Crocodile feeding in the impressive crocodile enclosure is by far the highlight of the day. Watch as the trainer holds a long pole over the water's edge while a croc emerges, leaps into the air, takes the dangling chicken from the end of the pole into its jaws, and thrashes back into the water again. The park supplies venoms to countries all over the world for antivenenes and other research. There are picnic and barbecue facilities, but note that the place is overrun by kangaroos, and the joy of their company can quickly turn into despair if one bounds up and then pinches your lunch while you pat her! The park is open daily 9am-5pm, ☎4340 1146, and is on the Pacific Highway, Somersby. Admission prices are ✪$16 adults, $8 children, $40 families.

The Starship Cruise & Ferry Service, 100 John Whiteway Drive, ☎4340 1146, has two venues for cruises. The *Lady Kendall* departs from Gosford Wharf, Wed, Sat & Sun to cruise on the Brisbane Waters, and the *Trinity Queen* leaves from The Entrance Wharf for cruising Tuggerah Lakes and Wyong River, Wed-Sat 10.15am and 1pm. Both vessels operate daily during school holidays.

The Fragrant Garden, 25 Portsmouth Road, Erina, ☎4367 7322, has a very large collection of fragrant plants, crafts, pot-pourri in an olde-worlde garden. There is a mud-brick gallery, waterfall and a herb roof, and souvenirs are for sale.

Central Park Family Fun Centre, The Entrance Road, Forresters Beach, ☎4386 2466, has something for everyone - ten-pin bowling, five giant waterslides, a mini golf centre, senior and junior Grand Prix cars, BMX track, maze, mini bikes, Sunday markets. Open daily 9am-5pm, Sat and holidays 9am-10pm.

Festivals

Gosford's Australian Springtime Flora Festival is held in September.

Facilities

Fishing, swimming, boating, diving, wind-surfing, water skiing, horse riding, ten-pin bowling, squash, lawn bowls, golf and tennis. The Tourist Information Centre will give you all the information for directions and bookings.

Outlying Attractions

Beaches

The coastal beaches in the Gosford area are Killcare, McMasters, Copacabana, Avoca, Terrigal, Wamberal and Forresters. They each have their own attractions, and all are patrolled on weekends from October to April, with daily patrols during the school holiday periods. Apart from McMasters and Forresters, they have a choice of takeaway food outlets close to the beachfront.

The crystal clear waters right along the Central Coast offer some of the best diving in Australia, and there are fascinating wrecks off Terrigal in reasonably shallow water. If you are interested in learning how to dive, the *Terrigal Diving Centre*, The Haven Terrigal, ©4384 1219, or *Pro Dive*, 96 The Entrance Road, The Entrance, ©4334 1559, are the places to visit. They teach diving, and after 5 days tuition, which costs around $450, you are awarded a C card. If you are already a qualified diver and have your certificate with you, a diving charter can be arranged instead. Fishing tours are also available for those

who prefer to catch fish rather than rub noses with them (unless you are one of those fanatics who performs this ritual *after* catching a fish); one option is *Haven Fishing Charters*, 12 Lexington Parade, Green Point, ©4369 5673. The **Blue Bead Arabian Stud**, ©4382 2346, is located at Razina Park in Picketts Valley Road, 5 minutes from Terrigal and Avoca Beaches. They have mountain trails for the experienced, and instruct beginners and improvers. Bookings are essential, and the stud is open 7 days.

Tuggerah Lakes

The administrative centre of the Tuggerah Lakes district is Wyong, 22km (24 miles) north of Gosford on the banks of the Wyong River. The Lake system extends from Killarney Vale in the south to the township of Lake Munmorah in the north, and consists of three lakes - Tuggerah, Budgewoi and Munmorah. The biggest lake is Tuggerah Lake, and it has the only opening from the ocean, appropriately enough, at The Entrance. There are no sharks in the lakes.

Characteristics

One of the most popular holiday places in New South Wales, Tuggerah Lakes has grown like Topsy. Once it was strictly a fisherman's paradise with basic fishing shacks. Now there are first class motels, hotels, restaurants and sporting facilities.

How to Get There

By Rail

There is a regular electric rail service from Sydney to Wyong, and local buses from the station to the other areas.

By Road

From Sydney, via the Pacific Highway, or the F3 from Hornsby to the various destination turnoffs.

Visitor Information

The Entrance Visitor Information Centre has its office in Marine Parade, and is ⏲open daily 9am-

5pm. It shares its contact details with the Gosford Visitor Information Centre.

Accommodation

As with any holiday centre, there is a great deal of accommodation to choose from in the Tuggerah Lakes district. Here is a selection with prices for a double room per night, not including GST, which should be used as a guide only. The telephone area code is 02.

Wyong

Central Coast Motel, cnr Pacific Highway & Cutler Drive, ©4353 2911. 17 units, swimming pool - ✪$60-80.

The Entrance

El Lago Waters Resort, 41 The Entrance Road, ©4332 3955. 40 units, licensed restaurant, swimming pool, spa, sauna, tennis - ✪$70-120.

Ocean Front Motel, 102 Ocean Parade, ©4332 5911. 31 units, barbecue, undercover parking - ✪$80-150.

Sapphire Palms Motel, 180 The Entrance Road, ©4332 5799. 20 units, swimming pool, spa, barbecue - ✪$55-95.

Tienda Motel, 309A The Entrance Road, ©4332 3933. 30 units, swimming pool, spa - ✪$55-110.

Lake Front Motel, 16 Coogee Avenue, ©4332 4518. 14 units, swimming pool, barbecue - ✪$55-110.

Blue Bay Camping and Caravanning Park, cnr Bay Road & Narrawa Avenue, ©4332 1991. (No dogs allowed), 48 sites - powered sites ✪$18-25 for two, on-site vans $40-60 for two, cabins $50-80.

Dunleith Caravan Park, Hutton Road, North Entrance, ©4332 2172. 180 sites - powered sites ✪$17-25 for two, cabins $50-120 for two.

Long Jetty

The Coachman Motor Inn, 33 Gordon Road, ©4332 3692. 7 units, swimming pool, barbecue - ✪$50-110.

Palm Gardens Resort, 44 Kitchener Road, ©4333 1000. 23 suites, swimming pool, spa, sauna, barbecue - ✪$70-170.

Buccaneer Motel, 398 The Entrance Road, ©4334 3100. 14 units, swimming pool, barbecue - ✪$68-120.

Jetty Motel, 353 The Entrance Road, ©4332 1022. 22 units, swimming pool, spa, barbecue ✪$60-110.

Bateau Bay

Palm Court Motel, 61 Bateau Bay Road, ©4332 3755. 10 units, unlicensed restaurant, swimming pool - ✪$60-110.

Bateau Bay Hotel/Motel, The Entrance Road, ©4332 8022. 6 units, licensed restaurant - ✪$60-70.

Sun Valley Caravan Park, Bateau Bay Road, ©4332 1107. (No pets allowed), 342 sites - powered sites ✪$19-25 for two, holiday flat $55-95 for two.

Budgewoi

Hibiscus Lakeside Motel, 2 Diamond Head Drive, ©4390 9100. 13 units, barbecue - ✪$65-110.

Sunnylake Caravan Park, 2 Macleay Drive, ©4390 9471. 130 sites - powered sites ✪$15 for two, cabins $45-50 for two.

Budgewoi Tourist Park, Weemala Street, ©4390 9019. (Pets allowed on leash), 380 sites, barbecue - powered sites ✪$10-17.

Noraville

Sea'n'Sun Motel, 115 Budgewoi Road, ©4396 4474. 12 units, mini golf, barbecue - ✪$55-100.

Toukley

Toukley Motor Inn, 236 Main Road, ©4396 5666. 13 units, swimming pool - ✪$56-80.

Twin Lakes Motor Inn, 57 Main Road, ©4396 4622. 11 units, swimming pool - ✪$50-85.

Eating Out

The district has several licensed RSL and bowling clubs, and these usually offer reasonably priced meals. There are also many takeaway and fast food outlets, both in the towns and on the beachfronts.

Rus Chinese Rendevous, 120 Railway Street, Wyong, ©4353 2494.

Wyong Golf Club Restaurant, Pacific Highway, Wyong, ©4352 1999.

Sounan Thai, 27 The Entrance Road, The Entrance, ©4332 8806. Fully licensed restaurant with waterside views. Open 6pm-11pm 7 days and midday-3pm Wed-Sun, closed Public Holidays.

Jetty Indian Tandoori, 509 The Entrance Road, Long Jetty, ©4334 2477.

Jans Chinese Malaysian Restaurant, Shops 5-6, 227-229 The Entrance Road, The Entrance, ©4334 1333.

Mantas Seafood Restaurant, 347 The Entrance Road, Long Jetty, ©4332 2548.

Beach Point, 19 Point Street, Bateau Bay, ©4334 5070.

Carmelos Italian Restaurant, 61 Bateau Bay Road, Bateau Bay, ©4334 5155.

Pizza Pit, 65 Scenic Drive Budgewoi, ©4399 1035.

Silver Moon Chinese Restaurant, 105 Scenic Drive, Budgewoi, ©4390 0489. Licensed, open 5pm-9pm 7 days and for lunch midday-2pm every day except Monday.

Cactus Blues Mexican Restaurant, 245 Main Road, Toukley, ©4397 1557.

Starfish Seafood Restaurant, 200 Main Road, Toukley, ©4397 1300.

Points of Interest

The Forest of Tranquility, Ourimbah Creek Road, Ourimbah, is the home of Willy Wombat's rainforest walk, the best walk in a rainforest in the Sydney environs. There are gas barbecues, a children's playground, and picnic area, and rainforest plants are for sale. ⊙Open Wed-Sun 10am-5pm and all public holidays, ©4362 1855.

Crackneck Lookout, in Hilltop Avenue, Bateau Bay, offers sweeping views of the coastline to Norah Head and Bungary Point, over the three lakes and the three power stations.

Bateau Bay Golf Practice Range, 468 The Entrance Road, ©4332 3277, is the largest golf range on the Central Coast, and venue of Australian Golf Schools. Practice facilities include grass tees, target greens, bunker and distance markers. ⊙Open 7 days.

Long Jetty Catamaran Hire, cnr Tuggerah Parade and Pacific Street, Long Jetty, ©4332 9362, hires out catamarans, sailboards, canoes and pedal boats. They also have lessons in water skiing, and sell fishing tackle and bait.

The Entrance Aquaslide, ©4334 3151, adja-

cent to the Lakeside Plaza carpark, 19 Taylor Street, The Entrance, has The Space Spiral, Outer Orbit and Cosmic Crusher rides, and the good news is, the pool is heated.

Each afternoon at 3.30pm, near the children's playground in the **Memorial Park**, The Entrance, everybody gathers to feed the pelicans.

The pelican has been adopted as the symbol of the tourist industry on the Central Coast, and the daily feeding ensures that this symbol doesn't disappear. There is no doubt that they are fascinating creatures, with wing spans up to 2m, and those incredible beaks, but there are many locals who are not exactly enamoured of them. To start with, they eat fish and are not well mannered enough to limit themselves to the afternoon meals supplied by humans, but tend to fish for themselves in the lakes. And, they are much better at it than those people sitting in boats and on the shore with hooks and lines. Then they have lice, which they shed in the water to bite anyone who dares to swim in the area. It is not that the pelicans do this on purpose, but try selling that to a kiddy who is suffering from itchy bites. Of course, the pelicans came before people starting feeding them, but not in such large numbers.

At **Dunleith Caravan Park**, Hutton Road, North Entrance, ©4332 2172, there is a Shell Museum, with an extensive display of shells and early photographs of the area, along with models of aquatic animals.

Norah Head Lighthouse, circa 1903, is open for visitors only by arrangement with the Visitor Centre. At Cabbage Tree Bay, the tiny settlement where the road to the light house commences, there are steps leading down to a lovely little rock pool, which is very popular with children. You can also drive down the steep road before the steps, but parking is usually a problem. There is a surfing beach alongside, but it is not patrolled, and there is a dangerous riptide.

Edward Hargraves Homestead, in Elizabeth Drive, Noraville, is not open for inspection, but can be viewed from the road. Edward Hargraves discovered gold near Bathurst in 1851, causing the first gold rush in Australia.

Toukley has a good-sized shopping centre, and the Toukley & District Senior Citizens Club in Hargraves Street, has loads of entertainment and things to do. Toukley RSL is also a very busy club, and visitors are always welcome, as they are at Toukley Bowling Club.

Warnervale Airfield, near the expressway (follow the road through Toukley, crossing the Pacific Highway) offers joy-flights every Sunday, and other days by appointment. Contact **Central Coast Helicopters**, Lot 1, Sparks Road, Warnervale, ©4352 2222, or **Warnervale Air**, Jack Grant Avenue, ©4392 5174.

Smokey Mountain Steam Railroad, in Mountain Road, Warnervale, offers a different day out for all the family with steam train rides through the surrounding picturesque valleys ©between 11am and 4pm. It operates on Sundays and public holidays from Boxing Day until the last Sunday in October, except Good Friday and days of total fire ban. For further information, contact them on, ©4392 7644.

Central Coast

Beaches

The coastal beaches in the Tuggerah Lakes area are: Bateau Bay; Shelly Beach; Toowoon Bay; The Entrance; North Entrance; Soldiers Point; Cabbage Tree Bay; Jenny Dixon; The Lakes Beach.

Jenny Dixon Beach and Cabbage Tree bay are not patrolled, and Jenny Dixon has some nude bathers, but the other beaches are patrolled every weekend, and all through the school holidays, and have handy food outlets. From the Lakes Beach, miles of sand and surf stretch northwards, but it should be remembered that the site of the beach club was chosen because it is the safest part of that stretch.

Chapter 19
Newcastle

Population 138,200
Newcastle is situated on the Hunter River, 171km (106 miles) north of Sydney, and 827km (514 miles) south of Brisbane.

Climate
Average temperatures: January max 27C (81F) - min 18C (64F); July max 17C (63F) - min 6C (43F). Average annual rainfall: 1134mm (45 ins), and the rain falls evenly throughout the year.

Characteristics
Newcastle is the second largest city in New South Wales, and the sixth largest in Australia. The site was discovered when Lt Shortland was searching for convict escapees in the late 18th century, and discovered coal, which together with steel dominated Newcastle to the mid-1960s.

Newcastle is a city with international-style hotels, motels and shopping centres. It is an ideal base for visiting the holiday areas of Lake Macquarie, Port Stephens and the Hunter Valley.

The city was hit by a shocking earthquake on December 28, 1989, with the loss of lives and many buildings. A swift Novocastrian recovery has meant that few signs of the disaster remain.

How to Get There
By Air
The Newcastle Airport is at Williamtown, 23km from the city, and there are plenty of taxis available for transport to the city centre.

Qantas, ©13 1313 have regular flights to Newcastle.
By Bus
Greyhound Pioneer, ©13 2030, and McCaffertys, ©13 1499, are among the coach companies that stop at Newcastle.
By Rail
Newcastle is on the Sydney/Murwillumbah line with regular services, and connections from Murwillumbah to Brisbane and the Gold Coast, ©13 2232.
By Road
From Sydney, via the Pacific Highway and the F3 Expressway.
From Brisbane via the Pacific Highway through Tweed Heads and along the coast, or via the New England Highway through Glen Innes and Armidale.

Visitor Information
The Tourist Information Centre is located at 363 Hunter Street, ©(02) 4974 2999 or ©1800 654 558. ☉Opening hours are 9am-5pm Mon-Fri and 10am-3.30pm on weekends. The internet references are ✔newtour@hunterlink.net.au or ✔mail@ncc.nsw.gov.au for email, and ☞www.ncc.nsw.gov.au for the website.

Accommodation
As with any large city, moderately-priced accommodation places are in the suburbs, and the Tourist Office has a complete list of what is available. Here is a selection with prices for a double room per night, which should be used as a guide only. The telephone area code is 02.
City
Holiday Inn Esplanade Newcastle, Shortland Esplanade, ©4929 5576. 72 rooms, licensed restaurant - ✪$170-260.
Junction Motel, 121 Union Street, ©4929 6677. 30 units, licensed restaurant, pool - ✪$130.
Ridges City Central Hotel, cnr King & Steel Streets, ©4926 3777. 122 units, 6 suites, licensed restaurant, swimming pool, gym, spa - ✪$120-160.
Noah's On The Beach, cnr Shortland Esplanade & Zaara Street, ©4929 5181. 90 units, 1 suite, licensed restaurant - ✪$140.
Novocastrian Motor Inn, 21 Parnell Place, ©4926 3688. 47 units, licensed restaurant - ✪140-200.
Newcomen Lodge, 70 Newcomen Street, ©4929 7313. 1 room, unlicensed restaurant, pool - ✪$115.

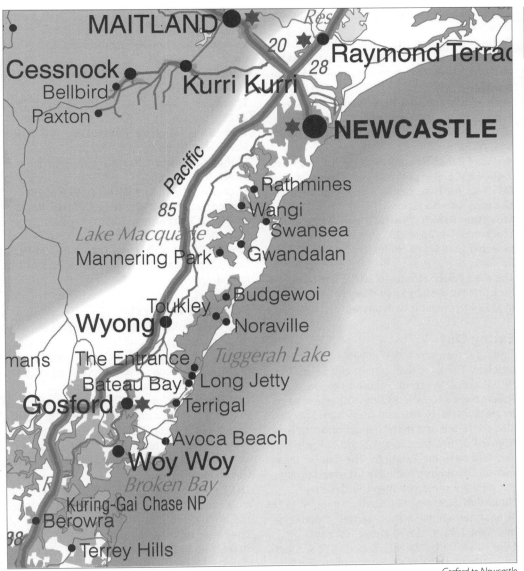

Gosford to Newcastle

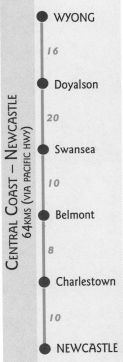

Newcastle

CENTRAL COAST – NEWCASTLE
64KMS (VIA PACIFIC HWY)

WYONG

16

Doyalson

20

Swansea

10

Belmont

8

Charlestown

10

NEWCASTLE

Suburbs

Apollo International Hotel, 290 Pacific Highway, Charlestown, ⓒ4943 6733. 42 units, 8 suites, tennis, swimming pool, barbecue - ✪$140-240.

Hospitality Motor Inn, 418 Maitland Road, Mayfield, ⓒ4967 1977. 28 units, licensed res-taurant - ✪$120-130.

Sovereign Motor Inn, 309 Maitland Road, Mayfield, ⓒ4968 4405. 34 units, licensed res-taurant, swimming pool - ✪$90-100.

Aloha Motor Inn, 231 Glebe Road, Merewether, ⓒ4963 1283. 29 units, barbecue - ✪$95-105.

Tudor Inn, cnr Tudor & Steel Streets, Hamilton,

©4969 2533. 31 units, unlicensed restaurant - ✪$90-100.

Panorama Motor Inn, 256 Pacific Highway, Charlestown, ©4943 3144. 33 units, licensed restaurant, barbecue, swimming pool - ✪$65-80.

Caravan Parks

Tomago Village Van Park, Pacific Highway & Tomago Road, Tomago, ©4964 8066. (No pets allowed) - powered sites ✪$19 for two, cabins $45-70 for two.

Redhead Beach Holiday Park, 1A Kalaroo Road, ©4944 8306. (No pets allowed) - powered sites ✪$19-25 for two, cabins $45-95 for two, on-site vans $45-55 for two.

Stockton Beach Tourist Park, Pitt Street, Stockton, ©4928 1393. (No dogs allowed) - powered sites ✪$16-20 for two, cabins $35-60 for two.

There is a **Youth Hostel** in 30 Pacific Street (cnr King Street), ©4925 3544. They have 22 rooms at ✪$24 per person twin share.

Eating Out

Finding somewhere to eat in Newcastle is not a problem. There are the licensed clubs (Newcastle Workers, Western Suburbs Leagues Club, Tubemakers Recreation Club, etc) which all offer restaurants, bistros and snack bars. There are also the hotels and motels, most of which have licensed or BYO restaurants, and coffee shops and takeaway food outlets. The Tourist Information Office has a complete list of restaurants, but here are some you might wish to try.

Hawaiian Sunsets, 171 Darby Street, ©4926 1264. International menu, licensed. Open 6pm-midnight 7 days, closed Public Holidays.

Lans, 146 Darby Street, ©4929 1565. Open 5pm-10pm every day except Mondays and Public Holidays (closed).

Delaney Hotel, 134 Darby Street, ©4929 1627. Open 10am-midnight Mon-Sat and Sunday midday-10pm.

San Marco on the Park, 10 Pacific Street, ©4926 3865. Fully licensed, open 12pm-3pm and 6pm-9pm Mon-Sat, closed Sunday.

Harry's on Hunter, 672 Hunter Street, ©4926 2165.

Mercury Cafe, Mercury Hotel, 23 Watt Street, ©4929 2025.

Queens Wharf Brewery Restaurant, 150 Wharf Road, ©4929 6333.

Signatures, Radisson Hotel, cnr King & Steel Streets, ©4926 3777.

Thara Tong Thai, 541 Hunter Street, ©4929 6722.

Taco Bills Mexican Restaurant, 80 Darby Street, ©4929 2971.

Maharaja Indian Restaurant, 653 Hunter Street, ©4926 1665.

Elizas, Shortland Esplanade, ©4929 5576.

Newcastle Happy Gardens Chinese Restaurant, 133 Scott Street, ©4926 2707.

McDonalds are on the corner of King & Steel Streets. KFC is at 227 Hunter Street and Pizza Hut is located at 500 Hunter Street, ©13 1166 for delivery.

Points of Interest

City Hall, in King Street, is the office of Newcastle's Lord Mayor, and is an impressive sandstone building with a tall clock tower. Opened in 1929, it was completely refurbished in 1970-80, and is now a Convention Centre.

Civic Park, opposite the City Hall, is a large park that is a favourite place for Newcastle's business people to relax during the lunchbreak. The special trees planted at the eastern and western ends are gifts from Newcastle's Sister City, Ube in Japan.

The Captain Cook Memorial Fountain forms a backdrop to Civic Park. It was built in 1966, and is illuminated at night.

The Newcastle Regional Art Gallery, in Laman Street, ©4974 5100, was opened in 1977 by Her Majesty, Queen Elizabeth II. It houses the city's Art Collection and features visiting exhibitions regularly. In front of the building is another gift from Ube, a stainless steel sculpture, 'Space Two'. The gallery is ⊙open Tues-Sun 10am-5pm and entry is free.

Christ Church Anglican Cathedral overlooks the city from the top of **the hill**, and can be seen from harbour, sea and suburbs. The foundation for the first cathedral was laid in 1817

City Hall

and was in use until 1884 when another (now the Cathedral Hall opposite) was erected. The present cathedral was dedicated in 1902, and was eventually completed, tower and all, in 1979. It is ⏱open from early morning until 6pm. Guides are available on Sat and Sun afternoons.
Hunter Mall became a pedestrian arcade in 1980, and is framed by fine Victorian and Edwardian buildings. As well as David Jones department store, it has many specialty stores.
Fort Scratchley, on Nobbys Road, is Australia's only fort that went to war. An historical fort, it was built in the mid-1880s near the site where Lt Shortland first landed on September 9, 1879. It is one of two remaining 19th century closed fort complexes in NSW. Believing that Newcastle was a place likely to be attacked from sea, the Government decided a major fort should be built on Signal Hill. It was largely completed in 1882. In June 1942, it was involved in an attack by a Japanese Submarine. The guns, now on display in the fort, returned the fire, causing the submarine to break off. This was the only time in Australian history that heavy guns were

fired in hostility from coastal defences. The fort houses the **Newcastle Region Maritime Museum**, which has many interesting exhibits, and is ⏱open week-ends and Public Holidays from midday-4pm.
The Ocean Baths, located at Newcastle Beach and at Merewether Beach, are the two largest saltwater baths in the Southern Hemisphere.
The Obelisk, up the hill just to the south of the city, is in the park bounded by Bindle Reserve Road, Ordnance Street & Wolfe Street. It marks the site of Newcastle's first windmill. The mill was erected in 1820 and became a navigational mark for ships approaching Newcastle. It was demolished in 1847, and the obelisk erected in 1850. In early 1987 it was struck by lightning, but has since been repaired.
The multi-million dollar **Queen's Wharf and Harbour** is a pleasant attraction. You can walk along the promenade, metres away from ships from all over the world, or hire a Daisy Trike or bike and pedal your way around. The complex is only 50m from the Hunter Mall, and includes a marina, a seafood restaurant, a boutique brew-

ery, the Tourist Information Centre and variety shops. From the top of the tower in the complex one has a view of the city, harbour and beaches north up to Port Stephens, and west to the Watagan Mountains. On weekends there are horse-drawn carriage rides available, bands playing, and a complete holiday atmosphere. Unique little 'shop barrows' are located along its foreshores.

At **Harbourside Markets**, cnr Wharf Road & Merewether Street, there's everything to buy, in the classic market style.

William the Fourth was the first Australian-built coastal steamship, and is now anchored at Queen's Wharf. It is available for historical cruises around Newcastle Harbour. See the Tourist Information Centre for all the details.

Newcastle Regional Museum, 787 Hunter Street, ©4962 2001, is the leading Regional Museum in the country. It features exhibits about the industrial and technological heritage of the surrounding region, its social history, lifestyle and environment. The redevelopment of the former Castlemain & Wood Bros Brewery into the museum was a major Bicentennial project. The museum is ©open Tues-Sun and public holidays 10am-5pm.

Supernova, Newcastle's Science and Technology Fun Centre is housed within the Regional Museum. It is hands-on science, a museum where kids are encouraged to touch the displays. Supernova is open the same hours as the Museum, and there is a moderate admission fee.

Nobbys Head was first described by Captain Cook as a "small clump of an island". It was reduced in 1826 by half its size to improve access by ships to the harbour. In 1846, it was connected to the mainland by the breakwater. On top of Nobbys is a lighthouse signal station, and Nobbys Beach is a popular surfing beach with the Novocastrians.

The Heritage Centre, ©4925 2265, next door to the Post Office in Hunter Street, is Newcastle's former Police Station (1859), and is operated by the Hunter Region National Trust. The centre features an environmental Gift Shop, ©open Mon- Fri 9am-5pm.

Beaches

Newcastle Beach offers safe swimming from the rocks at the northern end to the front of the club pavilion, and surfboard riding to the southern end. *Surfest*, one of the world's leading surfing events takes place here every November. The floodlit and patrolled Ocean Baths are here also.

Nobbys Beach is an excellent family beach. There is good surfing on the reef, at the northern end and at Cowrie hole to the south (patrolled).

Horseshoe Beach is Newcastle's only harbour beach, and is popular with trainers and their racehorses. It is also a good fishing spot.

Stockton Beach, is opposite the city, and offers safe swimming from the breakwater to Hereford Street, and good surfing from there to the north. The main beach is patrolled. Here you can check out the wreck of the *Sygna* (1974).

Bar Beach to the south of Newcastle Beach and the Bogey Hole, is also a good family beach with safe swimming from the northern end (Bar area) to the front of the pavilion, and surfboard riding from there to the southern end. There is plenty of parking. The beach is patrolled and floodlit.

Susan Gilmore Beach, is accessed from the extreme northern end of Bar Beach, via a path down the cliff face, or over the rocks at low tide. The beach was named after an American ship that was wrecked here. It is a nudist beach, and is not patrolled.

Merewether Beach is an excellent swimming beach with good beachbreak surfboard riding south of the club house. The beach is patrolled and floodlit. There are Ocean Baths here too.

Dixon Park Beach offers safe swimming in front of the clubhouse, and is good for surfing, board and ski, in front of the cliff. The beach is patrolled.

Burwood and **Dudley Beaches** are excellent for swimming and board riding, but these nudists beaches are not patrolled.

Out-of-City Attractions

Shortland Wetlands Centre. The Centre is situated on 65ha (160 acres) of wetland along Sandgate Road, Shortland on the edge of

Hexham Swamp. More than 170 species of birds have been recorded here, with at least 30 of these breeding. During the summer months, several thousand egrets nest in the paperbark trees in one of the shallow swamps. Facilities include a Visitors Centre with static and live animal displays and a souvenir shop that provides light refreshments; picnic tables; walking trails; and a bird observation tower. Canoes can be hired for exploring the 7km of waterways around Hexham Swamp. The Wetlands Centre is located less than 1km from the Shortland Shopping Centre along Sandgate Road, Shortland, and a 10 minute walk away from Sandgate Railway Station. The centre is ☾open daily 9am-5pm, with extended hours during holiday seasons. An small admission price applies. Phone ©4951 6466 for more information. The Information Centre in Newcastle can arrange half day tours and twilight walks to Shortland Wetlands.

Blackbutt Reserve. A reserve of approximately 180ha, Blackbutt is situated in the middle of Newcastle's suburbia. It consists of open forest land intersected by four valleys running from west to east. One of the area's greatest attractions, apart from vegetation, animals and uncommon birds, is its seclusion from the City around it. The Reserve is a popular spot with the locals and a source of interest for overseas tourists keen to observe the exhibition of Australian indigenous wildlife, including wombats, koalas, kangaroos, emus, wallabies and native birds. Families can prepare a meal, relax or play in the grounds with the barbecue facilities, children's playground, several quaint ponds and marked bushwalking tracks available. It is ☾open all year, 10am-5pm for the wildlife exhibits, and there is no admission fee. The Maritime Model Club launch their ships on the biggest pond every Saturday. The Tourist Office has a leaflet setting out the various bushwalks and all the attractions, or you can call direct on ©4952 1449.

Tours

The Tourist Office has details of tours in and around Newcastle, and of Hunter River and harbour cruises that are available. Here are two worth enquiring about:

Australian Scenic Tours, 50 Hunter Street, ©4929 4333.

Free Spirit Charters, Level 4, 175 Scott Street, ©4929 1908.

There are several helicopter flights over the city, the surrounding coastal areas, and further afield to the Vineyards and to Moffats Oyster Barn at Swan Bay. *Scenic Helicopter Flights*, cnr Hannel and Cowper Streets, Wickham, ©4962 2240, is one company operating in the area.

Daily departures from Newcastle, Maitland and Cessnock to the Vineyards are available, visiting a range of wineries from small family-owned to large commercial, with numerous tastings. Two of these tours are *Hunter Vineyard Tours*, ©4991 1659, and *The Wine and Cheese Tasting Tour*, ©4938 5031.

Festivals

The Matarra Festival is held each September.

Facilities

Newcastle has all the facilities you would expect of a city its size. Theatre and cinema programmes are in the daily newspapers, and the Yellow Pages Telephone Book has details of all sporting facilities. The Tourist Information Centre has all the details.

Chapter 20
Newcastle to Taree

Hunter Valley

Location and Characteristics
The beauty of the Hunter, with its rolling hills covered in rows of grape-vines and surrounded by tall mountains, surprises many visitors. There are over 1500ha (3705 acres) of vineyards under cultivation in the Lower Hunter-Pokolbin district near Cessnock, and more than 1600ha (3952 acres) planted in the Upper Hunter, centred around the towns of Muswellbrook and Denman.

Visitor Information
The main Tourist Information Centre for the area is in Cessnock, but there is another in Maitland, in King Edward Park, Banks Street East, ©(02) 4933 2611.

The Hunter Regional Tourism Organisation has a web page at ☞www.huntertourism.com/Online/home/main.html

Points of Interest
Renowned for the production of top quality table wines, the Valley's wineries range in size and production from small family affairs, where their entire vintage goes in their own tastings and cellar door sales, to large famous brand company bottlers whose award-winning labels have become household names.

In the last few decades, the rising popularity of the Hunter has produced a rapid development in ancillary visitor amenities with restaurants, craft shops, galleries and children's playgrounds becoming parts of many of the wineries.

Even if you are not in the grip of the grape, a day at Pokolbin Estate Vineyard, or Hungerford Hill wine village, is good fun for all the family.

Kurri Kurri

Population 12,500
Location and Characteristics
Kurri Kurri is the closest notable town in the Hunter Valley to Sydney (150km) and it lies fairly close to the end of the northern freeway, but really there are more picturesque places to stay in the region, so an extra drive is worth the time.

Accommodation and Services
If you do wish to spend some time here, the **Kurri Motor Inn**, is on the corner of Lang & Alexandra Streets, Kurri Kurri, ©4937 2222. They have 14 units and a pool - ✪$80-95.

Points of Interest
Near the town of Kurri Kurri is the **Richmond Vale Railway Museum** and the **Richmond Main Colliery**, but opening days are limited so phone ©4937 5344 or ©4936 1124 if you are fascinated by mid-nineteenth century mining and engineering accomplishments. The historic Kurri Kurri Hotel on the corner of Lang and Hampden Streets is also worth a visit.

Cessnock

Population 17,500
Location and Characteristics
The town of Cessnock is 52km (32 miles) from Newcastle and 185km (115 miles) from Sydney. It is the gateway to the wineries, with approximately 30 in the area.

Visitor Information
The Visitor Information Centre is in Turner Park, Aberdare Road, and ⊙opens 7 days, Mon-Thu 9am-5pm, Fri 9am-6pm, Sat 9.30am-5pm and Sunday and Public Holidays 9.30am-3.30pm. They can be emailed at ✎info@winecountry.com.au or visited at the website ☞www.winecountry.com.au

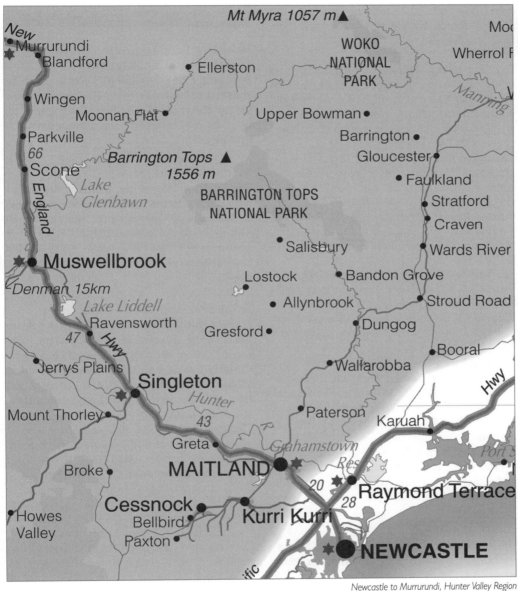

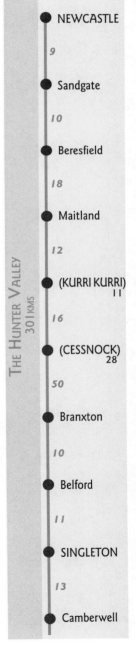

NEWCASTLE

9

Sandgate

10

Beresfield

18

Maitland

12

(KURRI KURRI)
11

16

(CESSNOCK)
28

50

Branxton

10

Belford

11

SINGLETON

13

Camberwell

THE HUNTER VALLEY
301 KMS

Newcastle to Murrurundi, Hunter Valley Region

Accommodation and Services

Cessnock is the major town in the area, but the satellite district of Pokolbin provides the real accommodation treats.

Cessnock

Aussie Rest Motel, 43 Shedden Street, ©4991 4197. 15 units, good room facilities, unlicensed restaurant, saltwater pool - ✪$180-120.

Cessnock Heritage Inn, 167 Vincent Street, ©4991 2744. 13 rooms, unlicensed restaurant, comfortable rooms - ✪$65-85.

Cessnock Motel, 13 Allandale Road, ©4990 2699. 20 units, good room facilities, solar heated pool - ✪$70-100.

**Newcastle
to Taree**

Royal Oak Hotel, 221 Vincent Street, ©4990 2366. 11 rooms, licensed restaurant, basic room facilities - $40-50.

Pokolbin

Cypress Lakes Resort, cnr McDonalds & Thompson Roads, Pokolbin, ©4993 1555 or ©1800 061 818 (toll free). 84 rooms, licensed restaurant, car parking, room service, gym, tennis, heated pool, spa, sauna, superb 18-hole golf course - ✪$249-309.

Casuarina Country Inn Guest House, Hermitage Road, Pokolbin, ©4998 7888. 8 rooms, licensed restaurant, tennis, pool, sauna - ✪$190-230.

Hunter Resort, Hermitage Road, Pokolbin, ©4998 7777. 35 units, licensed restaurant, barbecue, playground, tennis, pool, spa - ✪$140-190.

The Woods at Pokolbin, Halls Road, Pokolbin, ©4998 7368. 2 cottages, excellent room facilities, fireplace, car parking - ✪$100-165.

Vineyard Hill Country Motel, Lovedale Road, Pokolbin, ©4990 4166. 8 units, pool, spa - ✪$100-145.

Caravan Parks

Valley Vineyard Tourist Park, Mt View Park, Cessnock, ©4990 2573. (Pets allowed by arrangement) 90 sites, kiosk, barbecue, pool - powered sites ✪$20 for two, cabins $60-105 for two.

Southwood Park Village, Carrs Road, Neath, ©4930 4565. (Small dogs allowed) 112 sites, barbecue, pool - powered sites ✪$19 for two, cabins $60-75 for two.

Points of Interest

The Information Centre has a list of all the attractions in the town, and of the wineries which are open for tours and cellar door sales.

The historic village of **Wollombi**, 31km (19 miles) south-west of Cessnock, has a few interesting buildings worth visiting - the Court House, St John's Anglican Church and the two-storey Post Office.

Singleton

Population 12,500

Location and Characteristics

Back on the New England Highway we come to the geographical heart of the Hunter Valley, Singleton. It has the Hunter River flowing past its doorstep and irrigating the surrounding rich grazing land.

Visitor Information

The Singleton Information Centre at the southern entrance to the town, in the Shire Council, Civic Centre on Queen Street. They are ⏲open Mon-Fri 8.30am-4.30pm, ©(02) 6578 7267. The website is ✆www.singleton.nsw.gov.au and the email address is ✉ssc@singletoncouncil.nsw.gov.au

Accommodation and Services

Francis Phillip Motor Inn, 18 Maitland Road, ©6571 1991. 30 units, licensed restaurant, room service, undercover parking, pool - ✪$125-160.

Country Comfort Motel, cnr George & Hunter Streets, ©6572 2388 or ©1800 065 064 (toll free). 49 units, licensed restaurant, room service, pool - ✪$90-100.

The Royal Hotel Motel, 84 George Street, ©6572 1194. 7 units, licensed restaurant, basic room facilities, car parking - ✪$50-55.

Singleton Caracourt Caravan Park, cnr Bridgman Road, Dunolly, ©6572 2886. (Pets allowed by arrangement) 46 sites, playground, barbecue - powered sites ✪$13 for two, on-site vans $30 for two, cabins $45 for two.

Country Acres Caravan Park, ©Maison Dieu Road, ©6572 2328. (Pets allowed overnight) 88 sites, kiosk, playground - powered sites ✪$17 for two, cabins $45 for two, on-site vans $35 for two.

Points of Interest

Nearby **Lake St Clair** offers boating and fishing, and maps of the waterways are available from the Information Centre.

The **Singleton Army Camp** includes the Royal

Australian Infantry Corps Museum, which is ⏱open to visitors 9am-4pm Wed-Sun.

On the New England Highway, between Singleton and Muswellbrook, are the Liddell (✆6542 1611) and Bayswater (✆6542 1611) **Power Stations**, which are two of the biggest thermal power stations in the Southern Hemisphere. Visitor tours are available at certain times by arrangement.

Denman

Location and Characteristics
Situated in one of the most fertile areas of the Hunter Region, some 15km south-west of Muswellbrook off the New England Highway, Denman has many fine horse and cattle studs, and has become an acknowledged quality wine producing area.

Accommodation and Services
Denman Motor Inn, 8 Crinoline Street, ✆6547 2462. 10 units, playground, pool - ✪$70.
Denman Van Village, Macauley Street, ✆6547 2590. (Pets allowed under control) 58 sites, playground, basic facilities - sites ✪$17 for two, cabins $40-45 for two, on-site vans $30-40 for two.

Points of Interest
Vineyards in the area are: **Arrowfield**, ✆6576 4041, one of the largest in Australia; **Rosemount Estate**, ✆6549 6400; **McGuigan Wines**, ✆6547 2422; and **Horsehoe Vineyard**, ✆6547 3528.

The nearby **Widden Valley** is considered to be second only to America's famous Kentucky Blue Grass region for the breeding of racehorses.

Muswellbrook

Population 10,500
Location and Characteristics
The Muswellbrook area has benefitted in recent years with the growth of the mining and power industries, and as well, the wine industry. The major rural activity, though, is dairy farming. Produce is supplied through the Hunter Valley Co-operative Dairy Company's processing plant at Muswellbrook.

Visitor Information
For more information, the Muswellbrook Visitor Information Centre is in 87 Hill Street, ✆(02) 6541 4050. ⏱Open 9am-5pm daily. A web page lets you explore the area at 👁www.muswellbrook.org.au

Accommodation and Services
Baybrook Motor Inn, New England Highway, ✆6543 4888. 12 units, barbecue, pool - ✪$80-90.
Sovereign Inn, cnr New England Highway & Bell Street, ✆6543 1188. 37 units, licensed restaurant (closed Sunday), pool - ✪$75-90.
Red Cedar Motel, 12 Maitland Street, ✆6543 2852. 10 units, basic facilities - ✪$65-70.
Pinaroo Leisure Park, New England Highway, ✆6543 3905. (No pets allowed) 135 sites, playground, tennis half-court, pool - powered sites ✪$17, cabins $45-55, on-site vans $35-40.

Points of Interest
The area boasts a number of **Art and Craft Galleries**, and the **Rainbow Zone Fun Centre** in Industrial Close, ✆6541 4279.

Scone

Population 3400
Location and Characteristics
Scone was first settled during the 1830s by Scottish settlers who likened the countryside to their homeland, and named many spots after their birthplaces. The town is now a thriving commercial centre supporting important rural industries, and is well known for its thoroughbred horses, cattle and sheep from stud properties in the area.

Scone is also the inland gateway to the Barrington Tops region, via the Scone-Gloucester Road.

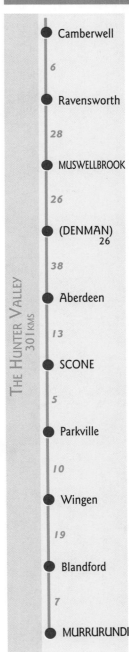

Newcastle to Taree

THE HUNTER VALLEY
301 KMS

● Camberwell
  6
● Ravensworth
  28
● MUSWELLBROOK
  26
● (DENMAN)
  26
  38
● Aberdeen
  13
● SCONE
  5
● Parkville
  10
● Wingen
  19
● Blandford
  7
● MURRURUNDI

Visitor Information

Scone has a Visitor Information Centre on the corner of Susan & Kelly Streets, ⏰open daily 9am-5pm. Email them at ✎ stic@scone.nsw.gov.au or phone them on ©(02) 6545 1526.

Accommodation and Services

Belltrees Country House, Gundy Road, ©6546 1123. 8 rooms, unlicensed restaurant, car parking, horse riding, bushwalking, tennis court, pool - ✪$410-500.

Airlie House Motor Inn, New England Highway, ©6545 1488. 26 units, licensed restaurant, room service, tennis court, pool - ✪$85-95.

Isis Motel, 250 New England Highway, ©6545 1100. 18 units, barbecue, pool - ✪$55-65.

Glenbawn State Park, Brushy Hill Road, ©6543 7193. (No pets allowed) 62 sites, golf, tennis court, playground, pool - powered sites ✪$17 for two, cabins $70-120 for two.

Scone Caravan Park, New England Highway, ©6545 2024. Kiosk, playground, barbecue - powered sites ✪$14 for two, cabins $40-50 for two.

Points of Interest

Nearby **Glenbawn Dam** is well stocked with freshwater fish, and is ideal for boating, yachting, water skiing and swimming.

The **Burning Mountain**, off the New England Highway between Scone and Murrurundi, turn-off just north of Wingen, has been burning for thousands of years. According to Aboriginal legend, a tribesman was lighting his fire on the mountainside when he was carried off into the earth by the evil one. Unable to escape, he used his fire sticks to set the mountain alight so that the smoke might warn others to keep away. Today the mountain is easily reached via a two kilometre walking track.

Travelling south through **Aberdeen**, which once housed a thriving abbatoir, one comes to Muswellbrook.

Murrurundi

Population 1000
Location and Characteristics

The town of Murrurundi on the Pages River occupies the northernmost point of the Hunter Valley, and has historic old buildings, many classified by the National Trust. Tales of bushrangers are intertwined with the region. Ben Hall was born here, and Thunderbolt roamed in the area in the latter part of the last century.

Accommodation and Services

Valley View Motel, New England Highway, ©6546 6044. 15 units, barbecue, playground, pool - ✪$60-65.

Murrurundi Motel, New England Highway, ©6546 6082. 16 units, barbecue, pool - ✪$55-60.

Points of Interest

Sheep, cattle and horse breeding are the major interests, and the mountain scenery of the Liverpool Ranges, at the town's doorstep, gives an unparalleled view of the valley.

Port Stephens

Location and Characteristics

Port Stephens is a 45 minute coastal drive north of Newcastle, and is regarded as one of the most attractive and unspoilt waterways anywhere in Australia. It proclaims itself as the 'Dolphin Capital of Australia', since more than 140 bottlenose dolphins reside in the port, which is more than twice the size of Sydney Harbour. Further upstream from where the Myall River flows into the Port are the Broadwater and the Myall Lakes systems with lovely waterways, tiny uninhabited islands, abundant bird life, a national park, and unpolluted beaches stretching north to the Smith's and Wallace Lakes systems.

What were once isolated fishing settlements around the Port's foreshores, have become connected with the influx of residents and tourist facilities. The main centres are Shoal Bay, Nel-

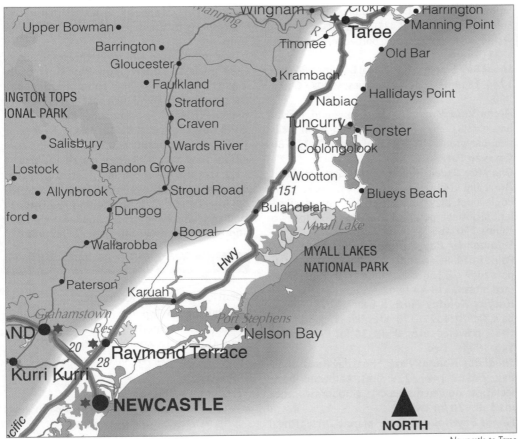

NORTH

Newcastle to Taree

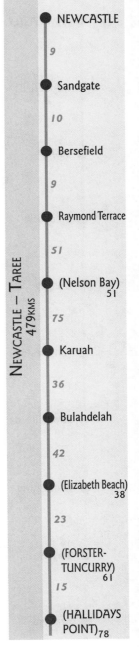

Newcastle to Taree

NEWCASTLE

9

Sandgate

10

Bersefield

9

Raymond Terrace

51

(Nelson Bay) 51

75

Karuah

36

Bulahdelah

42

(Elizabeth Beach) 38

23

(FORSTER-TUNCURRY) 61

15

(HALLIDAYS POINT) 78

NEWCASTLE – TAREE 479KMS

son Bay, Salamander Bay and Soldiers Point, and the smaller, and somewhat newer areas are Lemon Tree, Mallabula, Tanilba Bay and Oyster Cove.

On the waterway's northern reaches are the holiday centres of Tea Gardens and Hawks Nest, both offering good accommodation, beaches and facilities.

Visitor Information

The Port Stephens Visitor Information Centre is on Victoria Parade, Nelson Bay, ✆(02) 4981 1579 or ✆1800 808 900. It is 🕐open 9am-5pm Mon-Fri and 9am-4pm Sat, Sun and Public Holidays. You will find it at the drive-way entrance to the Marina. Email them at ✉ tops@hunterlink

.net.au or find the website at 👁www.port stephens.org.au

Accommodation and Services

There is plenty of accommodation in Port Stephens. Here is a slice of the seemingly endless variety.

Country Comfort - Port Stephens, 265 Sandy Point Road, Salamander Bay, ✆4984 1111 or ✆1800 065 064 (toll free). 30 units, licensed restaurant, room service, recreation room, playground, gym, tennis courts, mini golf, pool, spa - ✪$140-200 per person.

Nelson Towers Motel, 71A Victoria Road, Nelson Bay, ✆4984 1000. 16 units, room service, good facilities, pool - ✪$125-270.

**Newcastle
to Taree**

THE BARRINGTON TOPS 179KMS

● NEWCASTLE

37

● MAITLAND

8

● Seaham

25

● Brookfield

14

● Dungog

20

● (Chichester)
20

43

● Stroud Road

14

● Wards River

5

● Craven

4

● Stratford

Salamander Shores, 147 Soldiers Point Road, Soldiers Point, ✆ 4982 7210. 90 units, 2 licensed restaurants, room service, barbecue, sauna, pool - ✪$110-265.

Shoal Bay Motel, 59-61 Shoal Bay Road, ✆4981 1744. 18 units, cooking facilities, sauna - ✪$75-200.

Aloha Villa Motel, 30 Shoal Bay Road, Nelson Bay, ✆4981 2523. 16 units, good room facilities, playground, spa, heated pool - ✪$75-180.

Caravan Parks

One Mile Beach Holiday Park, Gan Gan Road, Anna Bay, ✆4982 1112. 217 sites, kiosk, tennis court, pool, playground, recreation room, excellent facilities - powered sites ✪$18-20 for two, cabins $50-165 for two.

Salamander Bay Caravan Park, 208 Soldiers Point Road, Salamander Bay, ✆4982 7287. (No pets allowed) 108 sites, minimal facilities - powered sites ✪$18 for two.

Halifax Holiday Park, 5 Beach Road, Nelson Bay, ✆4981 1522. 173 sites, kiosk, good facilities - powered sites ✪$19-30 for two, cabins $45-190 for two.

Shoal Bay Holiday Park, Shoal Bay Road, Shoal Bay, ✆4981 1427. 228 sites, barbecue, basic facilities - powered sites ✪$18-30 for two, cabins $30-170 for two.

Fingal Bay Holiday Park, Marine Drive, Fingal Bay, ✆4981 1427. (No pets allowed during holidays) 450 sites, recreation room, barbecue, playground, pool - unpowered sites ✪$19-30 for two, cabins $50-200 for two.

There is a **Youth Hostel** at 59-61 Shoal Bay Beachfront Road, Shoal Bay, ✆4984 2315. It has 4 rooms at ✪$23 per person for a double room.

Points of Interest

Lying only a couple of hours away from Sydney by car, this is a booming tourist area that bustles with visitors in the peak summer season. **Nelson Bay** is the Port Stephens service centre, with a variety of shops, a movie cinema, a supermarket, restaurants, banks, a pub, and plenty more. People flock to the scenic **Marina** for shopping, dining and entertainment.

There is no shortage of activities to occupy your time in Port Stephens, from all manner of watersports to a number of Hunter Valley wine tours.

Two golf courses will meet the standards of keen players. **The Nelson Bay Golf Club**, ✆4981 2073, is a 27-hole course nestling into the mountains behind the coast and carved out of lush bushland. In Salamander Bay, the **Horizons Golf Club**, ✆4982 4074, is a challenging 18-hole championship course in stunning condition. They have a pleasant restaurant here.

The area also has theme parks catering for children, including **Toboggan Hill Park** in Salamander Bay, ✆4984 1022; **Tomteland Australia** in Williamtown, ✆4965 1500; and **Oakvale Farm and Fauna World** in Salt Ash, ✆4982 6222.

Barrington Tops

Location and Characteristics

The Barrington Tops National Park is about 110km (68 miles) north-west of Newcastle, travelling through Raymond Terrace and Dungog. The area is on the World Heritage List.

Visitor Information

A wonderful website covers this area in great depth: ☞www.barringtons.com.au

Dungog Visitors Information Centre is on the corner of Dowling and Brown Streets, Dungog, ✆4992 2212, or email ✉ dungogvc@midac.com.au.

It is ⏰open Mon-Fri 9am-5pm and Sat-Sun 9am-3pm.

The Gloucester Visitor Information Centre is on the corner of Church & Denison Streets, Gloucester, ✆6558 1408, or email ✉ glosinfo @tpg.com.au. It is ⏰open 7 days 9.30am-4.30pm.

Accommodation and Services

Hookes Creek Forest Resort, 1800 Scone Road, Gloucester, ✆6558 5544. 10 rooms, licensed restaurant, playground, car parking, horse riding, tennis court, pool - ✪$340-420 including meals.

The Barringtons Country Retreat, Chichester

Dam Road, Chichester Dam, ℂ4995 9265. 21 cabins, licensed restaurant, cooking facilities, car parking, playground, tennis court, 2 pools - ✪$110.

Yeranda Cottages, 117 Skimmings Gap Road Main Creek, Dungog, ℂ4992 1208. 2 cottages, cooking facilities, barbecue, car parking - ✪$90-130.

Gloucester Cottage, ℂ61 Denison Street, Gloucester, ℂ6558 2658. 3 rooms, fireplace, car parking - ✪$75.

Gloucester Country Lodge, Bucketts Way, Gloucester, ℂ6558 1812. 25 units, car parking, barbecue, pool - ✪$80-90.

Tall Timbers Motel, 167 Dowling Street, Dungog, ℂ4992 1547. 12 units, licensed restaurant, cooking facilities - ✪$75-115.

Caravan Parks

Gloucester Holiday Park, Denison Street, ℂ6558 1720. (No pets allowed) 230 sites, recreation room, playground, barbecue, kiosk - powered sites ✪$16 for two, cabins $35-55 for two.

Riverwood Downs, Monkerai Valley, ℂ4994 7112. (Pets allowed) 80 sites, unlicensed restaurant, barbecue, basic facilities - powered sites ✪$24 for two, cabins $110-145 for two, bunkhouses $40 for two.

Points of Interest

The fabulous Barrington Tops landscape is the drawcard. It is very mountainous country, with many 4WD and hiking tracks, but care should be taken as many people have become lost wandering off the beaten track. There are many excellent places to spend a few days in this marvellous setting, suiting a wide range of budgets and tastes.

Forster/Tuncurry

Population 16,000

Location and Characteristics

North of Newcastle, about 161km (100 miles), are the twin towns of Forster and Tuncurry, which are the major tourist areas of the Great

Lakes, and are renowned for their beaches, fishing, seafoods and temperate climate all year around.

How to Get There

Follow the Pacific Highway north to Bulahdelah, then take The Lakes Way turnoff to the right a little further on. It is well signposted. On this coastal road, there are houseboats that can be hired for a few days of relaxed cruising on the Myall Lakes.

Visitor Information

Forster has the Great Lakes Visitor Centre located in Little Street, ℂ(02) 6554 8799 or ℂ1800 802 692. It is ⏱open Mon-Fri 9am-5pm. They have a web page at ☞www.greatlakes.org.au and an email address at ✉tourglc@tpgi.com.au

Accommodation and Services

The choice here is almost overwhelming! Following is a sample guide.

Forster

Tudor House Lodge, 1 West Street, ℂ6554 8766. 8 units, licensed restaurant, room service, pool, spa, sauna - ✪$125.

Fiesta Motel, 23-25 Head Street, ℂ6554 6177. 20 units, cooking facilities, spa, pool - ✪$80-125.

Forster Motor Inn, 11 Wallis Street, ℂ6554 6877. 24 units, licensed restaurant, undercover parking, heated pool - ✪$80-125.

Forster Palms Motel, 60 Macintosh Street,

THE BARRINGTON TOPS 179KMS

● Stratford

4

● Forbesdale

5

● Gloucester

Newcastle to Taree

NEWCASTLE - TAREE
479KMS

- (HALLIDAYS POINT) 78
- 2
- (DIAMOND BEACH) 80
- 98
- Wooton
- 9
- Coolongolook
- 18
- Nabiac
- 15
- Rainbow Flat
- 22
- (OLD BAR) 13
- 15
- (MANNING POINT) 28
- 30
- TAREE

☏6555 6255. 36 units, barbecue, pool - ✪$65-140.

Bella Villa Motor Inn, 19 Lake Street, ☏6554 6842. 23 units, pool, barbecue, cooking facilities - ✪$55-110.

Jasmine Lodge Motel, 18 Wallis Street, ☏6554 9838. 11 units, barbecue, pool - ✪$55-105.

Great Lakes Motor Inn, cnr West & Head Streets, ☏6554 6955. 27 units, barbecue, cooking facilities, pool - ✪$45-90.

Tuncurry

South Pacific Palms Motor Inn, 36 Manning Street, ☏6554 6511. 26 units, licensed restaurant, room service, heated pool - ✪$83-128.

Rest Point B&B, 35 Rest Point Parade, ☏6554 9051. 2 rooms, lounge, fireplace, barbecue - ✪$120-130.

Tuncurry Motor Lodge, 132 Manning Street, ☏6554 8885 or ☏1800 637 166 (toll free). 23 units, cooking facilities, recreation room, barbecue, pool - ✪$65-95.

Caravan Parks

Smugglers Cove Holiday Village, 45 The Lakes Way, Forster, ☏6554 6666. (No pets allowed) 235 sites, year-round entertainment, playground, recreation room, mini golf, kiosk, pool - powered sites ✪$20-35 for two, cabins $45-145 for two.

Forster Beach Caravan Park, Reserve Road, Forster, ☏6554 6269. (No dogs allowed) 283 sites, playground, barbecue - powered sites ✪$16-25 for two, cabins $35-165 for two.

Suncoast Caravan Park, 7 The Lakes Way, Forster, ☏6554 6591. (Pets allowed) 123 sites, shop, playground, pool - powered sites ✪$16-24, cabins $35-110, on-site vans $25-50.

Shangri-La Caravan Park, South Street, Tuncurry, ☏6554 8522. (No dogs allowed) 185 sites, barbecue, recreation room, kiosk, playground, pool - powered sites ✪$16-29, lodges $60-85, on-site vans $25-50.

Tuncurry Beach Caravan Park, Beach Street, Tuncurry, ☏6554 6440. (No dogs allowed) 360 sites, barbecue, playground - powered sites ✪$16-25, cabins $35-100.

There is a **Youth Hostel** at 43 Head Street, Forster, ☏6555 8155. It has 20 rooms at ✪$21 per person twin share.

Points of Interest

On land there is the **Booti Booti National Park** to explore, and the **Cape Hawke Bicentennial Walk** with its panoramic viewing platform. The popular beaches and lakes provide ample opportunites for swimming, fishing and sailing.

Hallidays Point/Diamond Beach

Population 600
Location and Characteristics
Midway between Taree and the Great Lakes region is the coastal area of Hallidays Point - Diamond Beach.

Accommodation and Services

Elga Black Head Motor Inn, Black Head Road, ☏6559 2649. 7 units, cooking facilities, barbecue, playground, pool - ✪$70-95.

Happy Hallidays Holliday Park, 146 Black Head, ☏6559 2967. (No pets allowed) 143 sites, recreation room, barbecue, kiosk, tennis court, pool - powered sites ✪$20-35 for two, cabins $50-160 for two.

Points of Interest

The Lands Department has established a **rainforest walk** encompassing the coastal landforms as well as rare tracts of coastal rainforest. The walk takes in two headlands, Black Head and Red Head, and is joined by Black Head Beach. The Visitor Information Centre in Taree has brochures on the Walk.

Nine Mile Beach stretches southwards.

Old Bar

Population 2600
Location and Characteristics
The town centre of Old Bar is only 16km (10 miles) from Taree's closest surfing beach.

Visitor Information

Full information on Old Bar is provided by the Tourist Information Centre in Taree (*see separate listing*).

Accommodation and Services

Accommodation is available in cabin style or a caravan park. Entertainment is provided in the Bowling Club and the Tavern.

Chiltern Lodge Country Retreat, 139 Metz Road, ©6553 3190. 4 cabins, cooking facilities, barbecue, car parking, pool, spa - ✪$150-200.

Old Bar Beachfront Holiday Park, Old Bar Beach, ©6553 7274. (No dogs allowed) 188 sites, kiosk, barbecue, pool - powered sites ✪$17-19 for two, cabins $45-85 for two.

Points of Interest

Old Bar's attractions, apart from the beach, are the mouth of the Manning River and the reserve/picnic area known as **Mud Bishops Reserve**, which offers shaded barbecue facilities.

Manning Point

Population 300

Location and Characteristics

The township is a little over 35km (22 miles) from Taree, and is located on an island near the mouth of the river.

Accommodation and Services

Accommodation is available at caravan parks.

Manning Point Ocean Caravan Park, Manning Street, ©6553 2624. (Pets allowed with security deposit) 149 sites, playground, kiosk, recreation room, pool - powered sites ✪$16-25 for two, cabins $45-145 for two, on-site vans $45-75 for two.

Weeroona Caravan Park, 21 Main Road, ©6553 2635. (Pets allowed) 170 sites, kiosk, playground, pool - powered sites ✪$14-22 for two, on-site vans $35-55 for two, cabins $50-95 for two.

Points of Interest

The sea and the north arm of the Manning River meet at Manning Point, with the ocean providing safe white sandy beaches for swimming, and the river providing excellent fishing.

Taree

Chapter 21
Taree

Population 16,700
Taree is located on the banks of the Manning River, 330km (205 miles) north of Sydney.

Characteristics
Taree is the commercial centre of the Manning Valley, which offers a diversity of natural attractions from scenic lookouts and waterfalls that plunge deep into a box gorge, to some of the cleanest, whitest beaches on the east coast of Australia.

Climate
Average temperatures: January max 29C (84F) - min 17C (63F); July max 18C (64F) - min 6C (43F). Average annual rainfall: 1171mm (46 ins).

How to Get There
By Air
Qantas, ✆13 1313, has flights from/to Sydney.
By Bus
McCaffertys, ✆13 1499, and Greyhound Pioneer, ✆13 2030, stop at Taree on their Sydney/Brisbane runs.
By Rail
There is an XPT Countrylink service from Sydney to Taree and the trip takes 5 hours, ✆13 2232.
By Road
From Sydney (310km) and Brisbane (8 hours), via the Pacific Highway.

Visitor Information
The Manning Valley Visitor Information Centre is on the Old Pacific Highway, Taree North, 3km north of the Taree Shopping Centre, ✆(02) 6552 1900 or ✆1800 801 522. They are ✆open 7 days a week 9am-5pm, and the complex includes a restaurant, public toilets, and a 70-seat theatrette showing an audio-visual presentation. The email address is ✉ manningvic@gtcc.nsw. gov.au and the web address is ✆www.gtcc.nsw.gov.au/tourism

Accommodation
Taree has many motels, a few caravan parks, and houseboats for hire (available from Manning River Holidays Afloat, 36 Crescent Avenue, Taree, ✆6552 3162). Here is a selection of accommodation with prices for a double room per night, which should be used as a guide only. The telephone area code is 02.
Riverview Motor Inn, Old Pacific Highway, ✆6552 2122. 21 units, 1 suite, licensed restaurant, swimming pool - ✿$100.
City Centre Motor Inn, 4 Crescent Avenue, ✆6552 5244. 20 units, swimming pool, barbecue - ✿$80-90.
Best Western Caravilla Motor Inn, 33 Victoria Street, ✆6552 1822. 27 units, licensed restaurant (closed Sunday), swimming pool - ✿$75-85.
In-Town Motor Inn, 77 Victoria Street, ✆6552 3996. 20 units, spa bath, barbecue - ✿$70-80.
Marco Polo Motor Inn, Pacific Highway, ✆6552 3866. 20 units, swimming pool, sauna, barbecue - ✿$100-110.
Agincourt Motel, 9 Commerce Street, ✆6552 1614. 21 units - ✿$45-65.
Jolly Swagman Motel, 1 Commerce Street, ✆6552 3511. 21 units, barbecue - ✿$55-90.
Chatham Motel, Pacific Highway, ✆6552 1659. 10 units - ✿$40-45.
Arlite Motor Inn, cnr Bligh Street & Pacific Highway, ✆6552 2433. 20 units, swimming pool - ✿$50.

Caravan Parks
Twilight Caravan Park, Pacific Highway, ✆0500 854 448. (Pets allowed under control), 65 sites - powered sites ✿$17-20 for two, on-site vans $30-40 for two, cabins $35-70.
Riverside Caravan Park, Reid Street, Croki, ✆6556 3274. (No pets), 38 sites, barbecue - powered sites ✿$15-18 for two, on-site vans $35 for two, cabins $35 for two.

Eating Out
The hotels all have restaurants and snack bars, and some of the motels have licensed or unli-

Jin Hong Chinese Restaurant, 91 Victoria Street, ✆6552 7199.
Seafood on Victoria, 166 Victoria Street, ✆6557 8111.
McDonalds is on the corner of the Pacific Highway and Manning Street. You will find KFC at 38 Victoria Street. Pizza Hut is in Manning Mall, Manning Street, ✆13 1166.

Points of Interest

Taree is, as we have mentioned, a holiday town, and there is not a great deal of sightseeing, just plenty of places to relax and take advantage of the river.
The riverside **Fotheringham and Queen Elizabeth Parks** offer the opportunity to feed the pelicans and seagulls, and to observe the river.
Manning River Cruises, ✆6557 4767, have a cruise boat on the Manning, with informative commentary to accompany your charter. There are regular departures during school holidays.
The Big Oyster, Pacific Highway, North Taree, is like the other striking and rather ludicrous 'Bigs' in the country.

Festivals

The Taree Aquatic Festival is held each January, and the Taree City Festival is held every two years in June.

Facilities

An 18-hole golf course, several tennis courts, 4 bowling clubs, BMX track, Olympic swimming pool, basketball stadium, indoor cricket stadium, squash courts, ten pin bowling, greyhound racing and horse racing, and facilities for rugby league, rugby union, soccer, hockey, and netball.
  The Manning Entertainment centre, ✆6551 0555, has a 505 seat auditorium, and local clubs have top local and interstate bands throughout the year. There is also a twin cinema.

A pelican takes to flight

censed restaurants. The local licensed clubs also have dining rooms and bistros. Here are some restaurants you might like to try.
Thai Tarni, Albert Street, ✆6552 2366. BYO dine-in or take-away. Open 5.30pm-9.30pm every day except Monday and for lunch 11.30am-2pm Tue-Fri.
Il Colosseo, 32 Oxley Street, ✆6552 6289. BYO, Italian, also offers free pizza delivery within a 10km radius. Open 6pm-10pm every day except Monday, and until midnight Fri-Sun.
Shades, 23-25 Oxley Street, ✆6552 1455. Fully licensed restaurant with an international menu. Open every day except Sunday 6pm-midnight.
Kowin Chinese Restaurant, 22 Chatham Avenue, ✆6552 3482. Licensed, open 7 nights 5pm-9pm.
East Court Chinese Restaurant, 73 Victoria Street, ✆6552 2465. Licensed, salad bar, banquets, open 7 nights 5pm-10pm.
Silhouettes, Shop 5, 103 Victoria Street, ✆6552 1393.
Pelican, Old Pacific Highway, ✆6552 2122.
Laurents, 33 Victoria Street, ✆6552 5022.

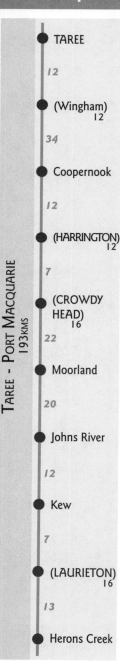

Taree to Port Macquarie

TAREE

12

(Wingham)
12

34

Coopernook

12

(HARRINGTON)
12

7

(CROWDY HEAD)
16

22

Moorland

20

Johns River

12

Kew

7

(LAURIETON)
16

13

Herons Creek

TAREE - PORT MACQUARIE 193KMS

Chapter 22
Taree to Port Macquarie

Wingham

Population 4500

Location and Characteristics

Situated 13km (8 miles) west of Taree, Wingham has a feeling of 'olde England', with its town common that is also the local cricket pitch. There are also about 13 buildings which have been classified by the National Trust for their historical significance, and most have been carefully reconstructed. They include the School of Arts, the Police Station and Court House, the Bank Building, Gibson & Skinner Butchery and the Australian Hotel.

Visitor Information

Use the resources of the Taree Information Centre to obtain further details of Wingham, ©6552 1900.

Accommodation and Services

Wingham Country Lodge Motel, Country Club Drive, ©6553 0300. 27 units, licensed restaurant, car parking, barbecue, pool - ✪$85-100.
Wingham Motel, 13 Bent Street, ©6553 4295. 14 units, cooking facilities, playground, pool - ✪$65-70.

Points of Interest

Manning Valley Historical Society's Museum, corner Farquhar & Bent Streets, ©6553 5823, ⏰open 10am-4pm, is also located within the town square area, and displays include Jimmy Governor's cell, together with various items relating to the history of the area.
Wingham Brush, located 500m from the shopping centre on Farquhar Street, is 7ha (17 acres) of coastal rainforest, with birds and native marsupials. The Brush is adjacent to the Manning River and has picnic tables, barbecues and boat launching facilities.

Forestry Drives:

Bulga Forest Drive is a scenic tour through timbered country north west of Wingham, passing the Ellenborough Falls near Elands. The round trip from Wingham takes visitors through three State Forests - The Bulga, Dingo and Knorrit.

Kiwarrak State Forest is 5km (3 miles) south of Taree, adjacent to the Pacific Highway. Highlights of this 16km (10 miles) sign-posted drive include the Pines picnic area and Breakneck Lookout.

Coopernook State Forest Drive includes Vincents Lookout, Newbys Creek Walk, Newbys Lookout, Starrs Creek, Big Nellie Mountain and Wautui Falls.

Middle Brother Forest surrounds Middle Brother Mountain (556m -1824 ft). Several walking trails have been established within the Forest, and attractions include the largest Blackbutt trees in the State.

Crowdy Head

Location and Characteristics

4km (2 miles) north-east of Harrington is the quaint village of Crowdy Head, the home of the local fishing fleet.

Visitor Information

The Harrington Crowdy Tourist Information Centre is at 85 Beach Street, Harrington, ©6556 1188.

Accommodation

There is little choice here. Head for the **Crowdy Head Motel**, 7 Geoffrey Street, ©6556 1206. They have 6 units, room service and barbecue, for ✪$65-85 a double per night.

Points of Interest

There's good fishing from the headland, and a co-op if you don't have any luck yourself. The **lighthouse** is easily reached by a sealed road, and gives excellent views of the coastline, both north and south.

Crowdy Beach sweeps in a long arc through to Diamond Head in the National Park, and offers safe swimming.

Harrington

Population 1400

Location and Characteristics

The northern arm of the Manning River reaches the ocean at Harrington, and a long breakwall provides excellent fishing. The town is about 5km south of the east-side turn-off on the Pacific Highway.

Visitor Information

The Harrington Crowdy Tourist Information Centre is at 85 Beach Street, Harrington, ✆6556 1188.

Accommodation and Services

Accommodation is available in motels and caravan parks. Here is a selection.

Harrington Village Motel, 255 Beach Street, ✆6556 1386. 9 units, cooking facilities - ✪$60-75.

Harrington Holiday Park, Crowdy Street, ✆6556 1228. (No pets allowed) 350 sites, playground, barbecue - powered sites ✪$14-25 for two, cabins $60-130 for two, bunkhouses $40-65 for two.

Oxley Anchorage Caravan Park, 71-83 Beach Street, ✆6556 1250. (No pets allowed) 96 sites, barbecue, pool - powered sites $16 for two, on-site vans $35-60 for two.

Points of Interest

Safe lagoon swimming is available, and there are barbecue and picnic areas.

From **Pilot Hill Lookout** there is a good view of the coastline. The graves near the lookout are those of pilots whose jobs were to guide the boats over the treacherous bar to enable the timber to be picked up at the ports of Wingham and Taree.

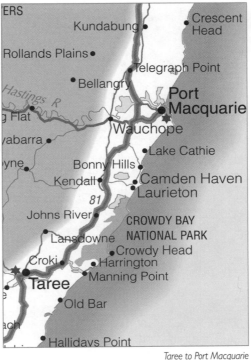

Taree to Port Macquarie

Laurieton

Location and Characteristics

Laurieton is south of Port Macquarie on Ocean Drive, and is part of Camden Haven. It is another popular holiday spot, with a range of accommodation, restaurants and clubs.

Visitor Information

The Camden Haven Neighbourhood Information Centre is in 1 Seymour Street, Laurieton, ✆6559 5676.

Accommodation and Services

Mariner Motel, 12 Kew Road, ✆6559 9398. 12 units, barbecue - ✪$60-95.

Carawatha Country Resort, 146 Ocean Drive, ✆6559 4209. 10 units, basic accommodation, cooking facilities, playground, barbecue, tennis, pool - ✪$65.

Laurieton Gardens Caravan Resort, 478 Ocean

Sailing on the Pacific

National Parks

Crowdy Bay National Park is located in the northern section of the Manning Valley, and covers some 6000ha (14,820 acres). Access to the park is via the Coralville Road at Moorland, some 35km (22 miles) north of Taree. Picnic and camping areas are available within the park and the main attractions are fishing and surfing. *Diamond Head* is the main camping area with barbecues and toilet facilities, however drinking water is not available within the Park.

Author Kylie Tennant often spent time at Diamond Head, where he built a hut from which he wrote *The Man on the Headland*. The hut was a gift to the National Park in 1976, and was restored in 1980.

Boorganna Nature Reserve is on the western edge of the Comboyne Plateau, 7km (4 miles) west of Taree. Access is along the Innes View Road from the Wingham/Comboyne Road. Brochures on both of these parks are available from the Tourist Information Centre in Taree.

Wauchope

Population 4600

Location and Characteristics

Wauchope is 19km (12 miles) west of Port Macquarie on the Oxley Highway. At the centre of the region's timber industry, this historic town draws visitor mainly to its Timbertown theme park.

Visitor Information

The Wauchope Information and Neighbourhood Centre is in Shop 3 Roland Plaza, 33 High Street, ©6586 4055.

Accommodation and Services

The Broad Axe Motel, Oxley Highway, ©6585 1355. 10 units, located next to Timbertown, barbecue, tennis, pool - ✪$60-80.
Wauchope Motel, 84 High Street, ©6585 1933. 12 units, barbecue - ✪$45-70.
The Broad Axe Caravan Park, Oxley Highway, ©6585 1355. (Pets allowed) 57 sites, kiosk,

Drive, ©6559 9256. 75 sites, kiosk, 2 pools, recreation room - powered sites ✪$16-25 for two, units $55-145 for two, cabins $35-90 for two, on-site vans $30-55 for two.
The Haven Caravan Park, Arnott Street, ©6559 9584. (No dogs allowed) 63 sites, barbecue, playground - powered sites ✪$15-21 for two, cabins $35-70 for two.

Points of Interest

This is a great area for fishing, and there are many good beaches to tempt you. The town is overlooked by **North Brother Mountain**, from which there are good views of the town and the coastline. **Kattang Nature Reserve**, a few kilometres east, and **Crowdy Bay National Park**, just south, are two pleasant natural features of the local environment.

pool, tennis - powered sites ✪$17 for two, cabins $45-80 for two.

Points of Interest

The main attraction is **Timbertown**, ✆6585 1866, an entire village recreated to demonstrate the struggles and achievements of the pioneers. It has a steam train, timber sawing, a bullock team, a woodturner and a general store selling the finished goods plus lollies from glass jars and licorice by the yard, amongst other things from 'the good old days'. There is also a bakery offering freshly baked damper with home-made jams, and Devonshire teas. The houses and the church have been faithfully reproduced in the manner of the era (1880-1910), many with fine furniture and utensils brought out from the home country. You should allow 4 hours minimum for a visit, maybe more if it's a hot day and you spend some time in the *Maul and Wedge Hotel*. Timbertown is ⏱open daily from 9am. It is 3km from Wauchope on the Oxley Highway.

Another attraction is the **Big Bull** in Redbank Farm, 50 Redbank Road, ✆6585 2044, just over the river. The Bull is 14m (46 ft) high, and in the complex there is a working dairy farm, an animal nursery, an educational display, hay rides, a restaurant, and a souvenir shop. It is ⏱open daily 9am-5pm.

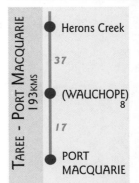

Taree to Port Macquarie

TAREE - PORT MACQUARIE 193KMS

Herons Creek

37

(WAUCHOPE)
8

17

PORT MACQUARIE

Chapter 23
Port Macquarie

Population 33,700

Port Macquarie is situated at the mouth of the Hastings River on the North Coast of New South Wales, 423km (263 miles) north of Sydney.

Climate

Average temperatures: January max 25C (77F) - min 18C (64F); July max 18C (64F) - min 7C (45F). Average annual rainfall: 1563mm (62 ins). The CSIRO suggests that Port Macquarie has the most ideal climate in Australia. A warm off-shore current combines with the surrounding barrier of hills to form a pocket, and produce this small range of temperature.

Characteristics

A major coastal tourist resort and retirement area, Port Macquarie is the most historically significant town along the coast between Newcastle and the Queensland border.

In October, 1818, John Oxley reached the mouth of the Hastings River and described the area as "... a beautiful point of land, having plenty of good water and grass, and commanding a fine view of the interior of the port and the surrounding country". He named the inlet Port Macquarie in honour of the Governor of the Colony of New South Wales.

In 1821, the settlement of Port Macquarie was established by a pioneer party of soldiers and convicts.

How to Get There

By Air

Qantas, ✆13 1313 provide flights from Sydney, Melbourne, Brisbane, Newcastle, Taree, Coffs Harbour, Lismore, Ballina and Coolangatta.

By Bus

Greyhound Pioneer, ✆13 2030, and McCaffertys, ✆13 1499 stop at Port Macquarie.

By Rail

The XPT service from Sydney stops at Wauchope and a coach service connects with Port Macquarie, ✆13 2232.

By Road

From Sydney, via the Pacific Highway on a 400km trip. From Brisbane, either the Pacific Highway along the coast (510 km), or the Cunningham Highway to Warwick, the New England Highway and then the Oxley Highway back to the coast.

Visitor Information

The Port Macquarie Visitor Information Centre is on the corner of Clarence and Hay Streets, ✆(02) 6581 8000 or ✆1800 025 935. Their ⏱opening hours are 8.30am-5pm Mon-Fri, 9am-4.30pm weekends. Their web page is at 🖳www.portmacquarieinfo.com.au and they can be emailed at ✉vicpm@midcoast.com.au

Accommodation

There is a lot to choose from in Port Macquarie itself, and then there are the nearby resorts of Lake Cathie, North Haven and Laurieton. It is still advisable to book well in advance during the Christmas and school holiday periods.

The prices listed here are for a double room per night, which should be used as a guide only. The telephone area code is 02.

Sails Resort, Park Street, ✆6583 3999 or ✆1800 025 271. 83 guest rooms and suites, spa, sauna, mini golf, tennis, waterfront restaurant, cocktail bar - ✪$150-315.

Country Comfort Port Macquarie, cnr Buller & Hollingworth, ✆6583 2955 or 1800 065 064. 61 units, licensed restaurant, swimming pool, spa, barbecue - ✪$115-165.

El Paso Motor Inn, 29 Clarence Street, ✆6583 1944 or ✆1800 027 965. 55 units, licensed restaurant, swimming pool, spa, sauna, barbecue - ✪$100-115.

Best Western Macquarie Barracks Motor Inn, 103 Hastings River Drive, ✆6583 5333 or ✆1800 622 511. 14 units, swimming pool, barbecue - ✪$100-170.

Aquatic Motel, 253 Hastings Drive, ✆6583

7388. 21 units, swimming pools, barbecue - ✪$80-150.

Rocky Beach Motel, 10 Pacific Drive, ✆6583 5881. 10 self-contained units, barbecue - ✪$65-90.

Arrowyn Motel, 170 Gordon Street, ✆6583 1633. 14 units, basic facilities, pool - ✪$55-95.

Port O'Call Motel, 105 Hastings River Drive, ✆6583 5222. 13 units, swimming pool, barbecue - ✪$70-115.

Narimba Lodge Motel, 4 Narimba Close, ✆6583 3839. 5 units with en suites and a range of facilities - ✪$55-80.

Holiday Units

Airlie Palms, 50 Pacific Drive, ✆1800 242 992. 6 units, air conditioning, comfortable facilities, barbecue, undercover parking - ✪$55-140.

Golden Sands Apartments, ✆6583 2067. 5 self-contained suites, barbecue, undercover parking, centrally located - ✪$50.

Blue Pacific Holiday Flats, 37 Pacific Drive, ✆6583 1686. Self-contained units, undercover parking - ✪$45-80.

Bed & Breakfast

Lighthouse Beach B&B Homestay, 91 Matthew Flinders Drive, ✆6582 5149. Self-contained, spa, swimming pool, barbecue, garage parking, guest library, adults only - ✪$110-150.

Belrina B&B, 22 Burrawong Drive, ✆6582 2967. Luxury accommodation with ensuite bedroom, barbecue, swimming pool - ✪$95-110.

Dolphin View B&B, 53 Matthew Flinders Drive, ✆6582 3561. Ensuite rooms, swimming pool, parking, adults only - ✪$110-145.

Joy's Doo Drop Inn B&B, 29 Laguna Place, ✆6583 3405. Situated on canal waters with private jetty available, solar heated swimming pool, barbecue - ✪$75-110.

Caravan Parks

Sundowner Breakwall Tourist Park, 1 Munster Street, ✆6583 2755. Swimming pool, games room, guest lounge, no pets allowed - powered sites ✪$19-32 for two, cabins $50-140 for two.

Hastings River Caravan Park, 268-270 Hastings River Drive, ✆6583 3387. En suite cabins, tent area, powered sites, barbecue, swimming pool - powered sites from ✪$18 for two, cabins from $45.

Lighthouse Beach Holiday Village, 50 Hart Street, ✆6582 0581. 24 self-contained cabins, 91 powered sites, no pets allowed - powered sites ✪$16-30 for two.

Melaleuca Caravan Park, 128 Hastings River Drive, ✆6583 4498. Budget to luxury accommodation, swimming pool and slide, barbecue, central location, no pets allowed - 81 powered sites ✪$18 for two, on-site vans $35-60 for two, cabins from $55-115.

There is a **Youth Hostel** at 40 Church Street, ✆6583 5512. It has 9 rooms at ✪$20 per person twin share.

Eating Out

There are many restaurants in the town, offering local seafood, French, Italian, Thai, Mexican, Chinese, Vegetarian and Aussie fare. Here are a few you might like to try.

Cray's Restaurant and Fish Cafe, 74 Clarence Street, ✆6583 7885. Seafood specialists, licensed, lunch and dinner, quality takeaway available.

Scampi's on the Marina, Park Street, ✆6583 7200. Seafood, dinner 7 days after 6pm, BYO, 'Seafood to Go' quality takeaway available for dinner 7 days.

Filou Restaurant, Mercure Sandcastle Motor Inn, 16-24 William Street, ✆6583 4646. Licensed, French cuisine, breakfast, lunch and dinner daily.

Zephyrs on Clarence, 2 Clarence Street, ✆6583 6822. Authentic Australian foods including crocodile, kangaroo and barramundi, licensed, open from 6pm.

Spinnakers Resort, Sails Resort, Park Street, ✆6583 3999. A la carte dining, licensed, breakfast, lunch and dinner.

Al Dente, 74 Clarence Street, ✆6584 1422. Licensed Italian restaurant on the waterfront, lunch and dinner.

Cafe 66, 66 Clarence Street, ✆6583 2484. BYO, Italian fare, from snacks to meals, open late.

Toro's Mexican, 22 Murray Street, ✆6583 4340. BYO, dine in or take away.

Pancake Place, cnr Clarence & Hay Street, ✆6583 4544. BYO, open seven days from 10am,

take-away and home delivery.
McDonalds is on the corner of Bay & Park Streets, opposite Settlement City and on the corner of the Pacific Highway and Oxley Street. *KFC* is on the corner of Horton and Hayward Streets. The phone number for *Pizza Hut* deliveries in the area is ✆13 1166.

Shopping
Two major shopping centres in the town are:
Port Central Shopping Centre, Horton Street, ✆6584 2988; and
Settlement City Shopping Centre, Bay Street, ✆6581 7377.

Points of Interest
Peppermint Park, cnr Pacific Drive & Ocean Street (near Flynn's Beach), ✆6583 6111, has landscaped parkland with water slides, pools, mini golf, aviaries, monkeys, 'Twista' Dodgems and roller skating. Barbecue facilities, a milk bar, and a fitness trail are other attractions. The Park is ⏰open Tue-Sun, and every day during school holidays. Adults ✪$14, children $14, pensioners $9, family $50.

Sea Acres Rainforest Centre, Pacific Drive, ✆6582 3355, has a 1.3km boardwalk within 6.2ha (15 acres) of coastal rainforest. There is also a theatre with continuous shows, a restaurant, gift shop and picnic area. The centre is ⏰open daily 9am-4.30pm. Adults ✪$10, children $6, pensioners $8, family $25.

The Church of St Thomas the Apostle, cnr Hay & William Streets, was built by convicts, completed in 1828, and has the original box pews made from local red cedar. In the church grounds is the old hospital dispensary, now a simple chapel. For a donation of a couple of dollars, two-hour tours are available on weekdays. The hospital was across the road, where St Agnes' Catholic Church now stands.

Fantasy Glades, Port Macquarie's Fantasy World, is in Parklands Close, off Pacific Drive, ✆6582 2506. Situated in 2.5ha (6 acres) of rainforest gardens, the Glades have ghosts, castles, dragons, witches, dwarfs, mini-cars and train

rides. There are also barbecue and picnic areas and a coffee shop. A wonderful attraction for families. ⏰Open daily from 9am-5pm. Adults ✪$9, children $6.

Kingfisher Park, Kingfisher Road, off the Oxley Highway, has a large collection of Australian fauna and farm animals. There is also a coffee lounge and barbecue facilities. ⏰Open daily from 9am, ✆6581 0783. Adults ✪$9, children $6, family $25.

Billabong Koala & Aussie Wildlife Park, near the intersection of the Pacific and Oxley Highways, ✆6585 1060, is another place where you can cuddle a koala or pat a kangaroo. There are also indoor and outdoor displays and activities, a souvenir and gift shop, a barbecue courtyard, and Matilda's Restaurant. The Park is ⏰open every day 9am-5pm. Adults ✪$9, children $5.

The **Hastings District Historical Museum**, in Clarence Street near the corner of Hay Street, ✆6583 1108, won the Museum of the Year Award way back in 1981 and 1982. Its 14 rooms are ⏰open Mon-Sat 9.30am-4.30pm, Sun 1.30-4.30pm.

Port Macquarie Observatory, in Rotary Park, William Street, allows visitors to observe the Solar System with the aid of a Planetarium and telescope. ⏰Open Wed and Sun 7.30-9.30pm (8.15-10pm during Daylight Saving).

Both the **Historic Cemetery Gardens** and **Kooloonbung Creek Nature Park** are situated at the southern end of Horton Street. The cemetery has many old graves dating back over 150 years, and the nature reserve has landscaped gardens and walks along the creek.

Tacking Point Lighthouse, at the end of Lighthouse Beach Road, is the third oldest in the country.

Macquarie Nature Reserve, Roto House off Lord Street, has an historic visitors' centre, and in the grounds you can picnic, spy on some healthy koalas, or visit some sick ones in the yard of the Koala Hospital a short distance away (the public is not permitted inside the complex itself). The koalas are fed daily at 8am and 3pm. The Koala Preservation Society of NSW is a voluntary organisation and your support will help save the koalas in Port Macquarie.

Old World Timber Art, 120 Hastings Drive, ℂ6583 2502, is where you can watch craftsmen creating hand-crafted woodware and souvenirs from beautiful Hastings timbers. The complex is ⏱open Mon-Fri 8.30am-5pm, and the showroom is open Sat-Sun 10am-4pm.

Thrumster Village Pottery, is a pottery and craft centre situated 9km (6 miles) west of Port Macquarie on the Oxley Highway. Pottery, leatherwork, copper enamelling, hand made glassware and hand-crafted works are on display. ⏱Open daily during school holidays, otherwise Thurs-Sun 9am-5pm, ℂ6581 0885.

Cassegrain's Hastings Valley Winery, Pacific Highway, is ⏱open daily 9am-5pm, ℂ6583 7777. They offer winery inspections, wine tasting and cellar door sales. There are also picnic and barbecue facilities, a children's play area, cooperage and souvenirs.

Surfing beaches are part of the city atmosphere. The best known is Lighthouse Beach, which has magnificent surf for boards and body surfing.

Tours

The Visitor Information Centre has details of many river cruises, boat hire outlets and deep sea fishing charter boats. They can also advise on bush and forest safaris. Here is a selection:

Port Explorer Bus, ℂ1800 025 935 for details. Town Tour, ✪$15 adults, $12 children, $13 pensioner.

Eagle Iron Motorcycle Tours, ℂ1800 025 935 for details. From ✪$34 for half an hour to $290 for a full day (7 hours).

At the southern end of Lighthouse Beach, **Camel Safaris**, ℂ6583 7650, offer camel rides lasting from 20 minutes (✪$14 adult, $9 child) to overnight camping safaris ($195pp).

Everglades Waterbus, ℂ6582 5009. 5 dolphin-spotting cruises on offer, from adult ✪$22 to $50.

Fantasea, ℂ015 256 742. Adults ✪$19, children $8, pensioners $17, family $48.

Macquarie Mountain Tours, ℂ1800 025 935 for details. Full day, adult ✪$85, child $50; River and Mountain Escape, adult ✪$80, child $40, Wine Tasting Tour, ✪$23.

Mansfield's Aussie Beach and Bush Tours, ℂ1800 025 935 for details. Full day with two meals provided, ✪$80.

Port Macquarie Canoe Safaris, ℂ1800 025 935. Short day tour, ✪$55 adult, $33 child. All day tour including lunch, ✪$85 adult, $45 child.

Port Macquarie River Cruises, ℂ1800 025 935 for details. A number of choices including a 2hr scenic cruise, ✪$17 adults, $17 child, $9 pensioner.

Queens Lake Cruiser, ℂ1800 025 935 for details. 2hr scenic cruise, adult ✪$16, child $8; 4hr lunch cruise, ✪$23 adult, $12 child.

Seaplane Joy Flights, ℂ1800 025 935 for details. From ✪$45 adult, $22 child.

Wingaway Air Scenic Flights, ℂ18000 025 935 for details.

Festivals

Port Macquarie has The Carnival of the Pines over the Easter period, and Wauchope (*see separate entry*) has Colonial Week in September.

Sports
Fishing

Mid Coast River Fishing Charters, ℂ1800 025 935 for details. 2 people full day, ✪$125.

Odyssey Charters, ℂ6586 3132. Long Day Reef/ Trolling ✪$155 (minimum 10 people), other packages available.

Port Macquarie Estuary Sportfishing Tours, ℂ6582 2545.

SeaQuest Fishing Charters, ℂ6583 3463. ✪$100 adult, $70 child.

Airborne

High Adventure Airpark, ℂ1800 025 935 for details. Microlite flight (✪$145 for 1hr), tandem hanggliding (✪$160 for 20mins) and tandem paragliding (✪$145 for 30mins) are a few of the activities available.

Skydiving, ℂ6584 3655. ✪$290 for a tandem jump.

Horse Riding

Cowarra Homestead Forest Trails, ℂ1800 025 935 for details. 1hr ✪$28, 2hrs $45, several

Port Macquarie

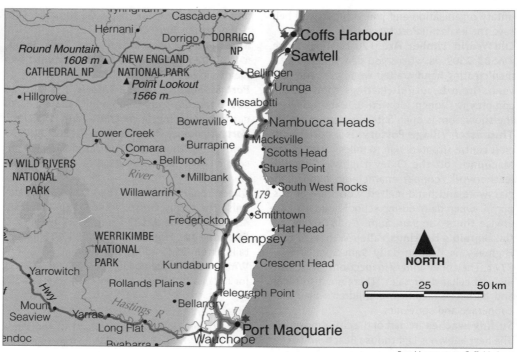

Port Macquarie to Coffs Harbour

routes to choose from.

Watersports

Port Macquarie Kayak Adventures, ℂ1800 025 935 for details. Half-day ✪$33.

Port Water Sports, ℂ1800 025 935 for details.

Parasailing ✪$50, coastal tour $39.

Golf

Supa Putt Golf, ℂ1800 025 935 for details. Adult ✪$7, child $5 for 18 holes.

Chapter 24
Port Macquarie to
Coffs Harbour

Kempsey

Population 8600
Location and Characteristics
Situated 48km (30 miles) north of Port Macquarie, Kempsey straddles the Macleay River and is the heart of a fast growing valley renowned for its natural beauty and stress-free lifestyle.

Visitor Information
The Kempsey Visitor Information Centre is on the Pacific Highway, South Kempsey, ⏰open Mon-Fri 9am-5pm, weekends 10am-4pm. ✆(02) 6554 8799 or ✆1800 642 480 or email at ✉ktic @midcoast.com.au

Accommodation and Services
All Nations Hallmark Inn, 320 Pacific Highway, ✆6562 1284 or ✆1800 066 139. 30 units, licensed restaurant, barbecue, playground, pool, spa, room service - ✪$85-105.
Skyline Motel, 40 Pacific Highway, ✆6562 4888. 11 units, undercover parking - ✪$50-85.
Fairway Lodge, 385 Pacific Highway, ✆6562 7099. 6 units, barbecue, car parking, playground, pool - ✪$45-50.
Moon River Motor Inn, 157 Pacific Highway, ✆6562 8077. 31 units, licensed restaurant, room service, pool - ✪$65-110.
Southside Caravan Park, 317 Pacific Highway, ✆6562 5275. (Pets allowed) 50 sites, barbecue, playground - powered sites ✪$14 for two, on-site vans $30-35 for two, cabins $40-50 for two.
Sundowner Caravan Park, 161 Pacific Highway, ✆6562 1361. (Pets allowed) 36 sites, barbecue, pool - powered sites ✪$17 for two, cabins $30-40 for two, on-site vans $35 for two.

Points of Interest
Attractions include: The **Macleay River His-**

torical Societies' Museum, which can be found in the Information Centre complex on the Pacific Highway, South Kempsey, ⏰open daily 10am-4pm; The **Kempsey Shire Library and Les Graham Art Collection**, Elbow Street, West Kempsey, ⏰open Mon-Fri 10am-6pm, Sat 9am-noon; and **Kempsey Saleyards**, Kemp Street.
There are many bushwalks and drives in the **Macleay Valley**.
The area has facilities for every kind of **sport** imaginable on land and water.
The beaches in the Kempsey Shire offer safe, patrolled sections for families. The village of **Stuarts Point** is the focal point for the beaches that stretch north from the mouth of the Macleay River to the Shire's boundary above Middle Head.
The coastal village of **Hat Head** is regarded as one of the top fishing spots on the coast of NSW, because of its close proximity to the continental shelf. Hat Head is situated in the heart of the **Hat Head National Park**, and is the perfect base for a quiet family holiday, a fishing trip or a nature-lover's excursion.

South West Rocks

Population 3500
Location and Characteristics
The largest seaside resort in the Kempsey Shire is South West Rocks, 32km (20 miles) north-east of Kempsey, near the mouth of the Macleay River. The town was so named because the pilot officer at Grassy Head, the old entrance to the river, advised masters of vessels to anchor in Trial Bay, south-west of the rocks to ensure their ships would be in deep water with room to manoeuvre under sail.

Accommodation and Services
Costa Rica Motel Resort, 134 Gregory Street, ✆6566 6400. 21 units, licensed restaurant, barbecue, tennis, squash, sauna, spa, pool - ✪$75.
South West Rocks Motel, 110 Gregory Street, ✆6566 6330. 22 units, licensed restaurant,

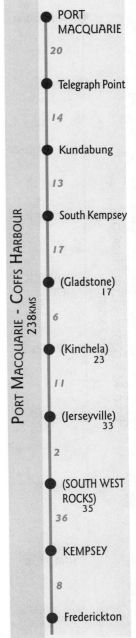

Port Macquarie to Coffs Harbour

PORT MACQUARIE

20

Telegraph Point

14

Kundabung

13

South Kempsey

17

(Gladstone)
17

6

(Kinchela)
23

11

(Jerseyville)
33

2

(SOUTH WEST ROCKS)
35

36

KEMPSEY

8

Frederickton

PORT MACQUARIE - COFFS HARBOUR 238KMS

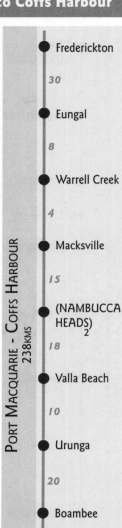

PORT MACQUARIE - COFFS HARBOUR 238KMS

- Frederickton
- *30*
- Eungal
- *8*
- Warrell Creek
- *4*
- Macksville
- *15*
- (NAMBUCCA HEADS) *2*
- *18*
- Valla Beach
- *10*
- Urunga
- *20*
- Boambee
- *6*
- COFFS HARBOUR

cooking facilities, room service, pool - ✪$55-95.

Horseshoe Bay Beach Park, Livingstone Street, ✆6566 6370. (Small pets allowed) 80 sites - powered sites ✪$18-28 for two, cabins $55 for two, on-site vans.

South West Rocks Tourist Park, Gordon Young Drive, ✆6566 6264. (Small pets allowed) 129 sites, recreation room, barbecue, pool - powered sites ✪$18-27 for two.

Points of Interest

There are many beaches in the area, and two interesting places to explore: Trial Bay Gaol and Smoky Cape Lighthouse.

Trial Bay Gaol, overlooking Trial Bay, was opened as a prison in 1886, and later during World War I was an internment centre for 500 Germans. Guided tours are available through the gaol, or you can browse through the complex, with its museum pieces and restored cells. The gaol is ⏱open 9am-5pm daily, ✆6566 6168.

Smoky Cape Lighthouse, on the border of Hat Head National Park, is the highest lighthouse on the NSW coast, standing 128m (420 ft) above sea level, and was opened in 1891. Visitors are welcome on ⏱Tuesdays and Thursdays, and you can chat to one of the lightkeepers, and admire the outstanding views.

On the shores of the beaches around South West Rocks there are many **wrecks** of vessels dating back to 1816.

Nambucca Heads

Population 6200
Location and Characteristics

Situated 114km (71 miles) south of Coffs Harbour, Nambucca Heads is another popular holiday resort, and has a wide range of accommodation from premier hotels to flats and caravan parks.

It is a farming and timber district, and there are facilities for boating, lawn bowls, fishing (river, rock, beach and deep sea), golf, surfing and tennis.

Visitor Information

The Nambucca Valley Visitor Information Centre can be found at 4 Pacific Highway. They are ⏱open 9am-5pm daily, ✆(02) 6568 6954 or ✆1800 646 587.

Accommodation and Services

Destiny Motor Inn, cnr Pacific Highway & Riverside, ✆6568 8044. 37 units, licensed restaurant, barbecue, room service, pool, spa, sauna - ✪$95-125.

The Nambucca Resort, Pacific Highway, ✆6568 6899. 27 units, licensed restaurant, recreation room, barbecue, playground, golf driving range, pool - ✪$90-100.

Nambucca Motor Inn, 88 Pacific Highway, ✆6568 6300. 12 units, licensed restaurant, recreation room, cooking facilities, car parking, pool - ✪$55-95.

Jabiru Motel, Pacific Highway, ✆6568 6204. 10 units, cooking facilities, undercover parking, tennis, pool - ✪$45-65.

Caravan Parks

White Albatross Holiday Centre, Wellington Drive, ✆6568 6468. (Pets allowed) 287 sites, licensed restaurant, playground, tennis, kiosk - powered sites ✪$16 for two, cabins $42-50 for two, on-site vans $25 for two.

Foreshore Caravan Park, Riverside Drive, ✆6568 6014. (No pets allowed) 135 sites, barbecue - powered sites ✪$14-18 for two, cabins $40-65 for two, on-site vans $25-40 for two.

Pacific Sands Caravan Park, Swimming Creek Road, ✆6568 6120. (Dogs allowed) 150 sites, recreation room, playground, pool - powered sites ✪$18 for two, cabins $55 for two.

Points of Interest

Attractions include the Nambucca Historical Museum; Mary Boulton's Pioneer Cottage; The Pub with No Beer; Taylor Arm - venue for the Easter Country Music Festival and Fair; the historical Star Hotel; Kew House Toy and Doll Museum; and the Worm Farm, Valla Road, Valla, which has worm picking, packing and racing.

Chapter 25
Coffs Harbour

Population 22,170
Coffs Harbour is situated on the coast of New South Wales, 578km (359 miles) north of Sydney and 427km (265 miles) south of Brisbane.

Climate

Average temperatures: January max 26C (79F) - min 19C (66F); June max 19C (66F) - min 9C (48F). Average annual rainfall: 1759mm (69 ins); wettest six months October to March.

Characteristics

Coffs Harbour is a popular year-round tourist destination. On one side there are the blue waters of the Pacific Ocean, while the western border area is the Great Dividing Range. The combination of golden sands, high mountains, dense luxuriant rainforests, steep banana plantations, clear rivers and streams make it a superb holiday area.

Coffs Harbour was originally called Korff's Harbour, named after Captain John Korff, who sheltered here in 1847. The harbour, being halfway between Brisbane and Sydney, was an extremely busy port facility for the many vessels plying the coastal trade. It was considered a dangerous port, however, and after a boycott by many ships' captains, the lighthouse was eventually built in 1878.

The surrounding lowlands and rolling hills were once a source of red cedar and other valuable timber when discovered some 150 years ago. The pastoralists followed in the tracks of the timber cutters and the area was given to cattle, dairying, vegetable growing and, of course, banana plantations.

How to Get There
By Air
The following airlines fly regional services into

Coffs Harbour: Qantas, ©13 1313 and Kendall, ©9670 2677.
By Bus
Interstate coach lines operate daily in Coffs Harbour. Contact Greyhound Pioneer, ©13 2030, or McCaffertys, ©13 1499.
By Rail
XPT services operate daily from Sydney and overnight expresses operate from Sydney and Brisbane, ©13 2232.
By Road
Travelling by the Pacific Highway, it is an 8 hour drive from Sydney, and about 6 hours from Brisbane.

Visitor Information

The Coffs Harbour-Tourism Holiday Coast Information Centre is located at the corner of Rose Avenue & Marcia Street, Coffs Harbour, ©(02) 6652 1522 or 1300 369 070. It is ©open 9am-5pm daily. Email them at ✉tourism@coffscoast. com.au or check out the website at ◉www. coffs.net

Accommodation

Coffs Harbour has resorts, motels, holiday apartments, caravan parks, hotels, cabins/lodges and hostels. Here is a selection with prices for a double room per night, which should be used as a guide only. The telephone area code is 02.
Aanuka Beach Resort, Firman Drive, Diggers Beach, ©6652 7555. 49 units, licensed restaurant, swimming pool, spa, sauna, gym, tennis, barbecue - ✪$205-400 including breakfast.
Coffs Harbour Motor Inn, 22 Elizabeth Street, ©6652 6388. 35 units, licensed restaurant, swimming pool, spa, barbecue - ✪$90-130.
Big Windmill Motor Lodge, 168 Pacific Highway, ©6652 2933. 39 units, licensed restaurant, swimming pool, spa, sauna, gym, barbecue - ✪$80-130.
Premier Motor Inn, Pacific Highway, ©6652 2044. 32 units, licensed restaurant (closed Sun), swimming pool, barbecue - ✪$160-120.
Coachmens Inn, 93 Park Beach Road, ©6652 2055. 41 units, swimming pool, spa - ✪$55-100.

Coffs Harbour

Matador Motor Inn, cnr Grafton & Albany Streets, ©6652 3166. 16 units, swimming pool - ✪$55-85.

Bananatown Motel, 15 Grafton Street, ©6652 4411. 13 units, swimming pool, barbecue - ✪$50-90.

Caravan Parks

Coffs Village Caravan Park, 215 Pacific Highway, ©6652 4633. (No pets allowed), 52 sites - powered sites ✪$17 for two, on-site vans $25 for two.

Bananacoast Caravan Park, Pacific Highway, ©6652 2868. (Dogs allowed by arrangement), 105 sites - powered sites ✪$17-26 for two, cabins $35-105 for two.

Split Solitary Caravan Park, Split Solitary Road, ©6653 6212. (No pets during holiday period), 125 sites - powered sites ✪$15-20 for two, cabins $40-75 for two.

There is a **Youth Hostel** in 110 Albany Street, ©6652 6462. It has 15 rooms at ✪$20-22 per person twin share.

Eating Out

Coffs Harbour has many restaurants and fast food outlets, particularly down on the Marina. The restaurants range from many international cuisines to the family type catered for by the local clubs. Many of the motels and hotels have restaurants and bistros, and here is a taste of what else is available.

The Fishermans Katch, 394 High Street, ©6652 4372. Seafood platters and steak. Open 6am-8pm daily, closed Public Holidays.

Tequila Mexican Restaurant, 224 High Street, ©6652 1279. Fully licensed open 5.30pm-8pm every day.

Stetsons Steakhouse & Saloon, cnr Pacific Highway & Bray Streets, ©6651 9166. Open 5.30pm-10pm 7 days, closed Public Holidays.

Sawan Thai Restaurant, 376 High Street, Coffs Jetty, ©6652 9699. Vegetarian food is a speciality, Open 5.30pm-10.30pm Mon-Sat, closed Sunday and Public Holidays.

Star Anise, 93 Grafton Street, open 6pm-9pm Wed-Sun, 11.30am-2pm Thursday and Friday, closed Monday and Tuesday with selected hours on Public Holidays.

The Dragon, 108 Grafton Street, ©6652 4187. Cantonese cuisine with a seafood emphasis.

Ocean Oyster & Steak Grill, 394 High Street, ©6650 0444.

Sands, cnr Park Beach Road & Ocean Parade, ©6652 2666.

Taruah Thai Restaurant, 360 High Street, ©6652 5992.

The Village, 97 Park Beach Road, ©6652 2055. McDonalds have a branch on the corner of the Pacific Highway and North Boambee Road and one in the High Street Mall. There is a Pizza Hut on the corner of High and Gordon Streets, and you can call them for delivery on ©13 1166.

Points of Interest

The Big Banana, Pacific Highway, ©6652 4355 is the landmark of Coffs Harbour, and is 3km north of the town. There you will find an audio-visual theatrette, Aboriginal Dreamtime Cave, historical exhibits, hydroponics glasshouse, banana packing shed, Triffid Forest, Time Tunnel, Future Culture Space Station, Greenhouse Food Fair/Souvenir complex, display gardens, machinery museum/ocean lookout, and a farmers' market.

Pet Porpoise Pool, ©6652 6133, in Orlando Street, has performing dolphins and sea lions, native fauna, marine animals, live sharks and reef tank, a kiosk and souvenir outlet. It is ⊙open daily 9am-5pm. Shows are at 10.30am and 2.15pm.

North Coast Regional Botanic Garden, ©6648 4188, in Hardacre Street in the centre of town, has 19ha (47 acres) featuring native and exotic plants, ⊙open daily.

Within an hour's drive of Coffs Harbour, and covered with magnificent rainforest, is **Dorrigo National Park**, which has many walking trails.

From Coffs Harbour there are a half-a-dozen **drives** that are recommended by the Tourist Office:

1 North along Pacific Highway, including the Big Banana, then continue north to Bruxner Park (Sealy Lookout) and Rainforest, back

south, left at the Big Banana through residential areas returning via Macauleys Headland.

2 Starting at the Post Office, go east to Beacon Hill Lookout then down to the harbour area, Muttonbird Island nature walk, out to Pet Porpoise Pool, Park Beach Surf Club development.

3 West along Coramba Road to Red Hill, Karangi, Coramba, Glenreagh, returning via Nana Glen, Lower Bucca and Moonee to Coffs Harbour.

4 South along Pacific Highway, turn left into Sawtell Scenic Drive, including Boambee Creek, Sawtell Beach and Bonville Lookout. Then on to Storyland Gardens, Pine Creek State Forest, Mylestom and Urunga then return.

5 South along Pacific Highway including Bellingen, Dorrigo National Park, Dangar Falls, and return via Thora to Coffs Harbour.

6 North along Pacific Highway including Big Banana, continue north to Kumbaingeri Wildlife Sanctuary, further north to Woolgoolga, see the Sikh Temple, Woolgoolga Art Gallery, return to Coffs via Lake Russell Gallery.

There are seven State Forests in the area. Sealy Lookout is a must when visiting Bruxner Park Flora Reserve, as it offers panoramic views of the city, Pacific coastline and banana-clad hillsides. The **Dorigo National Park and Rainforest Centre** is on the corner of Dome Road and Lyrebird Lane, ©6657 2309.

Several art and opal galleries are in and around the town. The Tourist Information Centre in Hickory Street, Dorrigo, ©6657 2486, can provide you with details if you are interested in browsing through these places.

Joy flights over Nambucca Heads, Bellingen, Orara Valley, Woolgoolga and the Solitary Islands, are available (**Skylink Helicopters**, Aviation Drive, ©6658 0899; **Wingaway Air**, Airport Drive, ©6650 0655), as are deep sea fishing trips (**Adriatic Fishing Trips**, Shop 5 International Marina, ©6651 1277; **Cougar Cat 12 Fishing Trips**, ©6651 6715).

Storyland Gardens, ©6653 1400, 10km south of Coffs Harbour on Lyons Road, Sawtell, has a giant Old Woman's Shoe, surrounded by popular fairytale settings such as Snow White and Little Red Riding Hood. It is ⏱open 10am-4pm Thu-Sun and every day during school holidays. And of course, there are the **beaches**. Coffs Harbour has many, and they range from those with full-blooded rolling surf that boardriders and body surfers love, to the sheltered, lagoon-type that are perfect for toddlers, to some secluded beaches used for nude bathing.

Festivals

The Agricultural Show is held in May.

Facilities

Two golf courses, five lawn bowling clubs, three surf clubs, a yacht club, a deep sea fishing club and racecourse. Tennis, squash, ten-pin bowling, croquet and indoor cricket facilities are available. An indoor stadium caters for basketball, badminton, indoor hockey and many other indoor sports.

Coffs Harbour to Lismore

COFFS HARBOUR - LISMORE
270KMS

- COFFS HARBOUR
- 3
- Korora
- 23
- WOOLGOOLGA
- 14
- Corindi Beach
- 45
- South Grafton
- 3
- (GRAFTON)
- 3
- 17
- Ulmarra
- 14
- Tyndale
- 10
- Maclean
- 6
- Harwood

Chapter 26
Coffs Harbour to Lismore

Woolgoolga

Population 3700
Location and Characteristics
Situated 25km north of Coffs Harbour, Woolgoolga has a large Sikh community and they have built a lavish temple, called Guru Nanak.

Accommodation and Services
Ocean Beach Motor Inn, 78 Beach Street, ℂ6654 1333. 10 units, barbecue, heated pool, spa - ✪$60-110.
Balcony View Motor Inn, 62 Beach Street, ℂ6654 1289. 10 units, barbecue, pool - ✪$55-100.
Woolgoolga Motor Inn, Pacific Highway, ℂ6654 1534. 10 units, playground, barbecue, pool - ✪$50-55.
Colonial Surfside Camping & Caravan Park, Pacific Highway, ℂ6654 1644. 120 sites, recreation room, barbecue, playground, kiosk, half tennis court, spa, heated pool - powered sites ✪$18-30, cabins $ 50-125, on-site vans $35-65.

Points of Interest
The **Raj Mahal Emporium**, ℂ6644 1149, an Indian Theme Park on corner of Pullen Street and the Pacific Highway, has Indian artefacts and food.
The **Woolgoolga Art Gallery**, Turon Parade, ℂ6654 1064, has a treasure trove of fine art, pottery, batikwork and woodcraft, and is ⏱open daily 10am-4pm.
Whitewater rafting on the **Nymboida River** is available for the adventurous.
George's Gold Mine, ℂ6654 5355, 782 Moleton Road, Moleton, is ⏱open Wed-Sun 10am-5pm, and has inspections of the Bayfield gold mine and original equipment. There are picnic and barbecue areas, and food is available.
Valery Trails, 758 Valery Road, Valery, ℂ6653 4401, offer escorted trail rides through the Pine Creek State Forest, catering for both experienced and inexperienced riders.

Grafton

Population 16,600
Location and Characteristics
Grafton huddles on both sides of the Clarence River, 40km (25 miles) inland from the coast and 106km south of Evans Head. There is en-ough here to appeal to day-trippers for a short exploration of the area.

Visitor Information
The Clarence River Tourist Association is on the corner of Spring Street and the Pacific Highway, ℂ6642 4277.
There is a current website with information on the town at ☞www.nnsw.com/grafton

Accommodation and Services
Reilley's Hideaway Grafton Farmstay, 218 Reilly's Lane off Pacific Highway, ℂ6642 6008. 3 rooms, cooking facilities, fireplace, playground, table tennis, pool, spa - ✪$110.
Bent Street Motor Inn, 62 Bent Street, ℂ6643 4500. 20 units, barbecue, licensed restaurant, car parking, spa, pool - ✪$70-90.
Abbey Motor Inn, 59 Fitzroy Street, ℂ6642 6122. 24 units, breakfast room service - ✪$65-70.
Fitzroy Motel, 27 Fitzroy Street, ℂ6642 4477. 21 units, spa, pool - ✪$70-105.
Hi-Way Motel, Pacific Highway, ℂ6642 1588. 31 units, playground, pool - ✪$55-75.
Roches Family Hotel, 85 Victoria Street, ℂ6642 2866. 14 rooms, licensed restaurant, barbecue - ✪$40.
Caravan Parks
The Gateway Village, 598 Summerland Way, ℂ6642 4225. 90 sites, pool, practice golf, barbecue - powered sites ✪$20 for two, cabins $60-85, on-site vans $40-45 for two.

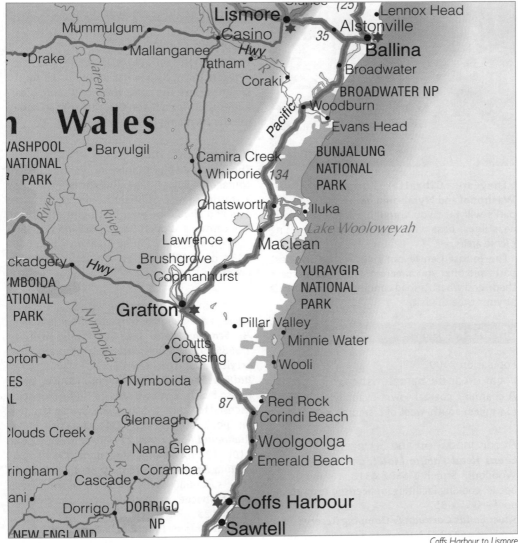

Coffs Harbour to Lismore

Grafton Sunset Caravan Park, 302 Gwydir Highway, ✆6642 3824. (Pets allowed by arrangement) 70 sites, barbecue, kiosk, pool - powered sites ✪$15 for two, on-site vans $30-35 for two, cabins $40-45 for two.

Points of Interest

Perhaps the city's most distinct feature is its scenic centre, filled with green parks and lined with thousands of trees. Other attractions include the **Anglican Cathedral** on the corner of Victoria and Duke Streets, the **Regional Art Gallery** in Prentice House, 158 Fitzroy Street (✆6642 3177), and the various **Heritage Walks**, about which the Tourist Centre can supply you information.

Four notable **National Parks** sprawl across the surrounding regions.

They are: **Gibraltar Range**, **Yuraygir**, **Washpool** and **Nymboida**. A drive through the parks will take you through rainforests, along coastlines, past wild rivers and into stunning picnic areas.

The Tourist Centre can give tips on the best parts and offer you directions on how to access them, and whether road conditions require 4WD at your time of visit.

Evans Head

Population 2300
Location and Characteristics
A charming coastal town, Evans Head is 55km (34 miles) south-west of Lismore.

Accommodation and Services
Evans Head Pacific Motel, cnr Davis Lane & Woodburn Street, ©6682 4318. 16 units, barbecue, cooking facilities, unlicensed restaurant, pool - ✪$50-85.
Silver Sands Caravan & Camping Reserve, Park Street, ©6682 4212. (No pets allowed) 632 sites, barbecue, playground, kiosk - powered sites ✪$16-20 for two, cabins $35-75 for two.

Points of Interest
North of the town is the Broadwater National Park, with unspoiled beaches and heathland that becomes a blaze of colour in spring. On the town's southern edge is the Bundjalung National Park, which is popular for surfing, boating, picnicking and bushwalking.

Ballina

Population 18,000
Location and Characteristics
A resort town, Ballina has all the usual tourist facilities. Take the coast road for a more pleasant drive to/from Byron Bay, rather than rejoining the Pacific Highway.

Visitor Information
The Ballina Visitor Information Centre is on the corner of La Balsa Plaza & River Street. They have a startling range of literature on tourist interests and should be your first point of contact. The centre is ◷open 9am-5pm Mon-Fri, 9am-4pm on weekends. Phone them on ©(02) 6686 3484 or email them at ⵍbalinfo@balshire. org.au

Accommodation and Services
There is a wide range to choose from in Ballina.
All Seasons Motor Inn, 301 Pacific Highway, ©6686 2922. 38 units, licensed restaurant, room service, pool, spa - ✪$105-150.
Ballina Beach Resort, Compton Drive, Lighthouse Beach, ©6686 8888. 46 units, barbecue, licensed restaurant, car parking, sauna, spa, tennis, pool, room service - ✪$110-215.
Richmond Motor Inn, 227 River Street, ©6686 9100. 13 units, car parking, pool - ✪$95-120.
Ballina Palms Motor Inn, cnr Bentinck & Owen Streets, ©6686 4477. 13 units, cooking facilities, barbecue, car parking, pool, playground - ✪$85-125.
Ballina Colonial Motel, cnr Bangalow Road & Skinner Street, ©6686 7691. 12 units, barbecue, pool - ✪$60-100.
Ballina Ferry Boat Motel, Pacific Highway, ©6686 2827. 13 units, car parking, playground - ✪$45-70.
Caravan Parks
Ballina Lakeside Holiday Park, Fenwick Drive, ©6686 3953. (No pets allowed) 245 sites, recreation room, barbecue, playground, pool, minigolf - powered sites ✪$23-28 for two, cabins $35-65 for two.

Sea Breeze Caravan Park, 344 South Beach Road, ℭ6686 3900. (Pets allowed by arrangement) 80 sites, kiosk, barbecue, pool - powered sites ✪$17-19, cabins $45-90.

Cedars Caravan Park, Pacific Highway, ℭ6686 3014. (No pets allowed) 62 sites, recreation room, barbecue, playground, pool - powered sites ✪$18-20, cabins $30-70.

There is a **Youth Hostel** in 36 Tamar Street, ℭ6686 6737. It has five rooms at ✪$18-22 per person twin share.

Points of Interest

The **Big Prawn** can be seen several kilometres from town.

The **Maritime Museum**, Regatta Lane, ℭ6681 1002, records the maritime history of the Richmond River and features the *Las Balsa Raft* which voyaged from South America to Ballina in 1973.

Shaws Bay Hotel, next to the caravan park, 2 Brighton Street, East Ballina, has a beautiful red cedar dining room and staircase which were carved in Spain, ⏰open daily 10am-10pm, ℭ6686 2034.

The **Broadwater Sugar Mill**, 19km (12 miles) south of Ballina, has tours during the crushing season (June to December).

Alstonville

Population 3600

Location and Characteristics

An attractive village that boasts a nice little bookshop, Alstonville is 19km (12 miles) from Lismore on the way to the coast.

Accommodation and Services

Garden Inn Wollongbar, cnr Bruce Highway & Smith Lane, ℭ6628 5666. 11 units, licensed restaurant, car parking, breakfast room service - ✪$75-120.

Alstonville Settlers, Bruxner Highway, ℭ6628 5285. 18 units, barbecue, pool - ✪$60-70.

Points of Interest

Near the village is the **Victoria Park Nature Reserve**, a remnant of the 'big scrub' which once covered most of the district.

The **Summerland House With No Steps**, Wardell Road, ℭ6628 0610, is a unique project providing job skills and training for the handicapped. It also has avocados, macadamia nuts, tropical stone fruit, custard apples, lychees and citrus fruits growing in plantations, and on sale, as well as a craft cottage, retail nursery and fruit packing house. Devonshire teas and light lunches are available ⏰daily 9am-5pm.

At Bexhill, 10km north-east of Lismore, is an **open-air cathedral**. The pews are fashioned from logs, whilst behind the stone altar and cross are magnificent views of the Corndale Valley.

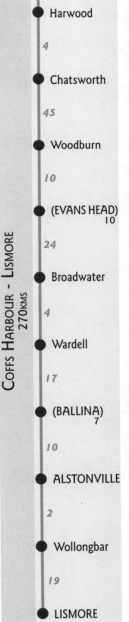

Coffs Harbour to Lismore

COFFS HARBOUR - LISMORE 270KMS

Harwood
4
Chatsworth
45
Woodburn
10
(EVANS HEAD)
10
24
Broadwater
4
Wardell
17
(BALLINA)
7
10
ALSTONVILLE
2
Wollongbar
19
LISMORE

Chapter 27
Lismore

Population 27,200
Situated between rainforest and sea, Lismore is in northern New South Wales, inland from Ballina on the Bruxner Highway.

Climate
Average temperatures: January max 30C (86F) - min 19C (66F); July max 20C (68F) - min 6C (43F). Average annual rainfall, 1349mm (53 ins); wettest months December-May.

Characteristics
The commercial, cultural and sporting capital of the North Coast region. Lismore is the administrative centre for Federal and State Government departments, as well as being the commercial and retail hub of the region. The surrounding countryside is extremely fertile and all types of agriculture are found in the region. Tropical fruits, such as bananas, avocados, pineapples and macadamia nuts, are widely grown. Dairying is also popular and the hills away from the coast are still timbered. There has been much controversy in past years over logging.

How to Get There
By Air
Hazelton Airlines, ©13 1713, fly to/from Sydney.
By Bus
Greyhound Pioneer, ©13 2030, stop at Lismore on their Sydney/Brisbane Pacific Highway route.
  Kirklands Coaches, ©1300 367 077, provide daily services to/from Brisbane and nearby regional centres.
By Rail
There is a regular Countrylink service from Sydney to Lismore, ©13 2232.
By Road
Via the Pacific Highway and the New England Highway from Sydney (787km - 489 miles) and Brisbane (222km - 138 miles).

Visitor Information
The Lismore Visitor Information Centre, cnr Ballina & Molesworth Streets (the main street), ©(02) 6622 0122 or ©1300 369 795, has literature, maps, souvenirs and accommodation booking services, and is ⏰open 9.30am-4pm Mon-Fri, 10am-3pm weekends and 9.30am-4pm on Public Holidays. The online references for more info are: email ✉tourism@liscity. nsw.gov.au and website ☞www.liscity.nsw. gov.au

Accommodation
Here is a selection of accommodation available in Lismore, with prices for a double room per night, which should be used as a guide only. The telephone area code is 02.
Sisleys Inntown Motel, 111 Dawson Street, ©6621 9888. 8 units, comfortable facilities - ✪$70-100.
Dawson Motor Inn, cnr Dawson & Orion Streets, ©6621 8100. 19 units, swimming pool - ✪$65-85.
Karinga Motel, 258 Molesworth Street, ©6621 2787. 31 units, licensed restaurant (Mon-Thurs) - ✪$65-80.
Arcadia Motel, cnr James Road & Ballina Road, Goonellabah (to the east of the city), ©6624 1999. 10 units, swimming pool - ✪$65.
McDermotts's B&B, cnr Dawson & Magellan Streets, ©6624 1158. 2 rooms, comfortable facilities - ✪$65-75.
Caravan Parks
Lismore Tourist Caravan Park, Dawson Street, ©6621 6581. (Pets allowed by discretion), 92 sites, barbecue - powered sites ✪$17 for two, on-site vans $30-35 for two, cabins $40 for two.
Lismore Lake Caravan Park, Bruxner Highway, ©6621 2585. (Pets on application), 138 sites, pool, barbecue - powered sites ✪$13 for two, cabins $35-45 for two.
Road Runner Caravan Park, Caniaba Road, ©6621 6705. (No pets allowed), 133 sites, tennis, pool - powered sites ✪$14 for two, cabins $40 for two.

Eating Out

The Gollan Hotel, cnr Woodlark and Keen Streets, serves meals, as do most of the hotels. For tasty and reasonably priced meals, try the Golf Club and the local RSL Club. A few additional suggestions are:

Mandarin Palace Chinese Restaurant, 153 Keen Street, 11.30am-2pm and 5pm-8pm 7 days, closed Public Holidays.

Ho Ho International, 67 Wyrallah Road, ©6621 5518. Chinese and international cuisine, open 11am-2pm and 5pm-9pm every day except Tuesdays.

Paupiettes, 56 Ballina Street, ©6621 6135. Open 6.30pm-9.30pm Tue-Sat only.

Mexican Magic, 6 Carrington Street, ©6621 8206.

Giorgios Vegetarian Italia, 73 Magellan Street, ©6622 3177.

The Tempted Palate, 34 Molesworth Street, ©6621 6566.

Lismore Seafood Inn, 25 Eggins Lane, ©6621 3736.

The Loft, 6 Nesbitt Lane, ©6622 0252.

Bangkok Lismore, 44 Ballina Street, ©6621 3375.

Thai Lotus Classic, 207 Ballina Street, ©6622 0062.

If the budget is wearing thin, look for *McDonalds* on the corner of Laurel Avenue and Brewster Street or call *Pizza Hut* on ©13 1166. Otherwise try another of the several take-away establishments in the city, most of which are on Keen, Ballina and Union Streets.

Points of Interest

Lismore was the queen of the river towns last century, as it was as far up river as the trading schooners could reach. The red cedar and other rainforest timber logs from 'The Big Scrub' were floated downstream to Lismore.

Cedar Log Memorial - a giant cedar log is displayed in the small park behind the City Hall as a permanent memorial to the first cedar loggers of the Richmond Valley.

Claude Riley Memorial Lookout, 3km north-east along the New Ballina Cutting, offers a fine view of the city.

Robinson's Lookout, also called Girard's Hill Lookout, is 2km south of the city centre. It offers views of the city, the river and the surrounding countryside.

There is a walking track that joins onto **Wilson's walk**, which starts at Albert Park and is 6.5km (4 miles) long. It takes you through Wilson's Park, a rainforest remnant with many trees identified by plaques where you can spot local bird life.

The Lismore Visitor and Heritage Centre, ©6622 0122, established during the Bicentennial Year, features an unusual walk-through, indoors 'rainforest experience'. Also incorporated in the centre are 'hands on' displays, models and photographic features of Lismore's history.

Lismore Lake is 2.5km from Lismore on the Casino road. There are gas barbecues and a swimming pool, children's playground and a BMX track. It is popular with water skiers.

Heritage Park, near the Visitors Centre, has toilets and gas barbecues.

The Richmond River Historical Society Museum, 165 Molesworth Street, ©6621 9993, contains a fascinating collection of Aboriginal artefacts and pioneer relics, as well as geological specimens.

The Regional Art Gallery, 131 Molesworth Street, ©6622 2209, houses fine collections of paintings, pottery and ceramics.

An **Aboriginal Bora Ring** adjoins Tucki Tucki Cemetery. The Ring overlooks the Steve King's Plain and the mid-Richmond valley. It is one of several tribal ceremonial grounds in the district, and has been fenced and marked with a description board.

Historic River Cruises aboard MV *Bennelong*, a fully licensed cruise boat, sail regularly from Lismore. For bookings, call into their office in Boat Harbour Road, Ballina, or ©0414 664 552 (mobile).

At Alphadale, on the eastern edge of the city, Cowlong Road, is **Macadamia Magic**. This is a macadamia nut processing complex where fac-

Lismore

tory inspections are welcome. The tourist annex specialises in macadamia products and provides refreshments and souvenirs daily, ©6624 2900. It is ⊕open 9am-5pm weekdays and 10am-4pm open weekends.

Festivals

September is the month when it's all happening: The Spring Orchid Show; The Lismore Cup, which is the highlight of the racing calendar in Lismore; The Cedar Guitar Awards; The Spring Greyhound Racing Carnival and the Annual Spring Garden Competition.

The North Coast National Show is held in the third week of October each year.

Facilities

Rolling skating at Summerland Skate Centre, North Lismore; Lismore Grand Prix, South Lismore, is a racing circuit where you are the driver, or where you can enjoy mini-golf.

You can learn to water ski at the Lismore Lake Ski School; The Lismore Bowl is ⊕open daily 9am-midnight for ten-pin bowling.

Lawn bowls, tennis, swimming, squash and golf are all catered for, as well as the traditional spectator sports and seasonal activities, such as the Speedway and Karting programmes.

Chapter 28
Lismore to Gold Coast

The Channon

Location and Characteristics
This is a charming village on Terania Creek, 20km (12 miles) north of Lismore.

Points of Interest
On the second Sunday of every month, the famous **The Channon Craft Market**, the original country market in the area, is held. Only hand-made articles and produce are sold. There is always a colourful crowd with buskers and street theatre, pony rides and games for the kids. Terania Creek, about which there was so much controversy in the 1970s, is now part of the **Nightcap National Park**, in which there are many walking tracks through tropical rainforest and to Protesters' Falls.

The **Wyymara Protea Plantation**, 8 Cooks Lane, Dalwood, ✆6629 5270, has 2000 protea shrubs in production, with many different varieties of fresh and dried protea flowers.

Nimbin

Location and Characteristics
Situated inland, in the centre of an area where the 'hippy' approach to life is very popular, one could say Nimbin was the birthplace of alternative lifestyle in Australia in the late 1960s. It is 30km from Lismore.

Visitor Information
The website at ☞www.nimbin.net will give you an idea of the limited facilities the town offers and a taste of the prevailing attitudes of this small rural community. The email address is ✉thecrew@nimbin.net.au

Accommodation and Services
Nimbin Caravan Tourist Park, 92 Sibley Street, ✆6689 1402. 38 sites, barbecue, car parking, playground - powered sites ✪$19, on-site vans $40.

Points of Interest
The town has a unique style and character of its own, and unusual local crafts may be purchased at the **Nimbin School of Arts Gallery**, 47 Cullen Street.

Nimbin Rocks, or Needles, are unusual rock formations 3km on the Lismore side of Nimbin. They are a sacred site of the Bundjalung Aboriginal Tribe.

The **Tuntable Falls**, 13km (8 miles) from Nimbin, can only be reached by a three hour return hike along the creek bed, and it is a walk only for the fit and healthy.

Kyogle

Population 12,500
Location and Characteristics
Kyogle is a small town 50km (31 miles) inland north-west of Lismore that is known as the Gateway to the Rainforest.

Visitor Information
The town has an Information Centre at the Shire Council in Strathedon Street, ✆(02) 6632 1611.

Accommodation and Services
The **Kyogle Motel** is at 295 Summerland Way, ✆6632 1070. There are 9 units here at ✪$60-80 per night for two.

Points of Interest
From the township it is an easy drive to the spectacular **Border Ranges National Park**.

Each November the town is filled with the excitement and colour of the **Fairymount Festival**.

Byron Bay

Population 5000

Location and Characteristics

42km (26 miles) from Lismore is idyllic Byron Bay - New South Wales' worst-kept secret. More than 500,000 tourists flock here each year, making it the most visited destination outside Sydney. The city is renowned for its relaxed, peaceful atmosphere, and has become a haven for a wide-range of individuals - from alternative youths to corporate high-flyers - retreating from modern life. Ironically, the town associated with serenity is becoming far less serene, unable to cope with the influx of visitors. Traffic during the peak season can be a nightmare in the centre of town. Locals feel suffocated by the tourist demand and have been fiercely battling corporate development in the area. There is even talk of actually *de-marketing* the tourist appeal of the city depite the fact that the industry is the region's major employer. Ultimately, the aim is to restore the calm atmosphere which locals believe is being steadily lost to a metropolitan congestion; which they deliberately left behind in major cities.

Some critics argue that the days of the city's pristine isolation are over and cannot be recovered. When you consider the enjoyment this part of the world offers (such as a stroll along the coastal seascape, kayaking with dolphins out in the bay or trying meditative yoga on a white beach at sunrise), it seems clear that Byron Bay's secret is out for good.

Visitor Information

For further details, the Byron Bay Visitor Information Centre is located at the Old Railway Cottage, Johnson Street, ✆(02) 6685 8050. It is ⏰open 9am-5pm daily. You will find a useful internet reference at 👁www.byronbayvbo.com

Accommodation and Services

There are many places to stay in Byron Bay, with plenty of variety. Here is a sample with prices for a double room per night. The area code is 02.

Beach Hotel, Bay Street, ✆6685 6402. 25 units, licensed restaurant, car parking, spa, heated pool - ✪$190-380.

Lord Byron Resort, 120 Jonson Street, ✆6685 7444. 29 units, licensed restaurant, security parking, heated pool, tennis, 2 spas - ✪$105-220.

Byron Hibiscus Motel, 33 Lawson Street, ✆6685 6195. 7 units,. cooking facilities - ✪$135-275.

Byron Central Apartments, Byron Street, ✆6685 8800. 26 units, barbecue, undercover parking, pool - ✪$65-150.

Byron Sunseeker Motel, 100 Bangalow Road, ✆6685 7369. 12 units, barbecue, recreation room, playground, pool - ✪$90-190.

Caravan Parks

Glen Villa Resort & Tourist Park, Butler Street, ✆6685 7382. (No pets allowed) 50 sites, spa, heated pool - powered sites ✪$20, cabins $80-195.

Clarks Beach Caravan Park, off Lighthouse Road, ✆6685 6496. (No dogs allowed) 134 sites, barbecue, playground - powered sites ✪$21-35, cabins $70-105.

Broken Head Beach Caravan Park, Broken Head Beach Road, ✆6685 3245. (No pets allowed) 115 sites, kiosk - powered sites ✪$22-34, park cabins $50-110.

There is a **Youth Hostel**, **J's Bay**, at 7 Carlyle Street, ✆6685 8853 or ✆1800 678 195 (free call). It has 25 rooms at ✪$25 per person twin share. Another, Cape Byron, is on the corner of Byron and Middleton Streets, ✆6685 8788 or ✆1800 652 627. It has 27 rooms at ✪$25-33 per person twin share.

Points of Interest

The focus here is on recreation and relaxation, so most of the town's services fall into one of these categories. Visit or contact the Information Centre to find the interests that most appeal to you.

Cape Byron is the most easterly point of Australia, topped by an extremely powerful lighthouse built in 1901. The Lighthouse is ⏰open daily 8am-6.30pm.

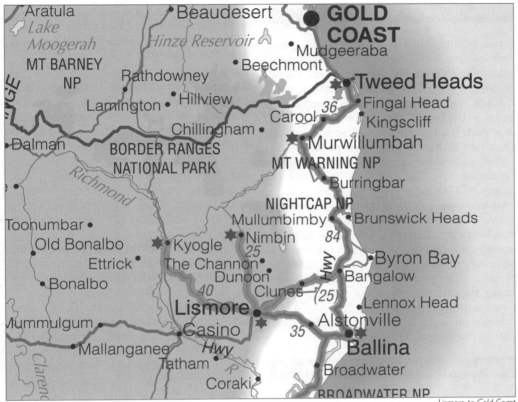

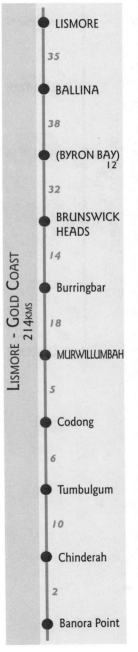

Lismore to Gold Coast

Brunswick Heads

Population 1600

Location and Characteristics

Going back to the coast, Brunswick Heads is a fairly quiet tourist resort. It is 21km (13 miles) from Byron Bay, and is popular with keen fishermen and families.

Visitor Information

When in town, drop into Brunswick Valley Coach and Travel, Park Street, ©6685 1385, for local information. There is a good website at 👁www.tropicalnsw/brunswickheads

Accommodation and Services

Heidleberg Holiday Inn, The Terrace, ©6685 1808. 12 units, licensed restaurant, pool - ✪$60-120.

Chalet Motel, Pacific Highway, ©6685 1257. 12 units, cooking facilities, pool - ✪$55-120.

Ferry Reserve Caravan Park, Pacific Highway, ©6685 1872. (No pets allowed) 142 sites, kiosk - unpowered sites ✪$13-20 for two, cabins from $40 for two.

Points of Interest

Apart from the attraction of the beaches, you will find a sub-tropical **Nature Reserve** located near the Brunswick River. Just north of the town is an alternative route along the coast, passing many popular surfing and fishing beaches, to Kingscliff.

Lismore to Gold Coast

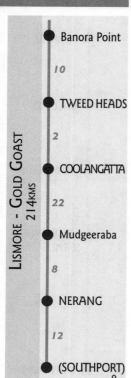

LISMORE - GOLD COAST
214KMS

- Banora Point
  - 10
- TWEED HEADS
  - 2
- COOLANGATTA
  - 22
- Mudgeeraba
  - 8
- NERANG
  - 12
- (SOUTHPORT)
  - 9

Murwillumbah Region

If you wish to visit the Murwillumbah region, drop into the World Heritage Rainforest Visitor Information Centre Murwillumbah, cnr Pacific Highway & Alma Streets, ⏰open Mon-Sat 9am-4.30pm, Sun 9.30am-4pm. They share a web page with Tweed Heads Information at ☞www.tactic.nsw.gov.au, and you can email them here at ✉info@tactic.nsw.gov.au

There is a **Youth Hostel** at 1 Tumbulgum Road, Murwillumbah, ✆6672 3763. They have 16 rooms at ✪$18 per person twin share.

Mt Warning, 1157m (3796 ft), which towers above the Tweed Valley behind Murwillumbah, dominates the scenery for miles around. It was named by Captain Cook in 1770. The area is a National Park, and a walking track winds its way to the top for panoramic views of the Tweed Valley and the coast. The lower slopes are rainforest with heathlands higher up. Ask at the Information Centre about where to start and the current conditions of the climb.

Coolangatta and Tweed Heads

Population 3500 and 55,900 respectively

Location and Characteristics

The twin towns of Coolangatta and Tweed Heads are the southern gateway to the Gold Coast, and occupy opposite headlands of the Tweed River, with Tweed Heads in New South Wales, and Coolangatta in Queensland.

Visitor Information

There is a Visitor Information Centre in Shop 14B, Beachhouse Plaza, Coolangatta Place, cnr Griffith & Warner Streets, Coolangatta, ✆(07) 5536 7765.

For more information on Tweed Heads, contact the Visitor Information Centre at 4 Wharf Street, ✆(07) 5536 4244 or ✆1800 674 414, ⏰open 9am-5pm Mon-Fri, 9am-12pm Saturday. You can email them at ✉info@tactic.nsw.gov.au or visit the web page at ☞www.tactic.nsw.gov.au

Accommodation and Services

Note that although the two towns are divided by a state border, the prefix for all phone numbers is the same: (07).

Coolangatta

Greenmount Beach Resort, 3 Hill Street, ✆5536 1222. 149 units, licensed restaurant (*Fagan's*, Australian and international/Mediterranean cuisine), swimming pool, spa, sauna - ✪$110-140. 2 patrolled beaches on the doorstep, walk to clubs and shopping centres, tours by arrangement, 10min from Gold Coast Airport.

Ocean View, cnr Clark & Marine Parade, ✆5536 3722. 19 units - ✪$55-130. Opposite the popular Twin Town Services Club and Greenmount Beach.

Outrigger Coolangatta Beach Resort, 88 Marine Parade, ✆5506 8787. 121 apartments, heated swimming pool, sauna, spa, secure parking, tennis, gym - ✪$145-285.

Bombora On the Park, Carmichael Close, Goodwin Park, ✆5536 1888. 34 units, licensed restaurant, swimming pool, barbecue - B&B ✪$100.

There is a **Youth Hostel** at 230 Cooloangatta Road, Bilinga, ✆5536 7644. They have 18 rooms at ✪$40-44 per person twin share.

Tweed Heads

Bayswater Motor Inn, 129-131 Pacific Highway, ✆ 5599 4111. 38 units, licensed restaurant, good room facilities, car parking, pool, spa - ✪$90-140.

Tweed Harbour Motor Inn, 135 Pacific Highway, ✆5536 6066. 16 units, basic facilities, pool - ✪$65-95.

City Lights Motel, 35 Old Pacific Highway, ✆5524 3004 or 1800 659 833 (toll free). 17 units, basic facilities, undercover parking, pool - ✪$45-100.

Tweed Fairways Motel, cnr Old Pacific Highway & Soorley Street, ✆5524 2111. 44 units, basic room facilities, pool - ✪$35.

Colonial Tweed Caravan Park, 158 Dry Dock Road, ✆5524 2999. (No pets allowed) 114 sites, kiosk, barbecue, playground, pool - powered sites ✪$18-22 for two, cabins $45-85 for two, on-site vans $30-55 for two.

Tweed Billabong Holiday Park, Holden Street,

©5524 2444. 187 sites, recreation room, barbecue, playground, kiosk, pool, tennis half-court - powered sites ✪$22-35 for two, cabins $50-135 for two.

For shopping, there is **Tweed Mall**, cnr Wharf & Bay Streets, Tweed Heads, ©5536 4066, with over 86 specialty shops. If you're in Coolongatta, the **Coolangatta Shopping Resort** is right on the beach. It is open seven days a week, and apart from the choice of shops, has four cinemas.

Points of Interest

A popular attraction in the Tweed Heads area is **Tropical Fruit World**, ©(02) 6677 7222. It is a tropical fruit plantation with 50 types of tropical and jungle fruit, overlooking the Tweed River, and is an ideal place for a picnic. Safaris, fruit-tasting, boat cruises and live shows are on offer. There is also a cafe. Tropical Fruit World is ⏰open daily 10am-5pm, ✪$25 adults, $14 children, $19 pensioners.

Close to Coolangatta is the lighthouse at **Point Danger**.

Both towns have holiday resort centres, shopping, restaurants and tour facilities, and opportunities for all water sports on the river and the beaches.

The Hinterland

Location and Characteristics

Away from the coastal plain of the Gold Coast, the terrain climbs steadily but steeply up over 1000m (3281 ft) into some of Australia's richest highlands, passing through rolling rural landscapes along the way.

The Hinterland is easily accessible by a number of roads, and offers spectacular views and walking trails into rainforests.

Visitor Information

For the Hinterland region, use the same contact and internet details as for the Gold Coast (*see separate chapter*).

Gold Coast Hinterland

Accommodation and Services

It you wish to spend some time in the mountains, accommodation is available at **Wantalanya Chalets**, Beechmont, ©5533 3520, with 4 units, basic facilities, for ✪$80 a double per night; and at **O'Reilly's Rainforest Guest House**, Lamington National Park Road, ©5544 0644, where accommodation includes all meals, activities, entertainment and tree top walk, and costs ✪$130-210 per person for first class accommodation, and $120 per person for budget rooms.

The town of Nerang is situated at the gateway to the Hinterland, on the Nerang River, and offers accommodation at the **Town & Country Motel**, 2 Nerang-Southport Road, ©5578 4488. There is a licensed restaurant, undercover parking, spa and heated pool for ✪$95-120 per night for two.

Further west is the **Kooralbyn Hotel**, Routley Drive, Kooralbyn, ©5544 6222. It is a leisure-oriented resort covering 25ha (62 acres), with three licensed restaurants, a choice of accommodation styles, spa, sauna, pool, golf, horseriding and more. Prices range from ✪$130-200 per night for two.

Points of Interest

One of the most popular lookouts is called '**The Best of All**' and is reached from Lyrebird Ridge Road. Good views can be also be obtained from **Purlingbrook Falls**, which cascade about 190m (623 ft) to the rocks below. You can walk to the base of the cliff and follow a track that leads behind the falls.

In the **Numinbah Valley**, just within the Queensland border, is the Natural Arch in the

**Lismore
to Gold Coast**

Ballooning over the Gold Coast Hinterland

Natural Arch National Park. Here there are several walks through rainforest, one of which leads to the stone archway through which a waterfall plummets to a rock pool below. There is also a **Glow Worm Cave** for walkers to discover.

Lamington National Park, 45km (28 miles) from the Coast, near the state border, is the largest preserved natural stand of sub-tropical rainforest in Australia, and the park has 160km (100miles) of graded walking tracks leading to many of its highlights, including Mount Merino, Echo Point, Coomera Gorge, Picnic Rock, and the Aboriginal Cooking Caves. In all the park has more than 500 waterfalls, and majestic blackbutt, bloodwood, and giant cedar trees.

Mount Tamborine is a plateau on the McPherson Ranges, 35km (22miles) west of the Gold Coast, and comprises seven small National Parks totalling 375ha (926 acres) of rainforest in which there are 15,000-year-old Macrozamia palms, said to be the oldest living things in the world.

St Bernards historic hotel, one of the mountain's oldest establishments, is famous for its smorgasbord lunches and beautiful gardens, and there are many other guest houses and restaurants in the area.

Other popular spots in the Hinterland are **Rosin's Lookout**, which overlooks the Numinbah Valley, and Mount Warning, off the Nerang-Beechmont Road. **Mount Warning** is the first point in Australia to be struck by the rays of the morning sun, and is an ideal place to unwind and enjoy the natural beauty at the *Springbrook Rainforest Cabins*, 317 Repeater Station Road, Springbrook, ©5533 5366. They have three cottages with full facilities for ✪$80-120 per person per night.

Chapter 29
Gold Coast

Population 275,000
The Gold Coast, Australia's most famous tourist destination, is situated in south-east Queensland.

Climate

Average Temperatures: January max 28C (82F) - min 20C (68F); July max 21C (70F) - min 9C (48F). Average annual rainfall: 1724mm (68 ins); driest months July-September.

Characteristics

The Gold Coast region is made up of the Gold Coast City, Albert and Beaudesert Shires. It covers 4254 sq km (1642 sq miles) and stretches 42km (26 miles) along south-east Queensland's world-famous, sun-drenched coastline and 100km (62 miles) inland into the Gold Coast Hinterland (*see separate listing*). The district has rolling surf, golden beaches, rainforest areas, non-stop entertainment, and millions of visitors every year.

How to Get There
By Air

Qantas, ©13 1313, services the Gold Coast frequently.

The closest airport is at Coolangatta, and there is no problem arranging coach transfers to your hotel anywhere in the Gold Coast area. The following regional services are available:
Coolangatta Airport Transfers, ©5588 8747;
Airporter, ©5588 8777;
SkyTrans, ©3236 1000;
Sunbus, ©5588 8740.
Coach Service to and from Brisbane City, ©13 12 30;
By Coach

Greyhound Pioneer, ©13 2030, and McCaffertys, ©13 1499, stop at the Gold Coast on their Sydney/Brisbane routes.

Greyhound Pioneer has a Brisbane/Gold Coast service, and McCaffertys has a Gold Coast/Toowoomba service.
By Rail

From Sydney, a train to Murwillumbah then a bus to the Gold Coast, ©13 2232.
By Car

From Sydney, via the Pacific Highway 900km (560 miles). From Brisbane, via the Pacific Highway, 79km (49 miles) to Southport, and 100km (62 miles) to Coolangatta.

Visitor Information

There is a Visitors Centre at Cavill Mall, Surfers Paradise, ©(07) 5538 4419, ⏰open 8am-4pm Mon-Fri and 8am-3pm Sat.

You will also find the head office of the Gold Coast Tourism Bureau in Surfers Paradise on Level 2, Ferny Avenue, ©5592 2699. They have a web site at ⊕www.goldcoasttourism.com.au and an email address at ✉info@gctb.com.au

If you require a money exchange facility, Kings Currency Services, Shop G21 Shopping Plaza, Elkhorn Ave, Surfers Paradise, ©5526 9599, places no charges on cash and is ⏰open 7 days, 8.30am-10pm.

Accommodation

Accommodation is not a problem on the Gold Coast. The motels, apartments, guest houses and camping grounds are more dense here than anywhere else in Australia. As a result of this, there is really no need to book in advance, except in school holidays.

Many airlines, bus companies, tour operators, travel bureaux and even the railways offer package holidays, which are very good value.

Here is a selection of accommodation with prices for a double room per night, which should be used as a guide only. The telephone area code is 07.
Coolongatta and Tweed Heads
See separate listing
Currumbin
Sand Castles, 31 Teemangun Street, ©5598

THE GOLD COAST 22KMS

● COOLANGATTA

10

● Burleigh Heads

10

● Surfers Paradise

2

● Southport

Gold Coast

Surfers Paradise

2999. 19 self-contained units, heated swimming pool, spa, barbecue, secure parking - ✪$85-185. Close proximity to Bird Sanctuary. Fronts Currumbin Beach.

Burleigh Heads

Outrigger Resort Gold Coast, 2007 Gold Coast Highway, Burleigh Heads, ✆5535 1111 or ✆1800 641 153 (toll free). 68 units, licensed restaurant, security parking, room service, pool, spa - ✪$90-140.

Fifth Avenue Motel, 1953 Gold Coast Highway (cnr Fifth Avenue), ✆5535 3588. 38 units, licensed restaurant (closed Sunday), swimming pool - ✪$100-180.

Casino Motel, 1761 Gold Coast Highway, ✆5535 7133. 12 units, swimming pool, barbecue - from ✪$45-110. Natural setting adjacent to Burleigh National Park. 250m from Burleigh Point, 300m from Burleigh central shops, 15km from Sea World, 35km from Movie World.

Elite Motel, 1935 Gold Coast Highway, ✆5535 2920. 8 units, barbecue - ✪$35-80.

Burleigh Beach Tourist Park, Goodwin Terrace, Burleigh Heads, ✆5581 7755. Pool adjacent to park, centralised location close to all facilities, 200m from Burleigh Beach, powered sites ✪$20-25 for two, cabins $80-125 for two.

Broadbeach

Conrad Jupiters, Broad Beach Island, ✆5592 1133. Several bars and restaurants including *Andamino's* for fine-dining Italian cuisine. Two-level casino open 24hrs, free admission. Recently renovated showroom: *Innuevre*. Monorail link to Oasis shopping centre and the beach. Hotel offers double rooms ✪$180 and suites $700-1100.

Grand Mercure Broadbeach, Surf Parade, ✆5592 2250. 298 rooms, licensed restaurant, swimming pool, sauna, gym, tennis, undercover parking - ✪$260.

Portobello Beachside, 2607 Gold Coast Highway, ✆5538 7355. 46 units, heated pool, spa, secure parking - from ✪$60-130.

Hi Ho Holiday Motel Apartments, 2 Queensland Avenue, ✆5538 2777. 20 units, swimming pool (heated), spa, barbecue, secure parking - ✪$80-90.

Montego, 2671 Gold Coast Highway, ✆5539 9956. 24 units, salt water pool - ✪$55-135.

Surfers Paradise

Sheraton Mirage Gold Coast, Sea World Drive, Main Beach, ✆5591 1488. 323 rooms, 45 suites, spa, pool, tennis court, gym - from ✪$470-700.

Sea World Nara Resort, Sea World Drive, Main Beach, ✆5591 0000. 391 rooms, heated pool, sauna, spa, gym, tennis court and jetty - ✪$200 (includes entry into theme park).

Surfers Paradise Marriott Resort, 158 Ferny Ave, Surfers Paradise, ✆5592 9800. 300 rooms, undercover parking, gym, heated pool, tennis court, sauna and spa - ✪$200-500.

Gold Coast International Hotel, cnr Gold Coast Highway and Staghorn Avenue, Surfers Paradise, ✆5592 1200. 296 rooms, 21 suites, gym, pool, sauna, spa, tennis half-court - ✪$210-230.

Courtyard by Marriott, cnr Gold Coast Highway and Hanlan Street, Paradise Centre, Surfers Paradise, ✆5579 3499. 405 rooms, tennis, pool (heated), gym, spa, undercover parking - ✪$110-310.

ANA Hotel Gold Coast, 22 View Avenue, Surfers Paradise, ✆5579 1000. 404 rooms, secure parking, tennis, swimming pool (heated), gym, sauna and spa - ✪$290-340.

Parkroyal, 2807 Gold Coast Highway, Surfers Paradise, ✆5592 9900. Security parking, heated pool - ✪$165-240.

Chateau Beachside, cnr The Esplanade & Elkhorn Avenue, Surfers Paradise, ✆5538 1022. 38 rooms, 58 suites, secure parking, pool, sauna, spa, gym - ✪$100-160.

Trickett Gardens Holiday Inn, 24 Trickett Street, Surfers Paradise, ⓒ5539 0988. 31 units, spa, heated pool secure parking, barbecue - ✪$100-135.

Bahia Beachfront Apartments (motel), 154 The Esplanade, Surfers Paradise, ⓒ5538 3322. 30 units, swimming pool, spa, sauna, barbecue - ✪$85-130.

Islander Resort, 6 Beach Road, Surfers Paradise, ⓒ5538 8000. 101 rooms, undercover parking, sauna, spa, tennis and squash, pool - ✪$85-105.

Iluka Beach Resort Hotel, cnr The Esplanade and Hanlan Street, Surfers Paradise, ⓒ5539 9155. 71 suites, 32 units, restaurant, secure parking, heated pool - ✪$80-100.

Pink Poodle, 2903 Gold Coast Highway, Surfers Paradise, ⓒ5539 9211. 21 units, spa, pool (salt water) - ✪$80-130.

Durham Court, 21 Clifford Street, Surfers Paradise, ⓒ5592 1855. 16 units, secure parking, swimming pool - ✪$50-150.

D'Arcy Arms Motel, 2923 Gold Coast Highway, Surfers Paradise, ⓒ5592 0892. 17 units, 1 suite, licensed restaurant (closed Sunday), swimming pool (heated), spa, barbecue - ✪$70-110.

Main Beach Tourist Park, Main Beach Parade, Gold Coast, ⓒ5581 7722. (No pets allowed) 170 sites, playground, pool - powered sites $20-23, self-contained sites $25-29.

There is a **Youth Hostel** in Mariners Cove, 70 Seaworld Drive, Main Beach, ⓒ5571 1776. They have 29 rooms at ✪$24 per person twin share.

Southport

Swan Lane Apartments, cnr Queens & Swan Lane, ⓒ5528 1900. 10 units, security parking, tennis pool (heated) - ✪$120.

Park Regis Hotel, 2 Barney Street, Southport, ⓒ5532 7922. 79 rooms, car parking, pool - ✪$210-280.

Earls Court Motor Inn, 131 Nerang Street, Southport, ⓒ5591 4144. 34 units, 3 suites, undercover parking, salt water pool - ✪$65-95 (unit), $75-120 (suite).

Southport Tourist Park, 6 Frank Street, Gold Coast Highway, Southport, ⓒ5531 2281. 55 sites, powered sites ✪$20-30 for two, cabins $45-100 for two, caravans $35-80 for two.

Broadwater Tourist Park, Gold Coast Tourist Highway, Southport, ⓒ5581 7733. 307 sites - powered sites ✪$30-35 for two.

Sanctuary Cove

Hyatt Regency Sanctuary Cove, Manor Circle, Casey Road, ⓒ5530 1234. 247 rooms, 24 suites, golf, gym, marina, pool, sauna and spa - ✪$200-240.

Sanctuary Shores Resort, 1 Pinnaroo Street, ⓒ5530 1111. 12 units, Putter's restaurant, spa, pool - ✪$80-95.

Outlying Areas

All Seasons Mermaid Waters Hotel, cnr Markeri Street & Sunshine Boulevard, Mermaid Beach, ⓒ5572 2500. 102 units, 14 suites, barbecue, room service, swimming pool - ✪$110-150.

Runaway Bay Motor Inn, 429 Oxley Drive, Runaway Bay, ⓒ5537 5555. 40 units, 3 suites, secure parking, swimming pool (heated, salt water) - ✪$105-170.

Coomera Motor Inn, Dreamworld Parkway, Coomera, ⓒ5573 2311. 31 units, heated pool, licensed restaurant, playground, room service - ✪$85-100.

Billinga Beach Resort, 281 Golden Four Drive, Billinga Beach, ⓒ5534 1241. 23 units, 3 divided rooms, pool, undercover parking - ✪$60-150.

Limassol, 109 Frank Street, Labrador, ⓒ5591 6766. 14 units, salt water pool - ✪$50-110.

Camden Colonial Motor Inn, 2371 Gold Coast Highway, Mermaid Beach, ⓒ5575 1066. 15 units, undercover parking, spa, salt water pool - ✪$60-110.

El Rancho, 2125 Gold Coast Highway, Miami, ⓒ5572 3655. 8 units, 1 suite, barbecue, pool, spa, playground - ✪$35-60.

Caravan Parks

Ocean Beach Tourist Park Miami, 2 Hythe Street, Miami, ⓒ5581 7711. Shared facilities, barbecue. 81 sites ✪$18-22, 58 powered sites $20-25.

Runaway Bay Caravan Park, 20 Bayview Street, Runaway Bay, ⓒ5537 1636. 83 powered sites ✪$19-21.

Miami Caravan Park, 2200 Gold Coast Highway, Miami, ⓒ5572 7533. Kiosk, barbecue, no pets allowed, 200 sites - powered sites ✪$16-19.

Gold Coast

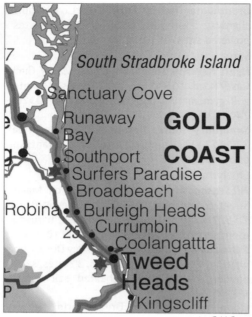

Gold Coast

Local Transport

Shuttle

There is an efficient and economical public transport system. Gold Coast Tourist Shuttle Bus Service, ✆1300 655 655 provides unlimited travel day or night for the one price. It travels from one end of the coastal strip to the other. 1 day pass: adult ✪$14, child $8, family $32. Theme park transfers also available.

Car Rentals

Car rental companies that have offices on the Gold Coast, include:

Red Back Rentals, ✆5592 1655. Open 7 days.

CY Rent A Car, Surfers International Arcade Shop 14, 9 Trickett Street, Surfers Paradise, ✆5570 3777.

Freeway Rent-A-Car, Zircon Avenue, ✆5591 1155. Open 7 days.

Network Car & Truck Rentals, cnr Gold Coast Highway & Palm Avenue, Surfers Paradise, ✆5538 2344.

A.B.L., Gold Coast Airport, ✆5598 3900. Open 7 days.

Tweed Auto Rentals, 4 Wharf Street, Tweed Heads, ✆5536 8000. Open 7 days.

Sunny Top, cnr Gold Coast Hwy & Surfers Ave, Mermaid Beach, ✆5578 6633. Open 7 days.

Suncoast, 3005 Gold Coast Hwy, ✆5592 4087.

Always Affordable, ✆5593 6026. Open 7 days.

Budget, cnr Ferry Ave & Norfolk Ave, ✆1300 362 848.

East Coast, 25 Elkhorn Ave, Surfers Paradise, ✆5592 0444.

Bargain Wheels, ✆5534 4544.

Costless, 3269 Gold Coast Hwy, Surfers Paradise, ✆5538 8400.

Anthony's Ezy-Drive, ✆5534 6022. Open 7 days.

Can Do, 3084 Gold Coast Hwy, Surfers Paradise, ✆55 925 887. Open 7 days.

Or you can rent a Pedicab, a moped (Moped Hire, cnr Hamilton Ave & Gold Coast Hwy, Surfers Paradise, ✆5592 4087) or a bicycle. At the other end of the scale, you can splurge and hire a stretch limousine.

For full information on all these options, contact the Tourist Information Centres, or browse the Yellow Pages telephone directory.

Combined Rail, Bus and Ferry

South East Explorer, ✆13 12 30. All day travel on participating services, Explorer ticket 1 - ✪$10, Explorer ticket 2 - ✪$16, Explorer ticket 3 - ✪$24.

Bus

Surfside Bus Timetables. For information on routes phone ✆ 13 12 30.

Coach

The following services are available:

Gold Coast Get Around, ✆1300 361 966;

Theme Park Transfers, ✆1800 426 224;

Coach Charter, ✆55 888 780.

Eating Out

The Gold Coast is said to have the largest collection of restaurants per square kilometre in Australia, and indeed there are more than 500 different restaurants on the coastal strip. You can eat and drink riverside, seaside, inside or outside. Almost every national cuisine is represented, and you can choose from licensed or BYO. The only problem is making up your mind which restaurant is going to get your patronage, and this is taken care of by phoning the Restaurant Infoline, ☎916 699, for information and bookings. Here is a taste of the wide selection, from low to lavish prices:

Four Winds Restaurant, in the Parkroyal, 2807 Gold Coast Highway. Surfers Paradise, ☎5592 9906. Seafood and Asian buffet, revolving restaurant 26 floors above the city, all-you-can-eat, open 7 days for lunch and 2 dinner sittings.

Rakugaki, 2nd Floor, Centre Arcade, Surfers Paradise, ☎5539 8741. BYO Japanese cuisine, lunch Mon-Fri (12pm-2pm), dinner Mon-Sat (6pm-10.30pm).

Hattie's Seafood Restaurant, ANA Hotel, 22 View Ave, Surfers Paradise, ☎5579 1000.

Cafe Carinya, ANA Hotel, 22 View Ave, Surfers Paradise, ☎5579 1000. Seafood buffet lunch 7 days a week - $25, huge seafood buffet nightly - $33.

Frenchy's Seafood Restaurant, Mariners Cove, Sea World Drive, Main Beach, ☎5531 3030. Licensed or BYO.

The Aztec, Victoria Square, Broadbeach Mall, ☎5538 8477. Mexican cuisine, licensed, open 7 days, lunch and dinner.

Montezuma's, Aloha Building, 8 Trickett Street, Surfers Paradise, ☎5538 4748. Mexican, licensed.

Pancakes in Paradise, cnr Gold Coast Hwy & Clifford St, ☎5592 0330. Licensed, open 7 days, lunch and dinner.

Bavarian Haus, cnr Cavill Ave & Gold Coast Hwy, Surfers Paradise, ☎5531 7150. German cuisine as well as steak, seafood, chicken and pasta, authentic Bavarian theme and atmosphere, live shows. Breakfast, morning & afternoon tea, lunch and dinner.

The Crab Cooker, cnr Gold Coast Hwy & Thornton St, Surfers Paradise, ☎5538 6884. Seafood and steak restaurant, licensed, indoor and outdoor dining, lunch and dinner.

Holy Mackeral, 174 Marine Pde, Labrador, ☎5531 1017. Seafood, licensed, open 7 days, lunch and dinner.

Times Cafe Restaurant, cnr Elkhorn Ave & Gold Coast Hwy, Surfers Paradise, ☎5538 3211. Steak, seafood and pasta, open 7 days. Breakfast, lunch and dinner

Mikado, cnr Elkhorn Ave & Gold Coast Hwy, Surfers Paradise, ☎5538 2788. Japanese cuisine including traditional sushi and teppanyaki dishes, open 7 days.

Imperial Palace, cnr Elkhorn Ave & Gold Coast Hwy, Surfers Paradise, ☎5538 9544, Chinese restaurant, open 7 days.

Mango's, Tiki Village, Cavill Avenue, Surfers Paradise, ☎5531 6177. Modern international cuisine with an emphasis on seafood, open 7 nights, dinner.

Grumpy's Wharf, Mariners Cove, 60-70 Seaworld Drive, The Spit, Main Beach, ☎5532 2900. Seafood, lunch Fri-Sun, dinner 7 days.

Rusty Pelican, cnr Orchid Ave & Elkhorn Ave, Surfers Paradise, ☎5570 3073. Lunch 11.30am-10.30pm, licensed until midnight, open 7 days.

Seashells Restaurant, at the Novotel Beachcomber, 18 Hanlan St, Surfers Paradise, ☎5570 1000. International seafood buffet.

Hard Rock Cafe, cnr Cavill Ave & Gold Coast Hwy, Surfers Paradise, ☎5539 9377. Restaurant open 7 days 12pm-late.

Cav's Steakhouse, 30 Frank St, Labrador, ☎5532 2954. Licensed, steak, seafood, pasta and salad. McDonalds is on the corner of Cavill Mall and The Esplanade. Pizza Hut is in Raptis Plaza, Cavill Avenue, ☎13 11 66. There is an abundance of fast food eateries in the area, and the selection will guarantee that you are not left wanting.

Entertainment

For after-dinner entertainment, you can choose between cabarets, discos, live bands, top international performers, sophisticated night clubs, poker machine palaces, and the world famous Jupiter's Casino. Or you can opt for something completely different - the bizarre Dracula's Cabaret restaurant. Here are a few venues:

Dracula's Cabaret Restaurant, 1 Hooker Blvd, Broadbeach, ☎5575 1000, comedy entertainment, dinner and show, bookings essential.

Inneuvre, at Conrad Jupiters Casino, ☎1800 074 144, live theatre, comedy, dance, music, circus acts.

Crazies Comedy Box, Sunshine Blvd, Broadbeach, ©5592 0755, dinner and live show.

Shopping

The Gold Coast is like one massive shopping centre, and in fact Surfers Paradise is known to some as 'Shoppers Paradise'. There are dozens of shopping centres, of every shape and size, and it is rumoured that some people never actually see the beach. To help you find your way through this consumers' paradise, the following list can be used as a guide:

On the Broadwater Spit is the stylish *Marina Mirage*, which offers good shopping, an aviary, and several food outlets including a 50s rock 'n' roll cafe with its own FJ Holden.

Sanctuary Cove, 20 minutes' drive north of Surfers, has the Marine Shopping Village, ©5577 6011, with over 80 specialty shops and its own brewery offering Bavarian style beer - Island Lager.

Australia Fair, Marine Parade, Southport, ©5532 8811. Over 230 specialty stores, ©open 7 days.

Pacific Fair Shopping Centre, Hooker Blvd, Broadbeach, ©5539 8766. Queensland's largest shopping centre with over 260 specialty stores and 12 cinemas, ©open 7 days.

Mariora Australia, 3290 Gold Coast Highway, Surfers Paradise, ©5538 9899. Opal retailer.

DFS Galleria, cnr Cavill Ave & Gold Coast Highway, Surfers Paradise, ©5570 9401. Duty free and tax free, ©open 7 days 8.30am-10pm

Nerang Disposals, 6 Spencer Rd, Nerang, ©5596 4434. Camping and outdoor store.

Carrara Markets, Nerang-Broadbeach Rd, along the road west of Pacific Fair. 500 stalls, open all day every Saturday and Sunday.

Fashion Factory Outlet, 4107 Ferry Rd, Southport, ©5531 1837. Ladies' fashion and lingerie, men's and children's fashion, swimwear, ©open 7 days 9am-5pm.

Marina Mirage, Sea World Drive, Main Beach, ©5577 0088. ©Open 7 days 10am-6pm.

Paradise Centre, Cavill Ave, Surfers Paradise, ©5592 0155. Over 120 shops, ©open 7 days.

Robina Town Centre, off Robina Pkwy, Robina,

©5575 0480. More than 200 specialty shops and 6 cinemas.

Raptis Plaza, Cavill Mall & The Esplanade, Surfers Paradise, ©5592 2123. Home to a full-size replica of Michelangelo's David, which stands in the Food Court. Open 7 days 10am-late.

The Oasis, Victoria Ave, Broadbeach, ©5592 3900. Over 100 specialty stores, direct link to Jupiters Casino via monorail.

Runaway Bay Shopping Village, Lae Drive, Runaway Bay, ©5537 2566. Over 100 specialty stores, Boardwalk Foodcourt, water views, ©open 7 days.

Sportsmans Warehouse, 32 Strathaird Rd, Bundall, ©5531 6511. Australia's largest sporting warehouse, free bus from Surfers Paradise, open 7 days.

Niecon Plaza, Broadbeach Central Mall, Victoria Ave, Broadbeach, ©5531 6659. Licensed bar, al fresco cafes.

Points of Interest

The main attractions are, of course, the beaches - and there are plenty of them, all offering clean, golden sand, and sparkling surf. But the Gold Coast has much more to offer, with special attractions in every town.

Southport

Situated across the Broadwater from The Spit, Southport was the first settlement in the Gold Coast, having been established in 1875. It is now the business and commercial centre for the region, along with neighbouring Labrador, Biggera Waters and Runaway Bay.

Inland from Southport, on the Pacific Highway, is the **Wet'n'Wild Water World**, ©5573 2255, with a giant fresh water wild wavepool that has one metre surf and its own lifeguards. The park also has Wild Billy the surfing kangaroo, white water twisters, and a breathtaking toboggan drop. The latest addition is the Super 8 Aqua Racer. The water park is ©open daily from 10am. Adults ©$31, children and pensioners $20.

Further north along the Pacific Highway brings you to **Koala Town**, where you can cuddle a koala and see the many animals that lived on

Old MacDonald's Farm. Also featured are sheep shearing and horse shoeing demonstrations.

Continuing north, you come to **Dreamworld**, Dreamworld Parkway, ☏5588 1111. It comprises 100ha (247 acres) of landscaped gardens and Australian bushland featuring nine wonderful worlds of fantasy, including 16 rides, seven live shows, a tiger exhibit, and the Imax Theatre with a six-storey high screen that creates an experience of light and sound which makes the viewer feel part of the film. The new Giant Drop and Tower of Terror are the fastest and tallest rides in the world. Dreamworld is ◷open every day, and is an experience that should not be missed. Adults ✪$52, children and concession $32.

Almost opposite Dreamworld is **Warner Bros Movie World**, ☏5573 8485, which is based on the world-famous Hollywood movie set. Terrific theme rides such as Lethal Weapon and Batman Adventure lead the attractions. Movie World has movie-making facilities, which are used for actual productions. Entry costs adults ✪$52, children and pensioners $33. The live shows are a must-see.

Lethal Weapon, Movie World

Further north is the **Le Mans Kart Racing Complex**, Pacific Highway, Pimpana Tourist Area, ☏55 46 6 566. There is a 700m circuit with fast karts and timed laps. No licence is necessary, but age restrictions do apply for safety reasons. The complex is ◷open 7 days 10am-5pm. ✪$28 for 7 laps, $33 for 10 laps.

Not far away, for those who are fascinated by (maybe obsessed with) the amber liquid, the **Carlton Brewhouse**, cnr Mulles Rd & Pacific Highway, Yatala, ☏3826 5858, offers 45min brewery tours at 10am, 12pm and 2pm - adults ✪$8, concession $3, children $3.

Surfers Paradise

The heart of the Gold Coast, Surfers Paradise is the ultimate tourist resort, and its malls and avenues are crammed with a multitude of places to eat, drink, shop, see and be seen. Condominiums abound, rising skyward one after another amid lush vegetation and island upon island reclaimed from the sea. It has been described as 'a pristine Miami Beach'.

For entertainment there are performances by international stars, spectacular revues, cabaret shows, top restaurants, intimate bars, discos, and dinner cruises departing from the Nerang River on the western side of Surfers. There are several different cruises, from a two-hour 'scones and cream' tour, to a tropical luncheon feast, a night shipboard cabaret, a twilight trip, or a raging disco.

For family fun, right in the centre of town is **Grundy's Paradise Centre**, with over 300 different activities in the one complex, ranging from games of skill to the latest electronic arcade machines.

In Raptis Plaza, Cavill Mall, there is the only Odditorium in the southern hemisphere, which in true **Believe It Or Not!** tradition has six-legged calves, bearded women, Siamese twins and many more exhibits. The museum is ◷open 7 days 9am-11pm, ☏5592 0040. Entry fees: adults ✪$12, concession $8, family discounts available.

The Centre, the Gold Coast's entertainment and arts complex, is on Chevron Island, and has all types of theatrical performances from opera to pantomime. There is also an Art Gallery which has changing exhibitions.

For a cool change to the typically humid climate, **Frozen World**, cnr Ocean Avenue & Gold Coast Highway, ☏5570 3922, offers mini-golf on ice, exhibitions of ice sculptures and carvers, a snow and ice playground, and a kids' club. Warm jackets are supplied for those who neglected to pack for snowy conditions on the Gold Coast. Adults ✪$17, children $9 (under 4 years free), conces-

Gold Coast

sion $12, family pass $42.

To the north of Surfers is **Main Beach**, fast becoming the 'best address' on the Coast, and nearby is the **Broadwater**, which offers still water swimming as an alternative to the open surf.

On Broadwater Spit is Australia's famous marine theme park, **Sea World**, ©5588 2205, which has the country's first monorail, the Three Loop Corkscrew, and Free Fall Water Slide, performing dolphins, killerwhales, sea lions, water skiing shows, and lots more. The most recent attraction is a 3D Pirate adventure. Sea World is ©open every day from 10am, and you are advised to get there early if you want to see and do everything available. Adults ✪$52, pensioners and children $33.

Another attraction on the Spit is **Fishermans Wharf**, which has a swimming pool, children's playground, and live band performances on the weekend.

Broadbeach

The town is internationally famous as the site of **Jupiter's Casino**, and the Gold Coast's first world-class hotel, the $185 million Hotel Conrad. A monorail links the casino with the Oasis-On-Broadbeach Shopping Resort and the Pan Pacific Hotel.

Burleigh Heads

Burleigh is the half-way point between Coolangatta and Surfers, and hosts one of the greatest week-long surfing events in Australia, held in March each year.

The town has a more relaxed atmosphere than Coolangatta or Surfers, and many people choose to stay here, and visit the other two when they want to get into the action. If you are into bushwalking, there is a 3km graded track that meanders among the habitat of koalas and bandicoots in the **Burleigh Heads National Park**.

The Gold Coast Highway then continues past the surfing beaches of Miami, Nobby's and Mermaid to Broadbeach.

Currumbin

Situated about 6km (4 miles) north of Coolangatta, past the settlements of Kirra, Bilinga and Tugun, Currumbin is home to the world-famous **Currumbin Wildlife Sanctuary**, Gold Coast Highway, Currumbin, ©5534 1266, a 20ha (50 acres) wildlife reserve with the the world's largest collection of Australian native fauna. The Sanctuary is visited every morning and afternoon by thousands of brightly coloured wild Rainbow Lorikeets, which don't need much encouragement to eat out of your hand, or sit on your head, and seem to love having their photographs taken. Also at the Sanctuary, which is ©open daily 8am-5pm, are waterfalls, rainforest pools, and 250 individual species of birdlife, including the glossy black cockatoo. Entry fees: adults ✪$18, children $22, under 4 years old free, family pass $48.

North of Currumbin are Pacific and Palm Beaches.

Festivals

January - The Magic Millions Horse Race Meeting. The Daikyo Palm Meadows Golf Cup.

July - Gold Coast International Marathon and Half-Marathon.

August - The Jupiter's Yacht Classic between Sydney and the Gold Coast.

November - The Queensland Open Golf.

Sports and Facilities ˙

The Gold Coast has all the facilities you could think of. You can play tennis, squash, golf, ten-pin bowling, lawn bowls or croquet, and go rollerskating or horseriding.

You can fish, swim, waterski, sailboard, sail, and more. There are also facilities for horse racing, greyhound racing, hot-air ballooning, mountain trekking, parasailing and many health and fitness centres.

Below are some of the sporting choices.

Golf

The Palms Golf Course, Santuary Cove, ©5577 6031.

Palm Meadows Golf Course, Palm Meadows Resort, Gooding Drive, Palm Meadows, ©1800 818 040.

Putt & Games, cnr Crescent Ave & Gold Coast Hwy, Mermaid Beach, ©5575 3381. ©Open 7 days.

Concept Golf Tours, ☎5578 8288, provide golfing packages from ❖$90 including green fees, cart hire and transfer to your desired resort course.

Shooting

Australian Shooting Academy, Lvl 1 Paradise Centre, Surfers Paradise, ☎5527 5100. ⏱Open 7 days, 10am-10pm.

Southport Indoor Pistol Club, Unit 1 76 Ferry Rd, Southport, ☎5531 1153. ⏱Open 7 days 10am-10pm.

Watersports

Shane's Watersports World, Harley Park, Labrador, ☎5591 5225. Paraflying, speedboat ride, jet ski ride.

Aussie Bob's Watersports, Berth 14D Marina Mirage, Sea World Drive, Main Beach, ☎5591 7577, parasailing, jet skis, speed boat rides, direct bookings only.

Fishing

Topline Sport Fishing Safaris, ☎5577 1953. Fresh and salt water fishing, tackle and refreshments provided, full day ❖$110pp, half day $60pp.

Paul Burt's Reel Action Fishing Charters, ☎5596 5546. Both deep sea reef (half day ❖$85pp, full day $125pp) and estuary (half day ❖$55pp, full day $105pp) fishing available.

Extreme Sports

Fly Coaster, Cypress Ave, Surfers Paradise, ☎5539 0474. Free-fall 11 stories on Australia's first extremist swing, ⏱open daily until 10pm.

Bungee Rocket, cnr Palm Ave & Gold Coast Hwy, Surfers Paradise, ☎5570 2700. Rocket to a height of 50m in just over a second, ⏱open 7 days 10am-10pm.

Tours and Cruises

If you have the time and desire to become intimate with the Gold Coast environment, the following selection of tours and cruises should cover all the aspects.

Tall Ship Sailing Cruises, Wharf D12 Marina Mirage, ☎5532 2444. Four different cruises, ship sails 9am daily.

Amphibious Aquabus Canal Cruises, Aquabus Safaris, 7A Orchid Ave, Surfers Paradise, ☎5539 0222, combined bus tour and canal cruise, bookings recommended, departs frequently throughout the day, 7 days, adults ❖$28, children $21, seniors $23.

Gold Coast Kayaking, ☎5527 5785. Offers morning tour or afternoon kayak snorkle tour, 9am-9pm, 7 days

Aries Tours, 16 Barnett Pl, Ernest, ☎5594 9933. Focus on eco-tourism, choices include a Southern Skytour (5.30pm-10.30pm nightly), a Kingfisher Hinterland Tour (8am-2pm daily) and a Night Safari Tour (5.30pm-10.30pm nightly).

Tweed Endevour Cruises, Tweed River Cruise Terminal, River Terrace, Tweed Heads, ☎5536 8800. Offers 4hr rainforest & river cruise or 1.5hr river and lake cruise, lunch included, bookings essential.

Island Queen Showboat Cruises, Marina Mirage, Main Beach, ☎5571 0219. A number of cruises with various destinations, lengths and themes, prices on application.

Whale Watch, Moreton Island, ☎5591 5599. Luxury coach transfers, meals provided on cruise.

Day Tours, ☎3236 4165. Various coach tours.

Chapter 30
Brisbane

Population 1,601,416
Brisbane, the capital city of Queensland, is situated on the banks of the Brisbane River, 32km (20 miles) upstream from Moreton Bay.

Climate

Average temperatures: January max 30C (86F) - min 19C (66F); July max 18C (64F) - min 6C (43F). Average annual rainfall - 1148mm (45 ins).

Characteristics

Brisbane, the capital of the Sunshine State, is a major international and interstate gateway to an exciting hub of tourism in the Pacific.

The sub-tropical city enjoys an easy-going, relaxed lifestyle, and offers the visitor a great introduction to the holiday resort destinations of the Gold Coast, and the less developed Sunshine Coast.

Just 20 minutes from the city centre you can see (and hold) koalas in their natural habitat at Lone Park Koala Sanctuary or watch sheep shearing at the Australian Woolshed. Brisbane Forest Park, with its abundant fauna and flora, not to mention rainforest, is right on the doorstep. So too are the islands of Moreton Bay - all 300 of them.

In the last decade, Brisbane has turned to the river, and fairly recent developments like Southbank and The Riverside Centre, famous for its popular Sunday craft markets, Waterfront Place, have changed the look of the city. A sightseeing cruise on the paddlewheeler, *River Queen*, is a highlight of any visit to the city.

How to Get There
By Air

As you would expect of a capital city, the Brisbane Airport is well-serviced.

International flights arrive direct from New Zealand, Asia & Pacific, Britain and Europe.

North America is linked via Sydney and Auckland.

The domestic carrier Qantas, ✆13 1313 has direct flights from/to Australian capital cities and selected major regional towns. At present, Virgin Blue, ✆13 6789, and Ansett, ✆13 1300, operate from eastern state capital cities only.

By Bus

Greyhound Pioneer, ✆13 2030, and McCaffertys, ✆13 1499, have the following return services: Brisbane/Sydney, Brisbane/Cairns with connections to Darwin and Alice Springs, and Brisbane/Melbourne.

By Rail

Queensland Rail, ✆13 2232, operates a Traveltrain service that links destinations around the state. Citytrains (✆131 230) run north from Brisbane to the Sunshine Coast and south to the Gold Coast. The Queenslander and Sunlander are two additional services connecting Brisbane to areas as far north as Cairns. The Capricornian links the capital city with Rockhampton.

From Sydney, Countrylink XPT trains run directly to Brisbane daily. Alternatively, you can take the XPT to Murwillumbah and change to a connecting coach to complete the journey.

From Melbourne, you must take a Countrylink train to Sydney and then change trains for the next leg of the trip.

By Road

From Sydney, via the Pacific Highway along the coast - 1001km (622 miles); or inland via the New England and Cunningham High-ways - 1033km (642 miles).

Visitor Information

The Brisbane Visitor Information Centre is situated in the Queen Street Mall, ✆(07) 3006 6290. It is ⏰open Mon-Fri 9am-5pm, Sat 9am-4pm, Sun 10am-4pm. Their email address is ✉enquiries@brisbanetourism.com.au and the website to visit is ☞www.brisbanetourism.com.au

The Queensland Travel Centre, 30 Makerston Street, ✆13 8833, is ⏰open Mon-Fri 8.30am-5pm, Sat 9am-1pm. They can be emailed at

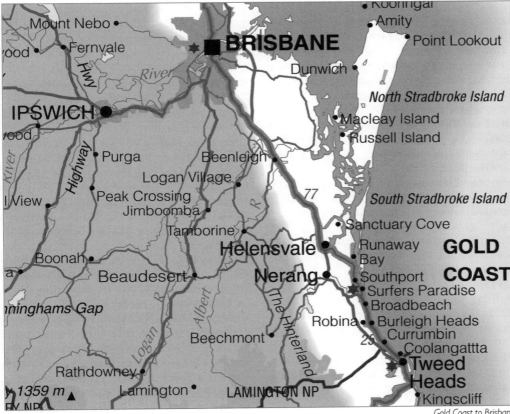

Gold Coast to Brisbane

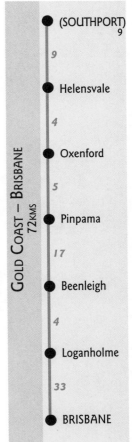

Brisbane

GOLD COAST – BRISBANE
72KMS

- (SOUTHPORT) 9
  - 9
- Helensvale
  - 4
- Oxenford
  - 5
- Pinpama
  - 17
- Beenleigh
  - 4
- Loganholme
  - 33
- BRISBANE

queensland@qttc.com.au or visited at the website www.tq.com.au

Tourism Queensland, Level 36, Riverside Centre, 123 Eagle Street, (07) 3406 5400, is open Mon-Fri 9am-5pm.

Two other internet addresses worth visiting are the Brisbane section of www.queensland-holidays.com.au or the local coucil website at www.brisbane.qld.gov.au

For Backpacker Budget Beaters, contact the Brisbane Visitor Information Centre. They offer a number of activities with reduced prices, such as $10 return ferry to nearby North Stradbroke Island, where you can go bushwalking and dolphin spotting.

The newspaper, the *Courier-Mail* publishes a travel section every Friday, which details drives, picnic and camping spots.

Emergency telephone numbers: Police, Fire Department, Ambulance - 000; Doctor - Travellers Medical Service - 3211 3611; Police Station - 3364 6464.

The Royal Automobile Club of Queensland has a breakdown service, 131 111.

Banks are open 9.30am-4pm Mon-Thu, and until 5pm on Fri. Major banks are are represented by branches in the city centre, chiefly on Queen and Adelaide Streets.

The Australian Foreign Affairs Department is in the Commonwealth Centre, 295 Ann Street, 3225 0122.

Accommodation

Brisbane has several 5-star international hotels, older style hotels, motels, guest houses, private hotels and many youth hostels. As with any large city, accommodation in the suburbs is often less expensive than in the city itself, and the Tourist Information Centres has a list of what is available.

Here we have a selection of city hotels and motels, with prices for a double room per night, which should be used as a guide only. The telephone area code is 07.

Brisbane Hilton, 190 Elizabeth Street, ©3234 2000 - 320 rooms, 6 suites, licensed restaurant, heated swimming pool, spa, sauna, gym, tennis - ✪$255-330.

Sheraton Brisbane Hotel & Towers, 249 Turbot Street, ©3835 3535. 410 rooms, 25 suites, licensed restaurant, bistro, swimming pool, spa, sauna, gym, squash - ✪$150-320.

Country Comfort Lennons Hotel, 66 Queen Street, ©3222 3222. 187 rooms, licensed restaurant, heated swimming pool, spa, sauna - ✪$125-180.

Holiday Inn Brisbane, Roma Street, ©3238 2222. 191 rooms, 27 suites, licensed restaurant, sauna, undercover carpark, spa, gym - ✪$105-150.

The Chifley on George, 103 George Street, ©3221 6044. 99 rooms, licensed restaurant, swimming pool, putting green, spa - ✪$120-140.

Metropolitan Motor Inn, 106 Leichhardt Street (cnr Little Edward Street), ©3831 6000. 54 units, licensed restaurant - ✪$90.

Astor Motel, 193 Wickham Terrace, ©3831 9522. 61 units, 17 suites - ✪$65-100.

Soho Motel, 333 Wickham Terrace, ©3831 7722. 50 units, licensed restaurant, undercover parking - ✪$80.

Ruth Fairfax House - QCWA Club (B&B), 89 Gregory Terrace, ©3831 8188. 36 rooms, communal tea making and refrigerator - ✪$70 including breakfast and dinner.

Acacia Inner City, 413 Upper Edward Street, ©3832 1663. 57 rooms - ✪$50-70.

The latest additions to the Brisbane skyline are:
Mercure Hotel Brisbane, 85 North Quay, ©3236 3300. 175 rooms, 15 suites, spa, sauna, licensed restaurant, room service, swimming pool - ✪$130-180.

The Point On Shaftson, 21 Lambert Street, Kangaroo Point, ©3240 0888. 106 rooms, gym, heated pool, tennis court, children's area - from ✪$110-180.

Caravan Parks

Colonial Village Motel, 351 Beams Road, Taigum, ©3865 0000. Licensed restaurant, tennis, pool - powered sites ✪$20 for two, cabins $55-65 for two.

Dress Circle Mobile Village, 10 Holmead Road, Eight Mile Plains, ©3341 6133. Pool, barbecue - powered sites ✪$30 for two, cabins $80-100 for two.

Sheldon Motel & Caravan Park, 27 Holmead Road, Eight Mile Plains, ©3341 6166. Pool, barbecue - powered sites ✪$16 for two, cabins $55 for two.

Gateway Village, 200 School Road, Rochedale, ©3341 6333. 148 sites, barbecue, pool, playground, recreation room - powered sites ✪$24 for two, villas $85-100 for two.

Durack Gardens Caravan Park, 758 Blunder Road, Durack, ©3372 7300. Tennis, pool, barbecue - powered sites ✪$17 for two, on-site vans $25 for two, cabins $45 for two.

There is a **Youth Hostel** at 392 Upper Roma Street, ©3236 1004. It has 52 rooms at ✪$22 per person twin share. **Palace Backpackers** is an alternative, located at 308 Edward Street, ©3211 2433.

Local Transport
Bus
Bus routes and timetables can be downloaded from the ◉www.transinfo.qld.gov.au webpage, or you can phone ©13 12 30 (interstate callers: ©07 3215 500).

As a basic guide, the CityCircle bus (333) is blue and white, and travels around the centre of the city frequently. The white and yellow Citybuses service the city and suburbs, with many stops in between. Buses with blue and yellow stripes are the Cityxpress buses, which have express routes every half hour from designated stops. Buses to most suburbs leave from the city terminal. Day Rover tickets are available for ✪$8, entitling you to unlimited trips on

Brisbane and the Brisbane River

all public buses, ferries and City Cats. Fare saver cards are also available. Buses to the Redcliffe Peninsula operate daily from outside the Transit Centre.

The *City Sights* tour is designed to familiarise visitors with the city so that they have an idea about what's on offer and can decide for themselves the places where they would prefer to spend some time. The tour costs ✪$20 and includes unlimited travel on buses and CityCats on the same day. Phone ©13 12 30 for more details.

Train

The new Airtrain now operates from Brisane Airport to the Gold Coast, stopping at Brisbane Central and Roma stations. For information, ring Transinfo ©13 12 30, interstate ©07 3215 5000, or visit the website at www.transinfo.qld.gov.au A suburban train service operates regularly throughout the city. The main city centre stations are Roma Street at the Brisbane Transit Centre, Central (next to the Sheraton Hotel on Turbot Street), and Brunswick Street Station in Fortitude Valley. For information, visit the same website listed above or call Transinfo on ©13 12 30.

Ferry

Regular commuter services operate daily on the Brisbane River. For details and City Cat and City Ferry timetables, explore the website mentioned above or phone ©13 12 30.

Taxi

Taxis may be hailed in the street, engaged at taxi stands, or at the front of the big city hotels, or you can book by phone. Two companies are: Yellow Cabs, ©13 1924 and Black & White Cabs, ©13 1008.

Car

Car hire companies are: Avis, ©13 6333; Budget Rent A Car, ©13 2727; Thrifty Car Rental, ©3252 5994; Abel Rent A Car, ©13 14 29; Hertz, ©13 30 39.

There are many parking stations in and around the city, and the Tourist Information Centre has a full list.

Eating Out

City centre restaurants, riverside bistros and off-the-beaten-track eateries provide a host of different menus from around the globe.

Queensland's famous mudcrabs are always a favourite with locals and visitors alike, as are the not-so-famous Moreton Bay Bugs, which are a cross between a lobster and a crab. Tropical fruits also feature prominently on most menus.

The Tourist Bureau has a full list of restaurants, both in the city and in the suburbs, but here are some you might like to try.

Summit, Sir Samuel Griffith Drive, Mt Coot-tha, ©3369 9922. Claims the best views over Brisbane, from the Mt Coot-tha Lookout. Licensed, Modern Australian cuisine. Open for lunch and dinner, brunch on Sundays. The Kuta Cafe and Kuta Gift Shop are nearby. Open daily.

Customs House Brasserie, 399 Queen Street, ©3365 8921. Overlooks the Story Bridge on the Brisbane River. Alfresco dining with a heritage theme. A wide international food selection, from Thai to Italian to Modern Australian influences. Open daily.

Romeo's, 216 Petrie Terrace, ©3367 0955. Award-winning traditional Italian restaurant with a Venetian emphasis. The interesting menu includes pastas, meats and seafood.

Spanish Garden Steakhouse, at the Breakfast

Creek Hotel, 2 Kingsford Smith Drive, Breakfast Creek, ✆3262 5988. Try the Steakhouse for the best steaks in town.

Wang Dynasty, Ground Level, Riverside, South Bank, ✆3844 8318. Most Asian styles are represented, including Chinese, Thai, Japanese and Singaporean, but there are a couple of surprises, like crocodile and kangaroo. It is open for lunch and dinner seven days, and has views of the river and parklands nearby.

Parklands Bar & Grill, at the Rydges South Bank Hotel, Grey Street, South Bank, ✆3364 0844. Live entertainment and the "Succulent Seafood and Pasta Buffet" (✪$58 adult) on Friday and Saturday nights. Family oriented, with a Kids Menu and amusement pack.

Cilantro, at the Novotel Hotel, 200 Creek Street, ✆3309 3364. This new restaurant provides Australian and Mediterranean cuisine with a-la-carte dining. It is licensed and open every day for breakfast, lunch and dinner.

Blu Poles, 6a, 110 Macquarie Street, Teneriffe, ✆3257 2880. Licensed restaurant offering an interesting and unusual menu, such as corn-fed duck livers. Lunch Wednesday to Sunday and dinner every day except Sunday.

Daniel's, 145 Eagle Street, ✆3832 3444. Licensed, open for lunch and dinner, sitauted on the banks of the Brisbane River, steak and seafood the specialities.

Captains Cove, 44 Ferry Street, Kangaroo Point, ✆3891 6644. River views, interesting menu, breakfast daily, dinner Monday to Saturday.

Picasso's, at the Carlton Crest Hotel, King George Square, ✆3222 1128. Licensed restaurant with a creative menu. Lunch and dinner served seven days.

McMahons, Quay West, 132 Alice Street, ✆3853 6000. Licensed, wide range of seafood, pasta and meats. Elegant dining overlooking the Botanic Gardens.

Cha Cha Char Grill, Eagle Street Pier, ✆3211 9944. Licensed restaurant, open for lunch and dinner, serving beef in all its forms for steaklovers.

Pancakes at the Manor, 18 Charlotte Street, ✆3221 6433. Enjoyable family dining, inexpensive meals of a good quality. Licensed and open 24 hours.

Big Fortune, Shop 8, Merthyr Road, New Farm, ✆3358 6633. Chinese restaurant also serving laksas and noodles. It is BYO and open for lunch and dinner 7 days.

Rosie's Tavern, 235 Edward Street, City, ✆3229 4916. International cuisine, moderate prices, open for lunch and dinner Mon-Sat.

Gertie's, 699 Brunswick Street, Fortitude Valley, ✆3358 5088. Licensed restaurant set in an area with a European atmosphere. Modern flavours are the focus.

Vroom, Shop 1, cnr James and Doggett Streets, Fortitude Valley, ✆3257 4455. This original Italian cafe is perfect for a light snack or meal.

Following is a list of additional international-style restaurants.

Fujiyama, cnr Ann & Duncan Streets, Fortitude Valley, ✆3252 3275. Traditional Japanese.

George's On Wickam, 256 Wickam Street, Fortitude Valley, ✆3854 1198. Thai and Filipino cuisine.

Govinda's, 99 Elizabeth Street, ✆3210 0255. Vegetarian fare.

Green Papaya, 898 Stanley Street, East Brisbane, ✆3217 3599. North Vietnamese menu.

King Ahirim, 88 Vulture Street, West End, ✆3846 1678. Lebanese selections.

Mirch Masala, 95 Turbot Street, ✆3220 0377. Indian food.

Also, keep in mind **Cafe 21** at the Treasury Casino for a cheap breakfast. You can get yourself a hot-and-hearty meal for less than ten dollars, which may be all you can scrape out of your pocket after an unlucky night in the gaming rooms next door.

McDonalds have branches in Queen, Albert (2), Ann, Eagle, Edward and Roma Streets, as well as many outlets further afield. KFC is in Roma, Albert and Eagle Streets, and adjoining areas. Pizza Hut is on the corner of Queen Street Mall and Albert Street, ✆3221 0199.

Entertainment

When the sun goes down over the city, Brisbane's hottest night spots begin to warm up. It may not be the city that never sleeps, but its people certainly stay out late, with some of the best music in town still going strong at 5am.

Nightclubs & Pubs

PJ O'Briens, 127 Charlotte Street, ©3210 6822. A new and dazzling addition to city-centre nightlife. The pub has an Irish theme, and the music and Guiness flow freely.

Loose Goose, in the Novotel Hotel, ©3309 3366. A two hour happy hour (5pm-7pm) every evening, live entertainment and no cover charge make this a popular destination.

Club Brazil, 79 Elizabeth Street, ©3221 4144. The club has a South American theme, a lively and upbeat atmosphere, and Happy Hour from 5pm-6.30pm Tuesday to Friday.

The Adrenalin Sports Bar, You will find in this shrine to sport a shark aquarium, a Formula One car, a hang glider and the Great Wall of Sport, among other memorabilia. Even the menu cannot escape the theme.

City Rowers, 1 Eagle Street, ©3221 2888. A famous and favourite spot, patronised by the Brisbane Broncos and other locals. It claims to be a 'Brisbane institution'.

Treasury Casino, Queen Street, at the south-western end of Queen Street Mall, ©3306 8888. Ironically, the casino was built in the former premises of the Government Treasury. The revenue-raising continues unabated - the only differences is that there are now neon lights and cocktails to disguise the process a little better. With 5 restaurants, 7 bars, over 100 gaming tables, 1100 machines, and open hours around the clock, the Casino will keep you entertained until you are unable to afford the taxi ride back to your hotel.

Cinemas

Myer Centre Cinemas, cnr Albert & Elizabeth Streets, City, ©3221 4199.

Village Twin Cinema, 701 Brunswick Street, New Farm, ©3358 2021.

Hoyts Regent Entertainment Centre, 167 Queen Street, City, ©3229 5544.

Hoyts - Southbank Cinemas, Grey Street, South Bank, ©3844 4222.

Dendy Cinemas, 346 George Street, ©3211 3244.

IMAX, cnr Ernest & Grey Streets, ©3844 4222.

Theatres

Arts Theatre, 210 Petrie Terrace, City, ©3369 2344.

Brisbane Entertainment Centre, Melaleuca Drive, Boondall, ©3265 8111.

Festival Hall, 65 Charlotte Street, City, ©3229 4250.

Cremorne Theatre, at the Performing Arts Complex, ©13 62 46.

Princess Theatre, 8 Annerley Road, Woolloongabba, ©3891 3800.

Queensland Cultural Centre, South Bank, ©3840 7100.

Metro Arts Theatre, 109 Edward Street, ©221 1527.

Queensland Theatre Company, Stanley Street, South Brisbane, ©3840 7000.

Opera Queensland, 114 Grey Street, South Bank, ©3875 3030.

Programmes for the above can be found in the entertainment pages of the daily newspapers, *The Courier-Mail* and *The Sun*.

Shopping

Whether you're after a souvenir, a gift for someone special, or just feel like shopping for yourself, Brisbane's malls, markets and arcades offer a cornucopia of good buys. There are nine city centre shopping arcades housing national department stores, specialty stores, Australiana and all sorts of welcome refreshment stops.

Shopping hours are:

City - ⏰Mon-Thurs 9am-5.30pm, Fri 9am-9pm, Sat 9am-5pm, Sun 10.30am-4pm.

Suburbs - ⏰Mon-Fri 8.30am-5.30pm, Sat 8.30am-4.30pm, Thurs 8.30am-9pm.

City Shopping

If you feel that a shopping tour might best overcome your unfamiliarity with the city's commercial centres, **The Brisbane Shopping Spree Company**, 2 Sheppard Street, ©3289 3367, offer a service that stops at bargain factory and warehouse outlets in the Brisbane area. They have included a buffet lunch at the Mt Coot-tha lookout.

Queen Street Mall

Queen Street Mall.
This colourful, lavish, modern and entertaining pedestrian mall contains more than 500 specialty shops, and is the premier shopping venue in Brisbane city. The department stores on the mall are David Jones and Myer, and there are a number of banks, fast cash services, buskers, flower sellers, and plenty of chances for alfresco eating. The mall stretches between George & Edward Streets.

Wintergarden on the Mall.
A three-storey complex housing a number of specialty shops, a food fair and five levels of parking. The emphasis here is on fashion. It extends from Queen Street to Elizabeth Street under the Hilton Hotel.

Myer Centre.
The vast Myer Centre joins Queen, Elizabeth and Albert Streets, and has been designed to reflect the Victorian age. It has six shopping levels with 200 stores, and houses the national department store, Myer, as well as numerous specialty shops, restaurants, delicatessens and cinemas.

Rowes Arcade.
The arcade is a mixture of old and new, with the restored cedar panelling of the Edward Street end and the contemporary Adelaide Street entrance, though it seems to have fallen on hard times in recent years. Two shopping levels contain up-market boutiques and designer wear outlets, and a very good coffee shop. The arcade runs towards Post Office Square.

Post Office Square.
Located opposite Anzac Square, and joining Adelaide and Queen Streets with an entrance to Rowes Arcade, Post Office Square has specialty shops, bookshops, coffee shops, delicatessens and a restaurant. Underground parking is available.

Riverside Centre.
Situated on Eagle Street, in the centre of Brisbane's financial district, Riverside is set back from the Brisbane River and has up-market restaurants and designer boutiques.

Brisbane Arcade.
This turn-of-the-century, heritage-listed arcade is full of up-market clothing and gift shops. It runs from Queen Street Mall to Adelaide Street.

T & G Arcade.
Halfway up Queen Street Mall is the T & G Arcade, whose shops specialise in designer fashions, shoes and accessories, jewellery, fine silver, ceramics, glassware and antiques.

Other Shopping Centres in the City

Chopstix.
Located in the heart of Brisbane's Chinatown, Fortitude Valley, this food and retail emporium is for lovers of the Orient, with specialty shops, kitchens and restaurants.

Paddington.
Only 3km from the city centre, Latrobe and Given Terraces are home to a collection of restored colonial buildings housing boutiques, cottage crafts centres, galleries, Australiana specialists and restaurants.

Savoir Faire.
An up-market shopping and eating experience on Park Road, Milton, ten minutes from the city centre. The shopping area features boutiques, open air restaurants, coffee shops and underground parking.

Suburban Shopping
Out of town there is even more shopping, with eight major everything-under-one-roof shopping centres, each featuring large department stores and a variety of specialty shops. The Brisbane City Council operated 'Great Circle Line' is the easiest way of getting to these centres.

Markets
Riverside Markets, Riverside Centre, Eagle Street, City, ✆3833 2400 - ⏰open every Sunday 8.15am-3pm.

"McWhirters" Marketplace, cnr Wickham & Brunswick Streets, City - ☉open daily.
Southbank Markets, Friday nights, Saturday and Sunday.

Points of Interest

The city centre is best seen on a walking tour, and the **Brisbane Transit Centre**, slightly to the northwest of your city, or your hotel are good places to start. It was opened in mid-1986 and is an integrated coach and railway terminal in Roma Street. The train service from Sydney comes right to the city centre at Roma Street Station, from where all the long distance country trains leave. The suburban electric trains also leave from here, as well as interstate, intrastate and local buses. There are also long and short term car parks, taxi ranks, a hotel, commercial offices, shops and a tourist information office (☏3236 2020). Queensland has an electric train service from Brisbane through Gladstone, Rockhampton, and inland to its central Queensland Coal Fields.

The newly opened **Roma Street parklands** have been built on the site of the old railway yards. You can enjoy several self-guided walks past the lake, over bridges, through palm forests and formal gardens.

It is a leisurely stroll from the Transit Centre, of some 15 minutes, to **King George Square** and **City Hall**. This imposing building is a combined cultural and community centre. An excellent view of the city can be obtained from the clock tower, but try to avoid being up there at noon, as it gets very noisy. Also facing the square is the **Albert Street Uniting Church**, dwarfed by the high rise office blocks around it. The church is in the Gothic revival style in red brick and white sandstone, and was opened in 1889.

Around the corner in Ann Street is the **Ann Street Presbyterian Church** which was opened in 1872. Continue along Ann Street and you will come to **Anzac Park** and the **Flame of Remembrance**, opposite Central Station. Walk down the stairs and through the park, across Adelaide Street, through the Post Office Square shopping complex, and you will come to the GPO in Queen Street, ☏3405 1202. There is a **Postal Museum** on the first floor which is ☉open Tues-Thurs 10am-3pm, and Mon-Fri during school holidays. Turn right and you will find yourself in **Queen Street Mall**. At the end you come to the former **Treasury** building (now facilitating the Casino) near **Victoria Bridge**. It is built around a central courtyard in Italian Renaissance style. Turn left into William Street, and head south for just over one hundred metres. On your right you will see the **Commissariat Stores**, now the site of the Royal Historical Society. This building is one of only two that were built for the initial settlement and still stand today. Continue along William Street until you reach the French Renaissance style **Parliament House**, whose ceremonial frontage overlooks the **Botanic Gardens**. After all that walking, the gardens will provide a spot for rest and recuperation, as well as a view of the Captain Cook and Story bridges. Or you can continue your walk over the newly-built Goodwill Bridge to Southbank Parklands and the Maritime Museum.

Following are some other sightseeing venues around the city:

The **Old Windmill Observatory**, on the hill to the north of the city in Wickham Terrace, was built as a windmill in 1829 by convict labour.

The Old Windmill Observatory

Brisbane

Due to defects it was never operational, and has been used as a treadmill, a signal post and a meteorological station. It is the other legacy of the first settlement.

The **Queensland Sciencentre**, in 110 George Street, ✆3220 0166, takes visitors through the weird world of science in a memorable, hands-on learning experience. ⏲Open 10am-5pm daily and admission is ➌$9 adults, $6 children and $28 for families.

To the west of the city the area has been totally redeveloped. Cross the Victoria Bridge and head west along Stanley Street, you will first pass the **Queensland Art Gallery** and Queensland Museum, then come to the **State Library of Queensland**. South, on Grey Street, and the **Queensland Cultural Centre**. The 1982 Commonwealth Games provided Brisbane with the opportunity to upgrade and improve its public transport and sporting facilities, and the 1988 World Expo, held on the south bank of the Brisbane River, saw the completion of the Queensland Cultural Centre. The Centre houses the Performing Arts Complex, and the annexed Art Gallery, Library and Museum. The Art Gallery, ✆3840 7303, has an extensive collection of Australian art from colonial times to the present, and is ⏲open daily 10am-5pm. The Performing Arts Complex, ✆3840 7444, is ⏲open daily 10am-5pm, and until 8pm on Wednesday. The Museum takes the visitor from the prehistoric age of dinosaurs up to Australia's colonial history, and is open daily, ✆3840 7555.

Further south of the Victoria Bridge is the extremely popular **South Bank Parklands** development. Restaurants, cinemas, parklands, exclusive restaurants, markets, subtropical gardens, lagoons, park areas, sightseeing attractions and Australia's only inland city beach (Breaka Beach), sprawl over 16 hectares. Just south of the Parklands is the **Queensland Maritime Museum**, which has on display a number of impressive vessels from varying eras. Admission is adults ➌$6, children $3, ✆3844 5361.

Close to the city the Brisbane River is spanned by five bridges, all of which have a unique architectural style and are worth seeing - the **Story Bridge**, the **Captain Cook Bridge**, the **Victoria Bridge**, the **William Jolly Bridge** and the **Goodwill Bridge**. East of the city at the mouth of the Brisbane River is the impressive **Gateway Bridge**, which was opened in 1986, and for a ➌$2 toll links the city with the Gold Coast and the Sunshine Coast. Travelling north from the Gold Coast, one can bypass Brisbane city by using this route.

The **Kookaburra River Queen** is one of Brisbane's most popular attractions, and a morning tea, luncheon or dinner cruise on this paddlewheeler is a delightful experience, and one of the best ways to view the city and its bridges. The main cruises are luncheon (from ➌$55 adults), city sights (from ➌$25 adults) and dinner entertainment (from ➌$75 adults). Phone ✆3221 1300 for bookings and departure times. Brisbane City Council, run **City Cat Cruises** which take you along the 19km length of the Brisbane River in 2 hours. If you are interested, information can be acquired and tickets purchased from the Council Customer Service outlets. The city branch is on the lower ground level of the Brisbane Administration Centre, 69 Ann Street, up near George Street, ⏲open Mon-Fri 8.15am-4.45pm; and the Fortitude Valley branch is in the TC Beirne Centre, Brunswick Street Mall, ⏲open Mon-Fri 9am-5pm. They are also at Embarkation Point on Eagle Pier.

Suburban Attractions

The Southern Cross, Sir Charles Kingsford Smith's plane, is preserved in a glass-walled building off Airport Drive at Brisbane Airport. Admission is free and the display is open daily. **New Farm Park** has almost 12,000 rose bushes and a Jacaranda and Poinciana avenue. Like the Botanic Gardens, it is situated on the riverbank, and although it can be reached by bus, a more scenic way to visit is by the City Cat Ferry. For ferry times, contact Transinfo, ✆13 12 30.

The **Mt Coot-tha Botanic Gardens** are only ten minutes' drive from the city, and have a large collection of Australian native plants, tropical plants, an arid-zone area and tropical plant display dome, ⏲open daily 8am-5.30pm. The Sir Thomas Brisbane Planetarium in the gardens is the largest in Australia. There is also a Japanese Garden, a Fragrant Plants and Herb Garden, and Australian rainforest. The picnic area at the top of Mt Coot-tha is a popular stop for a panoramic view of the city, day or night.

Lone Pine Koala Sanctuary, Jesmond Road, Fig Tree Pocket, ☎3278 1366, shouldn't be missed. It is situated on the banks of the river, and is best reached by boat - the Mirimar Boat Cruise departs from North Quay daily at 10am, ☎3221 0300. The Sanctuary is Australia's oldest, and also has a variety of native animals, reptiles and birds. It is ☉open daily 7.30am-4.45pm, and admission is ✪$14 adults, $7 children.

Temple of the Holy Triad, cnr Park & Higgs Streets, Breakfast Creek, is an historic Chinese Temple built in 1885, ☎3262 5588. The pillars of the building were set crookedly as a reminder to all that nothing in life is perfect.

Miegunya, 31 Jordan Terrace, Bowen Hills, was built in 1884, and is a good example of colonial architecture. It is dedicated to the pioneering women of Queensland.

Newstead House in Newstead Park, Breakfast Creek Road, Newstead, ☎3216 1846 or ☎1800 061 846, is Brisbane's oldest surviving residence. It is on the banks of the river near its junction with Breakfast Creek, and is ☉open Mon-Fri 10am-4pm, Sun 2-5pm.

The Queensland University at St Lucia, ☎3365 1111, is almost completely surrounded by the river, and has spacious parklands and sandstone buildings which are joined by sheltered walkways called The Cloisters. They are decorated with carvings of other universities' coats of arms, sculptures and grotesque faces and animals. Worth a visit if you are into varsity ambience and style.

Alma Park Zoo, Alma Road, Dakabin, ☎3204 656, features Australian and exotic fauna, tropical gardens, picnic and barbecue facilities. There are regular feeding times for a variety of animals. It is ☉open daily 9am-5pm. Admission is ✪$20 adults and $10 children. The zoo is located 28km (17 miles) north of Brisbane and takes about half an hour to reach.

Licoriceland, 21 Jijaws Street, Sumner Park, ☎3376 6945, is Queensland's only licorice factory. It is ☉open 9.30am-3.30pm Mon-Fri, except in January when it is closed to visitors. Tours are available, and there is also a sweet shop selling samples.

The Australian Woolshed, 148 Samford Road, Ferny Hills, ☎3872 1100, is a wonderful experience for people who don't have time to visit the great Aussie Outback. You can see seven different breeds of sheep, watch one being shorn, and then see the fleece spun into yarn. Once you've had a taste of Australia's rural backbone, you might like to expand your activities. Native animals are on display, waterslides are open at selected times for ✪$5 an hour, and a nine-hole round of mini golf is available for ✪$4. Every Saturday night there is a Woolshed dance which includes dinner. The Woolshed is about 20 minutes drive from the city centre and admission prices are ✪$18 adults and $11 children. A Park Package ticket is available, which includes a variety of these activites for ✪$20.

The **Boondall Wetlands** are a protected area maintained by Brisbane City Council, consisting of woodlands, tidal flats and swamp areas, north of Brisbane on the rim of Moreton Bay. The region can be explored on foot, bike or canoe, and birdwatching and exploration of Aboriginal culture are features. The Boondall Wetlands Visitor Centre has further details, ☎3865 5187.

Tours

Bus tours operate daily from Brisbane, taking in the very best of the city sights and venturing further afield to beautiful beaches and natural bushland. Following are some examples.

Brisbane Tours & Detours, ☎3830 4455: Koalas & Brisbane Parklands Tours, 2.15pm-4.15pm, ✪$50 adults; Highlights of the City, 9.15am-1.15pm, ✪$40 adults; Brisbane Moonlight Tour, 6.45pm-8.45pm, ✪$40 adults; Best of Brisbane - In a Day, 9.30am-5.30pm, ✪$75 adults.

Brian Ogdens Historical Walking Tours, ☎3217 3673.

The Mansions

Australian Day Tours, Level 3, Transit Centre, Roma Street, ✆3236 4155 or ✆1300 363 436 (free call):
Brisbane After Dark, 6pm-10pm, ✪$70 adults; Brisbane Sights Full Day, 9.30am-6.30pm, ✪$58 adults; City Sights, Woolshed and River Cruise, 9.30am-6.30pm, ✪$75 adults; Morning Tour, City Sights & South Bank, 9.30am-1.30pm, ✪$40 adults.
Brisbane Ghost Tours, ✆3344 7264:
An historical tour with a difference!
Mr Day Tours, Aminya Close, My Nebo, ✆3289 8364:
Afternoon Scenic Rainforest Drive, 12.30pm-4.30pm, ✪$70 adults; Brisbane and Its Outback Tour, 8am-6pm, ✪$135 adults; Morning Countryside Drive, 8am-12pm, ✪$75 adults.
Gray Line Tours, Level 3, Transit Centre, Roma Street, ✆3236 9444:
Best of Brisbane Cruise & Tour, 9.30am-6.30pm, ✪$95 adults; Mt Tamborine & Aussie Country Show, 7.30am-7.30pm, ✪$105 adults.
Rob's Rainforest Explorer Day Tours, 44 Felix Street, Lutwyche, ✆0409 49 6607:
Glasshouse Mountains & Kondalilla Falls, 8am-6pm, ✪$55 adults; Lamington/Springbrook National Parks, 8am-6pm, ✪$55 adults; Mt Glorious & Samford Valley Tour, 8am-6pm, ✪$55 adults.

See More Scenic Tours, 4 Mallee Street, Marsden, ✆3805 5588:
Glow Worm Express - Tambourine Mountain, 6pm-10pm, ✪$50 adults; Rainforest & Winery Tour, 8.30am-5.30pm, ✪$65 adults.
Sunrover Expeditions, 1 Eversleigh Road, Redcliffe, ✆3203 4241:
Moreton Bay Island Safari, 6.45am-6.45pm, ✪$135 adults.
Regular tours to Dreamworld, Sea World, Movie World, Wet'n'Wild, Gold Coast, Noosa and Sunshine Coast, Moreton Bay, Tamborine Mountains, Toowoomba and Darling Downs are also conducted.

Festivals
The Valley Fiesta held at Chinatown and Brunswick Street Malls is a multicultural music and arts festival held in July.
The Royal National Show (The Ekka) is held in the Brisbane Exhibitions Grounds, Fortitude Valley, over ten days in August.
The Spring Hill Fair is held in Water Street in September.
Brisbane River Festival is held from August to September.

Facilities
The Gabba is Brisbane's main cricket venue for International and interstate matches, and it is in Stanley Street, Woolloongabba, across the river to the south of the city centre, ✆3891 5464.
Horse races are held at Eagle Farm Racecourse, Lancaster Road, Ascot, ✆3268 2171, and Doomben Racecourse, 39 Brunswick Street, Fortitude Valley, ✆3268 6800.
The trotting venue is Albion Park Harness Racing, Amy Street, Breakfast Creek, ✆3262 2577.
The main football ovals are: Rugby League - Suncorp Stadium, Castlemaine Street, Milton, ✆3876 6511; Rugby Union - Ballymore, Clyde Road, Herston, ✆3352 8120; Australian Rules - The Gabba. There are also games of all three codes played at suburban grounds on the weekends in winter.
Baseball is also played at Suncorp Stadium, and for Basketball, the Brisbane Entertainment Cen-

tre, Melaleuca Drive, Boondall, is the home of the Brisbane Bullets.

For names and addresses of other sporting facilities, it is best to consult the Yellow Pages telephone directory.

Outlying Attractions

Moreton Bay and Island

The bayside suburbs of Wynnum, Lota, Manly, Wellington Point and Cleveland are great places for boating, and North Stradbroke and Moreton Islands are really worth a visit. They provide the opportunity for an island holiday without travelling far from Brisbane.

Moreton is the second largest sand island in the world (after Fraser Island), and much of it is National Park. There are unspoiled beaches, abundant birdlife, and the sand dunes are magnificent. In the centre, amongst the sand dunes where there is practically no vegetation, you can imagine that a camel train might arrive at any moment. Mount Tempest is one of the highest coastal sand dunes in the world. The **Wild Dolphin** resort at Tangalooma, the site of the old whaling station, offers standard and deluxe motel and cabin accommodation and a restaurant. Prices start from ✪$90 per person twin share in the peak season.

For those who prefer a simpler holiday, camping areas are found at **Accommodation Moreton Island**, The Strand Bulwer, ✆3408 3798. Facilities include water, toilets and showers. Moreton Island Tourist Information Services, located at The Strand Bulwer, can provide further details, ✆(07) 3408 2661.

Access to Moreton Island is by launch or air. The Tangalooma Flyer leaves Holt Street in Brisbane, with a courtesy coach transfer from the Transit Centre in Roma Street at 9am daily. The launch transfers cost ✪$33 return for adults. Air transfers are from Brisbane Airport to Moreton Island, a trip lasting about 15 minutes. Enquire about your preferred transfer method when booking your accommodation or by contacting the Visitor Information Centre.

North Stradbroke Island

North Stradbroke Island is larger and has more varied scenery than Moreton Island. There are mangrove swamps, lakes, bushland and great surfing beaches.

Accommodation is available at Amity Point and at Point Lookout, with campsites at Point Lookout and Dunwich. Vehicular ferries operate from Cleveland and Redland Bay.

The Stradbroke Island Tourist Information Centre is at the end of Middle Street, Cleveland, ✆3821 3821. Stradbroke Island Tourism is in Junner Street, Dunwich, ✆3409 9555 or email ✉redlands tourism@redlands.net.au

Beenleigh

If you are heading south to the Gold Coast from Brisbane, take time out to visit the Beenleigh Tavern at 124 Distillery Road, ✆3287 4777. It is ⏰open Mon-Fri 10.30am-10pm, Sat 11am until late, Sun 11am-6pm. For a moderate fee, tours are conducted between limited hours daily and include a tasting of Beenleigh rum (after all, that is why you came here).

Chapter 31
Sunshine Coast

Population 120,000
The Sunshine Coast stretches from Caloundra, 90km (56 miles) north of Brisbane, to Double Island Point in the north. It boasts 55km (34 miles) of white sandy beaches and rocky headlands.

Climate

Average Temperatures: January max 29C (84F) - min 20C (66F); July max 21C (70F) - min 7C (45F). Average annual rainfall -1776mm (70 ins). Driest months June-September. A lot of the summer rain falls in evening storms after hot sunny days.

Characteristics

The Sunshine Coast is rather like the Gold Coast was in the 1960s, but it has a friendlier, laid-back air with less razzamatazz. The beaches and surf compare favourably with the Gold Coast, and there are fewer high rise buildings that cast shadows on the beaches in the afternoons.

The high rocky headlands and areas of natural bushland divide the resorts, and afford the holiday maker the opportunity to walk along shady paths in the heat of the afternoon, or drop a fishing line into the shallow waters of the rivers and savour the peace and quiet.

There are still secluded beaches which can only be reached by narrow sandy paths meandering through sand dunes, and the mouths of the rivers are ideal places to fish, canoe, row or sail.

The Noosa River, which is navigable to near its headwaters at Tin Can Bay, is home to thousands of birds. The river flows through several lakes on its way to the sea, and many houseboats are to be found along its reaches. The pace is more relaxed than on the Gold Coast. There is plenty to entertain, and the area boasts of excellent restaurants.

How to Get There

By Air

The major airport for the region is the Sunshine Coast Airport, centrally located at Mudjimba, and equipped for jet aircraft.

Qantas, ©13 1313 flies directly from Sydney and Melbourne, with connections from other capital cities.

By Bus

Suncoast Pacific, ©5443 1011, and McCafferty's, ©13 1499, operate routes that service the Sunshine Coast frequently.

By Rail

Queensland Rail, ©13 2232, electric trains service the area from Brisbane to the main Sunshine Coast station at Nambour.

By Road

From Brisbane, via the Bruce Highway. The four lane section puts Caloundra within an hour's drive of Brisbane, and Noosa is only another 61km (38 miles), or 45 minutes, further on.

Visitor Information

Tourism Sunshine Coast Ltd, The Wharf, Parkyn Parade, Mooloolaba, ©(07) 5477 7311. The web site is ☞www.sunzine.net/suncoast/tsc/index.html and the email address is ✉tourism@sunzine.net

Maroochy Tourism and Travel, Sixth Avenue, Maroochydore, ©(07) 5479 1566, have an email facility at ✉admin@maroochytourism.com and a web page at ☞www.maroochy tourism.com

Caloundra City Information Centre, 7 Caloundra Road, Caloundra, ©(07) 5491 0202. Their web address is ☞www.caloundra.qld.gov.au and the email address is ✉c.stewart@caloundra.qld.gov.au

Tourism Noosa Information Centre, Hastings Street Roundabout, Noosa Heads, ©(07) 5447 4988. The web site is ☞www.tourismnoosa.com.au and you can email them here at ✉info@tourismnoosa.com.au

There is another outlet in the area: Noosa Junction Tourist Information Centre, Shop 5 The Oasis Centre, 20 Sunshine Beach Road, Noosa Heads, ©(07) 5447 3755.

NOOSA NATIONAL PARK
Noosa Head
Pomona 72 Tewantin
Cooroy
Eumundi **Noosa**
Sunshine Beach
Peregian Beach
35 *Coolum Beach*
Yandina
Kenilworth Mudjimba
Nambour **Maroochydore**
Mapleton *Point Cartright*
Buderim
Conondale 18 Kawana Waters
Maleny
Caloundra
CONONDALE
RANGE

ville
ore
Hwy Kilcoy
Hazeldean *Bribie Island*
Lake Somerset *Cape Moreton*
Woorim
Caboolture Bulwer
Bongaree
85 *Moreton Island*
Dayboro Tangalooma
Burpengary **Deception** *Moreton* **MORETON ISLAND**
Bay **NATIONAL PARK**
Redcliffe *Bay*
Lake Wivenhoe
Kooringal
Mount Nebo Amity
Lowood Fernvale **BRISBANE** Point Lookout

Brisbane to Sunshine Coast

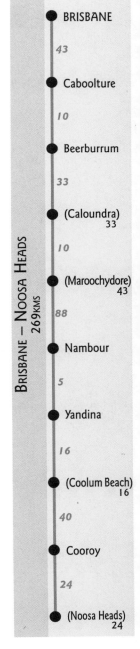

BRISBANE — NOOSA HEADS 269KMS

BRISBANE
43
Caboolture
10
Beerburrum
33
(Caloundra) 33
10
(Maroochydore) 43
88
Nambour
5
Yandina
16
(Coolum Beach) 16
40
Cooroy
24
(Noosa Heads) 24

Accommodation

A good variety of accommodation, ranging from caravan parks, motels, hotels, guest houses, self-contained units and five-star resorts are available throughout the coast from Noosa to Caloundra. For a copy of the *Sunshine Coast Accommodation Guide*, ©(07) 5477 7311.

Here is a selection, with prices for a double room per night, which should be used as a guide only. The telephone area code is 07.

Caloundra

Anchorage Motor Inn and Resort, 18 Bowman Road, ©5491 1499. 22 units, 4 suites, licensed restaurant, swimming pool, barbecue, tennis - ❂$75-125.

Altons Palm Breeze, 105 Bulcock Street, ©5491 5566. 19 units, 1 suite, swimming pool, barbecue - ❂$55-75.

Caloundra Suncourt, 135 Bulcock Street, ©5491 1011. 8 units, swimming pool, barbecue - ❂$65-120.

City Centre Motel, cnr Orsova Terrace & Minchinton Street, ©5491 3301. 8 units, undercover parking, barbecue - ❂$65-80.

Caloundra Motel, 30 Bowman Road, ©5491 1411. 14 units, swimming pool, barbecue, undercover parking - ✪$55-65.

Caravan Parks

Hibiscus & Tripcony Caravan Park, Bowman Road, ✆5491 1564. (No pets allowed) - powered sites ✪$20-26 for two, on-site vans $35-60, cabins $40-60 for two.

Danmira Tourist Park, 1 Onslow Street, Golden Beach, ✆5492 1731. 70 sites, barbecue, pool - powered sites ✪$20-25 for two, units $55-95 for two, cabins $40-85 for two.

Dicky Beach Family Holiday Park, Beerburrum Street, Dicky Beach, ✆5491 3342. 124 sites, tennis, swimming pool - powered sites ✪$18-30 for two, cabins $45-65 for two.

Maroochydore

Coachmans Courte Motor Inn, 94 Sixth Avenue, ✆5443 4099. 14 units, swimming pool, spa, undercover parking - ✪$90-95.

Heritage Motor Inn, 69 Sixth Avenue, ✆5443 7355. 18 units, swimming pool, spa - ✪$85-110.

Beach Motor Inn, cnr Sixth Avenue & Kingsford Smith Parade, ✆5443 7044. 18 units, swimming pool, barbecue - ✪$90-135.

Blue Waters, 64 Sixth Avenue, ✆5443 6700. 20 units, swimming pool, undercover parking - ✪$60-105.

Avenue Motor Inn, 106 Sixth Avenue, ✆5443 3600. 16 units, swimming pool, barbecue - ✪$85-115.

Maroochy River, 361 Bradman Avenue, ✆5443 3142. 8 units, swimming pool - ✪$55-95.

Caravan Parks

Alexandra Gardens Top Tourist Park, Okinja Road, ✆5443 2356. (No pets allowed) - powered sites ✪$19-24 for two, villas $50-100 for two, cabins $40-65 for two.

Maroochy Palms Holiday Village, 319 Bradman Avenue, ✆5443 8611. (No pets allowed) - powered sites ✪$26 for two, cabins $50-95, villas $65-125 for two.

Maroochy River Cabin Village & Caravan Park, Diura Street, ✆5443 3033. (Pets on application) - powered sites ✪$19-21 for two, on-site vans $40-55 for two, cabins $65-80 for two.

The Maroochydore **Youth Hostel** is in 24 Schirrmann Drive, ✆5443 3151. They have 9 rooms at ✪$19 per person twin share.

Noosa Heads

Netanya Noosa Motel, 75 Hastings Street, Laguna Bay, ✆5447 4722. 48 units, swimming pool, spa, sauna, gym, barbecue - ✪$200-600.

Noosa International, Edgar Bennett Avenue, ✆5447 4822. 65 suites, licensed restaurant, heated swimming pool, spas, saunas - ✪$165-210.

At the Sound, 119 Noosa Parade, Noosa Sound, ✆5449 9211. 22 units, undercover parking, swimming pool, barbecue - ✪$450-550.

Hotel Laguna, 6 Hastings Street, ✆5447 3077. 48 units, licensed restaurant, swimming pool, tennis, barbecue - ✪$110-330.

Noosa Parade Holiday Inn, cnr Noosa Parade & Key Court, ✆5447 4177. 11 units, heated swimming pool, spa, barbecue - ✪$100-140.

Chez Noosa Resort, 263 David Low Way, ✆5447 2027. 28 units, heated swimming pool, barbecue, undercover parking - ✪$70-120.

The Noosa Heads **Youth Hostel** is in 2 Halse Lane, ✆5447 3377. They have 26 rooms at ✪$22 per person twin share.

Eating Out

The Sunshine Coast is a gourmet's delight. Dozens of restaurants feature fresh local seafood complemented by delicious sun-ripened tropical fruit such as avocados, pineapples and pawpaws. Beach and river fronts are dotted with picnic tables where visitors can enjoy takeaway or picnic food. Here is an idea of what is available in each district.

Caloundra

Island Restaurant, at the Anchorage Moror Inn & Resort, 18 Bowman Road, ✆5491 1499. Licensed premises, steak and seafood are specialties, a-la-carte selection, cocktail bar. Opens at 6pm every night except on Public Holidays.

Trivolis of Pia Place, 118 Bulcock Street, ✆5491 1768. Licensed and BYO, seafood, a-la-carte dining. Open 10.30am-3pm and 6pm-midnight Mon-Sat, closed Sunday.

Chinese Holiday Restaurant, 106 Bulcock Street, ✆5491 6066.

Blue Orchid Thai Restaurant, 22 Bulcock Street, ℂ5491 9433.

Brunos Taverna Italian Ristorante, 725 Nicklin Way, ℂ5493 1806.

Bamboo Garden, 95 Bulcock Street, ℂ5491 2768.

Flower Lounge Indian Restaurant, Shop 4 The Strand, Bulcock Street, ℂ5499 7677.

You will find McDonalds on the corner of Erang Street & Nicklan Way and on the corner of Fourth Avenue & Bowman Road. KFC is at 73b Bowman Road. Pizza Hut is at 69 Bowman Road, ℂ5491 5100.

Maroochydore

Swells Restaurant & Bar, 6 Duporth Avenue, ℂ5443 6401. Fully licensed, open 11am-11pm every day.

Sun See Chinese Restaurant, Shop 1, 50 Aerodrome Road, ℂ5443 2636. BYO, wide range of cuisines with an oriental emphasis. Open 5pm-9pm every day.

Som Tam Thai Restaurant, cnr Fifth Avenue & Aerodrome Road, ℂ5479 1700. BYO (wine only), open 5pm-10pm 7 days and 12pm-2.30pm Fri-Sun, closed Public Holidays.

Waterfront, David Low Way, ℂ5448 4488.

Gauchos Mexican Restaurant, Kingsford-Smith Parade, ℂ5443 8877.

Jimmys Place, Shop 4, Broadmeadow Road, ℂ5479 2241.

Azzurro Ristorante Italiano, 93 Aerodrome Road, ℂ5443 3500.

Sizzler, cnr Fifth Avenue & Aerodrome Road, ℂ5443 4377.

Indian Hathi Restaurant, 37 Aerodrome Road, ℂ5443 5411.

McDonalds has two locations in Maroochydore: 14-18 Aerodrome Road and in Sunshine Plaza. Pizza Hut is on the corner of Horton Parade and First Avenue. Pizza Hut is at 153 Aerodrome Road, ℂ5443 4911.

Noosa Heads

Freshwater Bar & Grill, Edgar Bennett Avenue, ℂ5447 5900. Open 10am-midnight 7 days.

Riva Waterfront Restaurant & Bar, 10/1 Quamby Place, ℂ5449 2440. A-la-carte menu. Open midday-midnight 7 days.

Cocos, cnr Park Road & Mitti Street, ℂ5447 2440. Licensed restaurant open 8am-midnight.

Roma Pizza Restaurant, Sunshine Beach Road, ℂ5447 3602. Offers prawns, pizza, pasta and steak. Open 5pm-10pm.

Indian Empire, Shop 4 Noosa Wharf, Quambi Place, Noosa Sound, ℂ5474 5655.

Emerald House Chinese Restaurant, 11 Sunshine Beach, ℂ5447 3356.

Michels, 1 Hastings Street, ℂ5447 3880.

Lindonis Italian Ristorante, Hastings Street, ℂ5447 5111.

Sails, 75 Hastings Street, ℂ5447 4235.

Pommies, Quamby Place, Noosa Wharf Shopping Centre, ℂ5474 8600.

KFC is in 5 Sunshine Beach Road. Pizza Hut is on the corner of Lake Weyba Drive and Weyba Road, ℂ5449 7711.

Local Transport

Sunshine Coast Coaches operate daily bus services from Caloundra to Nambour, and Noosa District Bus Lines operate a daily service from Nambour to Noosa.

Points of Interest

Visitors to the area will quickly discover why it is one of Australia's premier tourist destinations. With golden beaches, scenic hinterland, lush rainforest, breathtaking mountain views,

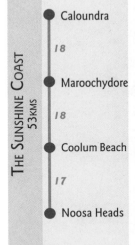

Sunshine Coast

THE SUNSHINE COAST
53KMS

● Caloundra

18

● Maroochydore

18

● Coolum Beach

17

● Noosa Heads

crystal-clear lakes and waterways, the Sunshine Coast has it all. For most visitors, the main attractions are sun, surf and sand.

The beaches stretch from Caloundra in the south to Double Island Point in the north, taking in popular holiday spots like Mooloolaba, Maroochydore, Coolum and Noosa.

Everyone, though, soon discovers that the hinterland also has much to offer, with its patchwork of tropical fruit farms, rainforests, State Forests and National Parks. It is the perfect complement to the coastal resorts. You can enjoy a bushwalk, while away the hours in one of the many arts and crafts galleries, sit down to a Devonshire tea, or take in the spectacular panoramic views.

Caloundra

Population 19,700

Caloundra City, at the southern entrance to the Sunshine Coast, is an attractive and affordable holiday destination. Located just an hour north of Brisbane by four-lane highway, it is the perfect place to shake the nine-to-five blues. Apart from 30km (19 miles) of beaches, Caloundra has a special attraction which makes it the envy of other coastal resorts - the Pumicestone Passage. It is a haven for a wide variety of water sports, is famed for its fishing and harbours as well as two of the safest swimming beaches on the Sunshine Coast - Bulcock Beach and Golden Beach.

Maroochy

Population 16,600

Mooloolaba, Alexandra Headland and Maroochydore are the main coastal townships of the Maroochy Shire.

Mooloolaba Beach, with Point Cartwright on the southern side and the Mooloolaba Harbour wall, is a protected beach which is popular with families and windsurfers. Mooloolaba is home to a large fishing fleet, and fresh fish can be purchased daily from the Mooloolaba Fisheries Co-operative.

Alexandra Headland is renowned for its great surf. In summer, board riders flock to the tiny cove every day.

Underwater World at the Mooloolaba Wharf is an enjoyable experience. The moving acrylic tunnel allows glass-housed sharks, stingrays, and fish to swim over and around the visitors. **Maroochydore**, at the mouth of the Maroochy River, is a thriving tourist and business centre. It has a fine surfing beach, and the river is a favourite spot for watersports and fishing alike.

Travelling north along the coast the major townships are Coolum Beach, Peregian Beach, Marcus Beach, Sunshine Beach and, finally, Noosa Heads.

Noosa

Population 6000

Noosa Heads, with its northerly facing beach, is protected from the prevailing south-easterly winds. Noosa has a cosmopolitan atmosphere, coupled with the natural beauty of the area. The headland is a National Park and there are several walks meandering through it to the various attractions, including Boiling Pot, Hell's Gates, Paradise Cave.

Noosa's boutiques and restaurants in Hastings Street are first class, and there is no shortage of entertainment.

The coloured sands at Teewah can be reached by 4WD from Noosa along the beach at low tide. Tours are available from Noosaville or Tewantin. Upstream from Tewantin, the Noosa River meanders through lakes which are surrounded by wetlands with prolific bird life. This area is the **Cooloola National Park**. In the 1870s, huge log rafts were guided down the river to Tewantin, where they were sorted before continuing their way to Brisbane. Five lakes are linked in a waterway network stretching for almost 80km (50 miles). Lake Cootharaba has a special area for learner water skiers, and many visitors spend holidays on houseboats wandering through the river system.

Inland is **Nambour**, the most southern of Queensland's sugar towns, where the old cane trolleys ramble across the main street to the Moreton Central Sugar Mill. Pineapple and other tropical fruit plantations are also found around the district.

At the Sunshine Plantation, 6km south of Nambour, you can see the **Big Pineapple**, Nambour Connection Road, Woombye, and take a tour of the plantation by train. It is ⏰open daily 9am-5pm, ✆5442 1333

Bli Bli has a **Fairytale Castle**, David Low Way, ✆5448 5373, a replica 11th century Norman Castle with moat, portcullis and drawbridge. Inside, fairytales are depicted in elaborate dioramas, and the castle is ⏰open daily 9am-5pm.

Nostalgia Town, 596 David Low Way, ✆5448 7155, is another attraction, just north of Bli Bli at Pacific Paradise. Call in and have a laugh at the past.

Big Cow Antique Centre, ✆5446 8477, home of the Big Cow, is 6km north of Nambour on the Bruce Highway, and milking demonstrations and feeding of nursery animals are some of the highlights.

Another 3km north at Yandina is **Gingertown**, Pioneers Road, ✆5446 8455, the largest ginger processing factory in the southern hemisphere. The ginger processed here is grown in rich red soil between the Blackall Range and the coast. On **Tanawha Forest Glen Tourist Drive**, visitors can visit three attractions:

Super Bee's Honey Factory near the Buderim turnoff, ✆5445 3544, has collecting demonstrations and is ⏰open daily 9am-5pm. Admission is free.

At the Forest Glen **Deer Sanctuary and Wildlife Park**, ✆5445 1274, free-roaming deer can be fed from your car. Koalas, kangaroos and emus can also be seen. It is ⏰open 9am-5pm, daily.

The **Moonshine Valley Winery**, Bruce Highway, ✆5445 1198, specialises in fruit wines. Free tastings are held daily.

BLACKALL RANGE
32KMS

● Nambour

10

● Mapleton

9

● Montville

13

● Maleny

Chapter 32
Sunshine Coast
to Maryborough

Blackall Range

Population 2066
Location and Characteristics
The Blackall Range, on Brisbane's Sunshine Coast, is a world apart, with its art and craft galleries, Devonshire teas, comfortable pubs, green fields, hedgerows, and a feeling of Olde England.

From high vantage points between Mapleton and Maleny, the small farms and cane fields of the coastal plain stretch out to join the blue Pacific, and south from Maleny are the dramatic Glass House Mountains.

Throughout the Blackall Ranges are national and forestry parks, offering superb walks through tropical rainforest, picnic spots beside waterfalls, and rock pools for swimming.

Visitor Information
The website to visit is ☞www.sunshinecoast.com/blackallranges.html

Accommodation and Services
Mapleton
Tanglewood Gardens, Montville Road, ✆5445 7100. 12 cabins, undercover parking, tennis, pool, sauna, spa - ✪$110-165.
Obilo Lodge B&B, Obi Obi Road, ✆5445 7705. 3 rooms, pool, restaurant, TV lounge - ✪&85-150.
Lilyponds Holiday Park, Warruga Street, ✆5445 7238. 45 sites, pool, recreation room, barbecue, playground, good facilities - powered sites ✪$17 for two, cabins $50-55 for two, units $65-70 for two.
Maleny
Tranquil Park Resort, 152 Mountain View Road,

✆5494 4544. 31 units, licensed restaurant, tennis, pool, undercover parking, recreation room - ✪$90-110.
Maleny Country Cottages, Cork's Pocket Road, ✆5494 2744. 4 cottages, undercover parking, barbecue, cooking facilities - ✪$95-175.
Maleny Hills, Montville Road, ✆5494 2551. 5 units, undercover parking, barbecue - ✪$60.
Cairncross Lodge, 33 Mary Cairncross Avenue, ✆5494 3633. 5 rooms, restaurant, recreation room - ✪$90-110.
Maleny Palms, 23 Macadamia Drive, ✆5494 2933. 42 sites, barbecue, pool - powered sites ✪$18-21 for two, cabins $55-70 for two.

Points of Interest
The scenic drive through the Blackall Range is one of the most popular day outings in southeast Queensland. The southern end of the range drive is little more than an hour north of Brisbane, and access is no more than half an hour from most Sunshine Coast resort towns.

Gympie

Population 11,800
Location and Characteristics
Gympie is a large township situated about halfway between Maryborough and Maroochydore on the Bruce Highway. Like many towns in the north of Queensland it was once known for its abundance of gold, after its discovery by James Nash. The town sprung up during a rush in 1868 and it didn't take more than a few months for 25,000 hopeful prospectors to cram the fields nearby.

Visitor Information
There are two places you can contact for further information: the Gympie Tourist Information Centre, Bruce Highway, Lake Alford, ✆(07) 5482 2847 or the Coloola Regional Development Bureau, 224 Mary Street, Gympie, ✆(07) 5482 5444.

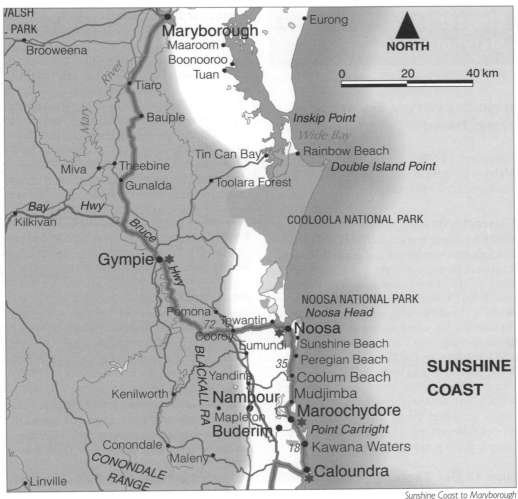

Sunshine Coast to Maryborough

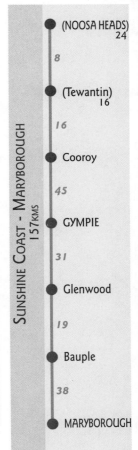

Accommodation and Services

Great Eastern Motor Inn, 27 Geordie Road, ©5482 7288. 32 units, 6 suites, conference centre, licensed restaurant, undercover carpark, room service, pool - ✪$85-100.

Gympie Motel, 83 Bruce Highway, ©5482 2722. 29 units, unlicensed restaurant, undercover carpark, room service, heated pool - ✪$55.

The Empire Hotel, 196 Mary Street, ©5482 8444. 12, double storey, licensed restaurant (closed Sunday) - ✪$30.

Gympie Caravan Park, 1 Jane Street, ©5483 6800. 106 sites, barbecue, kiosk, pool - powered sites ✪$16 for two, cabins $35-45 for two.

Silver Fern Caravan Park, Bruce Highway, ©5483 5171. 52 sites, barbecue, pool - powered sites ✪$12 for two, on-site vans $25 for two.

Points of Interest

Gympie's attractions are mainly historic, including The Gold and Mining Museum, the Woodworks Forestry and Timber Museum and a number of buildings reminiscent of the town's colonial heritage.

Chapter 33
Maryborough

Including Hervey Bay and Fraser Island

Population 25,500
Maryborough is 255km (158 miles) north of Brisbane, on the Mary River.

Characteristics

Maryborough is known as Heritage City due to its magnificent homes and public buildings.

Situated on a curve of the broad Mary River, close to 150 years of history can be found in the city. The Mary River was discovered by Andrew Petrie in 1842, and not long after a member of his party returned to establish sheep farming near Tiaro. However by March 1843, the venture had failed due to disease in the sheep and attacks by natives. In June, 1847, George Furber settled in one of the deserted outstations on the south bank and built a wharf, store and shanty. The schooner *Sisters* arrived in December to load wool from the stations and Maryborough became a wool port.

How to Get There
By Air
Sunstate Airlines, ©13 1313, have daily flights to/from Brisbane. Sunstate and Flight West, ©1300 130 092, both service Hervey Bay.
By Bus
McCafferty's, ©13 1499, Greyhound Pioneer, ©13 2030, and Suncoast Pacific, ©5443 1011, stop at Maryborough on their Brisbane-Cairns routes.
By Road
Maryborough is on the Bruce Highway, 255km (158 miles) north of Brisbane. The journey takes about 3 hours. Hervey Bay is a further 34km (half an hour's drive) north east.

Visitor Information

The Fraser Coast - South Burnett Regional Tourism Board. is located at 388-396 Kent Street, Maryborough, ©(07) 4122 3444. The web address is ☜www.frasercoast.org and the email address is ✍info@frasercoast.org

The Maryborough Tourist Information Centre is at 30 Ferry Street, Maryborough, ©4121 4111.

You will find the Hervey Bay Tourist & Information Centre at 353 The Esplanade, ©4124 4050. There is also an Information Centre at 63 Old Maryborough Road, Pialba, ©4124 9609.

If you wish to make bookings, the following two outlets will be able to assist you:

The Whale Booking Office, 419 The Eplanade, ©4125 3399, and Hervey Bay Accommodation Centre, 139 Boat Harbour Drive, Hervey Bay, ©4124 2424.

Accommodation

There is plenty of accommodation available in the South Burnett Region, and here is a selection with prices for a double room per night, which should be used as a guide only. The telephone area code is 07.

Maryborough

Susan River Homestead Ranch Resort, Fraser Coast Highway, ©4121 6846. 16 rooms, licensed restaurant, swimming pool, spa, sauna, tennis, water skiing, barbecue - ✪$122 twin share.

McNevins Parkway, 188 John Street, ©4122 2888. 15 units, licensed restaurant, swimming pool, spa, sauna - ✪$80.

Mineral Sands, 75 Ferry, cnr Albert Street, ©4121 2366. 20 units, licensed restaurant, swimming pool - ✪$70-75.

Cara, 196 Walker Street, ©4122 4288. 13 units, pool - ✪$60-75.

Arkana Inn, 46 Ferry Street, ©4121 2261. 32 units, licensed restaurant, swimming pool - ✪$60-70.

Spanish Motor Inn Maryborough, 499 Alice Street, ©4121 2858. 22 units, swimming pool - ✪$60-70.

Maryborough City, 138 Ferry Street, ©4121 2568. 17 units, licensed restaurant (closed Sun), swimming pool, barbecue - ✪$60.

Royal Centre Point, 326 Kent Street, ✆4121 2241. 18 units, licensed restaurant - ✪$55-80.

Caravan Parks

Wallace Units & Caravan Park, 22 Ferry Street, ✆4121 3970. Pool, barbecue - powered sites ✪$14 for two, units $50 for two, cabins $30 for two.

Huntsville Caravan Park, 23 Gympie Road, ✆4121 4075. (Pets allowed on application) - powered sites ✪$16 for two, on-site vans $25 for two, cabins $30 for two.

Maryborough Caravan Park, 209 Gympie Road, ✆4121 6379. 50 sites, barbecue, pool - powered sites ✪$14 for two, cabins, ✪$40 for two.

Country Stopover Caravan Park, Bruce Highway, ✆4121 2764. (Pets allowed on application) - powered sites ✪$17 for two, on-site vans $25 for two.

Hervey Bay

The accommodation for the Bay is in the towns of Torquay, Urangan, Pialba and Scarness.

Playa Concha Resort, 475 Esplanade, Torquay, ✆4125 1544. 40 units, 16 suites, licensed restaurants, heated swimming pool, spa, barbecue - ✪$75.

Reef, 410 The Esplanade, Torquay, ✆4125 2744. 25 units, swimming pool, barbecue - ✪$40-67.

Kondari Resort, 49 Elizabeth Street, Urangan, ✆4128 9702. 97 units, licensed restaurant, bistro, swimming pool, spa, playground, half-court tennis, barbecue - ✪$59-99.

Shelly Beach, 509 Esplanade, Urangan, ✆4128 9888. 13 units, barbecue, undercover parking - ✪$55-80.

Hervey Bay, 518 Esplanade, Urangan, ✆4128 9277. 18 units, swimming pool, barbecue - ✪$47-72.

Urangan Motor Inn, 573 Esplanade, Urangan, ✆4128 9699. 42 units, licensed restaurant, swimming pool, spa, barbecue - ✪$42-65.

Fraser Gateway Motor Inn, 68 Main Street, Pialba, ✆4128 3666. 28 units, licensed restaurant (Mon-Thu), swimming pool - ✪$75-80.

Hervey Bay Resort, 249 Esplanade, Pialba, ✆4128 1555. 24 units, licensed restaurant, swimming pool, spa - ✪$70-80.

Sunseeker Motel, 354 The Esplanade, Scarness, ✆4128 1888. 10 units, swimming pool, playground, barbecue - ✪$62-88.

Fairway, 29 Boat Harbour Drive, Pialba, ✆4128 1911. 10 units, swimming pool, barbecue - ✪$58-78.

Golden Sands Motor Inn, 44 Main Street, Pialba, ✆4128 3977. 10 units, swimming pool, barbecue - ✪$58-75.

Caravan Parks

Happy Wanderer Village Caravan Park, 105 Truro Street, Torquay, ✆4125 1103. 92 sites, pool, spa - powered sites ✪$21 for two, on-site vans $30 for two, cabins $45-55 for two.

Fraser Lodge, Fraser Street, Torquay, ✆4124 9999. Tennis, spa, pool - powered sites ✪$24 for two, cabins $50-55 for two.

Shelly Beach Caravan Park, 61 Ocean Street, Torquay, ✆4125 1105. (No dogs allowed) - powered sites ✪$17 for two, on-site vans $25-30 for two, cabins $40-45 for two.

Lazy Acres Caravan Park, 91 Exeter Street, Torquay, ✆4125 1840. 80 sites, pool, barbecue - powered sites ✪$15 for two, on-site vans $30 for two, cabins $60-70.

Torquay Beachfront Tourist Park, Esplanade, beach frontage, ✆4125 1578. (No dogs) - powered sites ✪$18-22 for two.

The Palms Caravan Park, cnr Roberts & Truro Streets, Torquay, ✆4125 1704. Pool, barbecue - powered sites ✪$17 for two, on-site vans $25-35.

Pier Caravan Park, 571 Esplanade, Urangan, ✆4128 9866. (Pets allowed on leash) - powered sites ✪$18, on site vans $25-35 for two, cabins $50-60 for two.

Anchorage Caravan Park, Boat Harbour Drive, Urangan, ✆4128 9286. Pool, barbecue - powered sites ✪$16-19 for two, on-site vans $35-40 for two.

Windmill Caravan Park, 17 Elizabeth Street, Urangan, ✆4128 9267. 60 sites, barbecue, pool - powered sites $18-20 for two, on-site vans $30-40 for two.

Hervey Bay Caravan Park, Margaret Street, Urangan, ✆4128 9553. Pool, barbecue - powered sites ✪$18-20 for two, cabins $60-70 for two.

Maryborough

Harbour View Caravan Park, Jetty Road, Boat Harbour, Urangan, ☏4128 9374. 80 sites, pool - powered sites ✪$16-18 for two, on-site vans $30 for two.

Pialba Beachfront Tourist Park, Esplanade, Pialba, ☏4128 1399. Powered sites ✪$18-22 for two.

Magnolia Caravan Park, cnr Boat Harbour Drive & Taylor Street, Pialba, ☏4128 1700. 53 sites, pool, barbecue - powered sites ✪$14 for two, on-site vans $30 for two.

Australiana Village, 295 Boat Harbour Drive, Scarness, ☏4128 2762. Pool, barbecue, excellent facilities - powered sites ✪$19-22 for two, on-site vans $35 for two, units $75-90.

Scarness Beachfront Tourist Park, Esplanade, Scarness, ☏4128 1274. (No dogs allowed) 160 sites - powered sites ✪$14 for two.

The Hervey Bay **Youth Hostel** is at Boat Harbour Drive, ☏4125 1844. They have 29 rooms ✪$18 per person twin share.

Fraser Island

Kingfisher Bay Resort and Village, North White Cliffs, ☏3032 2805. 19 units, licensed restaurant, pool, spa, tennis, fishing - ✪$280.

Fraser Island Retreat, Happy Valley, ☏4127 9144. 9 units, licensed restaurant, barbecue, pool - ✪$125-180.

Eurong Beach Resort, Eurong, ☏4127 9122. 59 units, pool - ✪$90-225.

Camping

Cathedral Beach Resort & Camping Park, Cathedral Beach, ☏4127 9177. (No pets, no permit required) 54 tourist sites, no power, hot showers, kiosk, barbecue - sites ✪$20 for two, on-site vans $50 for two, cabins $80-100 for two.

Queenslands Park & Wildlife Service, ☏4127 9128. (No pets) 250 camping sites, no power, hot showers, barbecue - ✪$16. Facilities vary, please check. 4WD vehicle access and a camping permit apply. Permit must be obtained prior to arrival. Available from Department of Environment & Heritage, Rainbow Beach, ☏ (07) 5486 3160 or ☏(07) 3227 7111 (Brisbane). Permit costs: ✪$30 per vehicle if pre-paid prior to arrival, $40 per vehicle on the island.

Eating Out

If you are having trouble deciding where to eat, here is a list of restaurants in the Maryborough area, with numbers and locations, from which you might like to make a choice. The telephone area code is 07.

Maryborough

China Dragon Restaurant, in the Central Hotel, 171 Adelaide Street, ☏4123 1399.

The Gardenia, 193 Adelaide Street, ☏4121 4967.

Muddy Water Cafe, 71 Wharf Street, ☏4121 5011.

Red Roo Hotel, 100 Adelaide Street, ☏4121 3586.

Colony Room Restaurant, cnr Ferry & Albert Streets, ☏4121 2366.

Casino Royale, 338 Kent Street, ☏4121 6225.

Lucky Chinese Restaurant, 302 Kent Street, ☏4121 3645.

McDonalds is on the corner of Quarry Road and the Bruce Highway, as well as on the corner of Alice and Ferry Streets. KFC is on the corner of Walker and Ferry Streets. Pizza Hut is on the corner of Alice and Ferry Streets, ☏13 1166.

Hervey Bay

The Deck, Hervey Bay Marina, Buccanneer Avenue, Hervey Bay, ☏4125 1155.

Don Camillo Ristorante Italiano, 486 Esplanade, Hervey Bay, ☏4125 5466.

Bay Central Chinese Kitchen, Boat Harbour Drive, Hervey Bay, ☏4124 1200.

Hervey Bay Chinese Restaurant, Shop A, 3 Fraser Street, Torquay, ☏4125 6906.

Aegean Waters French Restaurant, The Esplanade, Torquay, ☏4125 2232.

China Palace, 38 Torquay Road, Pialba, ☏4124 8808.

Curried Away, 174 Boat Harbour Drive, Pialba, ☏4124 1577.

Raphaels, 564 Esplanade, Urangan, ☏4125 2183.

Fryer Tucks, Urangan Plaza, 564 Esplanade, Urangan, ☏4125 5933.

Thai Diamond, 355 Esplanade, Scarness, ☏4124 4855.

Marty's on the Beach, 344 Esplanade, Scarness, ☏4128 1233.

KFC is on the corner of Torquay Road and Taylor Street in Hervey Bay. Pizza Hut is in Lot 2 Boat Harbour Drive, Pialba, ©13 1166.

Fraser Island

The resorts have restaurants and the camping grounds have barbecue facilities.

Points of Interest

Maryborough

The site of the original Maryborough township illustrated the real environs and features of early settlements in the then colony of New South Wales. Of particular relevance is the scale of the early settlement, with the landing, the inns, the sawpits, the water supply, trades and industries, and even the burial ground all within walking distance.

In the town there are two marked **Walking Routes** to see the attractions. For Route Number 1, start at the Information Centre and follow the Red Marker posts. Walk Number 2 branches from near the site of George Furber's Inn and returns past Baddow House.

Baddow House, 366 Queen Street, ©4123 1883, is one of Maryborough's most historic homes, and is fully furnished with authentic period furniture. It has exhibits of colonial and museum pieces, and is ©open daily 10am-4pm. Devonshire teas and souvenirs are available.

There are **Pioneer Graves** at the northern-most extremity of the original Maryborough township, in Aldridge Street, Baddow. The harshness and difficulties of frontier life ensured that the early township experienced loss of life, but death from natural causes or old age was virtually unknown.

Queens Park, Sussex Street, was established more than a century ago, and many of its huge trees were planted as experiments by the Acclimatization Society. Features of the park are the fernery, waterfall and lily pond, lace-trimmed band rotunda built in 1890, and the 13cm gauge model railway built by the Model Engineers and Live Steamers Association. On the last Sunday of the month the Association meets in Queens Park to relive the steam age.

Ululah Lagoon, Lions Drive, was originally the water supply in the early days of settlement. The lagoon is now a wildlife sanctuary where tame black swans, ducks and waterfowl can be hand fed. The lagoon is surrounded by tree-studded parkland with picnic tables and barbecues.

Bottlebrush Crafts (Maitlia Potters), 320 Albert Street, ©4122 2533, have sales and promotion of local crafts, regular exhibits and workshops. ©Open Mon-Fri 10am-3pm, Sat 10am-1pm.

Caltex Mountain View Roadhouse, Bruce Highway, Bauple, ©4129 2267, has an extensive range of rocks, minerals, gems and fossils, including thundereggs and petrified woods.

Macadamia Plantation, cnr Bruce Highway & Owanyilla Boundary Road, south of Maryborough, has brought the world of macadamia nuts to the public. Stage one of the complex, the processing and retail plant, is a major tourist attraction. Guided tours of the plantation aboard the Nutty Choo Choo, with running commentary, are very popular. There is also a shop selling unusual souvenirs, a kiosk with light refreshments, and barbecue lunches are available. ©Open daily 9am-5pm.

The **MV *Duchess*** has hourly cruises on the Mary River on Wed, Thurs and Sun afternoons. Her low profile design enables her to travel unrestricted up river under all the bridges, passing past and present sites of early industry and architecture, an island bat colony and much more. There is informative and humorous commentary. For more information contact the Maryborough Tourist Information Centre, ©4121 4111.

Hervey Bay

Situated 34km (21 miles) east of Maryborough, Hervey Bay is one of Australia's best value holiday destinations. It has a climate similar to that of Hawaii, and virtually year-round swimming in a safe and sheltered environment.

The Bay offers a variety of charter boats for fishing trips. These vary in length from a couple of hours out on the water to day/night trips. Most trips are out to the deep waters off Sandy Cape, Breaksea Spit, Rooney's and the gutters around Fraser Island. Reef fish which abound in the Bay's waters include Coral Bream, Blackall,

Maryborough

Snapper, Coral Trout and Cod. A few companies specialising in cruises are:

Lady Elliot Island Reef Resort Day Tours, ©1800 072 200 for reservations.

Splash Safaris, 6 Inman Street, Point Vernon, ©0500 555 580.

Stefanie Yacht Charters, 7 Burum Street, Hervey Bay, ©4125 4200.

Hervey Bay now has international recognition as one of the best vantage points for studying the **Humpback Whale**. From early August to mid-October, these gentle giants stop in at Hervey Bay on their return south to Antarctica. They frolic in the warm waters of the Bay, almost oblivious to the people watching eagerly from the safety of tour boats.

Some of the companies operating whale watch tours are:

Islander Whale Watch Cruises, Buccaneer Avenue, ©4125 3399.

Mimi Macpherson's Whale Watch Expeditions, 449 The Esplanade, Torquay, ©4125 1700 or ©1800 683 368.

Spirit of Hervey Bay Whale Watch Cruises, 864 Boat Harbour Drive, Urangan, ©4125 5131.

Whalesong Cruises, Torquay, Whale Watch and Dolphin Cruises, ©4125 6222.

For further details on tours and cruises, contact the Hervey Bay Tourist & Visitors Centre, 353 The Esplanade, © 4124 4050.

The **Whale Festival**, held in August, is a weekend full of activities to officially launch the whale watching season. Features include an aquatic carnival, illuminated procession of boats, the Princess of Whales competition, and the World Smiling Championships.

Hervey Bay Nature World, Maryborough Road, Pialba, on the main highway at the entrance to Hervey Bay, is an Australian theme park set in 15ha (37 acres) of bushland. Calling the place home are kangaroos, wallabies, wombats, emu, deer, buffalo, waterbirds and a large number of crocodiles. The crocodiles feed daily in summer and twice weekly in winter. Feeding time is 11.30am. Lorikeets feed daily between 3-4pm. There are free paddle boat rides, playground, barbecue and picnic areas, and toilets for the disabled. ©Open daily 9am-5pm. You can phone them on ©4124 1733.

Dayman Point features sweeping views of Great Sandy Strait, picnic facilities and two memorials: one to Z Force and their vessel *The Krait*; the other to Captain Matthew Flinders, who landed nearby on August 6, 1799, and Lt Joseph Dayman, RN who passed in the schooner *Asp* after making the first passage through Fraser Island (now Great Sandy) Strait in 1847.

Fraser Island

Fraser Island is the largest sand island in the world, a fishing paradise, and one of the world's last wilderness areas. It is 11km (7 miles) from Hervey Bay, and is composed almost entirely of siliceous sands which extend to more than 600m (1968 ft) below sea level. The only rock outcrops on the east coast are at Indian Head, Middle Rock and Waddy Point. On the west coast there is a small outcrop of hard rock at Bun Bun Rocks.

The island has an area of 184,000ha (454,480 acres), is 123km (76 miles) long, and has an average width of 14km (9 miles), ranging to 22km (14 miles) at its widest part. Dune heights reach to 240m (787 ft).

Most of the island is crown land, national park or State forest reserve. Five main tourist centres - at Eurong, Happy Valley, Orchard Beach, Cathedral Beach and Dilli Village - cater for those who like home comforts. If you prefer a real wilderness experience, you can camp in a secluded spot and explore the island by forest tracks, which are suitable for 4WD only.

All visitors to the island are required to have permits. The fee charged is used to provide facilities for visitors and to provide effective protection for the unique island environment. Permit costs are: ❂$34 per vehicle prior to arrival, ❂$45 per vehicle on the island. They are available from Department of Environment & Heritage, Rainbow Beach, ©(07) 5486 3160 or in Brisbane, ©(07) 3227 7111.

Fraser Island can be reached by sea and air. Cruises and vehicular barges operate from Hervey Bay, Mary River Heads and Rainbow Beach. Charter flights and tours are also available.

There are over 40 freshwater lakes on the Island. As well as the perched dune lakes, there are window lakes, formed when the shifting sand falls below the level of the island's dome-shaped water table. Remarkable is Lake Wabby, an easy walk from the ocean beach. It is the deepest of the island's lakes, and contains the greatest variety of fish, but it is dying, slowly being strangled by a sandblow that encroaches four metres each year.

Up to 72 different colours have been recorded in the sands on the island. The most famous area of coloured sand cliffs is **The Cathedrals** on the eastern side of the island midway between Happy Valley and Orchid Beach.

The island has hundreds of kilometres of white sand beaches, its own wreck (the *Maheno*, which beached during a cyclone 50 years ago) and countless freshwater streams.

Dingoes are also found on the island, not as pets or in cages, but living freely. It is generally accepted that if you leave them alone, they will leave you alone, but it is requested that you do not feed them. They find their own food, and do well without handouts.

Chapter 34
Maryborough to Bundaberg

Burrum Heads, Toogoom, Howard, Torbanlea

Population 1000
Location and Characteristics
Burrum Heads and Toogoom are two small coastal resorts located at the mouth of the Burrum River, both popular for their good fishing and relaxed atmosphere. In the winter months especially, fishermen come from miles around to catch whiting.

Burrum Heads is growing rapidly and is well serviced with shops. In September the area is vibrant with colourful wildflowers. Toogoom has plenty of good picnic spots, and over ninety species of birds have been identified in the area. Both of these resorts have caravan parks and holiday homes.

The Burrum River crosses the highway between Howard and Torbanlea. It is a picturesque waterway for boating, fishing and crabbing, and has a caravan park on its banks. Most houses in these two townships are the cool high-set timber Queenslander homes. Howard has all the facilities of an up-and-coming small town.

Approximately 20km north of Maryborough on the Bruce Highway, there is an exit for Burrum Heads.

Accommodation and Services
Burrum Sands, Burrum Street, Burrum Heads, ✆4129 5275. 8 units, self-contained, beachfront, undercover carpark, heated pool, barbecue - ✪$60-80.
San Marco Villas, 44 Esplanade, Burrum Heads, ✆4129 5224. 8 units, undercover carpark, barbecue, pool, spa - ✪$50-55.
Hillcrest Holiday Park, Howard Street, Burrum Heads, ✆4129 5179. 95 powered sites, kiosk, tennis courts, pool - powered sites ✪$15 for two, park cabins $25-65 for two, on-site vans $20-30 for two.

Childers

Population 1500
Location and Characteristics
Located 50km (31 miles) south of Bundaberg, Childers has rich red soil, and is famous for its avenue of leopard trees, colonial buildings, the Olde Butcher Shoppe and the Hall of Memories. It is on the Bruce Highway.

Accommodation and Services
Motel Childers, 136 Churchill Street (Bruce Hwy), ✆4126 1177. 14 units, unlicensed restaurant, undercover parking - ✪$65.
Gateway Motor Inn, Bruce Highway, ✆4126 1288. 19 units, dinner to unit , pool - ✪$60-70.
Sugar Bowl Caravan Park, Bruce Hwy, ✆4126 1521. 50 powered sites, barbecue, pool - powered sites ✪$16 for two, park cabins $45-50 for two, on-site vans $30 for two.

Points of Interest
Less than half an hour's drive away is Woodgate Beach and Woodgate National Park, which has many boardwalks allowing access to the swampy areas. There is also a special bird-watching shed. The beach is popular and stretches for about 16km (10 miles).

Biggenden

Population 1650
Location and Characteristics
Craggy, blue mountain ranges are the backdrop for Biggenden, 100km (62 miles) south-west of Bundaberg. Along with agricultural pursuits - beef, grain crops, dairying, citrus, piggeries, peanuts and timber - the area is rich in minerals.

Visitor Information
You will find tourist information at the Biggenden Shire Council, Edward Street, ✆(07) 4127 1177.

Accommodation and Services

Rocky Creek Farm Stay (B&B), 12km west on Ban Ban Springs Road then left, ©4127 1377. 3 rooms, farm style property, non smoking, various activities - ✪$220.

Biggenden Motel, 44 Walsh Street, ©4127 1301. 7 units with access of up to 4 people, undercover carpark, fuel, shop - ✪$55-60.

Mountain View Caravan Park, Walsh Street, ©015 155 743 (mobile). (Dogs allowed) 20 sites, barbecue - powered sites ✪$12 for two.

Points of Interest

Established in the goldrush of 1889, attractions include the historic Chowey Bridge, the old Mt Shamrock Gold Mine, the operational open-cut magnetite mine, the Coalstoun Lakes, Mt Walsh National Park and Mt Woowoonga Forest Reserve.

Gayndah

Population 3000

Location and Characteristics

Found 166km (103 miles) south-west of Bundaberg on the Burnett Highway, Gayndah is Queensland's oldest town, and was in the running with Ipswich and Brisbane for the title of State capital. In the 1840s Gayndah was originally settled as sheep country, and it wasn't until 1892 that William Seeney planted the first orchard, for which Gayndah is now famous. Even if you weren't aware of it before, you could hardly miss the Big Orange complex.

Visitor Information

The Golden Orange Hotel-Motel, Maltby Place, is the supplier of regional information for tourists, ©(07) 4161 1107.

Accommodation and Services

Gayndah Colonial Motor Inn, 62 Capper Street, ©4161 1999. 12 units, barbecue, dinner to unit, undercover carpark, spa, pool - ✪$65-70.

Gayndah Motel, 12 Maryborough Road, ©4161

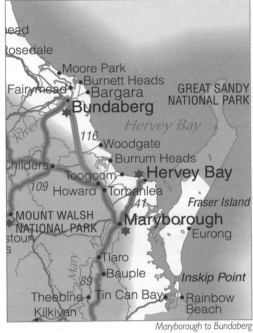

Maryborough to Bundaberg

2500. 9 units, barbecue, undercover carpark, pool - ✪$55-65.

Riverview Caravan Park, 3 Barrow Street, ©4161 1280. 47 sites, barbecue, kiosk - powered sites ✪$15 for two.

Mundubbera

Population 2300

Location and Characteristics

Mundubbera is situated on the banks of the Burnett River, 35km south-east of Eidsvold on the Burnett Highway. The River passes through the small sub-tropical valley of the Central Burnett. One-third of Queensland's citrus is produced here and the area is surrounded by orchards, and has the Enormous Ellendale (Big Mandarin). The Golden Mile Orchard has an extensive packing facility. The Auburn Falls National Park is 35km (22 miles) west, and has beautiful rock pools and formations.

Visitor Information

Tourist Information can be obtained from the

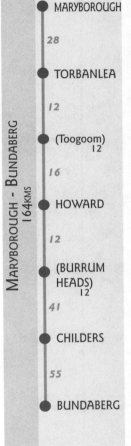

Maryborough to Bundaberg

MARYBOROUGH – BUNDABERG 164KMS

● MARYBOROUGH

28

● TORBANLEA

12

● (Toogoom) 12

16

● HOWARD

12

● (BURRUM HEADS) 12

41

● CHILDERS

55

● BUNDABERG

CHILDERS

30

Dallarnil

17

BIGGENDEN

20

Coalston Lakes

18

Ban Ban Springs

29

GAYNDAH

23

Binjour

23

MUNDUBBERA

36

EIDSVOLD

THE BURNETT HIGHWAY 196KMS

Big Mandarin complex in Durong Road, ℂ(07) 4165 4549.

Accommodation and Services
Billabong Motor Inn, Durong Road, ℂ4165 4533 or ℂ4165 4410. 2 units, barbecue, licensed restaurant, undercover parking, pool - ✪$70.

Mundubbera Motel, 42 Strathdee Street, ℂ4165 4399 or ℂ4165 4131. 12 units with access of up to 5 people, barbecue, dinner to unit, undercover parking, pool - ✪$65-80.

Citrus Country Caravan Village, Durong Road, ℂ4165 4549. 80 sites, barbecue, kiosk, spa, pool - powered sites ✪$13 for two.

Eidsvold

Population 1000
Location and Characteristics
Situated on the Burnett Highway 250km (155 miles) west of Bundaberg, via Gayndah, Eidsvold was established as a gold mining town in 1888

and is now a major producer of beef cattle. The town's past can be seen in the slab homestead 'Knockbreak' which is part of the Eidsvold Historical Museum.

Visitor Information
The Eidsvold Motel & General Store, 51 Moreton Street, can provide you with tourist information. ℂ(07) 4165 1209.

Accommodaiton
Eidsvold Motel, Moreton Street, ℂ4165 1209. 6 lodges for up to 3 people, unlicenced restaurant, self-contained facilities - ✪$40.

Eidsvold Caravan Park, Esplanade Street, ℂ4165 1168. 21 sites, barbecue - powered sites ✪$11 for two.

Points of Interest
Eidsvold has a unique museum housing the George Schaffer bottle, rock and gemstone collection - a display of unusual items gathered over one man's lifetime.

Chapter 35
Bundaberg

Population 54,800
Bundaberg is situated on the Burnett River, 378km (235 miles) north of Brisbane. Strictly speaking, it is not part of the Great Barrier Reef and in fact sits on the southern side of the designated boundary. If you are travelling along the coast in either direction, there are a number of factors which may encourage you to stop here.

Climate

Average temperatures: Jan max 30C (86F) - min 21C (70F); July max 21C (70F) - min 11C (52F). Average annual rainfall: 1149mm (45 ins); heaviest rainfall falls December-March.

Characteristics

The Bundaberg district grows approximately one-fifth of Australia's sugar crop, and in recent years has become a virtual salad bowl, growing large supplies of tomatoes, avocados, pineapples, beans and more. And, of course, the Famous Aussie Spirit, Bundaberg Rum, is produced here in this Sugar City.

How to Get There

By Air

Sunstate Airlines, ℂ13 1313, operate several flights daily to/from Cairns, Mackay, Rockhampton, Townsville and Gladstone.
Flight West, ℂ1300 130 092, operate a Brisbane to Bundaberg service 3 times a day.

By Bus

Greyhound Pioneer, ℂ13 2030, and McCafferty's, ℂ13 1499, stop at Bundaberg on their Brisbane/Cairns route.

By Rail

Bundaberg is on the main Brisbane/Cairns line. The Sunlander, Queenslander and Spirit of Capricorn all stop at Bundaberg, ℂ13 2235.

By Road

From Brisbane, Bundaberg is a 368km, four-and-a-half hour drive. Follow the Bruce Highway north to the turn-off at Childers.
It is 170km south of Gladstone, and the turn-off is at Gin Gin.

Visitor Information

Bundaberg District Tourism and Development Board is at the Hinkler Glider Museum, 271 Bourbong Street, next to the Base Hospital, ℂ4152 2333. ⏲Opening hours are Mon-Fri 8.30am-5pm, Sat-Sun 9am-5pm.

Accommodation

There are over 30 motels in Bundaberg as well as hotels, caravan parks and backpacker accommodation. Here is a selection, with prices for a double room per night, which should be used as a guide only. The telephone area code is 07.

City

Bert Hinkler Motor Inn, cnr Takalvan & Warrell Streets, ℂ4152 6400. 32 units, licensed restaurant, swimming pool, spa, sauna, half-court tennis - ✪$85-130.

Sugar Country Motor Inn, 220 Bourbong Street, ℂ4153 1166. 33 units, licensed restaurant, swimming pool - ✪$90-95.

Bundaberg City Motor Inn, 246 Bourbong Street, ℂ4152 5011. 17 units, swimming pool, spa, barbecue - ✪$85-95.

Acacia Motor Inn, 248 Bourbong Street, ℂ4152 3411. 26 units, undercover parking, swimming pool - ✪$80.

Alexandra Park Motor Inn, 66 Quay Street, ℂ4152 7255. 19 units, licensed restaurant, swimming pool - ✪$50-110.

Bundaberg Spanish Motor Inn, cnr Woongarra & Mulgrave Streets, ℂ4152 5444. 16 units, swimming pool, undercover parking, barbecue - ✪$75.

Butterfly Checkmate, 240 Bourbong Street, ℂ4152 2700. 18 units, unlicensed restaurant (closed Sun), swimming pool, barbecue - ✪$70.

Chalet Motor Inn, 242 Bourbong Street, ℂ4152

Bundaberg

9922. 14 units, swimming pool, spa - ✪$70-100.

Bourbong Street Motel, 265 Bourbong Street, ✆4151 3089. 17 units - ✪$55.

Lyelta Lodge & Motel, 8 Maryborough Street, ✆4151 3344. 20 rooms, undercover parking - ✪$35-40.

Caravan Parks

Oakwood Caravan Park, Gin Gin Road, ✆4159 9332. 86 sites, pool, barbecue, kiosk - powered sites ✪$15 for two, on-site vans $25-30 for two, cabins $40-45 for two.

Finemore Tourist Park, 33 Quay Street, ✆4151 3663. (No pets) 66 sites, barbecue, pool - powered sites ✪$14 for two, cabins $38 for two.

Cane Village Holiday Park, Twyford Street, ✆4155 1022. 84 sites, playground, barbecue, pool - powered sites ✪$17-16 for two, cabins $35-38 for two.

Coastal

Don Pancho Beach Resort, 62 Miller Street, Bargara, ✆4159 2146. 42 units, licensed restaurant, swimming pool, spa, barbecue, half-court tennis, gym - ✪$90-160.

Nieuport 54, 54 Miller Street, Bargara, ✆4159 2164. 6 units, sauna, spa - ✪$85-105.

Dunelm House Bed & Breakfast, 540 Bargara Road, Bargara, ✆4159 0909. 3 rooms, undercover parking, pool, spa - ✪$70-80.

Bargara Beach Motor Inn, 7 Bauer Street, Bargara, ✆4159 2395. 6 units, barbecue, undercover parking - ✪$55-95.

Pacific Sun Motor Inn, 11 Bauer Street, Bargara, ✆4159 2350. 10 units - ✪$50-65.

Caravan Parks

Absolute Ocean Front Tourist Park, 117 Woongarra Scenic Drive, Bargara, ✆4159 2436. 42 sites, barbecue, kiosk, spa, pool - powered sites ✪$14 for two, on-site vans $30-38 for two, cabins $40-47 for two.

Bargara Beach Caravan Park, Nielson Park, The Esplanade, Bargara, ✆4159 2228. (Pets on application) 300 sites, barbecue, playground, 2 tennis courts, kiosk - powered sites ✪$16 for two, on-site vans $28 for two, cabins $38-46 for two.

Eating Out

Bundaberg has an abundance of licensed and BYO restaurants, licensed clubs and hotels, and plenty of coffee lounges, takeaways and snack bars. If you wish, get in touch with the Tourist Information Centre, ✆4152 2333, for a list of culinary establishments and local advice on the best places to dine. If you're not in an adventurous mood, the major fast-food chains have branches in Bundaberg.

Beaches, at the Reef Gateway Motor Inn, 11 Takalvan Street, ✆4153 2255. Licensed a-la-carte dining, large seafood selection, cocktail bar. Open 6pm-10pm every day except Sunday (closed).

Spinnaker Stonegrill & Bar, 1a Quay Street, ✆4152 8033. Seafood and stonegrill selections, a-la-carte dining. Open midday to midnight 7 days, closed Public Holidays.

Rendezvous, 220 Bourbong Street, ✆4153 1747. Licensed, open 24 hours.

New China Dragon Restaurant, 32 Targo Street, ✆4151 1955. Seafood cuisine, BYO. Open 5am-9pm seven days and 11am-2.30pm Mon-Fri, closed Public Holidays.

The Strand, 55 Woongarra Street, ✆4151 2099. Curry a speciality on Sunday nights. Open 8am-midnight every day except Public Holidays (closed).

Codiannis, 66 Woongarra Street, ✆4153 0930.

Mexican Border, 27 Elliots Head Road, ✆4152 1675. Licensed, Mexican dishes.

Oriental Pearl Chinese Restaurant, 69 Takalvan Street, ✆4152 8655.

Zulus, 61 Targo Street, ✆4152 4691.

Numero Uno, 167a Bourbong Street, ✆4151 3666.

You will find *KFC* at 263 Bourbong Street, *McDonalds* on the corner of Woongarra and Targo Streets and *Pizza Hut* on the corner of Bourbong and Branyon Streets, ✆13 6611.

Local Transport

There are weekly bus services to North Bundaberg, South Bundaberg, Norville, West Bundaberg, Sugarland Shoppingtown, Bargara and Burnett Heads, Elliott Heads, South Kolan/ Bingera, Kepnock, Moore Park and Gin Gin - contact the Tourist Information Centre for details and timetables.

Points of Interest

A trip to the reef aboard the MV *Lady Musgrave* takes just over two hours from Bundaberg. The office is located in Shop 1 Moffat Street, Bundaberg Port Marina, ©4159 4519 or ©4152 9011.

Lady Musgrave Island, 49km (30 miles) from the coast, is a truly unspoiled, uninhabited coral atoll where you can stroll through the pisonia and casuarina trees and view the nesting seabirds. The launch trip includes morning and afternoon tea, smorgasbord luncheon, snorkelling gear and glass-bottomed boat rides. A fun day is assured. *(See separate listing.)*

Bundaberg has several memorials to its most famous son, Herbert John Louis Hinkler (*Bert Hinkler*) - locally he was known as 'Hustling Hinkler'. He was the first aviator to fly solo from England to Australia, in 1928. **Hinkler House**, Mt Perry Road, was transported brick by brick from Southampton, England, to Bundaberg in 1883, by a team of dedicated workers. Hinkler designed the house and lived in it from 1926-1933. It is now an aviation museum ☉open daily 10am- 4pm, ©4152 0222.

There are memorials to Hinkler in Buss Park beside the Civic Centre, at the southern end of the traffic bridge, and on the Hummock, 10km east of the city. The **Hinkler Glider Museum** contains a replica of Hinkler's glider which he successfully flew 35m from the sand dunes of Mon Repos Beach in 1912. The historical museum is in the same complex and contains a fascinating collection of domestic items and farm equipment. The **Botanical Gardens** and steam railway are also in the **Hinkler Rose Garden Tourist Complex**, along with the *Hinkler Rose Garden Restaurant*, ©4153 1477.

Bundaberg Rum Distillery, Whitred Street, ©4150 8686, has five conducted tours every weekday, which run for approximately one hour. You can see the rum being processed from raw sugar through to the bottled product - the 'Famous Aussie Spirit', although you will not get to sample the end product for free!

Schmeiders Cooperage & Craft Centre, 5 Alexandra Street, East Bundaberg, ©4151 8233 or ©1800 222 440, sells small handcrafted American Oak Casks. You can see the coopers at work making these casks in their workshops. Also in the Craft Centre are potters, a blacksmith, woodturner, artists and many more. There is a cafe as well, where you can grab a bite to eat.

Alexandra Park Zoo, is on the banks of the Burnett River, west of the main railway line. It is ☉open Mon-Fri 6.30am-3.30pm and admission is free.

The House of Dolls, Douglas Road, ©4159 7252, has a wonderful display of dressed dolls, in national and period costumes, and a display of the Royal Wedding.

Boyd's Antiquatorium, 295 Bourbong Street, ©4152 2576, has a collection of classic racing motorcycles, vintage cars, early cameras, farm machinery, a coin collection, and a great musical instrument display. The display is directed at all ages.

Take a stroll through the fragrant **Pennyroyal Herb Farm** which is a delightful place to visit. The display gardens are set in native Australian bush.

Bundaberg

Sugar cane fire

Avocado Grove, Douglas Road, ©4159 7367, has something for everyone. Exotic and sociable peacocks roam the grounds whilst many native birds live happily in aviaries amid the lush, sub-tropical gardens.

What caused those strange craters just north of Bundaberg? The **Mystery Craters** are said to be 25 million years old, and their origin remains unexplained. The fascinating area has a garden setting, observation tower, kiosk, rocks, souvenirs, currency display and playground. The area, in Lines Road, South Kolan, is ⏰open 8am-5pm. The admission fee is ✪$5 adults and $3 children, ©4157 7291.

For an unusual treat, stop and buy some tropical fruit wine at Bundaberg's unique **Winery** at 78 Mt Perry Road, ©4151 5993. Owners Carole and John Gianduzzo will explain the merits of the various wines. Another unusual facet is the large range of soft drinks now produced on the premises. It is ⏰open Mon-Sat 9am-5.30pm and 9am-midday on Sundays. Admission is free.

Bargara Beach is the aquatic playground for the sun and sea aficionados of Bundaberg. Just a 15 minute drive from Bundaberg, it offers safe surfing at Neilson Park. A very modern shopping centre known as 'Bargara Centrepoint' caters for everyone's needs. The town is serviced by a modern hotel/motel, motel and unit accommodation, caravan parks, TAB, convenience store, takeaway food outlets and fine restaurants. Kelly's Beach has a natural still-water tidal swimming pool and is a patrolled beach.

Mon Repos Beach, with magnificent sand dunes, is the largest and most accessible mainland turtle rookery in Australia. It is an environmental park and contains a magnificent Kanaka stone wall. It was the site of Bert Hinkler's first flights. The conservation park ⏰opens from 7pm onwards between November and March, and the Information Centre is open 8am-4pm March-October. Admission is ✪$5 for adults and $3 for children.

Burnett Heads, with **Oaks Beach**, is 18km (11 miles) from Bundaberg at the mouth of the Burnett River and has ample shops, a hotel and a couple of caravan parks. The lighthouse is located next to the hall and was taken out of service in 1972.

Moore Park, 21km (13 miles) north of Bundaberg, is an excellent seaside beach with 16km (10 miles) of firm sandy shores. Lifesavers patrol this beach throughout the surfing season. There is a motel and a caravan park.

The Town of 1770 (and Agnes Water to the south of Round Hill) was visited by Queensland's first tourist, Captain James Cook, in the *Endeavour* in May 1770. The small town takes its name from this event. Day trips to Lady Musgrave Island depart from the Town of 1770, and a bus pick-up operates from Bundaberg.

Chapter 36
Bundaberg to Rockhampton

Gladstone

Population 42,000
Location and Characteristics
Located 107km south of Rockhampton, Gladstone is a bustling port centre, one of the busiest and largest in the country. From its modest beginnings in 1847 as a small penal colony with a population below 200, it has grown to become home to more than 42,000 people.

Heron Island is only 73km off the coast of Gladstone.

How to Get There
By Air
Flight West, ©1300 130 092, and Sunstate, ©13 1313, service Gladstone Airport.
By Coach
McCaffertys stop off at Gladstone on their coastal route, ©13 1499.
By Rail
Gladstone Railway Station is on the Brisbane/ Cairns line, ©4972 4211. Queensland Rail can be contacted on ©13 2235.

By Car
Travel south from Rockhampton along the Bruce Highway for 100km until you reach the Gladstone turnoff (left) at Mt Larcom, then follow this until it terminates at Gladstone. Coming north, the town is 539km north of Brisbane and 170km north of Bundaberg.

Visitor Information
The Gladstone Area Promotion and Development Bureau is at Ferry Terminal, Gladstone Marina, Bryan Jordan Drive, ©4972 4000, and they will be able to assist you with enquiries. They have an online address at ☜www.gladstoneregion. com and email at ✉gapdl@gladstone region.org.au

Accommodation and Services
Gladstone is well-serviced for a town its size. Following is a selection of available accommodation, with rates representing a double room per night, which should be used as a guide only.
Country Plaza International, 100 Goondoon Street, ©4972 4499. 73 units, licensed restaurant, undercover parking, room service, pool - ✪$110.
Camelot, 19 Agnes Street, ©4979 1222. 16 units, 8 suites, licensed restaurant (closed Sunday), room service, pool - ✪$75, suites $95-120.
Gladstone Reef, cnr Goondoon & Yarroon Streets, ©4972 1000. 48 units, night club Friday and Saturday, licensed restaurant (closed Sunday), pool, room service - ✪$80-95.
Park View Gladstone, 42 Roseberry Street, ©4972 3344. 25 units, 1 suite, undercover parking, pool, sauna - ✪$60-65.
Sun Court Motor Inn, Far Street, ©4972 2377. 12 units, undercover parking, playground, pool, spa - ✪$65-70.
Mawarra, 6 Scenery Street, ©4972 1411. 32 units, cooking facilities, licensed restaurant (closed Sunday), undercover parking, playground, pool, room service - ✪$60-65.
Rusty Anchor Motor Inn, 167 Goondoon Street, ©4972 2099. 22 units, licensed restaurant (closed Sunday), room service, pool - ✪$60-70.
Queens, cnr Goondoon & Williams Streets, ©4972 6615. 13 units, licensed restaurant (closed Sunday) - ✪$50
Caravan Parks
Kin Kora Village Caravan Park, Olsen Avenue, Kin Kora, ©4978 5461. 70 sites, barbecue, pool, playground - powered sites ✪$17 for two, units $55 for two, on-site vans $30 for two.
Barney Beach Seabreeze Caravan Park, Friend Street, ©Barney Point, ©4972 1366. 64 sites, barbecue - powered sites ✪$18 for two, villas $55 for two, cabins $40 for two.
Eating Out
There are plenty of good places to dine in Gladstone.
For Chinese cuisine, try *China Garden*, 19 Tank Street, ©4972 5044 or *Dragon Garden*, 40 Tank Street, ©4972 9998.

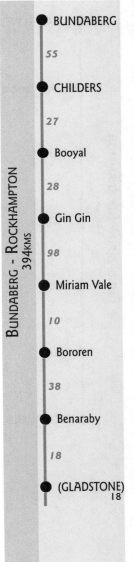

Bundaberg to Rockhampton

BUNDABERG ● BUNDABERG
55
● CHILDERS
27
● Booyal
28
● Gin Gin
98
● Miriam Vale
10
● Bororen
38
● Benaraby
18
● (GLADSTONE)
18

BUNDABERG - ROCKHAMPTON 394KMS

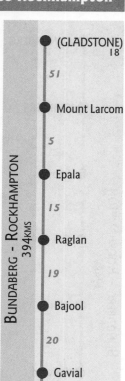

BUNDABERG - ROCKHAMPTON   394KMS

(GLADSTONE)	18
51	
Mount Larcom	
5	
Epala	
15	
Raglan	
19	
Bajool	
20	
Gavial	
14	
ROCKHAMPTON	

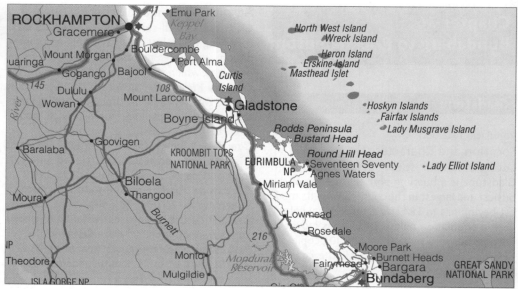

Bundaberg to Rockhampton

For Thai, there is the **Thai Classic** at 28 Tank Street, ©4972 1647.

If you are after Italian, **Amici's** is in 111 Tolooa Street, ©4972 2082 and **Fasta Pasta** is on the corner of Park Road and the Dawson Highway, ©4972 2577.

Flinders, on Flinders Parade, ©4972 8322, specialise in seafood.

Other choices include **Clancy's**, 19 Tank Street, ©4972 5044; **Kapers**, 124 Goondoon Street, ©4972 7902; **Klickity's**, cnr Far Street & Dawson Highway, ©4972 4322; and **Scottie's Bar & Restaurant**, 46 Goondoon Street, ©4972 9999.

Also remember that some of the hotels and motels serve adequate meals, which saves you the trouble of venturing far from your chosen accommodation - particularly appealing after a long drive.

Local Transport

The number for Blue & White Taxis in Gladstone is ©13 1008.

Points of Interest

The **Gladstone Art Gallery and Museum** is in Goondoon Street and ⏲opens 10am-5pm on weekdays and 10am-4pm on weekends. The building itself is a unique mix of architectural designs and complements the collection of Australian art and local memorabilia contained within. Admission is free.

The **Tondoon Botanic Gardens** cover 83ha and are considered the best of their type among Queensland's regional centres. The landscape is made up of lakes and forest and the fauna includes colourful birds and turtles. Access is between ⏲9am and 6pm in the summer months, and half an hour earlier (morning and evening) during winter. The Gardens can be entered through Glenlyon Road.

Just off the coast of Gladstone are the outlying **Curtis** and **Quoin Islands**.

Monto, 203km (126 miles) south west of Bundaberg, is the largest town of the North Burnett and the service centre for the surrounding dairy industry.

24km (15 miles) north-east is **Cania Gorge**, with its spectacular sandstone formations and crystal pools. Walkways and boardwalks extend well into the gorge. 8km further on is the massive Cania Dam, where there are attractive picnic areas. Gold was discovered at Cania in 1891, and some flecks can be panned from the streams even today.

If you wish to strike out west to get some dust in your hair and put paradise at your back, there are several highlights within 300km of Rockhampton. You will find historic mining towns and expansive outback landscapes to appreciate - in contrast to the lush rainforests, white sands, endless torquoise waters and vibrant coral formations of the Great Barrier Reef area.

Lady Elliot Island

Location and Characteristics
The most southerly of the islands of the Great Barrier Reef, Lady Elliot has an area of 0.42 sq km and has been nicknamed Queensland's "Shipwreck Island". This name is not unwarranted, as the wrecks of many ships can be seen littered around the island's shores. The first was probably in 1851, the *Bolton Abbey* cargo ship, and the latest was the *Tenggara II* which hit the reef in April, 1989.

The island is also popular with bird watchers as 57 species are known to flock here, with more than 200,000 birds nesting during the summer. Sea turtles also nest on Lady Elliot.

How to Get There
By Air
The island has an airstrip serviced by Whitaker Air Charters, ©1800 072 200 (free call), whose scenic flights operate daily from both Bundaberg and Hervey Bay.

These flights can be taken by resort guests, or by day-trippers for whom the fare includes the return flight, a picnic lunch, reef walking and snorkelling.

Visitor Information
Contact the resort on ©3348 8522 or ©1800 072 200 (free call). You can visit the web page at ☞www.ladyelliot.com.au or send an email to ✉info@ladyelliot.com.au

Accommodation
The *Lady Elliot Island Resort*, ©1800 072 200, is located on the beach front, and is rated at 2-star. There are 5 Island Suites, 24 Reef Units, 14 Tent Cabins and 6 Lodges.

The Resort has a licensed restaurant, cocktail bar, swimming pool, entertainment, novelty golf course, dive shop, resort shop, poolside bar and bistro, Reef Education Centre, glass bottom boat, baby sitting, snorkelling, scuba courses, guided eco tours, charter fishing boat, and a tour desk.

Units have private facilities, fans, balcony and maid service.

Prices per person per night, twin share, are:
Island Suite -   ✪$210 adults, $105 children
Reef Cabin -   ✪$185, $90 children
Tent or Lodge - ✪$140 adults, $70 children

Tariff includes accommodation, dinner, breakfast and snorkelling equipment.

Maximum occupancy of each unit is 4 persons (including children). Credit cards accepted: Visa, MasterCard, Bankcard, American Express, Diners Club.

Points of Interest
It only takes about an hour to walk around the entire island, and it is one of the least commercialised.
Diving
There are ten excellent diving sites that include Lighthouse Bommie, Coral Gardens, Moiri and Shark Pool. Visibility ranges from 80 to 25 to 50 metres. This island is also paradise for those who like exploring shipwrecks.

All equipment can be hired from the resort for around $60, and open water courses are available for ✪$550. Shore dives cost $30, boat dives $45 and night dives $60.

Lady Musgrave Island

Location and Characteristics
Lady Musgrave Island is part of the Capricorn Bunker Group, and is about 100km north-east of Bundaberg. It is a true coral cay, approximately 18ha in area, and rests on the edge of a huge coral lagoon that measures some eight kilome-

tres in circumference and covers an area of around 1192ha. The lagoon is one of very few on the Reef that ships can enter, making the island very popular with the yachting fraternity. Lady Musgrave is a National and Marine Park, and an unspoilt section of the Great Barrier Reef.

How to Get There

MV *Lady Musgrave* is a catamaran that sails from Port Bundaberg on Tues, Thurs, Sat and Sun, with extra services during school holidays. Even so, it is always advisable to book well ahead through Lady Musgrave Barrier Reef Cruises, Bundaberg Port Marina, Shop 1 Moffatt Street, Bundaberg, ✆4159 4519 or ✆1800 072 110. The trip out to the island takes about two-and-a-half hours, and passengers are allowed four hours on the island.

On reaching the island passengers are transferred to the semi-submersible for some coral viewing, and on returning to the catamaran a visit is made to the underwater observatory. Lunch is then served and afterwards passengers are taken ashore to explore the island. Snorkelling gear is provided for the day.

The cruise costs are ✪$180 for one certified dive, $205 for two dives, $195 for a diving introduction and $130 for snorkelling.

This cruise can also be used for people wishing to camp on Lady Musgrave.

Accommodation

There is no choice in this regard - if you wish to stay on Lady Musgrave Island you must camp. There are staff on-site, toilets and walking trails, and that is it. You have to first obtain a camping permit from the QNP&WS or Naturally Queensland, ✆3227 8187, and fees are ✪$3.50 per person per night.

Diving

The island is reputedly one of the finest dive sites on the Great Barrier Reef, and is home to around 1200 species of fish and 350 varieties of coral. The lagoon is reasonably shallow, allowing longer dives to be undertaken.

MV *Lady Musgrave* always has qualified diving instructors on board for the inexperienced, but they can also head certified divers in the best direction to get the most out of their trip.

Heron Island

Location and Characteristics

The island is about 72km east of Gladstone, roughly 100km from Rockhampton, and has an area of 19ha. It is a true coral cay that sits on the Tropic of Capricorn, surrounded by 24 sq km of reef.

It is possible to walk around the island in less than half an hour, and there is usually an organised beach and reef walk every day. Heron's eastern end has a track system that leads through dense pisonia forest and open grassy shrubland, with information posts along the way. In the summer months be sure to stay on the track, or you could destroy one of the many shearwater burrows that honeycomb the island.

The survey vessel *Fly* was the first to record the existence of Heron Island during its voyage of 1843. The captain named the island after the many reef herons, which are now known as reef egrets. Nothing much is recorded about visitors to the islands until around 1910 when birdwatchers and other naturalists came to explore. These groups did not usually have their bases on Heron, so their visits were only brief sojourns.

In the mid-1920s a canning factory was built where the resort office now stands, and turtle harvesting began. By the end of the decade the supply of turtles had dwindled and industry here ceased, although some turtles were caught here and sent south right up until they were declared a protected species in 1950. The clumsy creatures still come to Heron to lay their eggs.

In 1932, the canning factory was converted into a resort by Cristian Poulsen, and in 1936 he was granted the special lease on which the resort is built. Many facilities were added to the resort, and a regular flying-boat service was established before Poulsen disappeared from a dinghy near the island in 1947. The resort remained in the family until 1974.

The Heron Island research station commenced operations in 1951 and has an international reputation for coral reef research and education. In 1943 a national park was declared on Heron Island, and in 1974 Queensland's first marine National Park was declared over the Heron and Wistari Reefs. In 1979 the Capricornia section of the Great Barrier Reef Marine Park was declared under new federal government legislation.

How to Get There

Unfortunately, due to its distance from the mainland, Heron Island is one of the most expensive islands to visit.

By Air

Marine Helicopters, at Gladstone Airport, ©4978 1177, fly from Gladstone to Heron Island on a 30 minute trip. They don't have a regular schedule, but will meet flights into Gladstone to transfer passengers to the island. Obviously it is best to contact them before you arrive in Gladstone. Fares for adults are ✪$270 one-way, $440 return, half-price for children.

By Sea

A catamaran makes the trip from Gladstone to Heron in a little under two hours, but it can be a very choppy trip, so make sure you have some seasickness pills. It departs at 11am and returns about 3.45pm. Fares are ✪$85 each way (adult), $42 each way for children. Bookings can be made through the Resort.

Visitor Information

There is a website at ☞www.heronisland.com and email at ✉visitors@greatberrierreef.aus.net
The Resort can be phoned direct on ©132 469.

Accommodation and Services

The *Heron Island Resort*, ©4978 1488 or ©132 469, has 5 types of accommodation - 30 Turtle Cabins, 44 Reef Suites, 38 Heron Suites, 1 Beach House and 4 Point Suites.

The Cabins are budget bungalows, with basic facilities, shared bathroom and bunk sleeping arrangements. You may find yourself housed with strangers to make up numbers.

The Suites have a balcony and ensuite, and accommodate up to four people. The Point Suites are an extra-large version.

The Beach House occupies a premium beachfront position and has a balcony and ensuite. It accommodates two adults only.

Tarrifs per person per night are as follows:
Turtle Cabins - ✪$180 adults.
Reef Suites -   ✪$260 (adults, twin share).
Heron Suites - ✪$300 (adults, twin share).
Beach House - ✪$360.
Point Suites -   ✪$400 (adults, twin share).

These prices include all meals, and most activities.

Resort facilities are: restaurant, cocktail bar, coffee shop, tennis court, games room, two swimming pools, babysitting, discotheque, entertainment, reef walks, jumbo outdoor chess, dive shop, resort shop, SCUBA courses, snorkelling, Kids' Klub during school holiday and a semi-submersible reef viewer.

Rooms have private facilities, tea and coffee making facilities, refrigerator, mini bar on request, ceiling fans, daily cleaning service and inter-connecting rooms.

Credit cards accepted: Visa, MasterCard, Bankcard, American Express.

Diving

At other islands on the Reef it is sometimes necessary to travel 70 or 80 km for scuba diving and snorkelling, but at Heron the Reef is at the very foot of the white sandy beaches.

One of the most spectacular diving sites is the well-known Heron Bommie, a head of hard coral rising more than 18m from the seabed that is home to all kinds of fish and marine life.

All equipment can be hired from the resort's dive shop, and the six-day certificate diving course costs around ✪$450. Day dives, including all equipment, cost around $60.

Heron hosts a week-long Dive Festival in November each year, when divers from all over the world gather to swap knowledge and experience. There are those who think that this island rates highly among the world's premier dive locations, and given that there are twenty unique sites nearby, they are probably right.

Chapter 37
Rockhampton

Population 65,000
Gateway to the Capricorn Coast, Rockhampton is 660km (410 miles) north of Brisbane, on the Tropic of Capricorn. The city is situated on the Fitzroy River about 16km (10 miles) from the coast.

Climate

Average temperatures: January max 31C (88F) - min 22C (72F); July max 23C (73F) - min 9C (48F). Most rain falls between December and March - approximately 500mm (17 in).

Characteristics

'Rocky' is the heart of the beef cattle country. The main breeds are Santa Gertrudis, Hereford, Braford, Brahman, Africander and Zebu. Rockhampton also has two flour mills which process wheat from the Central Highlands around Emerald. Ever since Queensland became a separate state, there have been people politicising for the establishment of a separate North Queensland state.

How to Get There

By Air

Sunstate, ©13 1313, fly to/from Bundaberg, Gladstone, Mackay, Mary-borough, Townsville and Cairns, Great Keppel Island and Toowoomba. Eastern Airlines, ©13 1313, fly to/from the Gold Coast.
It is a good idea to check regional flight availability with your travel agent.

By Bus

Greyhound Pioneer, ©13 2030, and McCaffertys, ©13 1499, stop at Rockhampton on their Brisbane/North Queensland route.
McCaffertys have a daily service to/from Longreach.

Greyhound also have a Rockhampton/Longreach service departing 3 times weekly.

By Rail

Queensland Tilt Trains, ©13 2235, including The Spirit of Capricorn, service Rockhampton fairly frequently, with either day or overnight travel.
The Sunlander and the Queenslander both leave Brisbane in the early morning and stop at Rockhampton.

By Car

From Brisbane, via the Bruce Highway 660km (410 miles), or take the inland route via Esk and Biloela 758km (470 miles). Rockhampton is 1413km (878 miles) south of Cairns.

Visitor Information

Capricorn Tourism is at 'The Spire' in Gladstone Road, ©4927 2055, adjacent to the Tropic of Capricorn Spire. It is ⊙open 7 days a week and should be your first stop.
    The email address is ✎ captour@rocknet .net.au and the website is ⌖www.capricorn coast.com.au
    You will find the Rockhampton Tourist Information Centre in Quay Street, ©4922 5339.

Accommodation

Rockhampton has no shortage of motels, and there are plenty of older style hotels near the city centre. There is also no shortage of camping grounds. Below we have given a selection with prices for a double room per night, which should be used as a guide only. The telephone area code is 07.
Country Comfort Rockhampton, 86 Victoria Parade, ©4927 9933. 78 units, licensed restaurant, barbecue, swimming pool - ✪$105.
Ambassador on the Park, 161 George Street, ©4927 5855. 70 units, 3 suites, licensed restaurant, swimming pool - ✪$100-125.
Archer Park, 39 Albert Street, ©4927 9266. 26 units, licensed restaurant, swimming pool, undercover parking - ✪$80-85.
Sundowner Chain Motor Inns Rockhampton, 112 Gladstone Road, ©4927 8866. 32 units, licensed restaurant, swimming pool - ✪$65-110.

Rockhampton

Central Park, 224 Murray Street, ✆4927 2333. 26 units, licensed restaurant (closed Sun), swimming pool - ✪$70-85.

Leichardt Hotel Rockhampton, cnr Bolsover & Denham Streets, ✆4927 6733. 60 rooms, 8 suites, licensed restaurant and bistro - ✪$55-135.

Club Crocodile Motor Inn, cnr Albert & Alma Streets, ✆4927 7433. 44 units, licensed restaurant (closed Sunday), swimming pool - ✪$80-95.

Glenmore Palms, Bruce Highway, Glenmore, North Rockhampton, ✆4926 1144. 38 units, licensed restaurant, swimming pool, spa - ✪$80-100.

Centre Point Motor Inn, 131 George Street, ✆4927 8844. 48 units, licensed restaurant, heated swimming pool - ✪$100.

Golden Fountain Motel, 166 Gladstone Road, ✆4927 1055. 31 units, swimming pool - ✪$80-100.

Caravan Parks

Tropical Wanderer Resort, 394 Yaamba Road, ✆4926 3822. (No pets) 150 sites, licensed restaurants, barbecue, tennis (half court), pool - powered sites ✪$22 for two, cabins $55-65 for two.

Ramblers Motor Village, Bruce Highway, North Rockhampton, (opposite Shopping Fair), ✆4928 2084. (No pets) 60 sites, playground, pool - powered sites ✪$19 for two, units $55-60 for two, cabins $40-50 for two.

Southside Holiday Village, Lower Dawson Road, ✆4927 3013. 200 sites, heated pool, tennis (half court) - powered sites ✪$21 for two, on-site vans $30-40 for two, cabins $50-55 for two.

Riverside Tourist Park Rockhampton, Reaney Street, North Rockhampton, ✆4922 3779. (No pets allowed) 150 sites - powered sites ✪$16 for two.

Gracemere Caravan Park, Old Capricorn Highway, ✆4933 1310. 100 sites, barbecue, pool - powered sites ✪$13.

There is a **Youth Hostel** at 60 McFarlane Street, North Rockhampton, ✆4927 5288. They have 13 rooms at ✪$18 per adult per night twin share.

Eating Out

Most of the hotels serve casual counter meals, and the steaks in Rocky are particularly large, as this is the heart of the cattle country. The hotels, and several motels, also have licensed restaurants. A wide assortment of cuisine is available, from Chinese to seafood. Here are some names and numbers of establishments in the area:

Dragon Gallery, 295 Richardson Road, North Rockhampton, ✆4928 3399. Traditional Chinese cuisine.

Hogs Breath Cafe, Aquatic Place, North Rockhampton, ✆4926 3646. Hamburgers and steaks.

Hong Kong Seafood Restaurant, 98a Denham Street, Rockhampton, ✆4927 7144.

Pacinos, cnr Fitzroy & George Streets, Rockhampton, ✆4922 5833. Italian fare.

Thai Tanee Restaurant, cnr Bolsover & William Streets, Rockhampton, ✆4922 1255.

Wah Hah, 70 Denham Street, Rockhampton, ✆4927 1659. Chinese selections.

Sizzler, Rockhamtpon Shopping Fair, Rockhampton, ✆4926 1100. Australian steaks and salad.

Cravings Bar and Grill, cnr Water Street and Lakes Creek Road, North Rockhampton, ✆4928 5666.

Le Bistro on Quay, 194 Quay Street, Rockhampton, ✆4922 2019.

Cactus Jacks Restaurant, 243 Musgrave Street, North Rockhampton, ✆4922 2062.

Diamonds Down by the River, Quay Street, Rockhampton, ✆4921 1811.

Friends Bistro, 159 East Street, Rockhampton, ✆4922 2689.

Jans Restaurant, Pilbeam Theatre, Victoria Parade, Rockhampton, ✆4922 3060.

There are two McDonalds branches, one on the Bruce Highway in North Rockhampton and the other on the corner of George and Fitzroy Streets, Rockhampton. KFC also has two outlets, one at the corner of George and Arthur Streets, Rockhampton, and the other on the corner of Linnet Street and Queen Elizabeth Drive, North Rockhampton. Pizza Hut is on the corner of High

Street and Bruce Highway, North Rochampton, and on the corner of Denham Street and Bruce Highway in Rockhampton, ©13 1166.

Entertainment

Rockhampton has a three cinema complex in Shopping Fair, North Rockhampton, ©4926 6977, and indoor and outdoor concert venues.

There are three nightclubs in the city:

Strutters, cnr East & Williams Streets, ©4922 2882.

The Party Shack, cnr William & Alma Streets, ©4927 2005.

William Street Nite Club, 4 William Street, ©4927 1144.

The *Pilbeam Theatre* in Victoria Parade attracts regular performances by national and international artists, ©4927 4111.

For details of current entertainment programs at hotels, clubs, and so on, ask at the Visitor Information Centre.

Shopping

Rockhampton has never been described as a shopping capital, but the *Shopping Fair*, Yaaamba Road, North Rockhampton, ©4928 9166, was refurbished a few years ago and should cater to your basic needs. It has a department store, two supermarkets, over 100 specialty shops, a food court, and a licensed restaurant.

The *City Heart Mall*, in Bolsover Street, has local art and craft markets on Saturdays, ©4936 8481.

Points of Interest

Rockhampton was first settled in the 1850s by Charles and William Archer. Today, historic **Quay Street** contains over 20 buildings which have been classified by the National Trust.

The city is the commercial and administrative centre of central Queensland. Its wide streets are lined with trees and solid buildings, indicating a prosperity dating back to the early days. The Australian Estate Co Ltd offices were built in 1861, and the Customs House in 1901. It has a handsome copper dome and a striking semi-circular portico. Queens Wharf is all that remains of the quays of the port that was very busy un-

til silt caused the demise of the river trade. St Joseph's Cathedral (cnr Murray and William Streets) and St Paul's Anglican Cathedral are both built in Gothic Style from local sandstone. The Royal Arcade was built in 1889 as a theatre with a special feature - the roof could be opened on hot nights.

The Botanic Gardens in Spencer Street, ©4922 4347, are reputed to be one of the finest tropical gardens in Australia. Spreading over 4ha (10 acres), these gardens contain many native and exotic trees, ferns and shrubs, as well as a large walk-in aviary, orchid and fern house and a small Australian Zoo, which includes its own Koala Park. As part of a sister city agreement with Ibusuki City in Japan, separate Japanese Gardens were created in 1982. There are also paddle boat rides available on the lagoon. The gardens are open 6am-6pm daily and admission is free.

The Pilbeam Theatre, ©4927 4111 and **Art Gallery**, ©4936 8248, in Victoria Parade, form the cultural centre of Rocky. The Art Gallery has an extensive collection of Australian paintings, pottery and sculpture. The Pilbeam Theatre attracts regular performances by national and international stars.

St Aubin's Village, on Canoona Road beside the airport, consists of one of Rockhampton's oldest houses, and a number of gift shops specialising in cottage industries. It is open 9am-6pm Mon-Sat and on Sundays 9am-2pm. Admission is free.

Callaghan Park Racecourse, ©4927 1300, is Queensland's premier provincial racetrack. Thursday night has greyhound racing, Saturday evening has harness racing, and on Saturday afternoon it's the gallopers' turn.

Fitzroy River Ski Gardens, near the Barrage bridge, beside the boat launching facilities, has picnic facilities, a children's playground and electric barbecues.

Old Glenmore Homestead, ©4936 1033, through the Parkhurst Industrial Estate in the north of the city, is a 130-year-old complex consisting of a log cabin, slab cottage and an adobe house. Old Glenmore holds Queensland's first Historic Inn Licence, so visitors can sample some of the State's best fermented beverages in this pleasant old world setting. Bush dances and home-style cooking are also features. It is ⏱open only on Sundays between 11am and 3pm. Admission is ✪$7 for adults and $2 for children. Groups are allowed by appointment.

Cammoo Caves, ✆4934 2774, and **Olsen's Capricorn Caverns**, ✆4934 2883, approximately 23km (14miles) north of Rockhampton, are two cave systems which are open to the public. Cave coral, fossils and gigantic tree roots can be inspected in these dry, limestone caves. Cammoo Caves are ⏱open daily 8.30am-4.30pm and have conducted tours. Entry fees are adults ✪$8 and children $4. Olsen's, about 2km east of Cammoo, is privately owned, and 3 hour half-day tours into these caves cost ✪$33 adults, $16 children, departing from your accommodation in Rockhampton around 9am.

The Dreamtime Cultural Centre, ✆4936 1655, is a large Aboriginal Cultural Centre, and is on the Bruce Highway opposite the turn-off to Yeppoon. The centre is ⏱open daily 10am-5.15pm, with guided tours between 11am and 4pm (2 hours duration). Refreshments are available (eating bush tucker is not compulsory). Adults are charged ✪$13 and children $6.

Rockhampton Heritage Village is in Boundary Road, Parkhurst, ✆4936 1026. Attractions include a blacksmith's shop, wheel wrighting, dairy, fully furnished slab cottage, pioneering tools, vintage cars, horse-drawn vehicles, Hall of Clocks and a kiosk. Tours are conducted daily, and there are working demonstrations on the last Sunday of each month. It is ⏱open daily 10am-4pm and admission is ✪$12 adults and $7 children.

Koorana Crocodile Farm is in Koowonga Road, off Emu Park Road. This is a breeding farm, not a protective reserve, so don't be surprised when when you find crocodile kebabs on the menu, and crocodile skin shoes and purses for sale in the gift shop. The Crocodile Farm is ⏱open daily and costs adults ✪$15, children $7, and $12 per person for groups.

Sport

Rockhampton has all the usual facilities you would expect of a town of its size. To get to the beach, though, you have to drive 45km to the Capricorn Coast.

Diving

Capricorn Reef Diving, 189 Musgrave Street, North Rockhampton, ✆4922 7720, offer 5-day open water certificate PADI course. Classes are taken in Rockhampton, followed by 4 dives on the Keppel Island Group.

Tours

Rothery's Coaches, 13 Power Street, North Rockhampton, ✆4922 4320, offer tours of the city and to the Capricorn Coast, Koorana Crocodile Farm, Cooberrie Park, The Caves and the Dreamtime Culture Centre.

Duncan's Off Road 4WD Tours are in Kent Street, Rockhampton, ✆0418 986 050 (mobile).

Chapter 38
Rockhampton to Mackay

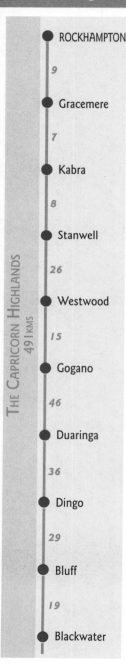

ROCKHAMPTON

9

Gracemere

7

Kabra

8

Stanwell

26

Westwood

15

Gogano

46

Duaringa

36

Dingo

29

Bluff

19

Blackwater

THE CAPRICORN HIGHLANDS
491 KMS

Capricorn Highlands

Location and Characteristics

The highlands stretch from Carnarvon to Clermont (Gregory Highway) and from Blackwater to Jericho (Capricorn Highway). The region is one of the most diverse and productive areas in the country. Coal, sapphires, cattle, sheep, wheat, sunflower, sorghum and cotton are but a few of the riches produced from around here. The Emerald Irrigation Scheme, along with the Fairbairn Dam, has increased rural productivity tenfold in the heart of the Highlands.

Visitor Information

Central Highlands Tourism Queensland can be contacted on ✆4982 4942 or emailed at ✉chtour@maxspeed.net.au. You will find plenty of useful information at ✇members.tripod.com/centralhighlands/

Points of Interest

A visit to this area can be a rewarding experience. The **Carnarvon Gorge** offers a breathtaking view of scenery, lush vegetation and Aboriginal art.

The town of **Springsure** has the famous Virgin Rock, and from **Emerald**, the hub of the Central Highlands, you can join a conducted tour of the **Gregory Coal Mine**, ✆4982 8200.

Travelling through **Capella** brings you to the township of **Clermont**, which was almost completely destroyed by a flood in 1916, and was moved to its present location with the aid of a huge steam engine. The engine has been preserved as a memorial in the centre of the town.

A National Park at **Blackdown Tablelands** offers camping facilities and good views.

After crossing the Drummond Range, the country opens out into Queensland's vast grazing lands, and towns like **Alpha** and **Jericho** are becoming increasingly popular stopovers for people visiting this outback area. It has become even more so since the opening in 1988 of the Stockman's Hall of Fame, ✆4658 2166, on the Landsborough Highway in **Longreach**.

The Central Queensland gemfields are a popular tourist spot in the Capricorn Region, and visitors come for a chance to 'stub their toe on a sapphire'. Towns such as **Anakie**, **Sapphire**, **Rubyvale** and the **Willows Gemfields** must be experienced to be fully appreciated. In Rubyvale you can visit a walk-in mine, called **Bobby Dazzler**, which has guided tours and is ☺open daily. It is in Main Street, ✆4985 4170.

Mount Morgan

Location and Characteristics

The historic township of Mount Morgan is 40km (25 miles) south of Rockhampton, and here you can tour through a 100-year-old mining town that is the real thing, not a reconstruction. Mt Morgan was listed as a Heritage Town by the Australian Heritage Commission in 1980, and by the National Trust of Queensland in 1981. The **Museum** on Morgan Street, ✆4938 4122, traces the history of the fabulously rich mine. Inspections of the mine are conducted by *Mt Morgan Mine Tours*, 38 Central Street, ✆4938 1081.

Whilst in town, you can call into the **Golden Nugget Hotel** on the Central Street, for a cool ale.

Mt Hay Gemstone Tourist Park

Location and Characteristics

It is 40km (25 miles) west of Rockhampton on the Capricorn Highway, Wycarbah. There you can fossick for 120 million-year-old Thundereggs. When the eggs are cut in the gemstone factory on the premises, beautiful agate patterns are exposed. Facilities here also include a swimming pool, craft and gift shop, barbecue facilities and powered caravan sites (✿$14 per night for two people), ✆4934 7183.

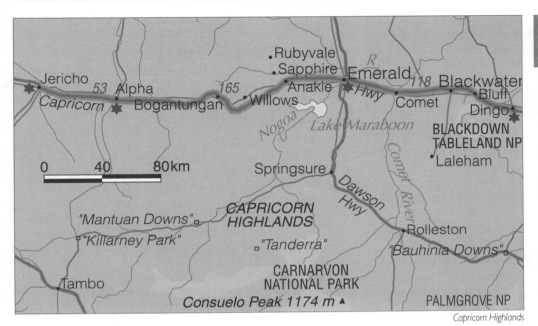

Capricorn Highlands

THE CAPRICORN HIGHLANDS 491 KMS

- Blackwater
- 35
- Comet
- 40
- Emerald
- 44
- Anakie
- 92
- Alpha
- 85
- Jericho

Great Keppel Island

Location and Characteristics

The island is a very popular tourist destination. Fringed by 17km (10 miles) of white, sandy beaches and offshore coral reefs, it provides an ideal setting for holiday makers and day trippers alike.

The Keppel Island group of 30 islands is situated 55km from Rockhampton, and 15km east of Rosslyn Bay on the Capricorn Coast. Great Keppel is the only island in the group to have been developed, and this is because of its permanent water supply as well as its size (14 sq km).

Some islands in the group are national parks - North Keppel, Miall, Middle, Halfway, Humpy and Peak - where camping is permitted, but numbers are limited. All drinking water has to be taken to these islands, but some have water for washing, and some have toilets, but it is best to get full information from either the Naturally Queensland Information Centre in Brisbane, ©3227 8187, or the QNP&WS branch on the corner of Yeppoon & Norman Roads,

Rockhampton, ©4936 0511, when applying for a camping permit. It is also wise to check on the fishing regulations for the area you are going to visit.

Great Keppel

In May 1770 Captain Cook sailed past Great Keppel and named it after Admiral Augustus Keppel, who later became the First Lord of the Admiralty.

A naturalist from the *Rattlesnake* is given the credit of being the first European to visit the island when he came ashore in 1847, but the Woppabura Aboriginal people had been living there for over 4,500 years. They called the island Wapparaburra.

The first European settlers arrived in 1906, but they could not live happily with the Aborigines and in fact treated them very badly. The Leeke family moved to the island in the 1920s and grazed sheep there until the 1940s. Their name is remembered in Leeke's Beach and Leeke's Creek, and the restored Homestead is where they lived. The resort opened in 1967.

Although not situated on the Reef, Great

Keppel is the gateway to the Outer Reef and North West Island, the largest coral cay in the Great Barrier Reef. It is a major breeding ground for Green Turtles, White Capped Noddy Terns, Wedge Tailed Shearwaters and Olive Head Sea Snakes.

Day trips to Great Keppel Island are available from *Keppel Tourist Services*, ✆4933 6744 or ✆1800 356 744 (free call). The trip lasts 8 hours and includes a cruise transfer from Rosslyn Bay, snorkelling and boom netting, buffet lunch and free time. The day trip costs ✪$80 adults, $45 children and $200 for families.

How to Get There
By Air
15 minute air transfers are available from Rockhampton Airport, ✆4936 8314 for more details. There are also coach transfers from the airport to Rosslyn Bay.
By Coach
If you are staying in Rockhampton, contact Rothery's Coaches, ✆4922 4320, or Young's Bus Service, ✆4922 3813, to check times for connecting bus services to Rosslyn Bay. The coach trip usually costs around ✪$28 for an adult.
By Sea
Ferries leave from Rosslyn Bay Harbour, south of Yeppoon.
Keppel Tourist Services, ✆4933 6744.
Capricornia Cruises, ✆4933 6730.
Australis Cruises, ✆0418 728 965.
Euphoria Catamaran Cruises, ✆1300 301 251
You can expect to pay upwards of ✪$70 for a family of four.
By Car
Visitors that have their own transport can enquire about long-term parking at Kempsea Car Park, 422 Scenic Highway, Rosslyn Harbour, ✆4933 6670, which is north of the harbour turn-off, on the main road, and has complimentary transport from there to the wharf.

Visitor Information
If you would like online details of the Great Keppel Island Resort, the web site is 👁www.

mpx.com.au/~adventures/gk/keppel.htm

Accommodation and Services
The *Great Keppel Island Resort*, ✆4939 5044, has over 190 units, labelled Garden, Beachfront or Hillside Villas. The Garden and Beachfront are rated 3-star, and the Villas are 4-star.

Resort facilities are: nightclub, live entertainment, 2 restaurants, bars, heated swimming pool, spa, kids' club, games room, squash, tennis courts, laundry/ironing, quick snack bar, fishing, babysitting, tube rides, golf, tandem- skydiving, cricket, waterskiing, parasailing, baseball, snorkelling, sailboarding, catamaran sailing, beach volleyball, SCUBA diving, cruising and coral-viewing, Barrier Reef trips and EFTPOS.

Unit facilities are: tea and coffee making facilities, refrigerator, ceiling fans (Garden and Beachfront) air-conditioning (Ocean View), colour TV, in-house movies, IDD/STD telephone, radio, inter-connecting rooms and a daily cleaning service.

Tariffs for a double room per night night are:
Garden -　　　　✪$170-330 adult
Beachfront -　　✪$220-410 adult
Hillside Villas - ✪$255-470 adult

The above rates are room only. Cheaper rates are available for longer stays, and packages are available which include meals.

Additional to the tariffs are: Barrier Reef trips, boom netting, cruising and coral viewing, deserted island drop-off, dinghies with outboards, fishing and yacht charters, island waterways cruise, kids camp-out (children 5-14 years), masseuse, scuba diving courses, scuba diving trips to the Great Barrier Reef, sunset cruise, tandem skydiving, tube rides, underwater observatory and waterskiing.

Reservations can be made by contacting the resort directly on ✆4939 5044. Credit cards accepted: Visa, MasterCard, Bankcard, Diners Club, American Express.

Keppel Haven, ✆4933 6744, have 12 cabins with cooking facilities, but bathrooms and laundry are shared. The room-only tariff is ✪$110 per night for a double.

Resort facilities include kiosk, gift shop, licensed restaurant, dive shop, jet ski and water sports hire.

There are also pre-erected tents that cost ✪$22 per person, in the Breeze Way section. There is undercover communal cooking and washing up, a refrigerator and barbecue, but no kitchen utensils.

And lastly, there is the Tent Village, where you must provide your own bedding and linen, and use common cooking facilities. There are units here for ✪$25 a night per person.

The **Great Keppel YHA Hostel**, ✆4927 5288, is a self-contained area within the Keppel Haven complex. It has 20 rooms in the main building, with a kitchen, bathrooms and a laundry. Tariffs are ✪$20 per adult twin share. Bookings and courtesy transfer arrangements can be made direct or through Rockhampton YHA, ✆4927 5288.

Local Transport

There are no motor vehicles on the island, so you can walk the many bush tracks or relax on the beach in peace.

Eating Out

Apart from the restaurants at the accommodation complexes, there are a couple of additional choices:

Between the Resort and Keppel Haven is the **Shell House**, ✆4939 1004, where you can get really tasty Devonshire tea, or pick up some scones and cakes for afternoon tea back at the tent or cabin. The place has, of course, a good shell collection, and contains information on the history of the island.

Nearby on The Esplanade is **Island Pizza**, ✆4939 4699, which also sells hot dogs, subs and pasta, all at reasonable prices.

Points of Interest

The **Middle Island Underwater Observatory** is a popular attraction. It is surrounded by natural coral, and the area teems with marine life of every type imaginable. A sunken wreck nearby also provides a haven for fish, sea snakes, turtles and a school of huge cod. The Underwater

Observatory is ⏰open daily 8am-5pm, if weather conditions are favourable, and admission charges are ✪$10 adults and $5 children.

There are ample opportunities for fishing, cruising, boom netting, windsurfing and bushwalking.

Diving

A glance at a map will show that the Great Barrier Reef is a long way from the mainland at this point, but there is some good diving closer to Great Keppel Island. Bald Rock and Man & Wife Rocks are popular diving venues, and between the southern end of Halfway Island and Middle Island Reef there is some good coral.

If the weather is calm there is good diving at Parker's Bombora, off the south-eastern tip of Great Keppel. It begins in water about 20m deep and is encircled by sea ferns, sponges, coral and hundreds of fish.

The outer islands of the Keppel group, particularly Barren Island, have deeper and clearer water than Great Keppel, so larger species of sea life are encountered, like turtles and manta rays.

All diving gear can be hired from the accommodation outlets on Great Keppel.

Yeppoon

Population 12,000

Location and Characteristics

A modern town with a population of approximately 12,000, Yeppoon nestles beside pineapple-covered hills on the shores of Keppel Bay. Palms and pines line the main street, and shady trees continue to line the road to Rockhampton. There is a 4m difference between high and low tide, so trawlers, yachts and dinghies are left high and dry.

Yeppoon is the main town on the Capricorn Coast and is one of the largest and fastest growing coastal communities in Queensland. It is a popular holiday spot, offering access to more than 40km of safe beaches.

How to Get There

By Coach

Young's Bus Service runs between Rockhampton

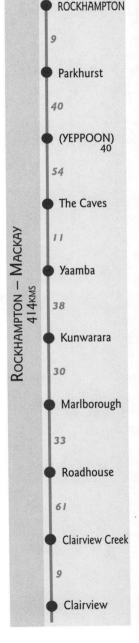

Rockhampton to Mackay

ROCKHAMPTON — MACKAY 414KMS

- ROCKHAMPTON
- 9
- Parkhurst
- 40
- (YEPPOON) 40
- 54
- The Caves
- 11
- Yaamba
- 38
- Kunwarara
- 30
- Marlborough
- 33
- Roadhouse
- 61
- Clairview Creek
- 9
- Clairview

and Yeppoon, ✆4922 3183 (Rockhampton) or ✆4939 3131 (Yeppoon).

By Car

If you have your own transport, the turn-off from the Bruce Highway for Yeppoon is just north of Rockhampton, and from there it is 40km (25 miles) towards the coast.

Visitor Information

The Capricorn Coast Tourist Organisation has an office at the roundabout as you drive into town (you can't miss it!) and it is ◷open daily 9am-5pm, ✆4939 4888.

Accommodation and Services

Here is a selection of available accommodation, with prices for a double room per night, which should be used as a guide only. The telephone area code is 07.

Rydges Capricorn International Resort, Farnborough Road, ✆4939 5111 or ✆1800 075 902 (toll free). 266 rooms, licensed restaurant, cocktail bar, swimming pool, sauna, spa, gymnasium, tennis golf, mini golf, archery, bowls, catamaran sailing, horse riding, scuba diving, volleyball, wind surfing, Kids Kapers, Teen Club - suites ✪$325-355.

Bayview Tower, cnr Adelaide & Normanby Streets, ✆4939 4500. 34 units, licensed restaurant, swimming pool, spa, sauna - ✪$75-105.

Blue Anchor, 76 Whitman Street, ✆4939 4288. 8 units, barbecue, playground, undercover parking, heated pool - ✪$65-80.

Driftwood, 7 Todd Avenue, ✆4939 2446. 9 units, undercover parking, pool - ✪$55-70.

The Strand, cnr Normanby Street & Anzac Parade, ✆4939 1301. 13 units, undercover parking, swimming pool - ✪$50.

Sail Inn, 19 James Street, ✆4939 1130. 9 units, cooking facilities, barbecue, undercover parking - ✪$60-85.

Tidewater, 7 Normanby Street, ✆4939 1632. 8 flats, cooking facilities, undercover parking, heated pool - ✪$45.

Caravan Parks

Poinciana Tourist Park, 9 Scenic Highway, ✆4939 1601. 60 sites, barbecue, recreation room - powered sites ✪$16-19 for two, cabins $35-55 for two.

Beachside Caravan Park, Farnborough Road, ✆4939 3738. (No pets allowed) 70 sites, barbecue - powered sites ✪$16 for two.

Blue Dolphin Caravan Park, 74 Whitman Street, ✆4939 3140. (Pets on application) 47 sites - powered sites ✪$16 for two, cabins $35 for two.

Eating Out

You can select from the following.

Happy Sun Chinese Restaurant, 34 James Street, ✆ 4939 3323. Open daily with a smorgasbord dine-in on Sunday.

Footlights Theatre Restaurant, 123 Old Rockhampton Road, ✆4939 2399. Fully licensed with great food and entertainment.

Yeppoon Galaxy, Shop 4, 26 James Street, ✆4939 1205. Chinese restaurant open daily.

Beaches, Rosslyn Bay Harbour, ✆4933 6300. Open daily 7am until late with live entertainment Wed to Sun, including Sunday lunch.

Local Transport

Capricorn Cabs can be contacted on ✆4939 1999.

Points of Interest

Cooberrie Park, 15km (9 miles) north of Yeppoon on Woodbury Road, is a bird and animal sanctuary with barbecue and picnic facilities. If you want to pat a kangaroo, this is the place to do it. They also have koalas and other native animals wandering freely through the parkland. It is ◷open daily 9am-4.30pm and costs adults ✪$12 and children $6, ✆4939 7590.

Byfield State Forest Parks are 17km (10 miles) north of Cooberrie Park, and are popular picnic areas. They include Stoney Creek, Waterpark Creek and Red Rock Forest Parks.

Nob Creek Pottery, ✆4935 1161, established in 1979, is located in the tropical Byfield Forest, and has gained a reputation as a quality cottage industry.

Wreck Point at Cooee Bay provides a spectacular view overlooking the Keppel group of islands.

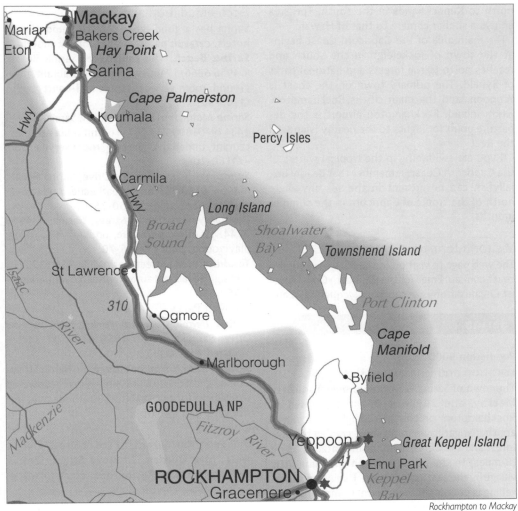

Rockhampton to Mackay

It is situated on the southern outskirts of Yeppoon.

Rosslyn Bay Boat Harbour is the base for a large fishing fleet, charter boats, *Keppel Isles Yacht Charters* (12 Poplar Street, Yeppoon, ©4939 4949), cruise boats and catamarans. Cruises available include coral viewing, boom netting and, weather permitting, a visit to Middle Island Underwater Observatory.

Emu Park, 19km (12 miles) south of Yeppoon and linked by the Capricorn Coast Scenic Highway, has an unusual memorial to Captain Cook - a singing ship. The mast, sail and rigging contain hollow pipes, and the ship 'sings' when the wind blows. This picturesque town is worth the short and scenic drive for a visit.

Capricorn Coast Tours are located at 50 McBean Street, Yeppoon, ©4349 1325.

Capricorn Coast

Location and Characteristics

The Capricorn Coast stretches some 48km (30 miles) from Yeppoon and the Byfield area in the

Rockhampton to Mackay

north to Keppel Sands in the south. The area enjoys a similar climate to that of Hawaii.

The main area of the Capricorn Coast begins at the town of Joskeleigh in the south and reaches north to the forests and national parks of Byfield. The primary town on the coast is Yeppoon, and the main city is Rockhampton, 41km inland. Rockhampton airport is the departure point for flights to the nearby islands of the Reef.

If you are swimming in the tropical waters of the Capricorn Coast, remember that deadly box jellyfish can be present in the sea anywhere north of the Tropic of Capricorn in the summer months.

Visitor Information

The web page to visit online is ☞www.capricorn coast.com.au. Email for the Capricorn Coast Tourist Organisation is ✎ capcoast@cqnet .com.au

Sarina

Population 9000

Location and Characteristics

The town of Sarina is 37km (23 miles) south of Mackay, and 296km (185 miles) north of Rockhampton, on the Bruce Highway. It is yet another sugar town in the area, cradled by rainforest and the Conners Range mountains. 13km (8 miles) to the north east is a charming little village by the sea, Sarina Beach. Fishing and snorkelling is popular in the tropical islands and reefs close to the mainland.

How to Get There

By Car

Sarina is on the Bruce Highway, 37km south of Mackay and 296km north of Rockhampton.

Visitor Information

Helpful local information is provided by the Sarina Tourist Art & Craft Centre, Lot 3 Bruce Highway, ©4956 2251.

Accommodation and Services

Sarina has a good range of accommodation in hotels, caravan parks and beachfront motels.

Sarina Beach, The Esplanade, Sarina Beach, ©4956 6266. 17 units, licensed restaurant, playground, room service, tennis half-court, pool - ✪$65-95.

Sarina Motor Inn, Bruce Highway, Sarina, ©4943 1431 or ©1800 248 087. 16 units, licensed restaurant, undercover parking, room service, pool - ✪$60-70.

Sandpiper, Owen Jenkins Drive, Sarina Beach, ©4956 6130. 23 units, barbecue, undercover parking, pool, spa - ✪$50-75.

Tramway, 110 Broad Street, Sarina, ©4956 2244. 12 units, barbecue, undercover parking, playground, pool - ✪$55-70.

Tandara, Broad Street, Sarina, ©4956 1323. 15 units, licensed restaurant, undercover parking - ✪$50-55.

Caravan Parks

Sarina Beach Caravan Park, Owen Jenkins Drive, Sarina Beach, ©4956 6130. 31 sites - powered sites ✪$17.

Sarina Palms Caravan Village, 11 Heron Street, Sarina, ©4956 1892. 38 sites, kiosk - powered sites ✪$15 for two, cabins $30-35 for two, onsite vans $25 for two.

Eating Out

Hideaway Restaurant, 22 Broad Street, ©4943 1431; ***Jake Garden***, 9c Broad Street, ©4956 2221; and ***Palms Restaurant***, The Esplanade, Sarina Beach, ©4956 6266.

Points of Interest

Broad Street, the main street of the town, is indeed broad with a median strip in the centre offering tables, park benches and public amenities, and best of all, shade.

There are plenty of sandy beaches and offshore islands to entice you to swim, jog, fish or go boating.

The **Dalrymple Bay Coal Exporting Facilities** at Hay Point, ©4943 8444, are the largest of their type in the Southern Hemisphere.

Chapter 39
Mackay

Population 58,600
Mackay is a coastal city, on the banks of the Pioneer River, 975km (606 miles) north of Brisbane.

Climate

Average temperatures: January max 31C (88F) - min 22C (72F); July max 23C (73F) - min 10C (50F). Average annual rainfall - 1672mm (66 ins), with over 1000mm (39 ins) falling January-March. The driest months are June-November.

Characteristics

Mackay is surrounded by miles and miles of sugarcane fields, which give the city its title of Sugar Capital of Australia. The district produces about one-third of Australia's total sugar crop, which is exported through the Port of Mackay.

Tram tracks meander through the fields, for the miniature engines that transport the cane to one of the seven sugar mills in the district. In some places the fields are torched between June and December, just before harvesting, and the night skies turn red with the reflections from the fires. These days this method is more frequently replaced by 'green harvesting', which involves cutting rather than burning. See under *Points of Interest* for details of a sugar farm tour.

North-east of Mackay, just off the coast from Shute Harbour, is the Whitsunday Group of Islands containing some of the most popular of the resort islands of the Great Barrier Reef. Although these islands are not coral cays, the scenery is similar to those featuring in your dreams of lazing on a palm-fringed beach on a tropical island.

The beautiful Eungella National Park, 84km inland from Mackay, has graded tracks leading through rainforest to waterfalls and cool pools (*see separate listing*).

How to Get There

By Air

The Qantas regional airlines of Airlink and Sunstate service Mackay, ✆131 313.

By Bus

Greyhound Pioneer, ✆13 2030, stops at Mackay on its Brisbane/Cairns route.

McCaffertys, ✆13 1499, also operates a Brisbane/Mackay service which takes the inland route from Rockhampton.

By Rail

Queensland Rail Travel Trains operate The Sunlander, The Queenslander and The Spirit of Tropics from Brisbane throughout the week, contact ✆13 2235.

The number for the Mackay Railway Station is ✆4952 7418.

By Road

From Brisbane, via the Bruce Highway, 975km (606 miles).

Mackay is 1079km (670 miles) south of Cairns.

Visitor Information

Mackay Tourism and Development Bureau Ltd is in 'The Mill', 320 Nebo Road, ✆4952 2677, and they are ☺open Mon-Fri 9am-5pm, Sat-Sun 9am-4pm. Their email is ✉ mtdb@mackay.net.au

Local Transport

Car Hire

The following companies operate in the area.
Avis, Mackay Airport, ✆4951 1266.
AAA Rental-U-Drive, 6 Endevour Street, ✆4957 5606.
Budget Rent-A-Car, 19B Juliet Street, ✆4951 1400.
Thrifty Car Rental, 3 Mangrove Road, ✆4957 3677.
Mackay Economy Rentals, 139 Sydney Street, ✆4953 1616.
Hertz Rentals, Mackay Airport, ✆4951 4685.
Network Rentals, 196 Victoria Street, ✆4953 1022.
Cut Rate Rentals, 105 Alfred Street, ✆4953 1616.

Mackay

Public Transport

Buses service the Mackay area on weekdays only, not on public holidays, ✆4957 8416 for time-table information from Mackay City Buses.

Taxis

Taxi Transit, Victoria Street, ✆4951 4990.
Mackay Taxis, Victoria Street, ✆13 1008.

Accommodation

Mackay has a wide range of accommodation, from international resort hotels and motels, to caravan parks and camping grounds. Here is a selection with prices for a double room per night, which should be used as a guide only. The telephone area code is 07.

Ocean International Hotel, 1 Bridge Street, ✆4957 2044. 46 rooms, licensed restaurant, swimming pool, spa, sauna, putting green, bar-becue - ✪$165-265.

Mercure Inn Mackay, 166 Nebo Road, ✆4951 1555. 34 units, 2 suites, licensed restaurant, undercover parking, pool - ✪$130.

Marco Polo Motel, 46 Nebo Road, ✆4951 2700. 30 units, licensed restaurant, swimming pool, spa, sauna, gym - ✪$100.

Shakespeare International, 309 Shakespeare Street, ✆4953 1111. 37 units, 17 suites, li-censed restaurant, swimming pool, spa, bar-becue - ✪$100.

White Lace Motor Inn, 73 Nebo Road, ✆4951 4466. 36 units, licensed restaurant, swimming pool, spa - ✪$90-120.

Sugar City, 66 Nebo Road, ✆4968 4150 or 1800 645 525 (toll free). 21 units, barbecue, licensed restaurant, playground, room service, car park-ing, pool - ✪$75-90.

Alara Motor Inn, 52 Nebo Road, ✆4951 2699. 34 units, licensed restaurant, swimming pool, spa, sauna - ✪$85-100.

Ocean Resort Village, 5 Bridge Street, ✆4951 3200 or 1800 075 144 (toll free). 34 units, kiosk, tennis half-court, undercover parking, 2 pools - ✪$80.

Coral Sands Motel, 44 MacAlister Street, ✆4951 1244. 46 units, 2 suites, licensed res-taurant (closed Sun), swimming pool, sauna, barbecue - ✪$70-75.

Country Plaza Motor Inn, 40 Nebo Road, ✆4957 6526. 38 units, licensed restaurant, un-dercover parking, pool, spa - ✪$75-80.

Paradise Lodge Motel, 19 Peel Street, ✆4951 3644. 12 units, undercover parking - ✪$60-65.

Pioneer Villa, 30 Nebo Road, ✆4951 1288. 18 units, licensed restaurant, swimming pool, bar-becue - ✪$65.

Hi Way Units, Nebo Road, cnr Webberley Street, ✆4952 1800. 7 units, undercover parking, swim-ming pool - ✪$50.

Bona Vista Motel, cnr Malcomson Street & Norris Road, ✆4942 2211. 18 units, licensed res-taurant, swimming pool, barbecue - ✪$45-55.

Boomerang, South Nebo Road, ✆4952 1755. 23 units, unlicensed restaurant, playground, pool - ✪$40-45.

Budget Accommodation

The places listed below offer double rooms at less than $50 per night:

Mackay Townhouse, 73 Victoria Street, ✆4957 6985.

International Lodge, 40 MacAlister Street, ✆4951 1022.

Austral Hotel, 189 Victoria Street, ✆4951 3288.

Taylors Hotel, cnr Wood & Alfred Streets, ✆4957 2500.

There is a **Youth Hostel** at 32 Peel Street, ✆4951 3728. 6 rooms at ✪$19 per person twin share.

Northern Beaches

Approximately 15 minutes drive north of Mackay.

Dolphin Heads Resort, Beach Road, Dolphin Heads, ✆4954 9666 or ✆1800 075 088 (free call). 2 units, licensed restaurant, swimming pool and spa, tennis court - ✪$165.

Ko Huna Beach, Homestead Bay Avenue, Bucasia, ✆5954 8555 or ✆1800 075 128 (toll free). 60 units, 2 licensed restaurants, swimming pool and spa, mini golf, tennis, watersport ac-tivities - ✪$98-130.

The Shores, 9 Pacific Drive, Blacks Beach, ✆4954 9444. 36 units, cooking facilities, undercover parking, 2 swimming pools, spa, tennis court - ✪$85-145.

Blue Pacific Village, 24 Bourke Street, Blacks Beach, ✆4954 9090. 38 units, licensed restaurant, barbecue, playground, undercover parking, cooking facilities, swimming pool, half-court tennis, heated pool, spa - ✪$83-130.

Pacific Palms Beachfront Units, Symons Avenue, Bucasia Beach, ✆4954 6277. 6 units, cooking facilities, swimming pool, undercover parking - ✪$62-69.

La Solana, 15 Pacific Drive, Blacks Beach, ✆4954 9544. 12 units, barbecue, playground, cooking facilities, swimming pool, half-court tennis - ✪$55-85.

Tropic Heart Units, 64 Waverley Street, Bucasia, ✆4954 6965. 7 units, barbecue, undercover parking, cooking facilities, swimming pool - ✪$44-65.

Hibiscus Coast

Approximately 40-45 minutes drive north of Mackay

See under *Cape Hillsborough* and *Halliday Bay*, which have separate listings.

Sarina

Approximately 30 minutes drive south of Mackay.

Sarina Motor Inn, Bruce Highway, ✆4943 1431 or ✆1800 248 087. 16 units, licensed restaurant, undercover parking, room service, pool - ✪$50-60.

Tramway, 110 Broad Street, ✆4956 2244. 12 units, cooking facilities, playground, undercover parking, pool - ✪$48-60.

Tandara, Broad Street, ✆4956 1323. 15 units, licensed restaurant, undercover parking - ✪$42-45.

Caravan Parks

Beach Tourist Park, 8 Petrie Street, Illawong Beach, ✆4957 4021 or 1800 645 111 (tollfree). (No pets allowed) 150 sites, playground, kiosk, pool - powered sites ✪$21 for two, villas $55-60, units $70 for two.

Andergrove Caravan Park, Beaconsfield Road, Andergrove, ✆4942 4922. (Pets allowed on application) 160 sites, barbecue, playground, pool - powered sites ✪$18 for two, on-site vans $35 for two, cabins $45 for two.

Tropical Caravan Park Melanesian Village, Bruce Highway, ✆4952 1211. (Pets allowed on application) 170 sites, barbecue, playground, kiosk, pool - powered sites ✪$19 for two, on-site vans $28 for two, villas $55-60 for two, units $45 for two.

Premier Van Park, 152 Nebo Road, ✆4957 6976. (No pets allowed) 42 sites, barbecue, kiosk pool - powered sites ✪$14 for two, cabins $30-35 for two.

Eating Out

Most of the motels have licensed restaurants, and many hotels serve inexpensive counter meals. Here are a few restaurants that you might like to try.

Pippi's Italian Restaurant, cnr Palmer & Grendon Streets, ✆4951 1376. BYO, Italian & Mediterranean, open Tues-Sat from 5.30pm.

Romeo & Juliet's Restaurant, 309 Shakespeare Street, ✆4953 1111. Licensed, a la carte - fresh local produce and fine Aussie wines are the specialties. Open nightly from 6.30pm.

The Beachhouse Seafood Restaurant, 2 Ocean Avenue, Slade Point, ✆4955 4733. Metres from the water's edge. Generous platters and Live Mud Crab Tank. Open for dinner seven nights, lunch Thursday, Friday and Sunday.

Valencia Restaurant, 44 MacAlister Street, at the Coral Sands Motel, ✆4951 1244. Licensed, a la carte, piano bar - open for dinner from 6.30pm, and for lunch Mon-Fri.

Toong Tong Thai Restaurant, 10 Sydney Street, Mackay, ✆4957 8051. Dinner 7 days from 5.30pm, lunch Mon-Fri 11.30am-2.30pm.

McDonald's is at the corner of Hicks Road and the Bruce Highway, ✆4942 3999. Pizza Hut has a free delivery service Mon-Thurs 4-11pm, Fri-Sun noon-11pm, ✆4957 2481.

Entertainment

If you fancy seeing a **movie**, head for the cinema complex in Gordon Street, ✆4957 3515.

For some **live entertainment** contact the *Mackay Entertainment Centre*, also in Gordon Street, ✆4957 1757 or ✆1800 646 574, to find out about current shows.

The *Conservatorium of Music*, 418 Shakespeare Street, has regular classical and jazz concerts, often featuring overseas artists, ✆4957 3727.

For night owls, there are a few **night clubs** where you can dance to the wee small hours:
Whitz End, The Whitsunday Hotel, 176 Victoria Street, ©4957 2811.
The Blue Moose Nightclub, 144 Victoria Street, ©4951 2611. ⏱Open Wed-Sun nights.
The Balcony, 144 Victoria Street, ©4957 2241.
Katie O'Reilly's Irish Bar & Restaurant, 38 Sydney Street, ©4953 3522.
The Saloon Bar, 99 Victoria Street, ©4957 7220.
If you are in town on a Thursday night you might like to go to the greyhound racing at the *Mackay Showground* in Milton Street, ©4951 1680.

Shopping

Centrepoint Shopping Centre, ©4957 2229, is in Victoria Street, in the heart of the city, where you will also find some good street shopping.
  Caneland Shoppingtown, ©4951 3311, is in Mangrove Road.
  Mt Pleasant Shopping Centre, Phillip Street, North Mackay, is more convenient for those staying to the north of the city.
Weekend markets are held as follows:
  The *Foundry Markets* on Harbour Road - ⏱Thursday, Sat-Sun 8am-4pm.
  Mackay Showground Markets in Milton Road - ⏱Sat 8am-1pm.
  Victoria Street Markets - ⏱Sun 8.30am-12.30pm.
  On the first Sunday of every month *Paxtons Markets* are held in River Street ⏱9am-1pm, and on most long weekends the *Eungella Markets* are staged at Dalrymple Heights Oval.

Arts & Crafts

Pioneer Potters in Swayne Street, North Mackay, ©4957 6255, has a good selection of handmade local pottery and sculpture. It is ⏱open Wed and Sat 10am-4pm.
The Beach Pottery, 6 Blacks Beach Road, Blacks Beach, offers functional stoneware pottery by local potters. It is ⏱open Mon-Thurs 10am-5pm, and weekends by arrangement.
Bucasia Gardens and Gifts, Bucasia Road, about ten minutes drive past Mt Pleasant Shopping Centre, has a wide selection of local pottery,
crafts, dried flowers and giftware. It is ⏱open daily 9.30am-5pm, ©4954 8134, and also has a coffee shop, plants and pots.
Homebush Store Pottery & Craft Gallery is situated 26km south-west of Mackay in an historic building, Sunnyside Road. Opening in the early 1900 as the local store for the people of Homebush and surrounding areas, it has now been restored and is operated as a pottery workshop. Also available are works of art, fibre arts, woodturned objects, hand painted T-shirts and handmade cane baskets. The Gallery is ⏱open Fri-Tues 9am-5pm, ©4959 7339.

Points of Interest

John Mackay discovered the Pioneer River Valley in 1860, but he named the river the Mackay. He returned with stock and registered "Greenmount" the first pastoral run in the district in 1862. Others followed and the settlement was named Mackay in his honour. The river's name, however, had to be changed to Pioneer because there was already a Mackay River.
  It was only a few years before sugar became the main industry, pioneered by the efforts of John Spiller, T. Henry Fitzgerald and John Ewen Davidson. Nowadays Mackay Harbour is home to the world's largest bulk sugar terminal.
  The port for Mackay was originally on the river, but because of the enormous tides (around 6.5m), a new port was built on the coast.
Tourism Mackay have put together a *City Walking Tour* that visits the historic buildings, including the Police Station (1885), Court House, Commonwealth Bank (1880), Town Hall (1912), Holy Trinity Church, Masonic Temple, National Bank, Mercury Building, Pioneer Shire Chambers, Post Office and Customs House (1901).
The closest beach to the city is **Harbour Beach**, on the southern side of the outer harbour wall. It has a children's playground, toilets and shady picnic areas, and is patrolled during summer by the Mackay Surf Club.
Queen's Park Orchid House, cnr Gordon & Goldsmith Streets, has an excellent display of native and foreign orchids.
Illawong Fauna Sanctuary, at Illawong Beach,

4km from Mackay centre, is a beachfront family recreation area amid tropical landscaping. There are kangaroos roaming free, a swimming pool, trampoline, video games and full catering facilities, as well as crocodiles (not roaming free). Feeding times are 9am, 11.30am and 3.30pm. For further information, ©4959 1777. The sanctuary is ☉open 9am-6pm daily, and until 10pm on Friday night.

You can get a good panoramic view of the city and the countryside from the **Mt Oscar Lookout** in Norris Road, North Mackay.

Tours of the **Racecourse Sugar Mill**, Peak Downs Highway, are conducted during the crushing season, from June to November, ©4953 8276 for more information.

Polstone Sugar Farm Tours, Masotti's Road, Homebush, adjacent to Orchid Way, conduct a 2 hour tour covering the history, equipment and process of growing and preparing sugar cane for the mill. Costs, including refreshments, are ✪$15 adults and $8 children, ©4959 7298.

North of Mackay are several popular beach resorts.

Blacks Beach is approximately 6km in length, and is probably the best beach in the area for swimming and fishing. **Bucasia** and **Eimeo** beaches are in the semi-rural area, about a 10 minute drive north of Mackay, and are long sandy beaches that are safe for swimming and have good play areas for kids. They also offer good views of the countryside and off-shore islands.

Beaches

Illawong (Far Beach) and **Iluka** (Town Beach) offer views of Flat and Round Top Islands and Dalrymple Bay/Hay Point coal loading terminal.

Harbour Beach has a surf lifesaving patrol, toilets, adventure playground and picnic area.

Lamberts Beach has a lookout that provides island views.

Blacks Beach is a long secluded beach with picnic facilities.

Dolphin Heads has accommodation available.

Eimeo Beach has a small picnic area next to an avenue of century old mango trees.

Sunset Beach has a shaded foreshore picnic area.

Bucasia Beach has a summer swimming enclosure, picnic area and views to Dolphin Heads and islands.

Shoal Point Beach has a picnic area, toilets and lookout. The Esplanade offers views of islands, Cape Hillsborough and Hibiscus Coast, and there is a causeway to Little Green Island.

South of Mackay

Twenty-five kilometres south of Mackay, at Hay Point, is the **Dalrymple Bay Coal Terminal Complex**, the largest coal export facility in the southern hemisphere. The wharves stretch 3.8km out to sea, and coal trains up to 2km long arrive at the port daily. The Port Administration Building has recorded information and a viewing platform, ©4943 8444.

The **Big Prawn** is at Lot 1, Grasstree Beach Road, Grasstree Beach, and is the only commercial hatchery in Australia that is open to the public.

The sugar town of **Sarina** is 37km south of Mackay. It has a population of around 9,000, some picturesque scenery, and some excellent beaches. *(See also separate listing.)*

Cape Palmerston National Park is 80km south of Mackay and has 4WD only access. It offers long sandy beaches, palm forests, freshwater lagoons and large stands of melaleuca. Attractions include Ince Bay to the north, Temple Island and the volcanic plug of Mt Funnel. There is camping, but facilities are very basic.

Beaches

Campwin Beach, 8.5km from Sarina, is home to a rich fishing and prawning industry. Boat launching and mooring facilities are available and there is easy access to nearby islands.

Armstrong Beach is 9.5km from Sarina and has a picnic and camping, and an orchid nursery that is open by appointment only.

Sarina Beach, 13km from Sarina, has a picnic area, store, boat ramp, and a surf lifesaving patrol. Coral Lookout is at the southern end of the beach.

Grasstree Beach, 13km from Sarina, has a picnic area and boat ramp in a wide sheltered bay.

Salonika Beach, 24km from Sarina, is a quiet sandy beach with an inland lagoon teeming with birdlife.

Mackay

Halftide Beach, 28km from Sarina, is home to the Tug Boat Harbour that services Hay Point Coal Terminal.

North of Mackay

Cape Hillsborough National Park, 45km (28 miles) north-east of Mackay, covers 830ha and features a variety of vegetation, elevated look-outs and peaceful beaches. It is not unusual to see a couple of kangaroos lazing on the beach undisturbed by humans doing the same thing.

Cathu State Forest is 70km (44 miles) north of Mackay. Drive along the Bruce Highway to 3km north of Yalboroo, turn left and continue for 12km (8 miles) along the gravel road to the Forestry Office. Within the forest is the Jaxut State Forest Park which has shaded picnic areas with friendly kangaroos, camping facilities and toilets.

Midge Point is reached by turning right off the Bruce Highway at Bloomsbury, and travelling 18km through the Condor Hill to the village of Midgetown. Named after a small survey vessel, the *Midge*, in the early 1920s, this area has been 'discovered' by developers, and has become a tourist destination.

Beaches

Roughly 25km north of Mackay, turn right onto Seaforth Road then travel 20km to the **Hibiscus Coast**. This includes the beachside settlements of Seaforth, Halliday Bay, Ball Bay and Cape Hillsborough. These beaches are all nesting sites for green and flatback turtles who lay their eggs during the three month period from October each year. The baby turtles hatch between late January and early April.

Halliday Bay has a sandy beach swimming enclosure, accommodation and a restaurant. It is reached from Cape Hillsborough Road.

Seaforth is 48km north-east of Mackay, and offers camping and picnic facilities overlooking the beach.

Belmunda Bay is reached by turning right about 5km along the Cape Hillsborough Road. The bay has secluded beaches with several fishing shacks. After rain has fallen, the nearby freshwater lakes are visited by crowds of water birds, including the brolga.

Festivals

The Sugartime Festival is held in the first week in September each year.

Sports

Golf

There are three golf courses within 40km of Mackay city:

Mackay Golf Club, Bucasia Road, Mackay, ☏4942 1362.

The Valley Golf Club, Leichhardt Street, Mirani, ☏4959 1277.

Sarina Golf Club, Golf Links Road, Sarina, ☏4956 1761.

Swimming

The *Memorial Swimming Pool*, Milton Street, is near Caneland Shopping Centre. It is ⏱open Tues, Thurs and Fri 5am-8.45pm, Wed, Sat and Sun 5am-6pm (closed June and early July).

Whitsunday Waterworld, Harbour Road, Mackay, ☏4955 6466, is a complex with waterslides, mini golf, pinball, video machines and kiosk. It is ⏱open Sat-Sun and school holidays 10am-10pm.

Indoor Sports

BG's Sports Centre on the Bruce Highway south of the City Gates, is one of the largest indoor recreational and fitness centres in Australia. It offers tenpin bowling, roller skating, squash and many other sports, ☏4952 1509. It is ⏱open daily 9am-midnight.

Diving

Following are a few diving tour operators.

The Diver Training Centre, ☏4955 4228, has a dive shop by the sea next to the departure point for Roylen Cruises, where you can hire snorkel and scuba gear. They also have 5-day dive courses.

Barnes Reefdiving, 153 Victoria Street, ☏4951 1472, offer diving trips to the Great Barrier Reef on Mon, Wed and Fri; Reef and Wreck Dive Trips on Tues; and Island Dive Trips on Thurs.

Mackay Diving, 1 Mangrove Road, ☏4951 1640, also offer gear hire and diving lessons.

Tours and Cruises

Natural North Discovery Tours, 11 Rafelo Drive, Farleigh, ©4952 2677 or ©4959 8360. Eungella National Park Tour - daily - 10 hours duration - ✪$80 adults, $55 children and $230 for families.

The Great Barrier Reef can be reached from Mackay by sea and air. Credlin Reef, one of the 2100 reefs that make up this coral colony, is only 2 to 3 hours from Mackay Harbour by high speed catamaran. There is a shaded pontoon, underwater viewing area and a seasub that make for excellent snorkelling, scuba diving and coral viewing.

Bushy Atoll, a half-hour seaplane flight from Mackay airport, is the only quay on the entire Reef to have an enclosed lagoon.

Elizabeth E II Coral Cruises, 102 Goldsmith Street, Mackay, ©4957 4281, offer trips from two to 21 days aboard their specially built monohull dive and fishing boat, *Elizabeth E II*. The boat is stabilised and has the latest navigation aids, as well as 240v throughout and a 110v charging system.

Accommodation for 12 to 28 passengers are in one double, 12 twin and two triple berths with en-suite facilities and unlimited fresh water. All meals are chef-prepared and snacks, weights, air and tanks are included in the charter costs.

Mackay Adventure Cruises, 320 Nebo Road, ©4952 2677. High-speed catamaran transport to the Credlin Reef pontoon for coral viewing.

Whitsunday Dreamer, ©4946 6611. Snorkelling and fishing. Stopovers to Daydream Island, Long Island and Sun Lovers coral reef.

Roylen Cruises, Harbour Road, ©4955 3066, have daily cruises to Brampton Island; Sat, Sun & Wed cruises to Lindeman and Hamilton Islands; Mon, Wed & Fri cruises to Credlin Reef; and 5-day luxury cruises through the Whitsunday Islands and to the Great Barrier Reef, all departing from the outer harbour. The 5-day cruise departs every Monday 1pm and returns Friday 4pm.

Scenic Flights

Horizon Airways, Casey Avenue, Mackay, ©4957 2446. Half-hour flights over Mackay.

Air Pioneer, Old Airport, Casey Avenue, Mackay, ©4957 6661. Offers flights to a coral atoll, then onto a glass-bottomed boat for touring plus snorkelling.

Whitsunday Helicopter Group, Mackay Airport, ©4953 3061. Joy flights over the Barrier Reef.

Fredericksons Air Services, 25 Norman Drive, Yeppoon, ©4938 3404. Includes 2-hour flights to Bushy Reef.

Chapter 40
Mackay to Townsville

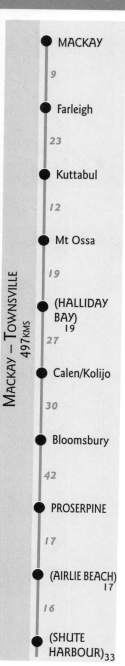

Halliday Bay

Location and Characteristics

Situated north of Mackay, near the town of Seaforth, Halliday Bay is noted for its white sandy beach and safe swimming enclosure.

The bay adjoins **McBride's Point National Park**, and has a shop and boat hire facilities. The Bay is named after Captain Halliday, whose century-old stone cottage is still standing.

Accommodation and Services

Halliday Bay, in Headland Drive, ✆4959 0322, have 54 units, a licensed restaurant, playground, tennis court, kiosk, sailing and a swimming pool - ✪$65. There are also 18 Holiday Units at $55 per night.

Cape Hillsborough

Location and Characteristics

Located 47km (29 miles) north of Mackay, the Cape Hillsborough National Park provides a beachfront picnic area with barbecue facilities. The park is relatively small (830ha - 2050 acres), but it is typical of the best of North Queensland, with rainforests, beaches and abundant wildlife. Walking tracks take you to billabongs, great lookouts and unusual volcanic formations. The fishing in the park is excellent.

How to Get There
By Road

To get to the park take the Bruce Highway north from Mackay, then turn right at The Leap.

Accommodation and Services

Cape Hillsborough Nature Resort, ✆4959 0262, offers 10 units at ✪$80 a double per night,

as well as 100 camping sites at $17 for two per night.

There is a licensed restaurant, barbecue area, undercover parking, good facilities and a pool.

Eungella National Park

Location and Characteristics

This stunning National Park is 84km (52 miles) inland from Mackay, and the bitumen road leading to it follows the Pioneer River and its tributaries up the valley past Finch Hatton, and through Eungella township at the top of the range. Finch Hatton Gorge has attractive mountain-fed waterfalls, a natural swimming pool, plus good walking tracks.

The Broken River area provides shady pools for swimming, and well marked bush walking tracks are a feature of the Park. If you are lucky you may see a platypus near the bridge.

Visitor Information

For information on all National Parks, the organisations to contact for information are the Environmental Protection Agency, ✆3224 5641, or the Queensland National Parks and Wildlife Service, ✆3227 8187 (Naturally Queensland). Connect online to 👁www.env.qld.gov.au

Accommodation and Services

Meals and accommodation are available at *Bro-*

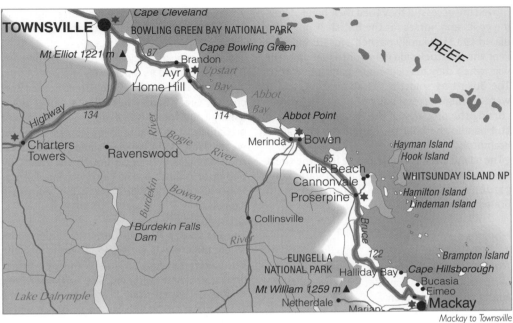

TOWNSVILLE

Cape Cleveland
BOWLING GREEN BAY NATIONAL PARK
Cape Bowling Green
Mt Elliot 1221 m ▲   87   Brandon   Upstart
Ayr   Bay
Home Hill   Abbot
Highway   134   Bay   Abbot Point
                                                      Merinda   Bowen
Charters   Bogie   River   Hayman Island
Towers   Ravenswood   River   Hook Island
                                                     65   WHITSUNDAY ISLAND NP
                    Burdekin   114   Airlie Beach
                    Bowen   Cannonvale   Hamilton Island
                                                   Proserpine   Lindeman Island
Burdekin Falls   Collinsville
Dam   River   Bruce
                                                              122   Brampton Island
                    EUNGELLA   Cape Hillsborough
                    NATIONAL PARK   Halliday Bay   Bucasia
Lake Dalrymple   Mt William 1259 m ▲   Eimeo
                    Netherdale •   Mackay
                              Marian

REEF

Mackay to Townsville

ken River Mountain Retreat, ℂ4958 4528. It has 4 units, guided activities including platypus viewing, a licensed restaurant, playground and pool - ✪$65-80.

At the top of the range at Eungella, the fully licensed *Historic Eungella Chalet Mountain Lodge*, ℂ4958 4509, has 12 rooms, a playground and pool - ✪$50-90.

A permit is required to **camp** in any of the local National Parks, and this can be obtained from the Ranger at Seaforth, ℂ4959 0410, the Ranger at Eungella, ℂ4958 4552, or from the Queensland National Parks and Wildlife Service, cnr Wood & River Street, Mackay, ℂ4951 8788. Typically, it costs ✪$3.50 per person per night to camp.

Brampton Island

Location and Characteristics
Brampton is not strictly in the Whitsunday region. It is part of the Cumberland Group of Islands about 32km north-east of Mackay, at the entrance to the Whitsunday Passage. The is-

land is a National Park, with an area of 4.6 sq km, and has unspoilt bush, lush tropical foliage, swaying coconut palms and many stunning and secluded beaches. It is connected to Carlisle Island and to Pelican Island by sand bars that can be crossed at low tide.

A mountainous island with lush forests, nature trails, kangaroos and emus, Brampton also has seven sandy beaches and is surrounded by coral reefs. The walk around the island is about 7km, takes around three hours, and is best done in a clockwise direction. There is a walk up to the island's highest point, Brampton Peak, beginning near the resort golf course and the round trip takes about two hours. Both walks offer great views.

Although Captain Cook was in the area, he either didn't see Brampton or he wasn't interested, because the island was not named and surveyed until 1879.

In the early 1900s the Queensland government used the island as a nursery for palm trees, which accounts for the abundance of those trees now.

The Busuttin family moved to Brampton in 1916 to breed chinchilla rabbits, and when this proved unsuccessful they tried their hand at raising goats and horses for the British Army in India. In 1933 the family opened a resort, but they kept the livestock side going until just after the war, when they needed more space for visitors. The Busuttins sold the resort in 1959, and it went through several pairs of hands before becoming the property of the Roylen group, who still handle the boat transfers from Mackay to Brampton.

The island is a 45 minute cruise from the Great Barrier Reef, but you can see underwater coral gardens and myriads of tropical fish off Brampton's East Beach.

How to Get There
By Sea
The *Spirit of Roylen* launch, ©4955 3066, departs daily from Mackay. Return fares are ✪$70 adults and $35 children.

Visitor Information
The contact number for the resort is ©4951 4097, and the website is ☞www.brampton islandresort.com

Accommodation and Services
Brampton Island Resort, ©4951 4097, has three styles of accommodation - 36 Ocean View Rooms, 56 Palm Rooms and 16 Carlisle Rooms.

Resort facilities are: restaurant, cocktail bar, two swimming pools, spa, games room, tennis courts, cafe, Kids' Club, surf skis, gymnasium, tube rides, golf, waterskiing, catamaran sailing, sail-boarding, beach volleyball, snorkelling, cruising and coral viewing, Barrier Reef trips and EFTPOS.

Room facilities are: balcony or verandah, tea and coffee making facilities, refrigerator, colour TV, in-house movies, IDD/STD telephone, radio, air-conditioning and a daily cleaning service.

Tariffs for one night per person/twin share are:
Ocean View - ✪$270 adult (child 3-14 years sharing with 2 adults - free)
Palm - ✪$240 adult (child - as above)
Carlisle - ✪$205 (child - as above)

The above rates include a full buffet breakfast, four course smorgasbord lunch and four-course dinner.

Maximum occupancy of all rooms is 3 persons (child is counted as a person).

Additional to the tariff are: Great Barrier Reef cruises, Great Barrier Reef flights, bullet rides, fishing trips, forest walks (day), Melaleuca Tour on Carlisle Island, scuba diving lessons and trips, water skiing, Whitsunday Island Cruises. Reservations can be made through the resort by phone or online. Credit cards accepted: Visa, MasterCard, Bankcard, Diners Club, American Express.

Eating Out
The **Bluewater Restaurant** is the dining room where main meals are taken. There is also the **Bluewater Lounge** for post- and pre-dinner drinks, with entertainment. The **Saltwater Cafe & Bar** is ⏱open from 11am-5pm and serves sandwiches, salads and light meals. This is where the day trippers usually stop for a bite to eat.

Points of Interest
Diving
There is nothing at Brampton itself to excite divers, but cruises from Mackay to Credlin Reef aboard the *Spirit of Roylen*, ©4955 3066, call in at Brampton to pick up and set down. Credlin Reef is in the Hydrographers Passage area, and there is a permanent pontoon over the reef, an underwater observatory and a semi-submersible. Resort diving courses are conducted on board the *Spirit of Roylen* in transit to Credlin Reef, or at the Resort by special arrangements.

The Whitsundays

Location and Characteristics
The Whitsundays consist of 74 islands from the Cumberland and Northumberland Island groups, and they form the largest offshore island chain on Australia's east coast.

The islands are the remains of a mountain range that was drowned when sea levels rose at the end of the last ice age. Most of them have Na-

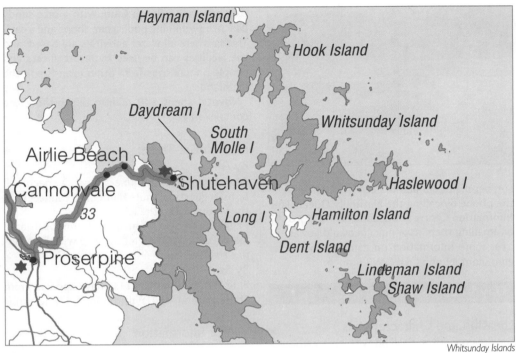

Whitsunday Islands

tional Park status, and all are situated in the marine park.

The islands were named by Captain Cook when he sailed through the passage on Whitsunday, 1770. Some like to point out that it was not actually Whitsunday, since the good old captain neglected to take into account the fact that he had crossed the international date line, and so was a day out. However, because he made so few nautical and mathematical errors on his journey, Captain Cook is usually forgiven his Whitsunday oversight.

Later, when European settlement began on several of the islands, there were some violent confrontations with the resident Aborigines which tarnish the history of this idyllic place.

Climate

This is a tropical, sub-rainforest region. Daytime temperatures April-October are 20 to 24C, night are 14 to 18C. During November-March, the "green season", daytime are 24 to 30C, and night are 18 to 26C. The water temperature remains 20 to 22C throughout the year.

Visitor Information

The Whitsunday Visitors and Convention Bureau, ©4946 6673, is found on the corner of Shute Harbour and Mandalay Roads, one kilometre from Airlie. They can be emailed at ✉tw@whitsundayinformation.com.au and have a web page at ☞www.whitsundayinformation.com.au

Alternatively, there is a website at ☞www.whitsunday.net.au

The Whitsunday Information Centre is on the Bruce Highway in Proserpine, ©4945 3711.

Camping

There are basic camping facilities on Hook, North Molle, Whitsunday, Henning, Border, Haslewood, Shaw, Thomas and Repulse Islands. These consist of toilets and picnic tables, with a ranger patrolling. Costs are ✪$3.50 per per-

Mackay to Townsville

son per night. All permits can be obtained over the phone by calling the Naturally Queensland Information Centre in Brisbane on ©3227 8197 or emailing them at ✒nqic@env.qld.gov.au

For more information on camping in the region, contact any QNP&WS branch.

Daydream Island

Location and Characteristics
Daydream is a small island with an area of just 17ha. It is a little over 1km long and no more than a couple of hundred metres at its widest point, but it has one of the largest resorts.

Originally known as West Molle, the island is the closest resort island to Shute Harbour. It was first settled in the 1880s by graziers, but the first resort was opened by Paddy Murray, who had purchased the island in 1933 and changed its name to Daydream after his boat.

Reg Ansett (later Sir Reginald), of airline fame, bought the resort in 1947 and ran it until 1953 when he pulled the whole lot down and transferred it to Hayman Island.

In the mid-1960s, a resort was established under the leadership of Bernie Elsey and it operated until destroyed by a cyclone in 1970. During this time Daydream's reputation was anything but squeaky clean - perhaps the 60s was not the decade to introduce topless bathing or illegal gambling.

The Jennings Group Ltd spent $100 million on a new complex at the northern end of the island and opened it in December 1990. Previous resorts had been at the southern end, but that part now has a Beach Club, with a nice sandy beach, a swimming pool, a bar, shops and a cafe. This is where all water activities are based, and the facilities can be used by resort guests and people on day trips from other islands and the mainland.

Novotel spent $40 million refurbishing the complex in 2001.

How to Get There
By Air
After flying to Proserpine airport, a coach will transfer guests to Shute Harbour to connect with the water taxi to the island.

Flights can also be made to Hamilton Island, followed by a (✪$45 return) trip with Blue Ferries to Daydream.
By Sea
Blue Ferries, ©4946 5111, have services from Shute Harbour to Daydream for ✪$18 return.

Visitor Information
Contact the resort on ©4948 8488 or ©1800 075 040 (reservations). The official web page is found at ✆www.daydream.net.au

Accommodation and Services
Daydream Island Resort accommodation is divided into three categories, all of which can accommodate up to 4 people: Ocean View Room, Garden View Room and Sunlover Room. Interconnecting rooms for larger families are available on request.

Resort facilities are: 3 restaurants, bakery/coffee shop, 4 bars, live entertainment, disco, spas, sauna, 2 swimming pools, 2 spas, gymnasium, aerobics, 2 tennis courts, windsurfing, catamaran sailing, paddle skis, snorkelling scuba diving and tuition, outer Reef excursions, waterskiing, parasailing, tour desk, laundry/ironing facilities, Kids' Club and child care.

Room facilities are: private bathrooms, mini bar, iron/board, hairdryer, tea/coffee making facilities, refrigerator, air-conditioning, colour TV, in-house movies, IDD/STD telephone, radio and daily cleaning services.

Tariffs for a double room per night are:

Garden View - ✪$290
Ocean View - ✪$320
Sunlover - ✪$460

The above rates include breakfast and use of most facilities. Not included are any sports that require fuel.

Reservations can be made online or through the resorts phone booking service, ✆1 800 075 040.

Points of Interest
Diving

Sunlover's Beach, at the north-eastern end of the island, behind the resort, has a 50m strip of sand and some good coral offshore for snorkellers. The Whitsunday tidal range does not affect Daydream as much as the other islands.

The Resort dive shop offers courses, and day cruises to Hardy Reef, about 50km offshore.

Hook Island

Location and Characteristics

Hook Island has an area of 53 sq km, some great beaches and some of the best diving sites in the Whitsundays, but it has one of the smallest resorts. The focus here is on the budget market, with a choice between camping sites, beachfront cabins and backpacker dorms.

Hook Island has two long, narrow bays on its southern end - Macona Inlet and Nara Inlet. Macona has a National Park camping site, and Nara has caves with Aboriginal wall paintings.

There is a variety of wildlife on the island, but one that can prove quite pesky is the large goanna. These have been known to chew through canvas to get to campers' stores.

How to Get There
By Air

Transfer by seaplane is an option, and it is best to enquire when making reservations at the resort for the best current prices.

By Sea

A catamaran service departs daily from Airlie Beach.

Visitor Information

The website is 🖳www.hookislandresort.com.au and the email address is ✉enquiries@hookis.com

The Wilderness Resort can answer any further enquiries, ✆4946 9380.

Accommodation and Services

The low-key **Wilderness Resort** has only three styles of accommodation - camping, cabins and dorms.

Resort facilities are: bar, coffee shop, gift shop, barbecue area, paddle skis and an on-site scuba instructor.

Beachfront cabins have private showers and a refrigerator, but toilet and cooking facilities are shared.

Dorms are shared accommodation facilities.

Camp sites are on the beachfronts, and have barbecues available for use.

Tariffs for a double per night are:

Cabins - ✪$95 adults
Dorms - ✪$20 adults
Camp Sites - ✪$13 adults

Reservations can be made through the Hook Island Wilderness Resort ✆4946 9380 or by phoning ✆4946 9925.

Points of Interest

The island is home to an underwater observatory that has an abundance of colourful corals and marine life. Though with so many trips available to the Outer Reef and the modern semi-submersible craft that tour operators use, you have to wonder why anyone would want to visit an underwater observatory. Still, it is popular with many visitors.

Diving

The northern end of Hook Island has some good diving and snorkelling sites - Pinnacle Point, Manta Ray Bay, Butterfly Bay and Alcyonaria Point. The resort can organise reef trips.

Hamilton Island

Location and Characteristics

Hamilton has an area of 6 sq km, and is home to

the largest resort in the South Pacific with its own jet airport.

The resort was the brain-child of Gold Coast entrepreneur Keith Williams, with help from friends such as Ansett Airlines. He had originally leased the island for deer farming, but converted this lease to one for tourism.

The workmen moved onto the island in 1982; parts of the complex were operational by 1984; and the entire resort was completed before the end of 1986. All this without interference from the Green Movement, even when the 15-storey condos went up and the airport runways were laid.

In the beginning it was a huge success, but disaster struck in ways that the management could neither foresee or control - firstly the domestic pilots' strike, then the international recession. Finally, in May 1992, Hamilton Island was placed in receivership, but in late 1993 it was successfully floated on the Australian Stock Exchange, and in March 1994 management of the resort was taken over by the Holiday Inn chain.

How to Get There
By Air
Qantas, ©13 1313, fly directly to Hamilton Island.
By Sea
Blue Ferries (Fantasea Cruises), ©4946 5111, operate a service to Hamilton from Shute Harbour for $38 return.

Visitor Information
An extensive website is provided at ⊛www.hamiltonisland.com.au

The Hamilton Island Resort can be contacted on ©4946 9999 or ©1800 075 110.

Accommodation and Services
There are four different types of accommodation from which to choose, all of which are part of the **Hamilton Island Resort**, ©4946 9999 or ©1800 075 110.

Beach Club Resort - 55 boutique-style rooms on Catseye Beach.

Reef View Hotel - 368 rooms and suites from Garden View to Presidential.

Whitsunday Holiday Apartments - 168 one bedroom apartments and 13 two bedroom apartments.

Coconut Palms bungalows and lodges - 50 free-standing Polynesian-style bungalows.

Resort facilities are: 6 swimming pools, 16 restaurants and take-aways, bars, shops and boutiques, tennis courts, squash courts, a gymnasium, aerobic classes, mini golf, live entertainment, parasailing, waterskiing, sailboards, SCUBA diving and lessons, catamarans and a free Kids' Club.

Room facilities are: private balcony, air-conditioning, fans, tea/coffee making facilities, ironing facilities, refrigerator and mini bar, colour TV, IDD/STD telephone and hairdryer.

Tariffs for a double room per night are:
Palm Terrace -   ✪$250
Reef View -   ✪$347-416
Whitsunday Apartments -   ✪$324-521
Beach Club -   ✪$486

The above rates are room only, and include use of most facilities. All other activities, meals and drinks are at the visitor's expense.

Bookings can be made online or through the resort. Credit cards accepted: all major cards.

Points of Interest
The resort is actually a small town with shops, restaurants and a 135-berth marina. There are a few walking tracks on the undeveloped parts of the island, and the main one leads up to Passage Peak (230m) the highest point on the island. To get around the island, you can rent a golf buggy and drive yourself. Hamilton even has island bus tours that operate daily.

There is a **Fauna Park** at the northern end of the island, with native animals, crocodiles and performing cockatoos.

4WD safari tours, go-karts and skirmish are further activities.
Diving
H2O Sportz, Front Street, Hamilton Island, ©4946 9888, is the only diving operation on Hamilton Island. A PADI 5-star Dive Centre, it

has all the services expected of a top dive facility. There is a wide range of diving options ranging from half-day trips to nearby fringing reefs, day trips on specialist dive boats, and large catamarans that sail to the Outer Reef.

H2O Sportz offer daily trips to the Outer Barrier Reef and visits such sites as Hook, Hardy, Black and Bait Reefs and the Whitsunday Island area. These are all Marine National Parks and offer some of the best diving in the area.

The one-day introduction program, Discover Scuba, costs ✪$205 and includes 2 escorted reef dives. A four-day open water course, with four-dives, is $500. The Advanced Diver Course is $450, with a 2-3 day duration and five ocean dives.

Hayman Island

Location and Characteristics

The island is a resort offering a balance between luxury living and natural beauty. Curving around the sandy shoreline of the blue lagoon on the south-western side of the island, Hayman looks out toward Langford Reef and an island called Bali Hai. All sports, both on land and water, are catered for at the resort.

Hayman Island has an area of 4 sq km, and is the most northerly of the Whitsunday resort islands. Its resort is one of the most luxurious on the Great Barrier Reef, and in fact is widely considered to be one of the top ten resorts in the world.

In 1866 the island was named after Thomas Hayman, navigator of the HMS *Salamander* which served in these waters for many years. In 1904 the island was leased by Thomas Abel for grazing his cattle, but he sold out in 1907. The first resort was established in 1935 by Bert Hallam and his brother, but this was a simple affair for fishing trips.

Reginald Ansett took over the island in 1947, and the fishing resort closed its doors in 1948, then in 1950 the Hayman Resort opened and remained so until 1985 when it was closed for a multi-million dollar rebuild.

There are several bushwalks on Hayman, including an 8km circuit and walks to Blue Pearl Bay or Dolphin Point. It is also possible to walk to nearby Arkhurst Island at low tide.

Visitor Information

Contact the resort or go to ◉www.hayman .com.au

Accommodation and Services

Hayman Island Resort, ©4946 1234, offers luxury of the highest quality. Antiques and treasures from around the world, as well as Australian works of art, can be found throughout the resort.

There are three main room categories - Rooms, Suites and Penthouses - with no less than 17 sub-categories, including Palm Garden, Beachfront, Contemporary, Californian, Japanese, Deco, Italian Palazzo, Moroccan and French.

Resort facilities are: six restaurants, cocktail bars, entertainment, pool bar, saltwater swimming pool, two freshwater pools, fully equipped health club, beauty salon, hairdresser, snorkelling, hobie cat sailing, windsurfing, beach volleyball, paddle skis, full and half court tennis, golf target range, lawn croquet, walking tracks, putting green, outdoor jacuzzi/spa, billiards room, table tennis, card and games room, badminton, new release movies on big screen, parasailing, water-skiing, water sleigh, yacht charter, Reef trips, dinghy hire, snorkelling excursions, picnics, tennis coaching, game/bottom and reef fishing trips and EFTPOS.

Rooms facilities are: air conditioning, ceiling fan, colour TV, video, IDD/STD telephone, hairdryer, mini bar, bathrobes, room safe, and rooms serviced daily.

Tariffs for a double room per night are:

Palm Superior -	✪$545
Pool Superior -	✪$795
Lagoon Superior -	✪$855
Beachfront -	✪$855
Pool Suites -	✪$1,485
Lagoon Suites -	✪$1,650
Contemporary Penthouse -	✪$1,870

Deco Penthouse -	✪$1,980
Italian Palazzo -	✪$2,200
English (2 bedroom) -	✪2,970
French (3 bedroom) -	✪$3,630

The above rates include breakfast only, and the rest of the meals don't come cheaply either. The wine list is extensive but expensive.

Activities not included in the rates are: parasailing, water skiing, water sleigh, yacht charter, Reef trips, dinghy hire, snorkelling excursions picnics, tennis coaching, game/bottom and reef fishing trips.

Reservations can be made through the website, or with the resort, ©4946 1234. All major credit cards are accepted.

Points of Interest
Diving
Hayman is closer to the outer Reef than other resort islands, and Hayman has a full-time dive boat to cater to every diver's desires. Thirty kilometres north-east of Hayman are the Hardy and Black Reefs.

Long Island

Location and Characteristics
The island is directly off the coast of Shute Harbour, and adjoins the Whitsunday Passage. It is deliberately underdeveloped, and the untamed tropical rainforest and protected Palm Bay Lagoon make for a very informal holiday.

There are 13km (8 miles) of well graded bushwalking tracks, and a variety of beaches for swimming and fishing.

Long Island is separated from the mainland by a channel that is only 500m wide, making it the closest resort island to the Queensland coast. It has an area of 12 sq km, but is about 11km long, so it is apparent that it is extremely narrow, only about 1.5km at its widest.

The island was originally called Port Molle, named after the Lieutenant Governor of the colony of NSW from 1814, who had his name liberally sprinkled on islands in the area. We still have North, Mid and South Molle, but there was also West Molle, which became Daydream, and this one whose name was changed to Long by Matthew Flinders.

The first resorts opened in the 1930s; one at Happy Bay, the other at Palm Bay. The Happy Bay establishment lasted up to 1983 when new buyers changed the name to Whitsunday 100 and tried to make it into another Great Keppel, but without much success. It was taken over and refurbished by Contiki in 1986 for their 18 to 35 clientele, then in 1990 new owners thought the name "The Island" would catch on, but in 1991 it became the Radisson Long Island Resort, and in January 1994, Club Crocodile.

Palm Bay Resort, in the southern part of the island, was devastated by a cyclone in the mid-1970s, but is back in operation as the Palm Bay Hideaway a low-key, old fashioned resort without all the commercial razzle-dazzle.

There was another resort at Paradise Bay, on the southern tip of Long Island, but it has never seemed to have the appeal of the others and has opened and closed several times.

Long Island has 20km of bush walks through the National Park, and there are some nice sandy beaches on its western side, but at Happy Valley the tidal variations cause the water to be so far from the beach that it is easier to swim in the pool. The box jellyfish makes its appearance in the vicinity from March to November. The beaches on the eastern side tend to be rocky and usually windy, but the dredging that has been undertaken at Palm Bay makes it ideal for swimming, and for mooring yachts.

How to Get There
By Sea
Access is daily by launch from Shute Harbour, and arrangements can be made through your selected accommodation.

Visitor Information
The Club Crocodile Resort can be contacted on ©4946 9233, and for a preliminary look at what

the island has to offer, follow the links to Long Island at ☞www.clubcrocodile.com.au

Accommodation and Services

There are two choices on Long Island:

Club Crocodile Long Island, ©4946 9400 (a sister to the Club Crocodile at Airlie Beach, Shute Harbour Road, ©4946 7155), has 54 garden rooms (3-star), 86 beachfront units (3-star) and 16 lodge rooms (2-star).

Resort facilities are: restaurants, cafe, barbecue, two bars, two swimming pools, spa, sauna, tennis courts, dance club and bar, extensive range of watersports, gymnasium, paddleboards, catamaran, coral viewing, resort store, games room, Kids' Club, laundry/ironing facilities and EFTPOS.

Room facilities are: private bathroom, air-conditioning (Beachfront), refrigerator, tea/coffee making facilities, radio, colour TV, balcony, ceiling fans, IDD/STD telephone and daily cleaning service.

Tariffs for a double room per night, full board, are:

Garden -   ✪$360
Beachfront -   ✪$410
Child rates, 3-17 years, ✪$45 per night.

Not included in the above rates are scuba diving, water taxi, fuel powered water sports or diving.

Contact the resort for reservations or book online. Credit cards accepted: American Express, Bankcard, Visa, MasterCard, Diners Club.

Palm Bay Hideaway accommodation consists of cabins and bures.

Resort facilities are: catamarans, windsurfing, volleyball, snorkelling gear, paddle skis, bar, dining room, hand line fishing gear, barbecue, swimming pool, spa, laundry/ironing facilities, lounge area, general store, outdoor dining terrace, tree house, open fireplace.

Room facilities are: private bathrooms, verandah, tea/coffee making facilities, ceiling fans, refrigerator, cooking facilities and utensils.

Tariffs for a double room per night are:

Cabin -   ✪$224.
Unit -   ✪$284.

Not included in the above rates are water taxi transfers or fuel powered water sports. Credit cards accepted: Visa, MasterCard, Bankcard, American Express.

The resort shop has food supplies for those wishing to utilise the kitchen facilities, but it will obviously be much cheaper to take your own provisions.

Points of Interest
Diving

Club Crocodile has a dive shop and can arrange trips out to the Reef.

South Molle Island

Location and Characteristics

The island covers 405ha (1000 acres) and is 4km long and 2.4km wide. It is situated in the heart of Whitsunday Passage, and offers fishing, golf, tennis, water skiing, coral viewing, scuba diving, parasailing and bushwalking.

South Molle has an area of 4 sq km, and is the largest of the Molle group. It is close to Mid Molle, and in fact you can walk from South Molle to Mid Molle at any time. Another island that is very close is Daydream.

The oldest of the resorts in the Whitsunday Group, South Molle is mostly national park and offers some good, if short, walks. The highest point is Mt Jeffreys (198m), and from it there are great views of the surrounding islands. Balancing Rock and Spion Kop also allow you to take in breathtaking vistas.

The first European settler was Henry George Lamond, who moved in with his wife and children in 1927 and stayed for ten years. There is a memorial to his son, Hal, on top of Lamond Hill.

South Molle is very much a family resort, there is even a pre-school nursery as well as activities for school-age children.

How to Get There
By Sea

Access is by launch departing daily from Shute Harbour, Blue Ferries (Fantasea), ©4946 5111.

A return fare is ✪$16.

Visitor Information

The resort can be contacted on ✆4946 9433. The web site is ⊚www.southmolleisland.com.au with an email service at ✎info@southmolleisland.com.au

Accommodation and Services

Accommodation is available at **South Molle Island Resort**, ✆4946 9433. 44 units, licensed restaurant, swimming pool, spa, sauna, tennis, squash, golf - full board ✪$310-390 a double per day.

The Resort has five different room categories, none of which are the most modern available in the Whitsundays, though they are definitely comfortable:

The Family rooms overlook the golf course and National Park, and have a double bedroom that can be shut off from the rest of the unit. These are ideal for a family of six.

Golf rooms also overlook the golf course and can accommodate a maximum of two.

Beachcomber units are freestanding and are located on the beachfront, with unobstructed ocean views. They can accommodate a maximum of four.

Reef units are set back 30-40 metres from the beach in a garden setting, and are handy to all facilities. They can accommodate four.

Whitsunday units have prime beachfront locations, facing the Whitsunday passage. Ground floor rooms have patios and those on the first floor have balconies. They can accommodate a maximum of four.

Resort facilities are: golf course, swimming pool, wading pool, kids' club, spa, sauna, beach towels, hairdresser, gift shop, coffee shop, live entertainment, disco, tennis, squash, volleyball, archery, gymnasium, snorkelling, scuba diving (tuition available), parasailing, water skiing, paddle skis, organised beach sports, windsurfers, catamarans, Great Barrier Reef cruises, day cruises to other islands and EFTPOS.

Room facilities are: private bathroom, ceiling fan, colour TV, refrigerator, IDD/STD phone, radio, tea/coffee making facilities, iron, ironing board and rooms serviced daily.

Tariffs for 2 adults and 2 children (minimum) are:

Family rooms - ✪$496 full board, $363 room only.

Tariffs for one night per person/twin share are:

Golf rooms - ✪$171 full board, $121 room only.

Beachcomber units - ✪$237 full board, $187 room only.

Reef units - ✪$193 full board, $149 room only.

Whitsunday units - ✪$215 full board, $165 room only.

The above rates include all meals. They do not include golf balls, tennis balls, squash balls or fuel powered watersports.

Reservations can be made through the resort, ✆4946 9433, or on the website. All major credit cards accepted.

Points of Interest
Diving

There is a Resort Dive Shop that offers short courses for beginners, and organises trips out to various parts of the reef. Contact the Resort for more information.

Lindeman Island

Location and Characteristics

The island has 20km (12 miles) of walking tracks that lead through 500ha (1235 acres) of National Park. There are seven secluded beaches, and at dusk from the top of Mt Oldfield, you can see the sun set over islands that stretch to the horizon in every direction.

Lindeman has an area of 8 sq km, most of which is national park, and was named after George Lindeman, whose job in the Royal Navy was to chart safe passages through the Whitsunday Islands.

The first resort was opened by Angus and Elizabeth Nicholson in 1923, and it stayed in their family until it was sold in 1979.

Lindeman has six beaches and 20km of walking

trails. Its highest point is Mt Oldfield, 210m. There is a resident Park Ranger who will advise and even accompany walkers.

How to Get There
By Air
Access is by air from Mackay or Shute Harbour, and can be included in room package rates on request.
By Sea
For a water taxi from Hamilton Island, ✆4946 9633 to make arrangements through the resort. Roylen Cruises, ✆4955 3066, have a launch service from Mackay.

Visitor Information
Contact the resort directly or follow the links to Lindeman Island at the Club Med website ☞www.clubmed.com.au

Accommodation and Services
Accommodation is available at **Club Med Lindeman Island**, ✆4946 9633, which opened its doors on Lindeman Island in 1992, and by 1994 had won the Hotel/Resort of the Year award.

Resort facilities are: boutique, restaurants, laundry, sports club-house, medical facilities, nightclub, recorded classical music concerts, card room, picnics, golf course (9-holes), tennis, aerobics, volleyball, basketball, archery, table tennis, football, cricket, badminton, hiking in the National Park, sailing, windsurfing, paddle skis, snorkelling, two swimming pools, seaboat trips, beach towels, Kids' Club.

Room facilities are: air-conditioning, private bathroom, balcony patio, TV, phone, bar fridge, tea/coffee making facilities, overhead ceiling fan.

Tariffs for one night per person/twin share (including light plane transfers from Mackay) are ✪$250 adults, $215 children 12-14; $130 children 4-11.

The above rates include all meals plus meal time drinks (beer, wine and juices). Cheaper packages include transfers from the Whitsundays. Enquire also about complete holiday packages, which include return air fares.

Not included in the tariffs are: the scuba diving course on the Great Barrier Reef, special excursions, and drinks at the bar.

Reservations can be made online at the Club Med website, or direct through the Resort, ✆4946 9333.

Credit cards accepted: American Express, Visa, Diners Club, MasterCard and Bankcard.

Points of Interest
Diving
There is not much here for scuba divers, but the Resort arranges diving trips out to the Reef. Snorkelling trips to Hardy Lagoon take place several days a week.

Whitsunday Island

Although Whitsunday is the largest of the island in the Whitsunday Group, it does not have a resort. But it does have Whitehaven Beach, the longest and best beach in the whole group, and the destination of many cruises. There is good snorkelling off the southern end of the beach.

There are several camping sites on the island, and more information can be obtained from Naturally Queensland, listed under *Camping* above.

Proserpine

Population 2800

Location and Characteristics
Proserpine, 127km (80 miles) north of Mackay, is mainly a sugar cane town. It serves as the centre of the Whitsunday region, in administrative terms, but most visitors by-pass its scenic charm on their way to the more seductive coastline. The town has full facilities and a good range of accommodation.

You may wish to stay close to the Bruce Highway on a northward/southward journey, but if you plan to be in the Whitsundays area for any

Mackay to Townsville

significant length of time, and are not planning to stay on an island resort, the coastal settlements of Airlie Beach and Shute Harbour have all the good views.

West of the town is Lake Proserpine, where waterskiing is a popular sport.

How to Get There
By Air
Sunstate, ©13 1313, have frequent flights to Proserpine.
By Rail
The Sunlander departs Brisbane for Proserpine every Tuesday, Thursday and Saturday, and departs Cairns on the return journey every Monday, Thursday and Saturday, ©13 2235.
By Coach
Both McCaffertys, ©13 1499, and Greyhound Pioneer, ©13 2030, stop at Proserpine.
By Road
Proserpine, on the Bruce Highway 127km (80 miles) north of Mackay, is the nearest major centre. Shute Harbour is a further 30km from there, and 8km from Airlie Beach.

Visitor information
The Whitsunday Information Centre on the Bruce Highway is in Proserpine, ©4945 3711.

Accommodation and Services
Laguna Quays, Kunapipi Springs Road, Repulse Bay, ©4747 7777 or ©1800 812 626 (toll free), is not strictly in Proserpine itself, but deserves a mention. It is on the coast 26km south of the town. There are 36 rooms, with 24 suites, 2 licensed restaurants, a playground, room service, bushwalking tracks, watersports, golf, tennis, a pool and sauna - ✪$275-400.
Proserpine Motor Lodge, 184 Main Street, ©4945 1788. 33 units, licensed restaurant, undercover parking, room service, pool - ✪$65.
Whitsunday Palms, Bruce Highway, ©4945 1868. 6 units, barbecue, undercover parking - ✪$55-65.
Reef Gardens Motel, Bruce Highway, ©4945 1288. 12 units, barbecue, playground, under-

cover parking - ✪$50-55.
Anchor Motel Whitsunday, Bruce Highway, ©4945 1200. 12 units, unlicensed restaurant, undercover parking - ✪$45.
Caravan Park
Golden Cane Caravan Park, ©4945 1540. 25 sites, barbecue, playground, kiosk, pool - powered sites ✪$14 for two, units $35 for two, cabins $45 for two.
Eating Out
Two places to dine at in Proserpine are *Proserpine Village Chinese Restaurant*, 13 Mill Street, ©4945 2589 and *Pioneer Bistro*, 140 Main Street, ©4945 3637.
Local Transport
Whitsunday Transit buses service the area, ©4952 2377 for schedule details.

Airlie Beach

Location and Characteristics
Airlie Beach, the main resort town on the Whitsunday coast, has a relaxed atmosphere, and is 8km (5 miles) from Shute Harbour, 24km (15 miles) from Proserpine.

The town borders the 20,000ha Conway National Park, and is the mainland centre for the Whitsundays.

Airlie Beach is a picturesque village and offers a lot to the holiday-maker on its own account, but when you add the close proximity of the Reef islands, it is not hard to figure out why some people choose to stay at Airlie and take day trips to the islands.

How to Get There
By Air
Sunstate, ©13 1313, have frequent flights to nearby Proserpine.

By Rail
The Sunlander departs Brisbane for Proserpine every Tuesday, Thursday and Saturday, and departs Cairns on the return journey every Monday, Thursday and Saturday, ©13 2235.
By Coach
Both McCaffertys, ©13 1499, and Greyhound

Pioneer, ©13 2030, stop at Airlie Beach.

By Road
Proserpine, on the Bruce Highway 127km (80 miles) north of Mackay, is the nearest major centre. From there it is 24km (15 miles) to Airlie Beach.

Visitor Information
The Airlie Tourist Information Centre is at 277 Shute Harbour Road, Airlie Beach, ©4946 6665, and can be emailed at ✉ abtic@whitsunday .net.au

Accommodation and Services
This is the major costal mainland accommodation centre for the Whitsundays. The area code is (07).

Whitsunday Vista Resort, 1 Hermitage Drive, ©4946 7007. 10 units, barbecue, undercover parking, pool, spa - ✪$150-250.

Mediterranean Resorts, Golden Orchid Drive, ©4946 6391. 12 units, undercover parking, spa, 2 pools - ✪$155-310.

Coral Sea Resort, 25 Ocean View Avenue, ©4946 6458 or ©1800 075 061 (toll free). 25 units, two licensed restaurants, room service, pool - ✪$50-270.

Airlie Beach Motor Lodge, Lamond Street, ©4946 6418 or ©1800 810 925 (toll free). 4 units, barbecue, undercover parking, pool, sauna - ✪$80-100.

Colonial Palms Motor Inn, cnr Shute Harbour Road & Hermitage Drive, ©4946 7166 or ©1800 075 114 (toll free). 30 units, licensed restaurant, undercover parking, room service, pool, spa - ✪$80-110.

Whitsunday Wanderers Resort, Shute Harbour Road, ©4946 6446 or ©1800 075 069. 104 units, licensed restaurant, barbecue, playground, table tennis, gymnasium, mini golf, volleyball, pool, 2 spas - ✪$100-150.

Airlie Beach Hotel/Motel, 16 The Esplanade, Airlie Beach, ©4946 6233. 30 units, pool - ✪$55-90. Every Tuesday and Thursday from 7.30pm the famous Charity Toad Races are held here. All proceeds are given to worthy causes, but you can win cruises and prizes at these family-fun nights.

The Islands Inn, Shute Harbour Road, ©4946 6755 or ©4946 6943. 32 units, barbecue, licensed restaurant, pool, spa - ✪$55-65.

Airlie Court Holiday Units, 382 Shute Harbour Road, ©4946 6218. 6 units, licensed restaurant, undercover parking - ✪$65-115.

Airlie Island Traders, Shute Harbour Road, ©4946 4056. 9 units, barbecue, playground, undercover parking, heated pool - ✪$55-75.

Caravan Parks
Airlie Cove Resort Van Park, cnr Shute Harbour & Ferntree Roads, ©4946 6727. (No dogs allowed) 64 sites, barbecue, playground, tennis, pool, spa - powered sites ✪$20 for two, cabins $45-95 for two.

Island Getaway Caravan Resort, cnr Shute Harbour & Jubilee Pocket Roads, ©4946 6228. 154 sites, barbecue, playground, shop, tennis and mini golf, pool, spa - powered sites ✪$20 for two, units $65 for two, cabins $50 for two.

Whitsunday Gardens Holiday Park, Shute Harbour Road, ©4946 6483. 40 sites, barbecue, kiosk, pool - powered sites ✪$16 for two, villas $65 for two, cabins $60 for two.

There is a **Youth Hostel** at 394 Shute Harbour Road, ©4946 6312 or ©1800 247 251. It has 17 rooms at ✪$21 per person twin share.

Local Transport
If you require local transport, the Whitsunday Taxi Service can be contacted on ©1800 811 388.

Points of Interest
The Barefoot Bushman's Wildlife Park, Lot 2, Shute Harbour Road, Cannonvale, ©4946 1480, has a terrific array of Australian wildlife with shows throughout the day. There are pythons, brown snakes, lizards, frogs, ducks, pelicans, owls, kookaburras, possums, wombats, fruit bats, native birds, doves, emus, dingoes and crocodiles, to name a few. Highlights include the Snake Show, where the world's deadliest snakes are put on display, and the Crocodile Feeding, where you can see these huge reptiles snapping up their lunch. The Wildlife Park is ⏰open 9am-4pm every day and admission is ✪$18 adults, $8 children and $45 for families.

Activities

Whitsunday Parasail, 25 Ocean View Avenue, Airlie Beach, ©4948 0000 - single flight ✪$45, tandem flight $90.

Brandy Creek Trail Rides, Lot 15 Brandy Creek Road, Cannon Valley, ©4946 6665 or ©4946 1121 - half-day escorted trail rides, departing daily 9am and 2.30pm - includes courtesy coach, billy tea and damper - proper clothing is supplied and horses are available to suit all riding expertise levels - ✪$45 adults and $40 children.

Charter Flights

Air Whitsunday Seaplanes, Air Whitsunday Drive, Airlie Beach, ©4946 9111, offer:

Panorama - two hours of snorkelling in lagoons only accessible by seaplane - a stop at Whitehaven Beach - champagne picnic at extra charge ($25) - 4 hours duration - ✪$280 adults, $140 children.

Reef Explorer - fly over all the Whitsunday Islands - land at Whitehaven Beach for two hours - 3 hours duration - ✪$200 adults, $128 children.

Reef Adventure - panoramic views of the Whitsunday Islands - land on the reef and board a coral viewing sub - snorkelling with tuition - 3 hours duration - ✪$225 adults, $140 children.

Hayman Day Trip - flight to Hayman Island - full use of resort facilities - return flight departs 4.30pm - 7 hours duration - ✪$145 adults, $105 children.

Cruises

There are countless companies operating cruise and sailing vessels through this coral paradise, and the Visitor Information Centre has more material than you will probably have time to read through. The choices are overwhelming, and may come down to the brochure with the brightest pictures!

The following details will give you a basis for comparison.

Fantasea Cruises, 11 Shute Harbour Road, Airlie Beach, ©4946 5811 or ©4946 5111 (bookings), offer:

Great Barrier Reef Day Cruise to Reefworld - semi-sub coral viewing, snorkelling equipment including hygienic mouthpiece, buffet lunch, morning and afternoon teas, fresh water showers and large sundeck area, courtesy pick-up from accommodation, large underwater viewing chamber - ✪$150 adults, $135 children (4-14), $350 for families - daily 8.15am-5.20pm from Shute Harbour.

Three Island Adventure - visit Whitehaven Beach, Hamilton and Daydream Islands - beach games at Whitehaven and pool facilities at Daydream, morning and afternoon tea, courtesy pick-up - ✪$85 adults, $40 children (4-14), $110 for families - departs Shute Harbour 8.45am, returns 5.20pm.

Hamilton Island Day Cruise - ✪$50 adults, $26 children - daily from Shute Harbour 8.15am, 9.15am, 10.15am or 11.15am.

Whitehaven Beach & Hamilton Island - ✪$68 adults, $33 children, $160 for families - departs Shute Harbour 8.45am.

Island Discovery Pass - one day pass for travel between Daydream, South Molle and Hamilton islands - ✪$50 adults, $26 children, $128 for families - departs Shute Harbour 8.45am.

Whale Watching Day Cruise - these are usually held July-September, depending upon the arrival and departure of these fascinating creatures - ©4946 5811 for seasonal prices and departure times.

Reefsleep - 2 days' and 1 night's accommodation at the Reefworld facility - snorkelling and scuba diving - underwater viewing - all meals - from ✪$330.

Fantasea has a website at ☞www.fantasea.com.au

Seatrek Whitsunday Cruises, Shop 1, 283 Shute Harbour Road, Airlie Beach, ©4946 4366 or ©4946 5255, offer:

South Molle Island Day Trip - includes windsurfing, catamarans, paddle skis, golf - daily ✪$35 adults, $28 children, $90 for families - departs Shute Harbour - 9am-5pm.

Whitsunday All Over Cruises, 398 Shute Harbour Road, ©4946 6900 or ©1300 366 494 (bookings), offer:

3 Islands in 3 Days - launch transfer between

Daydream, South Molle and Long Islands over a 3 day period - ✪$50 adults, $30 children.

Club Crocodile Long Island Adventure Pack - transfers from Shute Harbour to Long Island - lunch included - use of facilities at Club Crocodile - island exploration - ✪$40 adults, $18 children, $100 for families.

South Molle Island Day Trip - transfer to South Molle Island - lunch included - use of facilities - ✪$40 adults, $18 children, $100 for families.

Yellow Sub Cruise - includes courtesy coach, morning tea, picnic lunch, snorkelling gear, talk by marine biologist, guided island tours, guided coral viewing in an air-conditioned semi-submersible, visit to Daydream Island Beach Club for approximately an hour before returning to the mainland - ✪$75 adult, $40 child - $195 family - daily - departs Shute Harbour at 9.15am, South Molle at 9.30am - returns 5pm.

Mantaray Charters, 28 Jones Road, Cannonvale, ✆4946 4579 or ✆4946 6665 (bookings) - full day cruise taking in Whitehaven Bay and Mantaray Beach - diving and snorkelling - some equipment provided - ✪$65 adults, $35 children, $165 for families, tropical lunch an extra $10 adults and $6 children - departs Abel Point 9am.

Diving

Whitsunday Dive Charters, 5 Airlie Crescent, Airlie Beach, ✆4946 5366 - a fast dive vessel takes you out to Bait Reef for the day - departs Abel Point Marina 8.45am - from ✪$178 diving and $126 snorkelling.

Reef Dive Whitsundays, Shute Harbour Road, Airlie Beach, ✆4946 6508 or 1800 075 120 (free call) - live-aboard trip over 3 nights, with all meals and 10 dives (including 2 night dives) - ✪$490 per person.

Oceania Dive, 257 Shute Harbour Road, Airlie Beach, ✆1800 075 035 (enquiries) or ✆4946 6032 (bookings) - PADI open water courses - cruise to the edge of the Coral Sea, through the Whitsunday Islands - dive the Elizabeth and Stucco Reefs - from ✪$335 for a 4 day open water course - advanced courses, 3 days and 3 nights for $570.

Boats moored in Shute Harbour

Shute Harbour

Location and Characteristics
Shute Harbour is the focal point for departure of many tourist vessels cruising to the Whitsunday Islands. Not only is it the second busiest passenger port in Australia, it boasts the second largest bareboat industry in the world (a bareboat is a boat hired without a crew).

How to Get There
By Air
Sunstate, ✆13 1313, have frequent flights to nearby Prosperine.
By Rail
The Sunlander departs Brisbane for Proserpine every Tuesday, Thursday and Saturday, and departs Cairns on the return journey every Monday, Thursday and Saturday, ✆13 2235.

By Coach
Both McCaffertys, ✆13 1499, and Greyhound Pioneer, ✆13 2030, stop at nearby Proserpine.
By Road
Off the Bruce Highway 127km (80 miles) north of Mackay.

Visitor Information
Use the contact details for Whitsunday Tour-

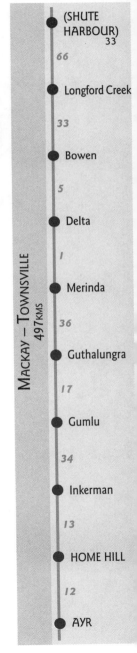

Mackay to Townsville

(SHUTE HARBOUR) 33

66

Longford Creek

33

Bowen

5

Delta

1

Merinda

36

Guthalungra

17

Gumlu

34

Inkerman

13

HOME HILL

12

AYR

MACKAY – TOWNSVILLE 497KMS

ism, listed under *Visitor Information* for Whitsunday Islands, or visit the Tourist Information Centre at Airlie Beach, 277 Shute Harbour Road, ©4946 6665.

Accommodation and Services

Shute Harbour is mostly a gateway for cruises out to the islands, and is one of the smaller satellite areas for Proserpine, as well as being superceded by Airlie Beach as an accommodation centre. Nevertheless, there are a couple of places to stay here.

Coral Point Lodge, Harbour Avenue, ©4946 9500 or ©1800 077 611. 10 units, views take in Shute Harbour and the Whitsunday Islands, unlicensed restaurant, undercover parking, transfers, pool - ✪$70-85.

Shute Harbour, Shute Harbour Road, ©4946 9131. 12 units, licensed restaurant, car parking, room service, pool - ✪$60-85.

Caravan Park

Flame Tree Tourist Village, Shute Harbour Road, ©4946 9388 or ©1800 069 388. 100 sites, barbecue, playground, shop, heated pool - unpowered sites ✪$17 for two, villas $55-65 for two, units $50-55 for two, cabins $40-45 for two, on-site vans $45 for two.

Eating Out

For decent meals at reasonable prices, try ***The Catalina Bistro Bar*** on Shute Harbour Road, ©4946 9797.

Bowen

Population 14,100

Location and Characteristics

Situated just north of the Whitsunday Islands, Bowen is a town where the ocean laps the edges of the main street. It is 210km (130 miles) south of Townsville on the Bruce Highway, and has one of the best climates in Australia.

The surrounding coast is indented with innumerable small headlands and quiet coral beaches. Inland, the Don River Plain is a fruit growing region.

How to Get There

By Rail

Bowen is accessible by rail, ©13 2235 for details, schedules and current fares.

By Coach

Greyhound Pioneer, ©13 2030, and McCaffertys, ©13 1499 service Bowen.

By Road

On the Bruce Highway, 210km south of Townsville.

Visitor Information

The Bowen Visitor Information Centre is on the Bruce Highway, Bowen, ©4786 4222.

Accommodation and Services

There is no shortage of accommodation here.

Castle Motor Lodge, 6 Don Street, ©4786 1322. 32 units, licensed restaurant, undercover parking, pool, spa - ✪$75.

Whitsunday Sands Resort, Horseshoe Bay Road, ©4786 3333. 14 units, barbecue, unlicensed restaurant (closed Sunday), playground, kiosk, pool - ✪$65.

Skyview Motel Family Units, 49 Horseshoe Bay Road, ©4786 2232. 14 units, playground, undercover parking, pool - ✪$65-80.

Queens Beach Motor Hotel, 101 Golf Links Road, ©4785 1555. 50 units, licensed restaurant, pool - ✪$55-70.

Big Mango Tree, Bruce Highway, ©4786 2499 or ©4786 2048. 11 units, playground, transfers, pool - ✪$50.

Ocean View, Bruce Highway, Gordon Beach, ©4786 1377. 12 units, barbecue, undercover parking, pool - ✪$60.

Caravan Parks

Horseshoe Bay Resort, Horseshoe Bay, ©4786 2564. 40 sites, licensed restaurant, barbecue, kiosk, mini-golf, pool, sauna, spa - powered sites ✪$14 for two, park cabins $40-45 for two, on-site vans $30 for two.

Bowen Village Caravan & Tourist Park, Bruce Highway (South) ©4786 1366. 75 sites, barbecue, playground, shop, pool - powered sites ✪$18 for two, cabins $40 for two, on-site vans

$25 for two.

Rose Bay Caravan Park, Rose Bay, ©4786 2388. 23 sites, barbecue, pool - powered sites ✪$13 for two, on-site vans $25 for two.

Eating Out

If you are interested in dining out, there is the *Peacock Restaurant* at 38 Williams Street, ©4786 1280, and *Fullagen's Irish Bar & Restaurant* at 37 Herbert Street, ©4786 1783.

Points of Interest

The Bowen Historical Society Museum, 22 Gordon Street, ©4786 2035. In it you will find shipwreck relics, information on early pioneers and indigenous artefacts. It is ⊙open 10.30am-4pm Mon-Fri and 10.30am-12pm Sunday and costs ✪$3 adults and $1 for children.

Bowen's stunning coastline encapsulates its attraction for visitors. Of particular note are idyllic **Horseshoe Bay** and **Murray Bay**. **Queens Beach** is also a popular haven.

In the southern area of Bowen, swimming, fishing, diving and snorkelling are year-round activities, and for those who prefer to stay on terra firma, there is fossiking for sapphires, amethysts, crystals and opalised woods.

Home Hill and Ayr

Population 8600 and 3300 respectivey.

Location and Characteristics

The twin towns of Home Hill and Ayr are 90km (56 miles) south of Townsville on the Bruce Highway, and sit either side of the delta of the Burdekin River, slightly inland from the coast. The Burdekin is the main waterway of the Magnetic North, and its catchment area includes the mountains to the north and the goldfields to the west.

How to Get There

By Coach

McCaffertys, ©13 1499, and Greyhound Pioneer, ©13 2030, service Ayr daily.

By Rail

The Ayr Railway Station is in Station Street, ©4783 2214, for current schedules.

By Road

Both towns are conveniently located on the Bruce Highway, 90km south of Townsville.

Visitor Information

The Burdekin Tourist Information Centre is in Plantation Park, on the Bruce Highway, Ayr, ©4783 5988.

Accommodation and Services

Accommodation is limited and far from flash in both of these towns, but here is a sample guide.

Ayr

Country Ayr, 197 Queen Street, ©4783 1700. 4 units, licensed restaurant (closed Sunday), undercover parking, pool - ✪$85-95.

Ayr Shamrock, 274 Queen Street, ©4783 1044. 10 units, undercover parking, pool - ✪$50-60.

Ayr Max Motel, 4 Edward Street, Bruce Highway North, ©4783 2033. 12 units, barbecue, undercover parking, pool, spa - ✪$60-65.

Tropical City Motor Inn, cnr MacMillan & McKenzie Streets, ©4783 1344. 16 units, licensed restaurant, undercover parking, room service, pool - ✪$55-70.

Caravan Parks

Silver Link Caravan Park, 34 Norham Road, ©4783 3933. 75 sites, barbecue, playground, kiosk, pool, spa - powered sites ✪$18 for two, villas $55-60 for two, cabins $40 for two, bunkhouses $28 for two.

Burdekin Cascades Caravan Park, 228 Queen Street, ©4783 1429. 42 sites, playground - powered sites ✪$16 for two, cabins $50 for two.

Eating Out

If you don't wish to eat at your motel, the *Burdekin Chinese Seafood Resturant* is at 110 Edward Street, ©4783 3444. There is also *Peppers on Queens*, 199 Queens Street, ©4783 1029 and *Charley's*, Queen Street, ©4783 4051.

Local Transport

You may require transport in the region, and in that case the Supreme Taxi Company can be contacted on ©4783 2244.

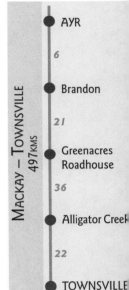

Mackay to Townsville

MACKAY – TOWNSVILLE 497KMS

- AYR
- 6
- Brandon
- 21
- Greenacres Roadhouse
- 36
- Alligator Creek
- 22
- TOWNSVILLE

**Mackay
to Townsville**

Home Hill

Burdekin Motor Inn, 14 Eighth Avenue, ℗4782 1511. 14 units, licensed restaurant (closed Sunday-Thursday), undercover parking, room service, pool - ✪$55.

Caravan Park

Bartons Caravan Park, Eighth Avenue, ℗4782 1101. 34 sites, playground - powered sites ✪$10-16 for two.

Points of Interest

The **Ayr Nature Display**, 119 Wilmington Street, Ayr, ℗4783 2189, has stunning displays ranging from reptiles to butterflies, birds to insects and fossils to shells. Admission is ✪$3 adults and $1.50 children, and the Nature display is ⌚open 8am-5pm daily.

The river and its tributaries offer some of the best **freshwater fishing** for barramundi, grunter and bream in Australia, while the river delta and Alva Beach tempt the salt water fisherman with whiting, flathead and salmon. The Burdekin River is also the hub of other river-based activities from water skiing to picnicking.

The wreck of the SS *Yongala* lies 20km (12 miles) out to sea and is a fine diving site.

Cape Upstart National Park, some 70km (43 miles) from town, is an imposing granite headland rising from the sea.

Chapter 41
Townsville

Population 140,000
Townsville is situated on the eastern coast of Australia, 1443km (897 miles) north of Brisbane.

Climate

Average temperature: January max 31C (88F) - min 24C (75F) and high humidity; July max 25C (77F) - min 15C (59F). Average annual rainfall is 1194mm (47 ins) - wettest months January-March, with an average of 873mm (34 ins).

Characteristics

The second largest city in Queensland and main commercial centre of northern Queensland, Townsville sprawls along the shores of Cleveland Bay and around the foot of Castle Hill. It offers not only easy access to the attractions of the Magnetic North and the Great Barrier Reef, but also all of the facilities of a major city.

Careful zoning has ensured that the city retains much of its original architecture and character. A walk around town will show you what makes North Queensland so different. Old wooden, highset houses stand everywhere, built to allow cooling breezes under the house and to provide a refuge during the heat of the day. In the gardens, mango, paw paw and banana trees seem exotic to the visitor, but are the normal homegrown product of the Townsville backyard.

Townsville is also a busy port that services Mt Isa, southern cities and south-east Asia. It has two metal refineries and other industrial enterprises.

How to Get There

By Air

Qantas, ©13 1313, have flights to/from Adelaide, Alice Springs, Brisbane, Cairns, Darwin, Gold Coast, Hobart, Launceston, Melbourne, Newcastle, Perth and Sydney.

Sunstate Airlines, ©13 1313, have flights to/from Brampton Island, Lizard Island, Mackay, Proserpine, Rockhampton and Thursday Island. Flight West, ©1300 130 092, is another airline that services Townsville.

Check other regional flights with your travel agent.

By Coach

Greyhound Pioneer, ©13 2030, and McCaffertys, ©13 1499, both stop at Townsville on their Brisbane-Cairns services.

By Rail

The Queenslander and the Sunlander services connect Townsville to both Brisbane and Cairns four times weekly, ©13 2235. Sleeping berths and motor rail facilities are available.

By Road

From Brisbane along the Bruce Highway, 1443km (897 miles); from Brisbane along the inland route, 1505km (935 miles). Townsville is 374km south of Cairns.

The Flinders Highway connects Townsville with Mt Isa and Alice Springs.

It is important to listen to a local radio station for reports on road conditions during wet weather, as roads in northern Queensland are often cut during heavy rain.

Visitor Information

The Townsville Enterprise Tourism Bureau is in Enterprise House, 6 The Strand, ©4771 3061. There is also a Visitors Information Centre in Flinders Mall, ©4721 3660, ©open 9am-5pm Mon-Fri and 9am-1pm Sat-Sun.

Accommodation

Townsville has over 30 motels, hotels, guest houses, hostels and half a dozen camping grounds. Here is a selection with prices for a double room per night, which should be used as a guide only. The telephone area code is 07.

Jupiters Townsville Hotel & Casino, Sir Leslie Theiss Drive, ©4722 2333, jupiterstownsville.com.au. 192 rooms, 16 suites, licensed restaurant, bars, swimming pool, spa, sauna, gym, tennis courts, casino - ✪$150.

Centra Townsville, Flinders Mall, ✆4772 2477. 158 rooms, licensed restaurants, bars, gym, rooftop swimming pool - ✪$220.

Aquarius on the Beach Townsville, 75 The Strand, North Ward, ✆4772 4255. 100 rooms, licensed restaurant (closed Sun), bistro, swimming pool - ✪$130.

Southbank Hotel, 23 Palmer Street, South Townsville, ✆4721 1474. 94 units, 4 suites, licensed restaurant, cocktail bar, swimming pool, spa, undercover parking - ✪$100-110.

Castle Lodge, cnr Warburton & McKinley Streets, North Ward, ✆4721 2290. 24 units, licensed restaurant (Mon-Sat), pool - ✪$95-105.

City Oasis Inn, 143 Wills Street, ✆4771 6048 or ✆1800 809 515 (toll free). 42 units, 2 suites, licensed restaurant, playground, pool, 2 spas - ✪$95-170.

Historic Yongola Lodge, 11 Fryer Street, ✆4772 4633. 8 units, licensed restaurant, pool, next to *National Trust* restaurant - ✪$90-110.

Shoredrive, 117 The Strand, ✆4771 6851. 30 units, unlicensed restaurant, pool - ✪$70.

Bessell Lodge, 38 Bundock Street, Belgian Gardens, ✆4772 5055. 50 units, licensed restaurant, cocktail bar, live entertainment, barbecue - ✪$85.

Aitkenvale, 224 Ross River Road, Aitkenvale, ✆4775 2444. 26 units, 2 suites, licensed restaurant, swimming pool, playground, undercover parking - ✪$65.

Hotel Allen, cnr Eyre & Gregory Streets, ✆4771 5656. 45 units, 5 suites, pool - ✪$70.

Adobi, 86 Abbott Street, ✆4778 2533 or ✆4778 2745. 12 units, pool - ✪$50.

Caravan Parks

Sun City Caravan Park, 119 Bowen Road, ✆4775 7733. 132 sites, pool, barbecue, playground - powered sites ✪$19 for two, on-site vans $35-40 for two, cabins $55-60 for two.

Magnetic Gateway Holiday Village, Bruce Highway, South Side, adjacent to Stuart Drive-in, ✆4778 2412. (No pets) 108 sites, barbecue, pool - powered sites ✪$17 for two, villas $55 for two.

Coonambelah Caravan Park, 547 Ingham Road, ✆4774 5205. (Pets on application) 75 sites - powered sites ✪$17 for two, on-site vans $35-40 for two, cabins $40-50 for two.

Town & Country Caravan Park, 16 Kings Road, ✆4772 1487. (No pets allowed) 72 sites, pool, barbecue, playground - powered sites ✪$18 for two, on-site vans $35 for two, cabins $55 for two.

Eating Out

Townsville has many hotels serving counter lunches and takeaways, and some good restaurants. The international hotels have at least one restaurant, and the staff where you are staying can probably recommend a restaurant on the basis of price or cuisine. Following is a broad sample for all tastes and budgets.

Scirocco Cafe Bar & Grill, 61 Palmer Street, ✆4724 4508. Mediterranean and Asian cuisine, alfresco dining. Open Tues-Sat 6pm-midnight, and for lunch from midday-2pm, 10am-4pm on Sunday, closed Monday and Public Holidays.

The Pier Waterfront Restaurant & Bar, Sir Leslie Thiess Drive, ✆4721 2567. Licensed restaurant with waterfront views. Seafood and steak, light lunches served. Open midday-2pm for lunch and 6pm-midnight for dinner 7 days.

Covers Restaurant, 209 Flinders Street, ✆4721 4630. Open 6pm-midnight Mon-Sat and for lunch Wed-Fri, closed Sunday and Public Holidays.

Flutes Restaurant, 63 The Strand, ✆4721 1777. Operates 24 hours a day, 7 days, in the Best Western Motel.

Hong Kong Restaurant, 455 Flinders Street, West Townsville, ✆4771 5818. A-la-carte menu with home-style cooking a specialty. Open 5pm-8pm Mon-Sat and for lunch Mon-Fri, closed Sunday and Public Holidays.

Wayne and Adeles Garden of Eating, 11 Allen Street, South Townsville, ✆4772 2984. Open 6.30-11pm Mon, Wed-Sat and Public Holidays, Sun 11am-3pm, closed Tuesday.

Metropole Hotel, 81 Palmer Street, South Townsville, ✆4771 4285. Seafood restaurant with gaming facilities and a beer garden in the complex. Open 24 hours, 7 days.

Taiping Chinese Restaurant, 350 Sturt Street, City, ✆4772 3619. A-la-carte, yum cha and buffet selections. Open midday-2pm and 5.30-midnight 7 days, closed Public Holidays.

Seagulls Resort, 74 The Esplanade, Belgian Gardens, ✆4721 3111. Open 6.30am-midnight every day.

Centra Townsville, Flinders Mall, ✆4772 2477. A-la-carte buffet menu and a cocktail bar. Open 7am-10pm every day.

Hogs Breath Cafe, 247 Flinders Street, ✆4771 5747. Open for lunch 11.30am-2.30pm and dinner 5.30pm-2.30am every day.

Pepperleaf at the Seaview, 56 The Strand, Townsville, ✆4771 5900.

McDonalds is on the corner of Flinders Mall and Denham Street. KFC is in the Nathan Plaza Stockland Shopping Centre. Pizza Hut is at 260 Ross River Road and on the corner of Charters Towers and Bayswater Roads, ✆13 1166.

Entertainment

First and foremost in this category would have to be the:

Sheraton Townsville Hotel & Casino, Sir Leslie Thiess Drive, ✆4722 2333. It was North Queensland's first licensed casino. Here you can try blackjack, the Sheraton wheels, two-up, roulette, keno, mini-dice, craps and mini baccarat. They also have video games and Sky Channel. To get the tourists in they offer a free courtesy bus service to most hotels and motels. The casino is ⏰open from noon to the early hours of the morning.

Townsville Civic Theatre is in 41 Boundary Street, South Townsville, ✆4727 9013 or ✆4727 9797 (box office), and can seat 1066 people. It offers culturally diverse programs.

The **Entertainment & Convention Centre**, ✆4771 4000, on Entertainment Drive, is primarily for indoor sport, such as basketball, but if a big-name performer or band hits town, this is where the concert will be.

Fisherman's Wharf in Ogden Street has live entertainment seven nights a week, a restaurant, coffee shop and a bar.

If you are in the mood for dancing, head for Flinders Street where there is a night club, *Bullwinkles*, ✆4771 5647.

For a pub night out try the *Great Northern Hotel* in 496 Flinders Street, ✆4771 6191.

Shopping

Flinders Street Mall has several boutiques and specialty shops and *Northtown on the Mall*, ✆4772 1566, but the big shopping centres are out of town.

At Aitkenville, 20 minutes from the city centre is *Stockland*, 310 Ross River Road, ✆4779 6033, which has David Jones department stores as well as specialty shops. Nearby is *K-Mart Plaza*, Nathan Street, ✆4779 9277, which has food shops and, of course, K-Mart.

The suburb of Pimlico has *Castletown*, 35 Kings Road, ✆4772 1699, which has a variety of chain stores, including Target. The suburb of Kirwan has *The Willows*, Thuringowa Drive, ✆4773 6333.

North Queensland's largest arts and crafts market is held in Flinders Mall every ☉Sunday 9am-1pm. Called *Cotters Market* it has pottery, jewellery, paintings, leadlighting, leatherwork, woodwork, crocheting and knitwear, original handicrafts, wooden toys, hats, homemade goodies, plants and preserves, islander crafts, timber, fishing lures, homemade chocolates, Devonshire teas, orchids, souvenirs, and seasonal fruit and vegies. What more could you want?

Points of Interest

Castle Hill (286m - 938 ft) offers a panoramic view of Townsville. It is topped by an octagonal restaurant which commands a 260 degree view of the town and the bay. Nearby **Mount Stuart** is also an excellent vantage point.

Flinders Mall is virtually the heart of the city. It is a landscaped pedestrian mall with a relaxed atmosphere.

The **Perc Tucker Regional Gallery** is in the mall, ✆4727 9011, and it houses an extensive collection of national and regional art in an impressive building that was originally a bank. It is ☉open Mon-Thurs 10am-5pm, Fri 10-6pm, Sat-Sun 10am-2pm, and admission is free. Nearby **St Joseph's Cathedral** in Fryer Street, North Ward, ✆4772 1973, is a reflection of the architecture of the past.

The Strand, Townsville's sea promenade, has many parks including the Sister Kenny Park, and the Anzac Memorial Park with its Centenary Fountains, waterfall and bougainvillea gardens. Also along The Strand is the Tobruk Memorial Swimming Pool.

Queen's Gardens next to Queen's Park, encompasses Kissing Point and Jezzine Army Barracks. An all-tide rock swimming pool, a restaurant and a kiosk are also in the gardens.

The Town Common Environmental Park is a flora and fauna sanctuary where visitors may see some rare water fowl, including the primitive magpie goose. In the winter months, at the height of the dry season, as many as 3000 brolgas, along with up to 180 other species of bird, flock to the Common's salt-marsh lagoons and waterholes. The brolga is famous for its courting ritual, and the park provides visitors with an excellent opportunity to see this dance at close quarters. The park is ☉open daily 6.30am-6.30pm and barbecue facilities are available.

Great Barrier Reef Wonderland in Flinders Street East, is one of the most popular attractions in Townsville. It features the **Great Barrier Reef Aquarium**, ✆4750 0891 - the world's largest living coral reef aquarium. Conceived and operated by the Great Barrier Reef Marine Park Authority, the aquarium includes a huge main tank containing a living coral reef, a smaller tank displaying sharks and other reef predators and an extensive area containing numerous display tanks, educational exhibits, a theatrette and a large touch-tank. You actually walk beneath the water through a transparent tunnel surrounded by hundreds of coral reef animals. Admission costs are ○$16 for adults, $8 children and $40 for families. This very popular attraction is ☉open 9am-5pm.

Wonderland also houses: the operational headquarters of the Great Barrier Reef Marine Park Authority, the federal government agency responsible for safeguarding the Great Barrier Reef Marine Park (Reef HQ); a licensed restaurant featuring tropical cuisine; a shop with a variety of souvenirs and educational material; a post office; and an information centre with all you need to know about national parks, marine national parks, camping permits and locations, walking trails, and wildlife.

An **Imax Theatre**, ✆4721 1481 is close to the aquarium, at 86 Flinders Street. The theatre is dome-shaped and uses a special type of projection so that the image is projected above and around the audience - a fascinating experience. The theatre seats 200 people, including facilities for the handicapped.

The **Museum of Tropical Queensland**, 78-102 Flinders Street, ✆4726 0600, has recently undergone a complete transformation. The former museum has been expanded and modernised into a new and improved complex, opened in June 2000. It has an extensive array of exhibits, from the life-cycle of the world's largest moth to various Aboriginal crafts, and is worth a visit.

From the Wonderland ferry terminal there are cruises leaving for Magnetic Island and the Great Barrier Reef throughout the day. And while you are waiting to pick up your cruise, or the next show at the theatre, you can spend some time in the specialty shops in the complex.

Pangola Park, Spring Creek, ✆4782 9252, between Giru and Woodstock, is about 40 minutes' drive from Townsville. It has ideal swimming spots and adjoins a National Park with mountain streams and waterfalls. There is good bushwalking, picnic areas, barbecues, caravan and camping sites, a licensed kiosk, fishing spots, minibikes, and conducted horse and pony rides on weekends and public holidays. The park is ☺open daily and an admission fee is charged. Camping and powered sites are available.

South of Townsville, in fact much closer to the town of Ayr, the wreck of the *Yongala* lies off Cape Bowling Green. A coastal steamer, she was bound for Cairns when a cyclone struck on March 14, 1911, and she went down with all hands - 121 people including officers and crew. The wreck was discovered in 1958, but has only been dived regularly since the 1980s. Diving the *Yongala* is rated as one of the best wreck-dive experiences in the world.

The wreck is 110m long, and supports a system of hard and soft corals and many different marine animals including pelagics, stingrays, gropers, turtles and sea snakes. She lies in 30m of water with her funnel only 15m below the surface. The *Yongala* is protected by the Historic Shipwreck Act as a memorial to all who went down with her, so nothing may be taken from the ship. This is a temptation as there are dinner plates, knives, forks, and some evidence of human remains, but where they are they must stay. See the Diving section under *Sport* for operators who will take divers to the wreck.

Sport
Swimming
There are three salt water mesh swimming enclosures, one at Rowes Bay, one at Pallarenda, and one next to the rock pool in Queen's Gardens. They provide safe sea swimming free from sharks, sea-stingers and other marine hazards.
Golf
Townsville Golf Club, Benson Street, Rosslea, ✆4779 0133. 27-hole championship course - equipment hire - ☺open 6.30am-6pm, clubhouse open 10am-8pm.
Rowes Bay Golf Club, Cape Pallarenda Road, Pallarenda, ✆4774 1288. 18-hole par 72 course - equipment hire - ☺open seven days.
Willows Golf Club, Nineteenth Avenue, Kirwan, ✆4773 4352 - 18-hole course - ☺open daily.
Horse Riding
Ranchlands Equestrian School, 83 Hammond Way, Kelso, ✆4774 0124 - ☺open week days and nights.
Saddle Sense Riding School, 95 Haynes Road, Jensen, ✆4751 6372 - trail rides and camping - ☺open Wed-Sun.
Fishing/Yacht Charters
Tangaroa Cruises, 19 Crowle Street, Hyde Park ✆4772 2127. 50ft motor cruiser available for extended cruises, social outings, fishing and diving trips - support vessel.
True Blue Charters, 65 Gilbert Crescent, North Ward, ✆4771 5474. Charter boat for reef and game fishing, diving, snorkelling, island cruising - maximum 8 passengers - full boat charter - half day and other charters on request.

Farr Better Yacht Charters, 76 Allen Street, South Townsville, ✆4771 6294. Yacht and boat charter - bare boat or with sail guide - *Hood* 23ft yacht and *Farr Star* 40ft yacht - sailing training (AF) - 7 days. Special weekend trips to Palm and Dunk Islands.

Diving

Diving courses are not cheap, and you should expect to pay at least ✪$400 for a comprehensive open water instruction program. If you are already a qualified diver, the cost for a guided dive is considerably less, and depends on the location and duration of the dive. Following are a few examples of companies operating in the area.

Mike Ball Dive Expeditions, 252 Walker Street, ✆4772 3022 - internationally acclaimed 5 star PADI dive centre providing PADI instruction from entry level to Dive career programs - expeditions to Yongala wreck and Coral Sea, also Cod Hole - ☼open Mon-Fri 8.45am-5pm, Sat 8.45am-noon.

The Dive Bell, 16 Dean Street, South Townsville, ✆4721 1155 - sport diving and dive shop - commercial diving school - diving trips to Yongala wreck and the reef - ☼open Mon-Fri 8.30am-5pm, Sat 9am-noon.

Pro-Dive Townsville, Great Barrier Reef Wonderland, Flinders Street, ✆4721 1760. PADI scuba diving school - 5 star Gold dive shop - charter boats, hire equipment, learn to dive - Yongala wreck dives (up to 3 days) - ☼open daily 9am-5pm.

Skydiving

Coral Sea Skydivers, Shop 3, 14 Plume Street, Townsville, ✆4772 4889. Tandem and accelerated free fall dives for beginners and experienced jumpers - souvenir videos, photos and certificates - Tandem Dives: 8,000 feet ✪$245; 12,000 feet $350 - Accelerated Free Fall Course: $500 - Complete Free Fall Course, including training and 12 jumps: $2400.

Tours

Detours, Shop 5, Great Barrier Reef Wonderland Complex, ✆4721 5977, offer the following trips.

Tropical Rainforest and Waterfalls - Mt Specs National Park, Balgal Beach, Little Crystal Creek rainforest walk, Frosty Mango fruit farm - 8 hours - ✪$80 adults, $35 children - 9am Tues, Thurs, Sat.

The Real Outback - Charters Towers and outback country - 8 hours - ✪$80 adults, $35 children - 9am Wed & Sat.

Billabong Sanctuary - wildlife sanctuary - 4 hours - ✪$38 adult, $18 child (includes entrance fee) - 10am daily.

Tropical City Tour - more than 9 points of interest visited - 2 hours - ✪$26 adult, $10 child - 11am weekdays.

Night Tour - Castle Hill, Casino, Entertainment Centre - 1 hour - ✪$20 adults, $7 children - 6pm-7pm Mon-Thu May-Oct.

Hinchinbrook Island - coach to Cardwell, cruise to Hinchinbrook, self-guided walk - 12 hours - ✪$115 adults, $50 children - 6am Tues, Thu & Sun.

Dunk & Bedarra Islands - Mission Beach to Dunk Island to Bedarra Island, lunch, boom netting, tropical fruit tasting - ✪$110 adult, $50 child - 6am Thurs & Sun.

Raging Thunder, 52 Fearnlet Street, Cairns, ✆4030 7990. Although based in Cairns, this company has a 5-day tour that departs Townsville and takes in the best of the Tropical North. The highlight of day one is 5 hours of Tully River rafting then transfer to Cairns. Day two comprises a 5 hour reef cruise. Day three begins with a Hot Air Balloon flight above the Atherton Tablelands, a visit to Kuranda Markets, then a return trip to Cairns on the Skyrail. Day four is an exploration of Cape Tribulation and Daintree, including a Crocodile Cruise on the river. On day five you are taken to Fitzroy Island to relax or take the optional tour, then return later to Cairns.

The cost of the tour is ✪$520 per person, but you must arrange your own accommodation for the duration of the tour.

Cruises

Coral Princess Cruises, Breakwater Terminal, Sir Leslie Thiess Drive, ✆4721 1673 or ✆1800 079 545 (free call), offer these trips.

Townsville/Barrier Reef/Islands - 4 days/3 nights Barrier Reef and Island cruise - departs Townsville 1pm - calls at resorts, uninhabited islands and reef - from ✪$1350 per person twin share. 8 day/

7 night cruise - combines 3 night Townsville with 3 night Cairns cruise - $2200 per person twin share.

Magnetic Island Ferry, Ross Street, South Townsville, ©4772 5422, offer:

Cruise to Magnetic Island - open return ticket, free pick up from accommodation - bus or mokes available - ✪$16 adult, $8 child.

Magnetic Island Cruise/Bus - open duration, pick up from accommodation, cruise and bus tour of island with commentary, exploring and swimming - ✪$28 adult, $14 child.

Cruise/Moke Hire - return ferry fare with moke hire on the island - includes insurance and island map - ✪$32 per person.

Pure Pleasure Cruises, Great Barrier Reef Wonderland, 4 The Strand, Townsville, ©4721 3555 or ©1800 079 797 (freecall), offer a:

Kelso Outer Reef Tour - 50 nautical miles north to Kelso reef on the Wave Piercer 2000 - includes swimming, snorkelling, fishing, glass bottom boat, buffet lunch, morning/afternoon tea all inclusive, bar and diving extra - ✪$135 adult, $68 child - departs 9am daily.

Scenic Flights

Townsville Aero Club, Townsville Aerodrome, Garbutt, ©4779 2069. Aircraft charter, joy flights, aerial tours.

Inland Pacific Air, Townsville Aerodrome, Garbutt, ©4775 3866 - twin engine aircraft charter 4 to 11 seats - 7 aircraft available including pressurised executive Cessna - available all hours to any destination.

Also at Townsville Airport are *Nautilus Aviation*, ©4725 6056, *Bluewater Aviation* ©4725 1888, and *Magnetic North Aviation*, ©4725 6227.

Festivals

Pacific Festival is held each September/October, and lasts for 10 days.

The Visitor Information Centre will advise on all current events at the time of your trip.

Chapter 42
Townsville to Cairns

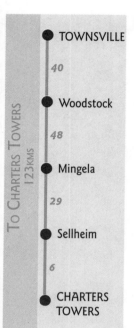

TOWNSVILLE

40

Woodstock

48

Mingela

29

Sellheim

6

CHARTERS
TOWERS

TO CHARTERS TOWERS
123 KMS

Charters Towers

Population 12,000
Location and Characteristics
The Outback is just on the other side of the mountains. If you wish to divert from your coastal holiday for a while, the old gold rush town of Charters Towers can be reached 123km (74 miles) south-west of Townsville on the Flinders Highway. Now a town of 12,000 people, Charter Towers was once home to more than twice this number.

Three itinerant prospectors discovered gold in 1871, and between then and 1911, some seven million ounces of gold were taken from the region. The memories may be growing dim, but the town looks much the same as it did a century ago. Historic buildings line the streets and remnants of the gold mining era dot the surrounding countryside.

In recent years a few small scale operations recommenced, and some gold was extracted from the area.

How to Get There
By Air
Charters Towers airport is serviced by small regional airlines, ©4787 3293.
By Rail
A railway network connects Townsville to Charters Towers. All travel arrangements and enquiries can be made through Traveland in Charters Towers, ©4787 2622.
By Bus
Buses run daily from Townsville to Charters Towers.
By Road
Follow the Flinders Highway west from Townsville for 135km.

Visitor Information
For more information contact the Charters Towers Dalrymple Tourist Information Centre, 74 Mosman Street, Charters Towers, ©4752 0314. You can email them at ✉ tourinfocentre@httech.com.au

Accommodation and Services
Charters Towers offers a wide range of accommodation in and around the city, from units to caravan parks, from modern hotels to original wooden hotels built during the gold rush. There is sufficient accommodation in this heritage town for a short stay, if you wish to take some time to view the restored historic buildings. The area code is (07).

Hillview, Flinders Highway, ©4787 1973. 11 units, playground, undercover parking, pool - ✪$70.

Cattlemans Rest Motor Inn, cnr Bridge & Plant Streets, ©4787 3555. 38 units, licensed restaurant (closed Sunday), undercover parking, room service, pool, spa - ✪$75.

Charters Towers Heritage Lodge, 79-97 Flinders Highway, ©4787 4088 or ©1800 880 444 (toll free). 17 units, playground, barbecue, undercover parking, room service, pool - ✪$80-100.

York Street Bed & Breakfast, 58 York Street, ©4787 1028. 5 rooms, pool - ✪$72.

Country Road, Flinders Highway, ©4787 2422. 18 units, barbecue, undercover parking, pool - ✪$55-65.

Caravan Parks
Dalrymple Tourist Van Park, Lynd Highway, ©4787 1121. 100 sites, barbecue, pool - powered sites ✪$17 for two, cabins $45-60 for two.

Charters Towers Caravan Park, 37 Mt Leyshon Road, ©4787 7944. 50 sites, barbecue, pool - powered sites ✪$17 for two.

Mexican Tourist Park, 75 Church Street, ©4787 1161. 22 sites, pool - powered sites ✪$15 for two, cabins $35 for two, on-site vans $30 for two.

Eating Out
Two restaurants worth dining at are *Lawsons*, 82- 90 Mosman Street, ©4787 4333, and *Gold City Chinese Restaurant*, 64 Mosman Street, ©4787 7609.

Points of Interest

The **Venus Gold Battery**, in Milchester Road, contains a restored gold crushing mill which operated for a century. It is ⏱open from 9am-5pm daily with guided tours available. Admission prices are ✪$4 adults and $2 for children.

The **Zara Clark Museum and Military Display** is at 36 Mosman Street. The aim of the complex is to enshrine the history of Charters Towers, particularly the nostalgia of its gold rush era. There is a range of memorabilia, and some interesting period photographs. It is ⏱open from 10am-3pm daily and costs adults ✪$4 and children $2.

Ravenswood is about 60km east of Charters Towers. It is also a heritage town and another centre of the gold rush. Although it once had no fewer than 55 pubs, it now has a population of less than one hundred. The town seems largely untouched by time.

Burdekin Falls Dam is a large catchment area that now provides the once dry cities of the coast with a plentiful water supply. Nearby, **Burdekin Dam Holiday Park Motel**, ✆4770 3178, offers accommodation and activities for patrons, $45-55 for two.

The Hinterland is to the north, sweeping towards the Gulf. Volcanoes once peppered the area, and the vast underground **Undara Lava Tubes** have become a notable attraction. The trip from Charters Towers to Undara covers a distance of about 380km (238 miles). From Charters Towers, take the Gregory Development Road north to Greenvale, then on to Lynd Junction, then a further 93km (58 miles) along the same road. Turn left onto the Gulf Development Road and travel towards Mt Surprise before taking another left turn at the signposted Undara turn-off. From there it is 15km (9 miles) to the **Undara Lava Lodge**, which has bed & breakfast for ✪$109 per person per night, ✆4097 1411. They offer several different tours of the Undara Experience, starting from ✪$33 adults, $16.50 children for two hours, up to a full day tour for $93 adults, ✆1800 990 992 for reservations.

There is a website at 🌐www.undara-experience. com.au, which you can check out beforehand to see if you think the attraction is worth the long drive.

Island Resorts

There are hundreds of islands in the bays of Magnetic North, many are ancient mountain tops, others are coral atolls. For tourists wishing to island-hop in comfort, small high-quality resorts have been built on Orpheus, Hinchinbrook, Dunk and Bedarra Islands. Many of the other islands are uninhabited, although some offer restricted camping facilities, ✆3227 8187.

Magnetic Island

Population 2200
Location and Characteristics
Magnetic lies 8km across Cleveland Bay from Townsville, fifteen minutes by catamaran. It is roughly triangular in shape and has an area of 52 sq km.

Townsville to Cairns

With 16 beaches, plenty of reasonably-priced places to stay, and an ideal climate, this is one of the most popular islands on the Reef.

The island's first visitor was Captain Cook in 1770, and he declared it Magnetic Island, believing that it had interfered with his compass. Magnetic's first European settlers were timber cutters at Nelly Bay in the early 1870s. A permanent settlement was not established until 1887 when Harry Butler and his family arrived at Picnic Bay. It was these people who began the tourist industry on the island and their story is told in *The Real Magnetic* by Jessie Macqueen, who was also one of the early settlers. At the end of the century Robert Hayles built a hotel at Picnic Point and introduced a ferry service to the island on an old Sydney Harbour ferry, *The Bee*. The island now has a permanent population of more than 2200 people, and draws millions of holiday-makers.

It is one of the largest islands on the Great Barrier Reef, and 70 percent of it is National Park. A high spine of mountains covered by forests of eucalypts and wattles, and strewn with granite boulders, runs across the island. Below the peaks lie sheltered white beaches, rocky coves and coral reefs.

More than 22km (14 miles) of walking tracks lead over and around hills to secluded coves and quiet bays. The four small settlements of Picnic Bay, Nelly Bay, Arcadia and Horseshoe Bay offer a plentiful range of services for the visitor. You will also find an aquarium and a koala sanctuary.

Box jellyfish are present around Magnetic between October and April, so during this time it is wise to swim only in the netted areas at Picnic Bay and Alma Bay.

The north coast of Magnetic is zoned Marine Park B, so fishing is not permitted.

There are quite a few good diving locations on the island's southern and eastern shores.

How to Get There
By Sea
Access is by cruises departing several times a day from Townsville.

Sunferries, ©4771 3855, have a high-speed catamaran offering family packages for the 25-minute trip to Magnetic Island. Return fares start from ✪$14 adults, $7 children and $29 for families. Magnetic Island Car & Passenger Ferry, Ross Street, South Townsville, ©4772 5422, run a car ferry to Arcadia from the south side of Ross Creek, but unless you are staying on the island for an extended period, a car is not really necessary.

Visitor Information
For details about other attractions on the island, contact either the Magnetic Island Tourist Information Bureau and Central Booking Office, 26 The Grove, Nelly Bay, ©4778 5596, or the Magnetic Island Holiday and Information Centre in Picnic Bay Mall, ©4778 5155. Between them, they know everything there is to know about Magnetic Island, and have some helpful brochures. They can advise on your tour bookings, accommodation, vehicle hire, travel arrangements and even the best way to climb Mt Cook (497m).

Accommodation and Services
There is a wide variety of accommodation including hotels, motels, luxury resorts, self contained holiday units, flats, backpacker hostels and camping facilities. Most accommodation is either beachfront, or close to it. The area code for Queensland is (07).

Hotels/Motels
Magnetic Island International Hotel, Mandalay Avenue, ©4778 5200 or ©1800 079 902 (toll free). 80 units, licensed restaurant, gym, tennis, pool - ✪$120 room, $160 suite.

Tropical Palms Inn, 34 Picnic Street, Picnic Bay, ©4778 5076. 14 units, pool - ✪$75-85 a double.

Arcadia Hotel Resort, 7 Marine Parade, Arcadia, ©4778 5177. 27 rooms, licensed restaurant, swimming pool, spa - ✪$75-100 a double.

Magnetic Island Tropical Resort, Yates Street, Nelly Bay, ©4778 5955. 30 units, licensed restaurant, spa, pool - ✪$55-105.

Self-Contained Units/B&B

Arcadia

Champagne Apartments, 38 Marine Parade, ©4778 5077. 11 units, secure parking, barbecue, spa bath, pool - ✪$140-160.

Magnetic Haven, 7 Rheuben Terrace, ©4778 5824. 7 units, playground, undercover parking, heated pool, spa - ✪$110.

Dandaloo Gardens, 40 Hayles Avenue, ©4778 5174. 8 units, barbecue, playground, pool - ✪$70-85.

Island Magic Apartments, Armand Way, ©4778 5077. 6 units, barbecue, undercover parking - ✪$100-110.

Marshalls Bed & Breakfast, 3 Endevour Road, Arcadia Bay, ©4778 5112. 4 rooms - ✪$60 a double.

Magnetic Retreat, 11 Rheuben Terrace, ©4778 5357. 7 units, undercover parking, transfers, pool, spa - ✪$95-120.

Magnetic North Holiday Apartments, 2 Endevour Road, ©4778 5647. 6 units, playground, undercover parking - ✪$600 for 7 days.

Nelly Bay

Island Leisure Resort, 4 Kelly Street, ©4778 5000. 17 units, licensed cafe, transfers, tennis, gym, pool, spa - ✪$120.

Island Palms Resort, 13 The Esplanade, ©4778 5571. 12 units, undercover parking, tennis half-court, pool, spa - ✪$85-100.

Palm View Chalets, 114 Sooning Street, Nelly Bay, ©4778 5596. 10 chalets, undercover parking, pool - ✪$50-75 a double.

Horseshoe Bay & Picnic Bay

Sails on Horseshoe, 13 Pacific Drive, Horseshoe Bay, ©4778 5117. 11 units, undercover parking, pool - ✪$205.

Magnetic Island Holiday Units, 16 Yule Street, ©4778 5246. 6 units, barbecue, undercover parking, transfers, heated pool - ✪$80.

There is a **Youth Hostel**, *Geoff's Place*, at 40 Horseshoe Bay Road, Horseshoe Bay, ©4778 5577 or ©1800 255 577 (toll free), with 30 rooms at ✪$20 per adult per night, twin share.

Two other venues for budget accommodation are for budget accommodation are **Centaur Guest House**, 27 Marine Parade, Alma Bay ©4778 568 or ©1800 655 680 (toll free); and *Forest Haven*, 11 Cook Road, Arcadia, ©4778 5153.

Eating Out

In addition to the restaurants you will find in a few of the hotel complexes, **Crusoe's Magnetic Island Restaurant** is at 5a The Esplanade, Picnic Bay, ©4778 5480. Alternatively, there is a small shopping centre in Arcadia and a general store in Horseshoe Bay where you can get supplies and cook for yourself.

Local Transport

Magnetic Island Bus Service, 44 Mandalay Ave, ©4778 5130, has a three hour tour with an all-day unlimited carousel bus trip around Magnetic Island and all its attractions, including a stop at Koala Park Oasis. Buses meet arriving ferries and depart from Picnic Bay, but do not pick up from accommodation. Note that the charge for the tour does not include entry into the Koala Park. Fares are ✪$30 adults and $15 children.

You can rent a moke for a novel way of moving around the island: Magnetic Island Rent-a-Moke are at 4 The Esplanade, Picnic Bay, ©4778 5377.

The area is also serviced by Magnetic Island Taxi, 25 Marine Parade, Alma Bay, ©13 1008. They operate 18 hours per day, seven days a week with pick-up and wheelchair facilities, bookings, ferry connections, tours and sightseeing in air conditioned cars.

Road Runner Scooter Hire, 3/4 The Esplanade, Picnic Bay, ©4778 5222. Single seat 50cc mopeds (scooter) hire. Open 7 days. Rates include helmet and free kilometres.

Points of Interest

Picnic Bay

This is where the ferry docks, and where many people choose to stay. A lookout above the town offers some good views, and to the west is Cockle Bay and the wreck of the *City of Adelaide*, which went aground in 1916. To the east is Rocky Bay, and a lovely secluded beach.

Nelly Bay

There is a pleasant beach with shade and barbecue facilities. At low tide the reef is visible.

Some graves are found at the end of Nelly Bay, and they mark the resting places of pioneers.

Arcadia

The next bay you come to is Geoffrey Bay, with a 400m low-tide reef walk that begins at the southern end of the beach. There's a signboard that marks the starting point.

The Arcadia Hotel Resort offers all kinds of entertainment for guests and visitors, but one that is strictly "Queensland-ish" happens every Wednesday at 8pm - **cane toad racing**. For the uninitiated, cane toads are repulsive creatures that were imported from Hawaii years and years ago to eat a bug that was causing trouble for sugar cane growers. When in Hawaii the toads loved the bug and couldn't get enough of it; once in Australia they couldn't have cared less about the bug, but found plenty of other things they did like to eat, and began to live happy and contented lives which, of course, resulted in more and more cane toads and eclipsed the initial problem of the bug.

Anyway, back to the races. The person in charge of the meeting catches at least twelve toads, paints a different coloured stripe on each of them and auctions them off to the highest bidders in the waiting crowd. The animals are then put into the middle of a circle and the first one to hop over the outside ring is declared the winner, and his 'owner' scoops the pool. At a 'serious' meeting this can make the owner several hundred dollars richer.

The **Arcadia Pottery Gallery** is 200m from the hotel at 44 Armand Way (Horseshoe Bay Road), ©4778 5600, and it is ⊙open daily 9am-4pm. It displays and sells work from dozens of potters and is worth visiting even if you are not intending to buy.

Continuing around the island the next bay is Arthur Bay, where there are reef fish caves, then Florence Bay, a sheltered shady beach where you can visit **"The Forts"**. These are relics of World War II and consist of a command post and signal station, gun sites and an ammunition store. The views from here are fantastic.

Then there is Balding Bay which can only be reached by walking track or by sea, and around

the point is Horseshoe Bay, home to the Koala Park Oasis, Horseshoe Bay Lagoon Environmental Park, water birds and a Mango farm. **The Koala Park Oasis**, in Pacific Drive, also has wombats, kangaroos, wallabies, emus and birds, and is ⊙open daily 9am-5pm. Admission is ✪$15 adult and $7 children, ©4778 5260.

Further around is Five Beach Bay, which is only accessible by boat, and West Point, a very secluded area that people say has the best sunsets ever seen.

Sport

There is a golf course at Picnic Bay, ©4778 5188, and horse riding at Horseshoe Bay - *Blueys Horseshoe Ranch Trail Rides*, 38 Gifford Street, ©4778 5109. ✪$50 for 2 hour bush and beach ride, $80 for half-day bush and beach (with morning tea). *Blueys* is ⊙open daily 7am-7pm.

Horseshoe Bay Watersports, 97 Horseshoe Bay Road, Horseshoe Bay, ©4758 1336, offer beach hire for paraflying, water skiing, jet skiing, catamarans, aqua bikes, boats and motors, free stinger suits and waverunners. ⊙Open daily, weather permitting.

Diving

Comprehensive diving courses are available. Some include diving theory, meals, training, reef dives, and provide you with an internationally recognised certificate. Be aware you may require a doctor's certificate to prove your fitness level, and 2 passport photos. Those who are already certified divers, or who wish only to snorkel among the coral, can take either short trips out into the reef, or expeditions that last for days. Tanks and weight belts are usually provided but additional gear may have to be hired.

Pleasure Divers, Arcadia Resort Shop 2, Marina Parade, Alma Bay, ©4778 5788, is a dive shop and dive school with scuba hire, snorkel hire, reef and island bookings, adventure bookings and Saturday night dives - from ✪$170 open Water PADI. ⊙Open daily 9am-4.30pm.

Alternatively, the *Magnetic Island Dive Centre* can be contacted on ©4758 1399.

Tours

Pure Pleasure Cruises, Great Barrier Reef Wonderland, 4 The Strand, Townsville, offer 9 hour tours from Townsville and Magnetic Island to Kelso Reef on the Wave Piercer 2001. The trip includes morning and afternoon tea, a tropical smorgasbord lunch, glass bottom coral viewing, swimming, snorkelling and scuba - ✪$125 adults, $60 children, ✆4721 3555 or ✆1800 079 797 (free call)

Adrenalin Jet Ski Tours, 89 Gifford Street, ✆4778 5533, take you around the island's coastal waters, with commentary.

Orpheus Island

Location and Characteristics

This island is mostly national park, but has a secluded resort at one end. Orpheus Island is encircled by wide beaches and a warm shallow sea. A fringe reef possesses a rich variety of marine life and provides excellent diving.

Orpheus Island has an area of 14 sq km and is the second largest in the Palm Island group. There are ten main islands in the group, but eight of them are Aboriginal reservations and permission must be obtained to visit. Orpheus is National Park while Pelorus, the other island not part of the reserve, is Crown Land.

The island is 80km north of Townsville and roughly 20km off Lucinda Point near Ingham. It was named in 1887, after the HMS *Orpheus* - the largest warship in Australia, which sank off New Zealand in 1863 with the loss of 188 lives. Orpheus is long and narrow and its fringing reef is probably the best of all the resort islands. It is heavily wooded and is home to a large population of wild goats. The goats were introduced many years ago as food for people who might be shipwrecked on the island, but they have obviously not been needed and have multiplied to the point where they are causing some problems.

There are a few beaches on the island, although some, such as Hazard Bay and Pioneer Bay, are only suitable for swimming at high tide. When the tide is out they become wading pools. Mangrove Bay and Yankee Bay are good places to swim at low tide.

As far as bushwalks are concerned, there is a shortage of them on this island. One traverses up to Fig Tree Hill, and the other winds from Hazard Bay through a forest to Picnic Bay.

There is a Marine Research Station, part of James Cook University, at Little Pioneer Bay, and it is engaged in breeding clams, both giant and other species, and transplanting them to other reefs where there is a shortage of them through overgathering. It is possible to visit the station, but prior arrangements should be made by contacting the station manager, ✆4777 7336.

The zoning for most of the water around Orpheus is Marine National Park B, although part of the south-west coast is zoned 'A'. So limited line fishing is allowed in the 'A' part, but collecting shells or coral is strictly forbidden.

How to Get There

By Air

Daily flight by seaplane from Townsville with Nautilus Aviation, ✆4725 6056. Return air fares are ✪$350 from Townsville and $550 from Cairns. You must book when you make a resort reservation.

Visitor Information

The number for the resort is, ✆4777 7377. The web page is ☞www.orpheusisland-australia.com/ with an email facility at ✉reserv@greatbarrier reef.aus.net

Accommodation and Services

The **Orpheus Island Resort**, ✆4777 7377, has 31 rooms that are rated 4-star.

Resort facilities are: restaurant, cocktail bar, lounge, barbecue area, entertainment, games room, tour desk, recreation room with television, gym equipment, two swimming pools, spa, boutique, tennis court, waterskiing, windsurfers, catamarans, snorkelling, paddleboards, boat charter, SCUBA diving, canoes, picnic lunches and laundry.

Room facilities are: private bathrooms, hairdryer, bathrobes, tea/coffee making facilities, refrigerator, mini bar, ceiling fans, radio/music, air-conditioning, non-smoking rooms, iron and a daily cleaning service.

The following tariffs are for one night per person/twin share:

Beachfront Terrace -	✪$510
Beachfront Studio -	✪$610
Beachfront Bungalow -	✪$685
Hillside Villa -	✪$715

These rates include all meals, snacks and most activities. Not included are those activities that require power. People under 15 years of age are not accepted at the Resort. Day trippers are not allowed in either.

Reservations can be made through the Resort or online. Credit cards accepted: American Express, Bankcard, MasterCard, Diners Club, Visa.

Camping

Camp sites are found at Pioneer Bay and Yankee Bay. They are patrolled, and have picnic tables, toilets and drinking water. For further information and booking, get in touch with the Rainforest and Reef Centre, Bruce Highway, Cardwell, ✆4066 8601, or call Naturally Queensland on ✆3227 8187.

Campers cannot buy meals at the Resort, and fires are not permitted on the island, so if you are intending to camp bring all your provisions, including water and a fuel stove.

Points of Interest

As mentioned previously, Orpheus has some of the best fringing reef of all the islands, and good reefs are also found off Pelorus Island to the north and Fantome Island to the south. The Resort dive shop offers local dives and diving courses, but remember that these activities are not included in the Resort tariff.

There are many opportunities for bush walking and rainforest study, and snorkelling, as always, remains popular.

Hinchinbrook Island

Location and Characteristics

Hinchinbrook is the world's largest island national park, with over 45,000ha (393 sq km) of tropical rainforests, mountains, gorges, valleys, waterfalls and sandy beaches. It is one of the most beautiful tropical islands in the world and offers some of the best bushwalking in Australia. A magnificent jagged mountain range drops to warm seas and coral reefs, dominating the skyline. The rainforests offer spectacular views.

The island is separated from the mainland by Hinchinbrook Channel, a narrow mangrove-fringed strip of water that is very deep. From further out at sea, the channel cannot be seen, and in fact, when Captain Cook sailed past he did not record the presence of an island.

Aborigines lived on the island and remains of their fish traps can be seen near the Scraggy Point camp site.

The best walk on any of the Great Barrier Reef islands is the three to four day walk along the eastern side of Hinchinbrook, but it is strongly recommended that information be obtained from the National Parks and Wildlife Service in Cardwell (near the jetty), ✆4066 8601, before setting out. They can advise you on facilities on the island, give tips for climbing the mountains and protecting your supplies from the local wildlife, and issue permits for camping.

Remember that marine stingers may be around in the October-May period, and that crocodiles may be found in channel waters and estuaries.

How to Get There
By Sea

Access is via boat from Cardwell. You can use Hinchinbrook Adventures & Ferries, Port Hinchinbrook Marina, Bruce Highway Cardwell, ✆4066 8270.

Visitor Information

For further information, contact the Development Bureau of Hinchinbrook & Cardwell Shires, 77 Townsville Road, Ingham, ✆4776 5381. Alternatively, call the Island Resort on ©4066 8585. Updated information is provided at ⊕www.hinchinbrookresort.com.au

Accommodation and Services

Hinchinbrook Island Resort, ©4066 8585, is a small resort located at Cape Richards to the north of the island.

It houses guests in 3 cabins and 15 treehouse units, all with their own bathrooms, tea/coffee making facilities and a refrigerator. The cabins have two bedrooms, and the newer treehouses have one or two. There is no TV or radio on the island, and only one telephone.

There is a licensed restaurant, a bar, a barbecue near the swimming pool, canoes, snorkelling gear, surf skis, fishing equipment, shop and a lending library. There is almost nothing in the way of night life, and even during the day there is not much organised activity. Hinchinbrook is the place to really 'get away from it all'.

Tariffs for one night per person are:
Cabins -   ✪$293 single, $248 share.
Treehouse Units -   ✪$364-409 single, $341-369 double.

These rates include all meals and use of most of the equipment (except those requiring power).

Camping

The island has limited camping at ✪$3.50 per person per night (permit required, ©4066 8601). **Macushla Camping Area** - patrols, picnic tables, shelter shed, toilets, fires prohibited. Walking tracks, ocean swimming beaches, fishing spots, rainforest areas.
Goold Island - patrols, picnic tables, shelter shed, toilets, fires prohibited. Fishing and swimming.

Bedarra Island

Location and Characteristics

Part of the Family Group of Islands, Bedarra lies about 6km south of Dunk Island and about 5km offshore. It is privately-owned and is shown on marine charts as Richards Island.

Bedarra has an area of one square kilometre, and is a rainforest with natural springs and plenty of water. It has some very good sandy beaches. Note that it has a very definite Wet Season from December to the end of March, when it can rain every day and sometimes all day.

Originally occupied by Aborigines, the island was purchased by Captain Henry Allason from the Queensland Land Department for £20, and they threw in Timana Island for good luck. He sold Bedarra to Ivan Menzies, in the 1920s, for £500, and it then passed through several pairs of hands until it reached Dick Greatrix and Pierre Huret, who established gardens at the sandspit end. A section of the island had been sold to Australian artist Noel Wood in 1936, and another artist John Busst, leased the south-east corner. His home became the Plantation Resort (Bedarra Bay), and in 1947, Geatrix and Huret sold out to him.

There is a walking track from Bedarra Bay to the resort, which is in fact the only walking track.

How to Get There
By Sea
Bedarra Island is reached via Dunk Island. The boat connects with flights to/from Dunk, and the water taxis between Dunk Island and the mainland. Enquire when making a reservation.

Visitor Information

The Bedarra Island Resort can be contacted on, ©4068 8233. There is a web page at ⊕www.bedarraisland-australia.com with an email address at ✉visitors@greatbarrierreef.aus .net

Accommodation and Services

Bedarra Island Resort is on the eastern side of the island. It has 15 villas with 5-star ratings.

Resort facilities are: restaurant, cocktail lounge, swimming pool, spa, floodlit tennis court, laundry service, dinghies with outboards, sailboarding, snorkelling, fishing equipment, EFTPOS.

Villa facilities are: bathroom with bath, hair

dryer and bath robes, queen size beds, refrigerator, mini bar, air-conditioning, ceiling fans, radio, telephone IDD/STD, daily cleaning service, beach towels, writing desk, separate living area, colour TV, video cassette recorder and private balcony.

Tariff for one night per person/twin share is ✪$840-950, which includes accommodation, all meals, drinks (including alcohol) and most activities.

Note that children under 16 years are not accepted at the Resort, and that maximum villa occupancy is 3 people.

Reservations can be made online at the website listed above, or over the phone.

Credit cards accepted: Visa, MasterCard, Bankcard, Diners Club, American Express.

Points of Interest
Activities which are not included in the tariff are: Great Barrier Reef trips, boutique/shop, float plains, game fishing charters, hair salon (available on Dunk Island), private boat charters, sailing charters.

Dunk Island

Location and Characteristics
Dunk Island, across the bay from Mission Beach, is mostly National Park land, but there is one luxury resort. The island is shaped by rolling hills and deep valleys. It is home to the famous Ulysses butterfly.

Dunk Island is also part of the Family group of islands, and its Aboriginal name is Coonanglebah which means "isle of peace and plenty". Captain Cook named it Dunk after Lord Montague Dunk, the Earl of Sandwich, who was the First Lord of the Admiralty at the time.

It is the largest island in the group and is sometimes called the Father of the Family Group (Bedarra is the Mother). The island's area is 10 sq km, but 7.3 sq km is national park. The Wet Season, when it is best not to visit, lasts from December to the end of March.

Cook recorded that Aborigines on these islands stood in groups and watched the *Endeavour* sail

past, but they have long gone from the area. The earliest long term European resident was E.J. Banfield, who lived there from 1897 to 1923. He was a journalist on *The Townsville Daily Bulletin* when his doctor told him to slow down and take it easy, or face the consequences. So he and his wife decided to get back to nature and live on Dunk, where they were apparently very happy. When he wasn't tending his garden, Banfield wrote articles for his old newspaper, or worked on his books - *Confessions of a Beachcomber* (1908), *My Tropic Isle* (1911), *Tropic Days* (1918) and *Last Leaves from Dunk Island* (1925), the last published after his death.

The Banfields' house became part of a small resort that was opened in 1934 by Spenser Hopkins, a friend of theirs, but a year later that part of the island was sold with Hopkins only keeping the section where the Artists' Colony is today.

During the Second World War a radar station was set up on Mt Kootaloo and proved its worth during the Battle of the Coral Sea. Its remains can still be seen.

Dunk is very much a family resort and it has some good high tide beaches, but at low tide they are too shallow and have a lot of weeds. The island doesn't seem to have a significant problem with box jellyfish, but it is wise to keep an eye out during the November-March period. There are 13km of walking tracks, and the 10km walk around the island rates among the best of any on the Barrier Reef islands.

How to Get There
By Air
Sunstate Airlines, ©13 1313, have flights to Dunk from Townsville and Cairns. Both flights take 45 minutes.
By Sea
Water taxis from Mission Beach to Dunk are operated by Dowd's Coaches & Water Taxi, © 4068 8968, and Mission Beach/Dunk Island Water Taxi, © 4068 8310.

Visitor Information
Contact the Dunk Island Resort directly on ©4068 8199, visit the website at ☜www.dunk

islandresort.com or email an information request at ✎visitors@greatbarrierreef.aus.net

Accommodation and Services

Dunk Island Resort, Dunk Island, ✆4068 8199 - all inclusive rates are ✪$340-520 per double, per day.

The Resort accommodation consists of 148 rooms divided into four categories: Bayview Suites (4-star); Beach Front Units (3-star); Garden Cabanas (3-star); and Banfield Units (3-star).

Resort facilities are: live entertainment, restaurant, brasserie, cocktail bar, games room, two swimming pools, spa, tennis courts, laundry/ironing, Kids' Club, babysitting, snorkelling, catamaran sailing, parasailing, sailboarding, fishing, cricket, waterskiing, horse riding, golf, archery, tube rides, clay shooting, squash, Barrier Reef cruises and air tours, cruising and coral viewing, SCUBA diving, tandem skydiving, beach volleyball and EFTPOS.

Unit facilities are: tea/coffee making facilities, refrigerator, colour TV, in-house movies, IDD/STD telephone, radio, air-conditioning, ceiling fans, daily cleaning service, balcony or verandah, and interconnecting rooms.

Tariffs for one night per person/twin share are:

Banfield -	✪$220 (child sharing with 2 adults - $40)
Beachfront -	✪$300 (child - as above)
Garden Cabana -	✪$260 (child - as above)
Bayview -	✪$176 (child - as above).

Note that a full breakfast is included in the daily rate.

Additional to the tariffs are: Artists' Colony visits, clay target shooting, game fishing, glass bottom boat tours, golf clinics, horse riding, massage therapist, nature walks and rainforest tours, outboard dinghies, reef cruises, scuba diving and lessons - resort and accredited courses and dive trips to the Great Barrier Reef, sunset cruises, tandem skydiving, tennis clinics, waterskiing.

Reservations can be made with the Resort over the phone, or online at the website listed under *Visitor Information* above.

Credit cards accepted: Visa, MasterCard, Bankcard, Diners Club, American Express.

Camping

Camping is permitted on the Foreshore reserve, and information and bookings can be obtained from the National Park Campsite, ✆4068 8199.

Fees are moderate and facilities include picnic tables, toilets, drinking water and showers. No fires are permitted.

Campers and day trippers are welcome to hire the Resort's equipment.

Points of Interest

Bruce Arthur's Artists' Colony
Situated just beyond the Resort garden, the colony's longest term resident is former Olympic wrestler Bruce Arthur, who produces large and beautiful tapestries. He and his cohorts lease the land, and have an open house ☉10am-1pm between Thursday and Sunday (small entry fee) when they chat about the island and their projects, and present their work for sale.

Diving

The Great Barrier Reef is an hour away by *Quickcat*, the high-speed catamaran, and there are four reefs to dive: Beaver, Farquharson, Yamacutta and Potter. They have some of the best coral and marine life on the Reef, and feature feeding stations, coral walls, caves, caverns and gardens. Trips to Beaver Reef include glass bottom boat, semi-submersible rides, lunch and onboard dive instruction.

All diving needs on Dunk are catered for by very experienced instructors. Training is available to international levels (PADI & NAUI) in a variety of courses from beginners to most experienced, including: Open Water Course, Advanced Rescue, Divemaster and specialist courses like night diving. Only the very latest equipment is available for hire at reasonable rates.

Paluma

Location and Characteristics

61km (38 miles) north of Townsville, and 40km (25 miles) south of Ingham on the Bruce High-

Townsville to Cairns

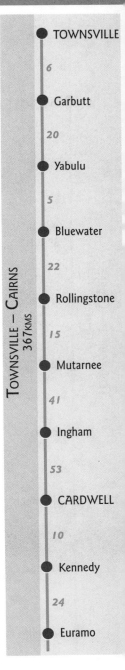

TOWNSVILLE

6

Garbutt

20

Yabulu

5

Bluewater

22

Rollingstone

15

Mutarnee

41

Ingham

53

CARDWELL

10

Kennedy

24

Euramo

TOWNSVILLE – CAIRNS 367 KMS

Townsville to Cairns

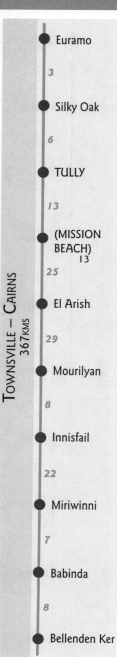

TOWNSVILLE – CAIRNS
367KMS

- Euramo
- 3
- Silky Oak
- 6
- TULLY
- 13
- (MISSION BEACH)
- 13
- 25
- El Arish
- 29
- Mourilyan
- 8
- Innisfail
- 22
- Miriwinni
- 7
- Babinda
- 8
- Bellenden Ker

way, the Mount Spec Road turns towards the mountains of the Paluma Range, following the southern boundary of Mount Spec National Park. The road was built mainly by hand during the Great Depression.

Accommodation and Services

23km (14 miles) further on is secluded **Hidden Valley**, with cabin accommodation at 46 Hidden Valley Road, including licensed facilities and a swimming pool, ✆4770 8088 - ✪$40-65.

Points of Interest

7km along the road lies **Little Crystal Creek**, with picnic, barbecue and toilet facilities, and deep pools for swimming.

18km (11 miles) from the highway, at about 900m (2953 ft) is **McClellands Lookout**, also with picnic, barbecue and toilet facilities. Near the lookout is **Paluma Village**, with its Ivy Cottage Tearooms, ✆4770 8533.

Also worth a visit is **Paluma Rainforest House** in Lennox Crescent, ✆4770 8560.

The Cassowary Coast

The Cassowary Coast incorporates the towns of Cardwell, Tully and Mission Beach, and is the stepping-off point for the great Hinchinbrook Channel, that is renowned for its barramundi, mangrove jack and many other table fish.

Ferries to Hinchinbrook Island National Park leave from Cardwell, and the town also offers estuary and reef fishing trips. You can also organise fully guided or self drive tours through world heritage forests, and scenic attractions such as the beautiful Murray Falls and the wild Blencoe Falls.

Tully is a sugar town that nestles at the foot of the mountain range. Quite close is the Tully River, famous for its whitewater rapids, and there are many operators in town that are ready to take you whitewater rafting.

Mission Beach has a cassowary reserve, great sandy beaches, and a water taxi service to nearby Dunk Island.

Cardwell

Population 8,800

Location and Characteristics

Cardwell is a fishing village situated between the mountains and the sea. It is in the middle of a natural wonderland, with world heritage rainforests, waterfalls, swimming holes, wilderness tracks, whitewater rafting, canoeing, crabbing, fishing and prawning. The Cardwell lookout offers panoramic coastal views and there are very scenic drives to Murray Falls, Blencoe Falls, the Edmund Kennedy National Park, Dalrymple's Gap Track and Cardwell Forest.

Cardwell is also the gateway to Hinchinbrook Island, the world's largest Island National Park.

How to Get There

By Rail

The Queenslander and Sunlander stop in Cardwell en route to Cairns, ✆13 2235.

By Coach

Greyhound Pioneer, ✆13 2030, and McCaffertys, ✆13 1499, pass through Tully on the Bruce Highway, stopping at the Cardwell Transit Centre.

By Car

Cardwell is on the Bruce Highway, about halfway between Tully and Ingham.

Visitor Information

For tourist information, contact the Development Bureau of Hinchinbrook & Cardwell Shires, 77 Townsville Road, Ingham, ✆4776 5381.

Accommodation and Services

Sunrise Village & Leisure Park, 43 Marine Parade, ✆4066 8550. 28 units, licensed restaurants (closed Sunday), undercover parking, pool, spa - ✪$70-80. Also has powered sites ✪$15 for two, villas $50-55 for two, cottages $40-55 for two, cabins $35.

Aquarius Motel and Holiday Units, 25 Bruce Highway, ✆4066 8755. 5 units, undercover parking, pool, spa - ✪$50-65.

Lyndoch Motor Inn, 215 Victoria Street, ✆4066

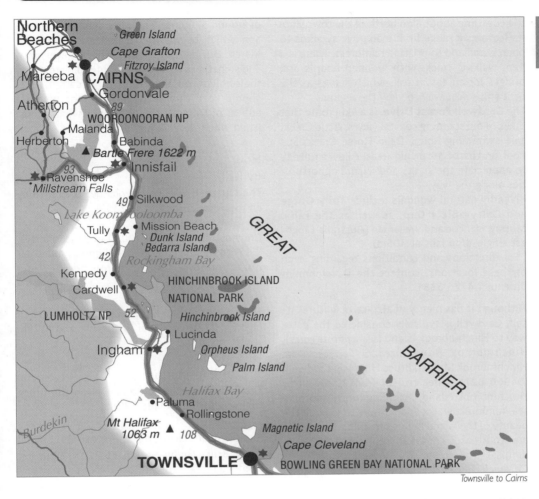

Townsville to Cairns

8500. 19 units, barbecue, licensed restuarant (closed Sunday), transfers, pool - ✪$33-60.
Marine, Victoria Street, ✆4066 8662. 8 units, licensed restaurant (closed Sunday) - ✪$45.

Caravan Parks

Kookaburra Holiday Park, 175 Bruce Highway, ✆4066 8648. 31 sites, barbecue, pool - powered sites ✪$13-15, cabins $80, units $55, on-site vans $32, bunkhouse $15.
Hinchinbrook Hop, Bruce Highway, ✆4066 8671. 34 sites, unlicensed restaurant, kiosk, pool - powered sites ✪$15 for two, cabins $30 for two, bunkhouses $12 for one.
There is a **Youth Hostel** at 175 Bruce Highway,

Cardwell, ✆4066 8648, with 28 rooms at ✪$20 per adult per night, twin share.

Eating Out

If you wish to eat out in Cardwell, there are a number of options, including **Beach Hut**, 93 Victoria Street, ✆4066 8080; **Muddies**, 219 Victoria Street, ✆4066 8907; and **Edward Kennedy**, 43 Marine Parade, ✆0417 771 975.

Local Transport

If you require local transport, Cardwell Taxis, ✆4066 8955, operate services in the area.

Points of Interest

Edmund Kennedy National Park, nestles into

the coastline about 4km north of the township. Its features a range from mangrove swamps to open woodland to pristine rainforest. There is a 3km walking track, with wooden boards and bridges for an easy stroll, which serves as the best and safest way to view the region.

The **Cardwell Forest Drive**, is a 9km route that takes in outstanding coastal views, Attie Creek, safe swimming holes, Dead Horse Creek, Spa Pool, and barbecue picnic areas. Allow a full day to appreciate the sights and leisure opportunities along the way.

Nearby natural wonders include **Tully Gorge** and **Dalrymple's Gap**, as well as the **Falls**: Murray, Blencoe and Wallaman (Australia's highest single-drop falls at 305m).

For directions and conditions regarding each of these locations, contact the Development Bureau, ©4776 5381.

Although it has plenty of attractive features itself, Cardwell is typically considered the gateway to Hinchinbrook Island (*see separate entry*). *Hinchinbrook Adventures & Ferries*, Port Hinchinbrook Marina, Bruce Highway Cardwell, ©4066 8270, offer cruises from Cardwell to Hinchinbrook Island, including lunch, morning tea, rainforest walks and 5 hours to explore the beauty of the island before returning. The cruise and tour costs are ✪$80 adults and $40 children.

Cardwell Air Charters, 22 Winter Street, ©4066 8468, have various scenic flights over rainforest and reef.

Tully

Population 3100
Location and Characteristics
With a population of around 3000, Tully is set at the foot of Mt Tyson, and is the centre of a large sugar cane and banana growing region. The Tully River rapids provide some very fine whitewater rafting and canoeing, and there is plenty of fishing for enthusiasts.

It should be noted that Tully has the highest annual rainfall in Australia (along with Innisfail)

of around 3700mm. There is a definite Wet Season which begins in December and peaks in March. During this period it can rain every day, and sometimes all day. People intending to spend their holiday on either Dunk or Bedarra Islands should keep this in mind, since the paradise appeal of tropical islands is somewhat diminished when the rain just doesn't stop.

How to Get There
By Rail
The Queenslander and Sunlander stop in Tully en route to Cairns, ©132 235.
By Coach
Greyhound Pioneer, ©13 2030, and McCaffertys, ©13 1499, use the Bruce Highway on their northbound/southbound journey to/from Cairns.
By Car
Tully is on the Bruce Highway 106km north of Ingham, 222km north of Townsville, and 152km south of Cairns.

Visitor Information
The Tully Information Centre, is on the Bruce Highway in Tully, ©4068 2288.

Accommodation and Services
Tully, Bruce Highway, ©4068 2233. 22 units, licensed restaurant, 9-hole golf course, undercover parking - ✪$35-65 per person.
Googarra Beach Caravan Park, Tully Heads Road, ©4066 9325. 50 sites, barbecue, pool - powered sites ✪$14 for two, cabins $40-45 for two.
Tully Heads Van Park, 56 Taylor Street, Tully Heads, ©4066 9260. 40 sites, barbecue, pool - powered sites ✪$16 for two, cabins $40 for two, on-site vans $30 for two.
Eating Out
For a bite out, there is the *Raging Thunder Cafe*, on the Bruce Highway, Tully, ©4068 3196.

Points of Interest
Between June and November, tours of the **Sugar Mill** can be arranged through the information

centre, ©4068 1222. They begin at 10am, 11am, 1pm and 3pm, and cost ✪$10 per person, $22 for families.

The **Kareeya State Forest** is accessible via a spectacular drive up the Tully River gorge.

The **Tully Country Club**, Pratt Street, Tully ©4068 1236, is an option for keen golfers.

Tours

Raging Thunder Adventures, 52 Fearnley Street, Cairns, ©4030 7900 or ©4030 7990 (reservations), offer rafting on the Tully River. An all day tour includes pick-up at local accommodation, lunch, dinner and 5 hours of action - ✪$160, departing Mission Beach at 8am and returning 5pm. Tours also depart Port Douglas, Townsville and Cairns at earlier times. Raging Thunder also have Barron River rafting, Heli Raft, Jetboat, Bungy, kayaking, ballooning and adventure holiday packages, as well as combinations of all these.

Mission Beach

Population 1,500
Location
At Mission Beach, about halfway between Townsville and Cairns, a chain of mountains runs down to the sea, and surrounds the small coastal settlements. Offshore lie the North and South Barnard, Dunk and Bedarra Islands, and beyond them, the Great Barrier Reef.

Mission Beach is set on a stretch of 14km of coastline that includes Garners Beach, Bingil Bay, Narragon Beach, Clump Point and Wongaling Beach. There is a daily water taxi service from Mission Beach to nearby Dunk Island, and many visitors choose to stay on the mainland and visit the islands, rather than pay resort prices.

The town is named after the Aboriginal Mission that was set up in 1912 at South Mission Beach, but the first settlers were the Cutten brothers who landed to the north at Bingil Bay in 1882 and founded a farming dynasty. They introduced pineapple growing to this part of Queensland and founded tea and coffee plantations. In 1918 the 'cyclone of the century' lev-elled the settlements and farms in the district.

Nowadays the main industries are banana and sugar-cane growing, and tourism.

Climate
Dry Season: April-October 18C-26C. Wet Season: November-March 20C-35C. Average annual rainfall, about 2500mm.

Characteristics
Four villages comprise the Mission Beach area: South Mission Beach, Bingil Bay, Wongaling Beach and Mission Beach. The region's attractions include 14km of pristine beaches, Dunk Island, the offshore Reef, rainforests, and rafting on the Tully River.

How to Get There
By Air
You can fly to Cairns then either rent a car or catch the Mission Beach Bus, ©4068 7400, and Coach Company service, which has regular day and night routes to the four villages. From Cairns, Transtate Airlines, ©13 1528, has a service to Dunk Island nearby.
By Coach
All major bus companies provide regular daily services between Townsville and Cairns, calling into the above towns.

Greyhound Pioneer, ©13 2030, has 2 southerly services to Wongaling Beach daily, and 3 going north.

McCaffertys, ©13 1499, services Mission Beach twice daily in both directions.
By Rail
The Queenslander, Sunlander and Spirit of the Tropics trains provide luxury services from Brisbane. For more information, ©13 2235.
By Car
Mission Beach is on a loop road that branches off the Bruce Highway at Tully and rejoins at El Arish.

Visitor Information
The Mission Beach Visitor Information Centre, Porter Promenade, ©4068 7066, can be found

TOWNSVILLE – CAIRNS
367KMS

- Bellenden Ker
  - 6
- Deeral
  - 6
- Fishery Falls
  - 15
- Gordonvale
  - 10
- Edmonton
  - 6
- White Rock
  - 7
- CAIRNS

100 metres from the post office. The Centre has a wealth of information on every part of the area. They can be contacted by email at ✏ visitors@znet.net.au

Accommodation

What follows is only a selection of accommodation available in Mission Beach and adjoining villages. The prices listed below should be used as a guide only. These figures generally represent an overnight stay for two people, and the range from budget to premium rates has been provided where possible. The area code is 07.

Castaways On The Beach Resort, cnr Pacific Parade & Seaview Street, ✆4068 7444. 37 units, licensed restaurant, undercover parking, pool, spa - motel ✪$130, suite $230.

Beaches, 82 Reid Road, Wongaling Beach, ✆4068 7411. 5 units, undercover parking, pool - ✪$100-160.

Mission Beach Resort, cnr Cassowary Drive & Wongaling Beach Road, ✆4068 8288. 75 units, undercover parking, pool - ✪$110.

Collingwood House, 13 Spurwood Close, Wongaling Beach, ✆4068 9037. 3 rooms, barbecue, pool - ✪$90-100

Bingil Bay Resort, The Esplanade, Bingil Bay, ✆4068 7208. 16 units, licensed restaurant, pool - ✪$65-80.

Liana Place, cnr Boyett Road and Porter Promenade, ✆4068 7411. 4 units, barbecue, playground, undercover parking, pool - ✪$60-100.

Sejala On The Beach, 1 Pacific Street, ✆4068 7241. 16 units, secure parking, air conditioning, pool - ✪$45-75.

Caravan Parks

Mission Beach Hideaway Holiday Village, 58-60 Porters Promenade, ✆4068 7104. 130 sites, playground, barbecue, pool - powered sites ✪$21 for two, cabins $55-65 for two.

Dunk Island View Caravan Park, 175 Reid Road, ✆4068 8248. 75 sites, pool, playground, barbecue - powered sites ✪$18 for two, units $55 for two.

There is a **Youth Hostel** in Bingil Bay Road, ✆4068 7137, which has 12 rooms at ✪$23 per person twin share.

Local Transport
Coaches

Coral Coaches, ✆4098 2600. Door to door shuttle service, routes from Cairns to Mission Beach, connects with boats to Dunk Island, bookings essential.

Mission Beach Bus Co, ✆4068 7400. Operates day and night, 7 days, service from Bingil Bay to South Mission, daily ticket ✪$9.

Water Taxi

Dunk Island Express, ✆4068 8310. Mission Beach to Dunk Island return, adult ✪$28, child $16, departs 6 times a day from Wongaling Beach.

Car Rentals

Sugarland Car Rentals, ✆4068 8272.

Taxi

Mission Beach Taxis, ✆4068 8155, run regularly 24hrs.

Eating Out

Here are some of the restaurants you will find in Mission Beach:

Friends Restaurant, Beachtown Porter Promenade, ✆4068 7107.

The Horizon at Mission Beach, Explorer Drive, ✆4068 8154.

The Shrubbery Taverna, 44 Marine Parade, ✆4068 7803.

Port O'Call Cafe, Shop 6 Porter Promenade, ✆4068 7390.

Piccolo Paradiso, David Street, Mission Beach, ✆4068 7008.

Wheats Steakhouse, The Village Green, Mission Beach, ✆4068 7850.

Cafe Coconuts, Porter Promenade, Mission Beach, ✆4068 7397.

Blarney's By The Beach, Wongalong Beach Road, Wongalong, ✆4068 8472.

Shopping

Markets are a popular form of trade in the Mission Beach area. *Monster Markets* are ⊙open every last Sunday of the month from April to November, and *Mission Beach Markets* are held on Porter Promenade opposite Hideaway Caravan Park ⊙every first Saturday and third Sunday.

Points of Interest

The main activities in Mission Beach involve water sports and reef viewing, so if you wish to view land-based attractions, you will have to travel a little further afield. Here are a few suggestions, and the Visitor Centre can provide you with detailed directions to each.

The **Australian Insect Farm**, Davis Road, Gurradunga, ©4063 3860, offers regular tours daily Tues-Sun, adults ✪$10, children $8.

Paronella Park, Japoonvale Road, Mena Creek, ©4065 3225, comprises historic rainforest gardens. It is ©open 9am-5pm and costs adults ✪$14, pensioners $10 and children $7.

The Australian Sugar Industry Museum, Bruce Highway, Mourilyan, ©4063 2656, has a wealth of memorabilia from old harvesters to historical photographs.

Johnstone River Crocodile Farm, Flying Fish Point Road, Innisfail, ©4061 1121, facilitates crocodile breeding and displays wildlife. It is ©open 7 days 8.30am-4.30pm, adults ✪$15, children $8, family pass $35.

In addition, trips can be taken to these popular environmental destinations: Tully Gorge, Hinchinbrook Island, Murray Falls and the Atherton Tablelands.

Festivals

The premier event in Mission Beach is the Aquatic Festival, held in October, ©4068 7066. Fishing and sailing competitions are organised regularly throughout the year.

Sports

Bush'n'Beach Horse Rides, ©4068 7893. 1 and a half hours ✪$38; half day (refreshments provided) $80.

Coral Sea Kayaking, Dunk Island, ©4068 9154. Including snorkelling and lunch ✪$80; half day coastal kayaking $40.

FNQ Fishing Adventures, ©4068 9000. Half day ✪$70; full day $125. Also sightseeing tours with crocodile and bird spotting.

Jump the Beach Skydiving, ©1800 638 005 (bookings). From ✪$240-325.

RnR Rafting Tully River, ©4051 7777. Full day rafting 8am-5pm, barbecue lunch, buffet dinner, ✪$140.

South Mission Beach Boat Hire, ©0419 651 288 (mobile). Dinghy hire, ✪$35 for the first two hours, $12 for each additional hour.

Mission Beach Dive and Tackle, Shop 4, The Hub Shopping Centre, Porters Promenade, ©4068 7294, offers bicycle hire.

Golfing enthusiasts can play rounds at the *El Arish Country Club*, Bruce Highway, El Arish, ©4068 5140.

For a game of squash, head to *Mission Fitness* at the Gymnasium Mission Trade Centre, Unit 7, ©4088 6555.

Tours and Cruises

Dunk Island Jet Ski Tours, ©4068 8699. A unique way to circumnavigate Dunk Island, ✪$200.

Friendship Cruises, Clump Point Jetty, Mission Beach, ©4068 7262. Great Barrier Reef Cruise, adults ✪$85, chidren $45.

Mission Beach Dive Charters, ©1800 700 112. Various dives and locations, from ✪$110-340.

Mission Beach Nature Tours, ©4068 8582. Canoe trip through the wet tropics rainforest, 8.30am-3.30pm, adults ✪$80, children $42, under 10 years $12.

Mission Beach Rainforest Treks, ©4068 7028. Guided rainforest walks, morning (adults ✪$36, children $18) and night ($22) tours.

Quickcat Cruises, ©1800 654 242. Dunk Island (adults ✪$35, children $22) and Outer Barrier Reef (adults $135, children $68), 10am-5pm.

Cardwell Air Charters, ©4066 8468. 5 flights, various locations, from ✪$45 to $250 for adults.

Fitzroy Island

Location and Characteristics

Fitzroy has an area of 4 sq km, and is situated 26km south-east of Cairns. It is only 6km from the mainland and was named by Captain Cook after the Duke of Grafton, a politician of the time.

In 1819 Phillip King reported that Welcome Bay, where the resort is, was a good anchorage for passing ships because of its fresh water and supplies of timber.

In 1877 Fitzroy was made a place of quarantine where Chinese immigrants were to stay for 16 days before completing their journey to the Queensland gold fields. At one stage there were 3000 of them in residence, which lead to near-riot conditions. *This* is the reason for the Chinese graves that are to be found at the site, not the Smallpox that the authorities feared.

How to Get There
By Sea
Since this is the only method of transport to the island, include fares in the budget for your trip.

Great Adventures, ✆4051 0455 or ✆1800 079 080, has a fast catamaran service that leaves Cairns three times daily and takes 45 minutes to reach the island. Fares are ✪$50 adult return, $30 child return.

Visitor Information
Contact the Fitzroy Island Resort on ✆4051 9588 or ✆1800 079 080 (toll free) or visit the website at ✎www.fitzroyislandresort.com.au

Accommodation and Services
The **Fitzroy Island Resort** has 8 cabins and 1 bunkhouse.

Resort facilities include: licensed restaurant, bar, kiosk, dive shop, laundry/ironing facilities, swimming pool, volleyball, boutique and EFTPOS.

Beach Cabin facilities are: private facilities, colour TV, hairdryer, tea/coffee making facilities, iron/board, refrigerator, ceiling fans, room serviced daily.

Beach Bunkhouse facilities are: shared rooms, shared bathrooms, linen and blankets, shared kitchen facilities and fans.

Tariffs for a double room per night are:
Beach Cabins - ✪$110 per person
Beach Bunkhouse - ✪$116 (private room)

Reservations can be made directly through the resort, ✆4051 9588 or ✆1800 079 080 (toll free).

Eating Out
The **Rainforest Restaurant** at the resort is open to guests, but it is not a cheap night out. There is a mini-market near the beach house bungalows which has a range of supplies for those who want to cook for themselves.

Points of Interest
Fitzroy Island is not a great place for swimming as the beaches tend to be corally rather than sandy, although Nudey Beach has some sand. There are a few walking trails - the round trip to the lighthouse; a short rainforest walk to the Secret Garden; and the walk to Nudey Beach.

Canoes and catamarans are available for use, and sailing is popular. There is good diving water right off-shore, and the Reef is not far away. The resort dive shop hires out all gear for snorkelling and diving, runs courses, and provides daily trips to Moore Reef.

Chapter 43
Cairns

Population 130,000
The Far North Queensland region extends from Cardwell in the south to the Torres Strait in the north, and west across the Gulf of Carpentaria to the Northern Territory border, an area of 377,796 sq km (145,829 sq miles) which is almost twice the size of the state of Victoria. Cairns, its major city and service, administration, distribution and manufacturing centre, has recorded the second highest percentage of population growth of any Australian city since 1979. In fact, it was named Australia's most livable regional centre back in 1995.

Climate

Average temperature: January max 32C (90F) - min 24C (75F); July max 25C (77F) - min 16C (61F). The humidity is high in summer, and the best time to visit is from May to October.

Characteristics

Cairns, in the heart of the tropical wonderland, is an international tourist mecca. It is a modern, colourful city situated on the shores of a natural harbour, Trinity Inlet, with a magnificent backdrop of rugged mountains covered with thick tropical rainforest.

The major glamour activity in Cairns is Big Game Fishing, and numerous fish over 450kg (992 lb) are caught each year. The game fishing season starts in early September and continues through to late November, however light game can be caught all year round.

As well as being a major city for tourism, Cairns is an important centre for the export of sugar and the agricultural products of the Atherton Tablelands.

The city was named after William Wellington Cairns, the third Governor of Queensland.

How to Get There

By Air

Qantas, ✆13 1313 have frequent daily flights to Cairns from major southern ports.

Sunstate Airlines, ✆13 1313, operate daily flights to/from Cairns, Cooktown and Thursday Island, along with scheduled services to other centres.

Flight West, ✆1300 130 092, is another option when travelling internally around northern Queensland.

Check with your travel agent about the availability of other domestic airlines.

Cairns International Airport accepts many international airlines including Qantas, Thai International, Air Nuigini, Continental, Air New Zealand and Japan Airlines.

Cairns' Domestic and International airports, ✆4052 9703, are approximately 6km from the centre of the city. Regular coach services depart from the domestic terminals for the city and the northern beaches, and there is also an inter-terminal coach service.

By Rail

The Queenslander and The Sunlander operate regular services from Brisbane to Cairns. Both services provide sleeping berths, sitting cars, dining and club cars, and a lounge car. Single economy fares for The Queenslander are ✪$142 adults and $71 concession, and passengers have the option of taking their private vehicles on this service. Single economy fares for The Sunlander are ✪$177 adults and $106 concession. The Brisbane to Cairns trip takes about 32 hours on these fast and luxurious trains. For more information, ✆132 235.

By Bus

Greyhound Pioneer, ✆13 2030, and McCafferty's, ✆13 1499, operate regular daily express coach services from major southern cities.

By Road

From Brisbane, via the Bruce Highway, it is a four day trip covering 1,720km (1,070 miles). From the north, access is via the Captain Cook Highway.

Cairns

Visitor Information

The Visitors Information Centre is on the Cairns Esplanade (near the pier complex). ⊕Open 7 days, 9.30am-5.30pm.

For information relating to all areas in North Queensland, contact Tourism Tropical North Queensland on ℂ 4051 3588 or at ✉ttnq@tnq.org.au

If you wish, visit the website at ☞www.tnq.org.au

The Great Barrier Reef Visitors Bureau has developed a web site encompassing the entire region, with detailed and up-to-date information on accommodation, sightseeing, tours and more for every major locality. The address is: ☞www.greatbarrierreef.aus.net with email at ✉visitors@greatbarrierreef.aus.net

Accommodation

The Cairns area has over 40 motels, as well as hotels, guest houses, holiday apartments and over 20 caravan parks. Prices vary considerably depending on the standard of accommodation and the season. Here we have a selection, with prices for a double room per night, which should be used as a guide only. The telephone area code is 07.

Radisson Plaza, Pierpoint Road, ℂ4031 1411. 219 rooms, 22 suites, licensed restaurants, swimming pool, spa, sauna, gym - ✪$370-405.

Hilton Cairns, Wharf Street, ℂ4050 2000 or ℂ1800 222 255 (toll free). 260 rooms, 5 suites, licensed restaurant, 3 cocktail bars, coffee shop, barbecue area, swimming pool, fitness centre, spa, sauna, beauty salon, shopping, tour desk, garage parking - ✪$230-320.

Holiday Inn Cairns, cnr Esplanade & Florence Street, ℂ4050 6070. 232 rooms, 6 suites, licensed restaurant, bars, swimming pool - ✪$260-290.

Cairns International Hotel, 17 Abbot Street, ℂ4031 1300 or ℂ1800 079 100 (toll free). 339 rooms, 18 suites, licensed restaurant (closed Sunday), cocktail bars, coffee shop, entertainment, barbecue area, swimming pool, fitness centre, spa, 2 saunas, beauty salon, shopping, tour desk - ✪$320-430.

Cairns and the Northern Beaches

Righa Colonial Club Resort, 18 Cannon Street, Manunda, ℂ4053 5111. 145 units, licensed restaurants, 3 swimming pools, tennis court, courtesy coach transfers and shuttle to and from the city - ✪$220.

Bay Village Tropical Retreat, 227 Lake Street, ℂ4051 4622. 63 rooms, licensed restaurant, room service, bar, swimming pool, courtesy coach to airport - ✪$125.

Club Crocodile Hides Hotel, cnr Lake & Shields Streets, ℂ4051 1266. 70 rooms with private facilities, some with shared facilities, swimming pool, spa, bistro, bars, 24 hour security - ✪$85-120 per person (including light breakfast).

Ocean Blue Resort Cairns, 702 Bruce Highway, ℂ4054 7383. 36 units, licensed restaurant, bar, swimming pool - ✪$110

Country Comfort Outrigger, cnr Abbott & Florence Streets, ℂ4051 6188. 90 units, licensed restaurant, bar, coffee shop, swimming pool, spa - ✪$110-130.

Acacia Court, 223 The Esplanade, ℂ4051 5011. 150 hotel style rooms, 16 motel units, licensed restaurant, lounge, bar, swimming pool - ✪$99-110.

Flying Horseshoe, 281 Sheridan Street, ℂ4051 3022. 51 units, licensed restaurant, swimming pool, spa, games room - ✪$90-105.

Cairns Holiday Lodge, 259 Sheridan Street, cnr Thomas Street, ℂ4051 4611. 35 units, licensed restaurant, swimming pool, courtesy bus - ✪$85-95.

G'Day Tropical Village Resort, 7 McLachlan Street, Manunda, ©4053 7555. 68 studio units, licensed restaurant, swimming pool - ✪$90.

Great Northern, 69 Abbott Street, ©4051 5966. 33 rooms, air conditioning, cooking facilities - ✪$90-120.

Cairns Tropical Gardens, 314 Mulgrave Road, ©4031 1777. 55 units, licensed restaurant open Mon-Sat, pool, spa, sauna - ✪$65-85.

A1 Motel, 211 Sheridan Street, ©4051 4499. 31 units, 1 suite, licensed restaurant and bar, swimming pool - ✪$70.

Adobe, 191 Sheridan Street, ©4051 5511. 15 units, licensed restaurant, room service, swimming pool - ✪$55-85.

Caravan Parks

Cairns Coconut Caravan Resort, cnr Bruce Highway & Anderson Road, ©4054 6644. (No pets) 279 sites, recreation room, barbecue, playground, cafe, transfers, tennis, pool, mini golf, basketball - powered sites ✪$28 for two, cabins $50-85 for two, units $80-95 for two.

First City Caravilla Caravan Park, Little Street, ©4054 1403. (No pets) 100 sites, barbecue, playground, kiosk, mini golf, pool - powered sites ✪$22 for two, cabins $50-75 for two.

Cairns Villa & Leisure Park, 28 Pease Street, Manunda, ©4053 7133. (No pets) 163 sites, recreation room, lounge, barbecue, playground, shop, pool - powered sites ✪$17-25 for two, units $55-70 for two, cabins $50-65 for two.

Crystal Cascades Holiday Park, Intake Road, Redlynch, ©4039 1036. 92 sites, recreation room, barbecue area, salt water pool, spa - powered sites ✪$21 for two; villas $65-80 for two. There are two **Youth Hostels** in the area:

Cairns Esplanade, 93 The Esplanade, ©4031 1919. 18 rooms, ✪$22 per person twin share; and **Cairns-McLeod Street**, 20-24 McCleod Street, ©4051 0772. 30 rooms - ✪$21 per person twin share.

Local Transport

There are public transport services to all Cairns city areas, suburbs and beaches. Timetables and routes are available at hotels and bus depots.

Cairns City Airporter, ©4031 3555, have an airport/city/airport service, and bookings are essential for trips to the airport. They also have vehicles available for charter.

Coral Coaches, ©4031 7577, have daily services between: Cairns, Hartley Creek, Port Douglas, Mossman, Daintree, Cape Tribulation, Bloomfield, Cooktown - Inland and Coast Road. They also have airport transfers to/from: Northern Beaches, Port Douglas, Mossman and Cape Tribulation.

Whitecar Coaches, ©4051 9533, service the Atherton Tabelands and Chillagoe.

Car Hire

Avis, 135 Lake Street, ©4051 5911, and Cairns International Airport, ©4035 9100.

All Car Rentals, 30 Grafton Street, ©4031 6322.

Cairns Tropical Rent-A-Car, 141 Lake Street, Cairns, ©4031 3995.

Hertz, 436 Sheridan Street, Cairns, ©4053 6701.

Mini Car Rentals, 150 Sheridan Street, Cairns, ©4051 6288.

Peter's Economy Rent-A-Car, 36 Water Street, Cairns, ©4051 4106.

Cairns Leisure Wheels, 314 Sheridan Street, Cairns, ©4051 8988.

National Car Rental, 135 Abbott Street, Cairns, ©1800 350 536.

Honeycombs Cars & 4WD's, 303-307 Mulgrave Road, Cairns, ©4051 9211.

Entertainment

Cairns has nightclubs, discos, karaoke bars, theatre restaurants, live theatre and cinemas. There are street musicians and all types of performing artists in and around the shopping areas, taverns and bars.

Club International & My Karaoke Bar, 40 Lake Street, ©4052 1480.

Sports Bar, 33 Spence Street, ©4041 2533.

The Beach Nite Club, 78 Abbott Street, ©4031 3944.

The Cat House Night Club, 78 Abbott Street, ©4051 6322.

Because the weather is quite warm at night there

are always lots of people to be found along the Esplanade, eating at pavement tables, or picnicking on the lawns.

Cairns also has a couple of clubs who welcome visitors and offer free temporary membership for those who live more than 40km from the club.

Brothers Leagues Club (Cairns), 99 Anderson Street, Manunda, ©4053 1053.

The Yacht Club, 4 The Esplanade (between Hilton Hotel and Great Adventures), ©4031 2750.

Shopping

There are plenty of shopping opportunities in Cairns. The large hotels have boutiques offering imported fashion items and jewellery, and then there is *The Pier Marketplace*, ©4051 7244, in Pierpoint Road. The Pier is a landmark in Cairns. The building contains the Radisson Plaza Hotel and a specialty retail leisure centre.

It has separate theme walkways, the most glamorous of which is the Governor's Way, where Cairns' best fashion stores and boutiques are found. The main entrance leads to Trader's Row, which has a colonial air and some appealing shops that are not the usual 'high fashion'.

The *Mud Markets* are held on Saturday and Sunday in the main amphitheatre of the specialty retail centre, and local artisans and artists set up stalls selling all sorts of interesting objects from handcrafts to glassware. Live entertainers roam around the markets, creating a really festive atmosphere.

The Pier Marketplace is ⊕open daily 9am-9pm, but most of the shops in the city centre are open Mon-Thurs 8.30am-8pm, Fri 8.30am-9pm, Sat 8.30am-5.30pm, Sun 3-8pm. Those in the suburbs have shorter hours with night shopping on one night only.

Eating Out

Cairns has some of the best eating places in Queensland. Most of the international standard hotels and motels have at least one restaurant as well as a bistro, or the like. There is also a good selection of restaurants, some of which can be found along the Cairns Esplanade, where you can enjoy both the meal and views of the natural harbour inlet. Here is a selection of restaurants in the area:

Tawny's Seafood Restaurant, Marlin Parade, ©4051 1722. Seafood specialists with an a-la-carte menu. Open 5.30pm-midnight 7 days, closed on Public Holidays.

Golden Sun Inn, 313 Kamerunga Road, Freshwater, ©4055 1177. Chinese cuisine, BYO and licensed. Open 5pm-10pm every day except Tuesday and Public Holidays.

Tandoori Oven, 62 Shields Street, ©4031 0043. Open 6.30pm-10.30pm daily, closed Sunday and Public Holidays.

Thai Pan Restaurant, 43-45 Grafton Street, ©4052 1708. Licensed and BYO, take-away and free home delivery available. Open 6pm-8pm every day.

Cosmo On The Bay, The Esplanade Centre, ©4031 5400. Cosmopolitan dining, seafood is a speciality. Open 5.30pm-11.30pm daily, and for lunch and extended hour on Thursdays, Fridays and Sundays.

Jango Jango Club Restaurant, Level 1 Palm Court, 34 Lake Street, ©4031 2411. Asian influenced fare and karaoke. Open 6pm-2am daily.

Brothers Leagues Club (Cairns), 99 Anderson Street Cairns, ©4053 1053. Betting and gambling facilities. Open 9am-11pm daily except on Public Holidays.

The Sorrento, 70 Grafton Street, ©4051 7841. Italian cuisine, pizza, seafood and steak.

Red Ochre Grill, 43 Shields St, ©4051 0100. Modern Australian cuisine with seafood and outdoor dining facilities. Open 10am-11pm Mon-Sat, 3pm-11pm Sunday and Public Holidays.

Aphrodisias Restaurant, 82 Sheridan Street, ©4051 5871.

McDonalds is in both the Cairns Central Shopping Centre and on the Esplande. KFC is at Shop 5, 71-75 The Esplanade and at the corner of Mulgrave and Florence Streets. Pizza Hut is on the corner of Aurnullar Street & Mulgrave Road, ©13 1166.

Points of Interest

There are no sandy beaches in Cairns itself, only mudflats, but prolific birdlife gathers here. Palms

Reef Hotel Casino

line many streets, with parks and gardens displaying a riot of colour from bougainvillaea, hibiscus, poinciana and other tropical blooms. The old part of town is to be found around Wharf Street and The Esplanade. The National Trust has put out a walking tour brochure about this part of town.

The Esplanade is 5km (3 miles) long and runs along the side of the bay. This park-like area is a very pleasant place to relax in the cooler part of the day.

The Flecker Botanic Gardens, Collins Avenue, Edge Hill, are ☺open daily and feature graded walking tracks through natural rainforest to Mount Whitfield. From here there are excellent views of the city and coastline.

The **Centenary Lakes**, Greenslopes Street, Cairns North, are an extension of Flecker Botanic Gardens and were created to mark the city's centenary in 1976. There are two lakes - one fresh water, the other salt. Bird life abounds and barbecue facilities have been provided. Mount Mooroobool (610m - 2000 ft) in the background is the city's highest peak.

The Pier Marketplace hosts live entertainment daily, and is the departure point for most reef cruises and fishing boat charters. Sit on the verandah for a quick snack or a delicious meal from one of the many food outlets, while checking out the magnificent views over Trinity Inlet.

The Royal Flying Doctor Base, 1 Junction Street, Edge Hill, ✆4053 5687, has fully guided tours, film shows, and displays of the history and present operations of this legendary service. ☺Open seven days.

Sugarworld Waterslides, Mill Road, Edmonton, ✆4055 5477, is 14km south of Cairns City centre, and has tropical horticulture, a licensed restaurant, tours, rides and waterslides.

The Reef Hotel Casino, 35-41 Wharf Street, ✆4030 8888, offers what all casinos offer: a glitzy way to part with your money.

The **Cairns Convention Centre**, cnr Wharf & Sheridan Streets, ✆4042 4200, may have a function on at the time of your visit.

Festivals

The festival season begins with the Mareeba Rodeo in early July and then onto the Cairns Show for three days of entertainment.

The Cairns Amateur Horserace Meeting is held in September, and the week-long Fun in the Sun Festival is in October.

Sports

All types of water sports are catered for, as well as the usual sporting activities.

Diving

The following companies in Cairns offer diving trips and lessons.

Pro Dive, 116 Spence Street, ©4031 5255. 5 day learn to dive courses are held 4 times weekly. 3 day/2 night liveaboard cruises 4 times weekly - PADI 5-Star facility.

Deep Sea Divers Den, Wharf Street, ©4031 5622. Dive and snorkel trips, dive courses (beginner to instructor level), diving/fishing charters on the Outer Barrier Reef.

Taka 2 Dive Adventures, 131 Lake Street, ©4051 8722. Offer dives in Cod Hole, Ribbon Reefs, Coral Sea - liveaboard, departs bi-weekly.

Great Diving Adventures Cairns, Wharf Street, ©4051 4444. PADI open water dive courses available on tropical Fitzroy Island, including accommodation, meals, transfers and certification - other great dive locations include Norman Reef and Michaelmas Cay, both on the Outer Barrier Reef.

Tours

Cairns is a staging place for tours to the Great Barrier Reef, the Islands, the Atherton Tablelands, the Barron Gorge, Cooktown and Cape Tribulation. Here are a few.

The *Cairns Explorer* bus leaves from Lake Street Transit Mall every hour 9am-4pm Mon-Sat. It visits Wescourt shopping, Earlville shopping, Freshwater swimming hole, Freshwater Connection, Mangrove Boardwalk, Botanical Gardens, Flying Doctor and Centenary Lakes. For bookings and enquiries, ©4033 5344.

Wait A-While Environmental Wildlife Tours, 5 Alkoo Close, Bayview Heights, ©4033 1153. Day/night wildlife tours - the best way to see the rainforest, birds and animals of North Queensland - small groups, 4WD, experienced guides - departs 2pm daily and costs adults ✪$145.

Tropic Wings Luxury Coach Tours, 278 Hartley Street, ©4035 3555. Specialise in day tours around Cairns and The Tropical North - Atherton Tablelands, Port Douglas & Daintree, Cape Tribulation, Chillagoe, 3 day Outback and Gulf.

Down Under Tours, Cairns, © 4035 5566. Offer tours to Kuranda, Daintree/Port Douglas, The Tablelands, Cairns and Orchid Valley, Weatherby Station (outback).

Australian Pacific Tours, 278 Hartley Street, Cairns, ©4041 9419 or ©1300 655 965 (reservations). They have an extensive range of half and full days tours, as well as extended tours from 2 to 12 days.

Wilderness Challenge, 15 Tranguna Street, Trinity Beach, ©4055 6504. 4WD adventure safaris from 1 to 14 days or charters - travel to Cape York, Hinchinbrook, Cooktown, Daintree, Kakadu, Lava Tubes, and more.

Billy Tea Bush Safaris, 94 Upper Richardson Street, Whitfield, ©4032 0077. 1 day to 14 day safaris available to Cape York, Alice Springs, Ayers Rock, and more.

Oz Tours Safaris, Captain Cook Highway, Smithfield, ©4055 9535. 7, 9, 10 and 12 day overland/air or 16 day all overland Cape York safaris. Both camping and accommodated options available - also Cairns-Cape York-Thursday Island.

Barrier Reef Cybertours, Shop 9, 7 Shields Street, ©4041 0666.

Cairns Eco-Tours, 85 Lake Street, ©4031 0334.

Cairns Harley Tours, ©0417 45 4962 (mobile).

Cruises

Sunlover Cruises, cnr Tingara & Aumuller Streets, ©4050 1333. Luxurious travel aboard Super-Cats to Moore or Arlington Reef - most innovative reef pontoons afloat, underwater theatre and marine touch tanks, free guided snorkelling tours, delicious buffet lunch - free semi-sub (Moore Reef), Supa Viewer (Arlington Reef), and glass bottom boat rides - all levels of diving catered for - optional helicopter and sea plane joyflights (Moore Reef only) - free guided rainforest walk on Fitzroy Island.

Ocean Spirit Cruises, 33 Lake Street, Cairns, ©4031 2920. Daily departures aboard the *Ocean Spirit I* or *Ocean Spirit II* sailing vessels, to either Michaelmas or Upolu Cay - delicious tropical seafood buffet available.

Big Cat, Pier Marketplace, ©4051 0444. Has cruises that depart daily from The Pier at 9am and travel to Green Island - snorkelling, glass bottom boat tours, lunch served on board, submersible reef coral viewer, guided snorkel tours - return Cairns 5pm - from ✪$70 adults.

Captain Cook Cruises, Trinity Wharf, © 4031 4433. Offer 3, 4 and 7 day Reef Escape cruises every week - cruise to Hinchinbrook and Dunk Islands, or Cooktown and Lizard Island.

Coral Princess Barrier Reef and Island Cruises, Shop 5, 149 Spence Street, ©4031 1041. Sails between Cairns and Townsville, calling at island resorts and uninhabited islands for beachcombing, swimming and a tropical barbecue.

Clipper Sailaway Cruises, 287 Draper Street, Cairns, ©4052 8300. Sail on SV *Atlantic Clipper* - a 140' sailing ship catering for 34 passengers - cruises from Cairns to Lizard Island, Great Barrier Reef, Cape York.

Seahorse Sail & Dive, B16 Marlin Marina, © 4041 1919. Snorkelling, diving, lunch included.

Auspray Seafaris, 125 Aumuller Street, ©4035 3931.

Sport n Game Fishing Charters, 23 Bolton Street, ©4053 1828.

Barrier Reef Luxury Cruises, Marlin Marina, ©4051 3555.

Blue Whaler Charters, Marlin Marina, ©4051 1414.

Scenic Flights

Tiger Moth Scenic Flights, Hangar 8, Tom McDonald Drive, Aeroglen, ©4035 9400 or ©4055 9814 (after hours).

Chapter 44
Cairns to Cape York

Marlin Coast - Northern Beaches

Location and Characteristics

The Marlin Coast area extends from Machans Beach, at the mouth of the Barron River 13km (8 miles) north of Cairns to Ellis Beach, passing by Holloways Beach, Yorkeys Knob, Clifton Beach, Palm Cove and Kewarra Beach.

Trinity Beach and Clifton Beach are popular holiday destinations, and Palm Cove and Kewarra Beach have international resorts.

How to Get There
By Bus

There are regular bus services from Cairns. The charter company, Marlin Sunbus, operates from the City Centre Bus Terminal in Cairns, ✆4057 7411.

By Car

The southern Marlin Coast settlements can be reached by turning east off the Captain Cook Highway at signposted points. The townships of Clifton Beach, Palm Cove and Ellis Beach lie on or near the highway, further north.

Visitor Information

Trinity Beach and Yorkeys Knob have their own web sites:
☛ www.trinitybeach.com and email at ✎ info@trinitybeach.com
☛ www.yorkeysknob.com and email at ✎ hmbr@internetnorth.com.au

For other information on the Marlin Coast, use the same contact details as those listed under Tourist Information for *Cairns.*

Accommodation and Services

There is plenty of accommodation along the entire stretch of the Marlin Coast settlements. Below is an overview of what is on offer. Area code 07.

Yorkeys Knob

Golden Sands Beachfront Resort, 12-14 Deauville Close, ✆4055 8033. 30 units, licensed restaurant, undercover parking, tennis court, pool - ✪$100-130.

Half Moon Bay Resort, 101 Wattle Street, ✆4055 8059 or ✆1800 810 010 (toll free). 19 units, undercover parking, pool, spa - ✪$95.

Villa Marine, 8 Rutherford Street, ✆4055 7158. 9 units, barbecue, pool - ✪$85.

Cairns Yorkeys Knob Beachfront Van Park, 73 Sims Esplanade, ✆4055 7201. 32 sites, barbecue - powered sites ✪$19 for two.

Eating Out

If you wish to eat out, there is the ***Blue Horizons Restaurant*** at the Golden Sands Boutique Resort, 12-14 Deauville Close, ✆4055 8633; ***La Provencal***, Deauville Close, ✆4055 8028; or ***Chinese & Thai Takeaway***, 455 Varley Street, ✆4081 0100.

Kewarra Beach

Kewarra Beach Resort, off Captain Cook Highway, ✆4057 6666. 76 units (four varieties), licensed restaurant, tennis court, swimming pool - ✪$230-370.

Trinity Beach

Coral Sands , cnr Trinity Beach Road & Vasey Esplanade, ✆4057 8800. Licensed restaurant, security parking, pool - ✪$160-320.

Marlin Gateway Apartments, 33 Trinity Street, ✆4057 7600. 16 units, undercover parking, pool - from ✪$120.

Tranquil Trinity, 154 Trinity Beach Road, ✆4057 5759. 3 rooms, parking, pool, spa - ✪$60.

Tropic Sun Holiday Units, 46 Moore Street, ✆4055 6619. 4 units, parking, pool - ✪$65-85.

Wintersun Caravan Park, 116 Trinity Beach Road, ✆4055 6306. 68 sites, pool - powered sites ✪$19 for two.

Eating Out

Restaurants in the area include, ***Avanti BYO Trattoria***, 47 Vasey Esplanade, ✆4057 7515; ***Blue Waters at the Beach***, 77 Vasey Esplanade, ✆4055 6194; and ***Chalet Swiss***, Shop 9,

Coastwatcher Centre, ©4055 6122.

Clifton Beach

Agincourt Beachfront Apartments, 69 Arlington Esplanade, ©4055 3500. 45 units, undercover parking, transfers, pool - ✪$130-155.
Kaikea, 16 Eddy Street, ©4059 0010. 2 rooms, spa, pool - bed & breakfast ✪$50-130.
Clifton Sands, cnr Guide Street & Clifton Road, ©4055 3355. 18 units, undercover parking, pool - ✪$65-85.
Paradise Gardens Caravan Resort, cnr Clifton Road & Captain Cook Highway, ©4055 3712. 80 sites, barbecue, playground, pool - powered sites ✪$21 for two, cabins ✪$40-50.
Billabong Caravan Park, Captain Cook Highway, ©4055 3737. 40 sites, barbecue, playground, pool - powered sites ✪$20, units $50-65.

Eating Out

You can dine out at *Clifton Capers Bar & Grill*, 14 Clifton Road, ©4059 2311; or *Serenata Pizza & Pasta*, Captain Cook Highway, ©4055 3699.

Palm Cove

Villa Paradiso, 111 Williams Esplanade, ©4055 3838. 19 units, cooking facilities, secure parking, spa, pool - ✪$280-380.
Novotel Palm Cove Resort, Coral Coast Drive, ©4059 1234. 343 rooms, 72 suites, licensed restaurant, playground, transfers, golf course, gym, squash, tennis courts, sauna, pool, spa, sailing, windsurfing - ✪$220-465.
Angsana Resort and Spa, 1 Veivers Road, ©4055 3000. 70 units, licensed restaurant, secure parking, pool, spa - ✪$330-800.
Palm Cove Beach Sarayi, 95 Williams Esplanade, ©4055 3734. 16 units, barbecue, playground, secure parking, air conditioning, restaurant - ✪$80-220.
Melalaeuca Resort, 85 Williams Esplanade, ©4055 3222. 22 units, barbecue, undercover parking, transfers, pool, spa - ✪$110-170.
Silvester Palms, 32 Veivers Road, ©4055 3831. 7 units, barbecue, pool - ✪$80-120.

Eating Out

Palm Cove has several restaurants, such as *Clippers*, 73 Williams Esplanade, ©4059 0013; *Far Horizons*, 1 Veivers Road, ©4055 3000; *Pisces Live Seafood Restaurant*, Paradise Village Shopping Centre, Williams Esplanade, ©4055 3200; and *The Coach House*, Captain Cook Highway, ©4055 3544.

Ellis Beach

Ellis Beach Oceanfront Bungalows & Leisure Park, Captain Cook Highway, ©4055 3538. 61 sites, barbecue, pool - powered sites ✪$19 for two, units $65 for two, cabins $55 for two.

Points of Interest

Two attractions are located on the magnificent Cook Highway, both of which are popular with tourists and locals alike.

40km north of Cairns is **Hartley's Creek Crocodile Farm**, ©4055 3576, where admission rates are ✪$16 for adults, $8 children and $40 for a family pass. **Wild World**, ©4055 3669 at Palm Cove along the same stretch of road 20 minutes north of Cairns, is a wildlife sanctuary with a hands-on approach. It is ⊙open daily 8.30am-5pm and costs ✪$22 for adults and $12 for children, with family passes available.

All beaches have picnic areas and regular bus services to and from Cairns. Palm Cove and Ellis Beach are regularly patrolled in the summer season by the local Life Saving Club members. Watersporters can hire catamarans, windsurfers and surf skis at most of the major beaches in the area. Countless cruises to the coral creefs are also available, and the Visitor Information Centre can advise.

Yorkeys Knob has the popular **Half Moon Bay Golf Course**, ©4055 8059, a pleasant 18-hole, par 67 course that costs ✪$25 for a full round, $30 to hire a cart, and $15 for clubs.

The Novotel Resort at Palm Cove also has a **Golf Course**. Here it costs ✪$30 for 18 holes, $20 to hire clubs and $30 for a motorised cart, ©4059 1234.

The Atherton Tablelands

Location and Characteristics

Inland from Cairns are the fertile Mareeba, Atherton and Evelyn Tablelands, rising in three gigantic steps from the coastal plains. Jungle-

Cairns to Cape York

fringed volcanic crater lakes, waterfalls and fertile farmlands, coupled with the only temperate climate in the Australian tropics, lure many visitors to the Tablelands each year. Views from the lookouts on the Kuranda, Gillies, Rex and Palmerston Highways are spectacular.

How to Get There

By Train

From Cairns, a steam train runs along a very picturesque route to the Kuranda Railway Station, ©4032 3964.

By Car

The major settlements are joined by major highways, and the Visitor Information Centre in Cairns will be able to provide you with clear and precise directions for your chosen destinations.

Visitor Information

The Tropical Tableland Promotion Bureau has an outlet at the Old Post Office Gallery Information Centre, Herberton Road, Atherton, ©4091 4222. They have a terrific website at ✍www.athertontableland.com and can be emailed at ✉info@athertontableland.com

Accommodation and Services

Kuranda

Kuranda Rainforest Resort, Kennedy Highway, ©4093 7555. 70 units, licensed restaurant, transfers, tennis, gymnasium, pool, spa - ✪$125-179.

Kuranda Rainforest Park, Kuranda Heights Road, ©4093 7316. (Pets allowed at owner's discretion) 60 sites, barbecue - powered sites ✪$17, cabins $65-70.

Eating Out

Here is a selection of good restaurants in the area: *Billy's Garden Bar & Barbecue*, Coondoo Street, ©4093 7203; *Clohesy Country Gardens*, Clohesy River, Kennedy Highway, ©4093 7859; and *Frogs*, 11 Coondoo Street, ©4093 7405.

Atherton

Lavender Hill Rural Stay, 1 Favier Road, ©4095 8384. Bed & breakfast - ✪$100.

Atherton, Maunds Road, ©4091 1500. 18 units,

licensed restaurant (closed Sunday), undercover parking, pool - ✪$70.

Hinterland, 44 Cook Street, ©4091 1885. 16 units, undercover parking - ✪$54.

Mountain View Van Park, 152 Robert Street, ©4091 4144. 42 sites, barbecue, playground - powered sites ✪$17-18 for two, units $40-50 for two.

Atherton Woodlands Tourist Park, 141 Herberton Road, ©4091 1407. (No dogs allowed) 60 sites, barbecue, playground, pool - powered sites ✪$18 for two, cabins $50 for two.

Eating Out

There are a few restaurants to choose from in Atherton, including *Atherton Chinese Restaurant*, 18 Main Street, ©4091 2585; the *Chatterbox Bistro*, 48 Main Street, ©4091 4388; the *Grill Room*, 77 Main Street, ©4091 1139; *Maree's*, 154 Robert Street, ©4091 4936; and *Sami's Cafe Theatre Restaurant*, 18 Main Street, ©4091 2585.

Malanda

Travellers Rest, Millaa Millaa Road, ©4096 6077. 6 units, barbecue, unlicensed restaurant, secure parking - ✪$80.

Fur n Feathers Rainforest Tree House, Hogan Road, Tarzali, ©4096 5364. 4 cottages, rainforest walks, wildlife sanctuary, undercover parking - ✪$135-225.

Malanda Lodge, Millaa Millaa Road, ©4096 5555. 17 units, licensed restaurant (closed Sunday), par 3 golf course, pool, spa - ✪$75.

Malanda Falls Caravan Park, 38 Park Avenue, ©4096 5314. 70 sites, barbecue, playground - powered sites ✪$14 for two, units $50 for two.

Eating Out

If you wish to eat out, try the *Diggers Den* in the RSL, 8 Catherine Street, ©4096 5901.

Millaa Millaa

Iskanda Park Farmstay, Nash Road, ©4097 2401. 1 cottage, standard facilities - ✪$120.

The Falls Holiday Park, Malanda Road, ©4097 2290. 22 sites, barbecue - powered sites ✪$15 for two, cabins $30-40 for two.

Eating Out

Christies, 19 Main Street, ©4097 2126; and *Falls Tea House*, Palmer-ston Highway, ©4097

2237, are two restaurants among a very limited variety.

Ravenshoe

Millstream Retreat, Kennedy Highway, ☏4097 6785. 2 cottages, undercover parking - ✪$110.

Possum Valley Rainforest Cottages, Evelyn Central, ☏4097 8177. 2 cottages, barbecue, car parking - ✪$75.

Tall Timbers, Kennedy Highway, ☏4097 6325. 4 units, unlicensed restaurant, undercover parking - ✪$50, powered sites in Caravan Park section $14.

Club, Grigg Street, ☏4097 6109. 8 units, licensed restaurant, under-cover parking, room service - ✪$50.

Points of Interest

Kuranda, a tiny mountain hamlet in the rainforest, is the first stop-off stage on the Tableland journey. The town can be reached by train from Cairns (☏4032 3964) and the ride passes waterfalls and stunning views to the coast before ending at picturesque Kuranda Station.

Kuranda has many attractions:

Pamagirri Dancers, Kennedy Highway, ☏4093 9033, is an Aboriginal theatre presenting daily shows based on Dreamtime legends.

Australian Butterfly Sanctuary, 8 Rob Veivers Drive, ☏4093 7575, is the largest butterfly farm in the world, listed in the Guinness Book of Records.

The **Kuranda Wildlife Noctarium**, 8 Coondoo Street, ☏4093 7334, provides a close-up look at the rarely seen nocturnal inhabitants of the rainforests, and guided walks into the jungle.

Kuranda Riverboat and Rainforest Tours, 24 Coondoo Street, ☏4093 7476 or ☏0412 159 212 (mobile), have tours of the Barron River and surrounding rainforest area.

The town's main street is lined with galleries, shops and restaurants. The terraced *Kuranda Markets*, at 5 Therwine Street, are considered the best in the north, ☏4093 8772.

The **Mareeba/Dimbulah** district, approximately 66 km (41 miles) west of Cairns, is the largest tobacco growing area in Australia.

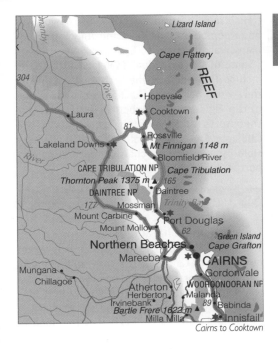

Cairns to Cooktown

Atherton, with its red volcanic soil, is the central town of the Atherton Tablelands. Maize silos dominate the skyline.

Malanda is situated in the heart of tropical Australia's only viable dairying district. The Malanda milk factory boasts the longest milk run in the world, which extends as far as Darwin in the Northern Territory.

Millaa Millaa is the waterfall capital of the Tablelands, taking in the Millaa Millaa, Zillie and Elinjaa Falls.

The **Millstream Falls**, south of Ravenshoe, when in flood are the widest waterfalls in Australia.

Herberton is the north's historic mining town, and tin is still produced in the area.

Irvinebank situated near Herberton, is steeped in history. Its tin crushing plant has been in operation since 1890, and it has other historic buildings.

Ravenshoe is situated on the western side of the Evelyn Tablelands, and is the gateway to the back country and gemfields of the north. It is a major timber town providing some of Australia's most beautiful woods. Close by you will find Koombooloomba Dam and Tully Falls, with many walking tracks to Eyrie Lookout.

Some of the individual Tableland attractions include Tinaroo Dam, the Crater National Park, the twin crater lakes of Eacham and Barrine, the Curtin Fig Tree and Herberton Tin Fields. Further north of the Evelyn Tablelands is the Chillagoe Caves National Park, which is accessible by road and air charter from Cairns Airport, ©4052 9703.

Green Island

Location and Characteristics

The island has an area of 15ha and is 27km north-east of Cairns. It is a true coral cay surrounded by coral reefs, and has the only 5-star resort on a coral cay in Great Barrier Reef Marine Park. Incidentally, this island was also named by Captain Cook, after his chief astronomer.

The island grew out of debris washed from its surrounding platform of coral, and is gradually being pushed north-west by prevailing currents. The waters abound with sea life, and the beach is quite beautiful. It only takes about 20 minutes to walk around the island, passing tropical vegetation, fringing casuarinas and pandanus.

Green Island's Underwater Observatory is well known. From 5m below the surface, the ever-changing panorama of marine life can be seen through portholes. Marineland Melanesia has been the island's main attraction for many years.

Green Island is very popular with day trippers.

How to Get There
By Sea

Great Adventures Outer Reef and Island Cruises, Wharf Street, Cairns, has a fast, daily catamaran service that departs from Cairns at 8.30am, 10.30am, 1pm, 3.30pm and 9.30pm (Tue, Wed & Fri). Fares are ✪$44 adults and $22 children. You can also visit the island as part of a cruise to Fitzroy Island and the Outer Barrier Reef. For enquiries, ©1800 079 080 and to book, ©4051

0455. Note that transfers are included in the tariff if you are staying at the resort.

Visitor Information

For information on Green Island, either contact the Green Island Resort directly, ©07 4031 3300, visit the web page at ☞www.greenislandresort. com.au or email them at ✉res@greenisland resort.com.au

Accommodation and Services

The **Green Island Resort** has deluxe guest rooms and reef suites.

Resort facilities are: restaurants, pool bar, two swimming pools, resort shops, dive centre, sailboards, snorkelling, surf skis, canoes, nature activities and a guest reception lounge in Cairns.

Unit facilities are: private bathroom with shower and bath, tea/coffee making facilities, air conditioning, ceiling fans, mini bar, refrigerator, colour TV, in-house movies, IDD/STD telephone, balcony, in-room safe and bath robes.

Tariffs for a double room per night are:
Island Suite - ✪$440
Reef Suite - ✪$550

The above rates are room only and include free use of beach hire equipment, guest library, underwater observatory, snorkelling equipment, fish feeding and activities, and transfers ex Cairns.

Points of Interest

Apart from the facilities and activities listed above, the island also has its own resident attraction. **Marineland Melanesia**, ©4051 4032, is an underwater observatory which also features Cassius, the largest salt water crocodile in captivity. It has interesting displays of Melanesian tribal art, and a collection of early Coral Sea sailing relics. Interest in the observatory draws many people out to Green Island for the day. There are shows at 10.30am and 1.45pm, daily. Marineland Melanesia is ⊙open 9.30am-4.30pm every day and costs adults ✪$8 and children $4.

Port Douglas

Population 1400

Location and Characteristics

The 83km (52 miles) drive north from Cairns to Port Douglas covers some of the most spectacular coastal strips and beaches in Australia. The Captain Cook Highway is wedged between towering, lush forest-covered mountains and the Coral Sea.

Situated 6km east of the highway, Port Douglas is one of the closest towns to the Great Barrier Reef. It has all the charm of a fishing port tastefully combined with modern tourism facilities.

The township was settled in 1877 as the main port for the Palmer River goldfields, and today it is a popular departure point for professional and amateur fishermen, for trips to the outer reef and islands, and for scuba diving and aquatic sports.

How to Get There

By Air

Sunlover Helicopters have transfer flights from Cairns Airport on arrangement, ©4035 9669. For details on Port Douglas airport services, make enquiries at the Information Centre, ©4099 5599.

By Coach

Coral Coaches, ©4099 5351, have a service to Port Douglas for ✪$25 one-way. Sun Palm Express, ©4099 4992, offer a return fare for $60.

By Road

Port Douglas is a short distance towards the coast from a signposted turn-off along the Bruce Highway.

Visitor Information

The Port Douglas Tourist Information Centre is in 23 Macrossan Street, ©4099 5599. The relevant website is ✪www.portdouglas.com and there is an email service at ✉reserv@great barrierreef.aus.net

Accommodation and Services

This place draws visitors like a magnet, but as long as you plan ahead there is little chance of you finding yourself without a bed in Port Douglas. Accommodation abounds, and all budgets are targeted. The area code is 07. Here is sample:

Sheraton Mirage Port Douglas, Port Douglas Road, ©4098 5885, www.sheraton-mirage.com. 297 rooms, luxurious facilities, beach frontage, licensed restaurant, golf course, spa, sauna, pool, gym, tennis - ✪$490-670 (3 suites - $1900-2100).

Balboa Apartments, 1 Garrick Street, ©4099 5222. 10 units, undercover parking, pool, spa - ✪$250-390.

Rydges Reef Resort, Port Douglas Road, ©4099 5577. 180 units, children's facilities, 2 licensed restaurants, playground, putting green, pool, tennis, gym - ✪$185-385.

Tropical Nites, 119 Davidson Street, ©4099 9666. 12 units, undercover parking, pool - ✪$110-170.

Port Douglas Tropic Sands, 21 Davidson Street, ©4099 4533. 14 units, pool, barbecue, secure parking - ✪$100-150.

Hibiscus Gardens, cnr Owen & Mowbray Streets, ©4099 5315. 34 units, undercover parking, barbecue, pool, spa - ✪$90-320.

Pelican Inn, 123 Davidson Street, ©4099 5266. 17 units, licensed restaurant (closed Sun), undercover parking, pool - ✪$100-120.

Coconut Grove, 58 Macrossan Street, ©4099 5124. 22 units, undercover parking, licensed restaurant, pool - ✪$85.

Caravan Parks

Glengarry Caravan Park, Mowbray River Road, ©4098 5922. 90 sites, barbecue, playground, pool - powered sites ✪$21 for two, cabins $70 for two.

Pandanus Van Park, 97-107 Davidson Street,

©4099 5944. 100 sites, pool, barbecue - powered sites ◕$19, cabins $55-75.

Eating Out

For Chinese dining, you can visit **Han Court**, 85 Davidson Street, ©4099 5007, or **Jade Inn**, 35 Macrossan Street, ©4099 5974. **Chief's**, 43 Macrossan Street, ©4099 4199, serves Mexican, while **Sardi's**, 123 Davidson Street, ©4099 5266, serves Italian cuisine and also has a bar.

Three other restaurants you may like to try are **Taste of Thailand**, 12 Macrossan Street, ©4399 4384, **Whispers**, 20 Langley Road, ©4099 3877 and **Nautilus**, 17 Murphy Street, ©4099 5330.

Points of Interest

Flagstaff Hill offers a great view over Four Mile Beach.

The **Rainforest Habitat** in Port Douglas Road, ©4099 3235, has over 300m of elevated walkways with thousands of butterflies, native birds, crocodiles, koalas and wallabies set among waterways and shaded tropical gardens. They have over 1,000 animals representing more than 140 species. *Breakfast With the Birds* and *The Koala Spot* are two popular attractions. The Habitat is ☉open daily from 8am-5.30pm, with admission prices at ◕$18 adults and $7 children.

Ben Cropp's Shipwreck Treasure Trove Museum, is located on Ben Cropp's Wharf, ©4099 5488, and houses nautical exhibits of historical significance, including Spanish galleons, a century-and-a-half-old wreck and a lost loot. It is ☉open daily 9am-5pm and admission is ◕$6 adults, $3 children.

The Bally Hooley Steam Express travels through Mossman and its countryside to the sugar mill. For more details, contact the Information Centre in Grant Street, ©4099 5051.

Tours and Cruises

Quicksilver Cruises offer voyages to Agincourt Reef on the Outer Barrier Reef, and to the Low Isles. Trips are made on a high-speed Wavepiercer Catamaran for the Outer Reef, on a Reef Platform for slow cruising and coral viewing, and on the 30m Wavedancer for sailing around the coral cays. Cruises depart Marina

Mirage at 10am daily. Outer Reef Cruises start from ◕$140 and include lunch, morning and afternoon tea, commentary, snorkelling equipment and coral viewing. Trips on the Wavedancer start from ◕$95. For information and bookings, ©4099 4455.

Quicksilver Connections also have day trip coach tours, including skyrail and cultural tours from ◕$40-85, ©4099 4455.

Helicopter flights with *Heli-Adventures* are available over reef and rainforest, and to golf courses and rafting expeditions, ©4034 9066.

A number of other tours may be taken from the town, including horsetrail riding (*Mowbray Valley Trails*, ©4099 3268) a regular catamaran service to Cooktown, rainforest hiking, 4WD safaris (*Australian Rainforest Safari*, ©4094 1388), coach trips and reef tours (*Synergy Reef Sailing*, ©4099 4696).

Mossman

Population 1850

Location and Characteristics

171km south of Cooktown and only 20km (12 miles) north of Port Douglas, Mossman is in the heart of the Mossman Valley. It is a sugar town surrounded by green mountains (highest is Mt Demi, 1159m-3802 ft) and fields of sugar cane. Mossman is fast becoming well-known as a centre for exotic tropical fruit growing, and a number of farms conduct tours and offer their products for sale.

How to Get There

By Air

Port Douglas has an airport, from which bus transfers can be arranged to Mossman. The Visitor Information Centre will assist you with arrangements, ©4099 5599.

By Bus

Coral Coaches, ©4098 2600, stop at Mossman on their Daintree route from Cairns.

By Road

The Bruce Highway passes through Mossman, about 75km north of Cairns.

Visitor Information

The Queensland National Parks and Wildlife Service has a branch at Mt Demi Plaza, on the corner of Front and Johnston Streets, ©4098 2188. They can assist you with local details and it should be your first stop if you wish to explore this area.

For more information, contact the Visitor Information Centre in Port Douglas (*see separate listing*).

Accommodation and Services

Here is a selection of accommodation. Prices are for a double room per night. Area code 07.

Demi View, 41 Front Street, ©4098 1277. 12 units, licensed restaurant, undercover parking, pool - ✪$75.

Silky Oaks Lodge, Finlayvale Road, Mossman River, ©4098 1666. 60 chalets, licensed restaurant, guided bushwalks, tennis, pool, breakfast included - ✪$430.

Caravan Parks

Mossman Bicentennial Caravan Park, Foxton Avenue, ©4098 2627. 43 sites, barbecue, standard facilities - powered sites ✪$12.

Eating Out

Three restaurants you might like to try are: **Chung Tai Chinese**, cnr Front Street & Johnston Road, ©4098 1102; **Jack High Bistro**, 6 Johnstone Road, ©4098 3166; and **Mojo's** 41 Front Street, ©4098 1202.

Points of Interest

The business centre of the Douglas Shire, Mossman has wide tree-lined streets, colourful gardens and a large sugar mill. Guided tours of the **Mossman Sugar Mill**, Mill Site, ©4098 1400, are conducted during the cane crushing season (June to December).

Australian Wilderness Safaris operate out of Finlayvale Road, Mossman, ©4098 1766.

A few minutes' drive from the township, a sealed road leads to the **Mossman Gorge** in Daintree National Park. This is a wilderness area of 56,000ha (138,320 acres), with crystal clear running streams, waterfalls, walking tracks through towering rainforest, barbecue picnic sites and a unique suspension bridge over a steep ravine.

Daintree and Cape Tribulation

Location and Characteristics

25km (16 miles) north of Mossman and about 146km (92 miles) south of Cooktown lies the township of Daintree, nestled in the heart of the Daintree River catchment basin, surrounded entirely by the rainforest-clad McDowall Ranges. The Daintree National Park lies to the west and Cape Tribulation National Park to the east; both have flourished largely unspoilt for millions of years. A World Heritage listing now ensures the continued preservation of this 17,000ha region.

The area has an abundance of native plant-life, birds and exotic tropical butterflies. Australia's prehistoric reptile, the estuarine crocodile, can be seen lurking in the mangrove-lined creeks and tributaries of the Daintree River.

Cape Tribulation, where the rainforest meets the reef, is an increasingly popular tourist area for both camping and day visits. Crystal clear creeks and forests festooned with creepers and vines, palm trees, orchids, butterflies and cassowaries, are part of the Cape Tribulation experience in one of the country's finest rainforest areas.

There are several resorts, hostels and camping grounds.

The atmosphere is relaxed and 'alternative' in this tropical rainforest retreat. It is a very popular haven for backpackers.

How to Get There

By Air

Daintree Air Services, ©4034 9300, operate from Cairns. In Cape Tribulation there is an airport at Cow Bay, serviced by Hinterland Aviation, ©4035 9323.

By Bus

Coral Coaches, ©4031 7577, can take you to Daintree for ✪$35 one way.

By Road

From Cairns, simply follow the Bruce Highway

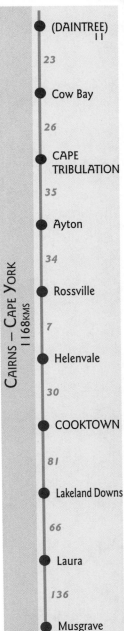

Cairns to Cape York

CAIRNS – CAPE YORK 1168KMS

- (DAINTREE) 11
- 23
- Cow Bay
- 26
- CAPE TRIBULATION
- 35
- Ayton
- 34
- Rossville
- 7
- Helenvale
- 30
- COOKTOWN
- 81
- Lakeland Downs
- 66
- Laura
- 136
- Musgrave

Four-wheel driving in the Daintree

north until it terminates at Daintree. Coming south from Cooktown, take the coastal road until it connects (and ends) with the Bruce Highway, then travel in a north-westerly direction for about 10km (6 miles) along the highway to Daintree. A vehicle ferry will take you across the Daintree River into Cape Tribulation.

It should be noted that caution must be exercised if driving a conventional vehicle, even one with high clearance, and during and after rain a 4WD vehicle is essential. The 32km narrow, unsealed Cape Tribulation/Bloomfield Road is recommended for 4WD only, and towing caravans should not be attempted.

Visitor Information

The Daintree Tourist Information Centre is in 5 Stewart Street, ©4098 6120. The Great Barrier Reef website has a section on Daintree at ☞www. greatbarrierreef.aus.net as does Tourism Tropical North Queensland at ☞www.tnq.org.au

Accommodation and Services

Accommodation is not abundant in the Daintree area, so it is advisable to book well in advance. Prices are for a double room per night. Area code 07.

Daintree Eco Lodge, Daintree Road, Daintree, ©4098 6100, www.daintree-ecolodge.com.au. 30 units, licensed restaurant, heated pool - ✪$435.

Bloomfield Wilderness Lodge, Weary Bay, Daintree National Park, ©4035 9166. 16 cabins, licensed restaurant, barbecue, pool, extensive package deals included in tariff, guided rainforest walks, Bloomfield River Cruise, all meals - ✪$from 210 per person.

There are also camping facilities for $20 per double per night.

Daintree Manor, 27 Forest Creek Road, North Daintree, ©4090 7041. 3 rooms, basic facilities - ✪$100.

Caravan Park

Daintree Riverview Caravan Park, 2 Stewart Street, ©4098 6119. 26 sites, basic facilities - ✪$15 powered sites, $35 on-site vans.

Lync Haven Rainforest Retreat, Cape Tribulation Rd, Alexander Bay, ©4098 9155. 31 sites, limited facilities - powered sites ✪$16, cabins $110. There is a **Youth Hostel** at Cape Tribulation, **Crocodylus Village**, Lot 5, Buchanan Creek Road, Cow Bay, ©4098 9166. There are 8 twin share rooms at ✪$37 per person per night.

Eating Out

If you plan to eat out, a selection of restaurants includes the **Big Barrumundi Barbecue Garden**, 12 Stewart Street, ©4098 6186; **Daintree Village**, 3 Stewart Street, ©4098 6173; and **Jacanas**, 1 Stewart Street, ©4098 6146.

Points of Interest

The township has art and craft centres, and the **Daintree Timber Museum & Gallery**, 12 Stewart Drive, ©4098 6166. The real attraction, however, is the National Park itself.

Given the majestic quality of the natural environment, the emphasis here is on eco-touring.

Several cruises operate on the Daintree River offering passengers a leisurely tour observing the beauty of the river and rainforest, and enjoying morning or afternoon tea. A few available are:
Daintree Dancer Sailing and River Cruises, Daintree Public Jetty, ©4098 7960;
Daintree Lady Cruise, 13-15 Osborne Street, ©4098 6138;
Electric Boat Cruises, Daintree Road, ©4098 6103;
Daintree Rainforest River Train, Bailey Creek Road, ©4090 7676.

There is a *Daintree Wildlife Safari* for the more adventurous explorers. They are located at 12 Stewart Street, ©4098 6125.

Adventure Connections, Clifton Beach, ©4059 1599, operate small tours that are designed to foster education and appreciation of the natural environment and its wildlife. They are run by people with botanical and zoological backgrounds who know what they are talking about. Prices start from ✪$110 per person. Nocturnal tours are also conducted for those who are interested.

The *Daintree River Ferry*, ©4098 7788, which operates daily, takes visitors into the world of wilderness and rainforest at Cape Tribulation and beyond.

The famous **"bouncing stones"** are just north of Thornton's Beach.

Cooktown

Population 1300
Location and Characteristics
Cooktown is 246km north of Cairns. Its close proximity to Aboriginal culture, diverse wildlife, rainforests, unique land formations and extensive surrounding savannah, means that it can be described as the geographical intersection of Reef and Outback. The town is clustered on the banks of the scenic Endeavour River.

Cooktown is etched in history, drawn from the early days of its Aboriginal inhabitants, to Captain Cook's forced landing, to gold rush times and the adventures of subsequent pioneers and explorers.

How to Get There
By Air
A flight to Cooktown takes just over half an hour from Cairns Airport. Transtate, ©13 1528, runs this service.
By Coach
Coral Coaches run from Cairns as far north as Cooktown, ©4031 7577.
By Car
From Cairns there are two options:

The direct route which follows the Bruce Highway (becomes the Captain Cook Highway out of Cairns) towards Mossman and Daintree, then turns right onto the signposted coastal road that passes Wujal Wujal, Rossville and Helensvale to Cooktown. Note that between Cape Tribulation and Helensvale the road is recommended for 4WD vehicles only.

Or you can take the winding inland route along part of the Peninsula Development Road, then turn right at Lakesland onto the connecting road which joins the coast road just north of Helenvale, then continue directly to Cooktown.

Visitor Information
The Cooktown Tourism Association can be contacted on ©4069 6100 or ©1800 001 770. They have a website at ☞www.cooktownau.com and their email address is ✉info@cooktownau.com

Accommodation and Services
There are sufficient motels, guest houses and caravan parks to accommodate a short stay. Following is a list of suggestions to give you an idea of what is on offer, with prices for a double room per night. Area code 07.

The Sovereign Resort, cnr Charlotte & Green Streets, ©4069 5400. 26 rooms, 3 suites, licensed restaurant, pool - ✪$110-135.

Seagrens Inn, 12 Charlotte Street, ©4069 5357. 7 units, licensed restaurant, pool, wonderful beach and river views - ✪$50-70.

Milkwood Lodge Rainforest Cabins, Annan Road, ©4069 5007. 6 cabins, good facilities - ✪$100.

Caravan Park
Cooktown Tropical Breeze Caravan Park, cnr Charlotte Street & McIvor Road, ©4069 5417. 45 sites, barbecue and pool - ✪$17 powered sites, $55-80 cabins.

There is a **Youth Hostel** on the corner of Boundary and Charlotte Streets, *Pam's Place*, ©4069 5166. It has 13 twin share rooms at ✪$25 per person per night.

Eating Out
If you plan to dine out, the **Burragi Floating Restaurant**, in Webber Esplanade, is recommended, ©4069 5956.

Points of Interest

Apart from the picturesque surrounds, it is worth exploring the historical buildings in Cooktown, including the old Post Office, Westpac Bank and the Sovereign Hotel. The **James Cook Historical Museum** is in Helen Street, ✆4069 5386. Cook's Monument, The Cannon, Grassy Hill and the Chinese Graveyard are additonal points of interest.

Cooktown Tours, ✆4069 5125, will take you by coach on a two-hour guided historical tour of the city for ✪$18 adults, $12 children, departing at 9am. Additional tours to nearby regions of natural or cultural interest are available:

Black Mountains & Lion's Den Tour, 4hrs, 9am departure, ✪$50 adults, $25 children.

Elim Beach and Coloured Sands, 5hrs, 9am departure, ✪$80 adults, $55 children.

Laura Aboriginal Rock Art Site & Lakefield National Park, 8hrs, 9am departure, ✪$110 adults, $80 children.

You can explore the coastal waters with *Cooktown Reef Charters*, ✆4069 5519.

Lizard Island

Location and Characteristics

With an international reputation as the place for big game fishing, Lizard Island is 97km (60 miles) north-east of Cooktown and is basically a 1000ha National Park boasting pristine natural beauty. It has an area of 21 sq km, and is the most northerly of the Barrier Reef resort islands. It is 240km from Cairns, but close to the outer Barrier Reef, and has 23 beaches that are good for swimming and snorkelling.

Captain Cook and Dr Joseph Banks landed on Lizard Island, after they had repaired the *Endeavour* at what is now Cooktown. They named it after the many large lizards they found there.

Shell middens found around the island testify to the fact that Aborigines had made it their home, and it is thought that parts of the island had some sacred meaning for them. This is given as the possible reason for the tragedy that occurred in the early 1880s. Robert and Mary Watson lived on the island and collected bechedemer (sea slugs), a Chinese delicacy. Robert left

Mary and her baby in the company of two Chinese servants while he went off in search of new fishing grounds. Whilst he was away some Aborigines arrived on the island and killed one servant and wounded the other. Mary decided to leave the island, so she loaded the baby and the remaining servant into an iron tank and set off for the mainland. They never made it, and their bodies were discovered some months later on one of the Howick islands.

It is thought that inadvertently the Watsons may have interfered with an Aboriginal sacred site, thus causing the attack. The ruins of the Watson's house can still be seen, near the top of Cook's Look.

Lizard has over 1000ha of National Park, and some good walks. The climb to the top of Cook's Look is the most popular, and is well signposted, and from the Resort it is a short walk to the ruins of the Watson's house. The waters around the island are home to coral reefs and countless tropical fish, including the renowned Black Marlin. From August to November it attracts fishermen worldwide.

Cooktown to Cape York

How to Get There

The Island is very remote and exclusive, with access only via a scenic air one-hour flight from Cairns Airport. You can make arrangements when booking accommodation.

There are no regular ferry or boat services to Lizard Island, but it is included as a destination in some of the cruises run by Captain Cook Cruises, ☎4031 4433.

Visitor Information

You can explore the website at ☞www.lizard islandresort.com or email them at ✎visitors@ greatbarrierreef.aus.net

The resort itself has all the facilities and information you require, so it is best to contact them directly with any queries.

Accommodation and Services

Accommodation is available in 40 well-appointed units facing the beach at the *Lizard Island Resort*, ☎07 4060 3999. Tariffs start from ✪$600 twin share per person per night in the Anchor Bay Rooms, to $800 for the Premium Sunset Point Villas. Enquire also about package deals on offer at the time of your trip.

The room facilities consist of a private bathroom, refrigerator, mini-bar, air-conditioning, IDD/STD telephone, ironing facilities, daily cleaning service, writing desk and private verandah. The deluxe suites have a separate living area.

The above rates include all meals and free use of snorkelling gear, water skiing, tennis, surf skis, windsurfers, catamarans, basic fishing gear and outboard dinghies. Not included in the rates are game fishing boats and dive facilities.

The standard and array of food in the restaurant is excellent, and the cost is included in the room tariff.

Note that children under 6 years of age are not catered for, but alternative arrangements may be made at the resort's discretion.

Camping is also available at Watson's Bay, by

application and with a permit. Facilities include toilets, drinking water, barbecues and picnic tables. Contact the National Parks and Wildlife Service in Cairns, ©4052 3096, for more information.

Points of Interest

The resort has a swimming pool, tennis court, a club-like lounge, a boutique, a small shop and a bar with a recorded history of the island's biggest catches.

The focus, however, is on getting wet, and there is a superb coral lagoon, shady white beaches (24 in total), good scuba diving areas, boating facilities and fishing opportunites. Available are paddle skis, outboard dinghies, catamarans, sailboards, snorkelling equipment, Outer Barrier Reef trips, eco tours, basic fishing gear, glass-bottom boat trips, scuba diving/training, waterskiis, boats and game fishing charters.

Diving

Some believe that Lizard Island has the best diving along the Great Barrier Reef, and in fact it is surrounded by excellent coral reefs.

The Ribbon Reefs lie only a 20 minute boat ride from the island. These are comprised of a string of ten coral ramparts that support an immense undersea world of living coral and sea animals, and the most spectacular underwater scenery. All the Ribbon Reefs are great, but following are a few highlights:

The Code Hole is world renowned and very popular. It is at the northern tip of Reef No. 10, and divers can hand feed giant Potato Cod, some over 2.5m in length.

Pixie Pinnacle is a coral bommie on the southern end of Reef No. 10. Here divers will find species of pelagic fish, black coral, and a host of tropical fish.

Dynamite Pass is a narrow area of water just north of Ribbon Reef No. 10. the depths range is from 4m to 40m below the surface, but visibility is about 30m and there is plenty to see.

Detached Reefs are located in the Coral Sea half-way between Cooktown and Cape York. Both reefs extend from a metre or so under the surface to the seabed some 500m below. This is sheer wall diving at its best with visibility extending more than 40m. Expect to see giant sponges, sea whips, Angelfish, Clownfish, Manta Rays, sharks and varieties of coral.

Cape York

Location and Characteristics

This remote mainland spur is Australia's northernmost tip, 2753km north of Brisbane. Like an outstretched finger the peninsula points towards the south coast of Papua New Guinea, just over 100km away on the other side of the Torres Strait. The Jardine National Park hugs the eastern portion of the Peninsula about 50km south of the Cape.

How to Get There

By Air

Qantas, ©13 1313, fly to Thursday Island, which is a short distance north-west of Cape York. Cape York Air Services, ©4035 9399, operate out of Cairns Airport.

By Car

From Cairns, the most direct route is by 4WD only via the Peninsula Development Road which cuts through the eastern side of the peninsula to Cape York. The journey is 861km on the direct route and 1062km if you weave through the National Parks. Road conditions vary with each Wet season, so it is essential that you check current road integrity with the Visitor Information Centre in Cairns, ©4031 4355, or visit the relevant web pages listed in the *Tourist Information* chapter.

Visitor Information

For a preliminary look, the web pages to explore are ☞www.tnq.org.au and ☞www.visitcape york.com

Additional information can be obtained from the Cooktown Tourism Association, ©4069 6100 or ©1800 001 770. Their email address is ✉info@cooktownau.com

Cape York swampland

Accommodation and Services

Accommodation is varied but limited. Area code 07. Here are a few examples:

The *Pajinka Wilderness Lodge* is only 400m south of Cape York, ©4031 3988. They have 24 units, resort facilities, a licensed restaurant and a pool - ✪$460-500 for two, for a three night minimum stay with all meals included.

You can camp in Bamaga, 30km south of the Cape, at the **Seisia Village Campground**, Koroba Road, ©4069 3243. It has 42 powered sites, a barbecue and an unlicensed restaurant open Mon-Sat - ✪$18 a double per night.

If neither of the above appeals, try the **Seisa Seaview Lodge**, also in Koroba Road, ©4069 3243. It has 6 lodges, good facilities, an unlicensed restaurant, horse riding and a pool - ✪$105 a double per night.

Points of Interest

Crocodile farming at the **Edward River Crocodile Farm,** ©4060 4177; pearl farming; black boar hunting; barramundi fishing, ©4031 3988; and Aboriginal Corroborees at **Bamaga Mission**, are just a few of the unique attractions Cape York has to offer.

Tours and Cruises

Last Frontier Safaris offer 1, 2 or 4 day wild pig hunts, so if this appeals to you, ©4098 8264.

Several cruises sailing to Cape York and the Torres Strait are available, and this is probably the best way to visit this remote region if you are not the rugged, adventurous type. *Kangaroo Explorer Cruises*, 2 Reservoir Road, Manunda, ©4032 4000, sail from Cairns to Thursday Island, or vice versa, and offer 4-7 day cruises starting from ✪$984 including airfares to departure points and all meals.

In Cape York, the Pajinka Wilderness Lodge runs a number of tours, *Pajinka Pastimes*, which include 4WD safaris, fishing trips, bridwatching, wilderness walks and self-guided tours, ranging from ✪$15 to $60, ©4031 3988.

From Cairns, *Quinkan Country Adventures*, 13 Shields Street, Cairns, ©4051 4777, operate tours to Aboriginal Rock Art sites in the Laura River Valley.

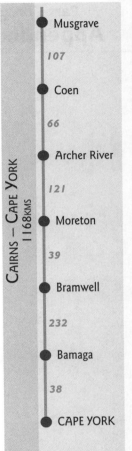

Cairns to Cape York

CAIRNS – CAPE YORK
1168KMS

Musgrave

107

Coen

66

Archer River

121

Moreton

39

Bramwell

232

Bamaga

38

CAPE YORK

Appendix

Part Three
Appendix

INTERNET INFORMATION

International Airlines

Air New Zealand
👁 www.airnz.com.au
✎ email service under *Contact Us* then *Online Booking Enquiries*
✆ 13 24 76

Ansett
👁 www.ansett.com.au
✎ email service under *About Ansett* then *Contacts*
✆ 13 13 00

British Airways
👁 www.british-airways.com
✆ 8904 8800

Canadian Airlines
👁 www.cdnair.ca
✎ comments@cdnair.ca
✆ 1300 655 767

Cathay Pacific
👁 www.cathaypacific.com/australia
✎ email service under *Feedback*
✆ 13 17 47

Qantas
👁 www.qantas.com.au
✎ email service under *Contacts* then *Enquiries and Feedback*
✆ 13 13 13

Singapore Airlines
👁 www.singaporeair.com.au
✎ info_syd@singaporeair.com.au
✆ 13 10 11

United Airlines
👁 www.unitedairlines.com
✎ email service under *Contact United*
✆ 13 17 77

Domestic Airlines

Airlink
👁 www.qantas.com.au/flights/regional/airlink.html
✆ 13 13 13

Ansett
👁 www.ansett.com.au
✎ email service under *About Ansett* then *Contacts*
✆ 13 13 00

Eastern Australia Airlines
👁 www.qantas.com.au/flights/regional/eastern.html
✆ 13 13 13

Flight West
👁 www.flightwest.com.au
✎ flightwest@fltwest.com.au
✆ 1300 130 092

Hazelton
👁 www.hazelton.com.au
✎ email service under *Customer Feedback*
✆ 13 17 13

Impulse Airlines
👁 www.impulseairlines.com.au
✆ 13 13 81

Kendell
👁 www.kendell.com.au
✎ kendell@kendell.com.au
✆ (03) 9670 2677

Qantas
👁 www.qantas.com.au
✎ email service under *Contacts* then *Enquiries and Feedback*
✆ 13 13 13

Sunstate
👁 www.qantas.com.au/flights/regional/sunstate.html
✆ 13 13 13

Virgin Blue
👁www.virginblue.com.au
✆13 6789

Inter- and Intrastate Rail Services

Countrylink
👁www.countrylink.nsw.gov.au
✉bookings@countrylink.nsw.gov.au
✆13 22 32
Great Southern Railway
👁www.gsr.com.au
✉salesagent@gsr.com.au
✆13 21 47
Queensland Rail Traveltrain
👁qroti.bit.net.au/traveltrain
✉qroti@proceed.com.au or
✉res.traveltrain@qr.com.au
✆13 2232
Rail Australia
👁www.railaustralia.com.au
✉info@railaustralia.com.au

Interstate Coach Services

Greyhound Pioneer
👁www.greyhound.com.au
✉express@greyhound.com.au
✆13 20 30
McCaffertys
👁www.mccaffertys.com.au
✉infomcc@mccaffertys.com.au
✆13 14 99

Overseas Visitors Information

Australian Tourist Commission
👁www.australia.com
✉email service under *Ask Us*
✆1300 361 650
Australian Quarantine
👁 www.aqis.gov.au
✆1800 020 504
Customs Australia
👁www.customs.gov.au
✆1300 363 263

Foreign Currency Exchange
👁www.xe.net/ucc
Telephone Numbers
👁www.whitepages.com.au
👁www.yellowpages.com.au
👁www.colourpages.com.au
✆1223

Visitor Information - Australia

Australian Tourist Commission
👁www.australia.com
✉email service under *Contact Us*
✆1300 361 650

Visitor Information - Queensland

General
Environmental Protection Agency
👁www.env.qld.gov.au
✆(07) 3224 5641
Naturally Queensland
👁www.env.qld.gov.au/environment/feature/nqic
✉nqic@env.qld.gov.au
✆(07) 3227 8187
Queensland Government
👁www.qld.gov.au
✆1800 803 788
Queensland Holidays
👁www.queensland-holidays.com.au
Tourism Queensland
👁www.qttc.com.au
or 👁www.tq.com.au
✉qttcinfo@qttc.com.au
✆(07) 3406 5400
Brisbane
Brisbane Local Coucil
👁www.brisbane.qld.gov.au
Brisbane Tourism
👁www.brisbanetourism.com.au
✉enquiries@brisbanetourism.com.au
✆(07) 3221 8411
Transinfo
👁www.transinfo.qld.gov.au
✆13 1230

Regional
Airlie Tourist Information Centre
✉ abtic@whitsunday.net.au
☎ (07) 4946 6665

Bedarra Island Resort
🌐 www.bedarraisland.com
✉ visitors@greatbarrierreef.aus.net
☎ (07) 4068 8233

Brampton Island Resort
🌐 www.bramptonislandresort.com
☎ 4951 4097

Caloundra City Information Centre
🌐 www.caloundra.qld.gov.au
✉ c.stewart@caloundra.qld.gov.au
☎ (07) 5491 0202

Cape York Tourist Info
🌐 www.visitcapeyork.com

Capricorn Coast Tourist Organisation
🌐 www.capricorncoast.com.au
✉ capcoast@cqnet.com.au
☎ (07) 4939 4888

Capricorn Tourism
🌐 www.capricorncoast.com.au
✉ captour@rocknet.net.au
☎ (07) 4927 2055

Central Highlands Tourism Queensland
🌐 members.tripod.com/centralhighlands/
✉ chtour@maxspeed.net.au
☎ (07) 4982 4386

Charters Towers Dalrymple Tourist
Information Centre
✉ tourinfocentre@httech.com.au
☎ (07) 4752 0314

Club Crocodile Resort Long Island
🌐 www.clubcrocodile.com.au
☎ (07) 4946 9233

Club Med Lindeman Island
🌐 www.clubmed.com.au
☎ (07) 4946 9633

Cooktown Tourism Association
🌐 www.cooktownau.com
✉ info@cooktownau.com
☎ 1800 001 770

Daintree Tourist Information
🌐 www.greatbarrierreef.aus.net
or 🌐 www.tnq.org.au

☎ (07) 4098 6120

Daydream Island Resort
🌐 www.daydream.net.au
☎ 1800 075 040

Development Bureau of Hinchinbrook &
Cardwell Shires
🌐 www.hinchinbrookferries.com.au
☎ (07) 4776 5381

Dunk Island Resort
🌐 www.dunkislandresort.com
✉ visitors@greatbarrierreef.aus.net
☎ (07) 4068 8199

Fitzroy Island Resort
🌐 www.great-barrier-reef.com/fitzroy
☎ 1800 079 080

Fraser Coast Tourism
🌐 www.frasercoast.org
✉ info@frasercoast.org
☎ (07) 4122 3444

Gladstone Area Promotion and
Development Bureau
🌐 www.gladstoneregion.com
✉ gapdl@gladstoneregion.org.au
☎ (07) 4972 4000

Gold Coast Tourism
🌐 www.goldcoasttourism.com.au
✉ info@gctb.com.au
☎ (07) 5592 2699

Great Barrier Reef Visitors Bureau
🌐 www.greatbarrierreef.aus.net
✉ visitors@greatbarrierreef.aus.net
☎ (07) 4099 4644

Great Barrier Reef Marine Park Authority
🌐 www.gbrmpa.gov.au
☎ (07) 4750 0700

Great Keppel Island Resort
🌐 www.mpx.com.au/~adventures/gk/keppel.htm
☎ (07) 4939 5044

Green Island Resort
🌐 www.greenislandresort.com.au
✉ res@greenislandresort.com.au
☎ (07) 4031 3300

Hamilton Island Resort
🌐 www.hamiltonisland.com.au
☎ 1800 075 110

Hayman Island Resort
👁www.hayman.com.au
✆(07) 4946 1234
Heron Island Resort
👁www.heronisland.com
✉visitors@greatbarrierreef.aus.net
✆132 469.
Hook Island Resort
👁www.hookislandresort.com.au
✉enquiries@hookis.com
✆(07) 4946 9380
Lady Elliot Island
👁www.ladyelliot.com.au
✉info@ladyelliot.com.au
✆1800 072 200
Lizard Island Resort
👁www.lizardislandresort.com
✉visitors@greatbarrierreef.net.au
✆(07) 4060 3999
Mackay Tourism and Development Bureau
✉mtdb@mackay.net.au
✆(07) 4952 2677,
Magnetic Island Tourist Information Bureau
👁www.magnetic-island.com.au
✆(07) 4778 5596
Maroochy Tourism
👁www.maroochytourism.com
✉admin@maroochytourism.com
✆(07) 5479 1566
Mission Beach Visitor Information Centre
✉visitors@znet.net.au
✆(07) 4068 7066
Noosa Information Centre
👁www.tourismnoosa.com.au
✉info@tourismnoosa.com.au
✆(07) 5447 4988
Orpheus Island Resort
👁www.orpheusisland.com
✉reserv@greatbarrierreef.aus.net
✆(07) 4777 7377
Port Douglas Tourist Information Centre
👁www.portdouglas.com
✉reserv@greatbarrierreef.aus.net
✆(07) 4099 5599
Sunshine Coast Tourism
👁www.sunzine.net/suncoast/tsc/index.html

✉tourism@sunzine.net
✆(07) 5477 7311
South Molle Island Resort
👁www.southmolleisland.com.au
✉info@southmolleisland.com.au
✆(07) 4946 9433
Stradbroke Island Tourism
✉redlandstourism@redlands.net.au
✆(07) 3409 9555
Tourism Tropical North Queensland
👁www.tnq.org.au
✉ttnq@tnq.org.au
✆(07) 4051 3588
Trinity Beach
👁www.trinitybeach.com
✉info@trinitybeach.com
Tropical Tableland Promotion Bureau
👁www.athertontableland.com
✉info@athertontableland.com
✆4091 4222
Whitsunday Visitors and Convention Bureau
👁www.whitsundayinformation.com.au
or 👁www.whitsunday.net.au
✉tw@whitsundayinformation.com.au
✆(07) 4946 6673
Yorkeys Knob
👁www.yorkeysknob.com
✉hmbr@internetnorth.com.au

General
Tourism New South Wales
👁www.tourism.nsw.gov.au
✉visitmail@tourism.nsw.gov.au
✆9931 1111
Sydney
Darling Harbour Tourism
👁www.darlingharbour.com.au
✆(02) 9286 0111 or 1902 260 568
CityRail
👁www.cityrail.nsw.gov.au
✉ysl@stellarcallcentres.com.au

☎131 500
Manly Council
👁www.manly.nsw.gov.au
✎vic@manly.nsw.gov.au
☎(02) 9977 1088
Manly Tourism
👁www.pcn.com.au
State Transit
👁www.sydneybuses.nsw.gov.au
✎info@sydneybuses.nsw.gov.au
☎131 500
Sydney City Local Government
👁www.cityofsydney.nsw.gov.au
✎jsmithers@cityofsydney.nsw.gov.au
☎(02) 9265 9653
Sydney City Search
👁www.sydney.citysearch.com.au
Sydney Sidewalk
👁www.sydney.sidewalk.com.au
Regional
Ballina Visitor Information
✎balinfo@balshire.org.au
☎(02) 6686 3484
Barrington Tops Information
👁www.barringtons.com.au
Blue Mountains Tourism
👁www.bluemountainstourism.org.au
✎info@bluemountainstourism.org.au
☎1300 653 408
Brunswick Heads
👁www.tropicalnsw.com.au/brunswickheads
☎(02) 6685 1385
Byron Bay Visitor Information
👁www.byronbayvbo.com
☎(02) 6685 8050
Central Coast Tourism
👁www.cctourism.com.au
✎thecoast@cctourism.com.au
☎(02) 4385 4430 or 1800 806 258
Cessnock Visitor Information
👁www.winecountry.com.au
✎info@winecountry.com.au
Coffs Harbour-Tourism Holiday Coast
👁www.coffs.net
✎tourism@coffscoast.com.au
☎1300 369 070

Dungog Visitor Information
✎dungogvc@midac.com.au
☎(02) 4992 2212
Eurobodalla Visitor Information
👁www.naturecoast-tourism.com.au
✎info@naturecoast-tourism.com.au
☎1800 802 528
Gloucester Visitor Information
✎glosinfo@tpg.com.au
☎(02) 6558 1408
Grafton
👁www.nnsw.com/grafton
☎(02) 6642 4277
Great Lakes Visitor Centre
👁www.greatlakes.org.au
✎tourglc@tpgi.com.au
☎1800 802 692
Hunter Regional Tourism Organisation
👁www.huntertourism.com/Online/home/main.html
✎huntertourism@bigpond.com
☎(02) 4929 1900
Kempsey Visitor Information
✎ktic@midcoast.com.au
☎1800 642 480
Kiama Tourism
👁www.kiama.com.au
✎kiamatourism@ozemail.com.au
☎(02) 4232 3322 or 1300 654 262
Lake Macqurie Tourism
👁www.infohunt.nsw.gov.au/lakemac
✎tourism@lakemac.nsw.gov.au
☎(02) 4972 1172
Lismore City
👁www.liscity.nsw.gov.au
✎tourism@liscity.gov.nsw.au
☎1300 369 795
Maitland Information Centre
👁www.maitlandtourism.nsw.gov.au
✎maitland.tourism@maitland.nsw.gov.au
☎(02) 4933 2611
Manning Valley Visitor Information
www.gtcc.nsw.gov.au/tourism
manningvic@gttc.nsw.gov.au
☎1800 801 522

Musswellbrook Visitor Information
👁www.muswellbrook.org.au
✆(02) 6541 4050
Narooma Visitor Information
✉eurovcn@acr.net.au
✆1800 802 528
Newcastle Tourism
👁www.ncc.nsw.gov.au
✉newtour@hunterlink.net.au or
mail@ncc.nsw.gov.au
✆(02) 4974 2999 or 1800 654 558
Port Macquarie Visitor Information
👁www.portmacquarieinfo.com.au
✉vicpm@midcoast.com.au
✆1800 025 935
Port Stephens Visitor Information
👁www.portstephens.org.au
✉tops@hunterlink.net.au
✆(02) 4981 1579 or 1800 808 900
Queanbeyan Visitor Information
👁www.queanbeyan.nsw.gov.au
✉tourist@qcc.nsw.gov.au
✆1800 026 192
Sapphire Coast Tourism
👁www.sapphirecoast.com.au
Scone Visitor Information
✉stic@scone.nsw.gov.au
✆(02) 6545 1526
Shellharbour Visitor Information
👁www.shellharbour.nsw.gov.au
✉tourism@shellharbour.nsw.gov.au
✆(02) 4221 6169
Shoalhaven Visitor Information
👁www.shoalhaven.nsw.gov.au
✉beverlyc@shoalhaven.nsw.gov.au
✆1800 024 261
Singleton Visitor Information
👁www.singleton.nsw.gov.au
✉ssc@singletoncouncil.nsw.gov.au
✆(02) 6578 7267
Southern Highlands Tourism
👁wingtour@wsc.com.au
✆(02) 4871 2888
Tourism Lake Macquarie
👁www.infohunt.nsw.gov.au/lakemac
✉tourism@lakemac.nsw.gov.au

✆(02) 4972 1172 or 1800 802 044
Tweed Heads Visitor Information
👁www.tactic.nsw.gov.au
✉info@tactic.nsw.gov.au
✆1800 674 414
Wine Country Visitor Information
👁www.winecountry.com.au
✉info@winecountry.com.au
✆(02) 4990 4477
Wollongong Tourism
👁www.wollongong.nsw.gov.au
✉tourism@wollongong.nsw.gov.au
✆(02) 4277 5545 or 1800 240 737

Visitor Information - Australian Capital Territory

Canberra
Canberra Visitor Information
👁www.canberratourism.com.au
✉canberravisitorcentre@msn.com.au
✆1800 100 660
Canberra City Search
👁canberra.citysearch.com.au
Action Buses
👁www.action.act.gov.au
✆13 17 10

Visitor Information - Victoria

General
V/Line
👁www.vline.vic.gov.au
✆13 61 96
Victoria Visitor Information Centre
✉melbourne@vic.gov.au
✆(03) 9658 9955
Victorian Tourism Operators Association
✉vtoa@vtoa.asn.au
✆(03) 9614 8877
Victrip
👁www.victrip.com.au
✉feedback@victrip.com.au
✆13 13 68

Tourism Victoria
👁www.tourism.vic.gov.au
✆13 28 42
Melbourne
City of Melbourne
👁www.melbourne.org
✆9658 9955
Melbourne City Search
👁melbourne.citysearch.com
Metropolitan Public Transport
👁www.met.vic.gov.au
Regional
Bairnsdale Visitor Information
👁bairnsdale@lakesandwilderness.com.au
✆(03) 5152 3444
Gippsland Tourism
👁www.gippslandtourism.com.au
👁information@gippslandtourism.com.au
Great Ocean Road Information
👁www.greatoceanrd.org.au
Lakes Entrance Visitor Information
👁www.lakesandwilderness.com.au
✉lakes@lakesandwilderness.com.au

✆(03) 5155 1966
Lorne Visitor Information
👁www.surfcoast.vic.gov.au
✉lornevic@primus.com.au
✆(03) 5289 1152
Phillip Island Visitor Information
👁www.phillipisland.net.au
✉info@phillipisland.net.au
✆1300 366 422
Penguin Parade Visitor Centre
👁www.penguins.org.au
✆(03) 5956 8300
Snowy River Visitor Centre
✉orbost@lakesandwilderness.com.au
✆(03) 5154 2424
Warrnambool Visitor Information
👁www.warrnambool.org
✆(03) 5564 7837

Independent Traveller Information

Youth Hostels Association Australia
👁www.yha.com.au
✉yha@nswyha.com.au
✆(02) 9261 1111

Budget Form

This budget form will help you budget your road trip.

Trip Description:		
Basic Distance:		km
Side Trips, etc. (allow 10%):		km
Additional Distances:		km
Total Distance:		km

TOWN	Distance	Fuel	Car Service	Accomm.	Food	Fees, Charges	Other Expenses
TOTAL							
GRAND TOTAL =							

NOTES:

Budget Form

This budget form will help you budget your road trip.

Trip Description:	
Basic Distance:	km
Side Trips, etc. (allow 10%):	km
Additional Distances:	km
Total Distance:	km

TOWN	Distance	Fuel	Car Service	Accomm.	Food	Fees, Charges	Other Expenses
TOTAL							

GRAND TOTAL =

NOTES:

Trip Log

List your expenditures here.

Date	Town	Speedo	Fuel $	Accom $	Meals $	Other Expenses $
	TOTALS=					

Photo Log

Roll 1	Roll 2	Roll 3
1	1	1
2	2	2
3	3	3
4	4	4
5	5	5
6	6	6
7	7	7
8	8	8
9	9	9
10	10	10
11	11	11
12	12	12
13	13	13
14	14	14
15	15	15
16	16	16
17	17	17
18	18	18
19	19	19
20	20	20
21	21	21
22	22	22
23	23	23
24	24	24
25	25	25
26	26	26
27	27	27
28	28	28
29	29	29
30	30	30
31	31	31
32	32	32
33	33	33
34	34	34
35	35	35
36	36	36

Index

Index

Index

Maps

Strip Maps

The perfect driving guide companion to **Doing the Coast...**

Australian Road Trips
35 Complete Holiday Drives Around Australia

35 easy-to-follow road trips take you on some of the most scenic drives around the country.

All the information you require about where to go, what to see, what to do, what to take and how to get there, developed for the average traveller.

Many peope have thought about taking an Australian road trip, but most aren't sure where to start. Other travel guides give information on towns and national parks, but fall short of detailing how to get there, while street directories show you the way but don't tell you why to go. **Australian Road Trips** is a comprehensive combination of the two. It's aimed at the average traveller who has little or no knowledge of extended touring by car, and who doesn't necessarily have a 4WD sitting in his or her driveway. The 35 road trips have been carefully selected to ensure that traveller's experience the true Australia, and most are suitable for conventional vehicles.

The author draws on his years of travel experience to give you a complete holiday package. All the trips have been laid out in an easy-to-read, step-by-step design, accompanied by detailed text on why the trip is worth doing, what you'll see on the way, where to stop overnight, how far you have to go and how long it will take. Other guides expect you to map out your trip, but **Australian Road Trips** does it for you, taking the major hassle – and the biggest obstacle to actually going – out of the planning stage. All the road trips interconnect, giving you the flexibility of deciding which path you want to take to your destination, or, if you have the time, on a loop around Australia by coast or through the centre. There are also side trips en route for the adventurous.

Australian Road Trips takes you out of the 'comfort zone' and into the inland areas, and the less-populated places of the north, south, west and upper-east coast. Spectacular routes take you through the Barossa Valley, Margaret River, along the Great Ocean Road, up to Cape York, into Uluru-Kata Tjuta National Park, Kakadu, the Kimberley, around Tasmania, and through hundreds of towns and countless scenic landscapes.

Australian Road Trips is everything you need to explore the continent. So you don't have to put if off any longer.

By Ian Read • 190 x 220mm • 432 pages • paperback with flaps • 2-colour text • 2-colour maps throughout •
Little Hills Press • ISBN 1 86315 169 9 • $34.95rrp

Trip Notes

Trip Notes

Trip Notes

Trip Notes

Trip Notes

Trip Notes

Trip Notes

Trip Notes